Lecture Notes in Artificial Intelligence 9319

Subseries of Lecture Notes in Computer Science

More information about this series at http://www.springer.com/series/1244

Andrey Ronzhin · Rodmonga Potapova
Nikos Fakotakis (Eds.)

Speech and Computer

17th International Conference, SPECOM 2015
Athens, Greece, September 20–24, 2015
Proceedings

 Springer

Editors
Andrey Ronzhin
SPIIRAS
St. Petersburg
Russia

Nikos Fakotakis
University of Patras
Patras
Greece

Rodmonga Potapova
Moscow State Linguistic University
Moscow
Russia

ISSN 0302-9743   ISSN 1611-3349 (electronic)
Lecture Notes in Artificial Intelligence
ISBN 978-3-319-23131-0   ISBN 978-3-319-23132-7 (eBook)
DOI 10.1007/978-3-319-23132-7

Library of Congress Control Number: 2015946768

LNCS Sublibrary: SL7 – Artificial Intelligence

Springer Cham Heidelberg New York Dordrecht London

Printed on acid-free paper

Springer International Publishing AG Switzerland is part of Springer Science+Business Media
(www.springer.com)

Preface

The Speech and Computer International Conference (SPECOM) is a regular event organized since 1996 when the first SPECOM was held in St. Petersburg, Russian Federation. It is a conference with a long tradition that attracts researchers in the area of computer speech processing (recognition, synthesis, understanding etc.) and related domains (including signal processing, language and text processing, multi-modal speech processing or human–computer interaction, for instance). The SPECOM international conference is an ideal platform for know-how exchange, especially for experts working on Slavic and other highly inflectional languages, and also know-how exchange between these usually less-resourced languages as well as standard, well-resourced languages.

The long history of the SPECOM conference has seen it being organized alternately by the St. Petersburg Institute of Informatics and Automation of the Russian Academy of Sciences (SPIIRAS) and the Moscow State Linguistic University (MSLU) in their home cities. Furthermore, it was organized in 1997 by the Cluj-Napoca Subsidiary of the Research Institute for Computer Techniques (Romania), in 2005 by the University of Patras (Greece), in 2011 by the Kazan Federal University (Russian Federation, Republic of Tatarstan), in 2013 by the University of West Bohemia (Pilsen, Czech Republic), and in 2014 by the University of Novi Sad (Serbia). The last conferences were organized in parallel with TSD 2013 and DOGS 2014 and they enjoyed great success and benefits of joining the various research teams.

SPECOM 2015 was the 17th event in the series. Ten years since it was first held here, the SPECOM conference returned to Greece and it was our great pleasure to host the SPECOM 2015 conference in Athens organized this time by the University of Patras, in cooperation with the Moscow State Linguistic University (MSLU), St. Petersburg Institute for Informatics and Automation of the Russian Academy of Sciences (SPIIRAS), and St. Petersburg National Research University of Information Technologies, Mechanics and Optics (ITMO University). The conference was held during September 20-24, 2015, in the conference center of the Titania Hotel situated in the heart of the historical and commercial centre of Athens.

During the conference the invited talks were given by Gerhard Rigoll (Head of the Institute for Human–Machine Communication, TU München, Germany), Yannis Stylianou (Professor at the Department of Computer Science, University of Crete, Greece), Murat Saraçlar (Professor at the Department of Electrical and Electronic Engineering, Boğaziçi University, Turkey) on the newest achievements in speech technologies and the relatively broad and still unexplored area of human–machine interaction. The invited papers are published in the first part of the SPECOM 2015 proceedings.

This volume contains a collection of submitted papers presented at the conference, which were thoroughly reviewed by members of the Program Committee consisting of 50 top specialists in the conference topic areas. A total of 59 accepted papers out of 104 submitted, altogether contributed by 159 authors and co-authors, were selected by the Program Committee for presentation at the conference and for inclusion in this book. Theoretical and more general contributions were presented in common (plenary) sessions. Problem-oriented sessions as well as panel discussions then brought together specialists in limited problem areas with the aim of exchanging knowledge and skills resulting from research projects of all kinds.

Last but not least, we would like to express our gratitude to the authors for providing their papers on time, to the members of the Program Committee for their careful reviews and paper selection, and to the editors for their hard work preparing this volume. Special thanks are due to the members of the local Organizing Committee for their tireless effort and enthusiasm during the conference organization. We hope that you benefitted from the event and that you also enjoyed the social program prepared by the members of the Organizing Committee.

July 2015   Andrey Ronzhin

Organization

SPECOM 2015 was organized by the University of Patras, Patras, Greece, in cooperation with the Moscow State Linguistic University (MSLU, Moscow, Russia), St. Petersburg Institute for Informatics and Automation of the Russian Academy of Science (SPIIRAS, St. Petersburg, Russia), and St. Petersburg National Research University of Information Technologies, Mechanics and Optics (ITMO University, St. Petersburg, Russia) The conference website is located at: http://specom.nw.ru/.

Program Committee

Etienne Barnard, South Africa
Laurent Besacier, France
Vlado Delić, Serbia
Olivier Deroo, Belgium
Christoph Draxler, Germany
Thierry Dutoit, Belgium
Nikos Fakotakis, Greece
Peter French, UK
Hiroya Fujisaki, Japan
Todor Ganchev, Bulgaria
Rüdiger Hoffmann, Germany
Oliver Jokisch, Germany
Slobodan Jovicic, Serbia
Dimitri Kanevsky, USA
Alexey Karpov, Russian Federation
Heysem Kaya, Turkey
Irina Kipyatkova, Russian Federation
Daniil Kocharov, Russian Federation
George Kokkinakis, Greece
Steven Krauwer, The Netherlands
Lin-shan Lee, Taiwan
Boris Lobanov, Belarus
Elena Lyakso, Russian Federation
Konstantin Markov, Japan

Yuri Matveev, Russian Federation
Konstantinos Moustakas, Greece
Iosif Mporas, Greece
Geza Nemeth, Hungary
Heinrich Niemann, Germany
Alexander Petrovsky, Belarus
Elias Potamitis, Greece
Dimitar Popov, Italy
Rodmonga Potapova, Russian Federation
Vsevolod Potapov, Russian Federation
Lawrence Rabiner, USA
Gerhard Rigoll, Germany
Andrey Ronzhin, Russian Federation
Murat Saraclar, Turkey
Jesus Savage, Mexico
Tanja Schultz, Germany
Milan Sečujski, Serbia
Pavel Skrelin, Russian Federation
Viktor Sorokin, Russian Federation
Eberhard Stock, Germany
Yannis Stylianou, Greece
Christian Wellekens, France
Miloš Železný, Czech Republic

Local Organizing Committee

Nikos Fakotakis *(Chair)*
Nikolay Bobrov

Evangelos Dermatas
Rania Doufexi

Alexey Karpov	Iosif Mporas
Otilia Kocsis	Rodmonga Potapova
Liliya Komalova	Alexander Ronzhin
Elias Kotinas	Andrey Ronzhin
Yuri Matveev	Anton Saveliev
John Mourjopoulos	Kyriakos Sgarbas
Konstantinos Moustakas	Mikhail Stolbov

Acknowledgements

Special thanks to the reviewers who devoted their valuable time to review the papers and thus helped to keep the high quality of the conference review process.

Sponsoring Institutions

Speech Technology Center Ltd.
ITMO University
International Speech Communication Association, ISCA

About Athens

Athens is the capital city of Greece with a metropolitan population of 4.7 million inhabitants. It is in many ways the birthplace of Classical Greece, and therefore of Western civilization. Athens is one of the world's oldest cities, with its recorded history spanning around 3,400 years. A centre for the arts, learning and philosophy, home of Plato's Academy and Aristotle's Lyceum, it is widely referred to as the cradle of Western civilization and the birthplace of democracy, largely due to the impact of its cultural and political achievements during the 5th and 4th centuries BC on the rest of the then known European continent. In modern times, Athens is a large cosmopolitan metropolis and central to economic, financial, industrial, maritime, political and cultural life in Greece. In 2012, Athens was ranked the world's by purchasing power.

The University of Patras presently stands well ahead of its original goal, which was to set "a firm model of an Academic institution providing Greece with a highly qualified Alumnae contributing to the society's development and growth". Today, the University of Patras enjoys recognition as Academic institution with a worldwide impact, attracting thousands of students and a large number of academic and research personnel actively involved in the cutting-edge science, innovation and excellence.

The Department of Electrical & Computer Engineering was founded as the first department of the School of Engineering in 1967. Initially its name was Electrical Engineering Department. It included eight chairs and five laboratories. In the following period up to 1982, eleven more chairs and five laboratories were established, while six chairs were transferred to other departments. In 1995 the Department of Electrical Engineering was renamed Electrical and Computer Engineering Department honouring its strong activity in the area of computers. The department now has 14 Professors, 13 Associate Professors, 12 Assistant Professors and 7 Lecturers. It offers instruction and conducts research in the fields of electric power, telecommunications, information technologies, computers, electronics, systems and automatic control.

Contents

Invited Talks

Multimodal Human-Robot Interaction from the Perspective of a Speech
Scientist.. 3
  Gerhard Rigoll

A Decade of Discriminative Language Modeling for Automatic Speech
Recognition 11
  Murat Saraclar, Erinc Dikici, and Ebru Arisoy

Conference Papers

A Bilingual Kazakh-Russian System for Automatic Speech Recognition
and Synthesis 25
  *Olga Khomitsevich, Valentin Mendelev, Natalia Tomashenko,
  Sergey Rybin, Ivan Medennikov, and Saule Kudubayeva*

A Comparative Study of Speech Processing in Microphone Arrays
with Multichannel Alignment and Zelinski Post-Filtering 34
  Sergei Aleinik and Mikhail Stolbov

A Comparison of RNN LM and FLM for Russian Speech Recognition 42
  Irina Kipyatkova and Alexey Karpov

A Frequency Domain Adaptive Decorrelating Algorithm for Speech
Enhancement 51
  Mohamed Djendi, Feriel Khemies, and Amina Morsli

Acoustic Markers of Emotional State "Aggression"................... 55
  Rodmonga Potapova, Liliya Komalova, and Nikolay Bobrov

Algorithms for Low Bit-Rate Coding with Adaptation to Statistical
Characteristics of Speech Signal 65
  Anton Saveliev, Oleg Basov, Andrey Ronzhin, and Alexander Ronzhin

Analysing Human-Human Negotiations with the Aim to Develop
a Dialogue System 73
  Mare Koit

Analysis of Facial Motion Capture Data for Visual Speech Synthesis 81
  Miloš Železný, Zdeněk Krňoul, and Pavel Jedlička

Auditory-Perceptual Recognition of the Emotional State of Aggression   89
Rodmonga Potapova and Liliya Komalova

Automatic Classification and Prediction of Attitudes: Audio - Visual
Analysis of Video Blogs   96
Noor Alhusna Madzlan, Yuyun Huang, and Nick Campbell

Automatic Close Captioning for Live Hungarian Television Broadcast
Speech: A Fast and Resource-Efficient Approach   105
Ádám Varga, Balázs Tarján, Zoltán Tobler, György Szaszák,
Tibor Fegyó, Csaba Bordás, and Péter Mihajlik

Automatic Estimation of Web Bloggers' Age Using Regression Models   113
Vasiliki Simaki, Christina Aravantinou, Iosif Mporas,
and Vasileios Megalooikonomou

Automatic Preprocessing Technique for Detection of Corrupted Speech
Signal Fragments for the Purpose of Speaker Recognition   121
Konstantin Simonchik, Sergei Aleinik, Dmitry Ivanko,
and Galina Lavrentyeva

Automatic Sound Recognition of Urban Environment Events   129
Theodoros Theodorou, Iosif Mporas, and Nikos Fakotakis

Automatically Trained TTS for Effective Attacks to Anti-spoofing System. . .   137
Galina Lavrentyeva, Alexandr Kozlov, Sergey Novoselov,
Konstantin Simonchik, and Vadim Shchemelinin

EmoChildRu: Emotional Child Russian Speech Corpus   144
Elena Lyakso, Olga Frolova, Evgeniya Dmitrieva, Aleksey Grigorev,
Heysem Kaya, Albert Ali Salah, and Alexey Karpov

Cognitive Mechanism of Semantic Content Decoding of Spoken Discourse
in Noise.   153
Rodmonga Potapova and Vsevolod Potapov

Combining Prosodic and Lexical Classifiers for Two-Pass Punctuation
Detection in a Russian ASR System   161
Olga Khomitsevich, Pavel Chistikov, Tatiana Krivosheeva,
Natalia Epimakhova, and Irina Chernykh

Construction of a Modern Greek Grammar Checker Through Mnemosyne
Formalism   170
Panagiotis Gakis, Christos Panagiotakopoulos, Kyriakos Sgarbas,
Christos Tsalidis, and Verykios Vasilios

Contribution to the Design of an Expressive Speech Synthesis System
for the Arabic Language   178
   Lyes Demri, Leila Falek, and Hocine Teffahi

Deep Neural Network Based Continuous Speech Recognition for Serbian
Using the Kaldi Toolkit   186
   *Branislav Popović, Stevan Ostrogonac, Edvin Pakoci, Nikša Jakovljević,
and Vlado Delić*

DNN-Based Speech Synthesis: Importance of Input Features and Training
Data   193
   Alexandros Lazaridis, Blaise Potard, and Philip N. Garner

Emotion State Manifestation in Voice Features: Chimpanzees, Human
Infants, Children, Adults   201
   Elena Lyakso and Olga Frolova

Estimation of Vowel Spectra Near Vocal Chords with Restoration
of a Clipped Speech Signal   209
   Andrey Barabanov, Vera Evdokimova, and Pavel Skrelin

Fast Algorithm for Precise Estimation of Fundamental Frequency on Short
Time Intervals   217
   *Andrey Barabanov, Alexandr Melnikov, Valentin Magerkin,
and Evgenij Vikulov*

Gender Classification of Web Authors Using Feature Selection
and Language Models   226
   *Christina Aravantinou, Vasiliki Simaki, Iosif Mporas,
and Vasileios Megalooikonomou*

Improving Acoustic Models for Russian Spontaneous Speech Recognition . . .   234
   *Alexey Prudnikov, Ivan Medennikov, Valentin Mendelev,
Maxim Korenevsky, and Yuri Khokhlov*

Information Sources of Word Semantics Methods   243
   Miloslav Konopík and Ondřej Pražák

Invariant Components of Speech Signals: Analysis and Visualization   251
   Valeriy Zhenilo and Vsevolod Potapov

Language Model Speaker Adaptation for Transcription of Slovak
Parliament Proceedings   259
   Ján Staš, Daniel Hládek, and Jozef Juhár

Macro Episodes of Russian Everyday Oral Communication: Towards
Pragmatic Annotation of the ORD Speech Corpus.   268
   Tatiana Sherstinova

Missing Feature Kernel and Nonparametric Window Subband Power
Distribution for Robust Sound Event Classification   277
   Tran Huy Dat, Jonathan William Dennis, and Ng Wen Zheng Terence

Multi-factor Method for Detection of Filled Pauses and Lengthenings
in Russian Spontaneous Speech   285
   Vasilisa Verkhodanova and Vladimir Shapranov

Multimodal Presentation of Bulgarian Child Language.   293
   Dimitar Popov and Velka Popova

On Deep and Shallow Neural Networks in Speech Recognition
from Speech Spectrum.   301
   Jan Zelinka, Petr Salajka, and Luděk Müller

Opinion Recognition on Movie Reviews by Combining Classifiers   309
   Athanasia Koumpouri, Iosif Mporas, and Vasileios Megalooikonomou

Optimization of Pitch Tracking and Quantization   317
   Oleg Basov, Andrey Ronzhin, and Victor Budkov

PLDA Speaker Verification with Limited Speech Data   325
   Andrej Ridzik and Milan Rusko

Real-Time Context Aware Audio Augmented Reality   333
   Gerasimos Arvanitis, Konstantinos Moustakas, and Nikos Fakotakis

Recurrent Neural Networks for Hypotheses Re-Scoring   341
   Mikhail Kudinov

Review of the Opus Codec in a WebRTC Scenario for Audio and Speech
Communication.   348
   *Michael Maruschke, Oliver Jokisch, Martin Meszaros,
   and Viktor Iaroshenko*

Semantic Multilingual Differences of Terminological Definitions
Regarding the Concept "Artificial Intelligence".   356
   Rodmonga Potapova and Ksenia Oskina

SNR Estimation Based on Adaptive Signal Decomposition for Quality
Evaluation of Speech Enhancement Algorithms.   364
   Sergei Aleinik and Mikhail Stolbov

Sociolinguistic Factors in Text-Based Sentence Boundary Detection   372
   Anton Stepikhov

Sparsity Analysis and Compensation for i-Vector Based Speaker
Verification   381
   Wei Li, Tian Fan Fu, Jie Zhu, and Ning Chen

Speaker Identification Using Semi-supervised Learning   389
  Nikos Fazakis, Stamatis Karlos, Sotiris Kotsiantis,
  and Kyriakos Sgarbas

Speaker Verification Using Spectral and Durational Segmental
Characteristics   397
  Elena Bulgakova, Aleksei Sholohov, Natalia Tomashenko,
  and Yuri Matveev

Speech Enhancement in Quasi-Periodic Noises Using Improved Spectral
Subtraction Based on Adaptive Sampling.   405
  Elias Azarov, Maxim Vashkevich, and Alexander Petrovsky

Sub-word Language Modeling for Russian LVCSR.   413
  Sergey Zablotskiy and Wolfgang Minker

Temporal Organization of Phrase-final Words as a Function of Pitch
Movement Type   422
  Tatiana Kachkovskaia

The "One Day of Speech" Corpus: Phonetic and Syntactic Studies
of Everyday Spoken Russian   429
  Natalia Bogdanova-Beglarian, Gregory Martynenko,
  and Tatiana Sherstinova

The Multi-level Approach to Speech Corpora Annotation for Automatic
Speech Recognition.   438
  Igor Glavatskih, Tatyana Platonova, Valeria Rogozhina,
  Anna Shirokova, Anna Smolina, Mikhail Kotov, Anna Ovsyannikova,
  Sergey Repalov, and Mikhail Zulkarneev

The Role of Prosody in the Perception of Synthesized and Natural Speech. . .   446
  Maja Marković, Bojana Jakovljević, Tanja Milićev, and Nataša Milievıć

The Singular Estimation Pitch Tracker.   454
  Daniyar Volf, Roman Meshcheryakov, and Sergey Kharchenko

Voice Conversion Between Synthesized Bilingual Voices Using Line
Spectral Frequencies   463
  Young-Sun Yun, Jinman Jung, and Seongbae Eun

Voicing-Based Classified Split Vector Quantizer for Efficient Coding
of AMR-WB ISF Parameters   472
  Merouane Bouzid and Salah-Eddine Cheraitia

Vulnerability of Voice Verification System with STC Anti-spoofing
Detector to Different Methods of Spoofing Attacks   480
    Vadim Shchemelinin, Alexandr Kozlov, Galina Lavrentyeva,
    Sergey Novoselov, and Konstantin Simonchik

WebTransc — A WWW Interface for Speech Corpora Production
and Processing   487
    Tomáš Valenta and Luboš Šmídl

Word-External Reduction in Spontaneous Russian   495
    Yulia Nigmatulina

Author Index   505

Invited Talks

Multimodal Human-Robot Interaction from the Perspective of a Speech Scientist

Gerhard Rigoll$^{(\boxtimes)}$

Institute for Human-Machine-Communication,
TU Munchen (TUM), Munich, Germany
`rigoll@tum.de`

Abstract. Human-Robot-Interaction (HRI) is a research area that developed steadily during the last years. While robots in the last decades of the 20th century have been mostly constructed to work autonomously, the rise of service robots during the last 20 years has mostly contributed to the development of effective communication methods between human users and robots. This development has been even accelerated with the advancement of humanoid robots, where the demand for effective human-robot-interaction is even more obvious. It is also amazing to note that, inspired by the success of HRI in the area of service and humanoid robotics, human-robot-interfaces become nowadays even attractive for areas, where HRI has never played a major role before, especially for industrial robots or robots in outdoor environments. Compared to classical human-computer-interaction (HCI), one can say that the basic interaction algorithms are not that much different in HRI, e.g. a speech or gesture recognizer would not work much differently in both domains. The major differences between HCI and HRI are more in the different utilization of modalities, which also depends very much on the type of employed robot. Therefore, the primary goal of this paper is the description of the major differences between HCI and HRI and the presentation of the most important modalities used in HRI and how they affect the interaction depending on the various types of available robot platforms.

Keywords: Human-robot interaction · Service robots · Humanoid robotics · Multimodal dialogue · Brain-machine interfaces

1 Introduction

Human-Robot-Interaction (HRI) is a research area that developed steadily with the rise of robotics and of multimodality in classical human-computer interaction (HCI) during the last decades. Looking at typical situations where robots are nowadays mostly deployed in industrial environments, such as manufacturing in the automotive industry, it is obvious that the direct communication between humans and robots have so far not yet played a major role in such environments. The same is true for the field of autonomous robotics, where robots navigate independently through complex environments. The importance of HRI

© Springer International Publishing Switzerland 2015
A. Ronzhin et al. (Eds.): SPECOM 2015, LNAI 9319, pp. 3–10, 2015.
DOI: 10.1007/978-3-319-23132-7_1

however changed dramatically, when the new research direction of service robotics became more and more popular. Service robots are designed to solve problems in cooperation with humans and therefore an effective communication between them is crucial in this case. In the first part of this paper, the major differences between classical human-machine communication and human-robot interaction will be discussed.

The remaining part will cover other important issues, e.g. the impact of modalities that play a less important role in classical HCI, such as e.g. the design of gaze, face or facial expressions as output modality. It will be shown that such modalities have a much more important impact in HRI, but that it depends very much on the current application and especially on the type of robot, which interaction scheme is possible and also effective. As a consequence of these considerations, a variety of different interaction schemes between humans and robots will be described, ranging from very simple, unimodal interaction up to much more complex, multimodal communication schemes with modalities that are quite unusual in classical HCI, but very useful in HRI. As an example, the figure below shows two different service robots, where on the left side, a more ancient robot with less sophisticated interaction capabilities is shown, whereas the robot on the right side, which has used in our European project ALIAS [3], enables a more advanced interaction mode consisting mainly of quite conservative interfaces, such as a touch screen or a microphone for voice input.

Fig. 1. Service robot in passive (left, [4]) and active (right, [3]) usage

2   Major Differences Between HCI and HRI

Although at the first sight, the problem of Human-Robot-Interaction (HRI) seems to be very similar to classical Human-Machine-Interaction (HCI), it turns out that in fact HRI is quite more complex, due to a few special circumstances that are specific for robotics. Looking at the (most important) disciplines that are involved in multimodal HRI, the following major research areas can be listed:

- Signal Processing;
- Pattern Recognition;
- Software/Realtime Development;
- Speech Processing;
- Image Processing;
- Neurocomputing;
- Psychology, Artificial Intelligence;
- Mechanical Engineering;
- Mechatronics;
- Automation & Control;
- Optimization & Path Planning;
- Sociology.

As many of these areas listed above are also crucial for the design and implementation of a classical user interface with related recognition algorithms (e.g. for voice or handwriting input), e.g. on a smartphone, HRI would require several additional skills and research areas that are listed above, such as Control or Mechatronics. The major reason for those additional areas is the fact that a robot typically is composed out of a complex mechanical body, it is therefore much more a physical device with many actuators that are very often also strongly involved in the interaction process, where in this case physical force is one major modality that is typically not used in classical software-based human-computer interaction. Additionally, a robot is in many cases a mobile device and thus interaction will be mostly carried out over a certain distance between human and robot. This involves in almost all cases a strong impact of robustness for every communication channel, especially for the acoustic interaction modality. An even more important difference is the already above mentioned "embodiment effect", because a robot has typically a body that can be more or less directly involved in the interaction process. One of the consequences is the option that it is not only possible to interact with robots similarly to e.g. interacting with smartphones, but instead to actively perform a physical joint cooperation with robots, e.g. carrying something together or mounting a heavy piece jointly with the robot. The embodiment has also other implications, e.g. concerning social behavior and acceptance issues, which is currently intensively investigated in the area of social robotics.

Generally, this implies that HRI can lead in many applications to a much more intensive physical coupling between machine and user. Whereas in classical HCI, the *dialogue* between a user and the machine is the most prominent issue in communication, this is replaced in many (mostly advanced) HRI scenarios by a *cooperation* between user and machine, i.e. the human and the robot are actively solving a joint task together (see e.g. [5]). Insightful examples for such situations are e.g. robots who act as assistant for humans to jointly carry with them a table, or to hold a heavy piece of machinery for the human to mount this workpiece. An example for an even closer cooperation would be e.g. a "dancing partner robot", leading to a very intensive physical interaction between human and robot. As it is straightforward to imagine, such applications imply a certain social component to HRI, on the one hand side because the robot can be perceived as "cohabitant" (e.g. especially in the example of the dancing robot before) and, on the other hand, because this close physical coupling does of course imply a certain danger of injury and mistreatment by the robotic partner.

Another difference to classical HCI is the fact that knowledge processing is becoming even more important in HRI than it is in HCI. Access to databases, websites or other knowledge bases became more important in classical HCI in recent years due to the rise of personal digital assistants, such as e.g. SIRI in the area of speech recognition. An efficient robot assistant might need access to similar knowledge bases, possibly also via Internet, if e.g. a human is asking a service robot at home to tell him about the weather or to arrange a phone call to a company to repair his refrigerator. Additionally, a robot might have to access a huge internal knowledge base, where e.g. the information about the household is stored, or where the knowledge about how to open a dish washer and move the items back to their original destination is contained. This is because the dialogue between the human and the robot is much more a joint cooperation than just a dialogue and thus implies much more complicated "dialogue actions" on the side of the machine, such as moving, fetching, holding or grasping.

From this description, it might also become obvious, that HRI involves partially different modalities compared to classical HCI and that some "less usual" modalities, such as e.g. force, haptics, gaze, or facial expressions have a stronger meaning in HRI. Since the employment of specific modalities is also quite much dependent on the specific type of robot selected for interaction, the next section lists the various types of robots and describes their impact on the typical interaction modalities.

3 Different Types of Robots and Resulting Implications for Interaction Schemes

Having a closer look at different fundamental types of robots, it becomes more obvious why there are quite many different degrees of complexity in HRI. The following is a listing of characteristic robots employed in typical HRI scenarios:

- Very simple industrial robots, often consisting only of an active arm, which could imply quite simple interaction via force (e.g. autotracking of the robot arm if slightly pulled by human) or more complex ones (e.g. grasping and reaching a tool).
- Classical industrial robots in manufacturing, e.g. for welding in the automotive industry. Communication with humans is here typically quite limited, since physical interaction would be too dangerous and typical multimodal interaction over speech or gestures are not very promising due to the adverse environment.
- Construction robots: They are employed in high story buildings for replacing workers in dangerous situations. HRI for these robots is not yet very popular.

– Outdoor robots, operating in extreme environments, such as underwater, in space, in contaminated areas or plants, or in the air as drones. For such robots, typically tele-operation is a very suitable interaction scheme, very similar to remote-control of machines or devices.

– Medical robots, mainly used for precise surgery and similar operations. Here, interaction is very recommendable, e.g. via voice for hands-free scenarios or remote control of hands and arms.

– Service robots, active in private households or in hospitals. The necessity of effective HRI is in this case absolutely obvious, since the direct purpose of such robots is the assistance to and cooperation with human users. Within this category, it is possible to distinguish several robot types, such as

1. Simple passive robots, typically used as walking aid for elderly people or similar. They often require some force to be applied by a user in order to move.

2. Active service robots, with their own motor drive, who would typically approach a person or would actively serve a user by bringing him a desired item, e.g. a drink. Both types of robots (1) and (2) are shown in Fig. 1.

3. Active "companion robots" that assist users in outdoor environments, e.g. by helping them in carrying shopping goods or guiding elderly persons through an unknown environment.

– Robots directly interconnected to users, such as e.g. so-called exoskeletons to support and protect a human's body. Interaction is always implicitly built-in through the direct connection between robot and human. This is often implemented through a neural interface or a brain-robot-interface and implies one of the most demanding interaction schemes for HRI.

– Humanoid robots that have a shape similar to human beings, as shown in Fig. 2 on the next page. This type of robot is technically probably the most demanding and has likely the highest potential for HRI. One might think that only a small fraction of special applications require the deployment of humanoid robots, however studies show that the percentage of applications involving humanoid robots is steadily rising and that users require more and more such robots in environments where no humanoids have been employed in the past.

For instance, one might imagine that a humanoid robot is not necessarily required in a household and that instead a service robot as displayed in Fig. 1 would be sufficient in such an environment. Nevertheless, it is a fact that many users would prefer a humanoid robot as personal assistant, because the dialogue with him would appear much more natural, with body language, a robot head displaying emotions or natural gaze. In a household with stairs, such a robot is much more mobile. Even in industrial applications, humanoid robots are considered to be the optimal choice in many environments, where e.g. a walking robot is superior to a robot on wheels, e.g. in airplane assembly. For a humanoid robot, one would also expect a very natural, basically human-like interaction scheme, which should be as close to human interaction as the robot's appearance is to a human. Therefore, one would expect from such a robot a close to perfect

Fig. 2. Humanoid Robots from [1]

replication of the human senses, like hearing, speaking or seeing, which directly implies a multimodal HRI scheme with all human modalities, also including haptics, force, motion, gaze and facial expressions. This leads to the next section, where the question is answered, which important basic interaction modes are established in HRI.

4   Basic Interaction Schemes in Human-Robot-Communication

As mentioned in the previous section, an interaction scheme in HRI is quite dependent of the robot type. Therefore, one can expect that the simplest type of robot also implies the simplest interaction scheme. Looking at the left side of Fig. 1, it may be obvious that simple force *interaction* might be the most primitive way of interacting between a human and a robot. There is only limited computational intelligence required in recognizing a certain force threshold that might lead the robot in one or the other direction. A different, but technically similar force interaction is employed in a scenario where only a robot arm is moved with little force applied in one direction, as in a typical servo-control application.

A more sophisticated version of force interaction is in scenarios of *reaching and grasping*, e.g. the robot hands over a tool to the user. Staying in the area of force-interaction, another classical scenario would be in *teleoperation*, where e.g. a remote robot arm in space is controlled by a lever operated by a human, very much like in a game controlled by a joystick. This kind of remote-interaction is already around since many years and therefore represents one of the earliest and most successful HRI schemes.

More sophisticated interaction is certainly realized if more complex modalities are considered, such as the typical human senses for hearing and vision, using speech recognition, gestures or face recognition. In most past applications, this used to be mostly a *unimodal interaction*, e.g. controlling a robot only via gestures or voice.

Then consequently, the next step in complexity would be a *multimodal dialogue*, typically using modalities such as speech and gesture in parallel. In many cases, it makes a lot of sense if such natural modalities are additionally extended by a simple communication channel, such as e.g. a touchscreen, which can also serve as fallback alternative in case of recognition problems. Such a typical multimodal system with additional simpler input device can be seen in Fig. 1 on the right side.

As already mentioned, for special cases, e.g. humanoid robots, a much more sophisticated multimodal communication scheme would be possible and desirable, involving many more modalities, also at the output side, such as the generation of motion (arms, hands, body), gaze, or facial expressions and audio-visual text-to-speech using an artificial humanoid head.

Another interesting variant is a *mobile interface*, e.g. implemented on a smartphone. This can be quite effective for HRI because a robot is in many cases also a mobile device and therefore it could be advantageous to interact with this device from different positions, partially quite far away. Also, in such a case, speech communication could be e.g. implemented directly on the mobile device to avoid the typical far distance problems in speech recognition. Mobile augmented reality could be used to enhance the view on the robot or display instructions to the users.

Certainly, one of the most complex interactions schemes is the active *joint cooperation* between user and robot, e.g. carrying a desk together and passing some stairs on the way. It is obvious that this implies very strong requirements for the human-robot interface, for several reasons: Firstly, the robot must react very sensitively to any human input, e.g. if the human suddenly reduces speed while descending the stairs. The robot should even be able to anticipate very quickly the humans intention, which would not be necessarily required in many other scenarios, but might be crucial for joint cooperation. Another issue here is that multimodality is almost compulsory, since in the above example, the robot has to communicate at least via force and vision in parallel, where only one modality (e.g. force coupling only) would not be sufficient to solve such a complex cooperation problem. Furthermore, such an example would involve a quite high accident risk, therefore the robot has to function almost perfectly, with close to zero failure rate, which is still quite difficult in pattern recognition these days.

Concerning safety issues, probably an even more demanding communication scheme is the one between humans and interconnected robots, such as exoskeletons or robots carrying humans. As it is easy to imagine, a failure in such a case can lead to the most possible serious injuries of the user. As already mentioned, in such cases there is often a direct neuronal coupling between human and robot, e.g. via neural implants which receive signals from the spine or the brain. The popular paradigm of *Brain-Machine Interfaces* (BMI) would be another possibility to realize such an interface in this case (see [2]).

Therefore, a very future-oriented vision of HRI could be that a paralyzed person can control a humanoid robot by BMI, where the robot could be of service to this person in all daily situations, not only bringing him some drinks or switching on some devices, but also helping him into the wheelchair or carrying him down the stairs.

5 Conclusions

In conclusion, the intention of this paper was to illustrate the amount of complexity that especially comes with advanced forms of Human-Robot-Interaction and to clarify that HRI can indeed be more complex than traditional HCI, although this is very much depending on the employed type of robot and the envisaged application as well as the environment in which the interaction occurs. Also the employed modalities can be even richer than in classical multimodal HCI, with a lot of more unusual modalities, especially on the output side, whereas modalities on the input side are more or less similar to interaction not involving robots, at least concerning their algorithmic implementation.

References

1. Darpa robotics challenge (2015). www.theroboticschallenge.org
2. Bell, C.J., Shenoy, P., Chalodhorn, R., Rao, R.P.: Control of a humanoid robot by a noninvasive brain-computer interface in humans. J. Neural Eng. **5**(2), 214 (2008)
3. Geiger, J., Leykauf, T., Rehrl, T., Wallhoff, F., Rigoll, G.: The robot alias as a gaming platform for elderly persons. In: Wichert, R., Klausing, H. (eds.) Ambient Assisted Living, pp. 327–340. Springer, Heidelberg (2014)
4. Hans, M., Graf, B., Schraft, R.: Robotic home assistant care-o-bot: past-present-future. In: Proceedings of the 11th IEEE International Workshop on Robot and Human Interactive Communication, pp. 380–385. IEEE (2002)
5. Rigoll, G.: Multimodal interaction techniques for joint cooperation between humans and cognitive systems. In: Proceedings of the 2nd IEEE International Conference on Intelligent Human Computer Interaction (IHCI 2010), Allahabad, India, pp. 32–41 (2010)

A Decade of Discriminative Language Modeling for Automatic Speech Recognition

Murat Saraclar[1][(✉)], Erinc Dikici[1], and Ebru Arisoy[2]

[1] Electrical and Electronics Engineering Department, Bogazici University,
34342 Bebek, Istanbul, Turkey
{murat.saraclar,erinc.dikici}@boun.edu.tr
http://busim.ee.boun.edu.tr/~speech
[2] Electrical and Electronics Engineering Department, MEF University,
34396 Sariyer, Istanbul, Turkey
ebruarisoy.saraclar@mef.edu.tr

Abstract. This paper summarizes the research on discriminative language modeling focusing on its application to automatic speech recognition (ASR). A discriminative language model (DLM) is typically a linear or log-linear model consisting of a weight vector associated with a feature vector representation of a sentence. This flexible representation can include linguistically and statistically motivated features that incorporate morphological and syntactic information. At test time, DLMs are used to rerank the output of an ASR system, represented as an N-best list or lattice. During training, both negative and positive examples are used with the aim of directly optimizing the error rate. Various machine learning methods, including the structured perceptron, large margin methods and maximum regularized conditional log-likelihood, have been used for estimating the parameters of DLMs. Typically positive examples for DLM training come from the manual transcriptions of acoustic data while the negative examples are obtained by processing the same acoustic data with an ASR system. Recent research generalizes DLM training by either using automatic transcriptions for the positive examples or simulating the negative examples.

Keywords: Automatic speech recognition · Discriminative training · Language modeling

1 Introduction

Discriminative language models (DLMs) have been part of ASR systems for over a decade and have been applied to tasks such as LVCSR [29], utterance and call classification [33], automatic transcription and retrieval of broadcast news [2], along with their use in parsing [37] and machine translation [24].

DLMs are typically formulated as a linear [8], log-linear [29] or an exponential model [41]. In this paper, we follow the linear model framework that reranks alternative hypotheses produced by a function $\mathbf{GEN}(\cdot)$ using the inner product of a feature vector $\mathbf{\Phi}$ and a weight vector $\mathbf{w}$ as a score.

© Springer International Publishing Switzerland 2015
A. Ronzhin et al. (Eds.): SPECOM 2015, LNAI 9319, pp. 11–22, 2015.
DOI: 10.1007/978-3-319-23132-7_2

The use of a feature representation allows DLMs to integrate many different sources (n-gram, morphological, syntactic, and semantic information) into a single mathematical structure. The details of various feature sets used in DLMs are given in Sect. 2.

The objective of DLM training is to estimate the model vector **w** by optimizing an objective function directly related to the word error rate (WER). DLM training algorithms can be categorized as classification and reranking approaches. While the classification approaches aim to improve the score of the least errorful hypothesis, the reranking approaches aim to adjust the scores so as to match the ordering of the hypotheses with respect to error rate. The perceptron algorithm is a popular method which formulates discriminative modeling as a structured prediction task [29]. It has also been adapted to reranking [37], which gives higher accuracies at the cost of a longer training duration [13]. Modifications of the perceptron optimization criterion have been proposed to make it more directly related to the WER [32,38]. Large margin methods such as the support vector machines (SVM) and the margin-infused relaxed algorithm (MIRA) [10] are among the other methods that are used to train a DLM. Classification and reranking variants of the SVM [16] have been used for tasks such as ASR [42], lexical disambiguation [4], parsing and machine translation [7]. The MIRA has also been applied to statistical machine translation [40] and parsing [27]. The details of DLM training algorithms are given in Sect. 3.

Traditionally, DLMs are trained in a supervised setting where the training data is composed of pairs of spoken utterances and corresponding manual transcriptions. DLM training requires a set of alternative hypotheses produced by a function **GEN**($\cdot$). In the supervised setting this represents the ASR system itself and produces lattices or n-best lists corresponding to the spoken utterances.

In cases where the data is not sufficient to train a DLM in a supervised manner, semi-supervised training techniques are applied. Here, the function **GEN**($\cdot$) generates alternative hypotheses from the transcriptions using a confusion model (CM). In [17] and [22], the CM is constructed using phonetic similarities estimated from an acoustic model. In [5] and [12], CMs based on words and different sub-word units are compared. Other approaches [25,39] make use of a machine translation system to learn phrase similarities as if the ASR outputs were translations of a source reference transcription. On the other hand, [41] finds competing words (cohorts) directly from the ASR outputs of untranscribed speech to form the CM. A comparison of these three main approaches is given in [31].

Unsupervised training of discriminative language models is a more recent area of interest. In this approach, DLMs are trained using examples without any reference. Like the supervised setting, the **GEN**($\cdot$) function is an ASR system producing the alternative hypotheses, however the reference is replaced by an automatically derived hypothesis. In [21] the reference is chosen according to the Minimum Bayes Risk criterion. Alternatively in [18], a weak acoustic model is used for generating alternative hypotheses and a stronger acoustic model is used to automatically derive the reference. Further details are given in Sect. 4.

2   Features

In DLMs, $\Phi_d(x, y)$ represents a particular sentence-level feature in the feature vector $\mathbf{\Phi}(x, y)$ extracted from the candidate hypothesis y for the utterance x. The most common feature type used in DLMs is the n-gram features [29] defined as the number of times an n-gram is seen in the candidate hypothesis y. In this case, the features do not explicitly depend on x, so the notation can be simplified to $\mathbf{\Phi}(y)$. For instance if the candidate hypothesis is *"in the paper"*, the feature corresponding to the bigram *"the paper"* is defined as follows:

$\Phi_d(y)$ = number of times *"the paper"* is seen in candidate hypothesis $y = 1$

Using word n-grams as features in discriminative language modeling outperformed the traditional generative n-gram language modeling approach for English [29] as well as Turkish [2] ASR systems.

This section reviews various feature sets used in DLMs. The features discussed in this section are linguistic, statistically derived, and acoustic features.

2.1   Linguistic Features

Linguistic features used in DLMs involve morphological and syntactic features as well as features extracted from the topic or the conversation context.

Morphology is an important information source for feature-based language modeling, especially for agglutinative or highly inflectional languages both in generative [20,35] and discriminative language modeling [3,32,36] frameworks. In the DLM framework, the words in the candidate hypotheses are parsed with a morphological parser and the features are extracted from these parses. Possible choices of DLM features are n-grams extracted from stem, ending and morphological tag sequences. In stem and ending features, the stem is extracted from the morphological decomposition and the remaining part of the word is taken as the ending. After converting all the hypotheses into stem and ending sequences, either in surface [3] or lexical form [32], the n-gram features are extracted in the same way as words, as if the stem and endings were words. The same procedure can also be applied to morphological tag sequences. Morphological n-gram features in DLMs have been shown to yield significant improvements on top of generative n-gram language models both for Czech [36], a highly inflectional language, and Turkish [3,32], an agglutunative language, ASR systems.

Syntax, the rules of sentence formation, is also an important information source for language modeling, especially for capturing long distance dependencies in addition to the previous n-1 words. Therefore, syntactic information has been incorporated into conventional generative language models [6,28] and feature-based conditional exponential language models [19,30]. In the DLM framework, the candidate hypotheses are parsed using a syntactic parser and the syntactic features are extracted from these syntactic analyses. For instance in [9], each candidate hypothesis received a Part-of-Speech (PoS) tag annotation and a parse tree annotation from a syntactic parser and the syntactic features were extracted from PoS tag and shallow parse tag sequences, again using the n-gram feature approach. Also [9] proposed syntactic features that make use of the full parse tree, such as context-free rule features and head-to-head dependency features. An example context-free rule feature is given as follows:

$\Phi_d(y) =$ number of times the context-free rule $S \rightarrow NP\ VP$ is seen in the parse tree of the candidate hypothesis y

Head-to-head features were also defined in the same way by using the lexical heads with their constituents and head-to-head dependencies. Among these proposed features, PoS tag n-grams yielded the most of the gain on top of the word n-gram features on an English ASR system [9].

In [3], these syntactic features were adopted for Turkish using the dependency parser output for the candidate hypotheses. Moreover, PoS speech tag n-gram features yielded the most of the gain, consistent with the findings of [9], on a Turkish Broadcast News (BN) transcription system.

Wider context in the form of trigger-based features that identify the reoccurrence of words within a conversation were utilized in the DLM framework [38]. Additionally, semantic context was incorporated as an additional information source using features based on automatically annotated topics for each utterance [3].

2.2   Statistically Derived Features

In addition to linguistic tools, useful information for DLMs can be derived statistically. For example, instead of using PoS tags for words, automatically derived word classes are used as DLM features in [3] resulting in similar gains.

Similar to the grammatically-driven sub-word units, such as morphemes or morpheme groupings (stems and endings), statistical sub-lexical units called morphs [11] can be obtained using statistical approaches. The n-gram DLM features can be directly extracted from the statistical morph sequences. Since, statistical morphs do not convey explicit linguistic information, features similar to PoS tags and trigger dependencies are obtained from morphs with statistical approaches [3]. For instance, automatically clustering morphs into syntactic categories and considering the cluster associated with a particular morph as the tag of that morph provide morpho-syntactic features that resemble the PoS tag features for words. It was shown that morph unigram features yield significant gains on top of the generative n-gram language model and automatic morph clusters give a significant additive gain on top of morph unigram features on a Turkish BN transcription system [3].

2.3   Acoustic Features

Acoustic features in DLMs incorporate acoustic state transitions and state durations in language modeling [23]. State and duration n-gram features are extracted from the clustered allophone state sequence obtained by the alignment of the hypothesis y to the acoustic input x, in contrast to extracting features directly from the hypothesis y. Considering the following clustered allophone state IDs "$\cdots$ 1000, 1000, 4546, 4789, 1000, 1000, 4546 $\cdots$" as a label sequence, state n-gram features are extracted in a similar way with word n-gram features. Duration features also take into account the consecutive occurrences of the same state in the feature definition. An example 4-gram duration feature extracted from this state sequence is as follows:

$\Phi_d(x, y)$ = the number of times "4546 4789 1000_2 4546" is seen in state sequence of (x, y)

State and duration n-gram features together with word n-gram features were shown to give a significant gain on a GALE Arabic transcription task [23]. Additionally, combining word cluster features with duration features yielded a significant gain on top of the generative language model on an English BN system [1].

3   Algorithms

In this section we first explain how the DLM is used at test time and then review the popular DLM training algorithms.

In the testing phase, the estimated model vector $\mathbf{w}$ is used to reweight the ASR hypotheses of a test utterance x. The final output is the hypothesis with the highest evaluation score: $y^* = \text{argmax}_{y \in \mathbf{GEN}(\cdot)} \left\{ w_0 \log P(y|x) + \langle \mathbf{w}, \mathbf{\Phi}(y) \rangle \right\}$. Here, $\log P(y|x)$ is the recognition score assigned to y by the baseline recognizer for x, and w_0 is a scaling factor optimized on a held-out set. The overall system performance is represented by the WER of all y^*s.

Discriminative language modeling for ASR can be viewed as a structured prediction or a reranking task. Structured prediction is a classification type of approach in which the aim is to pick the most accurate example (hypothesis) in the N-best list, in terms of the number of word errors (WE) with respect to the reference. Generally, this means training with one positive example against a representative or collection of negative examples. The reranking approach, on the other hand, learns from pairwise relationships between the examples. In this section, after reviewing the traditional training algorithms for DLM, namely the structured perceptron and global conditional log-linear model (GCLM), we will summarize some of the recently proposed algorithms for both structured prediction and reranking tasks.

Structured Perceptron (Per) [29] is an adaptation of the canonical perceptron algorithm for solving structured prediction problems. For each utterance in the training set $x_i, i = 1..I$, Per uses two hypotheses for training: y_i is the *oracle* hypothesis which has the least WE, and z_i is the *current-best* hypothesis which yields the highest inner product score, $\langle \mathbf{w}, \mathbf{\Phi} \rangle$, under the current model $\mathbf{w}$. Taking into account the fact that the oracle needs to have the highest inner product score in order to minimize the overall WER, the model weights are updated by favoring the features which occur in y_i and penalizing the ones which occur in z_i.

Global Conditional Log-Linear Model (GCLM) [29] aims to maximize the conditional log-likelihood of the training data under the parameters $\mathbf{w}$, given by

$$F(\mathbf{w}) = \sum_i \log p_{\mathbf{w}}(y_i|x_i) = \sum_i \log \frac{e^{\langle \mathbf{w}, \mathbf{\Phi}(y_i)\rangle}}{\sum_{y \in \mathbf{GEN}(\cdot)} e^{\langle \mathbf{w}, \mathbf{\Phi}(y)\rangle}}. \tag{1}$$

The numerator can be thought of as the score of the correct hypothesis while the denominator is a sum of the scores of all hypotheses. F is a convex function so the optimal parameters can be found using a simple gradient update $\mathbf{w} = \mathbf{w} + \eta \nabla F$, where

$$\nabla F = \mathbf{\Phi}(y_i) - \sum_{y \in \mathbf{GEN}(\cdot)} p_{\mathbf{w}}(y|x_i)\mathbf{\Phi}(y). \tag{2}$$

Thus, GCLM considers all alternative hypotheses in the parameter estimation, while the perceptron algorithm compares only the reference hypothesis and the current best hypothesis under the current model. The perceptron algorithm is typically used for feature selection and model initialization, and from that starting point, GCLM training with a zero mean Gaussian prior on the model parameters has been shown to further improve the model [29].

Ranking Perceptron (PerRank) [37] also considers all alternative hypotheses by comparing each and every pair of hypotheses a and b with the intention that if a has fewer word errors, it must have an inner product score significantly higher than that of b.

Figure 1 shows pseudocodes of the Per and PerRank algorithms as applied in this study. Both algorithms make several passes (T) over the data $(\{1 \leq i \leq I\})$ and in the end, the model weights obtained at each update step are averaged for robustness. The significance multiplier $g(\cdot, \cdot)$ in the update rule is implied by the optimization criterion. Defining this parameter as the edit distance between the two hypotheses leads to a word error rate sensitive update rule [32]. Some other parameters such as the margin constraint multiplier (τ), learning (η) and decay (γ) rates facilitate the convergence of the optimization procedure, and are determined by grid search on a held-out set. For more information on the selection of these parameters, the reader is referred to [12].

```
w = 0, w_sum = 0                    w = 0, w_sum = 0
for t = 1...T, i = 1...I do         for t = 1...T do
    z_i                  =            for i = 1...I do
    argmax_{z∈GEN(·)}⟨w,Φ(z)⟩            for (a,b) ∈ GEN(·) do
    w  +=  g(y_i,z_i)(Φ(y_i) −             if r_a ≻ r_b & ⟨w,Φ(a) − Φ(b)⟩ < τg(a,b)
    Φ(z_i))                                then
    w_sum = w_sum + w                          w += ηg(a,b)(Φ(a) − Φ(b))
return w_avg = w_sum/(IT)                  w_sum = w_sum + w
                                      η = η · γ
                                    return w_avg = w_sum/(IT)
```

Fig. 1. Per and PerRank algorithms

Margin Infused Relaxed Algorithm (MIRA) [10] is an algorithm which trains a model (so called the *prototype*) for each class such that the inner product score of an instance with its class prototype, $\langle \mathbf{w}_{c_i}, \mathbf{\Phi} \rangle$, is higher than the score with any other class prototype. For a two-class problem with $c_i \in \{\pm 1\}$, the binary MIRA iteratively updates a single prototype $\mathbf{w}$, just like the perceptron. The update rule is $\mathbf{w} = \mathbf{w} + \tau_i c_i (\mathbf{\Phi}(y_i) - \mathbf{\Phi}(z_i))$, where, unlike the perceptron, the learning rates τ_i are hypothesis-specific, and are found by solving a quadratic constrained optimization problem. More information on the application of the MIRA algorithm can be found in [13].

Ranking MIRA (MIRArank) [13] follows a similar procedure as in PerRank by updating for each pair of hypotheses that satisfy the margin criterion.

Support Vector Machine (SVM) is a binary linear classifier which aims to find a separating hyperplane that maximizes the margin between the nearest samples of two classes. The constrained optimization problem which covers all training examples j is defined as $\min_{\mathbf{w}} \frac{1}{2} \langle \mathbf{w}, \mathbf{w} \rangle + C \sum_j \xi_j$ subject to $c_j \langle \mathbf{w}, \mathbf{\Phi}(y_j) \rangle \geq 1 - \xi_j$, where $\xi_j \geq 0$ are the slack variables for violations of the margin constraints and C is a user-defined trade-off parameter for its smoothness. The labeling of training examples in an SVM setup is not straightforward. In our implementation, the positive class is composed of the hypotheses having the lowest error rate of their N-best list.

Ranking SVM (SVMrank) [16] is a modification of the classical SVM setup to handle the reranking problem. Here the optimization can be viewed as an SVM classification problem on pairwise difference vectors, $\mathbf{\Phi}(a) - \mathbf{\Phi}(b)$. In that sense, the algorithm tries to find a large margin linear function which minimizes the number of pairs of training examples that need to be swapped to achieve the desired ranking.

4   Training Approaches

The training approaches that will be explained in this section are evaluated on a broadcast news transcription task. Our Turkish Broadcast News Speech and Transcripts Database [2,34] is a collection of around 195 h of Turkish TV and radio channel recordings that are manually transcribed. We use 188 h of this collection for training, and about 3 h each as the held-out (parameter optimization) and test data.

The ASR hypotheses are organized in 50-best lists and represented in morphs as the language modeling unit. There are around 100k sentences and 46k unique morphs in our data set. The feature vector of the linear model, $\mathbf{\Phi}$, consists of morph unigram counts and therefore it is high dimensional but sparse. More information on our baseline system can be found in [2]. On the test set, the generative baseline WER is 22.4 % and the corresponding oracle rate is 13.9 %.

4.1   Supervised Training

The standard way to train a DLM is to use the supervised approach, where all acoustic training data are manually transcribed. In other words, the references

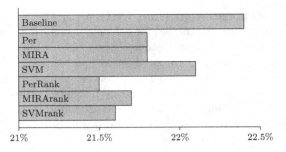

Fig. 2. Supervised training WER (%) for different training algorithms

of the ASR N-best hypotheses must be known beforehand. This allows us to determine their target ranks, which is the key factor in training.

We first examine the performance of supervised training, where DLM makes use of the 188 h of transcribed training data. Figure 2 shows the test set WERs of the six algorithms mentioned in Sect. 3, namely the classification and reranking versions of the perceptron, MIRA, and SVM. More information on how the algorithms are applied can be found in [13].

Figure 2 shows that the ranking variants of all three algorithms perform better than their classification variants, and that PerRank provides the lowest WER, with an improvement of around 1 % over the test baseline. SVMrank comes next, followed by MIRArank. We also see that the accuracies of Per and MIRA are very similar.

4.2   Semi-supervised Training

It is possible to increase the amount of training data by generating new artificial examples from some source text through confusion modeling. This approach as a whole is named semi-supervised training.

A confusion model (CM) is a model which represents the confusions (errors) made by the ASR system. In our study, we train the CM on pairs of the available ASR N-best hypotheses and their reference transcriptions [5]. Each hypothesis is aligned to its reference, resulting in a list of pairs confused by the ASR system together with the probability of confusion.

The artificial examples are generated from a text source which do not need to be associated with any acoustic component, thus is easier to obtain than manually transcribed recordings. Application of the CM yields a lattice of possible hypotheses that could be output by the ASR system if that sentence were to be uttered. The most probable N paths can be used as training data for the DLM training, along with their associated source text as the reference.

4.3   Unsupervised Training

In the case of having a large amount of untranscribed acoustic data, the class/rank of the hypotheses cannot be determined as there is no reference to be compared against. Unsupervised training approach helps DLM training in such a case.

The technique we employ in unsupervised training is to choose a *target output* sequence that will take over the missing reference, by observing the candidates in the N-best list. We explore three ways to generate or choose this word sequence. The first choice is to select the 1-best as the target output, and determining the WE of other hypotheses by aligning each to the 1-best. A second approach is to choose the target output by the Minimum Bayes Risk (MBR) formulation [14,26], which basically aims to determine the hypothesis which is closest to all the others in the N-best list [21]. As a third choice, the MBR approach can also be used on segments of each hypothesis instead of the whole hypothesis, which is named Segmental MBR after [15].

The target output selection approach can be used either to train a DLM or a CM. We refer to these two cases as Unsupervised DLM and Unsupervised CM, which are analogous to the supervised and semi-supervised training, respectively.

4.4 Summary of Experiments on Training Approaches

Table 1 is a summary of possible training approaches explained so far and their test set performances. The second and third columns show what kind of data is used to train the DLM, and if applicable, the CM. Here, A stands for acoustic data which are passed through the ASR system to obtain real hypotheses and T stands for their reference transcriptions. In our experiments, the artificial hypotheses are derived from the manual transcriptions instead of some other source text to be able to compare them to the real ones. The PerRank, which has shown the best performance in Fig. 2, is used for training and the training data is divided into two equal pieces, denoted by the numerical subscripts (A_1, T_2, etc.).

The first part of Table 1 presents the four basic scenarios whereas the second part shows their combinations. We see that the first three scenarios provide significant improvements over the baseline. This suggests that both the derived artificial hypotheses and the chosen target output are effective for training, if

Table 1. PerRank test WER (%) for different training scenarios.

Scenario	CM	DLM	Baseline
Supervised		$(AT)_2$	
Semi-Supervised	$(AT)_1$	T_2	
Unsupervised DLM		A_2	
Unsupervised CM	A_1	T_2	
Sup + Semi-Sup	$(AT)_1$	$(AT)_1 + T_2$	
Sup + Unsup DLM		$(AT)_1 + A_2$	
Unsup DLM + Unsup CM	A_1	$A_1 + T_2$	

21%   21.5%   22%   22.5%

not as effective as the real hypotheses and manual transcriptions. Unsupervised CM approach, on the other hand, does not provide a significant improvement.

The first two combination experiments suggest reusing the CM training data in DLM training, or combining transcribed and untranscribed data, and sets the WER below the 22.0 % line. The advantage of the third experiment is to be able to combine totally unmatched acoustic and textual sources, which still gives an improvement in WER.

5 Conclusion

In this paper we review a decade of discriminative language modeling and summarize the framework, training algorithms and possible training approaches. Discriminative language modeling outperforms the conventional approaches, partly due to the improved parameter estimates with discriminative training and partly due to using features that can reflect complex language characteristics, such as morphology, syntax and semantics. We present the classification and reranking variants of popular training algorithms in the literature, and discuss their advantages and disadvantages. There are several approaches of DLM training with respect to the availability of different data sources, and we investigate the supervised, semi-supervised and unsupervised cases. The results show that reranking techniques outperform classification techniques, and that it is possible to obtain improvements in WER even when the acoustic and text data are coming from different sources, without any manual transcriptions.

Acknowledgments. This research is supported in part by TUBITAK Project numbers 105E102, 109E142 and the Bogazici University Research Fund (BU-BAP) projects 07HA201D, 14A02D3 (D-7948).

References

1. Arisoy, E., Ramabhadran, B., Kuo, H.K.J.: Feature combination approaches for discriminative language models. In: Proceedings of Interspeech, Florence, Italy (2011)
2. Arisoy, E., Can, D., Parlak, S., Sak, H., Saraçlar, M.: Turkish broadcast news transcription and retrieval. IEEE Trans. Audio Speech Lang. Process. **17**(5), 874–883 (2009)
3. Arisoy, E., Saraçlar, M., Roark, B., Shafran, I.: Discriminative language modeling with linguistic and statistically derived features. IEEE Trans. Audio Speech Lang. Process. **20**(2), 540–550 (2012)
4. Bergsma, S., Lin, D., Schuurmans, D.: Improved natural language learning via variance-regularization support vector machines. In: Proceedings of CoNLL, pp. 172–181. CoNLL, Association for Computational Linguistics, Stroudsburg (2010)
5. Çelebi, A., Sak, H., Dikici, E., Saraçlar, M., Lehr, M., Prud'hommeaux, E., Xu, P., Glenn, N., Karakos, D., Khudanpur, S., Roark, B., Sagae, K., Shafran, I., Bikel, D., Callison-Burch, C., Cao, Y., Hall, K., Hasler, E., Koehn, P., Lopez, A., Post, M., Riley, D.: Semi-supervised discriminative language modeling for Turkish ASR. In: Proceedings of ICASSP, pp. 5025–5028 (2012)

6. Chelba, C., Jelinek, F.: Structured language modeling. Comput. Speech Lang. **14**(4), 283–332 (2000)
7. Cherry, C., Quirk, C.: Discriminative, syntactic language modeling through latent SVMs. In: Proceedings of the 8th AMTA Conference, Hawaii, pp. 65–74, October 2008
8. Collins, M.: Discriminative training methods for hidden Markov models: theory and experiments with perceptron algorithms. In: Proceedings of EMNLP, pp. 1–8 (2002)
9. Collins, M., Roark, B., Saraçlar, M.: Discriminative syntactic language modeling for speech recognition. In: ACL, pp. 507–514 (2005)
10. Crammer, K., Singer, Y.: Ultraconservative online algorithms for multiclass problems. J. Mach. Learn. Res. **3**, 951–991 (2003)
11. Creutz, M., Lagus, K.: Unsupervised morpheme segmentation and morphology induction from text corpora using morfessor 1.0. Technical report, Helsinki University of Technology, Palo Alto, CA, Publications in Computer and Information Science Report A81, March 2005
12. Dikici, E., Çelebi, A., Saraçlar, M.: Performance comparison of training algorithms for semi-supervised discriminative language modeling. In: Proceedings of Interspeech, Portland, Oregon, September 2012
13. Dikici, E., Semerci, M., Saraçlar, M., Alpaydın, E.: Classification and ranking approaches to discriminative language modeling for ASR. IEEE Trans. Audio Speech Lang. Process. **21**(2), 291–300 (2013)
14. Goel, V., Bryne, W.: Minimum bayes-risk automatic speech recognition. Comput. Speech Lang. **14**, 115–135 (2000)
15. Goel, V., Kumar, S., Byrne, W.: Segmental minimum bayes-risk ASR voting strategies. In: Proceedings of Interspeech, pp. 139–142 (2000)
16. Joachims, T.: Optimizing search engines using clickthrough data. In: ACM SIGKDD Conference on Knowledge Discovery and Data Mining (KDD), pp. 133–142 (2002)
17. Jyothi, P., Fosler-Lussier, E.: Discriminative language modeling using simulated ASR errors. In: Proceedings of Interspeech, pp. 1049–1052 (2010)
18. Jyothi, P., Johnson, L., Chelba, C., Strope, B.: Distributed discriminative language models for Google voice search. In: Proceedings of ICASSP, pp. 5017–5021 (2012)
19. Khudanpur, S., Wu, J.: Maximum entropy techniques for exploiting syntactic, semantic and collocational dependencies in language modeling. Comput. Speech Lang. **14**, 355–372 (2000)
20. Kirchhoff, K., Vergyri, D., Bilmes, J., Duh, K., Stolcke, A.: Morphology-based language modeling for conversational Arabic speech recognition. Comput. Speech Lang. **20**(4), 589–608 (2006)
21. Kuo, H.K.J., Arisoy, E., Mangu, L., Saon, G.: Minimum bayes risk discriminative language models for Arabic speech recognition. In: Proceedings of ASRU, pp. 208–213 (2011)
22. Kurata, G., Sethy, A., Ramabhadran, B., Rastrow, A., Itoh, N., Nishimura, M.: Acoustically discriminative language model training with pseudo-hypothesis. Speech Commun. **54**(2), 219–228 (2012)
23. Lehr, M., Shafran, I.: Learning a discriminative weighted finite-state transducer for speech recognition. IEEE Trans. Audio Speech Lang. Process. **19**(5), 1360–1367 (2011)
24. Li, Z., Khudanpur, S.: Large-scale discriminative n-gram language models for statistical machine translation. In: Proceedings of the 8th AMTA Conference, Hawaii, pp. 133–142, October 2008

25. Li, Z., Wang, Z., Khudanpur, S., Eisner, J.: Unsupervised discriminative language model training for machine translation using simulated confusion sets. In: Coling 2010, Posters, Beijing, China, pp. 656–664, August 2010
26. Mangu, L., Brill, E., Stolcke, A.: Finding consensus in speech recognition: word error minimization and other applications of confusion networks. Comput. Speech Lang. **14**, 373–400 (2000)
27. McDonald, R., Crammer, K., Pereira, F.: Online large-margin training of dependency parsers. In: Proceedings of ACL, pp. 91–98. ACL, Association for Computational Linguistics, Stroudsburg (2005)
28. Roark, B.: Probabilistic top-down parsing and language modeling. Comput. Linguist. **27**(2), 249–276 (2001)
29. Roark, B., Saraçlar, M., Collins, M.: Discriminative n-gram language modeling. Comput. Speech Lang. **21**(2), 373–392 (2007)
30. Rosenfeld, R., Chen, S.F., Zhu, X.: Whole-sentence exponential language models: a vehicle for linguistic-statistical integration. Comput. Speech Lang. **15**(1), 55–73 (2001)
31. Sagae, K., Lehr, M., Prud'hommeaux, E.T., Xu, P., Glenn, N., Karakos, D., Khudanpur, S., Roark, B., Saralar, M., Shafran, I., Bikel, D., Callison-Burch, C., Cao, Y., Hall, K., Hasler, E., Koehn, P., Lopez, A., Post, M., Riley, D.: Hallucinated N-best lists for discriminative language modeling. In: Proceedings of ICASSP (2012)
32. Sak, H., Saraçlar, M., Gungor, T.: Morpholexical and discriminative language models for Turkish automatic speech recognition. IEEE Trans. Audio Speech Lang. Process. **20**(8), 2341–2351 (2012)
33. Saraçlar, M., Roark, B.: Joint discriminative language modeling and utterance classification. In: IEEE International Conference on Acoustics, Speech, and Signal Processing (ICASSP), vol. 1, pp. 561–564, 18–23 March 2005
34. Saraçlar, M.: Turkish broadcast news speech and transcripts LDC2012S06, Philadelphia, Linguistic Data Consortium, Web Download (2012)
35. Sarikaya, R., Afify, M., Deng, Y., Erdogan, H., Gao, Y.: Joint morphological-lexical language modeling for processing morphologically rich languages with application to dialectal Arabic. IEEE Trans. Audio Speech Lang. Process. **16**(7), 1330–1339 (2008)
36. Shafran, I., Hall, K.: Corrective models for speech recognition of inflected languages. In: Proceedings of EMNLP, Sydney, Australia, pp. 390–398 (2006)
37. Shen, L., Joshi, A.K.: Ranking and reranking with perceptron. Mach. Learn. **60**, 73–96 (2005)
38. Singh-Miller, N., Collins, C.: Trigger-based language modeling using a loss-sensitive perceptron algorithm. In: Proceedings of ICASSP, vol. 4, pp. IV-25–IV-28, April 2007
39. Tan, Q., Audhkhasi, K., Georgiou, P., Ettelaie, E., Narayanan, S.: Automatic speech recognition system channel modeling. In: Proceedings of Interspeech, pp. 2442–2445 (2010)
40. Watanabe, T., Suzuki, J., Tsukada, H., Isozaki, H.: Online large-margin training for statistical machine translation. In: Proceedings of EMNLP-CoNLL, pp. 764–773, June 2007
41. Xu, P., Karakos, D., Khudanpur, S.: Self-supervised discriminative training of statistical language models. In: Proceedings of ASRU, pp. 317–322 (2009)
42. Zhou, Z., Gao, J., Soong, F., Meng, H.: A comparative study of discriminative methods for reranking LVCSR n-best hypotheses in domain adaptation and generalization. In: Proceedings of ICASSP, pp. 141–144 (2006)

Conference Papers

A Bilingual Kazakh-Russian System
for Automatic Speech Recognition and Synthesis

Olga Khomitsevich[1,2], Valentin Mendelev[1,2], Natalia Tomashenko[1,2]([✉]),
Sergey Rybin[2], Ivan Medennikov[2,3], and Saule Kudubayeva[4]

[1] Speech Technology Center, Saint Petersburg, Russia
{khomitsevich,mendelev,tomashenko-n,medennikov}@speechpro.com
[2] ITMO University, Saint Petersburg, Russia
rybin@speechpro.com
[3] STC-innovations Ltd., Saint Petersburg, Russia
[4] Kostanay State University named after A. Baytursynov, Kostanay, Kazakhstan
saule.kudubayeva@gmail.com

Abstract. The paper presents a system for speech recognition and synthesis for the Kazakh and Russian languages. It is designed for use by speakers of Kazakh; due to the prevalence of bilingualism among Kazakh speakers, it was considered essential to design a bilingual Kazakh-Russian system. Developing our system involved building a text processing and transcription system that deals with both Kazakh and Russian text, and is used in both speech synthesis and recognition applications. We created a Kazakh TTS voice and an additional Russian voice using the recordings of the same bilingual voice artist. A Kazakh speech database was collected and used to train deep neural network acoustic models for the speech recognition system. The resulting models demonstrated sufficient performance for practical applications in interactive voice response and keyword spotting scenarios.

Keywords: Speech recognition · Speech synthesis · ASR · TTS · Kazakh

1 Introduction

This paper describes an Automatic Speech Recognition (ASR) and Text-to-Speech (TTS) system designed for Kazakh speakers. Due to the fact that most Kazakh speakers are bilingual, and Kazakh texts and speech often contain fragments in Russian, we decided to create a bilingual Kazakh-Russian system. The TTS system we designed includes text processing and transcription modules capable of dealing with both Kazakh and Russian text, in particular with Russian borrowings in Kazakh. These modules are also used by the ASR system. We also created two TTS voices using the same bilingual female voice artist: a Kazakh voice and a Russian voice.

A Kazakh speech database, containing read and spontaneous speech, was collected and used to train a bilingual ASR system for Interactive Voice Response

© Springer International Publishing Switzerland 2015
A. Ronzhin et al. (Eds.): SPECOM 2015, LNAI 9319, pp. 25–33, 2015.
DOI: 10.1007/978-3-319-23132-7_3

(IVR) and Keyword Spotting (KWS) scenarios. The ASR system employs the TTS transcription module to generate phonetic transcriptions. A Context-Dependent Deep Neural Network Hidden Markov Models (DNN-HMM) architecture is implemented for acoustic model training.

This paper is organized as follows. Section 2 describes the challenges that the Kazakh language presents for the ASR and TTS tasks. Section 3 describes our TTS system. An overview of our ASR system and the results of recognition experiments are given in Sect. 4. Section 5 concludes the paper.

2   The Kazakh Language

Kazakh presents several challenges to Natural Language Processing (NLP) tasks and the development of speech technologies for this language. One is that few language resources, such as lexicons, corpora or NLP software, are available for Kazakh. It can thus be considered an underresourced language, and applications such as speech recognition and synthesis have to be built virtually from scratch (for instance, we could only find very basic Kazakh ASR systems described in the literature [1,2]).

Another, more important problem is the problem of bilingualism and interference with the Russian language. Kazakh is a Turkic language that is the state language of the former Soviet republic of Kazakhstan. The country gained independence in 1991 following the collapse of the Soviet Union, however Russian remains the second official language of the Kazakh state, and its role is still very prominent. Russian continues to be widely used in education, especially higher education, in the media, by state institutions, etc., and the majority of Kazakh speakers are bilingual [3,4].

The consequences of this sociolinguistic situation from the NLP perspective are twofold. Firstly, code switching and language interference are very common in Kazakh speech. It is typical for Kazakh texts or conversational speech to incorporate phrases in Russian or to switch from one language to the other, sometimes mid-sentence. This is an important challenge for speech recognition: an efficient ASR system for Kazakh designed to work in real-life situations needs in fact to be a bilingual system, recognizing both Kazakh and Russian speech without the need for special tuning in either case.

Secondly, Kazakh has accumulated a large amount of borrowings from Russian. That has especially important consequences for Kazakh TTS applications. Kazakh words follow the laws of vowel harmony, and for the overwhelming majority of word forms the stress is fixed on the final syllable of the word. Borrowed Russian words differ from Kazakh words in many respects. The most important one for us is that Russian does not have fixed word stress, in fact stress can fall on any syllable of the word. The unstressed vowels undergo both qualitative and quantitative reduction: in particular, the phonemes $/o/$ and $/e/$ are not pronounced in unstressed positions and are replaced by $/a/$ and $/i/$, respectively, though they are still written as $/o/$ and $/e/$. In contrast, Kazakh vowels do not undergo this type of reduction. It follows that Russian borrowings in Kazakh text need to be detected and transcribed accordingly. Russian words also contain phonemes not present in original Kazakh words, resulting in an increase in the number of phonemes needed for transcription. The way we deal with these problems is described in the next section.

3   Speech Synthesis and Transcription for Kazakh

Building a Kazakh TTS system involves a number of stereotypical steps. The text needs to be normalized, which means detecting words and sentences, processing non-standard words such as numbers, abbreviations, Latin script, etc. The resulting normalized text is then transcribed, and synthesized speech is formed. The Kazakh TTS system described here is a hybrid TTS system based on Unit Selection (US) algorithms and HMM intonation modeling [5,6], and is part of the VitalVoice TTS developed at Speech Technology Center Ltd. The text processing modules built for TTS, namely, text normalization and transcription, are also used in the ASR application. The tools we developed for these modules are described below.

3.1   Dictionary and POS Tagging

Kazakh belongs to Turkic languages and displays their typical properties [7,8]. It is an agglutinative language with highly regular morphology, where a sequence of affixes is added to a stem in strict succession in order to construct numerous inflectional forms. To help solve the task of text processing for Kazakh, we considered it essential to build a dictionary including a vocabulary of stems and an inventory of inflectional affixes. These tools are used in several ways. First, the affixes are added to non-standard words in writing (for example, 17-ші stands for он жетінші "seventeenth") so we need to detect them in order to process those words. Second, in most Kazakh words, stress falls on the final syllable, however a few affixes, such as the negative verb affix ма/ме/ба/бе/па/пе and its combinations, or the adjectival affix дай/дей/тай/тей do not take stress. Consequently, to predict stress placement, we need to detect affixes and also to resolve Part-of-Speech (POS) homonymy. Finally, common Russian borrowings need to be included in the dictionary; since they are routinely used with Kazakh affixes, it is also important to detect the affix for correct transcription.

Our Kazakh dictionary is organized in the following way. An entry in the vocabulary of stems contains the stem of a word together with its POS label or labels and, if applicable, the "Russian word" label, as well as the stressed syllable number for Russian words. As for affix detection, we should note that in Kazakh each grammatical function is represented by its own affix. The affix sequences can grow very long, and it is virtually impossible to compile a complete set of all possible combinations. However, for the sake of computational simplicity, we did not opt for a full morphological analysis, instead we made a list of common affix combinations and treated each as a separate affix. The affix lexicon thus contains a list of about 6700 affixes together with their POS labels. During text processing, each word form is split into stem and affix (if any) and assigned a POS label based on stem and affix label matching. Several basic context-based homonymy resolution rules are added to deal with remaining POS disambiguation.

3.2 Building Transcription Rules and Synthesizing Speech

Kazakh writing is based on the Cyrillic alphabet, with the addition of several specific letters [8]. It is a relatively straightforward phonemic orthography, so we decided to opt for rule-based transcription of Kazakh words. We developed a set of letter-to-phoneme rewriting rules, taking into account assimilation laws. It is important to note that these rules are only applicable to original Kazakh words. For Russian borrowings, a separate letter-to-phoneme transcription rule set had to be added, resulting in virtually two rule sets in one algorithm. The set of phonemes used in our TTS/ASR system consists of 59 phonemes, including both original Kazakh phonemes and those that only occur in Russian borrowings.

Consequently, an important step in our system is to determine which set of transcription rules we need to apply to a particular word, that is, whether or not it belongs to Russian borrowings. As noted in Sect. 3.1, frequently used Russian borrowings are included in the lexicon with the corresponding label. For out-of-vocabulary (OOV) words, this decision is made based on the letters and letter combinations occurring in the word. Thus, we look for specific letters that do not occur in original Kazakh words, such as ф, ч, э, for sequences of consonants at the beginning of the word, for consonant clusters typical for Russian, such as вск, ств, стр, and so on. Once the borrowed word is detected, a special tag is assigned to it for use in the subsequent processing modules.

An important issue is detecting the correct stress in Russian borrowings. We were not able to find any reference to this problem in the literature, which only describes stress in original Kazakh words. However, from our analysis and our interviews with Kazakh speakers we were able to conclude that the majority of Russian borrowings retain the stress they have in the source language. However, when a Kazakh affix is added to the Russian word, the rule that the stress shifts to the final syllable also applies. What happens is that the main stress remains on the stem, while the final syllable of the affix receives auxiliary stress, except for words that have the stress on the final syllable of the stem: in those cases the main stress shifts to the affix while the stem retains an auxiliary stress. We took this observation as the rule of thumb to be used in our TTS system, although this problem calls for further phonetic study. A remaining issue is detecting stress placement in OOV words detected as Russian borrowings. We developed a set of rules for stress placement in the detected Russian words based on the final combinations of letters in these words.

Finally, a few words need to be said about the recording process of the US database. We used a phonetically balanced Kazakh text that included a number of common Russian borrowings, and we also added a phonetically balanced Russian text to be read by the same voice artist (who was bilingual). The Russian borrowings and all the words in the Russian part of the voice database were then labeled with the special "ru" label. During synthesis, if a word in the input text

Table 1. Contents of recordings

Content	Type
Credit card numbers	Reading
Telephone numbers	Reading
Cities	Reading
Countries	Reading
Street names	Reading
Surnames	Reading
Commands	Reading
Dates	Reading
Phonetically rich sentences	Reading
Bio	Spontaneous
Current date and time	Spontaneous
General questions	Spontaneous

is detected as a Russian borrowing, the diphones from the "ru"-labeled words are preferably used for it in the Unit Selection process. In addition to that, a separate TTS voice was built using only the Russian part of the voice database. This voice can be used in conjunction with the Russian VitalVoice TTS engine if a purely Russian text needs to be synthesized using the same voice as in the Kazakh TTS.

4 Automatic Speech Recognition for Kazakh

4.1 The Speech Database

The Kazakh speech database used for ASR training was collected at Speech Technology Center Ltd. It comprises 780 sessions recorded over GSM and land-line telephone networks in Kazakhstan. Each session is approximately 15 min long and contains speech of one native Kazakh speaker. Each speaker participated in exactly one session, so the total number of speakers is 780, of which 392 were female and 388 were male. The contents of the recordings are described in Table 1. The total duration of the database is 147 h. About 120 h from this database were chosen for acoustic model training. The word "Bio" in Table 1 denotes the situation when the speaker was asked to produce a short spontaneous description of his or her biography.

4.2 Acoustic Models

In this section we present our setup for the acoustic models. We trained Deep Neural Network Hidden Markov Models (DNN-HMM) acoustic models [9], and followed the concept of cross-language knowledge transfer [10,11], in which we used the Russian speech corpus to improve the performance of Kazakh acoustic models. More specifically, the target language (Kazakh) network was initialized with an existing source (Russian) network. Our preliminary results showed that using both Russian and Kazakh datasets significantly improved the performance of acoustic models in comparison with the system trained only on the Kazakh dataset.

We trained all models using our proprietary tools and Kaldi speech recognition toolkit [12]. For each language, we first built two standard maximum-likelihood (ML) trained GMM-HMM systems, using 39-dimensional Mel-frequency cepstral coefficients (MFCC) features (C0-C12, with delta and acceleration coefficients). The number of context-dependent triphone states was 1500 for Russian, and 4100 for Kazakh. Then, using the obtained state tying [13] we trained two DNN-HMM models, as shown in Fig. 1. Input features for these DNNs were 13-dimensional MFCC with Cepstral Mean Normalization (CMN), spliced in time taking a context size of 31 frames (i.e., ±15). The resulting 403-dimensional features were used to train Russian and Kazakh DNNs.

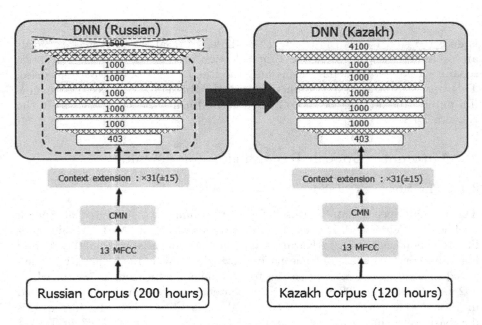

Fig. 1. DNN-HMM acoustic model training for Kazakh based on transfer learning using Russian speech data

The first DNN was trained using the data only from the Russian corpus. It had 5 hidden layers with 1000 neurons in each layer and a softmax layer with 1500 senons, corresponding to tied states of the Russian GMM-HMM. The DNN was trained with pre-training using the standard back propagation algorithm with cross entropy error criteria. Then the softmax layer of this DNN was replaced with the softmax layer (with 4100 senones) corresponding to the Kazakh language, and the resulting DNN was finetuned on the Kazakh corpus using several iterations of sequence-discriminative training with state-level Minimum Bayes Risk (sMBR) criterion [14].

4.3 Experiments

In this section we present the experimental results for the IVR and KWS scenarios. To test the system, 40 recordings from the recorded speech database were chosen randomly and were not used in training. In-grammar (IG) sets were composed from the test recordings for "Yes/No", "Cities" and "Surnames" grammars. All the grammars had a linear list structure and contained 2, 135 and 230 items respectively. Out-of-grammar (OOG) sets were made artificially to mimic real conditions. All sets except "Yes/No" included both Kazakh and Russian words. The results for the IVR scenario in terms of equal error rate (EER) are presented in Table 2. The network described in Sect. 4.2 is referred as DNN-2 in the tables below. For comparison purposes, we also trained another DNN acoustic model (denoted as "DNN-1") using only the Kazakh corpus. It had a topology similar to DNN-2, and was trained in a similar way, except the pre-training stage: layer-wise pre-training based on Restricted Boltzmann Machines (RBM) [15] was performed on Kazakh speech data.

Table 2. Equal error rates (%) for the IVR task

	Yes/no	Cities	Surnames
DNN-1	–	22	19
DNN-2	2,3	15	10

For the keyword spotting task, spontaneous parts of the test recordings were used with target word lists consisting of 10 and 100 items. The KWS results are presented in Table 3.

Table 3. Equal error rates (%) for the KWS task

	10 words	100 words
DNN-1	18	29
DNN-2	13	20

As evident from Tables 2 and 3, DNN-2 achieves significantly lower error rates compared with DNN-1. It should be noted that the observed Kazakh language ASR performance is weaker than that of our Russian language system but is high enough for practical applications.

5   Conclusions and Future Work

In this paper we presented a bilingual Kazakh-Russian TTS and ASR system. The TTS system includes both a Kazakh and a Russian voice based on the voice of the same bilingual voice artist, and tools for processing Kazakh and Russian text. The ASR system was trained on approximately 147 h of Kazakh speech and tested on IVR and KWS scenarios. The system is well suited for applications targeted at Kazakh speakers, who often use both Kazakh and Russian languages interchangeably.

In the future, we plan to record a second (male) Kazakh TTS voice for our system, and to continue enhancing the text processing and transcription modules of the TTS system in order to get rid of remaining processing errors. As for ASR, the development of a large vocabulary continuous speech recognition system for Kazakh language is the next obvious goal, and work in this direction is now in progress.

Acknowledgments. The work was financially supported by the Government of the Russian Federation, Grant 074-U01.

References

1. Karabalaeva, M., Sharipbaev, A.: Algorithms for phone-based recognition of kazakh speech in the amplitude-time space. In: Proceedings of 2nd All-Russian Conference "Knowledge-Ontology-Theories", Novosibirsk, Russia (2009) (in Russian)
2. Buribayeva, A., Sharipbay, A.: The advantage of interphoneme processing at diphone recognition of Kazakh words. Türkiye Bilişim Vakfı Bilgisayar Bilimleri ve Mühendisliği Dergisi 8(8) (2014)
3. Pavlenko, A.: Russian in post-Soviet countries. Russ. linguist. **32**(1), 59–80 (2008)
4. Pavlenko, A.: Multilingualism in post-Soviet countries: language revival, language removal, and sociolinguistic theory. Int. J. Biling. Educ. Biling. **11**(3–4), 275–314 (2008)
5. Chistikov, P.G., Korolkov, E.A., Talanov, A.O.: Combining HMM and unit selection technologies to increase naturalness of synthesized speech. In: Computational Linguistics and Intellectual Technologies: Proceedings of the International Conference "Dialog 2013", vol. 2, pp. 2–10 (2013)
6. Chistikov, P., Zakharov, D., Talanov, A.: Improving speech synthesis quality for voices created from an audiobook database. In: Ronzhin, A., Potapova, R., Delic, V. (eds.) SPECOM 2014. LNCS, vol. 8773, pp. 276–283. Springer, Heidelberg (2014)
7. Musaev, K.M.: The Kazakh Language. Russian Academy of Sciences, Moscow (2008). (in Russian)
8. Makhambetov, O., Makazhanov, A., Yessenbayev, Z., Matkarimov, B., Sabyr-galiyev, I., Sharafudinov, A.: Assembling the Kazakh Language Corpus. In: EMNLP, pp. 1022–1031 (2013)
9. Hinton, G., Deng, L., Yu, D., Dahl, G.E., Mohamed, A.R., Jaitly, N., Kingsbury, B.: Deep neural networks for acoustic modeling in speech recognition: the shared views of four research groups. IEEE Signal Process. Mag. **29**(6), 82–97 (2012)

10. Thomas, S., Ganapathy, S., Jansen, A., Hermansky, H.: Data-driven posterior features for low resource speech recognition applications. In: Proceedings of Interspeech (2012)
11. Huang, J.T., Li, J., Yu, D., Deng, L., Gong, Y.: Cross-language knowledge transfer using multilingual deep neural network with shared hidden layers. In: Proceedings of ICASSP 2013, pp. 7304–7308. IEEE (2013)
12. Povey, D., Ghoshal, A., Boulianne, G., Burget, L., Glembek, O., Goel, N., Vesel, K.: The Kaldi speech recognition toolkit (2011)
13. Chernykh, G., Korenevsky, M., Levin, K., Ponomareva, I., Tomashenko, N.: State level control for acoustic model training. In: Ronzhin, A., Potapova, R., Delic, V. (eds.) SPECOM 2014. LNCS, vol. 8773, pp. 435–442. Springer, Heidelberg (2014)
14. Kingsbury, B.: Lattice-based optimization of sequence classification criteria for neural-network acoustic modeling. In: ICASSP 2009, pp. 3761–3764. IEEE (2009)
15. Hinton, G.E.: A practical guide to training restricted Boltzmann machines. Technical Report UTML TR 2010–003, Deptartment of Computer Science, University of Toronto (2010)

A Comparative Study of Speech Processing in Microphone Arrays with Multichannel Alignment and Zelinski Post-Filtering

Sergei Aleinik[1(✉)] and Mikhail Stolbov[1,2]

[1] ITMO University, 49 Kronverkskiy Pr., St. Petersburg 197101, Russia
{aleinik,stolbov}@speechpro.com
[2] Speech Technology Center, Krasutskogo-4, St. Petersburg 196084, Russia

Abstract. In this paper we present the results of a comparative study of algorithms for speech signal processing in a microphone array. We compared the multichannel alignment method and two modifications of the well-known Zelinski post-filtering. Comparisons were performed using artificial and real signals recorded in real noisy environments. The experiments helped us to devise recommendations for choosing a suitable method of signal processing for different noise conditions.

Keywords: Microphone array · Zelinski · Post-filtering · Directivity pattern · Speech processing

1 Introduction

The Fixed Beam Forming (FBF) method is the basic method for controlling the look direction of microphone arrays [7]. FBF is usually provided by Delay & Sum (D&S) or Filter & Sum algorithms. It is well-known that FBF does not have the best characteristics when the signal being processed is speech [7]. As a result of that, many additional adaptive methods for speech signal processing in microphone arrays (MA) have been developed. These methods improve the MA directivity patterns (DP), increase the noise reduction (NR) level, etc. One of the widely used methods is Zelinski post-filtering [6,8,9,11]. It is claimed that Zelinski post-filtering is good for spatially uncorrelated noise suppression and works less well in the case of spatially correlated noise [6]. In [2,10] a novel method called "Multichannel alignment" (MCA) has been proposed and investigated in details. This method suppresses both spatially correlated and uncorrelated noises. In the present work we compare multichannel alignment method and two modifications of Zelinski post-filters (ZPF).

Let us define the implementation of the ZPF as it given in [6] (we changed some of the notation):

$$W_z(f,k) = \text{HR}\left\{ \frac{C_N Re\left[\sum_{n=0}^{N-2}\sum_{m=n+1}^{N-1}\langle \Phi_{Y_n Y_m}(f,k)\rangle\right]}{\frac{1}{N}\sum_{n=0}^{N-1}\langle \Phi_{Y_n Y_n}(f,k)\rangle + \delta} \right\}, \quad (1)$$

© Springer International Publishing Switzerland 2015
A. Ronzhin et al. (Eds.): SPECOM 2015, LNAI 9319, pp. 34–41, 2015.
DOI: 10.1007/978-3-319-23132-7_4

where: $W_z(f, k)$ is the filter transfer function; f is the discrete frequency index; k is the frame index; $Y_n(f, k)$ is the frequency-domain signal of the n-th microphone ($n = 0, N - 1$) at the output of the delay compensation block [2]; operator $\langle \cdot \rangle$ is the exponential smoothing over frames; $Re[\cdot]$ marks the real part; $HR\{x\} = \max\{x,\ 0\}$ is the rectification operator; and $C_N = 2/(N^2 - N)$ is the normalization factor.

The smoothed cross-spectra $\langle \Phi_{Y_n Y_m}(f, k) \rangle$ are calculated as follows [6]:

$$\langle \Phi_{Y_n Y_m}(f, k) \rangle = \alpha \langle \Phi_{Y_n Y_m}(f, k - 1) \rangle + (1 - \alpha) Y_n(f, k) Y_m^*(f, k), \qquad (2)$$

where $0 \leq \alpha < 1$ is the smoothing constant. The parameter δ in (1) is the small "regularization constant". This constant is absent in the Zelinski post-filter formula in [6], but it is common to add such a constant in the denominators "to prevent division by too small value" [1].

The frequency-domain output signal of the MA with a Zelinski post-filter $Z(f, k)$ is created by multiplication of the transfer function and the normalized sum of the $Y_n(f, k)$ signals, i.e. first the output of the FBF algorithm is calculated:

$$Y_{FBF}(f, k) = \frac{1}{N} \sum_{n=0}^{N-1} Y_n(f, k) \qquad (3)$$

and then the MA output $Z(f, k)$ is calculated as follows:

$$Z(f, k) = W_z(f, k) Y_{FBF}(f, k). \qquad (4)$$

In [9] it is claimed that using (1) "we get a good noise suppression but on the other hand a linear distortion of the desired signal". To avoid this effect, Simmer and Wasiljeff [9] proposed another formula:

$$W_{sw}(f, k) = \frac{C_N \sum_{n=0}^{N-2} \sum_{m=n+1}^{N-1} Re\left\{\Phi_{Y_n Y_m}(f, k)\right\}}{\left| \frac{1}{N} \sum_{n=0}^{N-1} Y_n(f, k) \right|^2} \qquad (5)$$

In (5) there is no smoothing and the operator $Re[\ \cdot\ ]$ is placed inside the sum, but these differences are not critical. The most fundamental differences are: first, in (5) there is no rectification $HR\{\cdot\}$; second, in (5) the denominator contains the power spectrum of the output FBF signal (3) (in contrast to (1) where the denominator contains the sum of the power spectra of the delayed input signals). In our opinion, in some cases these two differences lead to bad performance of (5).

Consider Fig. 1 which shows the DP for an 8-microphone MA (inter- microphone spacing is 5 cm) with FBF and Zelinski SW post-filtering [9]. The DP was obtained in simulation for an artificial harmonical input signal with the frequency of 2000 Hz. It can be seen that when the FBF output value is small (and, correspondingly, the denominator in (5) is small) the DP of the Zelinski SW method has high bursts of large amplitude, which is absolutely unacceptable. We found that the rectification operator $HR\{\cdot\}$ is able to improve (5). The fact is that the numerator of (5) becomes negative when the absolute value of the

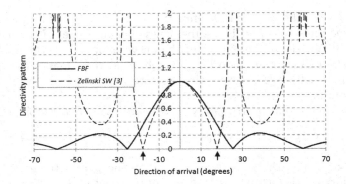

Fig. 1. Directivity patterns for an artificial harmonical input signal of 2000 Hz.

direction of arrival exceeds the "first DP null" angle (these angles are showed in Fig. 1 by the "up" arrows). Correspondingly, using HR{·} we set the Zelinski SW DP bursts to zero. Hence, we modified the Zelinski SW [9] (we added smoothing and a rectification operator, and left the power spectrum of the output FBF signal (3) in the denominator) as follows:

$$
W_{zm}(f,k) = \mathrm{HR} \left\{ \frac{C_N Re \left[\sum_{n=0}^{N-2} \sum_{m=n+1}^{N-1} \langle \Phi_{Y_n Y_m}(f,k) \rangle \right]}{\left\langle \left| \frac{1}{N} \sum_{n=0}^{N-1} Y_n(f,k) \right|^2 \right\rangle + \delta} \right\}, \qquad (6)
$$

In [2,10] a new multichannel alignment (MCA) method has been proposed. In this method, first, not a single but N transfer functions are calculated as follows:

$$
H_n(f,k) = \frac{\langle \Phi_{Y_n Y_{FBF}}(f,k) \rangle}{\langle \Phi_{Y_n Y_n}(f,k) \rangle + \delta}, \quad n = 0, N-1. \qquad (7)
$$

and then the frequency-domain output signal is calculated as:

$$
Z_a(f,k) = \frac{1}{N} \sum_{n=0}^{N-1} H_n(f,k) Y_n(f,k) \qquad (8)
$$

In the present paper we compare these three methods: (1), (6) and (7–8).

2   Experiments and Results

In our experiments we used the MA fully described in [2] an linear equidistant microphone array with 8 microphones and inter-microphone spacing of 5 cm (i.e. the total aperture length is 35 cm).We used sampling frequency of 16 kHz and the well-known Overlap-and-Add (OLA) technique with the frame length of 512 samples, 50 % overlapping and a Hann window. We chose the smoothing constant $\alpha = 0.75$. For every method we estimated:

1. MA directivity patterns for an artificial harmonical signal $f = 2000\,\text{Hz}$.
2. MA directivity patterns for artificial wide-band noise $f = [300, 5600]\,\text{Hz}$.
3. Spectrograms of the output signals in a real experiment with human speech and high-level coherent noise in an office.
4. Noise reduction level for artificial incoherent and real combined (coherent & diffuse) noise.

2.1 MA Directivity Patterns

MA directivity patterns for a harmonical signal with the frequency $f = 2000\,\text{Hz}$ for the FBF method and three adaptive methods (1), (6) and (7–8) are shown in Fig. 2.

All adaptive methods have better performance than FBF: the main lobes are narrower and the sidelobes are smaller. First we should point out that the MCA method [2, 10] gives the narrowest main lobe. Second, for both Zelinski post-filters (1) and (6) sidelobes are completely absent. This means that we have (starting from a certain angle) infinite suppression of spatially correlated harmonical interference.

The second conclusion is a surprise, because many authors claim that the Zelinski filter "is based on the assumption that the noise is spatially uncorrelated" [11], and further: "both filters (meaning (1) and (6) in the present paper) suffer from insufficient noise reduction in the case of correlated noises" [11]. The same property is described in [8] and many other papers.

On the other hand, physical causes of the "infinite suppression property" for a model harmonical signal are understandable. When such a signal comes from the look direction, there are no phase shifts between the signals from the microphones in the array. In this case $W_z(f, k) = W_{sw}(f, k) = 1$ and output signal suppression is absent. The more the look direction differs from the direction of arrival, the more phase shifts appear. Correspondingly, the value inside the braces in (1) and (6) is decreasing and at the end become negative. Thus the rectification operator $\text{HR}\{\cdot\}$ leads to $W_z(f, k) = W_{sw}(f, k) = 0$, i.e. to infinite suppression.

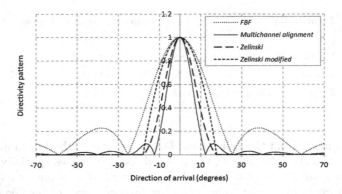

Fig. 2. Directivity patterns for an artificial harmonical input signal of 2000 Hz.

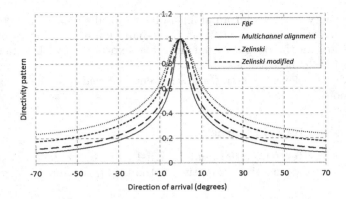

Fig. 3. Directivity patterns for artificial coherent wide-band noise.

DPs when the input signal is wide-band noise (we choose noise with a constant power spectrum in the range 300–5600 Hz) are shown in Fig. 3.

It can be seen that in the case of wide-band noise, the DP of a MA with MCA algorithm [2, 10] is the best in comparison with the remaining three methods. A MA with the Zelinski method gives slightly worse results. We can also see that because the phase of the signals on the microphones fluctuates randomly, there is no "infinite suppression property" in this case.

2.2 Incoherent and Coherent Noise Reduction Level

As a model of spatially incoherent noise we chose artificial independent white noise. To get "combined noise" we used music signals recorded in a real reverberant environment (see Sect. 2.3 for the description). Noise reduction levels are shown in Table 1.

Table 1. Noise reduction levels, dB.

Algorithm	Incoherent noise	Combined noise
FBF	9.03	8.11
Multichannel alignment	25.88	**14.13**
Zelinski	**39.58**	14.03
Zelinski modified	24.37	11.18

Table 1 confirms that the Zelinski method is the best method to suppress incoherent noise. On the other hands, the method also suppresses spatially coherent noise, but at a significantly lower level. In our opinion, it is necessary to agree with the statement in [7] that "The post-filter further enhances the beamformer's rejection of *coherent* correlated or uncorrelated noise sources not emanating from

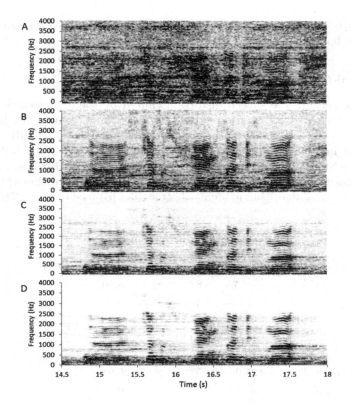

Fig. 4. Processing of speech + spatially coherent noise. (A) initial mixture, (B) FBF, (C) Multichannel alignment, (D) Zelinski method.

the steered direction", although in [7] the rectification operator HR{·} is also absent as in [9] and [8]. At the same time an MA with MCA method [2,10] demonstrates almost the same performance in coherent noise reduction, but is not so good for incoherent noise suppression.

2.3   Spectrograms of the Processed Speech Signal

In an office room (13 x 6 x 3 m, reverberation time 660 ms) we conducted the following experiment. The target speaker (male) was situated at $\varphi_s = 15°$ with respect to the perpendicular to MA and at a distance of $D_s = 4$ m. The interfering noise (music) was generated by a high quality load speaker ($\varphi_n = -56°$, $D_n = 5$ m). Signal-to-Noise ratio at the input of the MA was −6 dB. The signals from every MA microphone were sampled at the 16 kHz frequency and recorded on a computer hard drive. Then these signals were used as the input signals of the MA.

Spectrograms of the initial mixture and the processing results are shown in Fig. 4. It can be seen that MCA and Zelinski methods give almost similar results

(Zelinski is better for incoherent noise suppression – the spectrogram D has a lighter gray background).

2.4 Signal-to-Deviation Ratio

In order to measure the speech distortion caused by the enhancement process we evaluated Signal-to-Deviation ratio (SDR) as function of input Signal-to-Noise ratio (SNR) [5] (the higher is the SDR the better is the algorithm). SDR for different input SNR and enhanced algorithms is shown in Table 2. Table 2 confirms the statement given in [5] that in terms of signal distortion modified Zelinski algorithm (6) is better than "classical" Zelinski algorithm (1). On the other hands, MCA algorithm is slightly better than (6) when input SNR is small.

Table 2. Signal-to-Deviation ratio, dB.

Input SNR	FBF	MCA	Zelinski	Zelinski modified
$-15\,$dB	-1.75	5.84	5.12	5.10
$-10\,$dB	3.66	9.48	7.95	9.32
$-5\,$dB	9.13	12.95	11.10	13.35
$0\,$dB	14.57	16.53	14.63	17.37
$5\,$dB	19.90	20.36	18.59	21.54
$10\,$dB	25.09	24.57	23.06	25.94
$15\,$dB	30.15	29.13	28.04	30.54

3   Conclusions

In this paper we compare three methods for improvement of MA directivity and noise reduction level: Zelinski post-filtering [6] (1), modified Zelinski post-filtering (6) based on the method given in [9], and the MCA method proposed in [2,10]. We confirmed that Zelinski post-filtering gives the best result in incoherent noise suppression. At the same time Zelinski post-filtering demonstrates "infinite suppression property" for model harmonical signals and good performance in combined noise suppression. MCA has the best DP and gives the best results in combined noise suppression. We also conclude that modified Zelinski post-filtering (6) is worse than MCA and Zelinski methods. A more detailed study of these methods in relation to output speech quality (i.e. speech distortion level, etc.) as well as the study of the possibility of using MAs with the described methods in multimodal [3] or speaker verification [4] systems can be the subjects of future research.

Acknowledgements. This work was financially supported by the Ministry of Education and Science of the Russian Federation, contract 14.575.21.0033 (RFMEFI57514X0033), and by the Government of the Russian Federation, Grant 074-U01.

References

1. Bitzer, J., Brandt, M.: Speech enhancement by adaptive noise cancellation: Problems, algorithms, and limits. In: Audio Engineering Society Conference: 39th International Conference: Audio Forensics: Practices and Challenges. Audio Engineering Society (2010)
2. Borisovich, S.M., Vladimirovich, A.S.: Improvement of microphone array characteristics for speech capturing. Mod. Appl. Sci. **9**(6), p. 310 (2015)
3. Karpov, A., Akarun, L., Yalçın, H., Ronzhin, A., Demiröz, B.E., Çoban, A., Železný, M.: Audio-visual signal processing in a multimodal assisted living environment. In: Fifteenth Annual Conference of the International Speech Communication Association, pp. 1023–1027 (2014)
4. Kozlov, A., Kudashev, O., Matveev, Y., Pekhovsky, T., Simonchik, K., Shulipa, A.: SVID speaker recognition system for NIST SRE 2012. In: Železný, M., Habernal, I., Ronzhin, A. (eds.) SPECOM 2013. LNCS, vol. 8113, pp. 278–285. Springer, Heidelberg (2013)
5. Li, W., Itou, K., Takeda, K., Itakura, F.: Subjective and objective quality assessment of regression-enhanced speech in real car environments. In: Ninth European Conference on Speech Communication and Technology, pp. 2093–2096 (2005)
6. Löllmann, H.W., Vary, P.: Post-filter design for superdirective beamformers with closely spaced microphones. In: 2007 IEEE Workshop on Applications of Signal Processing to Audio and Acoustics, pp. 291–294. IEEE (2007)
7. McCowan, I.: Microphone Arrays: A Tutorial. Queensland University, Brisbane (2001)
8. McCowan, I., Bourlard, H., et al.: Microphone array post-filter based on noise field coherence. IEEE Trans. Speech Audio Process. **11**(6), 709–716 (2003)
9. Simmer, K., Wasiljeff, A.: Adaptive microphone arrays for noise suppression in the frequency domain. In: Second Cost 229 Workshop on Adaptive Algorithms in Communications. pp. 185–194 (1992)
10. Stolbov, M., Aleinik, S.: Speech enhancement with microphone array using frequency-domain alignment technique. In: Audio Engineering Society Conference: 54th International Conference: Audio Forensics. Audio Engineering Society (2014)
11. Wolff, T., Buck, M.: A generalized view on microphone array postfilters. In: International Workshop on Acoustic Signal Enhancement (2010)

A Comparison of RNN LM and FLM
for Russian Speech Recognition

Irina Kipyatkova[1,2]([⊠]) and Alexey Karpov[1,3]

[1] SPIIRAS, 39, 14th Line, St. Petersburg 199178, Russia
{kipyatkova,karpov}@iias.spb.su
[2] SUAI, 67, Bolshaya Morskaia, St. Petersburg 199000, Russia
[3] University ITMO, 49 Kronverksky Pr., St. Petersburg 197101, Russia

Abstract. In the paper, we describe a research of recurrent neural network (RNN) language model (LM) for N-best list rescoring for automatic continuous Russian speech recognition and make a comparison of it with factored language model (FLM). We tried RNN with different number of units in the hidden layer. For FLM creation, we used five linguistic factors: word, lemma, stem, part-of-speech, and morphological tag. All models were trained on the text corpus of 350M words. Also we made linear interpolation of RNN LM and FLM with the baseline 3-gram LM. We achieved the relative WER reduction of 8 % using FLM and 14 % relative WER reduction using RNN LM with respect to the baseline model.

Keywords: Recurrent neural networks · Language models · Automatic speech recognition · Russian speech

1 Introduction

Automatic recognition of continuous Russian speech is a very challenging task due to several features of the language. Russian is a morphologically rich inflective language. Word formation is performed by morphemes, which carry grammatical meaning. This results in increasing the vocabulary size and perplexity of n-gram language models (LMs). Word order in Russian is not strictly fixed that complicates creation of LMs and decreases their efficiency. The most widely used LMs are n-gram LMs. These models are good enough for languages with restricted word order (for example, English) but for the Russian language they are not so efficient.

At present, the usage of neural network (NN) for language modeling is very popular: both feedforward and recurrent NNs can be used. In feedforward NN, the input layer is a history of n-1 preceding words. Each word is associated with a vector, with length of V (vocabulary capacity). Only one value of the vector, which corresponds to the index of the given word, is equal to 1 and all other values are 0. The main drawback of feedforward NN is that they use preceding context of a fixed length for word prediction. Recurrent neural networks (RNN)

© Springer International Publishing Switzerland 2015
A. Ronzhin et al. (Eds.): SPECOM 2015, LNAI 9319, pp. 42–50, 2015.
DOI: 10.1007/978-3-319-23132-7_5

for the first time were proposed in [2]. In RNN, the hidden layer represents all preceding history, thereby the length of the context is not restricted.

In order to model morphologically rich languages factored language model (FLM) can be used. This model allows to include additional information in LM and thereby to improve performance of speech recognition system. For the first time this model was introduced in [1] for modeling Arabic language.

In our research we made a comparison of RNN LM with FLM for N-best list rescoring of automatic speech recognition (ASR) system. In Sect. 2 we give a survey of using NN for LM creation, in Sect. 3 we describe RNN LM, in Sect. 4 we present our baseline and RNN LMs, experiments on using RNN LM and FLM for N-best list rescoring for Russian speech recognition are presented in Sect. 5.

2   Related Works

The use of NN for LM training was firstly presented in [13]. In that paper, the comparison of NN LM with n-gram LM with Kneser-Ney discounting was made. Models were trained on the corpus of 600M words. NN LM was trained not for the whole vocabulary, but for the most frequent words. An algorithm for NN training using large training corpus was proposed. According to the algorithm, instead of performing several epochs over the whole training data, a different small random subset is used at each epoch. Speech recognition was carried out using the back-off LM, and NN LM was used for the lattice rescoring. WER reduction was 0.5 %.

RNN LM was firstly used in [11]; in that paper, it was proposed to merge rare words (the words, occurrence frequency of which is less than a threshold) into a special rare token for training optimization. Experiment on speech recognition was conducted using the baseline 5-gram model with Kneser-Ney discounting. RNN LM was applied for rescoring 100-best list. Perplexity reduction of RNN LM was almost 50 % and the WER reduction was 18 % comparing to the baseline model.

In [17], a comparison of LMs based on feedforward and recurrent NN is made. The following realizations of NN LMs were used: (1) the LIMSI shortlist feedforward NN LM software, (2) the RWTH clustered feedforward NN LM, (3) the RWTH clustered recurrent Long Short-Term Memory NN LM implementation. For NN LM training in-domain corpus of 27M words was used. For NN LM clustering 200 classes were precomputed based on relative word frequencies. Hidden layer size varied between 300 and 500 nodes, depending on the performance on the development data. NN LMs were interpolated with the n-gram model. Experiments on speech recognition showed that LMs based on RNN outperform feedforward NN LMs. On the test set RNN LM showed 0.4 % absolute WER reduction comparing to feedforward NN.

Three approaches for exploiting succeeding word information in RNN LMs were proposed in [14]. The first approach was forward-backward model that combines RNN LMs exploiting preceding and succeeding words. In this case both forward and backward RNN LMs were created, then interpolation of the models was carried out. The second approach was the extension of a Maximum Entropy RNN LM that incorporates succeeding word information. The third approach combined LMs using two-pass alternating rescoring. In this case, an N-best list was rescored using the conventional RNN LM, and a part of the N-best list ($\alpha \cdot N$, $\alpha \in (0,1)$) was selected. Then the obtained N-best list was rescored using RNN LM with succeeding word information, and a new N-best list was created. These steps were repeated until the best hypothesis was obtained. The models were trained on a corpus of 37M words with 195K vocabulary. After combination of the three approaches, the WER was reduced from 16.83 % to 14.44 %.

In [10], the strategies for NN LM training on large data sets are presented: (1) reducing of training epochs; (2) reduction of number of training tokens; (3) reduction of vocabulary size; (4) reduction of size of the hidden layer; (5) parallelization. It was shown that when data are sorted by their relevance the fast convergence during training and the better overall performance are observed. A maximum entropy model trained as a part of NN LM that leads to significant reduction of computational complexity was proposed. 10 % relative reduction was obtained comparing to the baseline 4-gram model.

In [3], RNN LM was applied in the first pass decoding for Bing voice search task. In the paper it was proposed to call RNN LM to compute LM score only if newly hypothesized word has a reasonable score. Also cache based RNN inference was proposed in order to reduce runtime. Using the RNN LM allowed to reduce the WER from 25.3 % to 23.2 %. RNN was also applied for lattice rescoring. The best results were obtained, when the lattice was created using the RNN LM interpolated with the baseline n-gram model in the first pass, and then rescored with the same model using interpolation weight of 0.3. In this case WER was equal to 22.7 %.

RNN LM for Russian was firstly used in [19]. RNN LM was trained on the text corpus containing 40M words with vocabulary size of about 100K words. An interpolation of the obtained model with the baseline 3-gram and factored LMs was carried out. Obtained LM was used for rescoring 500-best list that allowed to achieve WER relative improvement of 7.4 %.

NN are also widely used for acoustic models. For example, the use of deep NN in Russian ASR is presented in [18, 20].

3   Recurrent Neural Network Language Model Topology

We used the same architecture of RNN LM as in [11]; it is presented on Fig. 1. RNN consists of an input layer x, hidden (or context) layer s, and an output layer y. The input to the network in time t is vector $x(t)$. The vector $x(t)$ is a concatenation of vector $w(t)$, which is a current word in time t, and vector $s(t-1)$, which is output of the hidden layer obtained on the previous step. Size of $w(t)$ is equal to vocabulary size. The output layer $y(t)$ has the same size as $w(t)$ and it represents probability distribution of the next word given the previous word $w(t)$ and the context vector $s(t-1)$. Size of the hidden layer is chosen empirically and usually it consists of 30–500 units [11].

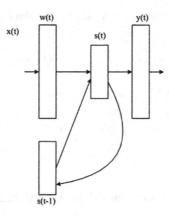

Fig. 1. Recurrent neural network topology

Input, hidden, and output layers are as follows [11]:

$$x(t) = w(t) + s(t-1), \ s_j(t) = f\left(\sum_i x_i(t)u_{ji}\right), \ y_k(t) = g\left(\sum_j s_j(t)u_{kj}\right),$$

where f(z) is sigmoid activation function:

$$f(z) = \frac{1}{1 + e^{-z}},$$

$g(z)$ is softmax function:

$$g(z_m) = \frac{e^{z_m}}{\sum_k e^{z_k}}.$$

NN training is carried out in several epochs. Usually, for training the back-propagation algorithm with the stochastic gradient descent is used.

4   Creation of Language Models for Russian ASR

4.1   Creation of the Baseline Language Models

For the language model creation, we used a Russian text corpus of a number of on-line newspapers [6]. The size of the corpus after text normalization and deletion of doubling or short (<5 words) sentences is over 350M words, and it has above 1M unique word-forms. As a baseline model we used 3-gram LM created using the SRI Language Modeling Toolkit (SRILM) [16]. We created 3-gram LMs with different vocabulary sizes using Kneser-Ney discounting method, obtained results are presented in Table 1. The experimental setup was the same as described in Sect. 5.1. The best speech recognition results were obtained with 150K vocabulary [7]. So, the same 150K vocabulary was chosen for the creation of FLMs and RNN LMs as well.

Table 1. Summary of the results on very large vocabulary Russian speech recognition using 3-gram LMs.

Vocabulary size, K words	# n-grams, M	Perplexity	OOV rate, %	n-gram hit, %	WER, %
110	94.4	516	1.9	56.4	26.85
150	99.5	553	1.1	56.2	**26.54**
219	104.1	597	0.6	56.0	26.78
303	106.6	630	0.5	56.0	27.34

4.2   Creation of Recurrent Neural Network Language Models

For creation of RNN LM we used Recurrent Neural Network Language Modeling Toolkit (RNNLM toolkit) [12]. In order to speedup training the factorization of the output layer was performed [10]. Words were mapped to classes according to their frequencies. At first, probability distribution over classes was computed. Then, probability distribution for the words that belong to a specific class was computed. We chose the number of classes equal to 100. We created three models with different number of units in the hidden layer: 100, 300, and 500. Perplexities of the obtained models computed on the text corpus of 33M words are presented in Table 2.

Table 2. Perplexities of RNN LMs.

Number units in hidden layer	Perplexity
100	981
300	1196
500	766

Then we made linear interpolation of the models with the baseline 3-gram model with different interpolation coefficients. Perplexities of the obtained models are presented in Table 3.

5   Experiments

5.1   Experimental Setup

For training the speech recognition system we used our own corpus of spoken Russian speech Euronounce-SPIIRAS, created in 2008–2009 in the framework of the Euro-Nounce project [4,5]. The speech data were collected in clean acoustic conditions, with 16 kHz sampling rate, 16-bit audio quality. A signal-to-noise ratio (SNR) at least 35–40 dB was provided. The database consists of 16,350 utterances pronounced by 50 native Russian speakers (25 male and 25 female).

Table 3. Perplexities of RNN LMs interpolated with 3-gram LM.

Language model	Interpolation coefficients		
	0.4	0.5	0.6
RNN with 100 hidden units + 3-gram LM	457	465	482
RNN with 300 hidden units + 3-gram LM	475	486	506
RNN with 500 hidden units + 3-gram LM	394	392	396

Each speaker pronounced more than 300 phonetically-balanced and meaningful phrases. Total duration of speech data is about 21 h. For acoustic modeling, continuous density Hidden Markov models (HMM) were used, and each context-depended phoneme (triphone) was modeled by one continuous HMM.

To test the system we used a speech corpus that contains 500 phrases pronounced by 5 speakers (each speaker said the same 100 phrases). The phrases were taken from the materials of the on-line newspaper that were not used in the training data.

For speech recognition we used Julius ver. 4.2 decoder [9]. The WER obtained with the baseline 3-gram language model was 26.54 %. We produced several N-best lists with different number of hypotheses and made their rescoring using FLMs and RNN LMs.

5.2 Experiments on Rescoring N-Best Lists Using FLM

For FLMs creation we used five factors: the word (W), its lemma (L), stem (S), part-of-speech (P), and morphological tag (M). The software VisualSynan from the AOT project [15] was used for obtaining morphological word features. We created models with the word plus one of the other factors using Kneser-Ney discounting method. We have tried 2 fixed backoff paths: (1) the first drop was of the most distant word and factor, then of the less distant ones; (2) the first drop was of the words in time-distance order, then drop of the factors in the same order. Our FLMs are described in detail in [8].

We made rescoring of several N-best lists using FLMs interpolated with the baseline model and the best speech recognition results were obtained after rescoring 20-best list. Recognition results are presented in Table 4. The lowest WER = 24.44 % was obtained after interpolation of the baseline model with the FLM created using the backoff path 1, in which word and morphological factors were used [8].

5.3 Experiments on Rescoring N-Best Lists Using RNN LM

For experiments of application of the RNN LMs for rescoring we used the same N-best lists as in previous experiments. Also we made rescoring of N-best list using RNN interpolated with baseline models with different interpolation coefficients. Obtained results are summarized in Table 5.

Table 4. Perplexities of RNN LMs interpolated with 3-gram LM.

Language models	10-best list		20-best list		50-best list	
	Path 1	Path 2	Path 1	Path 2	Path 1	Path 2
3-gram + WM	24.83	24.94	**24.44**	24.78	24.55	24.66
3-gram + WL	25.79	25.71	25.58	25.43	25.60	25.37
3-gram + WP	25.43	25.54	25.07	25.24	25.15	25.26
3-gram + WS	25.82	26.01	25.88	25.90	25.90	26.10

Table 5. WER obtained after rescoring N-best lists with RNN LMs (%).

Number units in hidden layer	Interpolation coefficient	10-best list	20-best list	50-best list
100	1.0	26.33	26.65	26.72
	0.6	25.13	25.06	24.98
	0.5	25.13	24.89	24.91
	0.4	25.06	24.72	24.72
300	1.0	26.39	25.82	25.82
	0.6	24.59	24.12	24.10
	0.5	24.51	24.03	23.90
	0.4	24.57	24.06	23.93
500	1.0	24.51	23.67	23.97
	0.6	23.76	23.07	22.96
	0.5	23.65	23.00	**22.87**
	0.4	23.82	23.26	23.24

From the table we can see that in the most cases rescoring decreased WER comparing to the recognition with the baseline model except the case of using RNN LMs with 100 hidden layers for 20 and 50-best list rescoring. Application of RNNs with 300 and 500 layers for N-best list rescoring gave better results than usage of FLMs. The lowest WER $= 22.87$ was archived using RNN LM with 500 hidden units interpolated with 3-gram model with interpolation coefficient equal to 0.5.

6   Conclusion

Statistical n-gram LMs do not have efficiency for Russian ASR because of almost free word order in Russian. RNN LMs are able to store arbitrary long history of a given word that is their advantage over n-gram LMs. In the paper we have investigated RNN LMs for Russian and made a comparison of them with FLMs. RNN LMs and FLMs were used for N-best lists rescoring. We have tried RNNs with various number of units in hidden layer and FLM with different factor sets, also we made the linear interpolation of the RNN LM and FLM with the baseline 3-gram LM. We achieved the relative WER reduction of 8 % using FLM and 14 % relative WER reduction using RNN LM with respect to the baseline model. In further research, we plan to interpolate RNN LM with FLM.

Acknowledgments. This research is partially supported by the Council for Grants of the President of Russia (Projects No. MK-5209.2015.8 and MD-3035.2015.8), by the Russian Foundation for Basic Research (Projects No. 15-07-04415 and 15-07-04322), and by the Government of the Russian Federation (Grant No. 074-U01).

References

1. Bilmes, J.A., Kirchhoff, K.: Factored language models and generalized parallel backoff. In: Proceedings of the 2003 Conference of the North American Chapter of the Association for Computational Linguistics on Human Language Technology, Companion Volume of the Proceedings of HLT-NAACL 2003-Short Papers, vol. 2, pp. 4–6. Association for Computational Linguistics (2003)
2. Elman, J.L.: Finding structure in time. Cogn. Sci. **14**(2), 179–211 (1990)
3. Huang, Z., Zweig, G., Dumoulin, B.: Cache based recurrent neural network language model inference for first pass speech recognition. In: 2014 IEEE International Conference on Acoustics, Speech and Signal Processing (ICASSP), pp. 6354–6358. IEEE (2014)
4. Jokisch, O., Wagner, A., Sabo, R., Jaeckel, R., Cylwik, N., Rusko, M., Ronzhin, A., Hoffmann, R.: Multilingual speech data collection for the assessment of pronunciation and prosody in a language learning system. In: Proceedings of the SPECOM, pp. 515–520 (2009)
5. Karpov, A., Kipyatkova, I., Ronzhin, A.: Very large vocabulary ASR for spoken Russian with syntactic and morphemic analysis. In: Twelfth Annual Conference of the International Speech Communication Association (2011)
6. Karpov, A., Markov, K., Kipyatkova, I., Vazhenina, D., Ronzhin, A.: Large vocabulary Russian speech recognition using syntactico-statistical language modeling. Speech Commun. **56**, 213–228 (2014)
7. Kipyatkova, I., Karpov, A.: Lexicon size and language model order optimization for Russian LVCSR. In: Železný, M., Habernal, I., Ronzhin, A. (eds.) SPECOM 2013. LNCS, vol. 8113, pp. 219–226. Springer, Heidelberg (2013)
8. Kipyatkova, I., Karpov, A.: Development of factored language models for automatic Russian speech recognition. In: Computational Linguistics and Intellectual Technologies: Papers from the Annual Conference "Dialogue", pp. 234–246 (2015)
9. Lee, A., Kawahara, T.: Recent development of open-source speech recognition engine Julius. In: Proceedings of APSIPA ASC 2009, 2009 Annual Summit and Conference on Asia-Pacific Signal and Information Processing Association, pp. 131–137. International Organizing Committee (2009)
10. Mikolov, T., Deoras, A., Povey, D., Burget, L., Černocký, J.: Strategies for training large scale neural network language models. In: 2011 IEEE Workshop on Automatic Speech Recognition and Understanding (ASRU), pp. 196–201. IEEE (2011)

11. Mikolov, T., Karafiát, M., Burget, L., Cernockỳ, J., Khudanpur, S.: Recurrent neural network based language model. In: INTERSPEECH 2010, 11th Annual Conference of the International Speech Communication Association, Makuhari, Chiba, Japan, pp. 1045–1048, 26–30 September 2010

12. Mikolov, T., Kombrink, S., Deoras, A., Burget, L., Cernocky, J.: RNNLM-recurrent neural network language modeling toolkit. In: Proceedings of the ASRU Workshop, pp. 196–201 (2011)

13. Schwenk, H., Gauvain, J.L.: Training neural network language models on very large corpora. In: Proceedings of the Conference on Human Language Technology and Empirical Methods in Natural Language Processing, pp. 201–208 (2005)

14. Shi, Y., Larson, M., Wiggers, P., Jonker, C.M.: Exploiting the succeeding words in recurrent neural network language models. In: INTERSPEECH, pp. 632–636 (2013)

15. Sokirko, A.: Morphological modules on the website. In: Proceedings of Dialog 2004 International Conference, pp. 559–564 (2004). www.aot.ru

16. Stolcke, A., Zheng, J., Wang, W., Abrash, V.: Srilm at sixteen: update and outlook. In: Proceedings of IEEE Automatic Speech Recognition and Understanding Workshop, p. 5 (2011)

17. Sundermeyer, M., Oparin, I., Gauvain, J.L., Freiberg, B., Schluter, R., Ney, H.: Comparison of feedforward and recurrent neural network language models. In: 2013 IEEE International Conference on Acoustics, Speech and Signal Processing (ICASSP), pp. 8430–8434 (2013)

18. Tomashenko, N., Khokhlov, Y.: Speaker adaptation of context dependent deep neural networks based on MAP-adaptation and GMM-derived feature processing. In: Fifteenth Annual Conference of the International Speech Communication Association (2014)

19. Vazhenina, D., Markov, K.: Evaluation of advanced language modeling techniques for Russian LVCSR. In: Železný, M., Habernal, I., Ronzhin, A. (eds.) SPECOM 2013. LNCS, vol. 8113, pp. 124–131. Springer, Heidelberg (2013)

20. Zulkarneev, M., Penalov, S.: System of speech recognition for Russian language, using deep neural networks and finite state transducers. Neurocomput. Develop. Appl. **10**, 40–46 (2013)

A Frequency Domain Adaptive Decorrelating Algorithm for Speech Enhancement

Mohamed Djendi$^{(\boxtimes)}$, Feriel Khemies, and Amina Morsli

Signal Processing and Image Laboratory (LATSI), University of Blida 1,
Route de Soumaa, B.P. 270, 09000 Blida, Algeria
m_djendi@yahoo.fr, f.khemies@outlook.fr, morsli.a@outlook.com

Abstract. In this paper, we propose a new frequency domain-symmetric adaptive decorrelating (FD-SAD) algorithm to cancel punctual noise components from noisy observations. The proposed FD-SAD is combined with the forward blind source separation (FBSS) structure to enhance the performances of the time-domain symmetric adaptive decorelating (TD-SAD) algorithm. The new FD-SAD algorithm shows a fast convergence speed and good tracking behaviour even in very noisy conditions.

Keywords: Speech enhancement · Decorrelation · Adaptive filtering

1 Introduction

In last year's, several speech signal enhancement algorithms have been proposed [1]. A large part of these algorithms are mainly based on the classical noise cancelling scheme with a noise reference sensor when significant leakage of the primary signal occurred onto the noise reference, this is mainly due to the primary and reference sensors spacing [2,3]. Recently, several two-sensors techniques combined with BSS have been proposed to overcome of this problem [4]. In this work, we focus on the forward BSS (FBSS) and propose a new FD-SAD algorithm to enhance noisy speech signal. The paper is organized as follows: Sect. 2 presents the mixing model. In Sect. 3, we present the proposed FD-SAD algorithm. The simulation results are presented in Sect. 4, and conclusion in Sect. 5.

2 Mixing Model

We consider the case of two sources and two sensors as given in Fig. 1 [A, in the left]. We use the model detailed in [4] to generate two noisy observations $m_1(n)$, and $m_2(n)$. In this model, we assume that the two source signals are: a speech signal $s(n)$, and a punctual noise signal $b(n)$. The two noisy observation signals are:

$$m_1(n) = s(n) + b(n) * h_{21}, \tag{1}$$
$$m_2(n) = b(n) + s(n) * h_{12}. \tag{2}$$

© Springer International Publishing Switzerland 2015
A. Ronzhin et al. (Eds.): SPECOM 2015, LNAI 9319, pp. 51–54, 2015.
DOI: 10.1007/978-3-319-23132-7_6

where $(.)^*$ represents the convolution operator. h_{21} and h_{12} are the impulse responses of the channels. $m_1(n)$ and $m_2(n)$ are the mixing signals [4]. L is the length of the real impulse responses. We assume that the two source signals s(n) and b(n) are statistically independent. i.e. $E[s(n)b(n - m)] = 0$.

3   Proposed Frequency Domain (FD-SAD) Algorithm

In Fig. 1 [B, in the right], we show a bloc diagram of the FD-SAD algorithm. In this Figure, the observations $m_1(n)$ and $m_2(n)$ are firstly transformed in the frequency domain by a short Fourier transform (SFT) at each frame k and then we obtain the frequency observation versions $M_1(w, k)$ and $M_2(w, k)$. The frequency filtering error $U_1(w, k)$ and $U_2(w, k)$ are given by:

$$U_1(\omega, k) = M_1(\omega, k) - W_{21}(\omega, k)M_2(\omega, k), \qquad (3)$$
$$U_2(\omega, k) = M_2(\omega, k) - W_{12}(\omega, k)M_1(\omega, k). \qquad (4)$$

The new proposed FD-SAD algorithm is based on a frequency domain implementation of the adaptive filters $W_{12}(\omega, k)$ and $W_{21}(\omega, k)$, which is updated by an adaptive algorithm on a frame-by-frame basis. To update $W_{12}(\omega, k)$ and $W_{21}(\omega, k)$, we have used the frequency domain LMS algorithm (FLMS) [5]. For each frame k, we propagate the following equation:

$$W_{12}(\omega, k) = W_{12}(\omega, k - 1) + \mu_{12}(\omega, k)\frac{U_2(\omega, k)M_1^H(\omega, k)}{DS_{M_1}(\omega, k)}, \qquad (5)$$

$$W_{21}(\omega, k) = W_{21}(\omega, k - 1) + \mu_{21}(\omega, k)\frac{U_1(\omega, k)M_2^H(\omega, k)}{DS_{M_2}(\omega, k)}, \qquad (6)$$

where $\mu_{12}(\omega, k)$ and $\mu_{21}(\omega, k)$ are two step-sizes control of the convergence behaviour of the two cross-adaptive filters $W_{12}(\omega, k)$ and $W_{12}(\omega, k)$, respectively. D is the length of the SFT (FFT). The 'H' symbol represents the Hermitian operator. The two parameters $S_{M_1}(\omega, k)$ and $S_{M_1}(\omega, k)$ represent the power spectral densities (PSDs) of the two observations $M_1^H(\omega, k)$ and $M_1^H(\omega, k)$ respectively. In order to get the enhanced speech signal at the output $U_1(\omega, k)$, we have used manual VAD system that controls, in the frequency domain, the filter $W_{21}(\omega, k)$ during noise-only periods. This adaptation mechanism achieves good convergence of the adaptive algorithms. To restor time domain output speech signal, an ovelap-add technique is used.

4   Simulations, Results, and Analysis

In this Section, we have evaluated The system mismatches (SM), and The segmental signal to noise ratio (SegSNR). Furthermore, we compare our proposed FD-SAD algorithm with its time domain version, i.e. TD-SAD. In this work, we

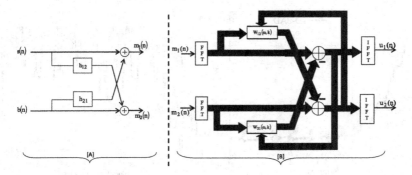

Fig. 1. Mixing model [in left, A], and proposed FD-SAD algorithm [in right, B]. FFT: means fast Fourier transform, and IFFT is the inverse of FFT

have used the specific model of [4] to generate the noisy observations. The punctual speech is an imbalance signal, and the punctual noise source is a correlated noise. These signals are taken form AUROA data-base. The input SNR is 0 dB at the two observations. The simulation parameters of each algorithm are given as follows: (1) the TD-SAD algorithm parameters [Step-sizes of the adaptive filters $w_{12}(n)$ and $w_{21}(n)$ are given, respectively by: $\mu_{12} = \mu_{21} = 0.9$]. In the proposed FD-SAD algorithms, the parameters are: [the frame length = 256; the SFT length = 512]. We note that the length of the adaptive filters are equal to that of the real ones, i.e. $L = 256$. the input SNRs at the two observations is 0 dB.

4.1   System Mismatch (SM) Evaluation

In this section, we have used the SM criterion which is evaluated according to the following expression (7):

$$SM_{dB} = 20 \lg \left(\frac{||h_{21} - w_{21}||}{||h_{21}||} \right), \tag{7}$$

where $w_{21}(n)$ and h_{21} are the adaptive and real filters of the Forward BSS structure. $||.||$ symbolizes the Euclidian norm, and lg is the logarithm of basis 10. The adaptive filter length is $L = 256$. The obtained results are reported on Fig. 2 [in the left]. From this figure, we note a faster convergence speed of the proposed FD-SAD in comparison with the TD-SAD.

4.2   Segmental SNR (SegSNR) Evaluation

We have evaluated the segmental SNR (SegSNR) given by (8), where $s(n)$ and $u_1(n)$ represent respectively the original speech signal and the enhanced one. The parameter Q is the mean averaging value of the SegSNR, i.e. $Q = 1024$.

$$SegSNR_{dB} = 10 \lg \left(\frac{\sum_{\lambda=0}^{Q-1} |s(\lambda)|^2}{\sum_{\lambda=0}^{Q-1} |s(\lambda) - u_1(\lambda)|^2} \theta(n) \right). \tag{8}$$

54   M. Djendi et al.

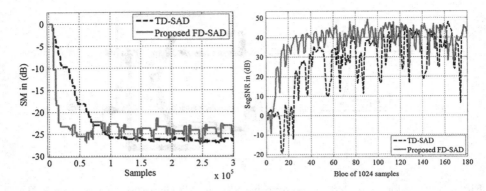

Fig. 2. Comparison of SM (in the left), and SegSNR (in the right) values obtained by TD-SAD (black) and proposed FD-SAD (green) algorithms with $L = 256$ (Colour figure online)

Figure 2 [in the right] shows the obtained results of the SegSNR with the two algorithms, i.e. TD-SAD and proposed FD-SAD algorithms. From this result, a good behaviour of the FD-SAD algorithm is noted with a slight degradation in the steady state.

5   Conclusion

In this paper, we have proposed a new frequency symmetric adaptive decorrelating (FD-SAD) algorithm for speech enhancement. The comparison between the FD-SAD algorithm and its time-domain SAD (TD-SAD) version has shown the superiority of the proposed one in terms of the System Mismatch (SM) and the Segmental SNR (SegSNR) criteria. The only drawback of the proposed FD-SAD algorithm is the degradation of its steady state values when the adaptive filters length is selected high. In a future work, we will propose a solution to this problem.

References

1. Loizou, P.C.: Speech Enhancement: Theory and Practice, 2nd edn. CRC Press and Taylor and Francis Group, Boca Raton (2013)
2. Van Gerven, S., Van Compernolle, D.: Signal separation by symmetric adaptive decorrelation: stability, convergence, and uniqueness. IEEE Trans. Signal Proc. **74**(3), 1602–1612 (1995)
3. Djendi, M., Scalart, P., Gilloire, A.: Analysis of two-sensors forward BSS structure with post-filters in the presence of coherent and incoherent noise. Speech Commun. **55**(10), 975–987 (2013)
4. Djendi, M., Gilloire, A., Scalart, P.: Noise cancellation using two closely spaced microphones: experimental study with a specific model and two adaptive algorithms. In: IEEE International Conference on ICASSP, vol. 3, pp. 744–747, Toulouse, France (2006)
5. Ferrara, E.R.: Fast implementation of LMS adaptive filter. IEEE Trans. Sig. Proc. **28**, 474–475 (1980)

Acoustic Markers of Emotional State "Aggression"

Rodmonga Potapova, Liliya Komalova[✉], and Nikolay Bobrov

Institute of Applied and Mathematical Linguistics,
Moscow State Linguistic University, Ostozhenka 38, Moscow 119034, Russia
{rkpotapova,genuinepr,arctangent}@yandex.ru

Abstract. The paper presents the results of comparison between auditory-perceptual and acoustic data obtained of the analysis of Russian, English, Spanish and Tatar speech produced in the emotional state of aggression [5]. Issues concerning the selection of relevant features in studies of the type are described. It is pointed out that the emotional state of aggression, as a special case of emotional state of physiological excitation, is characterized by acoustic markers that don't always conform to the common sense rule saying that the values being measured must correspond. In the concluding part of the paper preliminary approximate qualitative estimates of auditory-perceptual and acoustic characteristics describing the pronunciational manifestation of emotional state 'aggression' in the mentioned languages are presented.

Keywords: Speech acoustics · Speech perception · Semantic field 'aggression' · Cognitive mechanisms · Emotionally charged speech

1 Introduction

At present the problem of identifying "antidialogical relations" (this concept was introduced by R.K. Potapova to define destructive behavior implemented in written and oral discourse, see [4]) at early stages comes to the fore. They are determined among other things by different kinds of deprivation and can manifest themselves in the form of antisocial behavior as well as verbal and physical aggression [4].

The research presented in this paper is aimed at developing the typology of verbal and paraverbal determinants of human emotional and emotional-modal behavior, particularly the typology of emotional and emotional-modal variants of the state "aggression".

The subject matter of the research is written and spoken realization of the emotional state "aggression" in interpersonal communication. Due to the fact that the scope of the research include samples of spoken language of native speakers of Russian, American English, Castilian Spanish and Kazan Tatar languages taken from authentic movies and TV series, it would be more correct to speak not about the state of aggression (further on, SA) itself, but about a state

© Springer International Publishing Switzerland 2015
A. Ronzhin et al. (Eds.): SPECOM 2015, LNAI 9319, pp. 55–64, 2015.
DOI: 10.1007/978-3-319-23132-7_7

similar to the state of aggression (SSSA) (this concept was introduced by R.K. Potapova, see [8]).

"The state similar to the state of aggression is characterized by a complex of negative emotional and emotional-modal states experienced by the subject (a person) in the act of communication, which can lead to realization of aggressive behavior" [8].

2   Method and Procedure

The results of the study of written realization of the SA in digital media [6, 7, 9], in the setting of modelling the emotional state of "aggression" [1–3] as well as the results of the research of spoken realization of the SSSA [8] have been presented before. The current study presents the results of the acoustic analysis of the experimental data being compared with the results of the auditory-perceptual analysis conducted on the previous stage [5].

The goal of the acoustic analysis was to estimate the acoustic correlates of prosodic speech parameters of the speakers in the state of emotional arousal similar to the SA for Russian, English, Spanish and Tatar languages.

The following assumption was admitted as the hypothesis while formulating the problem of the research: *for all the above-listed languages it is possible to establish combinations of acoustic characteristics which correlate with auditory-perceptual parameters forming a set of attributes describing marked prosodic patterns different for each of the listed languages. These patterns correlate with manifestations of the speaker's negative psycho-emotional state, SSSA.*

The acoustic parameters constitute physical (i.e. amplitude, spectral and temporal) characteristics of the segments of the speech continuum. The perceptual parameters represent the verbal description of the properties of certain speech units identified through auditory perception [10]. According to R.K. Potapova and V.G. Mikhaylov, "the systems of perceptual and acoustic parameters turn to be in a complex interdependence" [10].

Among the acoustic characteristics analyzed in order to establish a correlation with the psycho-emotional state of the speaker, the most informative are the following:

– fundamental frequency (F_{0_i}):
  - $F_{0_{min}}$ and $F_{0_{max}}$ values for speech segments for phrases and phonoparagraphs;
  - the average $\overline{F_0}$ values for segments of the same syllable length;
  - the speech change rate V_{F_0} (from maximum to minimum values characterizing frequency variations within the same rhythmic structure and, in contrast, the existence of monotonous segments throughout the phrase);
– speech tempo T_i (the average number of syllables uttered per time unit);
– intensity level (I_i):
  - minimum I_{min} and maximum I_{max} values of the intensity level for segments from phrases to phonoparagraphs;
  - the average values of the intensity level I_i for segments of the same length;

- the change rate of the intensity level V_{I_i} (maximum and minimum values, characterizing sudden changes of the intensity level within one or two syntagmas or, on the opposite, the absence of significant changes of the intensity level throughout the phrase or phonoparagraph).

It should be noted that there is a certain restriction that is imposed on the use of data on intensity level variations and makes it difficult to correctly compare the values obtained for different phonograms. Since sound vibrations decay with distance, the energy measured depends on the distance between the microphone and the sound source. As this parameter is hard to control while recording the sound, the values of the intensity level obtained via mathematical processing of the phonograms can only be used for qualitative assessment and should be treated with extreme caution. Normalization methods involving the calculation of mean energy values on small segments (about 2–3 s, which approximately corresponds to a short phrase) can provide slightly more informative results with regard to their correlation with the phenomena on the prosodic level. However, they can bring about additional errors (artefacts), and in no way they eliminate other restrictions imposed on the use of the intensity level data.

According to R.K. Potapova, V.V. Potapov, the parameters of the speech pitch provide a high degree of emotional intensity of verbal expressions [11, 12], and therefore they appear to be informative when detecting emotional speech.

Along with the mentioned characteristics, there exist some other potential acoustic correlates of the state of emotional arousal of the speaker (particularly of the SA), such as the formant quality factor, as well as the change rate of the extrema positions in instantaneous spectra of the speech signal, obtained on the adjacent periods of the transition segments of the speech sounds (especially of vowels, sonorants and certain fricatives). These characteristics correlate with the degree of tension of the muscles of active and passive articulators and can be interpreted as correlates of articulatory tension, which is considered a part of psychosomatic manifestation of the state of emotional arousal and aggression. Careful investigation of speech phonograms obtained under laboratory conditions allows to provide the most detailed gradation while estimating the psychosomatic condition of the speaker (because among other things these characteristics are the least susceptible to random control). However, while analyzing the phonograms obtained in field conditions (including the type of recordings used in this study), it becomes difficult to accurately measure the spectral peaks due to large amounts of various kinds of noise, particularly, harmonic ones. Taking this into consideration, we decided not to analyze the spectral characteristics of the speech at this stage and focus on the acoustic characteristics listed above.

The traditional idea of the acoustic signature of the SSSA (i.e. the state of intense emotional arousal with predominant negative emotions accompanied by psychosomatic manifestations) is that this state is marked by the increase of all the values which correlate with the characteristics typical of this state: the fundamental frequency and the intensity level rise (speech turns into shouting), the change rate of both characteristics increases (the jagged uncontrolled speech prosody can be observed), speech tempo increases as well. However, the results obtained in this study argue against this point of view.

The SA as a specific instance of the state of emotional arousal is characterized on the acoustic level by a number of marked representations which do not always follow the intuitive rule of the increase of the measured characteristics values. Certain sets of features constituting these manifestations can depend on the psychosomatic state of the speaker (including the background state which overlaps with SA) as well as the speaker's speech habits and the intonation patterns which exist in the language system, used to convey a certain emotionally coloured expression. The latter tendency has not been studied sufficiently at present. The description of its particular manifestations with regard to English, Russian, Spanish and Tatar languages makes up one of the subsidiary issues in the experimental research being presented.

An important preliminary observation, which can be made on the basis of investigating the available information about the prosodic pragmatics of different languages and which can set the stage for the experimental work, involves the following:

– *intonational component* of an emotionally coloured expression, especially with predominantly negative emotions potentially representing the SA, is always marked;
– acoustic analysis of a phonogram containing an emotionally coloured expression, if the predominant emotion is negative and this emotion conveys the SA, can reveal *at least one acoustic feature correlating with articulatory or phonatory tension*;
– if the analysis of the spectrum or the waveform cannot detect articulatory and/or phonatory tension because of noise, the instability in the determination of other acoustic features (e.g. the fundamental frequency) can be regarded as indirectly indicating the presence of tension, unless these features are themselves influenced by the noise factor (if they are, the phonogram should be considered inadequate for analysis).

After conducting multiple experiments with Russian, English, Spanish and Tatar language material and comparing the results of auditory-perceptual and acoustic analysis, we discovered that the perceptual assessment 'the SSSA correlates with the high-pitched voice' correlates with the measured peak values of the fundamental frequency for the Tatar language. For other investigated languages there was found no correlation between peak values of the fundamental frequency and the results of auditory-perceptual analysis.

The measured values of the acoustic characteristic "peak signal intensity" correlate with the data, acquired in auditory-perceptual experiments, about the voice power as a possible feature of the SSSA only for Spanish. Some correlations between the abovementioned characteristics for the English phonograms are possible too. However, no explicit correlation has been observed. At the same time, there is still a possibility that Spanish intonation models may influence the prosodic system of American English.

Table 1. Perceptual and acoustic characteristics for different languages, %.

Russian phonograms #:	25	28	34	36	40	41	48	51	55	58
Deep voice	34	3	31	0	25	3	47	47	22	3
Middle voice	47	53	56	41	31	84	38	38	56	84
High voice	16	47	16	63	44	13	9	13	13	13
$F_{0_{max}}$ values, Hz	291	285	233	291	257	198	277	300	191	176
Weak voice	6	3	3	3	0	9	0	0	19	3
Moderate voice	41	19	25	22	16	56	50	25	59	53
Strong voice	56	81	75	78	88	34	53	78	19	47
$I_{i_{max}}$ values, dB	84	72	73	74	84	74	74	74	79	84
Smooth melodic pattern	16	9	19	6	6	28	6	16	66	38
Abrupt melodic pattern	84	88	78	94	97	56	88	88	19	63
Monotonous m.p	3	6	3	3	0	19	3	3	13	3
V_{F_0} values, Hz/s	387	868	786	634	893	589	228	1076	985	721
Slow tempo	6	0	6	3	0	9	6	3	47	0
Moderate tempo	53	19	41	44	22	78	53	47	38	56
Fast tempo	44	81	56	56	81	9	41	50	9	44
T_i values (syll./s)	6	7	5	5	6	5	5	7	5	6
English phonograms #:	10	19	26	32	33	37	38	45	77	118
Deep voice	41	31	6	44	28	47	44	31	41	34
Middle voice	59	50	72	50	47	28	34	34	56	44
High voice	0	19	25	9	28	25	22	31	0	0
$F_{0_{max}}$ values, Hz	172	334	320	304	291	353	381	284	308	122
Weak voice	19	0	0	3	0	9	6	0	6	13
Moderate voice	56	19	25	44	31	13	22	25	69	59
Strong voice	25	84	78	56	72	78	75	78	28	9
$I_{i_{max}}$ values, dB	90	90	72	75	78	75	72	79	72	73
Smooth melodic pattern	66	3	19	16	6	13	16	9	41	53
Abrupt melodic pattern	34	97	84	88	97	81	84	91	59	22
Monotonous m.p	6	0	0	3	0	6	3	3	3	9
V_{F_0} values, Hz/s	522	409	401	795	677	854	524	373	618	267
Slow tempo	28	0	3	6	6	0	13	0	0	31
Moderate tempo	59	47	25	28	44	16	50	34	41	47
Fast tempo	9	53	75	69	50	84	38	66	59	0
T_i values (syll./s)	5	5	3	4	5	5	4	4	4	6

(*Continued*)

Table 1. (*Continued*)

Spanish phonograms #:	4	8	30	53	57	61	66	132	134	137
Deep voice	28	22	28	31	9	34	9	25	19	31
Middle voice	34	38	50	63	75	53	75	47	63	63
High voice	41	38	22	3	13	6	16	28	3	3
$F_{0_{max}}$ values, Hz	230	280	272	307	293	189	284	311	189	192
Weak voice	0	0	0	9	6	25	0	0	13	3
Moderate voice	19	9	44	44	47	6	34	47	34	34
Strong voice	81	88	59	50	50	9	69	56	41	66
$I_{i_{max}}$ values, dB	88	88	74	76	63	69	77	68	64	62
Smooth melodic pattern	3	3	13	22	9	9	9	6	25	0
Abrupt melodic pattern	100	94	84	72	78	88	88	84	44	91
Monotonous m.p	0	3	3	9	13	6	3	13	13	13
V_{F_0} values, Hz/s	805	483	971	447	950	604	707	438	805	584
Slow tempo	0	0	3	0	6	0	6	3	3	0
Moderate tempo	9	3	16	50	16	47	16	3	9	41
Fast tempo	94	94	81	47	78	47	78	91	69	59
T_i values (syll./s)	6	5	6	6	6	8	7	5	10	7
Tatar phonograms #:	50	52	54	59	63	68	71	91	108	110
Deep voice	3	28	6	34	72	22	28	47	28	28
Middle voice	63	66	38	53	25	56	56	38	50	50
High voice	31	0	53	6	3	16	3	13	22	19
$F_{0_{max}}$ values, Hz	275	308	387	204	181	287	256	228	202	239
Weak voice	0	9	3	0	41	16	0	0	0	0
Moderate voice	31	44	19	63	56	44	69	44	53	44
Strong voice	72	47	81	34	6	41	25	56	53	59
$I_{i_{max}}$ values, dB	76	74	77	84	71	78	77	79	75	77
Smooth melodic pattern	6	6	25	16	53	13	13	3	9	6
Abrupt melodic pattern	88	84	75	81	38	84	75	91	78	84
Monotonous m.p	13	9	0	3	16	3	6	9	19	13
V_{F_0} values, Hz/s	605	403	380	476	385	907	488	559	243	459
Slow tempo	9	25	3	3	25	9	3	6	16	3
Moderate tempo	53	25	66	72	59	38	66	59	53	34
Fast tempo	41	47	31	22	16	50	22	34	34	63
T_i values (syll./s)	4	5	3	6	6	6	4	6	4	5

Table 2. Estimated acoustic "representations" of SSSA compared with neutral speech.

Markedness	Parameters	Language			
		English	Russian	Spanish	Tatar
+	$F0_{max} -' F0_{min}$	A small or a very wide range	A wide or a very wide range	A wide or a very wide range	A mid-frequency or a wide range
	V_{F0}	High or low change rate	High change rate or unstable change rate	High change rate	Average or high change rate
	$I_{max} - I_{min}$	A wide or narrow range	A wide or narrow range	A wide or narrow range	A wide range
	V_{I_i}	High or low change rate	High or low change rate	High change rate	Average or high change rate
−	$F0_{max} -' F0_{min}$	A wide range	A small range	A mid-frequency range	A small range
	V_{F0}	A small change rate, except nuclear tones	An average change rate	An average change rate	A small change rate
	$I_{max} - I_{min}$	A mid-range	A mid-range	A wide range	A mid-range
	V_{I_i}	Small change rate	Small or average change rate	Small or average change rate	Small change rate

In auditory-perceptual experiments, almost all listeners noted abrupt changes in the pitch mentioning it as one of the possible features of the SSSA, which has been confirmed by the acoustic analysis findings. The average values of the first time derivative of the F_0 for most of the phonograms range from 250 to 700 Hz, which corresponds to a high degree of lability of the fundamental frequency (as well as the auditory-perceptual pitch of the voice). It should be mentioned that with F_0 values circa 200 Hz typical for the majority of the investigated phonograms, such first derivative values ($\overline{V_{F_0}}$) indicate the change of the F_0 by more than one octave per second (12 semitones).

Some correlation is observed in the Russian and Tatar languages while comparing such a perceptual characteristic as speech tempo to the measured values of the number of syllables per second. For the Spanish material these values do not correlate at all, while in the English language an inverse correlation is partially observed: the rapid speech tempo is marked by the listeners in places where from 3 to 4 syllables are pronounced at the average; the medium speech tempo was marked with 5 syllables. This may indicate a special expectation effect in perceptual strategy of the listener, who perceives English speech material (as prosodic patterns of the speech represented in "slow" phonograms suggest slower pronunciation than it occurs in reality. It may be the cause spoken speech is perceived as fast one).

The results of the comparison between auditory-perceptual and acoustic data are presented in Table 1.

These qualitative characteristics can be illustrated with numeric data, yet the correctness of numeric data comparison in this case even on a qualitative level can be achieved only for small fractional groups of speakers.

In fact, the qualitative characteristics of 'wide' and 'narrow', 'high' and 'low' are relative here and they can be treated as 'more than k times' and 'less than l times', where k 2 and l 1.5 with the opportunity to normalize all the values by the average speaker considering intraspeaker and interspeaker (within a small group) variation.

The experimental determination of the parameters that correlate with the estimated preliminary qualitative characteristics of four representative groups of native speakers of English, Russian, Spanish and Tatar languages, makes up the objective of further research.

According to the results of the acoustic analysis of the phonograms, the perceived characteristics associated by the listeners with the manifestation of the SSSA, do not always correspond to the acoustic characteristics normally considered to be their correlates. Furthermore, the nature of the mutual correlation between these characteristics in most cases tends to depend on the language (Table 2).

3   Conclusion

Basing on the results of the acoustic measurements, the following qualitative regularities can be stated:

- the high values of the fundamental frequency correspond to the perceived characteristic of "a high-pitched voice" and are relevant for the perception of the SSSA from the speech only for *Tatar*;
- the high values of the fundamental frequency correspond to the perceived characteristic of "a strong voice" and are relevant for the perception of the SSSA from the speech only for *Spanish*;
- the acoustic data analysis confirms the auditory-perceptual data with respect to *the angularity of the melodic contour* for the vast majority of the phonograms;
- the high values of the measured characteristic of speech rate (the number of syllables per time unit) correspond to the perceived characteristic of "speech tempo" for *Russian* and *Tatar* languages, while for *Spanish* these characteristics do not correlate; in *English* a reverse correlation, connected with the expectation effect, may take place.

Thus, in order to reveal the features of SSSA by means of both auditory-perceptual and acoustic analysis (as well as to compare the auditory-perceptual and acoustic data) one should always take into consideration the specificity determined by complex systematic features of the language systems.

3.1 Prospects of Investigation

As part of further research it is planned to specify the obtained results in order to provide a more detailed description of the mutual correlation between auditory-perceptual and acoustic characteristics of the spoken speech presented in the phonograms containing expressions implemented by speakers in the SSSA, considering the possible dependence of this mutual correlation on the language of communication.

Acknowledgments. The survey is being carried out with the support of Russian Science Foundation (RSF) in the framework of the project No.14-18-01059 at Moscow State Linguistic University (scientific head of the project R.K. Potapova).

References

1. Komalova, L.R.: Repertuar Verbal'noy Realizatsii Otvetnoy Agressii v Situatsiyakh Statusno-Rolevoy Asimmetrii. Aktual'nye problemy literaturnogo perevoda. Vestnik MGLU, 9(695), 104–116. MGLU, Moskva (2014) (in Russian)
2. Komalova, L.R.: Stereotipnye Modeli Rechevoy Agressii Russkoyazychnoy Molodezhi. Odeskiy lingvistichny visnik 2, 46–58. Odeska yuridichna akademiya, Odessa (2014) (in Russian)
3. Komalova, L.R.: Verbal'naya Realizatsiya Otvetnoy Agressii v Situatsii Konflikta i Frustratsii. In: Problemy yazyka: Sbornik nauchnykh statey po materialam Vtoroy konf.-shkoly "Problemy yazyka: vzglyad molodykh uchenykh", pp. 187–198. IYaz RAN, Moskva (2013) (in Russian)
4. Potapova, R.K.: Sotsial'no-Setevoy Diskurs kak Objekt Mezhdistsiplinarnogo Issledovaniya. In: Materialy Vtoroj mezhdunarod. nauchn. konf. "Diskurs kak sotsial'naya deyatel'nost': prioritety i perspektivy", pp. 20–22. MGLU, Moskva (2014) (in Russian)
5. Potapova, R.K., Komalova, L.R.: Auditory-perceptual recognition of the emotional state of aggression. In: Ronzhin, A., Potapova, R., Fakotakis, N. (eds.) SPECOM 2015. LNCS (LNAI), vol. 9319, pp. 89–95. Springer, Heidelberg (2015)
6. Potapova, R.K., Komalova, L.R.: Lingua-cognitive survey of the semantic field "Aggression" in multicultural communication: typed text. In: Železný, M., Habernal, I., Ronzhin, A. (eds.) SPECOM 2013. LNCS, vol. 8113, pp. 227–232. Springer, Heidelberg (2013)
7. Potapova, R.K., Komalova, L.R.: Lingvokognitivnoe Issledovanie Sostoyaniya 'Agressiya' v Mezhyazykovoy i Mezhkul'turnoy Kommunikatsii: Pis'menny Tekst. Semioticheskaya Geterogennost' Yazykovoy Kommunikatsii: Teoriya i Praktika. Chast' II, 15 (675), 164–175. MGLU, Moskva (2013) (in Russian)
8. Potapova, R.K., Komalova, L.R.: O Vozmozhnosti Raspoznavaniya Slukhovogo Obraza, Assotsiiruemogo Retsipientami s Sostoyaniem Agressii. Sovremennoe rechevedenie - agregatsiya mezhdistsiplinarnykh znaniy. Vestnik MGLU, 13(699), 202–214, IPK MGLU, Moskva (2014) (in Russian)

9. Potapova, R.K., Komalova, L.R.: On principles of annotated databases of the semantic field "Aggression". In: Ronzhin, A., Potapova, R., Delic, V. (eds.) SPECOM 2014. LNCS, vol. 8773, pp. 322–328. Springer, Heidelberg (2014)
10. Potapova, R.K., Mikhaylov, V.G.: Osnovy Rechevoy Akustiki. IPK MGLU 'Rema', Moskva (2012) (in Russian)
11. Potapova, R.K., Potapov, V.V.: Rechevaya Kommunikatsiya: Ot Zvuka k Vyskazyvaniyu. Yazyki Slavyanskikh Kul'tur, Moskva (2012) (in Russian)
12. Potapova, R.K., Potapov, V.V.: Yazyk, Rech'. Lichnost'. Yazyki Slavyanskoy Kul'tury, Moskva (2006) (in Russian)

Algorithms for Low Bit-Rate Coding with Adaptation to Statistical Characteristics of Speech Signal

Anton Saveliev[1], Oleg Basov[2], Andrey Ronzhin[1,3(✉)], and Alexander Ronzhin[1,3]

[1] SPIIRAS, 39, 14th Line, Saint Petersburg 199178, Russia
{saveliev,ronzhin,ronzhinal}@iias.spb.su
[2] Academy of FAP of Russia, 35, Priborostroitelnaya, Orel 302034, Russia
oobasov@mail.ru
[3] SUAI, 67, Bolshaya Morskaia, Saint Petersburg 199000, Russia

Abstract. The article establishes the general trends of speech coding algorithms based on linear prediction. The task of adaptation of speech codec to the statistical characteristics of the coding parameters is set and accomplished. The main procedures of their forming are examined. The results of experimental studies of the developed adaptive low bit-rate coding algorithms are presented. The benefits of the quality of remade speech in comparison with algorithms on FS1015, FS1017 and FS1016 standards and Full-rate GSM are displayed.

Keywords: Speech coding algorithms · Near prediction · Statistical characteristics · Overrightarrowtor quantization · Code-excited linear prediction · Mixed-excitation linear prediction

1 Introduction

Modern means of cryptographic protection of information for conjugation with data terminal equipment still widely use interface S1-FL-BE. Corresponding signal-conversion equipment provides data transmission at speeds of $V = \{1, 2; 2, 4; 4, 8; 9, 6\}$ kbps by non-switchable voice-frequency channels [1]. Existing needs for enhancing quality of speech processing at mentioned speeds determine particular urgency of search in the sphere of developing new and upgrading existing methods and low bit-rate speech coding algorithms. At the concerned speed range (< 16 kbps) leading position among various methods is occupied by the coding based on the method of linear prediction (LP). Efficiency of coding with LP algorithms is limited by the lack of their adaptation to the statistical characteristics of the speech signal.

The paper presents the developed algorithms of coding/decoding the speech signal, providing high syllable intelligibility, natural speech sound and speech, and speaker recognition of the subscriber at the data transfer range of 1,2–9,6 kbps.

This paper is organized as follows. Section 2 discusses trends in the development of algorithms for low bit-rate speech coding. Section 2.1 describes structural

© Springer International Publishing Switzerland 2015
A. Ronzhin et al. (Eds.): SPECOM 2015, LNAI 9319, pp. 65–72, 2015.
DOI: 10.1007/978-3-319-23132-7_8

scheme of the hybrid MELP/CELP coder with adaptation to the statistical characteristics of coding parameters. Section 2.2 presents the experiments and results.

2   Related Works

Modern linear predictive vocoders have approached waveform coders regarding quality of synthesized speech; at the same time, they provide significally lower transmission speeds. Their analysis allows us to identify the dominant trends in improving parametric speech coding method based on linear prediction.

1. Predominant use for describing the current state of the vocal tract of M-dimensional overrightarrowtor of line spectral frequencies (LSF), which is the mathematical equivalent of the LP coefficients, but has a better resistance to channel errors.
2. Use at encoding speeds from 4, 8 to 16 kbps different variants of code-excited linear prediction vocoders (CELP codecs) [2], and at speed range of 0.6 2.4 kbps mixed-excited linear prediction vocoders (MELP codecs) [3].
3. Representation of the excitation signal by multicomponent model. In versions of CELP codecs two- and three-component models are becoming most popular, which include one or two stochastic excitation overrightarrowtors encoded with the use of a fixed codebook, as well as excitation overrightarrowtor, displaying the result of long-term linear prediction based on analysis of the dynamics of the speech signal pitch. In MELP codecs the excitation signal represents the sum of the periodic and noise components synthesized in the respective frequency bands on the length of the pitch period of the speech signal.
4. Wide use of varieties of overrightarrowtor quantization (VQ) for displaying the encoded speech parameters with the active use of intra-frame and inter-frame dependencies of the latter in order to maximize the possible exception of redundancy.
5. Multiplex parameter coding, which is determined by sufficient degree of statistical independence of the vocal tract transfer function and generating function (of excitation signal) of the used model of speech production.

At the same time, codecs based on the LP have not yet exhausted all the possibilities for speech compression with maintaining the required quality. Feasible degree of optimization of linear predictive vocoders is largely determined by the level of available a priori information on coding parameters and the degree of its algorithmic use. It is obvious that the use of a locally stationary model of speech does not eliminate existing a priori uncertainty about the statistical characteristics of the speech source with memory. Contradiction between the natural nonstationarity of SS (speech signal) and a locally stationary character of its model leads to significant variation range of coding parameters calculated on different frames of speech.

The results of comparison of the main ways to overcome a priori indeterminacy, as well as constancy of space structure of coding parameters of linear predictive vocoders indicate existing today possibility of increasing the degree of LP algorithms adaptation to the statistical characteristics of coding parameters.

2.1   Structural Scheme of the Hybrid MELP/CELP Coder

Taking into consideration mentioned trends, generalized structural scheme of the hybrid MELP/CELP coder with adaptation to the statistical characteristics of coding parameters was the subject of the study (see Fig. 1). In accordance with the scheme, many coding parameters of the speech signal were defined $\{\vec{X}_j\}$: $\vec{X}_1$ line spectral frequencies (LSF), X_2 pitch period values, X_3 existence of pitch period jitter, $\vec{X}_4$ degree of band vocalization, $\vec{X}_5$ values of the amplitude spectrum of prediction error signal, corresponding to pitch period harmonics, $\vec{X}_6$ values of the excitation signal amplifications (frame), $\vec{X}_7$ the excitation vector, $\vec{X}_8$ values of the excitation vectors amplifications. Below is the description of their estimation procedures on adopted duration of the analyzed speech frames equal to $\hat{E} = 160$ samples (20 msec).

The procedure of parameter identification of the vocal tract $\vec{X}_1$ is standard and does not require explanation. Parameter identification of the excitation vector according to reference models of code excitation and mixed excitation have common procedure for determining pitch period. For use in the presence of acoustic noise algorithm for determining the pitch period has been developed X_2 [4,5]. Evaluation values of the pitch period are used to determine the presence of pitch period jitter X_3. The degree of vocalization $\vec{X}_4$ of four frequency

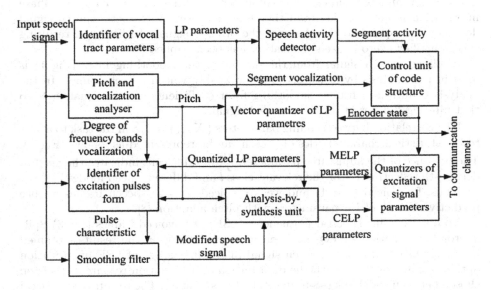

Fig. 1. Generalized structural scheme of the hybrid MELP/CELP coder

bands is (500–1000 Hz, 1000–2000 Hz, 2000–3000 Hz and 3000–4000 Hz) can be estimated on the basis of normalized autocorrelation function calculation [6].

In MELP codecs prediction error signal for voiced speech frames is represented by the values $\overrightarrow{X}_5$ of the amplitude spectrum at frequencies corresponding to pitch harmonics: $1/X_2T_d, 2/X_2T_d, \ldots, z/X_2T_d$, where T_d - the sampling period of the analog speech signal, z - number of harmonics, used for identifying forms of excitation pulses.

Amplification $\overrightarrow{X}_6$ of prediction error signal is determined twice per speech signal frame with the use of analysis interval adaptive to the pitch period [7].

The identification of the excitation vector $\overrightarrow{X}_7$ and corresponding to it amplification of $\overrightarrow{X}_8$ on the analysis interval is carried out by the known method of analysis through synthesis [6] in compliance with standard CELP model.

It is indicated that for coding:

– pause frames ($l = 0$) only service information about the state of the coder must be transmitted to the decoder;
– voiced frames ($l = 1$) a mixed excitation model should be used;
– weakly voiced frames ($l = 2$) we should use CELP coder with long-term predictor and algebraic codebook;
– unvoiced frames ($l = 3$) - CELP coder with stochastic codebook should be used.

However, CELP coder minimizes the error between the input and synthesized speech signal completely retaining its shape (including signal phase). In contrast, MELP coding is based on a minimizing the error between analyzed parameters $\overrightarrow{X}_j, j = 1, 6$ and parameters used in speech synthesis. In this case, the phase information is not encoded, and therefore the form of synthetic speech signal does not correspond to the shape of the original signal. To limit the resulting speech artifacts zero-phase equalization has been applied [7].

Modified speech signal from the output of the smoothing filter (Fig. 1) is used in the analysis-by-synthesis unit for weakly voiced speech frames. In the analysis of unvoiced frames smoothing filter coefficients are set equal to 1, so that filtering did not affect the encoded signal.

The correlation between coding parameters $\{\overrightarrow{X}_j\}, j = \overline{1,8}$ in the task to adapt to the statistical characteristics of speech can be represented as follows (Fig. 2). The presence of the adjustable parameter $o_j^{(l)}$ in table cells indicates the need to define j-th reflection F_j for the relevant class l and different speed modes V.

Thus, for voiced ($l = 1$) and weakly voiced ($l = 2$) speech frames we use predictive VQ F_1 of LP parameters with pitch adaption [8].

To quantize line spectral frequencies (LSF) of unvoiced frames ($l = 3$) Split Vector Quantization - SVQ has been used [6]. Basing on the results, obtained in [8], for use of unvoiced speech signal in the first stage of LSF quantization option of splitting 3-3-4 with the distribution of information resources has been chosen between codebook 6-8-9 (in total 23 bits/vector). The results of statistical studies of a large amount of speech material allowed us at the critical significance level $\alpha = 0,01$ to approximate the density function $p(X_2)$ of the distribution

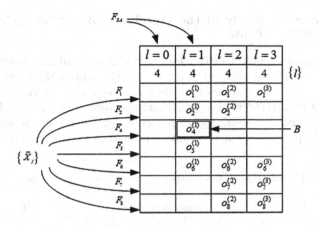

Fig. 2. Correlation between coding parameters

of pitch values by lognormal distribution with parameters $\mu = 4,0887$, $\sigma = 0,216752$ and calculate the parameters of the optimal scalar quantizer F_2 for pitch lag. At the same time, for a small number of quantization levels ($o_2 < 60$) a standard Maxs algorithm was used [9]. At the number of quantization levels $o_2 > 60$ we applied a method based on the use of asymptotically optimal compression characteristics of the form [10].

Iterative cluster algorithm K-means was used to construct VQ $\overrightarrow{X}_4$ parameters.

The results of experimental studies have shown that 10 pitch harmonics cover all or nearly all speech spectrum for voices of different speakers; therefore, for their quantization F_5 cascade VQ was used with weighing on the Bark scale [11].

Amplifications $\overrightarrow{X}_6$ for voiced ($l = 1$) and weakly voiced ($l = 2$) speech frames are scalarly quantized in the range from 10 to 77 dB with the use of an adaptive algorithm proposed in [3].

In the quantization F_7 and F_8 of parameters $\overrightarrow{X}_7$ and $\overrightarrow{X}_8$ of weakly voiced ($l = 2$) speech frames we use an algebraic codebook with four excitation pulses for each of the two analyzed subframes. On the duration of the analyzed speech signal frame $T_A = 20$ ms two gain values of the pitch predictor and two gain values of fixed (algebraic) codebook are scalarly quantized and transmitted to the decoder. For unvoiced ($l = 3$) speech frames search is implemented in stochastic codebook by displays F_7 and F_8; four indexes of code vector ($\overrightarrow{X}_7$) and their gain values ($\overrightarrow{X}_8$) are subjected to transmission to the decoder.

Introduced set of mappings F_j (Fig. 2) minimizes the speech signal distortion in the conditions of a selected number of classes ($l = 4$), method of their formation and adoption of classification decisions, while implementation of the control structure of codec F_{SA} on each interval of the speech signal analysis represents its adaptation to the statistical characteristics of coding parameters.

2.2 Experimental Study of the Developed Adaptive Hybrid MELP/CELP Coder

Implementation of coding algorithms for different transmission speeds $V \in \{V\}$ in accordance with a generalized scheme (Fig. 1) requires the determination of powers o_j for each j-th parameter and l-th class of its statistical characteristics (Fig. 2). Traditionally, the volume of information resources is generally measured in bits, so obtained distributions are presented in Table 1 in the form of $\log o_j$ bits / frame. In parentheses is the number of quantization steps for cascade VQ.

Table 1. Distribution of information resources over coding parameters.

№	V, kbit/s	l	Volume, bits/frame								Total, bits/frame
			l	$\vec{X}_1$	$\vec{X}_2$	$\vec{X}_4$	$\vec{X}_5$	$\vec{X}_6$	$\vec{X}_7$	$\vec{X}_8$	
1	1,2	0	2	-	-	-	-	-	-	-	2
		1	2	10(1)	5	2	-	5	-	-	**240**
		2	2	10(1)	5	2	-	5	-	-	
		3	2	17(1)	-	-	-	5	-	-	
2	2,3	0	2	-	-	-	-	-	-	-	2
		1	2	19(1)	7	4	8(1)	8	-	-	**48**
		2	2	19(1)	7	4	8(1)	8	-	-	
		3	2	23(1)	-	-	-	5	-	6	36
3	4,8	0	2	-	-	-	-	-	-	-	2
		1	2	32(2)	7	10	29(2)	16	-	-	**96**
		2	2	32(2)	7	-	-	8	38	9	
		3	2	23(1)	-	-	-	5	45	6	81
4	9,6	0	2	-	-	-	-	-	-	-	2
		1	2	54(3)	7	14	89(3)	26	-	-	**192**
		2	2	54(3)	7	-	-	16	83	12	174
		3	2	48(2)	-	-	-	8	96	9	153

In order to eliminate speech artifacts, especially seen at transmission speed of 9,6 kbps, algorithm № 4 (Table 1) provides for the encoding phase components of the spectrum of prediction error signal by SVQ-quantizer with the splitting scheme 14-13-13 bits. At that point, the values of the amplitude spectrum are quantized by cascade VQ with 8, 20 and 21 bits per cascade correspondingly.

Set of subjective evaluations (Table 2) shows that introduction of adaption procedure to LP coding algorithms ensured a high quality reconstruction of the speech signal for transmission speeds $\{V\}$. Furthermore, tests of the subjective listening of the speech signal, encoded (decoded) with the use of algorithms № 1-3, indicate marked superiority of intelligibility and naturalness of the synthesized speech. They also show superiority of the speaker's voice recognition in comparison with algorithms on FS1015 (1.2 kbps), FS1017 and FS1016 standards correspondingly; at the same time with the use of algorithm № 4 they point out quality, comparable to standard Full-rate GSM (13 kbps).

Table 2. Qualitative characteristics of the developed algorithms.

№	V, kbit/s	Quality of reconstructed speech			Q, MIPS	W, words
		Syllable intelligibility	Estimation by the method of pairwise comparisons	MOS		
1	1,2	86 %	2,9	3,2	19,2	16,44
2	2,4	92 %	3,5	3,7	28,4	20,5
3	4,8	94 %	4,2	4,2	24,1	29,2
4	9,6	96 %	4,6	3,5	26,7	37,4

Peak computational complexity Q of algorithms is calculated with allowance for the need to fulfill the required number of operations in real time for maximum volumes of VQ codebooks. The transition to the adaptive coding demanded substantial (about twice as much) increase in the amount W of stored information in memory devices due to the need to store the new program segments and additional variants of codebooks.

3   Conclusion

At the heart of improving the quality parameters of the developed algorithms is an in-depth analysis of the speech signal frame and adaption to their parameters, characterized by increased computational complexity of procedures for speech coding. At the hardware level the developed algorithms, in comparison with the similar standard algorithms, require increased efficiency of estimators and additional capacity of memory elements. The proposed speech coding algorithms will be implemented in developing peer-to-peer videoconferencing with serverless connections between clients and audiovisual data transmission by web application [12–14], as well as in developing services for smart meeting room [15–17].

Acknowledgments. This work is partially supported by the Russian Foundation for Basic Research (grants № 15-07-06-774-a, 13-08-0741-a); the scholarship of the President of the Russian Federation (project no. SP-3872.2015.5).

References

1. GOST 26532-85. Data transmission system signal conversion modulus for unswitched voice-frequency channels. Types and basic parameters. Moscow: GOST USSR (1985) (In Russia)

2. Trancoso, I.M.: An overview of different trends on CELP coding. In: Ayuso, A.J.R., Soler, J.M.L. (eds.) Speech Recognition and Coding: New Advances and Trends. NATO ASI Series, vol. 147, pp. 351–367. Springer, Heidelberg (1995)

3. Supplee, L.M., Cohn, R.P., Collura, J.S., McCree, A.V.: MELP: the new Federal Standard at 2400 bps. In: IEEE ICASSP-97 Conference, Munich, Germany, pp. 1591–1594 (1997)

4. Basov, O.O., Nosov, M.V., Shalaginov, V.A.: Pitch-jitter analysis of the speech signal. SPIIRAS Proc. 1(32), 27–44 (2014). (In Russian)

5. Basov, O.O., Saitov, I.A.: Basic channels of interpersonal communication and their projection on the infocommunications systems. SPIIRAS Proc. 7(30), 122–140 (2013). (In Russian)

6. Wai, C.C.: Speech Coding Algorithms: Foundation and evolution of standardized coders. Wiley, Hoboken (2003)

7. Stachurski, J., McCree, A., Viswanathan, V., Heikkinen, A., Ramo, A., Himanen, S., Blocher, P.: Hybrid MELP/CELP coding at bit rates from 6.4 to 2.4 kb/s. In: IEEE International Conference on Acoustics, Speech, and Signal Processing, pp. II-153–II-156 (2003)

8. Basov, O.O.: A conceptual model of multicriterion adaptation of the linear predictive voice coding procedure. Telecommun. Radio Eng. 68(10), 923–931 (2009)

9. Max, J.: Quantizing for minimum distortion. IRE Trans. Inform. Theory 6, 7–12 (1963)

10. Smith, B.: Instantaneous companding of quantized signals. Bell Syst. Tech. J. 36, 653–709 (1957)

11. Palival, K.K., Atal, B.S.: Efficient vector quantization of LPC parameters at 24 bits/frame. IEEE Trans. Acoustics Speech Signal Process. 1(1), 3–14 (1993)

12. Saveliev, A.I., Vatamaniuk, I.V., Ronzhin, A.L.: Architecture of data exchange with minimal client-server interaction at multipoint video conferencing. In: Balandin, S., Andreev, S., Koucheryavy, Y. (eds.) NEW2AN/ruSMART 2014. LNCS, vol. 8638, pp. 164–174. Springer, Heidelberg (2014)

13. Potapova, R., Sobakin, A., Maslov, A.: On the possibility of the skype channel speaker identification (on the basis of acoustic parameters). In: Ronzhin, A., Potapova, R., Delic, V. (eds.) SPECOM 2014. LNCS, vol. 8773, pp. 329–336. Springer, Heidelberg (2014)

14. Saveliev, A.I., Prischepa, M.: Architecture of lossless data exchange in pear-to-pear web application of videoconference. Proc. Tomsk State Univ. Control Syst. Radioelectronics 2(32), 238–245 (2014)

15. Ronzhin, A.L., Karpov, A.A.: A software system for the audiovisual monitoring of an intelligent meeting room in support of scientific and education activities. Pattern Recogn. Image Anal. 25(2), 237–254 (2015)

16. Ronzhin, A., Vatamaniuk, I., Ronzhin, A., Železný, M.: Algorithms for acceleration of image processing at automatic registration of meeting participants. In: Ronzhin, A., Potapova, R., Delic, V. (eds.) SPECOM 2014. LNCS(LNAI), vol. 8773, pp. 89–96. Springer, Heidelberg (2014)

17. Ronzhin, A.L., Ronzhin, A.L., Budkov, V.Y.: Methodology of facility automation based on audiovisual analysis and space-time structuring of situation in meeting room. In: Stephanidis, C. (ed.) HCII 2013, Part II. CCIS, vol. 374, pp. 524–528. Springer, Heidelberg (2013)

Analysing Human-Human Negotiations with the Aim to Develop a Dialogue System

Mare Koit$^{(\boxtimes)}$

University of Tartu, J. Liivi 2, 50409 Tartu, Estonia
mare.koit@ut.ee
http://www.cl.ut.ee

Abstract. We are studying human-human spoken dialogues in the Estonian dialogue corpus with the aim to design a dialogue system which carries out negotiation with a user in a natural language. Three sub-corpora have been analyzed: (1) telemarketing calls where a sales clerk of an educational company argues for taking a training course by a customer; (2) conversations between a travel agent and a customer who is planning a trip; and (3) everyday conversations where one participant argues for performing an action by the partner. A special case of negotiation – debate where the participants have contradicting communicative goals – has been implemented as an experimental dialogue system.

Keywords: Negotiation · Argument · Human-human conversation · Dialogue system

1 Introduction

Negotiation is a discussion between two or more participants who are trying to work out a solution to their problem [1]. While the speakers have interlocking goals that they cannot accomplish independently, they usually do not want exactly the same thing. This interdependence can be either win-win or win-lose in nature. Win-win outcomes occur when each side feels they have won. Win-lose situations result when only one side perceives the outcome as positive. Thus, win-lose outcomes are less likely to be accepted voluntarily [2].

Negotiation is an exchange of offers. Participants make offers that they find acceptable and respond to offers made to them. In argumentation-based negotiation, offers can be supported by arguments. "This permits greater flexibility than in other negotiation schemes since, for instance, it makes it possible to persuade agents to change their view of an offer by introducing new factors in the middle of a negotiation" [3].

Several researchers have been modelling argumentation on the computer. Overviews of the state of the art in modelling argumentation-based negotiation can be found e.g. in [4,5].

We are studying human-human dialogues in order to develop a dialogue system (DS) which interacts with a user in a natural language following norms

© Springer International Publishing Switzerland 2015
A. Ronzhin et al. (Eds.): SPECOM 2015, LNAI 9319, pp. 73–80, 2015.
DOI: 10.1007/978-3-319-23132-7_9

and rules of human communication. We consider the dialogue acts (DA) and the communicative strategies (CS) used by participants in conversation and the structure of dialogue. The dialogue manager of a DS will use information about the structure of interaction in order to interpret the user's utterances and to generate its own responses. On the other hand, automatic recognition of the dialogue structure formed by DAs and CSs can be considered as a sub-task of automatic pragmatical analysis of a dialogue text.

The rest of the paper is structured as follows. Section 2 introduces our empirical material: the Estonian dialogue corpus and software for its analysis. In Sect. 3 we analyze human-human argumentation-based dialogues in order to design negotiation on the computer. Section 4 discusses the lessons learnt from the analysis for creating a DS. In Sect. 5 we make conclusions.

2   Empirical Material and Used Software

Our study is based on the Estonian dialogue corpus (EDiC) [6]. It includes human-human spoken dialogues recorded in authentic situations and transcribed by using the transcription system of Conversation Analysis (CA).

DAs are annotated in the corpus by using a customized typology [6] which is based on CA. In the typology, the DAs are divided into two groups – adjacency pair (AP) acts where the first pair part expects a certain second pair part (like question-answer), and single acts which do not expect any response (like continuer *uhuh*). Names of the DAs consist of two parts separated by a colon: (a) the first two letters give an abbreviation of the name of an act-group, e.g. QU – QUestions, VR – Voluntary Reactions. The third letter is used only for AP acts – the first (F) or the second (S) pair part of an AP act; (b) the proper name of the act. Thus, there are acts as QUF: Wh-question, QUS: Giving information, VR: Neutral continuer, etc. The total number of the acts is 126.

CSs are annotated following the Constructive Dialogue Model (CDM) proposed by Jokinen [7]. CS is used by a participant to form his/her next turn as a response to the partner's previous turn. Four context factors with binary values (1 or 0) determine CSs in CDM which gives 16 CSs in total. Although Jokinen has used the CSs for the analysis of information seeking dialogues, they are applicable also for other kinds of dialogues. Still, the names of some CSs are not quite self-explaining.

We are using custom-made web-based software for annotation of dialogues [8]. The tool enables to annotate DAs and thereafter CSs in a dialogue text. Another custom-made software tool enables to calculate some statistics: the counts of utterances, words, different kinds of DAs, frequency of words and certain sequences of DAs, etc.

Here we study three subcorpora of EDiC: (1) telemarketing calls where sales clerks of an educational company are arguing for taking training courses offered by the company to customers (51 dialogues), (2) calls and face-to-face dialogues in travel agencies where customers are planning trips in collaboration with a travel agent (24 phone calls and 4 face-to-face conversations), and (3) everyday dialogues between acquaintances or friends where an action is negotiated and argued (22 phone calls and 22 face-to-face conversations). Our aim is to find out the typical structure of negotiations in the three types of dialogues as represented by DAs and CSs. Further, we attempt to design a general structure of argumentation-based negotiation.

3 Analysis of Human-Human Dialogues: Argument-Based Negotiation

3.1 Arguments and Negotiation in Telemarketing Calls

A sales clerk of an educational company initiates an interaction calling to a potential customer – a manager or personnel officer of another institution – and offers training courses (management, marketing, service, etc.) for employees of the institution. The selection of the institutions is based on a previous study carried out by the clerk. As a rule, more than one call is needed before a customer makes her decision about an offered course. In most of the analyzed calls, the participants only agree to continue negotiation afterward. The final decision (to take a course or not) has been made only in seven calls (among them are three positive decisions, i.e. to take a course, and four negative). Several phases can be distinguished in a telemarketing call [9].

The next examples demonstrate the usage of arguments in telemarketing calls. Here A denotes a sales clerk and B a customer. Transcription of CA is used in the examples. DAs are annotated by using our typology. CSs (in square brackets) are annotated following CDM. As we see, different DAs can express arguments – either AP acts or non-AP acts. For example, an assertion or opinion DA frequently used for presenting arguments are the first pair parts of an opinion AP, the notations are, respectively, OPF: Assertion and OPF: Opinion. The corresponding CSs are repeat-new or new-st-request. The second pair parts of this AP are OPS: Accept and OPS: Reject used by the partner for agreement or non-agreement with the argument (example 1).

(1)
A: ja saab seda:=m programmi nagu ju lähtuvalt teie vajadustest just (.) kohandada ka:.
And this programme can be adapted to your needs. OPF: Assertion [repeat-new]
B: jaa.
Yes. OPS: Accept [follow-up-old]

It is often the case that one utterance gets more than one DA tag in our annotation. In such a way, an utterance can be both the second pair part of a previous AP and the first pair part of a new AP, e.g. OPS: Accept and OPF: Opinion at the same time (example 2).

(2)
B: aga näiteks projektijuhtimist teil=ei ole, mida mina otsin tegelikult prae[gu.]
But you don't have project management what I'm looking for. OPF: Assertion [repeat-new]

A: kui keegi=on=meie käest projektijuhtimist küsinud, .hhh[h sii]s tegelikult
But if someone will order project management then we actually OPS: Reject + OPF:
Assertion [new-st-request]
B: [mhmh]
Uhuh. VR: Neutral continuer [continue]
A: meil=on=need vahendid olemas.
we are able to teach it. OPS: Limited accept + OPF: Assertion [new-st-request]

Some non-AP acts are also used as arguments: DAs of additional information
(AI: Justification, AI: Specification, AI: Explication) and a primary single act of
giving information (PS: Giving information). The corresponding CSs are backto,
follow-up-new or follow-up-old. As said above, non-AP acts do not expect any
reaction of the partner, in such a way, these acts are used as 'soft' arguments
which don't necessarily to be disproved. If the partner anyway attempts to rebut
the argument then s/he has to use either the first pair part of a new AP or
another non-AP act.

A typical structure of the main part of a telemarketing call can be represented
as follows. (*A* – sales clerk, *B* – customer. The winding brackets '{' and '}'
connect a part that can be repeated; round brackets connect a part that can be
missed; names of CSs are given in square brackets; ' |' separates alternatives; '-!'
starts a comment.)

A: DIF: Proposal [finish/start]
{
-! Finding out what *B* needs
A: QUF: Wh-question [repeat-new]
B: QUS: Giving information [follow-up-old]
{*A*: QUF: Wh-question [backto]
B: QUS: Giving information [follow-up-old]}
-! Argumentation
A: OPF: Assertion |QUF: Offering answer [repeat-new] -! <argument>
-! if collaboration
B: OPS: Accept |QUS: Yes [follow-up-old]
{*A*: OPF: Assertion |QUF: Offering answer [backto] -! <argument>
(AI: Justification [backto] |PS: Giving information [follow-up-old]) -! <argument>
B: OPS: Accept |QUS: Yes [follow-up-old]
(AI: Justification [follow-up-new] |PS: Giving information [follow-up-old]) -! <argument>}
-! if confrontation { *B*: OPS: Reject + OPF: Assertion [new-st-request] -! <argument>
A: OPS: Accept + OPF: Assertion [new-request] -! <argument>}
}
-! Decision
B: DIS: Accept |Deferral [follow-up-old] |DIS: Reject [continue]

We can see that a sales clerk gives his arguments by using the first pair parts of
APs therefore a customer could protest them (choosing the corresponding second
pair part). Nonetheless, the sales clerks have been able to choose such arguments
which have mostly been accepted by customers. A customer usually represents her
counter-argument (if any) by a non-AP act not expecting refutation.

The situation is different if the customer takes antagonistic position (in a few of dialogues) – then she uses the first pair parts of the opinion AP for her arguments (OPF: Assertion, OPF: Opinion) and the sales clerk has to react to them. Polite and friendly sales clerks always accept the arguments but also present their own (counter)arguments.

3.2 Negotiation in Travel Dialogues

Differently as compared with telemarketing calls, a customer initiates conversation with a travel agent and requests information. A travel agent is expected to give information, maybe after asking some adjusting questions. In this way, our analysed travel dialogues are first of all question-answering dialogues where both participants can ask and answer questions. The further communicative goal of a customer is to book a trip. This also is the goal of a collaborative travel agent therefore the agent could afford to argue for the pleasantness and usefulness of a certain trip. Still, argumentation for a trip has only been found in five dialogues (out of 28). Final decision (to take a trip or not) has not been made in these dialogues.

Arguments have mostly been represented as giving information what was not asked by the partner, by using a non-AP act PS: Giving information, example 3 (A – agent, B – customer). Justification (a non-AP act AI: Justification), assertion or opinion (the first pair parts OPF: Assertion or OPF: Opinion of an AP) have also been used.

(3)

A: ää: (2.0) sis kindlasti tasub teada=et=õ (0.4) pealelõunal (.) peetakse siestat?
You should definitely know that they have siesta in the afternoon. PS: Giving information [follow-up old]
(.) et kõik kauplused=ja: (0.3) ee kõik teeninduskohad on suletud?
That all the shops and services are closed. PS: Giving information [follow-up old]

While argumentation in telemarketing calls alternates with asking questions by an agent (and answering by a customer) then argumentation in travel dialogues alternates with answering the questions asked by a customer (and answered by the agent). The structure of a travel dialogue can be represented as follows.

-! Requesting information
B: DIF: Request |QUF: Wh-question [finish/start]
-! Adjusting the conditions of answer
{A: QUF: Offering answer |Closed yes-no [sub-question, X]
B: QUS: yes [follow-up-old]}
-! Giving information
{A: DIS |QUS: Giving |Missing information [follow-up-old] |[continue]
(PS: Giving information [follow-up old] |AI: Justification [follow-up-new]) -! <argument>
-! Specifying the answer
B: QUF: Wh-question [sub-question, X]}

A customer initiates a dialogue with a request for information. A travel agent gives information and sometimes (in a few of dialogues) he also argues for a trip by adding information which was not explicitly asked by the customer. The participants are cooperatively working for a common goal.

3.3   Arguments and Negotiation in Everyday Dialogues

All the analyzed everyday conversations include argumentation-based negotiation. That is different as compared with travel dialogues. The participants are acquainted or friends and the initiator A makes a proposal to his partner B to perform an action. Positive decision has been achieved in 25 cases and negative in one case. The remaining dialogues (out of 44) finish with the postponement of the decision. Several DAs and CSs are used for giving arguments: non-AP acts as well as AP acts like in the case of telemarketing or travel dialogues (examples 4, 5).

(4)
A: et ma mul on näiteks tollega see jama et ma saaks tulla pühappäeval.
I could only come on Sunday. PS: Giving information [follow-up old]

(5)
A: [oota, ei tegelt ta] on ikkagi:::: jõega ühenduses=ju.
Actually, the channel is connected with the river. OPS: Refusal + OPF: Assertion [new-st-request]
B: ei=ole jõega ühenduseses vaata.
No, it's not, you see. OPS: Refusal + OPF: Assertion [new-st-request]

The initiator A attempting to convince B to perform an action presents his (soft) arguments by non-AP acts (PS: Giving information, AI: Justification |Specification |Explanation) and does not expect the reaction of the partner. If the partner B is collaborative then she does not present counterarguments. On the contrary, if she is antagonistic then she takes over the initiative and presents her arguments as the first pair parts of the opinion AP (OPF: Assertion |Opinion) expecting A's counter-arguments. The general structure of an everyday negotiation can be represented as follows.

A: DIF: Proposal [finish-start] (PS: Giving information [follow-up-old] |AI: Justification [backto] -! <argument>)
-! if collaboration
{B: DIF: Request |QUF: Wh question [backto]
(PS: Giving information [follow-up-old] |AI: Justification [backto] -! <argument>)
A: DIS: Giving information [follow-up-old]
(PS: Giving information [follow-up-old] |AI: Justification [backto] -! <argument>)}
(-! if confrontation
B: OPF: Assertion [repeat-new] -! <argument>
A: OPS: Reject + OPF: Assertion [new-st-request] -! <argument>
{B: OPS: Reject + OPF: Assertion [new-st-request] -! <argument>
A: OPS: Reject + OPF: Assertion [new-st-request] -! <argument >})
-! Decision
B: DIS: Accept |Deferral [follow-up-old] |DIS: Reject [continue]

4 Discussion

The analysed dialogues represent different negotiations. In travel dialogues, the participants have the same communicative goal. The interaction is collaborative, few arguments for a certain trip have been presented by a travel agent. When giving arguments, an agent uses mostly non-AP acts that don't expect reaction of the partner, giving information which has not been asked by the customer.

Telemarketing calls are different because a customer may not be interested in taking a proposed course. However, the participants interact cooperatively in most cases and present such arguments which do not evoke rejection of the partner. Both participants can use non-AP acts as well as opinion AP acts. In a few calls the participants are explicitly antagonistic. Then the customer takes over the initiative and presents her arguments as assertions or opinions which expect reaction. A sales clerk always agrees with the arguments of a customer but he also proposes his own (counter)arguments. More opinion APs are used in the case if a telemarketing call finishes with a clear refusal of the customer to take a course. The arguments of sales clerks are mostly presented by a non-AP act giving information. Therefore, a customer presents strong arguments (opinions which expect reaction) while a sales clerk presents soft arguments (non-AP acts) that don't awake protest of the partner.

Everyday negotiations are similar with the telemarketing calls in this sense that the participants can be either collaborative or antagonistic. Similar DAs and CSs are used as compared with telemarketing calls with the difference that here the initiator mostly does not agree with the counterarguments of the partner.

Taking into account the results of the analysis, we can represent the general structure of argumentation-based negotiation where performing an action is discussed as a sequence of DAs:

proposal {question giving-information} {assertion |justification |giving-information accept |justification |giving-information |reject+assertion} accept |reject

or as a sequence of CSs:

finish/start {repeat-new follow-up-old} {backto follow-up-old}{new-st-request new-request} follow-up-old |continue.

Brackets '{' and '}' are used for a cycle and round brackets for a sequence that can be missed; '|' separates the alternatives.

If the participants are collaborative then they accept arguments of each other (using DA 'accept' and CS 'follow-up-old'). If they are confrontational then at least one of them rejects arguments of the partner and presents his or her own arguments (using DA 'reject' and CS 'new-request').

An experimental dialogue system has been created which carries out debates with a user about performing an action and presents counter-arguments to the arguments given by the user [10]. Both the computer and the user can choose their arguments from given sets of sentences. Interaction is text-based but our further goal is to implement also speech-based interaction.

5   Conclusion

We analyse three kinds of human-human negotiation dialogues with the aim to find the general structure of argumentation-based negotiation. We use dialogue acts of a customized typology as well as communicative strategies in order to represent the structure. This structure can be taken as a basis of the dialogue manager when developing a DS which interacts with the user in a natural language. We believe that such a DS can help to train the user's argumentation skills when carrying out negotiation.

Our further aim is to implement the results of the study in a DS for training argumentation abilities.

Acknowledgments. This work was supported by the European Regional Development Fund through the Estonian Centre of Excellence in Computer Science (EXCS) and the Estonian Research Council (grant IUT20-56).

References

1. Lewicki, R.J., Saunders, D.M., Minton, J.W.: Negotiation, 3rd edn. Irwin McGraw-Hill, San Francisco (1999)
2. Burgess, H., Burgess, G.: Encyclopedia of Conflict Resolution, 306–307, 309–310, Denver, ABC-CLIO (1997). http://www.amazon.com/Encyclopedia-Conflict-Resolution-Heidi-Burgess/dp/0874368391
3. Amgoud, L., Parsons, S., Maudet, N.: Arguments, dialogue, and negotiation. In: ECAI-2000, pp. 338–342. IOS Press, Berlin (2000)
4. Chesnevar, C., Maguitman, A., Loui, R.: Logical models of argument. ACM Comput. Surv. **32**(4), 337–383 (2000)
5. Besnard, P., Hunter, A.: Elements of Argumentation. MIT Press, Cambridge (2008)
6. Hennoste, T., Gerassimenko, O., Kasterpalu, R., Koit, M., Rääbis, A., Strandson, K.: From human communication to intelligent user interfaces: Corpora of spoken Estonian. In: LREC 2008, ELRA, Marrakech, Morocco (2008). www.lrec-conf.org/proceedings/lrec2008
7. Jokinen, K.: Cooperative response planning in CDM: reasoning about communicative strategies. In: TWLT11 Dialogue Management in Natural Language Systems, pp. 159–168. Universiteit Twente, Enschede (1996)
8. Aller, S., Gerassimenko, O., Hennoste, T., Kasterpalu, R., Koit, M., Laanesoo, K., Mihkels, K., Rääbis, A.: Software for pragmatic analysis of dialogues (in Estonian). Estonian Papers in Applied Linguistics, 23–36 (2014)
9. Koit, M.: Towards automatic recognition of the negotiation strategies. In: INISTA-2014, pp. 170–176. IEEE (2014)
10. Koit, M., Õim, H.: Modelling debates on the computer. In: KEOD-2014, pp. 361–368. SciTEC Publications (2014)

Analysis of Facial Motion Capture Data for Visual Speech Synthesis

Miloš Železný[(✉)], Zdeněk Krňoul, and Pavel Jedlička

Faculty of Applied Sciences, University of West Bohemia,
Univerzitní8, 306 14 Plzeň, Czech Republic
{zelezny,zdkrnoul,jedlicka}@kky.zcu.cz

Abstract. The paper deals with interpretation of facial motion capture data for visual speech synthesis. For the purpose of analysis visual speech composed of 170 artificially created words was recorded by one speaker and the state-of-the-art face motion capture method. New nonlinear method is proposed to approximate the motion capture data using intentionally defined set of articulatory parameters. The result of the comparison shows that the proposed method outperforms baseline method with the same number of parameters. The precision of the approximation is evaluated by the parameter values extracted from unseen dataset and also verified with the 3D animated model of human head as the output reproducing visual speech in an artificial manner.

Keywords: Visual speech synthesis · Facial animation · Data acquisition · Motion capture

1 Introduction

The current motion capture methods are very robust and precise to provide high quality motion data in 3D space. There are very powerful techniques to reconstruct face shape as well as its 3D movements that can be successfully applied in specialized assistive technologies or in the domain of entertainment. Furthermore, current research on the visual speech synthesis provides methods to create visual or audiovisual speech utterance in an artificial form from the text input [1]. The approaches do not omit visual/acoustic synchronization [2] or modeling of co-articulation effects [3]. The methods are often data-driven using some parametrization of the visual speech. The interpretation of the data capturing visual speech is one of important issues contributing to naturalness and intelligibility of synthesized speech.

The commercial optical capture systems are based on special cameras to track active or passive markers in 3D space (e.g. Vicon, Vicon Cara, Qualisys, OptiTrack, Optotrak). One category of problems is capturing motion of humans' face. There are methods based on markers fixed on speaker's face or marker-less techniques tracing the face by algorithms of image processing gray, color and/or depth data (e.g. faceshift[1] based on depth camera as the MS Kinect).

---

[1] www.faceshift.com.

© Springer International Publishing Switzerland 2015
A. Ronzhin et al. (Eds.): SPECOM 2015, LNAI 9319, pp. 81–88, 2015.
DOI: 10.1007/978-3-319-23132-7_10

There are several approaches of visual speech synthesis that can be divided into rule based or data-driven ones. The latter consider motion capture data to set free parameters of the synthesis system. Proper identification of the systems often requires large speech corpora consisting of hundreds sentences. In general the synthesis methods use certain parameterization as an approximation of mouth shape or entire face. The parameterizations are often based on Principal component regression (PCR) as a simple linear form of the approximation [4], each of them being a subject to the particular training data set.

In general there are also other linear techniques, e.g. Least-squares estimation, or Maximum-likelihood estimation. Nonlinear techniques can be nonparametric and constructed according to the information derived from the data such as Decision tree learning algorithms [5], or Gaussian process regression, where a Gaussian prior is assumed for the regression curve [6].

The structure of this paper is as follows: Sect. 2 describes recording method and collection of visual speech data, in Sect. 3 we propose the method for data approximation and interpretation by 3D animation head model. The Sect. 4 summarizes precision of the proposed method and shows interpretation of the parameters and paper concludes in the Sect. 5.

2   Speech Data and Collection

The visual speech data was collected by the Vicon Cara motion capture system. The system provides state-of-the-art tracking and reconstruction method for recording motions of human face in 3D space. In general, the system consists of four grayscale 720p cameras with up to 60 fps equipped by 3 mm F2.0 IR filtered lenses fixed to speaker's head through the special helmet base. The cameras are connected with the base by two arms facing 30 cm in front of the speaker's face.

The text material of the speech data consists in an input set of artificially created VCVCV words. The speech data are collected by one female speaker, age 25. There are 85 words from combination of five vowels V= (a, e, i, o, u) and 17 consonants C= (p, t, ť, k, f, s, š, c, č, ř, m, n, ň, l, j, r, ch). In total, 170 words were composited by repeated recording of the input set. Only the visual speech data was collected in this recording setup.

The visual speech data consists of 3D (x, y and z) positions of 46 passive markers that were glued on speaker's face, see Fig. 1 on left. The markers are distributed over lower part of the face thus the 3D shape of outer lip contour, skin of chin/jaw and cheeks is well approximated. 24 auxiliary markers of helmet brim are used by the capture system to correct position of each of the camera relatively to the helmet. The correction is determined for each captured data frame. The helmet base and speaker's skull is considered as a rigid body.

3   Methods

3.1   Interpretation of Speech Data by Animation Model

The speech data are interpreted by the 3D head model of an animated character, see Fig. 1 on right. The head model is a part of the 3D character model

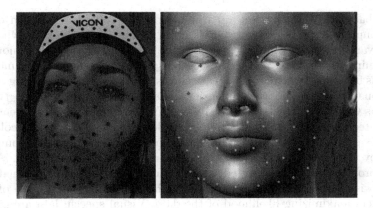

Fig. 1. On left: preview of 46 black markers glued on speaker's face captured by one of the Vicon Cara cameras. On right: the light points as a 3D reconstruction of the makers fitted to the head model, the dark points are the "facial" bones linked with the markers.

created by Autodesk character generator[2]. The facial animation (movements) of the head model is controlled through 21 auxiliary facial "bones" defined in the model. It uses the standard skinning method of facial animation where transformation of each bone is weighted and affects vertices of the mesh surface around. In general, the areas are overlapped to reach smooth deformation in-between neighboring bones.

In the context of visual speech we assume 10 bones: six bones to model lip shape (left/right lip corner, left/right lip upper, left/right lip lower); two bones for movements of cheeks, a jaw bone to rotate skin of the lower part of a face and one bone for movement of nostrils, see the dark points in Fig. 1 on right.

Each of the bones is fixed to a 3D position in the mesh surface of character's face. In general the 3D positions are different than the positions of the markers describing the visual speech data. Thus we assume weighted interpolation of the 3D position from 3D positions of the markers rather than to change definition of the facial bones and re-skinning the mesh surface. For this purpose *position constraints* for cheek- and lip-bones were defined. The constraint defines affected bone as a constrained object and one or more of the markers as source objects.

For the experiment the speech data was interpreted just by one animation model only and thus manual retargeting of motion capture data to the character's face was a convenient practice. As a result all the markers were transformed to correct positions of the character's face as close as possible. The retargeting, the constraints, and rendering of the visual speech data was implemented by the professional 3D character animation software Autodesk MotionBuilder.

3.2   Approximation of Speech Data

Gaussian process (GP) is a powerful multivariate interpolation technique for learning tasks in both unsupervised (e.g. manifold learning [7]) and supervised

---

[2] Available at https://charactergenerator.autodesk.com/.

(e.g. probabilistic classification [6]) frameworks. To solve the problem of non-linear nonparametric regression, GP is often defined over the time where the random variable is the time. We suppose the random variable to be more general, defining a latent space $\mathbf{X}$ in R^D as the space of articulatory parameters.

In this framework the regression task consists of recovering measuring of high-dimensional data $\mathbf{y}$ from lower-dimensional manifold $\mathbf{x}$ in the form $\mathbf{y} = f(\mathbf{x}) + \epsilon$, defined as GP on training set $\{\mathbf{x}_i, \mathbf{y}_i\}$ $i = 1..N$. Every point in the latent space is associated with a normally distributed random variable and a finite collection of those variables has a multivariate Gaussian distribution. GP is completely defined by the covariance and mean function as $f(\mathbf{x}) \sim GP(m(\mathbf{x}), k(x, x'))$.

The problem can be interpreted as a mapping from the low-dimensional latent space of visual speech parameters to the high-dimensional data space of facial 3D markers maximizing likelihood of the data. Visual speech data are given as matrix $\mathbf{Y}$, where each row is one observation (frame of motion capture data) defined as vector concatenating x, y and z coordinate of position of all affected 3D markers, where $D = 138$ is dimension of $\mathbf{y}$ and $N = 3360$ is the number of observations. The data in the matrix $\mathbf{Y} = [\mathbf{y}_1...\mathbf{y}_N]^T$ are centered so that each column has the zero mean. The mean vector is stored apart and describes mean shape of the affected part of speaker's face.

Linear Mapping. Principal component analysis (PCA) is considered the baseline method for analysis of visual speech data. PCA is defined as orthogonal linear transformation that transforms data in high dimension to a new coordinate system of linearly uncorrelated variables (principal components) maximizing the variance of the data.

In this work we assume probabilistic framework of PCA (PPCA) [8]. In our assumption the data $\mathbf{y}_n$ have multivariate normal distribution and denote the latent variable associated with the latent point $\mathbf{x}_n$ in the low dimension Q. The PPCA model marginalizing $\mathbf{x}_n$ and putting a Gaussian prior on $\mathbf{W}$ can be expressed as:

$$p(\mathbf{y}_n|\mathbf{W}, \beta) = \int p(\mathbf{y}_n|\mathbf{x}_n, \mathbf{W}, \beta)p(\mathbf{x}_n)d\mathbf{x}_n, \tag{1}$$

where $p(\mathbf{y}_n|\mathbf{W}, \beta)$ is likelihood for the observation n, $\mathbf{W} \in R^{D \times Q}$ is the transformation matrix, precision is given by β, $N(\mathbf{y}_n|\mathbf{W}\mathbf{x}_n, \beta^{-1}\mathbf{I})$ denotes the distribution function of a multivariate normal distribution for $p(\mathbf{y}_n|\mathbf{x}_n, \mathbf{W}, \beta)$, and $p(\mathbf{x}_n) = N(\mathbf{x}_n|\mathbf{0}, \mathbf{I})$.

The solution for $\mathbf{W}$ is found by maximizing the likelihood of the data $\mathbf{Y}$:

$$p(\mathbf{Y}|\mathbf{W}, \beta) = \prod_{n=1}^{N} p(\mathbf{y}_n|\mathbf{W}, \beta). \tag{2}$$

Nonlinear Mapping. We consider nonlinear mapping as GP [9], where $p(\mathbf{W}) = \prod_{i=1}^{D} N(w_i|0, \alpha^{-1}\mathbf{I})$ is a prior distribution and w_i is i-th row of the matrix $\mathbf{W}$. By marginalizing $\mathbf{W}$ we get likelihood for $\mathbf{Y}$ as:

$$p(\mathbf{Y}|\mathbf{X},\beta) = \frac{1}{(2\pi)^{\frac{DN}{2}}|\mathbf{K}|^{\frac{D}{2}}} \exp(-\frac{1}{2}tr(\mathbf{K}^{-1}\mathbf{Y}\mathbf{Y}^T)), \tag{3}$$

The covariance function is evaluated at each data point. We assume the covariance function to be in the form of Radial Base Function (RBF) kernel matrix $\mathbf{K}$ where n-th and m-th element is given as:

$$k_{n,m} = \alpha \exp(-\frac{\gamma}{2}(x_n - x_m)^T(x_n - x_m)) + \delta_{n,m}\beta^{-1}. \tag{4}$$

γ is scale parameter and $\delta_{n,m}$ is the Kronecker function.

Nonlinear optimization by scaled conjugated gradients (SCG) technique is used to optimize free parameters of the kernel function (4). The gradients of the kernel function are optimized corresponding to maximize likelihood (3).

Note that this approach differs from GPLVM [9] in fact that we do not want optimize positions of latent variables $\mathbf{x_n}$, but just the free parameters of the kernel function.

Visual Speech Parameters. Latent variables for the nonlinear optimization can be shared with the latent variables defined by PPCA. Using PPCA, 93 % of total variance of the data is expressed by three latent variables ($Q = 3$) and 95 % for $Q = 4$. However, for the experiment we consider the latent variables $\mathbf{x}$ to be more intuitive than its interpretation by PCA. Therefore three new parameters: *jaw rotation*, *upper lip*, and *mouth width* are experimentally defined to cover basic articulation variability and to be independent on total variance of the training set.

The aim is to have more consistent parameters defining a simple base for interpretation of visual speech for training visual speech synthesis methods and on the other hand being more easily extracted from speaker's face. Thus we assume *upper lip* describing vertical (y coordinate) displacement of the upper lip center, *jaw rotation* extracted from vertical displacement of the chin center and *mouth width* as horizontal displacement (x coordinate) of lip corners with respect to the mouth center. Note that the parameters describe lip shape in frontal 2D projection (the z coordinate is not used).

As an input the latent variables are extracted from spatial trajectories of 3D markers of the motion data $\mathbf{Y}$ as matrix $\mathbf{X}$ (3360×3) where rows are latent points $\mathbf{x}_n$ normalized on zero mean and unit variance.

4   Evaluation

4.1   Objective Evaluation

To evaluate precision of mapping from the defined latent spaces to the data space, the first set (85 VCVCV) words are used as a training set for both the PPCA and GP models. The second set (repeated recording of the VCVCV words) was not used to train and is used to evaluate precision of the nonlinear GP model.

Table 1. Comparison of the proposed approximation model based on Gaussian process with RBF kernel using three latent variables. The performance of proposed model is evaluated on the test set.

| | train, $N = 3360$ | | | | test, $N = 3514$ | |
| | PPCA ($Q = 4$) | | GP-RBF ($Q = 3$) | | GP-RBF ($Q = 3$) | |
	NRMSE [%]	$\rho_{Yf(X)}$	NRMSE [%]	$\rho_{Yf(X)}$	NRMSE [%]	$\rho_{Yf(X)}$
VCVCV	5.5	0.82	4.87	0.81	7.89	0.72
aCaCa	5.3	0.8	4.7	0.78	7.5	0.67
eCeCe	5.6	0.81	5.3	0.78	8.2	0.67
oCoCo	4.9	0.84	4.7	0.83	7.9	0.76
uCuCu	5.8	0.87	4.4	0.86	6.6	0.81
VCVCV C = (m,p)	5.4	0.86	5.0	0.83	7.77	0.72
VfVfV	5.7	0.74	5.1	0.76	7.29	0.63
VCVCV C = (s,c)	6.1	0.8	5.5	0.79	7.77	0.72
VCVCV C = (š,č)	5.6	0.84	5.2	0.83	7.75	0.73

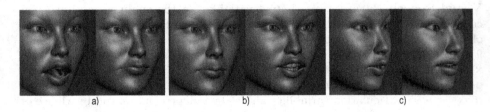

Fig. 2. The limit values of the considered articulatory parameters: (a) *jaw rotation*, (b) *upper lip* and (c) *mouth width*, on left/right panel is minimum/maximum of the latent point transformed to the data space by the proposed model and interpreted by the 3D animation model.

Pearson's linear correlation coefficients and the normalized RMSE (root mean squared error) between the captured data $\mathbf{Y}$ and the transformed data were calculated for each word and dimension D. Normalization of RMSE (NRMSE) facilitates the comparison between different variance in each dimension of the data. For example small variance in lip closure having high impact on intelligibility of bilabial stops will influence the evaluation. A normalization factor is range of maximum minus minimum values of each dimension.

The Table 1 shows comparison of the proposed model with the baseline model as the mean value over all words and over selected subsets. Next, prediction errors of the model for the testing set is added.

4.2 Verification by Animation Model

The defined articulatory parameters are verified by the 3D animation model described in Sect. 3.1. Firstly, a range of values between defined limits is artificially generated separately for each of the proposed parameters as a latent point test set. Next, the latent points are used to approximate shape of speaker's face in the high dimension and afterwards interpreted by 3D animation model, Fig. 2.

5 Conclusions

We propose the nonlinear model for approximation of high-dimensional facial motion capture data using Gaussian process (GP) and predefined articulatory parameters that are usable mainly for visual speech synthesis. For the experiment, visual speech composed from 170 artificial meaningless VCVCV words was recorded by one speaker by the state-of-the-art face motion capture device Vicon Cara.

The proposed model (GP-RBF) on the training part outperforms the baseline model (PPCA) with same number of parameters and is slightly better (for NRMSE) in comparison with the baseline model using one more parameter. PPCA - 3 parameters: NRMSE= 6.1 %; $\rho_{Yf(X)} = 0.78$, PPCA - 4 parameters: NRMSE= 5.5 %; $\rho_{Yf(X)} = 0.82$ and GP-RBF - 3 parameters: NRMSE= 4.87 %; $\rho_{Yf(X)} = 0.81$.

The approximation error of the proposed model is also evaluated by values of the defined articulatory parameters extracted from unseen data, GP-RBF - 3 parameters: NRMSE= 7.89 %; $\rho_{Yf(X)} = 0.72$. In this consideration, values for PPCA are not be extracted by this way. Furthermore, the proposed parameters are verified by the 3D animation model of head and the rendered animation shows meaningful interpretation of each of the parameters in high-dimensional data of a face.

Acknowledgements. This research was supported by the Technology Agency of the Czech Republic, project No. TA01011264.

References

1. Mattheysesa, W., Verhelsta, W.: Audiovisual speech synthesis: an overview of the state-of-the-art. Speech Commun. **66**, 182–217 (2015)
2. Karpov, A., Tsirulnik, L., Krňoul, Z., Ronzhin, A., Lobanov, B., Železný, M.: Audio-visual speech asynchrony modeling in a talking head. In: Proceeding of the International Conference INTERSPEECH 2009, Brighton, UK, pp. 2911–2914 (2009)
3. Beskow, J.: Trainable articulatory control models for visual speech synthesis. Int. J. Speech Technol. **4**, 335–349 (2004)
4. Badin, P., Bailly, G., Revéret, L., Baciub, M., Segebarthc, C., Savariauxd, C.: Three-dimensional linear articulatory modeling of tongue, lips and face, based on MRI and video images. J. Phonetics **30**(3), 533–553 (2002)
5. Breiman, L., Friedman, J.H., Olshen, R.A., Stone, C.J.: Classification and Regression Trees. Wadsworth & Brooks/Cole Advanced Books & Software, Monterey (1984). ISBN: 978-0-412-04841-8
6. Rasmussen, C.E., Williams, C.K.I.: Gaussian Processes for Machine Learning. MIT Press, Cambridge (2006). ISBN: 0-262-18253-X

7. Bishop, C.M.: Pattern Recognition and Machine Learning. Springer, New York (2006). ISBN: 0-387-31073-8
8. Tipping, M.E., Bishop, C.M.: Probabilistic principal component analysis. J. Roy. Stat. Soc. B **6**(3), 611–622 (1999)
9. Lawrence, N.D.: Learning for larger datasets with the Gaussian process latent variable model. In: Proceedings of the Eleventh International Workshop on Artificial Intelligence and Statistics, pp. 21–24. Omnipress (2007)

Auditory-Perceptual Recognition
of the Emotional State of Aggression

Rodmonga Potapova and Liliya Komalova[✉]

Moscow State Linguistic University,
Moscow, Russia
{RKPotapova,GenuinePR}@yandex.ru

Abstract. The authors propose several stages to research verbal-cognitive mechanisms regarding the formation and development of verbal realization of the emotional state of aggression. This paper describes an experimental study which investigates the auditory-perceptual analysis of male scenic speech experiencing the emotional state of aggression (for Russian, English, Spanish and Tatar languages). The results statistically confirm the detected auditory-perceptual "passports" of the emotional state of aggression and demonstrate differences in auditory perception of verbal aggressive behavior by groups of male and female listeners.

Keywords: Aggression · Verbal aggression · Prosody · Speech · Verbal-cognitive mechanism · Verbal behavior · Social learning theory

1   Introduction

Aggressive behavior as a whole communicative process requires interaction of an actor and a recipient. Thereupon carrying out an investigation of aggression a researcher should analyze not only the mechanisms of cognitive-communicative behavioral patterns of an aggressor but also peculiarities of perceptual sphere of a victim, observant and the aggressor itself. Social psychologists confirm that an act can be considered aggressive as well as the recipient perceives it aggressive, which means this particular communicative or physical act corresponds with ascriptions of aggression in recipients point of view [2, p. 113–156].

For example, "there are different rules for interpreting verbal abuse as opposed to physical abuse. < ... > It appears that people perceive verbal aggression differently when not paired with other types of aggression" [4, p. 76]. Also "past behavior as a predictor of future behavior is a central tenet of behavioral psychology with empirically demonstrated applicability to intimate partner violence and other forms of aggression" [15, p. 29]. Meanwhile, "age and educational level were both negatively related to tolerance for aggression, and Anglo vs. Hispanic ethnicity was also associated with perceptions of aggression" [5, p. 1] and "the subjective perception of aggression from others appears to be more strongly influenced by the gender role, rather than gender, of an aggressor" [3, p. 441].

© Springer International Publishing Switzerland 2015
A. Ronzhin et al. (Eds.): SPECOM 2015, LNAI 9319, pp. 89–95, 2015.
DOI: 10.1007/978-3-319-23132-7_11

2   Method, Procedure, and Results

We continue our survey of verbal-cognitive mechanisms of formation and development of the emotional state of aggression by auditory-perceptual and quantitative analyses.[1] The purpose of the present stage of the study is to determine similar and specific prosodic characteristics that can be used as support in recognition of the emotional state of aggression (on the material of Russian, American English, Castilian Spanish and Kazan Tatar languages).

The hypothesis of the research is that representing a complex of negative emotional and emotional-modal states of a person from any lingua-culture aggression might have similar prosodic features with reference to languages from different language families.

Native Russian speakers (n = 50, 19–23 years old, humanitarian students, study linguistics and understand English) were asked by method of auditory perception to analyze 40 samples of authentic speeches of males delivered in scenic situations modeling the emotional state of aggression.[2] Ten samples of male monologues in each of the languages under investigation were selected. There were two stages of the experiment.

At the first stage we were interested in quantitative description of emotional-modal complex aggression. The listeners were divided in two groups: the first one was given instructions to mark phonograms containing representations of the emotional state of aggression. The second group was asked to designate what emotional and emotional-modal state speakers experienced on the same phonograms.

The experiment showed that on average in 98 % of cases the listeners of both groups recognized that the speakers manifested one or another type of aggression (99,69 % of matches for Russian phonograms, 97,5 % for American English, 98,13 % for Castilian Spanish, and 99,06 % for Kazan variant of Tatar language).

We assume that the background for the emotional-modal complex aggression is formed of the emotional state of irritation that in combination with anger and malice provokes rage. On the whole this complex in the aggregate with other states-satellites (such as causticity, guilt, disgust etc.) is evaluated by the listeners as aggressive verbal behavior.

At the second stage of the experiment the listeners were asked to evaluate the same 40 phonograms based on prosodic characteristics of speakers (pitch,

---

[1] Results of previous stages of the survey see in [7,8]. Results of acoustic analysis see in [10]. For more details about auditory-perceptual method regarding audio-visual analysis of emotional foreign speakers speech see [11].

[2] Phonograms are taken out of the data base of recordings of modern authentic scenic speech in Russian, English, Spanish and Tatar languages in conditions of family violence, criminal behavior, and corporative conflicts (author L.R. Komalova 2013). Each sample is a fragment of sound-tracks from a movie or TV-series without visual support, accompanied with script of actors speech; playing time varies from 10 to 90 s. The database consists of samples of male and female speeches: monologues, dialogues and polylogues.

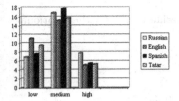

Fig. 1. Average evaluations of auditory-perceptual analysis of pitch

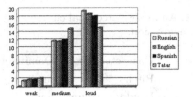

Fig. 2. Average evaluations of auditory-perceptual analysis of loudness volume

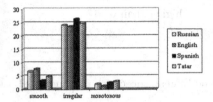

Fig. 3. Average evaluations of auditory-perceptual analysis of melodic contour

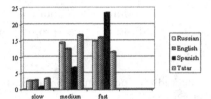

Fig. 4. Average evaluations of auditory-perceptual analysis of speech tempo

loudness volume, melodic contour of pitch, rhythm, tempo, speech breathing, duration of pauses etc.). We also asked the listeners to mark prosodic features which influence evaluation of the experimental material. The results of analysis are presented in Figs. 1, 2, 3, 4, 5, 6, 7 and 8.

As shown on the figures, both male and female listeners tend to perceive the emotional-modal complex of aggression in speech of male speakers in Russian, English, Spanish and Tatar languages without any visual support as loud, irregular, with indistinct rhythm, fast tempo, normal breathing and short pauses. Previously we revealed similar peculiarities researching conflictive communication [6,9]. We also have to mention that indicators that help the listeners recognize types of the emotional state of aggression differ: analyzing samples in native language (Russian) and the language they study (English) the listeners are guided by both prosodic and speech parameters, but analyzing unknown languages such as Spanish and Tatar they mostly take into account only prosodic parameters.

Then we proved our calculations with non-parametrical criteria: tendency L-criterion by Page and T-criterion by Wilcoxon to check validity of experimental evaluations concerning each parameter for each language under investigation; tendency S-criterion by Jonkir and Mann-Whitney U-test to check validity of distribution of dominant evaluations for Russian, English, Spanish and Tatar languages in comparison. The results are presented in Tables 1, 2, 3 and 4.

Table 1. Auditory-perceptual characteristics of male Russian speech for the emotional state of aggression.

Characteristics	Dominant parameter	$\rho \leq$
Pitch	medium	0,05
Loudness volume	loud	0,001
Melodic contour	irregular	0,001
Tempo	medium	0,01
Pauses	short	0,001
Rhythm	indistinct	higher than 0,05
Breathing	normal	higher than 0,05
Indicators	prosodic and speech	0,01

Table 2. Auditory-perceptual characteristics of male English speech for the emotional state of aggression.

Characteristics	Dominant parameter	$\rho \leq$
Pitch	medium	0,001
Loudness volume	loud	0,001
Melodic contour	irregular	0,001
Tempo	fast	0,001
Pauses	short	0,001
Rhythm	indistinct	higher than 0,05
Breathing	normal	higher than 0,05
Indicators	prosodic	0,01

Table 3. Auditory-perceptual characteristics of male Spanish speech for the emotional state of aggression.

Characteristics	Dominant parameter	$\rho \leq$
Pitch	medium	0,001
Loudness volume	loud	0,001
Melodic contour	irregular	0,001
Tempo	fast	0,001
Pauses	short	0,001
Rhythm	indistinct	higher than 0,05
Breathing	normal	higher than 0,05
Indicators	prosodic	0,01

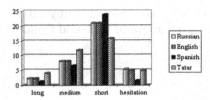

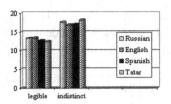

Fig. 5. Average evaluations of auditory-perceptual analysis of pause duration

Fig. 6. Average evaluations of auditory-perceptual analysis of speech rhythm

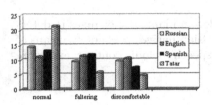

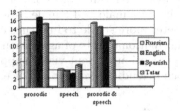

Fig. 7. Average evaluations of auditory-perceptual analysis of speech breathing

Fig. 8. Average evaluations of auditory-perceptual analysis of speech and prosodic indicators

Table 4. Auditory-perceptual characteristics of male Tatar speech for the emotional state of aggression.

Characteristics	Dominant parameter	$\rho \leq$
Pitch	medium	0,001
Loudness volume	loud	0,001
Melodic contour	irregular	0,001
Tempo	medium	0,001
Pauses	short	0,001
Rhythm	indistinct	higher than 0,05
Breathing	normal	higher than 0,05
Indicators	prosodic	0,01

As we can see the quantitative and comparative analyses statistically confirmed validity of the majority of results of the auditory-perceptual analysis. The validity of the obtained data was also confirmed for four languages under investigation (it's marked with italic type in the tables).

To specify our findings and exclude possible mistakes we divided the data into two groups of listeners by gender (5 males and 27 females) for each language. The discovered differences were analyzed using two-stages experiment procedure described below. As a result of the analysis we didn't find any statistically valid differences in perception of male aggressive speech by groups of male and female listeners.

3   Conclusions

Thus, based on results of the auditory-perceptual experiments we can conclude that emotional-modal complex "aggression" for Russian, American English, Castilian Spanish and Kazan variant of Tatar language is characterized by medium pitch of voice, loud voice, irregular melodic contour, short pauses, indistinct speech rhythm, and normal speech breathing. These parameters are similarly fixed by male and female listeners.

Parameter more stable to influence of gender and language changes in detection of the emotional state of aggression by Russian native speakers by means of auditory perception without visual support is speech melodic contour; and more varying one is loudness volume of voice.

4   Discussion

As any experimental research our investigation has limitations. The listeners analyzed the whole phonogram without differentiation to initial, medium and final part of the statement [12–14]. We also took average evaluations of auditory-perceptual analysis that can modify the obtained data. We involved only Russian speakers of one age group.

Owing to the fact that movie and TV-speech is usually considered only as imitation of speech in real conditions, the results of the experiment can't be simply extrapolated when detecting the state of aggression of male speech in real conditions. But in defense of utility of our research says the Social Learning Theory of A. Bandura. It postulates that "learning is a cognitive process that takes place in a social context and can occur purely through observation or direct instruction, even in the absence of motor reproduction or direct reinforcement" [1]. As applied to our investigation, it's possible to learn (and subsequently reproduce) aggressive verbal patterns through auditory perception of models of aggressive verbal behavior of movie- and TV-actors.

5   Prospects of Investigation

Undoubtedly, it would be interesting to continue our investigation with auditory-perceptual analysis of the same samples but involving English (American and British), Spanish (Castilian regions and Latin America) and Tatar native speakers as listeners, males and females of different ages. Also it will be interesting to reveal whether the auditory perception of female actors voice and speech in state of aggression is similar for listeners of different gender, age and linguacultures under investigation.

Acknowledgments. The survey is being carried out with the support of Russian Science Foundation (RSF) in the framework of the project #14-18-01059 at Moscow State Linguistic University (scientific head of the project R.K. Potapova).

References

1. Bandura, A.: Social Learning and Personality Development. Holt, Rinehart, and Winston, New York (1963)
2. Berkowitz, L.: Aggression: Its Causes, Consequences, and Control. McGraw-Hill, New York (1993)
3. Borhart, H.M., Terrell, H.K.: Perceptions of aggression are colored by gender roles. Psychol. Rec. **64**(3), 441–445 (2014)
4. Brandt, D.C., Pierce, K.J.: When is verbal abuse serious? In: The Impact of Relationship variables on Perceptions of Severity, pp. 71–78 (2000). http://murphylibrary.uwlax.edu/digital/jur/2000/brandt-pierce.pdf
5. Harris, M.B., Knight-Bohnhoff, K.: Gender and aggression. In: Perceptions of aggression. Sex Roles **35**(1–2), 1–25 (1996)
6. Komalova, L.R.: Lingvisticheskiy Aspekt Konfliktologicheskoy Kompetentnosti, Moskva (2009) (in Russian)
7. Potapova, R., Komalova, L.: Lingua-cognitive survey of the semantic field "Aggression" in multicultural communication: typed text. In: Železný, M., Habernal, I., Ronzhin, A. (eds.) SPECOM 2013. LNCS, vol. 8113, pp. 227–232. Springer, Heidelberg (2013)
8. Potapova, R., Komalova, L.: On principles of annotated databases of the semantic field "Aggression". In: Ronzhin, A., Potapova, R., Delic, V. (eds.) SPECOM 2014. LNCS, vol. 8773, pp. 322–328. Springer, Heidelberg (2014)
9. Potapova, R.K., Komalova, L.R.: Rechevoy Portret Kommunikantov v Usloviyakh Konflikta-Konsensusa. In: 14th International Conference Speech and Computer (SPECOM 2011), pp. 43–51. MGLU, Kazan (2011) (in Russian)
10. Potapova, R.K., Komalova, L.R., Bobrov, N.V.: Acoustic markers of emotional state of aggression. In: Ronzhin, A., Potapova, R., Fakotakis, N. (eds.) SPECOM 2015. LNAI, vol. 9319, pp. 55–64. Springer, Heidelberg (2015)
11. Potapova, R., Potapov, V.: Auditory and visual recognition of emotional behaviour of foreign language subjects (by native and non-native speakers). In: Železný, M., Habernal, I., Ronzhin, A. (eds.) SPECOM 2013. LNCS, vol. 8113, pp. 62–69. Springer, Heidelberg (2013)
12. Potapova, R.K., Potapov, V.V.: Pragmaphonetic Features of Oral Academic Genre (on the Basis of German University Lectures). The Phonetician. A publication of International Society of Phonetic Sciences (ISPhS), 109–110, 43–54 (2014)
13. Potapova, R.K., Potapov, V.V.: Yazyk. Rech. Lichnost, Yazyki Slavyanskoy Kultury, Moskva (2006) (in Russian)
14. Potapova, R.K.: Rech: Kommunikatsiya. Informatsiya. Kibernetika. Librokom, Moskva (2015). (in Russian)
15. Schumacher, J.A., Leonard, K.E.: Husbands and wives marital adgustment, verbal aggression, and physical aggression as longitudinal predictors of physical aggression in early marriage. J. Consult. Clin. Psychol. **73**(1), 28–37 (2005)

Automatic Classification and Prediction of Attitudes: Audio - Visual Analysis of Video Blogs

Noor Alhusna Madzlan[1,2], Yuyun Huang[1]([✉]), and Nick Campbell[1]

[1] Speech Communication Laboratory, Trinity College Dublin, Dublin, Ireland
{madzlann,huangyu,nick}@tcd.ie
[2] ELLD, Faculty of Languages and Communication, UPSI, Tanjong Malim, Malaysia

Abstract. This paper reports a study of automatic attitude recognition from a collection of over 500 segments of our video blog data. We annotated and analysed 3 different attitudinal states of the speakers. Following that, we extracted and analysed prosodic and visual features relevant to the classification task. We use machine learning methods and techniques to attain better understanding of the feature sets and their contribution to the prediction model.

Keywords: Attitude prediction · Audio and visual feature analysis · Machine learning · Random forest · LibSVM

1 Introduction

Attitudes, mood and affect are integral depictions of human behaviour. Attitudes are conscious outward representation of affective states which are commonly expressed through several modalities during the communicative process. Our study is concerned with the explicit expression of attitudinal states of the speakers and not of their inner feelings or emotional states. Current research in multiple fields of study has shown vast interest in the understanding of attitudes and affect [1–4]. Bomeister and Finkel [4] perceive attitudes as general evaluations individuals have regarding the self, people, objects and issues. Explicit attitudes are indicative of speakers' evaluative expression of socio-affective states. The dynamics of attitude expression are expressed through multimodalities. Mac et al. [3] analysed attitude perception and production across two cultures; Vietnamese and French, by means of audio-visual modalities. Treating Vietnamese as the native language, they found that Interrogation and Infant-Directed Speech were perceived correctly by native speakers, while Declaration and Positive Surprise were perceived by both native and non-native groups. Henrichsen and Allwood [2] investigated attitude prediction in the NOMCO speech corpus and developed a standard A10 attitude annotation scheme by means of multimodal speech cues. The ten attitudes are Amused, Bored, Casual, Confident, Enthusiastic, Friendly, Impatient, Interested, Thoughtful and Uninterested. They found that acoustic parameters;

© Springer International Publishing Switzerland 2015
A. Ronzhin et al. (Eds.): SPECOM 2015, LNAI 9319, pp. 96–104, 2015.
DOI: 10.1007/978-3-319-23132-7_12

Fundamental Frequency and Intensity are robust features for the prediction of attitudes. For semantic representation and consideration, this paper adopts part of the standard A10 Attitude annotation system by using both acoustic and visual parameters for automatic detection of attitudinal states.

With increasing interaction through social media, people create innovative channels of communication. A popular medium of self-expression is through video blogs. Video blogs are pre-recorded, online personal diaries shared to the larger public in the form of videos covering current issues, personal thoughts and events [5]. Video blogs consist of a single person talking in front of a webcam and are recorded at informal settings such as the bedroom to give the impression of familiarity to the audience. A popular channel for sharing and managing video blogs is YouTube. We consider video blogs as a unique form of speech. They are semi spontaneous combining both broadcast and spontaneous speech as content is pre-planned, but the delivery is conducted in a spontaneous manner.

There are numerous studies on video blogs [6–8]. Morency et al. [7] conducted sentiment analysis of speakers from YouTube videos. They study sentiment expressions through multimodal channels. They analysed polarized words, smile, eye gaze, pauses and pitch. Findings suggested that polarized words were big indicators of sentiment while visual parameters provide information on positive utterances and audio features indicate neutral utterances. Biel et al. [6] examined personality impressions of video bloggers through non-verbal modalities. They associate vloggers' non-verbal behaviour with the Big Five personality traits; Extraversion, Agreeableness, Conscientiousness, Emotional Stability and Openness. Acoustic features used in the study include: speaking time, voicing rate, energy, pitch and autocorrelation peaks while visual features involved the use of weighted motion energy images which measure mean, median, entropy and centre mass of body activity. A step-wise linear regression model was used to measure the predictive power of the nonverbal signals for personality detection. The predictive model attained 34 % prediction variance. Vloggers with high levels of Extraverted, Openness and Conscientiousness traits received a higher level of social attention. Madzlan et al. [8] conducted a study on attitudes of video bloggers. They exploited prosodic and visual features to evaluate predictive power of the features to the model. Audio signals such as pitch, intensity and voice quality were included in the prosodic features while visual features were extracted using Active Appearance Model (AAM) algorithm. Prosodic features that contributed most to the predictive power of the model were voice quality and pitch while the eyebrows, jaw and nose from the visual features proved quite useful for providing predictive power to the classifier.

Extending the works on video blogs and attitude recognition, this paper describes a rich source of attitudinal representations from our video blog dataset. We propose improved prosodic and visual analyses to achieve a higher predictive power for our classification model. From past research [8], visual feature selection focused on the average movement of visual landmarks. We propose an additional feature contribution which is the directionality of visual landmarks that could significantly contribute to an improved prediction model. We also report use of different classifiers and compare their predictive power using selected prosodic and visual features. We list the contributions of this paper as follows: *(1) collection of video blog dataset and (2) feature selection and their contribution to the classifier.*

2   Methodoloy

2.1   The Vlog Corpus

In studying the pragmatic aspect of video blogs as a means of dynamic attitude expression, we collected 250 video blogs from a popular video sharing website[1] from ten different speakers[2]. For ease of analysis, speaker selection was done according to the following characteristics; Native American English male speakers aged between 18–25 years old. Videos from each speaker were then selected according to viewership. High viewership is likely to be selected in comparison to lower viewership videos. Example of video blogs is illustrated in Fig. 1.

2.2   Attitude Annotation

Attitudes are evaluative representations of affect and emotion. We identify three main attitudinal states of the speaker. These attitudes are based on a subset of the A10 attitude annotation scheme [2]. In preliminary studies, we adopted five of Henrichsen and Allwood's [2] standard attitude scheme which are Amusement, Friendliness, Frustration, Enthusiasm and Impatience. In this paper, we clustered

Fig. 1. Instance of a video blogger

---

[1] http://www.youtube.com.
[2] https://www.youtube.com/user/nigahiga,
   https://www.youtube.com/user/JustinJamesHughes,
   https://www.youtube.com/user/uncuthashbrown,
   https://www.youtube.com/user/kevjumba,
   https://www.youtube.com/user/tyleroakley,
   https://www.youtube.com/user/ConnorFranta,
   https://www.youtube.com/user/TimothyDeLaGhetto2,
   https://www.youtube.com/user/DavidSoComedy,
   https://www.youtube.com/user/michaelbalalis,
   https://www.youtube.com/user/shane.

Table 1. The attitude annotation scheme we adapted

Attitude	Specific attitudes	Description	No. of segments
Positive	Amusement	Speaker laughs, chuckles	207
	Enthusiasm	Speaker appears excited	
Neutral	Friendliness	Speaker smiles, greets the audience	101
Negative	Frustration	Speaker sighs, appears 'defeated'	205
	Impatience	Speaker shouts, appears annoyed, harsh	

Table 2. Prosodic parameters

Prosodic features	
Fundamental Frequency (f0) - mean, max, min	Voicing
Shape of pitch contour	Intensity - mean, max, min
Peak position of power (ppct)	Voice Quality - h1, a3, h1h2, h1a3
Duration	

the attitudinal representations into Positive Attitude, Negative Attitude and Neutral Attitude. We found these classes most useful to attain robustness to our classification system. Annotation by two expert annotators was conducted over a period of six weeks using Wavesurfer. To indicate reliability of the annotation, we used Cohen's Kappa and obtained 75 % inter-annotator agreement. We collected over 500 labelled video segments containing the three attitudinal classes. Table 1 indicates our annotation scheme with the total number of segments.

In the annotation stage, we labeled the start and end times for each attitude label and automatically segmented the attitude chunks. For the audio files, each audio segment was automatically segmented using a TCL/TK script whilst a trim tool in Windows Live Movie Maker was used for video files.

2.3 Multimodal Feature Extraction

Prosodic Features. We selected 14 salient features that best represent prosodic characteristics of the attitude labels. Automatic feature extraction was conducted using a TCL/TK script. These features are listed in Table 2:

Visual Features. To measure the facial dynamics in speakers' attitude expression, we implemented an image processing technique using the Active Appearance Model (AAM). This process involved automatic extraction of 67 data points of the facial contour. A summary of this is listed in Table 3.

We used different techniques for calculating the AAM facial landmarks by measuring their average distance and movement. We also calculated the directionality or velocity of two visual landmarks. Distance, Movement and Directionality are used as visual features for training our classifiers.

Table 3. Visual parameters

Visual features	
Eyes (left, right, upper, lower, iris of the eyes)	Nose (bridge, tip, wing, bottom)
Mouth (corner, top, bottom, inner)	Chin (left, right, bottom)
Eyebrows (corner, middle)	Nasolabial Fold (upper, lower)
Face Contour (left, right, upper left, upper right)	Face

3 Attitude Classification Model

3.1 Feature Analysis

Prosodic Features. Prosody is the best indicator for the expression of attitudes and emotions [2]. As described in the previous section, we extracted 14 acoustic parameters to indicate attitudinal states of the speakers and their contribution to the attitude model. In this study, we conducted ANOVA test on the speech features and results showed Pitch as a feature that depicts a significant difference compared to other features with a p-value of 0.001. Figure 2a indicates distribution of Pitch for all three attitudinal states of the speakers. Neutral Attitude (Type 2) showed a normal distribution of pitch range while Negative Attitude (Type 3) showed the largest varying degree of pitch level. Neutral attitude showed a symmetric distribution as friendliness (associated with neutral attitude) is expressed with a relatively level pitch of the voice. In contrast, Negative Attitudes (Type 3) showed greater variance in pitch range such is the case of anger and frustration.

Visual Features. We extracted 67 facial landmarks using the AAM facial tracking model. We conducted ANOVA test on the visual features. We found movement of the Eyebrows as the most salient signal with a p-value of 0.001.

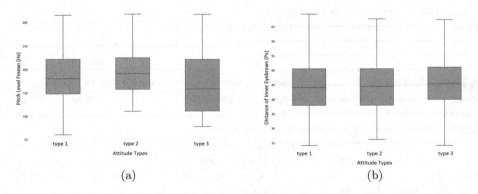

Fig. 2. (a) Results for prosodic features (b) Results for visual features

Table 4. Prediction by prosodic means

Attitude	Precision	Recall
Positive	0.58	0.61
Neutral	**0.79**	**0.71**
Negative	0.61	0.61

Distribution of Eyebrow movement between the 3 attitude classes is shown in Fig. 2b. We found that there is little variance in the distribution of Eyebrows for all attitude classes. Negative Attitude (Type 3) however showed greater variance range compared to the other attitude classes. This occurs because subsets within the Type 3 labels themselves have varying prosodic and visual characteristics.

3.2 Prediction by Prosodic and Visual Features

Prediction by Prosodic Features. We extracted and analysed 14 prosodic features listed in the previous section. We used these features to train our classifier in order to obtain correct classification rates using machine learning methods. We used Random Forest for the classification task and obtained 63.3 % accurate prediction of the 3 attitude classes. This result is indeed quite promising as it exceeds the confidence threshold or baseline $(1/3 = 33\%)$. Our confusion matrices showed Neutral Attitude with the least number of misclassifications through prosodic modality. Details of attitude prediction using prosodic signals and the confusion matrix are reported in Tables 4 and 5:

Prediction by Visual Features. We used eyebrow and head distance, movement and directionality measurements of the visual landmarks to become visual features. Directionality here refers to the direction of motion of the facial points, either vertical or horizontal. For the classification task, we conducted analysis with LibSVM [12] using a 10-fold cross validation technique. Results obtained from the classifier indicated 51.4 % of prediction accuracy. The feature that was most useful to the classification task is the combination of head and eyebrow movement. Detailed results are in Table 6:

Classifier Results. We used different classifiers to train the attitude classes. We used Random Forest (RF) and Support Vector Machine (LibSVM) to observe difference in the prediction rate. Results of the classification models are indicated

Table 5. Confusion Matrix of Attitudes

Classified \ Annotated	Positive	Neutral	Negative
Positive	128	11	68
Neutral	19	72	10
Negative	72	8	125

Table 6. Result of visual prediction

Visual features	Percentage
Eyebrow distance	50.9 %
Head and eyebrow movement	**51.4%**
Head movement	50.3 %
Direction	50.1 %

Table 7. Classification results

Modality	Baseline	Random forest	LibSVM
AUDIO	33.3 %	**63.3 %**	40.7 %
VISUAL	33.3 %	50.9 %	**51.4 %**

in Table 7. This indicates different types of classifiers that we used in our attitude detection model. We found Random Forest to be the most robust classifier for the prosodic features but LibSVM proved to give better classification for our visual feature set.

4   Discussion

This study presents speech and visual feature contributions for development of an automatic attitude recognition system. From analysis, speech features contributed greatest to the classification system compared to visual features. The reason for this is our visual feature sets may not be sufficient to measure speaker attitudes. We believe detailed visual information such as head rotation and shape of facial landmarks can potentially improve this classification model. This will be part of our planned future work. For classification using prosodic features, the feature that best contributes to the overall system is Pitch. Further analysis presents Negative Attitude as having the widest range of pitch distribution. This is the case where attitudinal classes within the class itself have varying acoustic characteristics. Frustration, a subset of the Negative attitude class shows lower pitch range in contrast to Impatience (another subset of negative attitude) which has a higher pitch range.

Visual feature analysis indicated Eyebrows as the most significant feature for attitude recognition. This is not a novel observation [9,10] but in our case, it is an important result that contributes to the classifier's reliability. We observe trends that Negative Attitude class showed greatest variance compared to other classes. This is because the variance within the class itself contributed to such results. For instance, Eyebrows moved closer together when the speaker shows impatience while there is little eyebrow movement when the speaker is frustrated. Thus, we find Negative Attitudes have greater variance both prosodically and visually. Finer analysis will be conducted on the attitude classes in future work.

We trained the classifiers using Random Forest (RF) and Support Vector Machine (SVM). Training on the prosodic features using RF showed a significant difference compared to SVM. This indicates that classification using RF is more robust in detecting attitudes through prosodic modality. Our visual features however, worked well with the SVM classifier compared to RF. But there was little difference between the two classifiers, hence we believe both classifiers are good for detecting attitudes through visual means. We also report several techniques used in measuring the visual points. We calculated the distance, movement and directionality of the visual points. Directionality improved the performance of the classifier compared to distance and movement, thus finding this feature most reliable for attitude detection. As mentioned in [11], directionality facilitates attentional selection. We find this true for attitude detection as reported in this paper. In future work, we intend to explore other visual information such as shapes of the facial landmarks and head rotations. Other works also include fusion of multimodal features for our attitude classification model.

5   Conclusion

In this paper, we described a rich source of attitudinal signals from our video blog corpus. We performed a multimodal feature analysis and found two significant features, Pitch and Eyebrow movement that contributed most to our attitude classifier. We described greater variance of these features in the Negative Attitude class compared to other classes. We compared average distance, movement and directionality of the visual features and found directionality of the visual signals as a better method of measurement for our attitude classification model.

Acknowledgments. This work is supported by the English Language and Literature Department, UPSI, Ministry of Education Malaysia, Center for Global Intelligent Content (CNGL) at TCD and the Speech Communication Laboratory at TCD.

References

1. Gobl, C., Ní Chasaide, A.: The role of voice quality in communicating emotion, mood and attitude. Speech Commun. **40**(1–2), 189–212 (2003)
2. Henrichsen, P.J., Allwood, J.: Predicting the attitude flow in dialogue based on multi-modal speech cues. In: NEALT Proceedings Series (2012)
3. Mac, D.-K., et al.: Cross-cultural perception of vietnamese audio-visual prosodic attitudes. In: Speech Prosody (2010)
4. Baumeister, R.F., Finkel, E.J.: Advanced Social Psychology: The State of the Science. Oxford University Press, USA (2010)
5. Wen, G., et al.: A survey of videoblogging technology on the web. ACM Comput. Surv. (CSUR) **42**(4), 15–78 (2010)
6. Biel, J.I., Aran, O., Gatica-Perez, D.: You are known by how you vlog: personality impressions and nonverbal behavior in YouTube. In: ICWSM (2011)
7. Morency, L.P., Mihalcea, R., Doshi, P.: Towards multimodal sentiment analysis: harvesting opinions from the web. In: Proceedings of the 13th International Conference on Multimodal Interfaces, pp. 169–176 (2011)

8. Madzlan, N., et al.: Automatic recognition of attitudes in video blogs - prosodic and visual feature analysis. In: INTERSPEECH (2014)
9. Ekman, P.: About brows: emotional and conversational signals. In: von Cranach, M., Foppa, K., Lepenies, W., Ploog, D. (eds.) Human Ethology, pp. 169–249. Cambridge University Press, Cambridge (1979)
10. Sadrô, J., Jarudi, I., Sinhaô, P.: The role of eyebrows in face recognition. Perception 32(3), 285–293 (2003)
11. Anllo-Vento, L., Hillyard, S.A.: Selective attention to the color and direction of moving stimuli: electrophysiological correlates of hierarchical feature selection. Percept. Psychophys. 58(2), 191–206 (1996)
12. Chih-Chung, C., Chih-Jen, L.: LIBSVM: a library for support vector machines. ACM Trans. Intell. Syst. Technol. 2(3), 27:1–27:27 (2011)

Automatic Close Captioning for Live Hungarian Television Broadcast Speech: A Fast and Resource-Efficient Approach

Ádám Varga[1], Balázs Tarján[1,3]([✉]), Zoltán Tobler[1], György Szaszák[1,3],
Tibor Fegyó[2,3], Csaba Bordás[4], and Péter Mihajlik[1,3]

[1] THINKTech Research Center, Budapest, Hungary
varga@thinktech.hu
[2] SpeechTex Ltd., Budapest, Hungary
[3] Department of Telecommunications and Media Informatics,
Budapest University of Technology and Economics, Budapest, Hungary
{tarjanb,mihajlik}@tmit.bme.hu
[4] Media Service Support and Asset Management Fund (MTVA), Budapest, Hungary

Abstract. In this paper, the application of LVCSR (Large Vocabulary Continuous Speech Recognition) technology is investigated for real-time, resource-limited broadcast close captioning. The work focuses on transcribing live broadcast conversation speech to make such programs accessible to deaf viewers. Due to computational limitations, real time factor (RTF) and memory requirements are kept low during decoding with various models tailored for Hungarian broadcast speech recognition. Two decoders are compared on the direct transcription task of broadcast conversation recordings, and setups employing re-speakers are also tested. Moreover, the models are evaluated on a broadcast news transcription task as well, and different language models (LMs) are tested in order to demonstrate the performance of our systems in settings when low memory consumption is a less crucial factor.

Keywords: Speech recognition · LVCSR · Broadcast news · Broadcast conversation · GMM · DNN · Hungarian · Kaldi · Limited resources

1 Introduction

Automatic speech transcription systems built and evaluated on broadcast audio have long been researched. Most experiments focus on broadcast news (BN) data, since the acoustic environment, the relatively low perplexity of the task, and the coordinated speech of news presenters provide adequate conditions for the training of recognition models that result in low error rates. Broadcast conversation (BC) speech, on the other hand, proves to be a more challenging task. This is caused by the higher level of spontaneity in utterances which increases the number of errors and pauses, and the time when more speakers talk simultaneously. Based on our data, in certain television programs this latter condition

© Springer International Publishing Switzerland 2015
A. Ronzhin et al. (Eds.): SPECOM 2015, LNAI 9319, pp. 105–112, 2015.
DOI: 10.1007/978-3-319-23132-7_13

may occur up to one third of the total time which may significantly decrease the performance of systems operating on BC audio. On the other hand, the task of close captioning BC programs has a high priority, since there are no transcriptions available for these shows in case of live broadcasting.

Our ongoing project with the Hungarian *Media Service Support and Asset Management Fund* (MTVA, Hungary's public service broadcaster) is to develop transcription systems that are capable of live close captioning of BC. This project poses several challenges: firstly, **the error rates have to be kept at a tolerable level**. Secondly, the decoding has to be performed in **real time** and with minimum (about 1 s) latency since delays between the broadcast sound and its corresponding transcription are not allowed. Finally, the **computational resource need** (especially the memory requirement) of the recognition has to be kept at a relatively low level. These latter two factors are seldom taken into consideration when conducting research on broadcast data, although they are key elements when building real-time automatic close captioning systems.

Section 2 reviews the international results achieved on similar BN and BC automatic speech recognition (ASR) tasks. Section 3 describes the experimental setup used for building and decoding the systems introduced in this paper. Section 4 presents and discusses the results of the experiments. Firstly, the *direct transcription* task of BC data is tested with two different decoders and three acoustic models (ACMs), and the setup most suitable for the purpose of close captioning television programs in real time is chosen. The speech recognition chain of BC data often employ *re-speakers*, where broadcast audio is re-spoken by a qualified person eliminating some of its imperfections, like noise, hesitation, simultaneous speech, etc. Experiments on re-spoken BC data are also discussed.

2   Related Work

Most research studying recognition of television broadcast programs focuses on the BN domain. The research group having the most results in Hungarian BN recognition [7–9] used 10 to 50 h of manual transcriptions of broadcast speech and texts from the web to train their transcription system, and reported 21–27 % WER on various test sets. Their best results were achieved with subword based LMs. In contrast [4] investigated unsupervised training methods on a Hungarian task and reported 24 % WER. However, the test set having been a mix of BC and BN speech makes it hard to compare with former results. The lowest WER (17 %) for Hungarian BN was shown in [10], where a web corpus based LM was combined with a deep neural network (DNN) based ACM.

There are only a few papers investigating BC-domain ASR that points out to the challenging nature of the task. The only study we found about transcription of Hungarian BC is [8], where a Gaussian mixture model (GMM) based ACM trained on 50 h of broadcast speech was combined with a web corpus based LM. Unfortunately, the reported WER was very high (about 50 %). The international results in the BC domain lie between 20 % and 30 % for other languages [2,6,11]. These systems, however, used much more acoustic training data (between 300 and 500 h), and only the Japanese system [2] was able to operate in real time.

3 System Description

3.1 Training Data

The acoustic training of our Hungarian broadcast speech transcription system was based on 64 h of manually transcribed television news programs. MTVA provided us with closed captions closely related to our current recognition tasks (BN, BC). The resulting training text consisted of 17 million tokens altogether. In the later part of our paper a background LM is also introduced that was trained on a 63 million token corpus gathered from the most popular news websites of Hungary. All acoustic and textual training data was dated prior to the test set.

3.2 Language Modeling

On the collection of closed captions first text normalization was performed: sentence segmentation and recomposition, decapitalization of non-proper names at sentence-initial position and the expansion of non-lexical items to their verbal form. This latter was to enable phonetization of non-lexical items. Note that a deverbalization process takes place at the end of decoding, thus non-lexical items appear on screen in their original form.

Based on the verbal expanded training corpus a word based 3-gram model was estimated with the SRI Language Modeling toolkit (SRILM) [5] by using modified Kneser-Ney smoothing method. Neither LM pruning, nor vocabulary cutoff was applied. Subword-based LMs were trained on morph segmented versions of the word based training texts. Word-to-morph mapping was carried out with the Morfessor Baseline algorithm [1]. We used here 4-gram models with non-initial tags for word boundary reconstruction.

3.3 Acoustic Models

Acoustic modeling was implemented in the HTK [12] and Kaldi [3] speech recognition toolkits. GMMs were trained in both frameworks, whereas DNN models were built in Kaldi. The models were trained on 39 dimensional MFCC (Mel-Frequency Cepstral Coefficients) feature vectors (including first and second order delta components and energy). CMVN (Cepstral Mean and Variance Normalization) was omitted in order to enable online usage, the feature vectors were normalized with blind equalization. DNN models were trained on features with LDA (Linear Discriminant Analysis) and MLLT (Maximum Likelihood Linear Transformation).

The position-independent triphone GMM trained in Kaldi consisted of 9453-state Hidden Markov Models (HMMs) with a total of 110214 Gaussians and 5-state silence models. The HTK model contained 7972 states with 79720 total Gaussian count and used 3-state silence models. DNNs trained on this dataset had 4 hidden layers with 1024 neurons per hidden layer using the *pnorm* ($p = 4$) activation function. For the re-speaker tests, the GMM was adapted to the speakers of the test set using maximum a posteriori adaptation (MAP).

3.4   Test Data and Decoding

BC-domain tests were executed on 2.75 h of BC programs. An additional set of 1 h of BC audio was evaluated both by directly decoding the recordings and by using re-spoken versions of the same data. The BN test set comprises 10 television news (3 h altogether).

During the experiments, the speed and memory need of two different weighted finite state transducer (WFST) based decoders are compared. Firstly, the decoder of the Kaldi toolkit and secondly, VOXerver [8], a decoder provided by SpeechTex Ltd. Memory need is a crucial factor in this particular industrial setting, considering that in some cases all five television channels operated by MTVA have to be transcribed simultaneously. The virtual machine allocated for running our close captioning system on had 24 GBs of memory available, allowing a maximum of 4.8 GB memory need per thread when performing live captioning on all channels. All RTFs were measured on a 3.4 GHz *Core i7* CPU.

4   Results

4.1   Broadcast Conversation

Direct Transcription. The best results achieved on the BC test set are shown in Table 1. There are significant differences between the performance of the two decoders examined: although the WER values are the same in the saturation point, it takes more than two times longer for the decoder of Kaldi to achieve this result. It also has to be pointed out that by decoding with VOXerver the amount of memory used by one thread is significantly lower than in Kaldi (1 GB vs. 5.9 GB). VOXerver's higher resource efficiency compared to Kaldi originates in the difference of their data storage and decoding strategy. In VOXerver, acoustic transitions are not included in the WFSTs, but ACMs and a CLG level WFST (composition of WFSTs representing the phonetic context, lexicon, and grammar, respectively) is stored in a special, binary data structure. This structure was designed for fast access, optimal cache utilization and extremely compact representation of recognition models.

In order to examine the performance of the different GMMs and decoders more thoroughly, tests with different beam parameters were performed. The

Table 1. Best WER results achieved on the direct transcription task of BC audio.

Model	Decoder	WER	RTF	Memory
HTK GMM	VOXerver	36.8 %	0.60	1.0 GB
Kaldi GMM	Kaldi	36.1 %	1.23	5.9 GB
	VOXerver	36.1 %	0.50	1.0 GB
DNN	Kaldi	31.6 %	1.03	5.9 GB
	VOXerver	30.6 %	0.71	1.0 GB

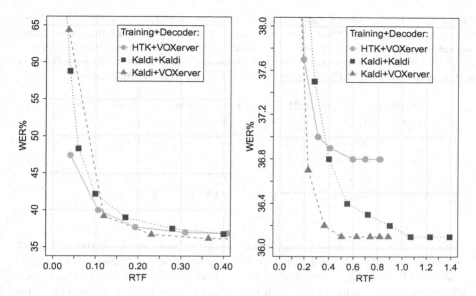

Fig. 1. WER vs. RTF in three configurations with two different axis scalings.

results of the three configurations (HTK model decoded in VOXerver, and Kaldi model decoded in VOXerver and Kaldi) are shown on Fig. 1 with two different resolutions. As discussed above, the same error rate is obtainable by decoding the Kaldi model in both decoders, however, the saturation occurs at a much lower RTF value when using VOXerver. The GMM trained in HTK produces higher error rates than the one built in Kaldi, although the difference is not remarkable and DNN models show about 12 % relative WER improvement over GMM architectures. Considering these results, it can be concluded that decoding Kaldi models with VOXerver is the optimal configuration in real time low memory-need BC transcription situations (the 5.9 GB of memory used by Kaldi exceeds the 4.8 GB limit described in Subsect. 3.4).

The results achieved in the direct transcription BC setup overperform previously reported error rates on Hungarian direct BC transcription tasks [8]. This might be because of the more in-domain data available to our experiments on the one hand, and more advanced acoustic modeling (e.g. DNNs) on the other.

Re-speaking. Although the WERs reported in this study are the lowest ever measured in Hungarian BC recognition tasks, they might prove to be too high for close captioning. Hence we decided to investigate the potentials of the re-speaking approach. Our partner MTVA provided us with re-spoken versions of some of their BC programs. However, it is important to note that these recordings were made with non-professional re-speakers, who were instructed to re-speak the BC programs strictly in the same words (as opposed to summarizing them), which made it even harder to accomplish their task precisely.

Table 2. WERs of direct and re-spoken audio transcription of various BC shows. Show and speaker IDs (*Show/Spk.*) are indicated with Arabic and Roman numerals respectively. Direct transcription with both GMM and DNN models (*GMM (dir.)*, *DNN (dir.)*) and re-spoken transcription with an unadapted DNN (*DNN (rsp.)*) model, and a GMM adapted to the re-speakers (*GMM+MAP (rsp.)*) are displayed.

Show/Spk	GMM (dir.)	DNN (dir.)	DNN (rsp.)	GMM+MAP (rsp.)
1/I	31.5 %	23.4 %	20.5 %	19.2 %
2/I	30.7 %	24.8 %	23.4 %	18.8 %
3/II	33.6 %	25.4 %	18.1 %	17.6 %
4/III	34.1 %	26.8 %	26.2 %	25.1 %
Avg.	**32.5 %**	**25.1 %**	**22.1 %**	**20.2 %**

Results of four different transcription configurations are displayed in Table 2. The setups were tested on 4 different BC programs, and assigned to 3 different speakers. The benefits of employing re-speakers are clear, although the achievable improvement highly depends on the actual television program and the quality of the re-spoken speech: relative error rate improvements vary between 2 % and 30 % when using unadapted models. The GMM adapted to the re-speakers produces the most accurate transcriptions: compared to the unadapted DNN, it shows an 8.5 % average relative WER improvement. It should be noted, however, that model adaptation requires additional data from the re-speakers.

4.2   Decoding with Advanced Language Models

During the tests presented above, a smaller LM was used in order to facilitate memory-efficient transcription. When the amount of memory used is not a key aspect, more advanced LMs (MTVA captions + background LM) can also be used. The extended LMs were tested with the VOXerver decoder only, because Kaldi would use up to 27 GB of memory at decoding and even more for building the WFST network. Word error rates can be decreased further this way, there are 4 % and 12 % relative improvements on BC and BN data respectively, see Table 3. The memory consumption, on the other hand, is increased by 400 % (from 1 GB to 5 GB). In the view of this, models with lower resource need and slightly lower accuracy might be the best options in real time close captioning systems. In [8], subword-based LMs provided the lowest error rates for broadcast speech transcription, hence we also tested LMs built on unsupervised derived [1] morphs. Morph based LMs turned out to be beneficial only in better acoustic conditions and if less training data was used (see "BN, closed captions" in Table 3). This matches with the findings in [7].

The best model-decoder configurations tested on the BC task were also evaluated on BN recordings with different LMs. This was done in order to examine their applicability in settings where the transcription of news programs might be necessary. The best result with the GMM is 12.6 % WER using the morph based

Table 3. Results achieved in the BC and BN domain with different LM configurations. The relative improvement achieved with morph based modeling (*Rel. improvement*) compared to word based LMs is also displayed.

Domain	ACM	Training text	WER		Rel. improvement
			Word LM	Morph LM	
BC	GMM	Closed captions	36.1 %	36.5 %	−1.1 %
		+ background text	34.6 %	34.8 %	−0.6 %
	DNN	Closed captions	30.6 %	30.6 %	0.0 %
		+ background text	29.3 %	29.2 %	0.3 %
BN	GMM	Closed captions	14.5 %	13.8 %	**4.8 %**
		+ background text	12.7 %	12.6 %	0.8 %
	DNN	Closed captions	11.9 %	11.6 %	**2.5 %**
		+ background text	10.5 %	10.6 %	−1.0 %

expanded LM. With the DNN setting the WER is further improved by a relative 17 % as it lies at 10.5 %. The performance of the systems are in accordance with the international results of BN ASR tasks and are significantly lower than any other published Hungarian BN result.

5 Conclusions and Future Work

This paper introduced automatic transcription systems operating in the broadcast domain, focusing on broadcast conversation captioning tasks in the Hungarian language. Various acoustic models have been developed and their performances were compared along with two WFST based LVCSR decoders. The proposed decoder called VOXerver proved to be prominent to Kaldi's fast decoder: it was almost 2 times faster and 6 times more memory efficient than the latter one in our test configuration. The best results on BN and BC data were 10.5 % and 29.2 % WER respectively, which are the lowest error rates achieved for Hungarian in both domains to the best of our knowledge.

In order to further decrease the error rate we investigated the potential in employing re-speakers instead of direct transcription of the BC programs. By combining DNN acoustic models and re-speaking the recognition error rate could be significantly reduced (∼20 % WER). However, the re-spoken BC results are still far from the level of BN results. Our conviction is that the obligation for word by word re-speaking and the lack of training for the re-speakers made the recognition task unnecessarily difficult.

Future research includes the application of speaker adaptive training (SAT) along with DNN as well as the investigation of semi-supervised training methods. Furthermore, we expect further improvement by employing better qualified re-speakers and by using conversational speech data for building acoustic models.

Acknowledgement. This research has been partially funded by the PIAC_13-1-2013-0234 (Patimedia) and KMR_12-1-2012-0207 (DIANA) projects. The authors would also like to thank MTVA for their support towards this work.

References

1. Creutz, M., Lagus, K.: Unsupervised morpheme segmentation and morphology induction from text corpora using Morfessor 1.0. Publications in Computer and Information Science, Report A81 (2005)
2. Kobayashi, A., Oku, T., Imai, T., Nakagawa, S.: Risk-based semi-supervised discriminative language modeling for broadcast transcription. IEICE Trans. **95**-**D**(11), 2674–2681 (2012)
3. Povey, D., et al.: The kaldi speech recognition toolkit. In: IEEE 2011 Workshop on Automatic Speech Recognition and Understanding. IEEE Signal Processing Society, Hilton Waikoloa Village (2011)
4. Roy, A., et al.: Some issues affecting the transcription of hungarian broadcast audio. In: 14th Annual Conference of the International Speech Communication Association (Interspeech 2013), pp. 3102–3106 (2013)
5. Stolcke, A.: SRILM - an extensible language modeling toolkit. In: Proceedings of International Conference on Spoken Language Processing, pp. 901–904. Denver (2002)
6. Sundermeyer, M., et al.: The RWTH 2010 Quaero ASR evaluation system for English, French, and German. In: 2011 IEEE International Conference on Acoustics, Speech and Signal Processing (ICASSP), pp. 2212–2215 (2011)
7. Tarján, B., Mihajlik, P.: On morph-based LVCSR improvements. In: Proceedings of the 2nd International Workshop on Spoken Language Technologies for Under-resourced Languages, pp. 10–15 (2010)
8. Tarján, B., Mihajlik, P., Balog, A., Fegyó, T.: Evaluation of lexical models for hungarian broadcast speech transcription and spoken term detection. In: 2nd IEEE International Conference on Cognitive Infocommunications, pp. 1–5 (2011)
9. Tarján, B., Fegyó, T., Mihajlik, P.: A bilingual study on the prediction of morph-based improvement. In: Spoken Language Technologies for Under-Resourced Languages, pp. 131–138 (2014)
10. Tóth, L., Grósz, T.: A comparison of deep neural network training methods for large vocabulary speech recognition. In: Habernal, I. (ed.) TSD 2013. LNCS, vol. 8082, pp. 36–43. Springer, Heidelberg (2013)
11. Winebarger, J., Nguyen, B., Gehring, J., Stüker, S., Waibel, A.: The 2013 KIT Quaero speech-to-text system for French. In: Proceedings of the 10th International Workshop for Spoken Language Translation (IWSLT 2013) (2013)
12. Young, S.J., et al.: The HTK Book, Version 3.4. Cambridge University Engineering Department, Cambridge (2006)

Automatic Estimation of Web Bloggers' Age Using Regression Models

Vasiliki Simaki$^{(\boxtimes)}$, Christina Aravantinou, Iosif Mporas,
and Vasileios Megalooikonomou

Multidimensional Data Analysis and Knowledge Management Laboratory
Department of Computer Engineering and Informatics,
University of Patras, 26500 Rion, Greece
{simaki,aravantino,vasilis}@ceid.upatras.gr, imporas@upatras.gr

Abstract. In this article, we address the problem of automatic age estimation of web users based on their posts. Most studies on age identification treat the issue as a classification problem. Instead of following an age category classification approach, we investigate the appropriateness of several regression algorithms on the task of age estimation. We evaluate a number of well-known and widely used machine learning algorithms for numerical estimation, in order to examine their appropriateness on this task. We used a set of 42 text features. The experimental results showed that the Bagging algorithm with RepTree base learner offered the best performance, achieving estimation of web users' age with mean absolute error equal to 5.44, while the root mean squared error is approximately 7.14.

Keywords: Author's age estimation · Text processing · Regression algorithms

1 Introduction

The extensive growth of the web and the plethora of options that social media provide, have resulted in the increase of the web users population, especially in the most developed countries. This reality results to the production of large amounts of written web posts on a daily basis. The automatic extraction of information from these online data is related not only to the text itself but also to the gender, age and other demographic characteristics of the user that are essential in the e-government, security and e-commerce market.

The detection of demographic information and more specifically the detection of age, among social media users may be important not only for commercial and sociological purposes, but also for security reasons. Teen users are allowed to use social media without often being supervised by adults, a situation that can be fatal in extreme conditions. It is thus important to be able to automatically estimate the age of an internet user from his/her writing input on the web. Except security, the estimation of the user's age can be important in detecting

© Springer International Publishing Switzerland 2015
A. Ronzhin et al. (Eds.): SPECOM 2015, LNAI 9319, pp. 113–120, 2015.
DOI: 10.1007/978-3-319-23132-7_14

the different trends, opinions, political and social views of each age group. This can enable social scientists to derive important clues about the anthropography among social media users, and how different age groups behave online. Market analysts and advertisers may also be interested in this kind of studies, in order to promote their product or a service in an age-targeted way according to their expressed interests and opinions.

Most studies on age identification treat the issue as a classification problem. In this article, instead of following an age category classification approach, we investigate the appropriateness of several regression algorithms on the task of age estimation of bloggers, dealing with a numerical estimation problem. We relied on several text-based features that have been widely used in the literature for text classification, authorship attribution, gender and age identification, in order to evaluate the performance of regression methods. The remainder of this paper is organized as follows: Sect. 2 presents the state-of-the-art in theoretical and automatic age estimation. Section 3 describes the followed methodology for age estimation from web posts. Section 4 presents the experimental setup and the achieved results. Finally Sect. 5 concludes this work.

2   Background Work

People of different age, gender, educational level, professional activity and geographical orientation make various linguistic choices, due to these social factors [1]. The matching of a linguistic attitude to the corresponding social group is one of the objectives of sociolinguistics. Several sociolinguistic studies in age variation [2,3] observed that teenagers use the language in a more creative and non-contractual way, by producing new forms, when adults prefer more standard types. Semantic neologisms, slang types, loanwords and code expressions are produced by teens, when adults tend to have a more conservative linguistic attitude. This can be explained after the social role in the production/work cycle and the family responsibilities that adulthood occurs, when teens and older people let to a more "loose" use of language [4].

Whilst sociolinguistic researches in age variation stand on theoretical and empirical findings, recent studies in text mining use machine learning algorithms and natural language processing methods for the automatic estimation of the authors' age. Schler et al. [5] create the "Blog Authorship Corpus" in order to identify the author's age and gender. They used style-related features and content-based characteristics in order to detect the gender and the age. They observed that specific forms and unigrams are more frequent in young bloggers, the blogging style and topics are different among 10's, 20's and 30's. Argamon et al. [6] used the corpus from their previous study [5], in order to go deeper in the gender and age mining from text. They used stylistic and content-based features in order to demonstrate the significant variation between different genders and ages in blogging. Goswami et al. [7] performed a stylometric analysis in terms of gender and age by using non-dictionary forms and the sentence length as features. The slang, smileys, out-of-dictionary words, chat abbreviations, on the one hand, and the sentence length on the other, proved to be highly distinctive among different ages and gender. Tam and Martell [8] performed age classification experiments, using Bayesian and SVM classifiers. They extracted character n-grams and word meta-data features, in order to classify the "NPS Chat Corpus" into five age groups. In their work, Peersman et al. [9], implemented age classification in small texts, using chat words as features, along with character-based features, achieving more than 88 % of accuracy. Other studies in age prediction [10,11], proved that content and stylistic features are extremely significant, and when the online users' activity is added, the classification accuracy increases approximately to 80 % [10]. In their overview of PAN 2013, Rangel et al. [12] presented the different feature sets that the participants in the Author Profiling Task used, which were finally grouped into stylistic-based, content-based, n-grams-, IR-, and collocations-based. Many of the participants dealt with the age detection, and Flekova & Gurevych [13] focused on age and gender using surface, syntactic and punctuation, readability, semantic, content, lexical and stop words features. They observed eventually that the age and gender profiling are not independent issues, but they are determined by the same features. Rangel & Rosso [14] used the PAN-AP-13 dataset in order to perform classification experiments in terms of age and gender, using though features based in cognitive traits of neurology studies. Their approach was more efficient in age than gender prediction and they proved the differences in language use of different ages, in English and Spanish. [15] is a quite integrated study in personality, gender and age detection of Facebook users. Standard approaches were implemented and a particular method was proposed for linguistic analysis and evaluation in terms of personality, age and gender with reliable results, contribution to interdisciplinary researches, and suggestion of new hypotheses and insights. Nguyen et al. [16] performed a study in language use among different age categories of Twitter users. Their analysis showed that differences in style, references, conversation and sharing depended not only on the age category estimation, but also on the life stage and the actual age of the user. Lately, the authorship profiling has become a task about multilingual efforts and [17] is one of the several studies implemented in a non-English corpus for stylometric research and possibilities to perform age, gender, opinion, authorship and personality experiments.

3   Proposed Age Estimation of Web Bloggers Using Regression Models

The estimation of the age of an author is a numerical estimation problem. Although some of the related work found in the literature targets at identifying the age class the author belongs to, according to some quantization of the age scale to age intervals of interest, we target at the direct estimation of the age value of the web blogger (i.e. the author). Thus the problem is formulated as follows: We consider a representation of each web blog post with a feature vector V_n, for the nth post with $1 \leq n \leq N$. A machine learning regression algorithm, f, is used as a numerical estimator, for assigning an age estimation, u, to each feature vector V_n, i.e. $u = f(V_n)$.

For the representation of each web blog post with a feature vector, we used a number of well-known and widely used in text-based analyses features, which have been used in the tasks of author, gender and age identification, they are normalized and they are presented in Table 1. The resulted feature vector has length equal to 42, i.e. $V_n \in \Re^{42}$.

Table 1. The description of features used in our study.

# of characters	# of the "hapax legomena"
# of alphabetic characters	# of the "hapax dislegomena"
# of upper case characters	# of pronouns
# of digit characters	# of function words
# of space characters	average # of sentences per paragraph
# of tab ("\t") characters	average # of characters per paragraph
# of occurrence of each alphabetic character	# of words starting with a capital
# of occurrence of special characters	# of punctuation symbols
# of words	# of capitalized types
# of words with length less than 4 characters	std of the word length
# of characters per word	max length word
average word length	min length word
# of sentences	# of future tense types
# of paragraphs	# of hyperlinks
# of lines	# of self-references
average # of characters per sentence	# of nouns
average # of words per sentence	# of proper nouns
# of unique words	# of adjectives
# of articles	# of prepositions
# of adverbs	# of emoticons
# of interjections	# of verbs

For the regression stage, we relied on a number of dissimilar machine learning algorithms, which have extensively been reported in the literature. In particular, we used:

- The multilayer perceptron neural network (MLP) with three layers which is capable for numerical predictions [18], since neurons are isolated and region approximations can be adjusted independently to each other,
- The support vector machines (SVM) for regression using the sequential minimal optimization algorithm and two different kernels, the radial basis kernel (rbf) and the polynomial kernel (poly),
- The M5 model tree (M5P) algorithm, which is a rational reconstruction of M5 method,
- The K-nearest neighbors algorithm (IBk),
- The RepTree, a fast decision tree learner, which builds a decision/regression tree using information gain/variance and prunes it using reduced-error pruning (with back-fitting). RepTree only sorts values for numeric attributes once

and missing values are dealt with by splitting the corresponding instances into pieces (i.e. as in C4.5),

- The Additive regression meta-classifier that enhances the performance of a regression base classifier along with DecisionStump, SVMs with polynomial and radial basis kernel and REPTrees,
- The bagging algorithm combined with REPTree and SVMs with polynomial and radial basis kernel, aiming to reduce variance,
- The M5Rules, which generates a decision list for regression problems using separate-and-conquer. In each iteration, it builds a model tree using M5 and makes the "best" leaf into a rule.

All regression algorithms were implemented using the WEKA machine learning toolkit [19].

4   Experimental Setup and Results

For the present evaluation we used the "Blog Authorship Corpus" [5], a collection of blog posts from 19,320 bloggers which have posted in their blogs. These blog posts were gathered from blogger.com in August 2004. The size of the corpus is 681,288 posts and over 140 million of words, which corresponds to 35 posts and 7,250 words per person. The bloggers fall into three age categories: 10's, 20's and 30's. The 10's age group is constituted of 8,240 blogs whose authors are between 13 and 17 years. The 20's is constituted of 8,086 blogs of 23–27 years old authors. Finally the 30's age group contains 2,994 blogs produced by bloggers between 33 and 47 years. Each blog is structured in a separate file containing the bloggers' posts, the bloggers' id number, his/her gender, his/her exact age and in many cases other anonymised personal pieces of information.

The "Blog Authorship Corpus" was evaluated on the task of age estimation, using the features described in the previous section. The performance of the evaluated regression algorithms was measured using the mean absolute error (MAE) and the root mean squared error (RMSE) of the difference (i.e. the error) between the actual and the estimated age of each web blogger. In order to avoid overlap between training and test subsets, a 10-fold cross validation evaluation protocol was followed. The experimental results for the evaluated regression algorithms in terms of MAE and RMSE are tabulated in Table 2. The best performance for each of the above metrics is indicated in bold.

As can be seen in Table 2, the best performing algorithm was the Bagging implemented with the RepTree base learner, achieving MAE and RMSE equal to 5.44 and 7.15, respectively. The second and third best performance was achieved by the RepTree regression algorithm and the Additive Regression algorithm with the RepTrees regression base classifier with MAE approximately equal to 5.67. The results show the appropriateness of RepTree regression algorithm for the task of age estimation from web blog posts, since it outperforms all the other algorithms either as a base learner within a meta-classification scheme or as a standalone regression algorithm. The superiority of the RepTree regression algorithm is not restricted only in the MAE criterion, but is also presented in

Table 2. Age estimation MAE and RMSE per regression algorithm.

Regression Algorithm	MAE	RMSE
MLP	8.013	10.2701
SVM-poly	5.8917	7.6787
SVM-rbf	6.0666	7.7548
IBk	7.5044	10.2675
Add. Regression (SVM-poly)	5.8702	7.6929
Add. Regression (SVM-rbf)	5.6772	8.0213
Add.Regression (RepTrees)	5.6741	7.5382
Bagging (SVM-poly)	5.9164	8.053
Bagging (SVM-rbf)	6.7432	8.345
Bagging (RepTrees)	**5.4407**	**7.1457**
M5Rules	24.5921	1196.7574
M5P	18.864	863.185
RepTrees	5.6695	7.464

the RMSE criterion, which shows that RepTrees offer the minimum outliers in terms of age estimation comparing to the rest of the evaluated algorithms.

The only regression algorithm which was found to have performance comparable to RepTrees was the SVM with polynomial kernel, performing slightly worse both as standalone and as base learner of a meta-classification algorithm. The good performance of the SVM algorithm is probably owed to the fact that they don't suffer from the curse of dimensionality. The worse performance was achieved by the M5Rules and M5P regression algorithms, which are model trees in contrast to the best performing RepTree which is a regression tree. Their low performance is probably owed to the fact that they leverage potential linearity at leaf nodes and the fact that they construct hard-decision rules based on the best leaf.

5   Conclusion

We presented an evaluation of regression algorithms for the estimation of web bloggers' age. For the estimation of the age we relied on a number of text-based characteristics, which are typical in text classification tasks related to gender and age identification, and constructed one feature vector for each blogger's post. The evaluation results showed that by using regression methods, age estimation can be adequately performed. The RepTree algorithm proved to outperform all the evaluated regression algorithms, and achieved accurate age estimations both when used as main regression algorithm and as a base learner of a meta-classification method. The application of regression algorithms on age categories dramatically increased age estimation accuracy both in terms of mean absolute error and in terms of root mean square error, which indicates that the combination of age category classification followed by age regression per category would offer robust estimation of the web bloggers' age.

References

1. Labov, W.: Sociolinguistic Patterns (No. 4). University of Pennsylvania Press, Philadelphia (1972)
2. Trudgill, P.: The social differentiation of English in Norwich, vol. 13. CUP Archive, Cambridge (1974)
3. Eckert, P.: Age as a sociolinguistic variable. In: Coulmas, F. (ed.) The Handbook of Sociolinguistics. Blackwell, Oxford (1997)
4. Labov, W.: Principles of linguistic change, cognitive and cultural factors, vol. 3. John Wiley & Sons, New York (2011)
5. Schler, J., Koppel, M., Argamon, S., Pennebaker, J.W.: Effects of age and gender on blogging. In: AAAI Spring Symposium: Computational Approaches to Analyzing Weblogs, vol. 6, pp. 199–205 (2006)
6. Argamon, S., Koppel, M., Pennebaker, J.W., Schler, J.: Mining the blogosphere: age, gender and the varieties of self-expression. First Monday, 12(9) (2007)
7. Goswami, S., Sarkar, S., Rustagi, M.: Stylometric analysis of bloggers' age and gender. In: Third International AAAI Conference on Weblogs and Social Media (2009)
8. Tam, J., Martell, C.H.: Age detection in chat. In: IEEE International Conference on Semantic Computing, ICSC 2009, pp. 33–39. IEEE (2009)
9. Peersman, C., Daelemans, W., Van Vaerenbergh, L.: Predicting age and gender in online social networks. In: Proceedings of the 3rd international workshop on Search and Mining User-Generated Contents, pp. 37–44. ACM (2011)
10. Rosenthal, S., McKeown, K.: Age prediction in blogs: a study of style, content, and online behavior in pre-and post-social media generations. In: Proceedings of the 49th Annual Meeting of the Association for Computational Linguistics: Human Language Technologies, vol. 1, pp. 763–772. ACL (2011)
11. Nguyen, D., Smith, N.A., Ros, C.P.: Author age prediction from text using linear regression. In: Proceedings of the 5th ACL-HLT Workshop on Language Technology for Cultural Heritage, Social Sciences, and Humanities, pp. 115–123. ACL (2011)
12. Rangel, F., Rosso, P., Koppel, M., Stamatatos, E., Inches, G.: Overview of the author profiling task at PAN 2013. Notebook Papers of CLEF (2013)
13. Flekova, L., Gurevych, I.: Can we hide in the web? Large scale simultaneous age and gender author profiling in social media. In: CLEF 2012 Labs and Work-shop. Notebook Papers (2013)
14. Rangel, F., Rosso, P.: Use of language and author profiling: identification of gender and age. Natural Language Processing and Cognitive Science, 177 (2013)
15. Schwartz, H.A., Eichstaedt, J.C., Kern, M.L., Dziurzynski, L., Ramones, S.M., Agrawal, M., Ungar, L.H.: Personality, gender, and age in the language of social media: the open-vocabulary approach. PloS one 8(9), e73791 (2013)
16. Nguyen, D., Gravel, R., Trieschnigg, D., Meder, T.: "How old do you think i am?"; A study of language and age in twitter. In: Proceedings of the Seventh International AAAI Conference on Weblogs and Social Media. AAAI Press (2013)
17. Verhoeven, B., Daelemans, W.: CLiPSStylometry Investigation (CSI) corpus: a Dutch corpus for the detection of age, gender, personality, sentiment and deception in text. In: Proceedings of the 9th International Conference on Language Resources and Evaluation (2014)

18. Chester, D.L.: Why two hidden layers are better than one. In: Proceedings of the International Joint Conference on Neural Networks, vol. 1, pp. 265–268 (1990)
19. Witten, I.H., Frank, E.: Data Mining: Practical Machine Learning Tools and Techniques, 2nd edn. Elsevier, Morgan-Kaufman Series of Data Management Systems, San Francisco (2005)

Automatic Preprocessing Technique for Detection of Corrupted Speech Signal Fragments for the Purpose of Speaker Recognition

Konstantin Simonchik[1,2], Sergei Aleinik[1]([✉]), Dmitry Ivanko[1], and Galina Lavrentyeva[1,2]

[1] ITMO University,
49 Kronverkskiy Pr., St. Petersburg 197101, Russia
{simonchik,aleinik,lavrentyeva}@speechpro.com
[2] Speech Technology Center,
Krasutskogo-4, St. Petersburg 196084, Russia

Abstract. In this paper we propose a preprocessing technique which allows to detect clicks, tones, overloads, clipping, etc., as well as to discover the parts of good-quality speech signal. As a result the performance of the speaker recognition system increases significantly. It should be noted that when describing noise detectors we aim only to provide a full list of algorithms we used as well as their parameters that we obtained in our experiments. The main goal of the paper is to demonstrate that using a set of simple detectors is very effective in detecting speech for speaker recognition task under the conditions of real noise.

Keywords: Preprocessing · Speaker recognition · Speech processing

1 Introduction

At the input of a speaker identification system we often have a mixture of distorted speech signal with various additive noises. Two classic approaches to handling this problem are well-known. The first is increasing the algorithms robustness: feature compensation, model adaptation, score normalization, etc. The second is using different noise cancellation techniques at the input stage. In practice that real-world audio signals in many cases are only partially (not totally) corrupted. For example, GSM-bursts or telephone bells are short-time noises that may be detected easily. So it is clear that a preprocessing technique which detects corrupted (i.e. distorted or with a high level of noise) fragments of input signals and then remove them from the next stages of processing may be useful for the automatic speaker recognition.

2 Preprocessing Technique

The structure of the proposed preprocessing is presented in Fig. 1, and contains different components, such as three levels of detectors, two resampling units and

© Springer International Publishing Switzerland 2015
A. Ronzhin et al. (Eds.): SPECOM 2015, LNAI 9319, pp. 121–128, 2015.
DOI: 10.1007/978-3-319-23132-7_15

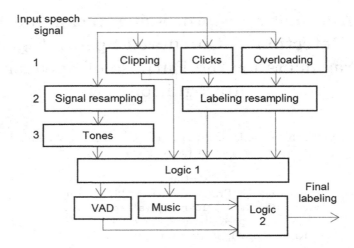

Fig. 1. Proposed preprocessing structure. The numbers on the left signify the detection levels

two logic units. An important point is that the goal of the order and connection of the detectors is to avoid the effects of mutual and resampling influence. Indeed, resampling smoothes short impulses and sharp power bursts, which leads to poor clipping, clicks and overloadings detection.

On the other hand, resampling does not have much influence on the detection of tones and music. Furthermore, signal overloading (as well as click, tone and beep sounds) may be classified as "speech" by voice activity detector (VAD), so the corresponding detectors have to be used before VAD. Additionally, in our technique every detector generates its own labeling. For example, the clipping detector marks clipped fragments of the processed signal, the click detector marks clicks, etc. The corresponding labelings are combined in logic units for the next stages of processing.

The workflow of the preprocessing system, based on our technique, is easy to understand via Fig. 1. The only unusual unit here is "labeling resampling". As mentioned above, clipping, clicks and overloading have to be detected and labeled at the input stage of the system. Then the signal resampling is provided and the subsequent detectors process the resampled signal. As a result the first and the next levels labelings have different time scales. The labeling resampling unit transforms labelings to the equal time scale. Logic unit 1 performs output signal using logical disjunction: a signal fragment is marked as distorted if one or more detectors mark it as distorted. Logic unit 2 provides the audio signal fragment to the next stage of processing only if human speech has been detected and a music signal has not been detected by the corresponding detectors. Detailed descriptions of the detectors are provided below. Some of the detectors are well known and we only evaluated their parameters in our experiments, using known sound and noise databases (TIMIT and NOISEX-92, respectively) as well as our databases of the typical signal distortions. Some of the detectors are our own developments. For example, we propose our own new clipping detector and a new modification of music detector based on spectral flux analysis.

3   Preprocessing Technique

3.1   Click Detector

A classic method to detect a click in a small signal block is [2]

1. Divide the analyzed signal block into an odd number of sections (usually 3 or 5).
2. Evaluate some signal parameter(s) in the central section and in the other sections of the signal.
3. Calculate the relation of the evaluated parameter(s) as a target value.

We calculate the following target value (Fig. 2):

$$V_{cl}(t_c) = \left(2(t_1 - t_0) \sum_{t=t_1}^{t_2} x^2(t) \right) \bigg/ \left((t_2 - t_1) \left(\sum_{t=t_0}^{t_1} x^2(t) + \sum_{t=t_2}^{t_3} x^2(t) \right) \right), \quad (1)$$

where $x(t)$ is input signal; $V_{cl}(t_c)$ is the target value at the time $t_c = (t_3 + t_0)/2$. Then the decision may be obtained: if $V_{cl} > Tr_{cl}$ then click is detected. The fixed threshold level Tr_{cl} value as well as time intervals have been obtained in our previous experiments: $Tr_{cl} = 2$; short time interval (t_1, t_2) is equal to 5 ms; long time intervals (t_0, t_1) and (t_0, t_1) are equal to 60 ms.

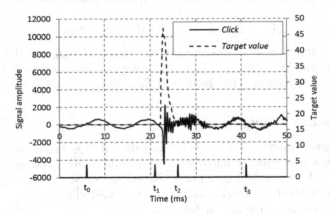

Fig. 2. An example of a typical click and the corresponding target value

3.2   Overloading Detector

We consider here "overloading" as "sharp sign changing" caused by integer overflow. In practice, one of the most frequently used quantization in digital audio processing is 16-bits quantization. So every digital signal sample is 16-bits integer value within the fixed limits: [-32768, 32767]. In this case if we process our signal in floating point format, and the result is out of the above range we will get sign changing when we try to transform our signal to 16-bits integer value at the output stage. For example value 32768.0 will be transformed into the negative value -32768; -32769.0 will be changed into 32767 , etc. Typical overloading is presented in Fig. 3.

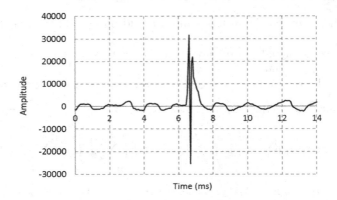

Fig. 3. An example of a typical overloading

The common overloading detection algorithm calculates the following target value:

$$V_{ov}(i) = (|x(i) - x(i - 1)|)/(x_{max} - x_{min}),\qquad(2)$$

where $x(i)$ is input signal at discrete time i; x_{max} and x_{min} are the maximum and minimum possible values of the signal, respectively. In our experiments we estimate the corresponding threshold level Tr_{ov} as equal to 0.7.

3.3   Clipping Detector

Clipping detector is fully described in [1]. In a digital clipping signal a number of samples are grouped near the maximum and/or minimum of the signal dynamic range borders. A typical histogram of a clipped speech signal (Fig. 4) has some narrow peaks on the tails which can be used to detect clipping.

The target value for clipping detector is:

$$V_{cg} = 2\max(Dl, Dr)/(x_{max} - x_{min}),\qquad(3)$$

where: $x_{max} - x_{min}$ is the range of x-axis; Dl and Dr are the "maximal distance between the tails local maximum and the point where the histogram ordinate is greater than this local maximum" for left and right half of the histogram, respectively. It is clear that $V_{cg} \in [0, 1]$ and the more signal is clipped, the close

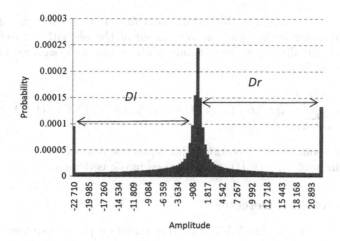

Fig. 4. An example of clipped speech signal histogram

V_{cg} to 1. Our experiments shows that for number of signal samples $N > 5000$ and number of histogram bins $K = 300$ the corresponding threshold level Tr_{cg} is equal to 0.6 [1].

3.4 Tones Detector

Tones are well-known single-tone or dual-tone harmonical impulses used for dialing and/or signaling within the telephone network. An important point is that the amplitude of these signals are high and the frequencies of carrier harmonic(s) is very stable (in contrast to a speech signal). In our preprocessing system there is algorithm based on the constancy of the maximums' spectral amplitudes. We analyze two magnitude spectrums calculated sequentially (in discrete time $i - 1$ and i), find theirs maximums $S_{\max}$, then calculate the target value:

$$V_{to}(i) = |S_{\max}^i - S_{\max}^{i-1}|/S_{\max}^{i-1}. \tag{4}$$

If $V_{to}(i) > Tr_{to}$ then tone signal is detected. We evaluate the value of the threshold level $Tr_{to} = 0.01$.

3.5 Music Detector

In our preprocessing we use music detection algorithm [5] based on modified spectral flux analysis fully described in [4]. Firstly, we calculate signal spectrogram: $X(t, f)$. Secondly we transform the spectrogram to detect the frequency domains that contained peaks of spectral density. In order to do that, we subtract its trend $Td(t, f)$ from the source spectrogram:

$$X'(t, f) = H(|X(t, f)| - Td(t, f)), \tag{5}$$

where $H(x) = (x + |x|)/2$ is the rectification function. Thirdly, we apply normalization in order to increase the invariance of the algorithm to changes in signal volume. Finally, we trace not only positive but also negative changes of the spectrogram bins:

$$SF'(t) = \sum_{k=-N/2}^{N/2-1} [(|X'(t,f) - X'(t-1,f)|) / (X'(t,f) + X'(t-1,f))] \quad (6)$$

The decision about music detection is based on the result of comparison with a predefined threshold. If $SF'(t) > Tr_{sf}$ then music is detected.

3.6 Voice Activity Detector

In our preprocessing we use VAD algorithm based on power envelope dynamics fully described in [6].

4 Experimental and Results

To evaluate the quality of the preprocessing modules we used our database with speech, tonal noises, clicks, overloads, etc., (evaluation data set was different from the development set, used for thresholds estimation). The total number of test phono-grams was 78. Signals segmentation was done manually. We calculated false acceptance (FA) and false rejection (FR) rates for each detector, mentioned above. To study how our preprocessing technique influences the speaker recognition system quality we carried out a series of experiments. In our experiments we used i-vector based speaker recognition system [3]. Proposed preprocessing technique was used for speech/non-speech segmentation. The front-end computed 13 mel-frequency cepstral coefficients, as well as the first and second derivatives, to yield a 39 dimensional vector per frame. We also applied a cepstral mean subtraction (CMS) and did not apply Feature Warping for the cepstral coefficients.

We used a gender-independent UBM with 512-component GMM, obtained by standard ML-training on the telephone part of the NIST's SRE 1998–2010 datasets (all languages, both genders). We also used a full-covariance GMM UBM. The i-vector extractor was trained on more than 60000 telephone and microphone recordings from the NIST 1998–2010 comprising more than 4000 speakers' voices.

For testing the speaker recognition system and preprocessing technique we took the database of typical telephone conversations (587 phonograms of 57 speakers), recorded via office telephones at the Speech Technology Center company. This database contained music signals, tones, DTMF signals, switching clicks and overloaded signals. The duration of speech in the recordings ranged from 3 sec to 5 min. The speaker recognition experiment was repeated several times with different sets of preprocessing detectors. Equal error rate (EER) was used as a measure of preprocessing system performance. It is understandable that

Table 1. EER for preprocessing detectors, Separate detectors trial.

Clicks	Clipping	Overloading	Music	Tones	VAD	EER %
-	-	-	-	-	-	11,69
-	-	-	-	-	ON	9,94
-	-	-	-	ON	ON	9,85
-	-	-	ON	-	ON	7,49
-	-	ON	-	-	ON	9,94
-	ON	-	-	-	ON	9,85
ON	-	-	-	-	ON	9,94

Table 2. EER for preprocessing detectors. The combination of detectors trial, part 1.

Clicks	Clipping	Overloading	Music	Tones	VAD	EER %
ON	-	-	-	-	ON	9,94
ON	ON	-	-	-	ON	9,85
ON	ON	ON	-	-	ON	9,85
ON	ON	ON	ON	-	ON	7,35
ON	ON	ON	ON	ON	ON	7,26

there are many combinations of the 6 detectors, so Tables 1, 2 and 3 present only a limited set (symbol '-'means "off" for the corresponding detector).

Tables 1, 2 and 3 show that:

1. The worst (highest) EER is when no detectors are used (trivial).
2. Significant increase in speaker recognition accuracy is achieved when VAD is used (even single).
3. The best combination of two detectors is VAD + Music detector.
4. Other detectors give less positive effects in "VAD + single detector" mode, but increases performance of speaker recognition.
5. The best results are obtained when all detectors are set to "on".

Table 3. EER for preprocessing detectors. The combination of detectors trial, part 2.

Clicks	Clipping	Overloading	Music	Tones	VAD	EER %
-	-	-	-	-	-	11,69
-	-	-	-	-	ON	9,94
-	-	-	-	-	ON	9,85
-	-	-	ON	ON	ON	7,40
-	-	ON	ON	ON	ON	7,36
-	ON	ON	ON	ON	ON	7,35
ON	ON	ON	ON	ON	ON	7,26

5   Conclusions

In this study we presented an automatic preprocessing technique for corrupted audio signal detection. The experimental results prove the efficacy of the proposed algorithms and methods. The preprocessing technique is suitable for situations where our input audio signal is partially corrupted (clipped, overloaded) and/or mixed with different interfering signals, such as clicks, tone impulses, music etc. Our research shows that the performance of a speaker recognition system may be improved by the use of the proposed technique. We demonstrate a synergetic effect of joint use of simple detectors of typical noises for effective speech detection in real telephone signals. However, it should be kept in mind that the proposed algorithms are basic and can be considerably improved by future research.

Acknowledgements. This work was financially supported by the Ministry of Education and Science of the Russian Federation, contract 14.575.21.0033 (RFMEFI57514X0033), and by the Government of the Russian Federation, Grant 074-U01.

References

1. Aleinik, S., Matveev, Y.: Detection of clipped fragments in speech signals. Int. J. Elect. Electron. Sci. Eng. **8**(2), 74–80 (2014)
2. Chandra, C., Moore, M.S., Mitra, S.: An efficient method for the removal of impulse noise from speech and audio signals. In: Proceedings of the 1998 IEEE International Symposium on Circuits and Systems, ISCAS 1998, vol. 4, pp. 206–208. IEEE (1998)
3. Kozlov, A., Kudashev, O., Matveev, Y., Pekhovsky, T., Simonchik, K., Shulipa, A.: SVID speaker recognition system for NIST SRE 2012. In: Železný, M., Habernal, I., Ronzhin, A. (eds.) SPECOM 2013. LNCS, vol. 8113, pp. 278–285. Springer, Heidelberg (2013)
4. Lokhanova, A., Simonchik, K., Kozlov, A.: Music detection algorithm in problems of speech processing. In: Proceedings of 12th International Conference and Exhibition Digital Signal Processing and its Applications (DSPA 2010), vol.1, pp. 210–213 (2010)
5. Seyerlehner, K., Pohle, T., Schedl, M., Widmer, G.: Automatic music detection in television productions. In: Proceedings of the 10th International Conference on Digital Audio Effects (DAFx 2007), pp. 10–15. Citeseer (2007)
6. Simonchik, K., Galinina, O., Kapustin, A.: Voice activity detector based on pitch statistics for speaker recognition. Nauchno-tekhnicheskie vedomosti SPbGPU 103.4, pp. 7–11 (2010)

Automatic Sound Recognition of Urban Environment Events

Theodoros Theodorou[1]([✉]), Iosif Mporas[1,2], and Nikos Fakotakis[1]

[1] Artificial Intelligent Group, Wire Communication Laboratory,
Department of Electrical and Computer Engineering, University of Patras,
26500 Rion-patras, Greece
{theodorou,imporas,fakotaki}@upatras.gr
[2] Computer and Informatics Engineering Department,
Technological Educational Institute of Western Greece,
30020 Antirio, Greece

Abstract. The audio analysis of speaker's surroundings has been a first step for several processing systems that enable speaker's mobility though his daily life. These algorithms usually operate in a short-time analysis decomposing the incoming events in time and frequency domain. In this paper, an automatic sound recognizer is studied, which investigates audio events of interest from urban environment. Our experiments were conducted using a close set of audio events from which well known and commonly used audio descriptors were extracted and models were training using powerful machine learning algorithms. The best urban sound recognition performance was achieved by SVMs with accuracy equal to approximately 93 %.

Keywords: Automatic sound recognition · Urban environment · Dimensionality redundancy

1 Introduction

Over the last years, the recognition of person's communication activities (mostly phenomena with cognitive index like speech, gesture and node) through an increasing number of areas of interest drove the automatic processing tools to incorporate analysis about person's surrounding. One of the common audio surroundings is the urban environment. The researchers of article [20] divide the urban events according to their origin (humane, biological and geophysical) and host conclusions about their affect on peoples' health, psychology, economic and lifestyle behavior, cognitive needs and etc.

An analytic taxonomy of the urban soundscape is presented in article [18]. Reviewing the bibliography, many tasks have investigating the audio events occurring in urban environments [2,5,8,15,21,23]. Article [12] examines the landscapes as an importance parameter of study. Event of urban origin can also be sought in other studies [4,6,9–11,14,16,17,22]. As can be seen, events related to the transportation system of a city [8,10,14,15,18,23] and to weather phenomena

© Springer International Publishing Switzerland 2015
A. Ronzhin et al. (Eds.): SPECOM 2015, LNAI 9319, pp. 129–136, 2015.
DOI: 10.1007/978-3-319-23132-7_16

[9,10,14,15,18] are quite common in recordings. Typical for an urban environment (in addition to rural and non-industrial environments) is the occurring construction activity [18] which includes interesting events of the urban soundscape. Moreover, people ability to be sound as crowd noise (in terms of acoustics) [10,14,15,17,23] and the vocalizations of domestic animals and urban wildlife [4,11,16,18,23] can easily be captured in audio recordings. Local customs, traditions and the technology (like horn/siren, phone ring and bell) [4,11,18,22] are also related to acoustic phenomena of the urban soundscape.

There are several works that proposed architectures that address unexpected audio events occurring on urban surrounding in speech or communication audio signals. In those architectures sound recognition precedes all other stages, and thus sound recognition stands as cornerstone of the audio processing. Typical sound recognition consists of short-time analysis in time and frequency domain, dividing the audio sequence into intervals. Audio descriptors are used to represent those intervals and pattern recognition algorithms build models to categorize those intervals with sound label from the set of events of interest.

Seeking for audio descriptors to distinguish the characteristics of urban events, several parameters of both time and frequency domain have been proposed. The zero crossing rate [9,14,17] and the Mel Frequency Cepstral Coefficients [10,15,18,22] are correspondingly typical examples of time and frequency domain that commonly have been used. Meanwhile, several studies presented a variety of descriptors, like the MPEG-7 descriptors [6,11,15], the Perceptual Wavelet Packets [15], the Linear Prediction Code [8,10], the Matching Pursuit [10], the pitch [17] and the spectral statistics [9,14,17].

A variety of deterministic and probabilistic machine learning algorithms have been selected to evaluate experimental frameworks of urban environment events. Some of the well known and commonly used algorithms are the Neural Networks [8,10,21], the Support Vector Machine [6,17,18,22,23], the decision trees [17,18], the k-nearest neighbors [10,17] and the hidden markov models [4,6,11].

In this work, we present a sound recognition methodology for distinguishing audio events of the urban environment based on widely known and commonly used audio descriptors. We combine them with a data-driven ranking algorithm for investigating their necessity and relevance to our audio task. Consequently, we were concentrating on our framework hypotheses about the coping of our classifiers with the dimensionality redundancy and changes in classifier's effectiveness while irrelevant to the task descriptors haven't been discarded.

The rest of the article is organized as follows. In Sect. 2 we present an analytic architecture. In Sect. 3 we introduce the experimental framework and derive details about the database, the audio descriptor and recognizer selection and the ranking technique. In Sect. 4 we described the experimental results. Finally, Sect. 5 follows with the conclusions.

2 System Description

In the proposed scheme the architecture for distinguishing audio events, found in urban environment recordings, relies on short-time analysis in both time and fre-

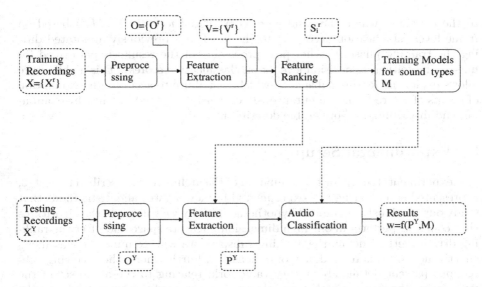

Fig. 1. General architecture of the scheme for distinguishing events from urban environments using feature subspaces.

quency domain. A ranking technique is applied to the audio descriptors to score their discrimination ability with respect to the events of interest in this task. The scheme of this architecture appears in Fig. 1. As it seems, the architecture is divided into training and testing phase.

During the training phase, the training set of recordings $X = \{X^r\}, r \in [1, R]$, which is previously be annotated with label tags and includes the whole and close set of events of interest of urban environment origin, are sequentially driven though the stages of short time analysis. Initially, the preprocessing stage frame blocks the recordings into sequences of overlapping frames with constant length and time-shift $O = \{O^r\},$. Afterwards these frame sequences are decomposed using a close set of audio descriptors, provided in the feature extraction stage. The outcome feature vector sequence $V = \{V^r\}$, consists of N feature in frame level organized in feature vectors $V^r = \{V_i^r\}, i \in [1, N],$. Thereafter, the ranking score measures the discrimination ability of each feature. The output rankings S_i^r are used to create feature subspaces. Within the sequence is discarded from those features with less significance. The threshold D that defines the boundary of necessity of a feature is manually defined or determined by data-driven criteria. The new sequences $P^r = g(V^r, S_i^r, D)$ are driven into the training steps of the classification. Within model M^D is trained from the sequence P^r. During the testing phase, the examining audio file X^Y is pre-processed with the frame block procedure to be similar to the one of the training phase producing the frame sequence O^Y. Afterward the selection of features which was done during the training phase is feeding the feature extraction block in order to decompose the frame sequence with only those descriptors attached to the working subspace. The extracted sequence $P^Y = g(O^Y, S_i^r, D)$ is finally driven to the classifier, where the results are constructed $w = f(P^Y, M^D)$ based on frame level classification according to the label tags previously annotated during the training phase. Further post processing of the results is performed for fine-tuning (either on decision level or on classification scores). This architecture allows exploiting feature subspaces, which contribute to accurate discrimination of events of interest with simultaneously dimensionality redundancy by examining and discarding non-preferable descriptors.

3   Experimental Setup

The experimental setup for the evaluation of the architecture described in Sect. 2, is presented here. During this experimental framework we validate methods that study our previously mentioned hypothesis. Initially we will study the algorithms that could outperform in our high dimensional feature space and after the ranking driven method define the working subspace we will examine the classifier's effectiveness on this redundancy of dimensions. Furthermore, the following subsections present details about this framework, relating to the audio set of the evaluation, the feature extraction algorithms, the ranking procedure and the selection of classifiers.

Table 1. Duration Distribution of our events of interest in the collected audio

Sound Type	Duration (in seconds)
Alarm	218.92
Motor Engines	76.10
Horns	160.30
Rain	149.82
Thunder	86.51
Wind	155.72
Railway	110.45
Bells	86.48

3.1   Audio Data Description

The evaluation of the experimental framework is relied on a collection of audio events commonly found in urban environments. Due to lack of a commonly used and appropriate for discriminating urban events database we turn into the BBC FX Library [1] from which we collect recordings, of total duration equal to 1,044.3 sec. These recordings represent common urban events. Their duration distribution is illustrated in Table 1. All data were stored in single-channel audio files with sampling frequency 16 kHz and resolution analysis 8 bits per sample and manually annotated from an expert audio engineer.

3.2   Feature Extraction

The audio events occurred in the urban environment varying on their time and frequency characteristis. Thus in the literature, a variety of proposed audio descriptors is presented. In this study, we rely on the OpenSmile [7] framework to extract well known and commonly used features, related to general audio processing and sound event distinguishing. The overall structure of our short-time analyis is relied on frame-blocking the audio sequence to overlapping frames of constant length of 25 msec with time shift of 10 mses, an 1st order FIR pre-emphasis filter followed by Hamming windowing and a variety of audio descriptors extracted in frame level. The parametrization and the feature extraction are illustrated in Fig. 2.

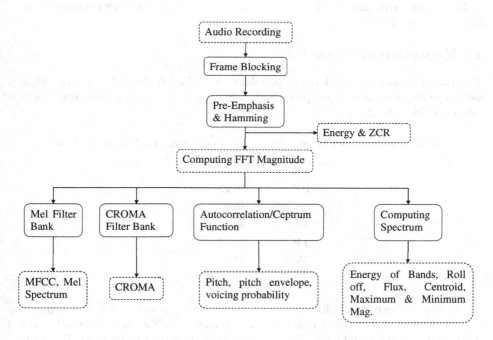

Fig. 2. Diagram of parameterization and feature extraction.

In details, we extract (a) the zero-crossing rate (ZCR), as it's a quite common time domain feature. Moreover, we extract, using suitable filter banks, (b) the Mel frequency cepstral coefficients (MFCC) [19], (c) the chroma coefficients (Chroma) [3,13] and (d) the Mel Spectrum. Thereafter, we extract (e) the energy, (f) the pitch, (g) the pitch envelope, (h) the voicing probability and some spectrum statistics' (i) the energy of 4 bands, (j) the roll off, (k) the flux, (l) the centroid, (m) the frequency of maximum magnitude and (n) the frequency of minimum magnitude. Finally, their values are concatenated to feature vector which was expaned with (o) first and second derivatives (delta and delta-delta coefficients).

3.3   Classification

The construction of the sound type classification models was achieved using the WEKA software toolkit [24]. The selection of classifiers was based on well-known and widely used algorithms in audio processing tasks. Thus we select: the k-nearest neighbors classifier with linear search of the nearest neighbor and without weighting of the distance – also known as instance based classifier (IBk), the Bayes network (BayesNet), with Simple Estimator (alpha = 0.5) and the K2 search algorithm (maximum number of parents = 1), a 3-layer Mulilayer perceptron (MLP) neural net-work, a pruned C4.5 decision tree (J48), a support vector machine with sequential minimal optimization (SMO) algorithm and RBF kernel. The training/testing frame-work was the same for all algorithms in order to have direct comparison of results. Moreover, the models were performed on the sound types of Table 1.

4   Experimental Results

The urban sound recognition methodology described in Sect. 2 was evaluated using the experimental setup presented in Sect. 3. The experimental results are tabulated in Table 2.

Table 2. Duration Distribution of our events of interest in the collected audio

Algorithm	Accuracy
IBk	89.22
BayesNet	86.05
MLP	90.59
J48	88.47
SVM	92.73

As can be seen in Table 2, the best performing algorithm was the support vector machines with radial basis function kernel, which achieved classification performance equal to 92.73 %. The second best performing was the MLP neural network with 90.59 % accuracy. The results show that the two evaluated discriminative algorithms outperformed the rest of algorithms.

In terms of sound types, the most misclassified sound type pairs were the wind sound and the motor engines sounds, which for the best performing SVM algorithm were found to be misclassified by approximately 5 %. All the rest misclassified sounds were found in less than 2 % for all cases.

5   Conclusions

The increasing influence of speaker's surroundings drove the interest of the scientific research interest towards to sound recognition of events from person's environment. Since urban environment is a quite common environment, it becomes into cornerstone of environments of interest. In the present work, we studied a methodology of automatic sound recognition with a short-time analysis framework using urban environment events. After computing a large set of audio descriptors we applied an ranking algorithm to score the descriptors' discrimination ability, in terms of necessity and relevance on the current task. With some well known and commonly used machine learning algorithms we evaluate this framework. Our results point out that SVMs managed to outperform all other algorithms with accuracy equal to 92.73 %. Also the sequential expansions of the working descriptor space with unnecessary dimensions don't significantly affect the effectiveness of the machine learning algorithms.

References

1. The BBC sound effects library original series. http://www.sound-ideas.com
2. Aucouturier, J.J., Defreville, B., Pachet, F.: The bag-of-frames approach to audio pattern recognition: a sufficient model for urban soundscapes but not for polyphonic music. J. Acoust. Soc. Am. **122**(2), 881–891 (2007)
3. Bartsch, M.A., Wakefield, G.H.: Audio thumbnailing of popular music using chroma-based representations. IEEE Trans. Multimedia **7**(1), 96–104 (2005)
4. Casey, M.: General sound classification and similarity in MPEG-7. Organised Sound **6**(02), 153–164 (2001)
5. Couvreur, L., Laniray, M.: Automatic noise recognition in urban environments based on artificial neural networks and hidden markov models. InterNoise, Prague, Czech Republic, pp. 1–8 (2004)
6. Dogan, E., Sert, M., Yazici, A.: Content-based classification and segmentation of mixed-type audio by using mpeg-7 features. In:First International Conference on Advances in Multimedia, MMEDIA 2009, pp. 152–157. IEEE (2009)
7. Eyben, F., Wöllmer, M., Schuller, B.: Opensmile: the munich versatile and fast open-source audio feature extractor. In: Proceedings of the international conference on Multimedia, pp. 1459–1462. ACM (2010)
8. Fernandez, L.P.S., Ruiz, A.R., de JM Juarez, J.: Urban noise permanent monitoring and pattern recognition. In: Proceedings of the European Conference of Communications-ECCOM, vol. 10, pp. 143–148 (2010)
9. Huang, R., Hansen, J.H.: Advances in unsupervised audio classification and segmentation for the broadcast news and NGSW corpora. IEEE Trans. Audio Speech Lang. Process. **14**(3), 907–919 (2006)
10. Khunarsal, P., Lursinsap, C., Raicharoen, T.: Very short time environmental sound classification based on spectrogram pattern matching. Inf. Sci. **243**, 57–74 (2013)
11. Kim, H.G., Moreau, N., Sikora, T.: Audio classification based on MPEG-7 spectral basis representations. IEEE Trans. Circuits Syst. Video Technol. **14**(5), 716–725 (2004)
12. Kinnunen, T., Saeidi, R., Leppänen, J., Saarinen, J.P.: Audio context recognition in variable mobile environments from short segments using speaker and language recognizers. In: The Speaker and Language Recognition Workshop, pp. 301–311 (2012)
13. Lee, K., Slaney, M.: Automatic chord recognition from audio using a HMM with supervised learning. In: ISMIR, pp. 133–137 (2006)

14. Lu, H., Pan, W., Lane, N.D., Choudhury, T., Campbell, A.T.: Soundsense: scalable sound sensing for people-centric applications on mobile phones. In: Proceedings of the 7th international conference on Mobile systems, applications, and services, pp. 165–178. ACM (2009)

15. Ntalampiras, S.: Universal background modeling for acoustic surveillance of urban traffic. Digital Signal Process. **31**, 69–78 (2014)

16. Ntalampiras, S., Potamitis, I., Fakotakis, N.: Exploiting temporal feature integration for generalized sound recognition. EURASIP J. Adv. Sig. Process. **2009**(1), 807162 (2009)

17. Patsis, Y., Verhelst, W.: A speech/music/silence/garbage/classifier for searching and indexing broadcast news material. In: 19th International Workshop on Database and Expert Systems Application, DEXA 2008, pp. 585–589. IEEE (2008)

18. Salamon, J., Jacoby, C., Bello, J.P.: A dataset and taxonomy for urban sound research. In: Proceedings of the ACM International Conference on Multimedia, pp. 1041–1044. ACM (2014)

19. Slaney, M.: Auditory toolbox. Interval Research Corporation. Technical report vol. 10 (1998)

20. Smith, J.W., Pijanowski, B.C.: Human and policy dimensions of soundscape ecology. Global Environ. Change **28**, 63–74 (2014)

21. Torija, A., Diego, P.R., Ramos-Ridao, A.: Ann-based m events. a too against envi environment (2011)

22. Tran, H.D., Li, H.: Sound event recognition with probabilistic distance SVMs. IEEE Trans. Audio Speech Lang. Process. **19**(6), 1556–1568 (2011)

23. Valero, X., Alías, F., Oldoni, D., Botteldooren, D.: Support vector machines and self-organizing maps for the recognition of sound events in urban soundscapes. In: 41st International Congress and Exposition on Noise Control Engineering (Inter-Noise-2012). Institute of Noise Control Engineering (2012)

24. Witten, I.H., Frank, E.: Data Mining: Practical Machine Learning Tools and Techniques. Morgan Kaufmann (2005)

Automatically Trained TTS for Effective Attacks to Anti-spoofing System

Galina Lavrentyeva[1](✉), Alexandr Kozlov[1], Sergey Novoselov[1],
Konstantin Simonchik[1,2], and Vadim Shchemelinin[1,2]

[1] Speech Technology Center Limited, Saint Petersburg, Russia
{lavrentyeva,kozlov-a,novoselov,simonchik,shchemelinin}@speechpro.com
[2] ITMO University, Saint Petersburg, Russia

Abstract. This article is the proceeding of the priority research direction of the voice biometrics systems spoofing problem. We continue exploring speech synthesis spoofing attacks based on creating a text-to-speech voice. In our work we focused on the completely automatic way to create new voices for text-to-speech system and the investigation of the state-of-art spoofing detection system vulnerability to this spoofing attacks. Results obtained during our experiments demonstrate that 10 seconds of speech material is enough for EER increasement up to 19.67 %. Considering the fact, that automatic method for synthesis voiced training allows perpetrators to increase the amount of spoofing attacks to biometric systems, we raise the issue of relevance of a new type of spoofing attack, and development of the effective methods to detect it.

Keywords: Spoofing · Anti-spoofing · Speaker recognition · TTS

1 Introduction

Due to the growing interest in reliable authentication methods for restricting access to informational resources, biometrics authentication has improved significantly in recent years. For example, speaker recognition systems are widely used in Internet banking systems, customer identification during a call to a call center, as well as passive identification of a possible criminal using a preset "blacklist" [1,2]. For instance, the latest overviews of speaker recognition systems show that EER is down to 1.5 - 2 % for text-independent [3] and down to 1 % for text-dependent [4] speaker recognition systems in various conditions. Although text-dependent systems propose better performance for authentic purposes, text-independent systems, that do not need any specific vocal password, are also used in specific scenarios, for example, in IVR (Interactive Voice Response) systems in call-centers for telephone banking.

Text-independent automatic speaker verification (ASV) systems, as well as text-dependent, are widely acknowledged to be vulnerable to spoofing attacks. A multitude of different effective spoofing methods were proposed in literature in recent years. For example, [5] describes methods based on "Replay attack",

© Springer International Publishing Switzerland 2015
A. Ronzhin et al. (Eds.): SPECOM 2015, LNAI 9319, pp. 137–143, 2015.
DOI: 10.1007/978-3-319-23132-7_17

"Cut and paste", "Handkerchief tampering" and "Nasalization tampering". [1] additionaly observe spoofing attacks based on "Speech synthesis" and "Voice conversion" as being the most potential spoofing attacks.

In response to potential threat of spoofing attacks, many researches were focused on detection of the most effective anti-spoofing countermeasures [1] and investigation of the ASV systems vulnerability. Several papers on the ASV system robustness evaluation against spoofing attacks [5–7] showed the high importance of new robust anti-spoofing countermeasures.

One of the most successful spoofing methods is Text-To-Speech (TTS) synthesis based on the target speakers voice. [6] examines the method of spoofing which is performed using a hybrid TTS method that combined Unit Selection and Hidden Narkov Models (HMM). Authors showed that the likelihood of false acceptance when using high-quality speech synthesis and a speech database recorded with studio quality can reach 98 %. [6] explored the robustness of text-dependent verification system against spoofing based on the described synthesis method using an automatically labeled "free" speech recorded in the telephone channel and achieved 10.8 % False Acceptance error. In this case perpetrator does not need the expert knowledge for preparing a synthesized voice. Because of that this method is more likely to be used by criminals.

In this paper we focused on the investigation of the anti-spoofing system (ASS) introduced on the Automatic Speaker Verification Spoofing and Countermeasures (ASVspoof) Challenge 2015 [8] as the primary system [?]. The aim of this research was to detect robustness of this ASS system against attack scenario based on Text-to-Speech (TTS) synthesis with automatically labeled speech and detect the dependency of ASS system Equal Error Rate (EER) of acceptance of a spoofed speech and rejection of a human speech. For this purpose we considered speech databases, recorded in telephone channel.

2   Anti-spoofing System

Spoofing detection method was firstly introduced in the ASVspoof Challenge 2015 and achieved 0.008 % EER for known spoofing attacks and 3.922 % EER for unknown types of spoofing attacks [9]. It should be mentioned that for the HMM-based spoofing attacks of the ASVspoof Challenge evaluation base zero error of spoofing detection was achieved. That was the motivation to include anti-spoofing system to detect impostors in ASV system.

This ASS consists of three main components:

– Pre-detection
– Acoustic feature extractor
– TV i-vector extractor
– SVM classifier

Pre-detector was used to check if the input signal has zero temporal energy and in this cases declared signal as spoofing attack. Otherwise acoustic features were extracted from signal.

As front-end acoustic features we used: 12 Mel-Frequency Cepstral Coefficients (MFCC), 12 Mel-Frequency Principal Coefficients (MFPC) and 12 Cos-Phase Principal Coefficients (CosPhasePC) based on phase spectrum with its first and second derivatives. To obtain these coefficients Hamming windowing was used with 256 window length and 50 % overlap.

For the acoustic space modelling we used the standard TV-JFA approach, which is the state-of-the-art in speaker verification systems [3,4,10]. According to this version of the joint factor anlysis, the i-vector of the Total Variability space is extracted by means of JFA modification, which is a usual Gaussian factor analyser defined on mean supervectors of the Universal Background Model (UBM) and Total-variability matrix T. UBM is represented by the Gaussian mixture model (GMM) of the described features. The diagonal covariance UBM was trained by the standard EM-algorithm.

In our ASS UBM was represented by a 1024-component Gaussian mixture model of the described features, and the dimension of the TV space was 400.

All i-vectors derived from different extractors were concatenated in one common i-vector, that was used after on the classification step by SVM classifier.

3   Spoofing Attack Modelling

To model spoofing attacks to our ASS system we choosed method of TTS voice synthesis, based on previously prepared free speech of the ASV system user with its segmentation. The scheme of such spoofing attack is shown on the Fig. 1.

This ASS used a hybrid TTS system developed by Speech Technology Center Ltd (STC), that was based on HMM and Unit Selection [11]. Authors of [6] demonstrated that in cases of the synthesized voice, built using 8 min of free speech recorded in a studio environment and manually labeled, the spoofer can achieve 19.1 % of false acceptance rate. In our work we used STC-base of the free speech recorded in telephone channel in order to evaluate the effectiveness

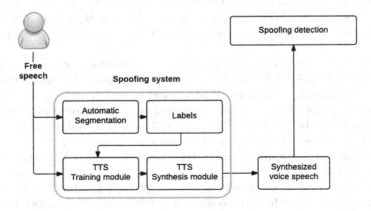

Fig. 1. The sceme of spoofing using TTS method

of this synthesis for spoofing aims. The segmentation of this base was obtained by STC automatic speech recognition (ASR) module [13].

For labeling we used automatic labeling module, which included automatic F0 period and phone labeling. This was done by automatic speech recognition (ASR) module, based on HMM. Phone labeling was based on forced alignement of the transcription and the signal. Details of this can be found in [13].

The process of automatically building a TTS voice is described in [14].

4   Experiments

4.1   TTS Training Database

As it was mentioned before we used STC base of monologues recorded in telephone channel as prepared bases for TTS voice construction. These base contains Russian speech records of 60 speakers with 3–6 records for each. In order to achieve good quality of synthesis speech we took only those speakers, whose speech time was more than 10 seconds. Thus we got 16 voices for telephone channel. By these voices we processed train and test bases. Each of them consists of 20 records for each voice of possible phrases during interaction with IVR system. Examples of this phrases include: "Listen to the information on the capabilities of the new system. All categories. Sort by popularity.", "Find the nearest flight to Brazil. Departure from Moscow. Airfare. Hand luggage. One ticket.", "Get the buying rate of the pound sterling on 3 May 2014." and etc. Original recorded phrases were included in the test database.

For each speaker, attempts to access the ASV system with ASS were made using generated records.

4.2   Evaluation Results

Our experiments were focused on the evaluation of vulnerability of the described ASS to proposed spoofing method, based on TTS voice construction and compare it to the vulnerability of this system to effective Hidden Markov model (HMM) and TTS based speech synthesis spoofing attacks from ASVspoof Challenge 2015.

In Table 1 the evaluation EER results for new spoofing type are introduced, in comparisson with EER for the spoofing types, proposed by ASVspoof Challenge 2015. Here: $S3$ is the Hidden Markov model based speech synthesis system using speaker adaptation techniques [15] and only 20 adaptation utterances. $S4$ is the Hidden Markov model based speech synthesis system using speaker adaptation techniques [15] and only 40 adaptation utterances. $S10$ is a speech synthesis algorithm implemented with the open-source MARY Text-To-Speech system (MaryTTS) [16].

It can be seen that obtained results for proposed automatically trained TTS based spoofing method are comparable with result for MaryTTS spoofing attacks, that turned out to be the most powerful spoofing attack during

Table 1. *EER* of ASS for spoofing algorithms based on TTS.

Spoofing algorithm	*EER* (%)
TTS-based	19.667
S3	0.000
S4	0.000
S10	19.571

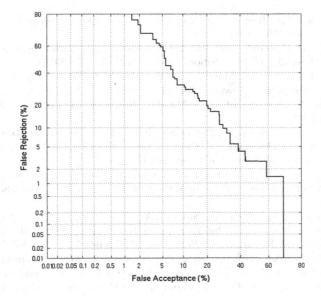

Fig. 2. DET curve of ASS against TTS based spoofing attack

ASVspoof Challenge. According to the obtained results it can be suggested that hybrid speech synthesis system is more threatful.

Figure 2 introduces the DET curve of ASS for spoofing atacks based on automatic training TTS.

5   Conclusion

In this paper we produced the investigation of the automatic TTS training method. During our research we compared hybrid TTS with MaryTTS and got comparable results confirming that proposed automatic method is suitable for effective spoofing attacks on the spoofing detection system and even 10 min of speech material is enough to increase EER of anti-spoofing system up to 19.67 %. This results prove that it is highly important to improve spoofing detection methods against speech synthesis spoofing atacks.

In future work we intent to use these results to improve our anti-spoofing system to make it robust to automatic trained TTS based spoofing attacks.

Acknowledgments. This work was partially nancially supported by the Government of Russian Federation, Grant 074-U01.

References

1. Wu, Z., et al.: Spoofing and countermeasures for speaker verification: a survey. Speech Commun. **66**, 130–153 (2015)
2. Matveev, Y.N.: Biometric technologies of person identification by voice and other modalities. Vestnik MGTU. Priborostroenie **3**(3), 46–61 (2012)
3. Kozlov, A., Kudashev, O., Matveev, Y., Pekhovsky, T., Simonchik, K., Shulipa, A.: SVID speaker recognition system for NIST SRE 2012. In: Železný, M., Habernal, I., Ronzhin, A. (eds.) SPECOM 2013. LNCS, vol. 8113, pp. 278–285. Springer, Heidelberg (2013)
4. Novoselov, S., Pekhovsky, T., Simonchik, K.: STC speaker recognition system for the NIST i-vector challenge. In: Proceedings of the Odyssey 2014 - The Speaker and Language Recognition Workshop (2014)
5. Villalba, E., Lleida, E.: Speaker verification performance degradation against spoofing and tampering attacks. In: Proceedings of the FALA 2010 Workshop, pp. 131–134 (2010)
6. Shchemelinin, V., Topchina, M., Simonchik, K.: Vulnerability of voice verification systems to spoofing attacks by TTS voices based on automatically labeled telephone speech. In: Ronzhin, A., Potapova, R., Delic, V. (eds.) SPECOM 2014. LNCS, vol. 8773, pp. 475–481. Springer, Heidelberg (2014). (including subseries Lecture Notes in Artificial Intelligence and Lecture Notes in Bioinformatics)
7. Marcel, S., Nixon, M.S., Li, S.Z.: Handbook of Biometric Anti-spoofing: Trusted Biometrics Under Spoofing Attacks. Springer, New York (2014)
8. Wu, Z., et al.: ASVspoof 2015: the first automatic speaker verification spoofing and countermeasures challenge 2015. http://www.spoofingchallenge.org/is2015_asvspoof.pdf
9. Novoselov, S., et al.: STC Anti-spoofing systems for the ASVspoof 2015 challenge. http://ris.ifmo.ru/wp-content/uploads/2015/06/Technical_report_ASVspoof2015_STC.pdf
10. Dehak, N., et al. : Support vector machines versus fast scoring in the low-dimensional total variability space for speaker verification. In: Proceedings of the Interspeech, pp. 1559–1562 (2009)
11. Chistikov, P., Korolkov, E.: Data-driven speech parameter generation for russian text-to-speech system. computational linguistics and intellectual technologies. In: Proceedings of the Annual International Conference "Dialogue", Issue 11(18), vol. 1. pp. 103–111 (2012)
12. Simonchik, K., Shchemelinn, V.: "STC SPOOFING" database for text-dependent speaker recognition evaluation. In: Proceedings of SLTU-2014 Workshop St. Petersburg, Russia, pp. 221–224 (2014)
13. Tomashenko, N.A., Khokhlov, Y.Y.: Fast algorithm for automatic alignment of speech and imperfect text data. In: Železný, M., Habernal, I., Ronzhin, A. (eds.) SPECOM 2013. LNCS, vol. 8113, pp. 146–153. Springer, Heidelberg (2013)

14. Solomennik, A., Chistikov, P., Rybin, S., Talanov, A., Tomashenko, N.: Automation of new voice creation procedure for a russian TTS system. Vestnik MGTU. Priborostroenie **2**, 29–32 (2013)
15. Yamagishi, J., et al.: Analysis of speaker adaptation algorithms for HMM-based speech synthesis and a constrained smaplr adaptation algorithm, IEEE Trans. Audio, Speech Lang. Process. **17**(1), 66–83 (2009)
16. Wu, Z., et al.: A study on replay attack and anti-spoofing for text-dependent speaker verification. In: Proceedings of the Asia-Pacific Signal Information Processing Association Annual Summit and Conference (APSIPA ASC) (2014)

EmoChildRu: Emotional Child Russian Speech Corpus

Elena Lyakso[1]([⊠]), Olga Frolova[1], Evgeniya Dmitrieva[1], Aleksey Grigorev[1], Heysem Kaya[2], Albert Ali Salah[2], and Alexey Karpov[3,4]

[1] The Child Speech Research Group, St. Petersburg State University,
St. Petersburg, Russia
lyakso@gmail.com
[2] Department of Computer Engineering, Bogazici University, Istanbul, Turkey
heysem@boun.edu.tr
[3] St. Petersburg Institute for Informatics and Automation of RAS,
St. Petersburg, Russia
[4] ITMO University, St. Petersburg, Russia
karpov@iias.spb.su

Abstract. We present the first child emotional speech corpus in Russian, called "EmoChildRu", which contains audio materials of 3–7 year old kids. The database includes over 20 K recordings (approx. 30 h), collected from 100 children. Recordings were carried out in three controlled settings by creating different emotional states for children: playing with a standard set of toys; repetition of words from a toy-parrot in a game store setting; watching a cartoon and retelling of the story, respectively. This corpus is designed to study the reflection of the emotional state in the characteristics of voice and speech and for studies of the formation of emotional states in ontogenesis. A portion of the corpus is annotated for three emotional states (discomfort, neutral, comfort). Additional data include brain activity measurements (original EEG, evoked potentials records), the results of the adult listeners analysis of child speech, questionnaires, and description of dialogues. The paper reports two child emotional speech analysis experiments on the corpus: by adult listeners (humans) and by an automatic classifier (machine), respectively. Automatic classification results are very similar to human perception, although the accuracy is below 55 % for both, showing the difficulty of child emotion recognition from speech under naturalistic conditions.

Keywords: Emotional child speech · Perceptual analysis · Spectrographic analysis · Emotional states · Computational paralinguistics

1 Introduction

Speech databases are an indispensable part of speech research. Their structure and technical characteristics depend on specific tasks and on the aims of the investigation for which the data are collected. One of the important areas of

© Springer International Publishing Switzerland 2015
A. Ronzhin et al. (Eds.): SPECOM 2015, LNAI 9319, pp. 144–152, 2015.
DOI: 10.1007/978-3-319-23132-7_18

speech studies is the detection of the speakers emotional state in voice and speech. Emotions play an important role in communication, being one of the major factors of human behavior and indicative of a person's mental states.

For the study of emotional speech, it is necessary to use special corpora. There are very few child emotional speech databases available for child speech research community. For example, such corpora exist for English, German, Italian, and Swedish [1] pre-school and school children. There is also a child speech database containing a large vocabulary rated on emotional valence (positive, neutral, and negative) by French children, differing in both age (5–9 years old) and sex (girls and boys) [13]. However, there are no databases containing emotional child speech material produced by Russian children.

For the Russian language studies, we created the corpus called "INFANTRU", which is the first database containing vocalizations of infants and children for a Slavic language [7]. The database contains 2967 recordings (70 h) of 99 children aged between 3 to 36 months. For 76 children, the corpus contains the longitudinal vocalization data from 3 to 36 months. A second corpus, called "CHILDRU", stores speech material for 4 to 7 year old Russian children. This database holds 28079 recordings (20 h in total) of 150 Russian children: 142 children growing in families and 8 orphans, growing in a child care facility [7].

Creation of a corpus of child emotional speech is more difficult than the construction of corpora of emotional speech of adults. In the case of adults, actors are often involved to portray the necessary emotional conditions [5], or records of patients from a psychiatry clinic are used. Such approaches cannot be used for children. It is necessary to model communicative tasks in which the child is not conscious of being recorded to produce veridical emotional reactions. The creation of the corpus should be based on a verified and clear method of obtaining spontaneous speech manifestations of certain emotional reactions. By nature, collection of child emotional speech data is 'in the wild'.

It is well known that acoustic and linguistic characteristics of child speech are widely different from those of adult speech. The child speech is characterized by a higher pitch value, formant frequencies and specific indistinct articulation with respect to the adult speech. It was recently shown that adult Russians could recognize 60 % to 100 % of 4–5 years old children's words and phrases during calm, spontaneous speech, and the amount of words recognized by adult native speakers does not increase much for children's speech from 4–5 to 7 years [4]. It is obvious that analysis of child speech must be separately investigated. The contributions of our current work are: 1) the collection of emotional speech material for 3–7 year old children in the form of a corpus and 2) a preliminary analysis of these data for studies of emotion development.

2 Emotional Child Russian Speech Corpus - EmoChildRu

2.1 Data Collection

"EmoChildRu" is the first database containing emotional speech material from 3–7 year old Russian children. The database includes 20.340 recordings (30 h) of

100 children growing in families. All children were born and live in the city of St. Petersburg (parents of the children were also born in St. Petersburg, or have been living there for more than 10 years). Places of recording were at home, in laboratory and kindergarten. The three different recording conditions are playing with a standard set of toys, repetition of words from a toy-parrot in a game store setting, and watching a Russian cartoon called "Masha and bear" from iPad and the retelling of the story, respectively. All experiments had a duration of 2 min. Every record is accompanied by a detailed protocol and video recording of child's behavior in parallel. The speech materials are grouped based on the protocol and the recording situation, in accordance with underlying base emotions: sadness, anger, fear, gladness. So far, about 10 % of the data are annotated for emotional states. The database contains additional information about the child's psychophysiological condition before and after speech recording. Original EEG and evoked potential (EP) records (visual stimuli images of the facial expression of infants and 3–4 year old children), dialogue descriptions, speech developmental and cognitive scale data are included in the database whenever available. The recordings were made with a "Marantz PMD660" digital recorder and with a single "SENNHEISER e835S" external microphone. The speech sounds were analyzed by experts, using Syntrillium's "Cool Edit Pro" sound editor. Stressed vowels were selected from all phrase's stressed words. The pitch as well as the vowel duration and phrase prosody were calculated.

2.2 Corpus and Software Structure

The corpus and accompanying software package includes the database, as well as a shell component to navigate, browse and search information in the database. The database stores information about files (file type, size in bytes, duration in minutes and seconds, name, description, etc.) and their relationships. Speech files are in Windows PCM format, 22050 Hz, 16 bit per sample.

A software tool was developed for enabling the experts to work with the "EmoChildRu" corpus. The shell component is developed in Microsoft Visual C#, and it is designed to enable working with the database under Windows operating system. This software also allows choosing speech material using a query interface, along dimensions such as a type of emotional state, child age and gender. It allows choosing any or each available feature, including speech material and acoustic characteristics of speech in different emotional states, video elements of nonverbal behavior, evoked potentials data on visual "emotional stimuli", or ECG data; filtered for all children of a certain age or gender.

3   Data Analysis

Three test sequences were formed from the speech material of 30 children aged from 3 to 7 years. The test sequences were composed into three groups (3–4 year old, 5 year old, 6–7 year old children) and every test sequence includes 10 phrases uttered by children in a comfortable emotional state, 10 phrases in a discomfort state and 10 phrases in a neutral (calm) state. We have used 90 sequences in total for testing. The child's emotional state was revealed based on the recording setting and by analysis of the video fragments by five speech experts. The test sequences were presented to 100 adults (native Russian speakers) for perceptual analysis. Thus, each phrase was evaluated by 100 auditors, and the correctness of auditors in correctly recognizing the emotional state on the base of speech samples (perception rate) was calculated. The aim of the perceptual analysis was to investigate how correctly the child's emotional state was perceived by native speakers. Spectrographic analysis of speech samples from the test sequences was also carried out.

4   Experimental Results

4.1   Human Recognition of Emotional States

At first, we studied recognition of a child's emotional state in speech material by humans. In average, adult native speakers correctly recognized less than 50 % of speech material samples in the test sequences (Fig. 1A).

Both discomfort and comfort conditions in the speech of 3–5 year old children were recognized by adults with the perception rate of 0.75-1.0 better compared to the neutral condition. Humans' emotion recognition rate for the 6–7 year old children was higher than for the 4 year old children, as shown in Fig. 1B ($p < 0.01$, Mann-Whitney test).

Spectrographic analysis revealed that speech samples interpreted by humans as discomfort, neutral and comfort are characterized by specific sets of acoustic features (Fig. 2). Discomfort speech samples are characterized by phrase duration lengthening; highest pitch values (comparatively) in phrase and in stressed vowels selected from stressed words in the phrase ($p < 0.05$ - vs. neutral state, Mann-Whitney test); an increase of minimum pitch value in phrases; an increase of

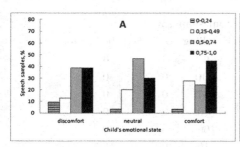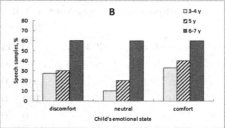

Fig. 1. Percentages of emotional child speech samples perceived by adult native speakers: A - correctly recognized as discomfort, neutral and comfort with the perception rate of 0-0.24 (horizontal hatch), with the rate of 0.25-0.49 (white color bar), with the rate of 0.5-0.74 (light gray) and with the rate of 0.75-1 (black); B - correctly recognized with the rate of 0.75-1.0 at different childrens ages: 3–4 years (light gray), 5 years (sloping hatch), 6–7 years old (grey).

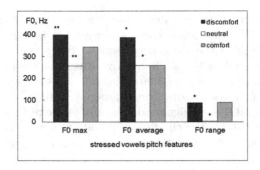

Fig. 2. The pitch values and the duration of vocalizations recognized by auditors as different emotional infants and chimpanzees states.

the pitch range in stressed vowels of stressed words in the phrase ($p < 0.05$ - vs. neutral state); falling pitch contour of stressed vowels of stressed words in the phrase. Comfort speech phrases have short duration, together with long stressed vowel duration; pitch values of phrases are increased, but less so compared to discomfort samples; pitch range in the stressed vowels is similar to discomfort samples; rising pitch contours of stressed vowels. Neutral speech samples are characterized by lowest values of vowel duration, stressed vowels' pitch and pitch range; and flat pitch contour is dominated as well (Fig. 2, Table 1).

Most speech samples that were correctly recognized by humans in the experiment have a complex shape of phrase pitch contours ($> 70\%$ samples). The analysis of features of all stressed vowels from stressed words revealed that discomfort speech samples have mainly a falling shape, while comfort speech samples have a rising shape (Table 1).

Table 1. Distribution of pitch contour shapes for correctly recognized speech samples

Children's state	Age, Year	Pitch contour shape, %				
		flat	rising	falling	U-shaped	bell-shaped
discomfort	3-4	0	33	**67**	0	0
	5	0	0	**100**	0	0
	6-7	33	0	**67**	0	0
neutral	3-4	100	0	0	0	0
	5	0	0	100	0	0
	6-7	67	0	16.5	0	16.5
comfort	3-4	0	**67**	0	33	0
	5	0	**75**	25	0	0
	6-7	17	50	0	33	0

Almost all neutral speech samples have flat, falling and bell-shaped pitch contours, and the first two patterns are the most common. U-shaped pitch contour is revealed in comfort speech samples only. Variety of pitch contour shapes in stressed vowels increases by 6–7 years, compared to younger children. It was revealed that the duration of phrases increases, and the duration of stressed vowels and pitch values decreases with increasing age of the children. The differences in the acoustic characteristics of speech samples correctly recognized as discomfort, neutral and comfort are more expressed at the age of 3–5 years. Correctly recognized speech samples of 6–7 years old children do not differ significantly in acoustic features. Adult listeners mostly rely on the meaning of the phrase. Analysis of speech samples correctly recognized by adults revealed that detection of word meanings from these phrases improved with increase of child's age: meaning of words from 57 % of child's phrases were detected at the age of 3–4 years, 86 % - at the age of 5 years, 100 % - at the age of 6–7 years.

4.2 Automatic Classification of Emotional States

Automatic processing of child speech is tackled in many recent studies, but automatic detection and classification of emotional states in children's speech in the wild is a new direction of research. As our perception analysis reveals, the recognition of children's emotions from speech is hard, even though some discriminative prosodic patterns can be discerned. The overall human recognition accuracy is about 50 % for the three-class problem.

In the second experiment, we employ an objective, automatic classification algorithm. For this purpose, we use a subset of the corpus, where all speech files have 1 to 5 sec of speech and all five child speech experts agree on the emotion annotation. Note that the annotation is done on the audio-visual material, including the linguistic information, although only acoustic features are used for automatic classification. The subset is collected from 50 children, and the number of speech files per child ranges from 1 to 78 (11.7 files on average, with a standard deviation of 12.5) increasing the difficulty of age/gender balanced partitioning, as well as recognition. There are 23 boys and 27 girls in the selected set, Meanstd age is 5.1 ± 1.1 years. Trying to keep the distribution of emotion labels as balanced as possible, we obtain the partitioning shown in Table 2. We report training and testing classification results in terms of accuracy and Unweighted Average Recall (UAR), which is introduced as performance measure in the INTERSPEECH 2009 Emotion challenge [12]. UAR is used to overcome the biased calculation of accuracy towards the majority class. It also gives a chance-level baseline performance as $1/K$, where K is the number of classes. In our case the chance-level is 33.3 %.

We extract openSMILE [2] features using a configuration file used in the INTERSPEECH (IS) ComParE Challenges in 2010 [10] and 2013 [11]. These feature sets contain 1582 and 6373 suprasegmental features, respectively. Utterance features are obtained by passing descriptive functionals (e.g. moments, percentiles, regression coefficients) on the Low Level Descriptors (e.g. pitch,

Table 2. Distribution of classes and gender (M/F) in train and test partitions

	M/F	Comfort	Neutral	Discomfort	Total
Train	16/20	144	164	52	**360**
Test	7/7	90	88	47	**225**
Total	**23/27**	**234**	**252**	**99**	**585**

MFCC 1-14, jitter, etc.). For classification, we use Linear SVM implementation from the WEKA data mining tool [3] and train models with the Sequential Minimal Optimization Algorithm [8]. To avoid over-fitting, we leave the SVM complexity parameter at its default value of 1. The classification can be thought of as a three-state valence classification problem. It is well known that valence classification from acoustics is poorer compared to arousal classification, and is at almost chance level in challenging conditions without adaptation (e.g. cross-corpus setting) [9]. In Table 3, we observe better classification performance with IS 2010 features compared to IS 2013 features, and the automatic approach performs better than human perception.

Table 3. Classification results for 3 valence states of comfort, discomfort, and neutral

	IS 2010 features		IS 2013 features	
Preprocessing	**Accuracy**	**UAR**	**Accuracy**	**UAR**
Z-norm	**53.3 %**	**55.0**	46.7 %	45.3
Minmax-norm	52.4 %	50.0	47.1 %	45.7

5   Discussion

The results of our previous study [6] showed the extent of the ability of adults in proper recognition of emotional states of infant vocalizations. Speech experts recognize discomfort vocalizations of infants better than vocalizations that reflect a comfortable condition. In the present study, we aimed to analyze the emotional speech of children 3–7 years of age. Choosing the age range as 3–7 years is due to the evolution of the grammatical skills of speech at 4 years and the ability of effective communication of a child with an adult, including regulation of emotional expressions, the "truth" of emotion and the contribution of society in the organization of the child's behavior is comparatively small. The upper bound age of 7 years is associated with the end of the preschool time of children in the Russian Federation. There is still no systematic training of kids at school, but more stable brain activity, compared to the earlier ages. There are only a few databases with emotional speech of children before 4 years of age [1].

The presented experimental results show that lexical information has more discriminative power in recognition of valence compared to acoustic features for speech samples of 6–7 year old children. Human perception of emotion is higher in the speech of older children, which has several implications. It is harder to recognize sentiment with younger children, since linguistic and acoustic control skills are not mature enough. Despite this issue, analyzing/monitoring child emotion in early ages is important not only for linguistics, but also for analysis of neurological development/disorders. The preliminary automatic classification study reveals very close performance to human perception, which can be taken as a gold standard. As in cross-corpus acoustic emotion recognition [9], we observed improved performance due to within-set normalization scheme.

6   Conclusions

In this paper, we introduced the EmoChildRu corpus that has been designed to study the reflection of the emotional state in the characteristics of voice and speech and for studies of the formation of emotional states in ontogenesis. From our point of view, child emotional speech material in our database can be the basis for scientific projects on how the Russian language is mastered by children and on the emotional development of children. This corpus can also be used for the research and development of automated child speech recognition systems.

Acknowledgments. This study is financially supported by the Russian Foundation for Humanities (project # 13-06-00041a), the Russian Foundation for Basic Research (projects # 13-06-00281a, 15-06-07852a, and 15-07-04415a), the Council for grants of the President of Russia (project # MD-3035.2015.8) and by the Government of Russia (grant No. 074-U01).

References

1. Batliner, A., Blomberg, M., D'Arcy, S., Elenius, D., Giuliani, D., Gerosa, M., Hacker, C., Russell, M.J., Steidl, S., Wong, M.: The pf_star children's speech corpus. In: INTERSPEECH, pp. 2761–2764 (2005)
2. Eyben, F., Wöllmer, M., Schuller, B.: Opensmile: the munich versatile and fast open-source audio feature extractor. In: Proceedings of the International Conference on Multimedia, pp. 1459–1462. ACM (2010)
3. Hall, M., Frank, E., Holmes, G., Pfahringer, B., Reutemann, P., Witten, I.H.: The weka data mining software: an update. ACM SIGKDD Explor. Newslett. **11**(1), 10–18 (2009)
4. Lyakso, E., Frolova, O., Grigoriev, A.: Acoustic characteristics of vowels in 6 and 7 years old russian children. In: Proceeding International Conference INTERSPEECH, pp. 1739–1742 (2009)
5. Lyakso, E.: Study reflects the voice of emotional states: comparative analysis chimpanzee, human infants and adults. In: Proceeding XVI European Conference on Development Psychology ECDP-2013 (2013)

6. Lyakso, E., Grigorev, A., Kurazova, A., Ogorodnikova, E.: "INFANT. MAVS" - multimedia model for infants cognitive and emotional development study. In: Ronzhin, A., Potapova, R., Delic, V. (eds.) SPECOM 2014. LNCS, vol. 8773, pp. 284–291. Springer, Heidelberg (2014)
7. Lyakso, E.E., Frolova, O.V., Kurazhova, A.V., Gaikova, J.S.: Russian infants and children's sounds and speech corpuses for language acquisition studies. In: Proceeding International Conference INTERSPEECH, pp. 1878–1881 (2010)
8. Platt, J., et al.: Fast training of support vector machines using sequential minimal optimization. Advances in kernel methods: support vector learning 3 (1999)
9. Schuller, B., et al.: Cross-corpus acoustic emotion recognition: variances and strategies. IEEE Trans. Affect. Comput. $1(2)$, 119–131 (2010)
10. Schuller, B., et al.: The interspeech 2010 paralinguistic challenge. In: INTERSPEECH, pp. 2794–2797 (2010)
11. Schuller, B., et al.: The interspeech 2013 computational paralinguistics challenge: social signals, conflict, emotion, autism (2013)
12. Schuller, B., Steidl, S., Batliner, A.: The interspeech 2009 emotion challenge. INTERSPEECH **2009**, 312–315 (2009)
13. Syssau, A., Monnier, C.: Children's emotional norms for 600 french words. Behavior Res. Methods **41**(1), 213–219 (2009)

Cognitive Mechanism of Semantic Content Decoding of Spoken Discourse in Noise

Rodmonga Potapova[1](✉) and Vsevolod Potapov[2]

[1] Institute of Applied and Mathematical Linguistics,
Moscow State Linguistic University, Ostozhenka 38, Moscow 119034, Russia
rkpotapova@yandex.ru
[2] Faculty of Philology, Lomonosov Moscow State University,
GSP-1, Leninskie Gory, Moscow 119991, Russia

Abstract. This paper discusses the results of experimental research in the field of auditory recognition of the semantic content of Russian spoken discourses in noise. Some spoken discourses in noise were presented to listeners for auditory perception and then recognition of main topics and subtopics of the stimuli. The research included the following questions: is it possible to define topics and subtopics of spoken discourse in noise; does the quality of speech recognition and understanding depend on a subject of spoken discourse; how do these factors correlate. Statistical analysis revealed that there is a main effect of the semantic content recognition of spoken text/discourse in noise (some kinds of signal-noise ratio) by listeners.

Keywords: Speech perception · Speech recognition · Topic · Subtopic · Listener · Speaker · Noise · Spoken discourse · Semantic content

1 Introduction

Influence of acoustic noise on the perception of speech has been studied deep enough for some decades, both in our country and abroad, primarily in connection with the testing of quality of speech signal transmitting tracts. Its known that speech can be distorted in many ways. It was noted that adding noise, band-pass filtering, or clipping the signal reduces the intelligibility of speech [4]. This interdisciplinary research area has developed mainly in the context of vocoder telephony, whose main subject is the companded speech signal with regard to a particular natural language, such as Russian [5,7,9]. Speech recognition was defined as a system of text information processing mechanisms, which leads to text understanding. These processes progress simultaneously at several levels of speech recognition, interacting with each other [1].

The essence of the research was to reveal the mechanisms of masking the acoustic signal, which is determined by the change in the threshold of audibility of speech compared to its perception in the absence of noise, interference and distortion. If we consider the dynamics of the research in this area with regard to

© Springer International Publishing Switzerland 2015
A. Ronzhin et al. (Eds.): SPECOM 2015, LNAI 9319, pp. 153–160, 2015.
DOI: 10.1007/978-3-319-23132-7_19

the Russian language, it can be pointed out that the original primary objective was to assess the quality of the speech transmission paths. In this regard, the development of research in the second half of the XX century has been headed to find a solution to the problem of determining the criteria if intelligibility of Russian speech in noisy environments. In cooperation with linguists, communication experts developed special tables of Russian speech intelligibility [8]. Much later, attempts were made to study the problems of language and speaker identification in heavy noise conditions. These two tasks proved much more difficult than the problem of intelligibility itself.

Training-related improvements in listening in noise and the biological mechanisms mediating these improvements have been investigated [10]. The goal of another study was to evaluate the intelligibility of synthesized speech in noise. An algorithm was proposed that improved speech intelligibility in noise for normal-hearing listeners [3]. At the beginning of the XXI century studies have been performed concerning not only the abovementioned tasks, but also the possibility of decoding of the semantic content (topics, subtopics exc.) of speech messages in difficult noise conditions. The main aim of another investigation was to examine the influence of semantically related and unrelated three-word text cues on the intelligibility of complete natural sentences in stationary noise with different noise levels. The researchers observed facilitative effects of relevant semantic contextual information on the perception of speech in noise [5].

2   Method and Experiment

Our research included studies of auditory perceptual features and reconstruction of semantic content of Russian speech in white noise. The studies involved different types of spoken language and different speech production situations: reading, monologue, dialogue, polylogue. The research was conducted in several stages: formation of the special corpus of experimental texts for reading and conversation (monologues, dialogues, polylogues); formation of the corpus of Russian native speakers and listeners; recording native Russian speakers in an anechoic chamber; adding different levels of white noise on the signal ($-10\,$dB, $-12\,$dB); auditory-perceptual analysis of phonograms with signal-noise ratio ($-10\,$dB, $-12\,$dB); creating a database of results. The data obtained were studied taking into account the factors of noise levels and speech production situation types regarding all types of speech activities. Such an approach to solving the problem it was necessary to determine not only the number of recognized lexical units, their attribution to grammatical classes of spoken language, but also to decode the recognized fragments of texts and topics of these texts in noise conditions.

The next step is analyzing spoken texts regarding the distribution of perceived units and their relations with the findings of experimental data on the immediate constituents (IC). Immediate constituents are a basic term in grammatical analysis for a linguistic unit which is a functional component of a larger construction. In an alternative formulation, a constituent is a set of nodes ultimately dominated by a single node [2]. During the studying all the sentences of texts in Russian being read and perceived by the listeners in noisy conditions (signal/noise ratios −10 and −12 dB) were analyzed in terms of immediate constituents.

During analysis different variants of auditory-perceptual recognition of verbal units revealed: elements precisely identified by listeners (coincidence one to one); those recognized by listeners, but to a lesser degree of precision; those replaced by listeners basing on meaning similarities. The original text and text recordings with noise ratio and the results of the auditory-perceptual decoding of these texts by listeners were analyzed to identify coincidences in the responses of listeners with the material of the original text, which they had listened to. A table of coincidences was composed, which reflects what words and phrases of the original text had been recognized by the listeners. Words recognized by the listeners can be divided into 3 groups: a full match, partial coincidence (for phonetic composition); replacement by meaning.

For each text the frequency of various parts of speech and the percentage of recognized words were also calculated in accordance with the above classes. For example, in the perception of the Text 1 with noise-ratio of −10 dB the listeners recognized 160 units (words and phrases). Of these, in 43 % there is a full match of units, and in 37 % there is a coincidence for the phonetic composition. Semantic coincidence is observed only in 3 %. Also mixed cases were identified where in the recorded phrase some words coincide exactly/fully, while some others that coincide only by phonetic composition (9 %). In 7 % it was impossible to determine the original word or phrase and identify the basis of replacement (Figs. 1 and 2).

With full matches most often adverbs (22 %), adjectives (20 %) and nouns (22 %) are encountered, verbs account for 11 %, of function parts of speech most precisely conjunctions were recognized - 14 % (among them the largest portion contain conjunctions *that* and *and*). In case of coincidence by phonetic features, more frequently autonomous parts of speech are encountered, there are virtually no conjunctions and prepositions.

The phonetic basis for replacement is most often presented by fricative consonants (30 %), the sounds [n] and [m] (25 %); also often replacement by parts of words is observed (17 %). In the perception of the text 2 the listeners recognized

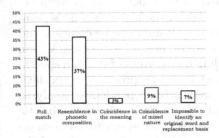

Fig. 1. Types of recognition of words and phrases (text 1; −10 dB)

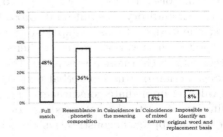

Fig. 2. Types of recognition of words and phrases (text 2; −10 dB)

93 verbal units (unit meant words and phrases). The full match is observed in 48 %. Coincidences by phonetic composition are encountered in 36 %. Semantic coincidence was identified in 3 %. Also mixed cases were identified where in the recorded phrase some words coincide exactly/fully, while some others coincide only by phonetic composition (5 %). In 8 % it was impossible to determine the original word or phrase and identify the cause of replacement. Thus, the full match of adverbs accounted for 35 %; verbs - 24 %; pronouns - 22 %; adjectives - 13 % and nouns - 7 % of cases. Among the function parts of speech most precisely conjunctions were recognized -14 % (among them the largest portion contain conjunctions *that* and *and*, *if*). In case of the coincidence by phonetic features, more frequently autonomous parts of speech are encountered, there are virtually no conjunctions and prepositions. The phonetic basis for replacement is most often presented by fricative consonants, the sounds [n] and [m]. Also often replacement by parts of words is observed.

The results of this analysis allow to conclude that most of the speech units recognized by the listeners are characterized with the noise of -10 dB and -12 dB, but with the noise of -12 dB it is impossible to find a coincidence to what was heard by the listeners in the original text. This means that they were able to identify only the presence of speech and the meaning of what they heard was not recognized. With the noise of -10 dB the listeners heard some words, some of them - quite precisely, others more or less precisely, on the basis of phonetic similarity. But in this case recognized words could not help determine the overall thematic dominant of the text, because the words are too dissipated and are often only phonetically similar to the original word.

The analysis of the two texts allows to conclude that the number of recognized words depends on the listener. Some of the listeners recognized words better than others, with the complete coincidence in the two texts, while others only heard fragments of words and the coincidence took place mainly by phonetic features. Further issues involved the reconstruction of the general semantic content perceived in the difficult conditions of the speech material that has been associated with a number of cognitive-semantic difficulties. To solve this problem, we developed a new integrated approach that allows for realizing the transition from the results on speech intelligibility to the reconstruction of semantic information and links in semantic gaps basing on the data obtained from perceptual analysis of speech in noise. To do this, we proposed a method that includes a hierarchy of iterations: auditory recognition of prosodic models of the syntactic and semantic segmentation of Russian spoken texts (discourse); auditory recognition and interpretation of various types of theme-rheme-structures/of utterances within perceived speech fragments; applying the rhythm/metric rules of Russian speech; reconstruction of Russian verbal text structures based on predicative and lexical valence; immediate constituents analysis; predicative dependencies analysis; definition of units characterized as contextually dependent using probabilistic forecasting approach; construction of probabilistic model of syntactic and semantic relations of the reconstructed spoken text; general semantic decoding of the reconstructed text to a required degree of accuracy of semantic reconstruction [6]. It is only those linguistic characteristics of the text which significantly affect the measure of adequacy of his interpretation by the recipient that can be considered informatively marked, or pragmatically relevant. Not all kinds of linguistic analysis provide semantically relevant information.

3 Discussion

Conceptual and linguistic organization of the spoken text, as well as some of its very specific verbal characteristics (organization of its syntactic and semantic structure, semantic focus of the text etc.) are considered informative, or interpretive for text properties, which manifest themselves in the process of semantic interpretation and can be established experimentally. The macrostructure of the spoken text can be presented as a hierarchy of semantic blocks of different order predications, where the first-order predicates are the linguistic means which transmits the main idea of the message, as predicates of the second, third, etc. order are the language means that transmit the total of its contents. The microstructure of the spoken text can be presented as a complete set of intratext relationships connecting main semantic text nodes. Such semantic support can be singled out in the text by using a special technique. They form a logical and factual chain, which represents the basic semantic content of the text.

The sequence of the facts (semantic reference nodes) in the chain may reflect either the logic of the author's intention deployment in the hierarchy of communicative and cognitive programs, or the logic of the deployment of the text production plan (speech incarnation of the semantic information), regardless of the specified hierarchy. There are two methods of singling out the logical content in the text: the first one requires the knowledge of the goal of the message and can be used only after a detailed preliminary study of the text, while the second one does not assume any familiarity with the text of the recipient and can be used off-hand when perceiving or reading the text. The process of cognitive decoding of the content of a text perceived in noisy conditions appears more complex and multi-layered. We propose the original concept of the step-by-step process of speech perception understanding regarding to speech in noise: (a) disruption of speech perception: only noise is perceived; (b) false guessing of some words of perceived spoken utterances; (c) fragmentary perception of verbal communication involving the perception of only some of the really uttered words and phrases, including some of the semantic keys; (d) pseudo-understanding of messages inaccurate or false prediction of the theme of the text on the basis of real and false semantic keys; (e) general understanding of the spoken text an adequate definition of the topic and the general meaning of the text with incomplete recovery of verbal material; (f) detailed understanding of the spoken text the result is almost verbatim decoding of phonograms; (g) understanding of the text. The proposed MRA text assessment method is based on this idea of the meaning level decoding of the speech in noise, a scale of meaning reconstruction adequacy (MRA) was designed, which determines the degree of reliability of the forecasts of an expert as to the semantic content of the phonogram [6].

3.1   MRA Text Assessment Method

Expert working with the soundtrack does not have any a priori knowledge about the content of the analyzed material. Therefore, an attempt was made to approach the problem of assessing the possibility of adequate understanding without involving cumbersome procedures of semantic analysis (method should be simple and accessible).

Using of the resulting speech material includes the following procedures: grouping words into semantic fields; definition of topics (themes); rearrangement of words according to the degree semantic closeness to the theme; determining the values of semantic features; assigning an MRA grade to the text; semantic grouping of words in the slots. There are words, phrases or sentences in the text that can be linked together by meaning. Expert puts these elements of the text in some meaningful groups, each of which has its own semantic core.

Definition of the subject

The theme is considered a phenomenon, event or thing the text describes. The theme can be expressed in a word or phrase from the recovered text, but sometimes the expert has to formulate a theme on their own based on the general meaning of the recovered material. The texts can contain several topics. Such texts are better divided into fragments that are to be analyzed separately and later combined into larger fragments if necessary. When analyzing a track of very poor quality, expert can presume there are a number of topics, even if they seem to contradict with one other. Rearrangement of words according to the degree of semantic closeness to the topic. At this stage, the units of all semantic groups are divided into three types: (a) words, phrases and phrases directly related to the subject; (b) those possible for a given topic; (c) those that do not comply with this topic. In the case of predicting several topics in one fragment of text or low quality soundtrack expert makes a set of different rearrangements to check all the projected themes.

Determination of semantic features

In MRA text assessment four semantic features are used: concreteness of the theme; word coefficient k_1; word combination coefficient k_2; phrase coefficient k_3. The parameter concreteness of the theme can assume one of the following values: $-T$ - the theme is not determined, $\varnothing T$ - the theme is formulated by the expert in their own words, $0.5T$ - the theme is partly expressed in the words of the text $+T$ - topic completely expressed in the words of the analyzed text.

It is only a value of $0.5T$ that requires an additional remark. The parameter takes this value when the expert includes both words from the text and their own words in the definition of the theme. Coefficients (verbal and phrasal ones and phrases) reflect the level of decoding of content of the text (single words, phrases, sentences) and indicate the degree of reliability of the identification of the theme. When one selects multiple topics in a single fragment of text or low quality recording, semantic characteristics are determined for all the suggested themes. The topic whose semantic parameters take values closer to 1 is considered real. In case of absence of phrases or sentences in the test material, the corresponding coefficients take the value (k_2 or k_3). In other cases the coefficients are calculated using a simple formula, and can range from a negative number to 1.

Assignment a MRA Grade to the Text

The scale of semantic decoding has six grades (evaluation of the level of critical understanding, obviously, is not included in the range of problems faced by an expert who analyzes the reliability of the restoration of the text). Each grade corresponds to a set of certain statistically significant semantic parameter values:

- disruption of speech perception - no semantic features are available;
- pseudo-perception of speech: the values of semantic parameters: $-T$ or $\varnothing T$; $k_1 \leq 0.3$; k_2 to ≤ 0.3;
- fragmentary perception of verbal communication: the values of semantic parameters: $\varnothing T$ or $0.5T$; $k_1 = 0.4$; $k_2 \leq 0.5$;
- pseudo-understanding of messages: the values of semantic parameters: $0.5T$ or $+T$; $k_1 = 0.5$, $k_2 = 0.5$, k_3 varies from negative to 1;
- general understanding of the text: the values of semantic parameters: $+T$, $k_1 > 0.5$, $k_2 > 0$, $k_3 = 1$;
- detailed understanding of the text: the values of semantic parameters: $+T$, $k_1 = 1$ or $\varnothing k_1$; k_2 varies from negative to 1 or $\varnothing k_2$, $k_3 = 1$.

Grades 2 and 3 show the unreliability of the reconstruction of the meaning of the text. Grade 4 indicates 50 % accuracy of semantic prediction. Phonograms graded 1–4 are unlikely to be useful, and when working with grade 5 texts, one should take into account the gaps in its semantic structure [6].

4 Conclusion

On the basis of the multi-stage experimental study an attempt was made to determine the specificity of cognitive functioning linguistic mechanism with respect to decoding semantic information in verbal and cognitive human activities in difficult (noise) conditions. There are no analogous methods of approach concerning cognitive auditory perceptual recognition of speech semantics in noise. It is assumed that the process of perception, cognitive analysis, semantic interpretation and "recovery" of spoken and written texts with regards to its media- and macrosegmentation activates different levels of verbal and cognitive processes, which calls for a cognitive reflection and communicative activity approach to the issue. The variability of mediasegmentation of reconstructed texts is significantly lower than that of macrosegmentation. On the basis of quantitative probabilistic frequency analysis we can conclude that the demarcation of semantic segments of the quasi-text has probabilistic nature. The localization of boundaries and the variability of ways of marking them are determined by the choice of a particular marker type and the semantic structure of the text. The data obtained indicate that the ratio of the number of markers of media- and macrosegmentation varies depending on the characteristics of auditory perception peculiarities. However, some observations are to be made. Two strategies of semantic decoding of spoken texts in difficult conditions have been revealed. One relies mainly on the grammatical level information, while the other clings to semantics. Further on, the analysis of the segmentation of telephone conversation texts (viewed as distant mediated communication case) revealed that the markers boundaries identified by the subjects should be classified into three groups: nuclear, intermediate and marginal, which directly depends on the frequency of their occurrence in a particular area of the text in noise. Thus, noise in the transmitting tract causes distortion of the final product of semantic decoding of the transmitted information and leads to the emergence of negative ergonomic effects not only of auditory or perceptual, but also of cognitive nature.

Acknowledgments. This research is supported by Ministry of Education and Science of Russian Federation. Project No. 3118, state assignment 2014/102 at Moscow State Linguistic University (scientific head of the project R.K. Potapova)

References

1. Borsky, M., Mizera, P., Pollak, P.: Noise and channel normalized cepstral features for Far-speech recognition. In: Železný, M., Habernal, I., Ronzhin, A. (eds.) SPECOM 2013. LNCS(LNAI), vol. 8113, pp. 241–248. Springer, Heidelberg (2013)
2. Crystal, D.: A Dictionary of Linguistics and Phonetics, 6th edn. Blackwell publishing, USA-UK Australia (2009)
3. Kim, G., Lu, Y., Ha, Y., Philipos, C.: An algorithm that improves speech intelligibility in noise for normal-hearing listeners. J. Acoust. Soc. Am. **126**, 1486–1494 (2009)
4. ÓShaughnessy, D.: Speech Communication. Human and Machine. Addison-Wesley Publishing Company, Reading (1987)
5. Potapova, R., Potapov, V.: Auditory recognition of speech semantic content (on the Basis of Spoken Discourse in Noise). In: Vestn. Mosk. Gos. Linguist. Univ; Ser. Linguistics. Moscow: Moscow State Linguistic University, **13**(699), 11–20 (2014)
6. Potapova, R., Potapov, V.: Theoretical basis for a new approach to the reconstruction of the semantic content of a noisy speech russian. In: V Mezhdunarodny Kongress "Russkiy Yazyk: Istoricheskie Sudby i Sovremennost". Trudy i Materialy. CD-ROM. Moskva, pp. 577 (2014). (in Russian)
7. Potapova, R.K., Mikhailov, V.G.: Osnovy Rechevoy Akustiki. IPK MGLU Rema, Moskva (2012). (in Russian)
8. Potapova, R.K., Potapov, V.V.: Rechevaya Kommunikatsiya: ot Zvuka k Vyskazyvaniyu. Yazyki slavyanskih kul'tur, Moskva (2012). (in Russian)
9. Song, J.H., Skoe, E., Banai, K., Kraus, N.: Training to improve hearing speech in noise: biological mechanisms. Cereb. Cortex **22**(5), 1180–1190 (2012)
10. Zekveld, A., Rudner, M., Johnsrude, I., Festen, J.M., van Beck, J.H.M., Roehnberg, J.: The influence of semantically related and unrelated text cues on the intelligibility of sentences in noise. Ear. Hear. **32**(6), 16–25 (2011)

Combining Prosodic and Lexical Classifiers for Two-Pass Punctuation Detection in a Russian ASR System

Olga Khomitsevich[1,2], Pavel Chistikov[1], Tatiana Krivosheeva[3], Natalia Epimakhova[3], and Irina Chernykh[2,3](✉)

[1] Speech Technology Center, Saint-Petersburg, Russia
olgahom@yandex.ru, chistikov@speechpro.com
[2] ITMO University, Saint-Petersburg, Russia
[3] STC-Innovations Ltd, Saint-Petersburg, Russia
{krivosheeva,epimakhova,chernykh-i}@speechpro.com

Abstract. We propose a system for automatic punctuation prediction in recognized speech using prosodic, word and grammatical features. An SVM classifier is trained using prosody, and a CRF classifier is trained on a large text dataset using word-based features. The probabilities are then fused to produce a joint decision on comma and period placement, with a second classification pass for question mark detection. Training two classifiers separately enables us to avoid data sparseness for the lexical classifier, and to increase the overall robustness of the system. This works well for Russian and could be applied to other inflected languages. The system was tested on different speech styles. On manual transcripts, we achieved an F-score of 50–71 % for periods, 46–66 % for commas, 19–47 % for question marks, and 77–87 % for "mark/no mark" classification. The results for recognizer output are 46–66 % for periods, 43–60 % for commas, 10–38 % for questions, and 64–80 % for "mark/no mark".

Keywords: Punctuation prediction · Sentence boundary detection · Speech recognition · Conditional Random Fields · Support Vector Machine · Russian

1 Introduction

Automatic punctuation prediction is a necessary step for processing recognized speech in state-of-the-art automatic speech recognition (ASR) systems, and a lot of work has been done on this task. The systems proposed in the literature are usually based on lexical features of the recognized words and prosodic features extracted from the speech signal. For instance, [1] uses an n-gram language model based on word and POS features to predict boundaries in recognized speech. In [2] lexical features and pause duration features are used for building a Maximum Entropy model which predicts commas, periods and question marks. A detailed case for employing various prosodic features, such as pause, F0, and

© Springer International Publishing Switzerland 2015
A. Ronzhin et al. (Eds.): SPECOM 2015, LNAI 9319, pp. 161–169, 2015.
DOI: 10.1007/978-3-319-23132-7_20

phone duration features, is made in [3], which uses a decision tree-based classifier. As demonstrated in [4], it is possible to build a simple sentence segmentation system based on only acoustic features; despite a relatively high error rate, that solution was useful for applications such as topic classification [5]. Most systems combine prosodic and lexical features while experimenting with various classifiers, for instance, a Multi-Layer Perceptron and a Finite State Model in [6], Dynamic Conditional Random Fields in [7], a Hidden Event Language Model in [8], etc. Question mark detection is usually reported to be the most challenging subtask in punctuation mark detection [2,6,9], and the best results are achieved by classifying manually labeled sentences into questions and statements [10,11].

In this paper we present a novel punctuation prediction system based on fusing probabilities from two classifiers and using a two-pass system to improve question mark detection. An important development is combining word features with a large number of morphological tags containing grammatical information about word forms, which provides an advantage over simple POS features for an inflected language like Russian. The system detects commas, periods and question marks and is designed for use in an Automatic Speech Recognition (ASR) system.

2   System Overview

Our system incorporates two classifiers which deal separately with two types of features: prosodic and lexical. A Support Vector Machine (SVM) classifier is trained on a dataset of speech recordings using a number of prosodic features. A Conditional Random Field (CRF) classifier is trained on a large text dataset and uses lexical features, which include word identities and morphological (POS-based) features. The probabilities generated by the two classifiers are combined to make the final decision about the punctuation mark after each word. The main reason for using two classifiers, rather than training one classifier using all types of features, is to increase the robustness of the lexical classifier by training it on a very large text dataset. Since Russian is a highly inflected language, large amounts of data are needed for n-gram training to counteract the data sparsity problem. Another reason is that by using two different classifiers and then combining their results we also increase the overall robustness of our system.

The system works in two passes. At the first pass, only commas and periods are detected. We use a second pass to identify question marks, that is, we classify all detected sentence boundaries (periods) into statements (ending with a period) and questions (ending with a question mark).

2.1   The Lexical Classifier

Lexical Features. Word context provides crucial information for the task of punctuation detection. In order to utilize this information, we trained a classifier on a large text dataset using a set of lexical features. The lexical features for each word are the word itself and its morphological tag. The morphological tag includes part of speech as well as more specific grammatical features (for example, case and gender) and a few semantic features (such as first name or geographical name). Grammatical features are especially important for highly inflected languages such as Russian and other Slavic languages, and they allowed us to obtain about 4 percent absolute gain in F-score compared to part-of-speech-only tags. The morphological features were calculated using the Russian POS tagger developed at Speech Technology Cetner Ltd for use in text-to-speech, speech recognition and other applications. Overall, the resulting morphological tag set for the training database consisted of 887 individual tags.

The CRF Classifier. We used the Linear-Chain Conditional Random Field (CRF) classifier for predicting punctuation based on lexical features. This classifier models conditional probability for sequential data labeling. It can be defined as:

$$p(\overrightarrow{y}|\overrightarrow{x}) = \frac{1}{Z(\overrightarrow{x})} \exp(\sum_{j=1}^{n} \sum_{i=1}^{m} \lambda_i f_i(y_{j-1}, y_j, \overrightarrow{x}, j), \tag{1}$$

where $Z(\overrightarrow{x})$ is the normalization factor, λ_i are the learnable weights, f_i are the feature functions, $\overrightarrow{y}$ is the punctuation labels sequence, $\overrightarrow{x}$ is the input sequence, n is the input sequence length, m is the feature function number.

We found that the most useful feature context was a 6 word window for words and a 3 word window for morphological tags. We set a cut-off threshold of 4 for feature occurrences, which allowed us to fit the requirements for time and computing resources for CRF model training. We used the CRF++ open source implementation for this project [12]. The model was trained on a dataset consisting of about 135 million words, built from literary works of various authors and genres.

2.2 The Prosodic Classifier

Prosodic Features. We calculated a set of prosodic features for each word boundary in the dataset. The features were calculated both over the duration of the word before/after the boundary, and over a time window (a 200 ms window was used). It is worth noting that in some research, prosodic features are normalized for each speaker in the dataset. However, our system is intended for use in real-time ASR applications where calculating speaker characteristics may not be possible, so we did not perform such normalization. Overall, 60 prosodic features were used, such as pause duration, F0 features, energy and duration features.

The SVM Classifier. For the prosodic classifier, we used an SVM classifier with a radial basis function kernel. The training procedure consisted of two steps. First, the optimal cost (C) and gamma (γ) parameters were estimated. For this purpose we used 20 % of all training data. Then the SVM model was trained for each value of the parameters, where $\log_2 C \in [1; 15]$ and $\log_2 \gamma \in [-15; -1]$

with the step of 0.5. To train the model we used 80 % of available data and the other 20 % were used to evaluate the classification accuracy. We used the average F-score of each class as the accuracy measure. Finally, the model was trained on all the data using the optimal parameters C and γ.

The classifier was trained on a dataset of audiobook-style read speech. Even though our system was tested on different types of data, we found that training the prosodic classifier on read speech gave the best results, presumably because the data were less noisy and easier to classify. The training dataset consisted of 21.5 hrs of speech (260 k words) recorded by professional voice artists in a studio environment, transcribed and labeled manually by expert linguists.

2.3   The Combined Model

The fusion of probabilities generated by the two classifiers was done using logistic regression. We use a dedicated binary-class model for each punctuation label (including the no-punctuation label). The fused probabilities were normalized to sum up to one. The final decision about the punctuation label was made by comparing the sum of punctuation mark probabilities with the probability of the no-punctuation label multiplied by a coefficient. We used the sum of punctuation probabilities because often, different types of punctuation are possible in the same position, so the probability is spread between those punctuation marks. In such cases the probability of zero punctuation may be greater than any of the punctuation mark probabilities, but smaller than the probability of "any punctuation". In terms of the readability of the resulting text, it is better to predict the wrong punctuation mark than to predict no punctuation at all where it is needed. Using a coefficient helps to keep the balance between the overall labeling precision and recall and provides a simple way to fine-tune our model for specific tasks.

The fusion model was trained on a dataset of telephone conversations (duration about 21.7 hrs) and their manual transcripts; the dataset was labeled automatically using forced alignment of the transcripts.

2.4   Second Pass for Question Mark Detection

At the second pass the algorithm tries to predict the positions where periods should be replaced by question marks. Our preliminary experiments demonstrated that this approach results in greater accuracy of question mark detection compared to a system where all punctuation is detected in one pass (about 14 % absolute F-score gain for question marks).

Both the lexical and the prosodic classifier were trained specially for the second pass. The question mark probabilities were combined by the fusion method described above. For the second CRF pass, several additional lexical features were added, such as the presence of a keyword, the first word after the closest preceding comma, and the number of words and comma-separated blocks in the sentence. Two question keyword lists (sentence beginning keywords and general keywords) were automatically built using statistical significance of words for interrogative sentences and postprocessed by an expert. They included wh-words, interrogative particles and other "trigger" words like the verb "tell" in the imperative form. The training dataset for the CRF model consisted of literary works selected so that at least 10 % of sentences in the data ended with a question mark (about 154 million words in total).

The second pass of the prosodic classifier was trained using the same training set as the first pass, with some additional read speech material included in order to increase the proportion of questions in the dataset. The combined duration of the dataset was about 24 hrs of speech. The same feature set as for the first pass was used.

3 Experimental Setup

3.1 The Datasets

We tested our system on three test cases: radio and TV interviews, telephone conversations, and read speech, so we used three test datasets collected at Speech Technology Center Ltd. The Interviews dataset (duration 5.5 hrs, transcripts 43.4 k words) consists of interviews and conversations broadcast on Russian radio and TV, and comprises spontaneous speech recorded in various environments, including noisy conditions. The Telephone dataset (11.4 hrs, 54.2 k words) consists of customer calls to a contact center. Finally, the Read Speech dataset (5.1 hrs, 34.7 k words) consists of literary works recorded by professional voice artists in a studio environment. All datasets contain around 10 % of interrogative sentences.

All the datasets were manually transcribed by experts, and the sound files were labeled with words, word boundaries and punctuation marks. The Read Speech dataset was labeled manually, and forced alignment was used for the other datasets.

3.2 ASR Setup

To test our punctuation detection system on recognizer output, we used the speaker-independent continuous speech recognition system for Russian developed at Speech Technology Center Ltd. [13,14] which is based on a CD-DNN-HMM acoustic model [15]. The basic tandem model was trained on LC-RC features [16]. For Interviews and Read Speech datasets we used a general language model (LM) trained on a 6GB text corpus of news articles (300 k words, 5 million n-grams), which provided recognition accuracy for these datasets of 75 % and 78 %, respectively. The ASR system used for recognizing telephone conversations included interpolation of a general LM with a thematic language model trained on a set of text transcripts of contact center calls (70 MB of training data). Recognition accuracy for the Telephone dataset was thus the highest, at 80 %. We used Good-Turing smoothing (cutoff = 1 for all orders of n-grams).

4 Results and Discussion

The results of our experiments are presented in Tables 1, 2 and 3. In order to demonstrate the input of each classifier, we provide the results for the lexical and prosodic classifier separately (Tables 1 and 2, respectively), as well as the final fusion results (Table 3). The tables show Precision, Recall and F-score values for periods, commas, question marks, as well as for all punctuation (in the latter case, only the presence or absence of punctuation is tested, without distinguishing between different punctuation marks). We show results both for manual transcripts and for the recognizer output.

The results show that, taken on its own, the lexical classifier shows a better overall performance than the prosodic classifier. Good performance of the prosodic classifier on Read Speech can be explained by the fact that it was trained on the same type of data, as well as by the nature of read speech which has a slow tempo and displays regular prosodic patterns. Nevertheless, adding prosodic information improves the accuracy of punctuation detection compared to the lexical classifier. The F-score for the "all punctuation" metric improves by 3–11 % absolute. A similar improvement is observed for all punctuation types; even question mark detection is improved by the addition of prosodic information, though on its own the prosodic classifier does poorly at question detection.

Overall, our results compare well with those reported in the literature; for instance, the recent paper [17] reports 46–65 % F-score for commas, 61–67 % for periods, and 20–41 % for questions on various English datasets. The results also reflect differences in our datasets. Thus, periods are detected better than commas for the Telephone dataset, and vice versa for the Intervews dataset. Analysing the transcripts shows that the former dataset has shorter sentences (around 8 words

Table 1. Lexical classifier results.

Dataset	Punctuation	Manual transcripts			Recognizer output		
		% P	% R	% F	% P	% R	% F
Read speech	Full stop	62.5	50.6	55.9	56.1	45.2	50.1
	Comma	72.5	51.1	59.8	66.7	46.2	54.8
	Question	56.4	24.8	34.4	58.3	19.0	28.7
	All	91.1	67.1	77.3	83.0	59.9	69.6
Interviews	Full stop	44.1	47.4	45.7	40.1	40.5	40.3
	Comma	75.6	51.5	61.3	70.3	42.6	53.0
	Question	31.9	11.9	17.3	20.0	4.0	6.6
	All	85.0	67.0	75.0	73.0	52.0	60.8
Telephone	Full stop	56.1	43.5	49.0	52.2	34.3	41.4
	Comma	55.5	35.7	43.5	50.8	30.1	37.8
	Question	30.1	14.1	19.2	30.2	8.0	12.6
	All	85.4	59.3	70.0	69.8	42.3	52.7

Table 2. Prosodic classifier results.

Dataset	Punctuation	Manual transcripts			Recognizer output		
		%P	%R	%F	%P	%R	%F
Read speech	Full stop	75.3	75.0	75.2	76.3	67.3	71.5
	Comma	52.0	53.9	52.9	53.9	48.9	51.3
	Question	31.1	2.8	5.1	43.5	4.0	7.3
	All	84.2	81.5	82.8	86.6	73.7	79.7
Interviews	Full stop	36.6	22.5	27.8	35.0	30.8	32.8
	Comma	28.3	20.7	23.9	38.4	29.1	33.1
	Question	4.4	1.2	1.9	3.0	1.2	1.7
	All	57.2	39.1	46.5	54.1	42.3	47.5
Telephone	Full stop	49.5	32.1	38.9	54.4	30.1	38.8
	Comma	25.0	22.1	23.5	31.0	20.5	24.7
	Question	8.4	13.2	10.2	10.0	11.6	10.7
	All	67.3	54.5	60.3	67.9	43.3	52.9

Table 3. Combined model results.

Dataset	Punctuation	Manual transcripts			Recognizer output		
		%P	%R	%F	%P	%R	%F
Read speech	Full stop	68.2	74.7	71.3	64.4	67.8	66.1
	Comma	73.2	60.1	66.0	68.4	53.9	60.3
	Question	56.6	39.6	46.6	55.7	29.2	38.3
	All	90.5	84.1	87.2	85.2	75.4	80.0
Interviews	Full stop	47.4	52.5	49.8	42.7	48.7	45.5
	Comma	72.3	53.7	61.6	67.8	44.6	53.8
	Question	29.9	13.9	19.0	18.9	6.7	9.9
	All	85.7	72.0	78.3	72.6	57.3	64.1
Telephone	Full stop	60.2	63.0	61.6	56.6	59.5	58.0
	Comma	58.2	37.7	45.8	55.9	34.5	42.7
	Question	29.2	20.8	24.3	27.9	21.1	24.0
	All	85.2	70.8	77.3	78.1	63.9	70.3

per sentence, as opposed to 16 words per sentence in Interviews). To counteract such differences in speech style we plan to use a coefficient that can give more weight to either commas or periods. It is used as a multiplier for the comma probability when choosing between comma and period during classification, and can be tuned for different use cases if we need to predict comparatively more commas or more periods.

5   Conclusions and Future Research

To sum up, the proposed system successfully detects most punctuation mark positions in Russian speech. Even though results deteriorate for recognized speech as opposed to manual transcripts, the recognizer output is rendered much more readable with the addition of punctuation.

In the future, we plan to continue developing our system in several directions. First, we plan to include phone boundary labels in the prosodic classifier input, so as to be able to calculate duration features more accurately. Another improvement would be using POS information in prosodic question prediction. For instance, in general questions phrasal stress often falls on the verb, and it is there that a raising tone is realized. Second, the lexical classifier may be improved by using the results of a syntactic parser (as reported, for instance, in [18]).

Acknowledgements. The work was financially supported by the Ministry of Education and Science of the Russian Federation, Contract 14.579.21.0008, ID RFMEFI57914X0008, and by the Government of the Russian Federation, Grant 074-U01.

References

1. Stolcke, A., Shriberg, E.: Automatic linguistic segmentation of conversational speech. In: Proceedings of the Fourth International Conference on Spoken Language, ICSLP 96, vol. 2, pp. 1005–1008 (1996)
2. Huang, J., Zweig, G.: Maximum entropy model for punctuation annotation from speech. In: Proceedings of ICSLP, pp. 917–920 (2002)
3. Shriberg, E., Stolcke, A., Hakkani-Tr, D., Tr, G.: Prosody-based automatic segmentation of speech into sentences and topics. Speech Commun. **32**(1), 127–154 (2000)
4. Chistikov, P., Khomitsevich, O.: Online automatic sentence boundary detection in a Russian ASR System. In: Proceedings of the 14th International Conference Speech and Computer - Specom 2011, pp. 112–117 (2011)
5. Korenevsky, M., Ponomareva, I., Levin, K.: Online topic segmentation of russian broadcast news. In: Proceedings of the 14th International Conference on Speech and Computer - SPECOM 2011, pp. 373–378 (2011)
6. Christensen, H., Gotoh, Y., Renals, S.: Punctuation annotation using statistical prosody models. In: ISCA Tutorial and Research Workshop (ITRW) on Prosody in Speech Recognition and Understanding (2001)
7. Wang, X., Ng, H.T., Sim, K.C.: Dynamic conditional random fields for joint sentence boundary and punctuation prediction. In: INTERSPEECH 2012 - Proceedings of th 13th Annual Conference of the International Speech Communication Association, pp. 281–286 (2012)
8. Hasan, M., Doddipatla, R., Hain, T.: Multipass sentence end detection of lecture speech. In: INTERSPEECH 2014 - Proceedings of the 15th Annual Conference of the International Speech Communication Association (2014)

9. Kolar, J., Lamel, L.: Development and evaluation of automatic punctuation for french and english speech-to-text. In: INTERSPEECH 2012 - Proceedings of the 13th Annual Conference of the International Speech Communication Association (2012)

10. Boakye, K., Favre, B., Hakkani-Tr, D.: Any questions? Automatic question detection in meetings. In: ASRU 2009 - IEEE Workshop on Automatic Speech Recognition & Under-standing, pp. 485–489 (2009)

11. Margolis, A., Ostendorf, M.: Question detection in spoken conversations using textual conversations. In: Proceedings of the 49th Annual Meeting of the Association for Computational Linguistics: Human Language Technologies, vol. 2, pp. 118–124 (2011)

12. Kudo, T.: CRF++: Yet another CRF toolkit (2005). http://crfpp.sourceforge.net

13. Chernykh, G., Korenevsky, M., Levin, K., Ponomareva, I., Tomashenko, N.: State level control for acoustic model training. In: Ronzhin, A., Potapova, R., Delic, V. (eds.) SPECOM 2014. LNCS, vol. 8773, pp. 435–442. Springer, Heidelberg (2014)

14. Tomashenko, N., Khokhlov, Y.: Speaker adaptation of context dependent deep neural networks based on MAP-adaptation and GMM-derived feature processing. In: INTERSPEECH 2014 - Proceedings of the 15th Annual Conference of the International Speech Communication Association, pp. 2997–3001 (2014)

15. Dahl, G.E., Yu, D., Deng, L., Acero, A.: Context-dependent pre-trained deep neural net-works for large-vocabulary speech recognition. IEEE Trans. Audio, Speech and Lan-guage Proc. **20**(1), 30–42 (2012)

16. Schwarz, P.: Phoneme recognition based on long temporal context. Doctoral thesis, Brno, Brno University of Technology, Faculty of Information Technology (2008)

17. Ueffing, N., Bisani, M., Vozila, P.: Improved models for automatic punctuation prediction for spoken and written text. In: INTERSPEECH 2013 - Proceedings of the 14th Annual Conference of the International Speech Communication Association (2013)

18. Zhang, D., Wu, S., Yang, N., Li, M.: Punctuation prediction with transition-based parsing. ACL **(1)**, 752–760 (2013)

Construction of a Modern Greek Grammar Checker Through Mnemosyne Formalism

Panagiotis Gakis[1,2,3]([✉]), Christos Panagiotakopoulos[1,2],
Kyriakos Sgarbas[1,2], Christos Tsalidis[2,3,4], and Verykios Vasilios[3,4]

[1] Department of Primary Education, University of Patras, Patras, Greece
[2] Department of Electrical and Computer Engineering,
University of Patras, Patras, Greece
[3] Neurolingo Company, Athens, Greece
[4] Open University, Patras, Greece
gakis@sch.gr, {cpanag,sgarbas}@upatras.gr,
tsalidis@neurolingo.gr, verykios@eap.gr
http://www.elemedu.upatras.gr/english/
http://www.ece.upatras.gr/en/
http://www.neurolingo.gr

Abstract. The aim of this paper is to present a useful and friendly electronic tool (grammar checker) which will carry out the morphological and syntactic analysis of sentences, phrases and words in order to correct syntactic, grammatical and stylistic errors. We also present the formalism used (the *Mnemosyne's Kanon*) and also the particularities of the Greek language that hinder the computational processing. Given that the major problem of modern Greek is the lexical ambiguity we designed the Greek tagger grounded on linguistic criteria for those cases where the lexical ambiguity impede the imprint of the errors in Greek language. The texts that were given for correction to the grammar checker were also corrected by a person. In a very large percentage the grammar checker approximates in accuracy the human-corrector.

Keywords: NLP · Greek language · Grammar checker · Mnemosyne · Unification grammars · Kanon

1 Introduction

Computational linguistic deals with the development of computational models to process information expressed in natural language. This paper presents the design and implementation of a useful and friendly electronic tool (the grammar checker) which will carry out morphological and syntactic analysis of sentences, phrases and words in order to correct syntactic, grammatical and stylistic errors. Given that such tool is not available for the Greek language, the development of the grammar checker is based on the detailed recording, analysis and standardization of errors of written speech and then on the formalism selection. In order to

---

P. Gakis—This paper is part of P. Gakis PhD. thesis.

© Springer International Publishing Switzerland 2015
A. Ronzhin et al. (Eds.): SPECOM 2015, LNAI 9319, pp. 170–177, 2015.
DOI: 10.1007/978-3-319-23132-7_21

construct the Greek Grammar Checker we used the *Mnemosyne environment*, a complete natural language processing system used for information retrieval and information extraction in free text. The *Mnemosyne System*[1] constitutes a complete NLP system that incorporates advanced linguistic resources and computational tools aiming at the automatic extraction of structured information from unstructured electronic documents. It is mainly used for automatic processing of free text documents. It ensures processing of big volumes of information, high precision in the recognition of named entities and events, as well as the possibility of adding new sources of information with low cost.

2   Particularities of Modern Greek Language

Natural language processing systems incorporate notoriously complex algorithmic processes which become even more complicated as far as Modern Greek language is concerned. The declinable parts of speech produce a huge set of morphological word forms, since Modern Greek is a highly inflectional language. The vocabulary of Modern Greek also includes words that are borrowed from other languages.

Moreover, Modern Greek is a *free word order* language and allows the speaker to form phrases in various ways. These variations however are big challenges for computational linguistics [8].

3   Lexical Ambiguity in Modern Greek

Lexical ambiguity is also an important phenomenon in Modern Greek. It occurs when a word type has more than one corresponding lexical entries (lemmas) or when the word is used with a different meaning in figurative sense. Lexical ambiguity has direct relation to the reconstruction and set-up of lexicological entries [1] and usually implies semantic ambiguity. As a result, we have to deal with a great number of words with an ambiguous meaning, and unless their meaning is resolved by the context, this ambiguity may carry over to phrases or even whole sentences. The lexical ambiguity is experienced when a word has more than one lexical entries or when it is used with different meanings in transposition. Jan van Eijck [13] defines the lexical ambiguity as the lack of information about the word meaning. John Lyons [6] describes the term *grammatical ambiguity* as the ambiguity that is observed generally in the language.

During natural language processing by computational systems, syntactic structures are represented by phrase structure rules [2]. However there are many cases in which ambiguity is introduced as a part of speech - which is a major

---

[1] The **MNEMOSYNE** system constitutes a complete NLP system that incorporates advanced linguistic resources and computational tools aiming at the automatic extraction of structured information from unstructured electronic documents. It is mainly used for automatic processing of free text documents (www.neurolingo.gr, www.neurolingo.com).

feature [10] - such as an individual morphological attribute that a lexical type may have. When the part of speech is ambiguous, the parser is forced to examine many more syntactic rules and, eventually, produce all the phrasal structures that these rules dictate, with the hope that one analysis will finally prevail.

The statistical processing of the inflectional types of electronic *Neurolingo Morphological Lexicon*[2] -the lexicon of grammar checker [4] - produced the following statistics for the words with unique morphological characteristics and for these that are ambiguous (Table 1).

Ambiguous words come after recalling the types of lexicon with common orthographic representation.

Table 1. Part of Speech frequencies

Part of Speech	Number of word forms
Number of unique inflected word forms	873701
Ambiguous word forms (from different Lemmas)	39119
Ambiguous word forms(from the same Lemma)	4758
Total number (for all ambiguous words)	182188

A tagger clarifies the morphosyntactic attributes and imputes the correct one. Clarification of lexical ambiguity is one of the most important issues in the text processing and is divided generally into two categories:

1. According to the linguistic approach, rules are manually based on generalizations clarifying examples, which are usually collected from corpus that is morphosyntactically labeled [9].
2. Following the approach of machine learning, a statistical model exists in order to solve automatically the problem from a corpus that is morphosyntactically labeled.

The tagger is oriented to the removal of lexical ambiguity in Greek. It isn't based on statistics but on equivalent context of words. The implementation of the tagger is geared to the needs of the following grammar checker levels. That means that the system faces the tagger as a supportive but absolutely necessary resource and does not analyze all forms of ambiguity.

Mnemosyne supports the complete removal of lexical ambiguity only with linguistic information as the only tool that manages ambiguous words only by their context.

The tagger of Mnemosyne aims not only at removing part-of-speech ambiguity such as the ambiguity met within the gender and case of ambiguous. The performance of the correct morphological characteristics is needed in gender, number or case agreement examined at the level of parsing.

Avoidance of lexical ambiguity examine both previous words -in number up to 4 tokens - and/or the following -in number up to 4 tokens.

---

[2] http://www.neurolingo.gr/en/technology/lexica/morpholexicon.jsp.

4 Features of the Grammar Checker

This tool is innovative and necessary for Modern Greek, both for students and for common users. Examines and verifies each word not only separately but also in relation to its context, e.g. the preposition with the noun, the article with the adjective and the noun, the verb with pronouns and complements etc. The grammatical test focuses primarily on the detection of the words or/and phrases described as problematic (morphological or stylistic). If the word or phrase has the required characteristics, it is considered correct. Otherwise, the grammar checker suggests the user use either the right type (e.g. the same word in another case: e.g. πληγέντων περιοχών [=affected areas] is corrected in πληγεισών περιοχών) or another word with the right characteristics (e.g. πιο καλύτερος will be corrected to: πιο καλός).

This tool is designed to mark the stylistic differentiation of word types. This means that the grammar checker is based on the electronic morphological lexicon where the inflectional generation of each lemma leads to morphological. In this way the user can choose in hindsight the style he prefers and, therefore, the analogous style checked by the grammar checker.

The grammar checker offers the user the ability to be informed about the meaning of a homonymous word or a word deriving from semantic confusion and, therefore, used incorrectly in a specific context. Moreover, checker extends the functionality of the word level at the sentence level, data that increases the complexity of such a tool.

The main areas of grammatical errors [12] the grammar checker addresses are: 1. punctuation problems, 2. final -ν, 3. stylistic issues (verb forms in cases of duplicates, inflectional types), 4. standardization issues (stereotyped phrases, words of literary origin), 5. inclination issues (incorrect declension of names or verbs either through ignorance or because of confusion), 6. vocabulary issues (cases of conceptual confusion, Greek translation of foreign words, redundancy and use of incorrect word or phrase), 7. orthographic confusion issues (homonymous words), 8. agreement issues (cases of elements of nominal or verbal phrase disagreement),9) syntax issues (verbs) and 9. cases of errors that require more specialized management of the spelling correction.

5 Implementation of Software

The formalism used in Mnemosyne (called *Kanon*) obeys the logic of Unification Grammars. Unification Grammars have a powerful and efficient representation of linguistic information and describe much more complex phenomena than the Context-Free Grammars [5]. The structure resulting from this operation contains the information synthesis and brings the two original structures together. The basic idea of the Unification Grammar formalism is simple. The sentence analyzer contains technical performances of semantic features (e.g. the case, etc.) of each component of a sentence [11].

In this analysis the parser clarifies the morphological ambiguity. The error description is done through a unification grammar that allows context-sensitive morphosyntactic grammars to be defined [7].

Mnemosyne is a complete, complex natural language processing system used for both information retrieval and information extraction in free texts. Its main advantage is that it incorporates data with linguistic information. It has already been used in applications with large quantity of items with very good results on the size of the input data, processing speed and output accuracy. In https://ws.neurolingo.gr/WebCleansing/GGC.html the templates of the grammar checker are shown in a friendly environment. The ultimate goal is to integrate the package in office applications.

6   "Kanon" Formalism

The syntactic parser consults the grammatical rules based on templates. It is responsible to check the correct command syntax and consists of approximately 2,600 rules. In no case the grammar checker attempts to resolve extreme language manifestations that cause doubts.

Initially the parser *reads* the tokens one by one, ascribing their morphological attributes. The result of this morphological analysis is: 1. the location of errors (grammatical and semantic) which are defined in grouping rules levels (rules flow) and 2. the recording of the tree production that reflects the part of the syntactic analysis that is problematic. This tree will provide the material for the next phase of analysis, the semantic analysis.

The Kanon formalism is able to exploit the morphological and stylistic attributes of words that have been described in an electronic morphological lexicon. Through this formalism identifies polylectic (multi-word) terms and - in an automated way- derives the phrase or word with the wrong information. It is worth noting that in all cases, any error will be examined separately and a set of corrective action is defined for its management. Each syntactic rule has five elements:

1. The head of a rule, left side of the symbol "=>", for example [VTEXT="$μήνας$"] or [VTEXT="$ρήμα$"]. This determines the replacement of the identified expression of one or more virtual items or rules. Thus the learned expression: $αυστηρώς$ $ακατάλληλον$ [strictly not appropriate] is replaced by the virtual text [VTEXT="__ancient_phrase__"].
2. The corresponding word or phrase or lemma that is being considered exists between the symbols '\' and '/'.
3. The left part of the expression before the symbol '\' is a set of words, phrases, and other tokens that is useful for expression determination but it is not replaced by the head of the rule.
4. Similarly the right of the expression following the '\'. e.g.
   [LEXY->HasMAttrs([MASC,SING,ACC]),ORTHO>AnyOfOAttrs Style2])]
   and denotes any word having morphological characteristics *(Male, Singular*

Accusative) and belong to a group of words specified by the first letter *[Style2]*. The right side also remains unchanged in case of grammar rules application.

5. The type of rules that lies within the symbols "and", before the left panel. This part is not necessary, but there is in each rule and is used to categorize errors.

The grammar checker rules are banded together in categories: 1. Error rules (`event.wrong`) 2. Warning rules (`gevent.warning`) and 3. Info rules (`gevent.info`).

The error-rules contain the errors that are not accepted by the grammar and therefore should not be present in a text (e.g. the final -*ν*), the warning-rules contain these errors that inform the user for possible error (e.g. homonymous words, wrongly used in corresponding words context). Moreover this rule category informs for the interpretation of the corresponding token and the user either confirms the proper use of the lemma or selects the entry that is suitable. The info-rules describe (a) the stylistic information of a word (e.g. oral type) and (b) foreign words. The user accepts or rejects the lemma, depending on the selected style. He may, earlier, determine the style he prefer to apply selecting the corresponding option.

Each word is defined by a sequence of values surrounded by the symbols '[' and ']'. Thus, the expression `ORTHO->AnyOfOAttrs` (`[WthSmbs]`) defines a condition that must be accepted by the rule and notes that the token's orthography contains one or more symbols (non-alphabetic characters).

The condition `ORTHO->AnyOfOAttrs` (`[NrWrd]`) means that the word must be normal Word (word with letters of the alphabet).

The condition `LEXY->HasMAttrs` (`[ADJ,...,ACC]`) means any entry that has certain morphological attributes (in this case: adjective ... accusative). Respectively may include the condition `LEXY->HasMAttrs([ADJ,...,ACC])` means any entry that has not the certain morphological attributes.

The condition `TTEXT->Match("γκαρσόν")` defines words that have the specific character sequence (capital letters ($ΓΚΑΡΣΟΝ$) or/and small letter ($γκαρσόν/Γκαρσόν$), stressed or unstressed: $γκαρσον$), while the more "strict" form is defined by `[TTEXT=="επιστήμων"]` which includes only the specific type: $επιστήμων$. These rules have the opportunity to define the prefix `[TTEXT->Prefix("εξεφώνησ")]` which includes all the generated words with the prefix "$εξεφώνησ$". Under circumstances the rules define the suffix of any word `TTEXT ->Suffix("ουνα")` which includes all the generated words with the suffix -"$ουνα$". Both cases support additional information by the definition of additional morphosyntactic attributes, to avoid identification of the type with another word with the same suffix and different morphological attributes. Thus, the rule:

`[TTEXT->Suffix("ουνα"), LEXY->HasMAttrs([V, A_P, SING])]`

defines words with suffix and morphosyntactic attributes [Verb,1st person, singular]. The condition `[LEXY->HasLemma3("γράφω")]` defines the specific lemma (all tenses, moods, persons, voices), while for more limited search is used the condition [LEXY->CanMatch("$\psi\eta\lambda\acute{o}\varsigma$",[FEM]) in which is defined only the female of the adjective: $\psi\eta\lambda\acute{o}\varsigma$. These conditions can be additionally determined by agreement conditions [ONTO?=$x:GNC_Agreement(1,[ADJ])] in many levels: Agreement in gender, number and case [ONTO?=$x: GNC_Agreement(1)], Agreement in number and case [ONTO ?= $x: GNC_Agreement(2)], Agreement only in number [ONTO?=$x:GNC_Agreement(3)] or Agreement only in case [ONTO?=$x:GNC_Agreement(4)].

Grammar checker has 4 levels of analysis. This function allows the phrases replacement by VTEXT. The necessity of levels becomes visible in the following analysis problem. Specifically, the particle $\mu\eta\nu$ is not converted into $\mu\eta$ in a specific context (style1: the first letter is κ, π, τ, etc.), while in another context remains (style2: the first letter is β, γ, δ, etc.). This rule does not apply to learned participles still in use in spoken language. In the first level, therefore, when the particle $\mu\eta$ is found in context consisting of learned participle is replaced by a virtual text, the [VTTEXT = "-archaiametochi-"]. Applying this approach, independent of the first letter of the learned participle, the rule concerning the final -ν is not executed. The statement of the rule has the following form:

```
/* GGC_TELIKO_N_remove_n_12 */
{1}
[ARULE="GGC_TELIKO_N_remove_n_12",VTEXT="_learn_par_"] =>
    \

        [LEXY->CanMatch("μη",[PARTICLE])]

    /
    [LEXY->HasMAttrs([LEARNED])]       |
    [LEXY->HasMAttrs([PART, LEARNED])]       ;
```

At the second level, however, the rule applies to all cases that are analyzed. This rule determines as error more specific events e.g. the particle $\mu\eta\nu$ in front of learned participles and therefore is replaced by the particle $\mu\eta$. At the end of this process, there is the final analysis, the dumper. The dumpers transfer the results of processing in detail and extract and record all the features (sentence analyzer, tagger, rules flow, rules) in the appropriate position. Export and analysis files are XML and Apache Lucene (http://lucene.apache.org) All dumpers have a certain common formalism format: {$ info} {analysis (options)} where {} means 0 or more than one items enclosed in {}.

7   Evaluation

In this work an electronic grammar checker presented. The tool can carry out morphological and syntactic analysis of sentences, phrases and words in order to correct syntactic, grammatical and stylistic errors. The grammar checker is supported by the Mnemosyne, the mechanism for the formalization of modern Greek, and by the Greek tagger, which deals with the most significant problems

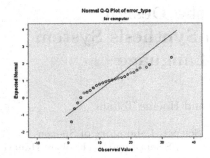

Fig. 1. Human correction

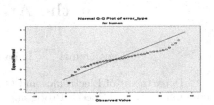

Fig. 2. Grammar checker correction

in natural language processing, the lexical ambiguity. Evaluation procedures showed that the results obtained by the tool are fully comparable with those obtained by a human editor Figs. 1 and 2.

References

1. Boguraev, B., Pustejovsky, J.: The role of knowledge representation in Lexicon design. In: Proceedings of the 13th Conference on Computation Linguistics, Finland, pp. 36–41 (1990)
2. Chomsky, N.: Aspects of the Theory of Syntax. MIT Press, Cambridge (1965)
3. Gakis, P., Panagiotakopoulos, Ch., Sgarbas, K., Tsalidis, Ch.: Design and implementation of an electronic lexicon for modern Greek. Literary Linguist. Comput. 27(2), 155–169 (2012)
4. Gakis, P., Panagiotakopoulos, Ch., Sgarbas, K., Tsalidis, Ch.: Analysis of lexical ambiguity in Modern Greek using a computational lexicon. Literary Linguist. Comput. 27(2), 1–15 (2013)
5. Kermanidou, K.: Learning of syntactic dependencies and the Grammatical development of the Greek Language, Ph.D. thesis, University of Patras (2005)
6. Lyons, J.: Semantics, vol. 2. Cambridge University Press, Cambridge (1977)
7. McCord, M.: Natural Language Processing in Prolog, Knowledge Systems and Prolog. Addison-Wesley, Benjamin (1987)
8. Orphanos, G.: Computational morphosyntactic analysis of Greek, Ph.D. thesis, University of Patras (2000)
9. Orphanos, G., Tsalidis, Ch.: Combining handcrafted and corpus-acquired Lexical knowledge into a Morphosyntactic tagger. In: Proceedings of the 2nd CLUK Research Colloquium, Essex, UK (1999)
10. Pollard, C., Sag, A.: Information-Based Syntax and Semantics, vol. 1. CSLI Publications, Stanford (1987)
11. Savranidis, X.: Teaching language with the support of computer. Sentence analyzer (1998)
12. Triantafyllidis, M.: Modern Greek Grammar, 3rd revised edition. Thessaloniki: Manolis Triantafyllidis Foundation (1991). (in Greek)
13. Van Eijck, J., Jaspars, J.: Ambiguity and reasoning. Technical report CS-R9616. Dutch national research institute for mathematics and computer science (1996)

Contribution to the Design
of an Expressive Speech Synthesis System
for the Arabic Language

Lyes Demri$^{(\boxtimes)}$, Leila Falek, and Hocine Teffahi

Department of Electronics and Computer Science, Laboratory of Spoken
Communication and Speech Processing, University of Science and Technology Houari
Boumediene, El-Alia 32, 16111 Algiers, Algeria
{ldemri1987,lfalek}@hotmail.fr, hteffahi@gmail.com

Abstract. In this paper we will present a contribution to the design
of an expressive speech synthesis system for the Arabic language. The
system uses diphone concatenation as the synthesis method for the
generation of 10 phonetically balanced sentences in Arabic. Rules for
the orthographic-to-phonetic transcription are detailed, as well as the
methodology employed for recording the diphone database. The sentences were synthesized with both "neutral" and "sadness" expressions
and rated by 10 listeners, and the results of the test are provided.

Keywords: Arabic expressive speech synthesis · Diphone concatenation · Voice transformation · Orthographic-phonetic transcription

1 Introduction

Expressive speech synthesis is the synthesis of spoken utterances that contain, in
addition to the semantic information of the uttered text, some emotional information that must provide a new layer of information to the listener. The field
of expressive speech synthesis/recognition is part of the larger field of Affective Computing that aims to develop systems and devices that can recognize,
interpret, process, and simulate human affects [1].

Despite the amount of effort put into the synthesis of expressive speech,
it seems that very few languages have benefited from most of it, i.e. English,
Japanese, Chinese and a few European languages. Arabic, despite being spoken
by a very large proportion of the world population, is one of the languages for
which little work has been done. The first study on Arabic expressive speech
synthesis seems to be the work of Al-Dakkak et al. in 2005 [2,3]. Al-Dakkak
recorded sentences in various emotional states, and analyzed them via a statistical study of the pitch, intensity, and duration (speech rate), in order to extract
rules to be applied to the synthesized speech, e.g. for anger: "F0 mean increases
by 40–75 %, F0 slope increases, intensity mean decreases", and so on. Using these
rules, the authors were able to produce sentences in Anger, Joy, Sadness, Fear

© Springer International Publishing Switzerland 2015
A. Ronzhin et al. (Eds.): SPECOM 2015, LNAI 9319, pp. 178–185, 2015.
DOI: 10.1007/978-3-319-23132-7_22

and Surprise, with acceptable recognition rates. More recently, Al Azmy used a unit selection approach to synthesize 3 expressions (neutral, sad and "question") [4,5]. An Arabic speech database consisting of 10 h of neutral speech and one hour of recordings for 4 different emotions (sadness, happiness, surprise, and "questioning") was recorded. The 10 h of neutral speech were further examined by an automatic emotion recognition system in order to further increase the amount of emotional utterances. The synthesized sentences were then presented both to an automatic emotion recognition classifier (Emovoice) and to human evaluators. The results are average but encouraging.

In this paper, we propose to contribute to the effort of Arabic expressive speech synthesis. We present the methodology employed to create an Arabic text-to-speech system using diphone concatenation. The emotion will be produced by selecting diphones from the corresponding diphone database and copying the prosody of the expressive sentence.

2 System Description

The Arabic text to be synthesized is inputted by the user. It is transformed into a phonetic string via an orthographic-to-phonetic module. This phonetic string is transformed into a list of diphones which is sent to a concatenation module that will use the diphones from a diphone database embedded into the system to produce an audio signal of the synthesized speech. This audio signal lacks prosody, i.e. all syllables have the same duration and pitch. The proper prosody for the synthetic speech therefore has to be applied using a voice transformation module that requires explicit values for the prosody parameters. These values are derived from the analysis of an expressive/emotive speech database. The system thus outputs expressive speech as an audio output signal. This section will detail the development of the various modules described above.

2.1 Orthographic-to-Phonetic Transcription

The first step in the concatenative synthesis of speech is to translate the inputted text into a list of units (diphones in our case). For this study, our focus is the production of expressive speech. We therefore simply created hand-written rules for the orthographic-to-phonetic transcription. All of these rules were created by examining 10 example sentences. Obviously, a lot of examples used for establishing these rules have counter-examples in which the rule should not or must not be applied. The current trend for orthographic-to-phonetic rules is to use statistical training on large amounts of text for a given language and to create CART models [6]. However, we feel it is equally important to try and deduce as many orthographic-to-phonetic transcription rules by hand as possible, as it deepens our understanding of the target language and also has the potential of enhancing the statistical training methods. The steps and rules used for the orthographic-to-phonetic transcription in our study are as follow:

2.1.1 Arabic to Latin Transcription

The inputted text being in Arabic, the first step is merely a transcription of the Arabic symbols into Latin characters. This will make the programming easier for the following steps. For this step, we created a dictionary in which each Unicode value from the inputted text is assigned a latin character, e.g. "a" for the Arabic letter "أ", "b" for the Arabic letter "ب", etc. The latin characters do not necessarily match phonetic symbols, and some Arabic letters may be represented by 2 latin characters, such as "th" for the letter "ث", or when one Unicode Arabic symbol represents 2 phones as in the diacritics "ً", "ٌ" and "ٍ", (respectively transcribed as "èn", "un" and "in").

2.1.2 Removing and Replacing Symbols

Some symbols such as "ْ" (*sukun*) and "ّ" (*shedda*) cannot be transcribed into any particular phone sound because they represent the absence of a phone or the insistence on a consonant. These symbols are represented in the dictionary by their name and later processed according to simple rules, e.g. remove all "*sukuns*" from the string obtained after the Latin transcription, and replace any "*shedda*" by the consonant preceding it. Similar processing is also performed for the symbols "أ", "ؤ" and "ئ" (replaced by "-" (silence stop)), as well as "آ" (replaced by "èè").

2.1.3 Handling "iy" Combinations

In situations where the consonant "ي" is preceded by a *kasra* ("ِ"), but not followed by a vowel (e.g. in the word "كَبِيرٌ", "kèbiirun") the "ي" will not be treated as a diphthong but as a prolongation of the "i" sound. Therefore, whenever this happens, the "y" sound (denoting the diphthong) is simply replaced by another "i".

2.1.4 Handling "è" Vowels

During the Arabic to Latin transcription, every "َ" symbol is simply transcribed as "è" (representing the phonetic sound "ϵ" as in "man"). However depending on the context, the "َ" vowel can be read either as "a" or "ϵ". We therefore have to analyze the location and the context of the "è" symbol and deduce whether it has to be transformed into a "a" sound. In our case the following rules were applied:

- If there are one or more consecutive "è" symbol(s) at the end of a word, except for the Arabic word "وَ" (meaning "and"), transform them into "a". (e.g. "مَنْزِلِهَا", "mènzilihaa").
- If a "è" symbol is located between a "r"(transcription for letter "ر") and a "i", "u", or "-"(or a word boundary), transform it into "a".

2.1.5   Pharyngalized Vowels

The presence of the consonants "ط", "ظ", "ص", or "ض" in a word induce the neighboring vowels to become pharyngalised. Pharyngalised vowels are denoted by the symbols "â", "û" and "î" in our programming scheme. If one of these consonants is located in a word, all the vowels located between the letter and a word boundary or a "-" become pharyngalized.

2.1.6   Handling Spaces and Sandhis

Spaces between words are not necessary when the objective is to produce a phonetic string representing a sentence to be synthesized. All spaces are therefore removed from the string. Furthermore, when a word ends with a vowel and the next one starts with the definite article "èl" , the "è" of the definite article is omitted and the 2 words are simply phonetically fused together.

2.1.7   Handling "èèn", "uun", "iin"

Certain Arabic words end with a long vowel that also have a nunation symbol, such as "وَالِيًا". In these cases, the vowel is not read as a long vowel. In such cases, we therefore remove the first vowel from the end of the word, i.e. "èèn" becomes just "èn".

2.1.8   Separating Phones

It has been mentioned above that certain Unicode Arabic symbols are sometimes transcribed in the dictionary as 2 consecutive phones. This is the case for nunation diacritics "ً", "ٌ" and "ٍ". These are written as "èn", "un", and "in" in the dictionary, but we prefer the phonetic string to be a simple list of phones. These phone combinations are therefore separated as "è" and "n", "u" and "n", and "i" and "n", respectively.

2.1.9   Phrase Boundaries Silences

For better synthesis results, we include silence symbols "-" at the beginning and end of the resulting phonetic string.

These rules were sufficient to produce correct phonetic strings for the 10 example sentences mentioned above. After the phonetic string is obtained, a final step is to convert it into a list of diphones by simply reading each character in the string and the one immediately following it.

2.2   Diphone Database

It is commonly accepted - and also reasonable - that the number of possible diphones for a language is the square of the number of phones for that language; however, many of these diphones do not occur naturally. For this study, more than 149 diphones were necessary to create 10 phonetically balanced sentences. It should be noted here that silence, denoted as "-" in our programming scheme, was treated as a possible phone unit, as this enhances the synthesis results but is also necessary for the synthesis of Arabic.

Two versions of the diphone database were created, one with "neutral" voice quality and the second with a "sad" voice quality. First, a list of necessary diphones was created by simply running the orthographic-to-phonetic algorithm on each sentence and converting the obtained phonetic string into a list of diphones as mentioned above. The diphones were then recorded using a simple headset's omnidirectional microphone with foam on GoldWave®. For each voice quality, the speaker simply uttered all the diphones consecutively with a monotone voice and constant "syllable" rate. In order to keep the background noise level consistent as well as the speech amplitude, all the diphones were recorded in one sitting.

A common approach for the recording of diphones is to include the desired diphone as the middle syllable of a nonsensical word. Our approach was to form a nonsensical word for each consonant (or silence), with each of the Arabic vowel sounds included in that word. For instance, for letter "ب" (Arabic sound "b"), the nonsense word would simply be "babubibɛb", for letter "ت", "tatutitɛt", and so on. All of the syllables are unstressed and the nonsense words are uttered with constant F0, syllable duration and amplitude.

All of the diphones are recorded in an audio file at 16 kHz. This file is then annotated by manually creating a Matlab®MAT-file containing the beginning and ending points of each diphone. These points are chosen so that the transition between the two phones is as close to the center of the diphone as possible. Furthermore, every diphone is 3200 samples wide.

2.3   Diphone Concatenation

With the orthographic-to-phonetic transcription and the diphone database in place, the system can already take in Arabic text as input from the user and as long as all necessary diphones are present and annotated in the diphone database, it will concatenate the diphones into a monotone audio output signal, where all syllables have the same duration and fundamental frequency. For good quality concatenation, however, it is not sufficient to simply concatenate the diphone waveforms without some processing. To ensure good quality concatenation between 2 consecutive units, the cross-correlation is computed between the end of the first diphone and the beginning of the following diphone. The 2 diphones are then concatenated at the point where the cross correlation is at its peak value, and after multiplying the ending of the first diphone by a decreasing ramp function, and the beginning of the following diphone by an increasing ramp function. This method is explained in [7] and allows the diphone concatenation to be much more smooth and natural sounding.

2.4   Voice Transformation

Last but not least in concatenative synthesis is the transformation of the monotone voice produced by the concatenation system into a sentence with the desired prosodic features. This step is typically performed by using machine learning techniques for the prediction of prosodic events that might be described or categorized in a given framework, such as the famous ToBI (Tones and Break Indices) labels [8]. Examples of this approach can be found in [9,10].

It is also possible to try and create rules for prosodic events manually; the Arabic rules for the stressing of syllables, for instance, seem pretty straightforward, as suggested in [11,12].

For this study, this step was done manually by copying the desired prosody from a recorded version of the sentence. The durations and F0 contours were copied as accurately as possible via the PSOLA algorithm using Praat. Four versions of the sentences were created:

- Neutral prosody + neutral voice quality
- Neutral prosody + sad voice quality
- Sad prosody + neutral voice quality
- Sad prosody + sad voice quality

The reason for doing this was to evaluate the naturalness of each of the versions of the sentences. It was expected that the "Neutral Prosody + neutral voice quality" and "Sad prosody + sad voice quality" would be the most natural. We also wanted to compare the relative importance of the voice quality and the pitch, as there is still a lack of consensus about this question in the literature.

3   Experiments and Results

As described above, 4 sets of 10 sentences were synthesized by combining 2 types of prosodic style with 2 types of voice quality. The resulting sentences were uploaded on a website and evaluated by 10 listeners that were asked to rate the naturalness and the expressivity of the speech signals on scales from 1 to 5. For the degree of expressivity (sadness), 1 corresponds to a completely neutral utterance and 5 to a completely sad utterance. For the rating of naturalness, 1 is a very robotic and unnatural voice, and 5 is a very "human" and natural voice. The results are summarized by Tables 1 and 2.

Table 1. Mean expressivity ratings for the various combinations of speech parameters.

Expressivity	Neutral Prosody	Sad Prosody
Neutral V.Q	1.49	2.15
Sad V.Q	2.88	4

Table 1 shows that the expressivity is better recognized when the voice quality matches the prosody. The ratings are closer to 1 when the neutral prosody is used in conjunction with a neutral voice quality, and they are closer to 5 when the

Table 2. Mean naturalness ratings for the various combinations of speech parameters.

Naturalness	Neutral Prosody	Sad Prosody
Neutral V.Q	3.83	3.19
Sad V.Q	3.25	3.06

sad prosody is used in conjunction with a sad voice quality. The ratings for the combinations "sad prosody + neutral V.Q." and "neutral prosody + sad V.Q." are in between these two mean ratings, which was predictable. However, it seems that voice quality plays a slightly more important role in conveying "sadness" than prosody, as the mean for "sad V.Q. + neutral prosody" is slightly closer to 5 than the "neutral V.Q. + sad prosody" combination. This is in agreement with previous studies such as [13].

Regarding naturalness (Table 2), the mean ratings are close to each other, with "Neutral prosody + neutral V.Q" being the most natural utterance and "Sad prosody + sad V.Q." being the least natural. This might be because the production of sadness required more processing during the transformation phase using Praat.

4   Conclusion and Future Works

This modest contribution can evidently be improved on many aspects. First, the orthographic-to-phonetic transcription works for the 10 selected sentences, however it should be able to produce correct phonetic strings for any inputted Arabic text. This is not a simple task. Therefore, the use of statistical training methods might be implemented for this task in future works, even though we find it interesting to simultaneously study the Arabic language for the establishment of more general hand-written rules.

A second way of improving this work is to record diphones for more types of expressive speech, such as anger, happiness, surprise, etc. Before doing this it would be worthwhile to reflect on the usability of certain diphones for more than one type of emotional speech, e.g. is it necessary to record diphones for surprise when the diphones for fear might already possess the required voice quality?

Another idea to improve the naturalness of the synthesized speech would be to record each diphone at multiple fundamental frequencies in order to minimize the use of the PSOLA algorithm. A similar idea can be applied for the diphone durations.

The biggest challenge at the moment is to predict the prosody in an automatic way. However, we are encouraged by the presented results as the synthesized speech sounds natural enough, and we will therefore look for ways to solve the issues discussed here in future works. We will also investigate on the ways to achieve various degrees of expressivity using the diphone synthesis method.

References

1. Picard, R.W.: Affective Computing, MIT Media Laboratory Perceptual Computing Section Technical report no. 321 (1995)
2. Al-Dakkak, O., Ghneim, N., Zliekha, M.A., Al-Moubayed, S.: Prosodic feature introduction and emotion incorporation in an arabic TTS. In: 2nd Information and Communication Technologies, ICTTA 2006, vol. 1, pp. 1317–1322. IEEE (2006)
3. Al-Dakkak, O., Ghneim, N., Zliekha, M.A., Al-Moubayed, S.: Emotion inclusion in an arabic text-to speech. In: 13th European Signal Processing Conference (2005)
4. Azmy, W.M., Abdou, S., Shoman, M.: Arabic unit selection emotional speech synthesis using blending data approach. Int. J. Comput. Appl. **81**(8), 22–28 (2013)
5. Azmy, W.M., Abdou, S., Shoman, M.: The creation of emotional effects for an arabic speech synthesis system. In: The Egyptian Society of Language Engineering, International Workshop, ESOLE 2013 (2013)
6. Black, A.W., Lenzo, K.A.: Building synthetic voices. Language Technologies Institute, Carnegie Mellon University and Cepstral LLC (2003)
7. Dutilleux, P., De Poli, G., Zlözer, U.: In: Zölzer, U. (ed.) DAFX - Digital Audio Effects, pp. 208–211. Wiley, Sussex (2002)
8. Silverman, K.E., Beckman, M.E., Pitrelli, J.F., Ostendorf, M., Wightman, C.W., Price, P., Hirschberg, J.: TOBI: a standard for labeling English prosody. In: ICSLP, vol. 2, pp. 867–870 (1992)
9. Xydas, G., Spiliotopoulos, D., Kouroupetroglou, G.: Prosody prediction from linguistically enriched documents based on a machine learning approach. In: Proceedings of the 6th International Conference of Greek Linguistics (2003)
10. Qian, Y., Wu, Z., Ma, X., Soong, F.: Automatic prosody prediction and detection with Conditional Random Field (CRF) models. In: 7th International Symposium on Chinese Spoken Language Processing (ISCSLP), pp. 135–138. IEEE (2010)
11. Assaf, M.: A Prototype of an Arabic Diphone Speech Synthesizer in Festival. Master thesis, Uppsala University (2005)
12. Youssef, A., Emam, O.: An arabic TTS system based on the IBM trainable speech synthesizer. Autom. Process. Arab. EHD T-ALN **2**, 1921 (2004)
13. Grichkovtsova, I., Lacheret, A., Morel, M.: The role of intonation and voice quality in the affective speech perception. In: Interspeech, pp. 2245–2248 (2007)

Deep Neural Network Based Continuous Speech Recognition for Serbian Using the Kaldi Toolkit

Branislav Popović$^{(\boxtimes)}$, Stevan Ostrogonac, Edvin Pakoci, Nikša Jakovljević, and Vlado Delić

Faculty of Technical Sciences, University of Novi Sad, Novi Sad, Serbia
bpopovic@uns.ac.rs

Abstract. This paper presents a deep neural network (DNN) based large vocabulary continuous speech recognition (LVCSR) system for Serbian, developed using the open-source Kaldi speech recognition toolkit. The DNNs are initialized using stacked restricted Boltzmann machines (RBMs) and trained using cross-entropy as the objective function and the standard error backpropagation procedure in order to provide posterior probability estimates for the hidden Markov model (HMM) states. Emission densities of HMM states are represented as Gaussian mixture models (GMMs). The recipes were modified based on the particularities of the Serbian language in order to achieve the optimal results. A corpus of approximately 90 hours of speech (21000 utterances) is used for the training. The performances are compared for two different sets of utterances between the baseline GMM-HMM algorithm and various DNN settings.

Keywords: Kaldi speech recognition toolkit · Continuous speech recognition · Deep neural networks · Serbian

1 Introduction

During the last decade, a number of speech and language resources, mathematical models, expert and machine learning systems for the Serbian language have been created [1]. Serbian belongs to the group of highly inflective languages. Words are modified in order to express a wide range of grammatical categories, e.g., person, number, gender, tense and case, resulting in extremely large vocabularies. The only CSR system for Serbian was GMM-HMM based, i.e., HMM states were represented as GMMs, and each Gaussian was represented by a mean vector and a diagonal covariance matrix. Tree based clustering (TBC) algorithm was used in order to train the acoustic models [2]. The language model was a combination of 3 N-gram models (based on tokens, lemmas and class N-grams). However, the performances of such an approach were poor for a large vocabulary continuous speech recognition task [3].

Kaldi is an open-source speech recognition toolkit written in C++ [4]. It incorporates OpenFst for the finite-state transducers (FST) framework [5]

© Springer International Publishing Switzerland 2015
A. Ronzhin et al. (Eds.): SPECOM 2015, LNAI 9319, pp. 186–192, 2015.
DOI: 10.1007/978-3-319-23132-7_23

and an extensive linear algebra support through a matrix library that wraps the standard BLAS [6] and LAPACK [7] routines. The complete, flexible and clearly structured recipes for the development of speech recognition systems are provided. Commonly used feature extraction approaches, such as cepstral mean and variance normalization, vocal tract length normalization (VTLN), linear discriminant analysis (LDA), maximum likelihood linear transform (MLLT), and others are supported. Model adaptation, i.e. maximum likelihood linear regression (MLLR), as well as feature space adaptation, i.e. constrained MLLR, are provided. Hidden Markov model (HMM) topology can be specified separately for each context-independent phone. Decision-tree roots can be shared among the phones and among the individual states of phones. Consequently, Kaldi was selected among other speech recognition candidates for the development of a LVCSR system for the Serbian language [8].

The paper presents a set of experiments on the DNN based LVCSR system for the Serbian language, developed using the Karel's DNN Kaldi setup [9]. The DNNs are used to provide pseudo-likelihoods for the HMM states, represented as GMMs. The RBMs are employed in a pre-training phase. The DNNs are trained to classify the individual frames based on a cross-entropy criterion. The results are compared to the baseline GMM-HMM Kaldi algorithm, on a train set of about 90 hours of speech, using 2 different test sets. The recipes are modified in order to address the particularities of the Serbian language.

The paper is organized as follows. In Sect. 2, the baseline GMM-HMM recipe is described. In Sect. 3, different DNN settings are provided. Section presents the results of our experiments. In Section, the conclusions are provided, based on the considerations from the previous sections.

2   GMM-HMM Recipe

Baseline GMM-HMM systems are trained on 13 Mel-frequency cepstral coefficients (MFCC), calculated by using a filter-bank of 22 overlapping triangular windows, along with the normalized energy and their first and second order derivatives. The feature vectors were extracted on 30 ms frames, with 10 ms frame shift. The recipe starts with the training of monophone models on a subset of 1000 utterances from the training set, using flat start and 40 iterations. The total number of Gaussians was set to 1000, and it was increased during the first 30 iterations. After the monophone training, 2 triphone training steps were performed, using 35 iterations and the alignments from the previous steps. The first triphone pass comprises 1800 regression tree leaves and 9000 Gaussians. The second triphone pass comprises 3000 regression tree leaves and 25000 Gaussians. The number of Gaussians was increased during the first 25 iterations. Maximum mutual information (MMI), as well as boosted MMI [10], were applied on top of the second triphone pass, using 3 or 4 iterations. This was the optimal configuration among all tested configurations for the given training database [8]. Several additional steps, i.e., LDA, MLLT, minimum phone error (MPE, [11]), speaker adaptive training (SAT, [12]), subspace Gaussian mixture models (SGMM, [13]), and different combinations of the above mentioned transforms, were removed from the original recipe, bearing in mind the fact that these steps were very time consuming and have not resulted in any noticeable improvements.

3   DNN Recipe

The DNNs are trained using the modified Karel's setup [9] on a single CUDA GPU (GeForce GTX 980). The training is completed in two separate phases. During the first pre-training phase, the RBMs are trained in a greedy layerwise fashion using the Contrastive Divergence algorithm with 1-step of Markov chain Monte Carlo sampling [14] and the same kind of features that were already used for the GMM-HMM recipe (13 MFCCs, the energy and their first and second order derivatives). The first RBM has Gaussian-Bernoulli units and it was trained with an initial learning rate of 0.01. The other RBMs have Bernoulli-Bernoulli units and they were trained with a learning rate of 0.4. The training was unsupervised, the number of iterations was set to 3, the number of hidden layers to 6 and the number of units per layer to 2048.

During the second phase, the DNNs are trained using 90 % of the training data for training and the remaining 10 % for evaluation. The stacked RBMs from the previous phase are used to initialize the DNNs, and a cross-entropy criterion is applied to classify individual frames into triphone-states. The optimization is conducted using the standard error backpropagation procedure, by mini-batch stochastic gradient descent (SGD). In order to prevent over-fitting, the objective function is measured on the cross-validation set and early stopping criterion is provided. The cross-entropy between the distribution represented by the reference labels and the predicted distribution is defined as:

$$\mathcal{F}_{CE} = \sum_{u=1}^{U} \sum_{t=1}^{T_u} \log y_{ut}(s_{ut}) \tag{1}$$

where s_{ut} is the reference state label for utterance u at time t and $y(s)$ is the output of the DNN for the HMM state s. The gradients are calculated in a back-propagation procedure with respect to the activations at the output layer corresponding to state s, $a_{ut}(s)$:

$$\frac{\partial \mathcal{F}_{CE}}{\partial a_{ut}(s)} = -\frac{\partial \log y_{ut}(s_{ut})}{\partial a_{ut}(s)}. \tag{2}$$

Sigmoid hidden units and Softmax output units were used. The initial learning rate was set to 0.008, and the minibatch size to 256. The input to the network was an 11 frame context window (the current frame and 5 frames on each side of the current frame). Each hidden layer had 1024 neurons and the number of hidden layers varied between 0 and 4.

4 Data Preparation

The database consists of various kinds of personal advertisements, spoken over the public telephone line, sampled at 8000 Hz, 16 bits per sample, mono PCM. The training database contains about 90 hours of speech (about 21000 utterances). The testing database (T1) contains about 5 hours of speech (more than 1000 utterances). Silence and noise marks were removed from the test transcriptions prior to determination of the word error rate (WER). The test vocabulary consists of about 14000 words. The results were confirmed by using about 1000 utterances (1.5 hours) from another SpeechDat database (T2). Silence and both types of noises, i.e., spoken and non-spoken noise, were replaced by !SIL, meaning that they share the same language model. Damaged words were replaced by a sequence of !SILs. The number of consecutive !SIL marks was determined depending of the number of phones from the original damaged word.

ARPA language model was used for both DB1 and DB2 experiments. The grammar was created by converting the appropriate language model into the weighted finite state transducer (an acceptor) [5]. The language model used for the experiments with DB1 was based on trigrams. It was built based on the training database (450000 tokens, personal advertisements, so the number of word forms was limited), and additional 270000 sentences from the Serbian journalistic corpus (6300000 tokens, consists of newspaper articles, books etc.), using the SRILM toolkit [15] and the Kneser-Ney smoothing method [16], without pruning. In case of DB2, the language model was used to verify the efficiency of the trained acoustic models for the GMM-HMM and DNN respectively. Therefore, a zero-probability unigram language model was employed.

The pronunciation dictionary contains more than 22000 words, including words from both training and testing sets and words from the Serbian journalistic corpus included in the language model. The aim was to compare the acoustic models for GMM-HMM and DNN approach. Therefore, we removed out-of-vocabulary words, although we were aware of the fact that the results would be optimistic. The number of words in the test set was several times smaller than 22000, so there were a lot of impostors. Vowels and their stressed versions share the same tree root. This was done in order to provide a robust estimation in case of lack of data. 3-state left-to-right topology is used to represent non-silence phones. Silence phones are represented by 5 emitting states and the morphology is somewhat more complex, i.e., it contains initial emitting state, 3 emitting states in the middle and an ending emitting state. Position dependency marks were used to designate different positions of the phones (_B for the phones at the beginning of a word, _E for the phones at the end of a word, _I for word-internal phones, and _S for singletons). The decision tree was built according to more than 200 manually created questions, according to the acoustic similarity between the phones and the particularities of the Serbian phonology.

5   Experimental Results

In Fig. 1, the results are presented in terms of the word error rate (WER) for the GMM-HMM recipe. The results are labeled in the following way: training of monophone models (mono), the first (tri1) and the second (tri1) triphone pass, the MMI (mmi) and boosted MMI (mmi_b) step. The best result was 2.19 % WER for 3 iterations of boosted MMI step, with boosting factor set to 0.05.

In Fig. 2, the results are given for DNN configurations, using 0 to 4 hidden layers. The optimal result of 1.86 % WER was obtained for 3 hidden layers, and it was an improvement compared to the boosted MMI step.

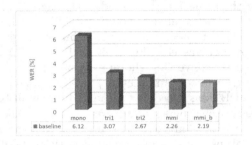

Fig. 1. GMM-HMM recipes, test set T1

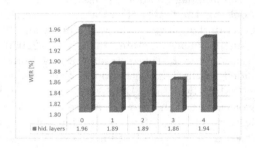

Fig. 2. DNN per number of hidden layers, test set T1

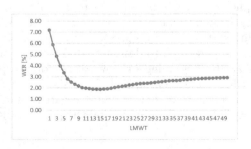

Fig. 3. DNN with 3 hidden layers per LMWT, test set T1

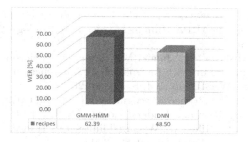

Fig. 4. DNN vs. GMM-HMM, test set T2

Figure 3 shows the results for the DNN with 3 hidden layers versus the language model weight (LMWT). The optimal result is obtained for the LMWT factor set to 15.

In Fig. 4, the results are presented for the GMM-HMM recipe (boosted MMI step) versus the DNN with 3 hidden layers for the second testing set (T2), using zero-probability unigram language model. Even with such language model, a notable improvement over the baseline algorithm is obtained (48.50 % for the DNN vs. 62.39 % WER for the GMM-HMM).

6   Conclusion

Based on the results from the previous section, for any number of hidden layers, DNN recipes provide an improvement over the baseline GMM-HMM setup. In both cases, we used 13 MFCCs, calculated by using a filter-bank of 22 overlapping triangular windows, normalized energy, and their first and second order derivatives. These were the "optimal" parameters for our training set, for the GMM-HMM case. The results were additionally confirmed on a separate test database, using a zero-probability unigram language model, in order to test the applicability of the trained acoustic models between the GMM-HMM and the DNN recipes. In both test cases, a noticeable improvement was obtained using the DNN over the baseline GMM-HMM algorithm.

Acknowledgments. The work described in this paper was supported in part by the Ministry of Education, Science and Technological Development of the Republic of Serbia, within the project TR32035: "Development of Dialogue Systems for Serbian and Other South Slavic Languages".

References

1. Delić, V., Sečujski, M., Jakovljević, N., Pekar, D., Mišković, D., Popović, B., Ostrogonac, S., Bojanić, M., Knežević, D.: Speech and language resources within speech recognition and synthesis systems for Serbian and kindred south slavic languages. In: Železný, M., Habernal, I., Ronzhin, A. (eds.) SPECOM 2013. LNCS, vol. 8113, pp. 319–326. Springer, Heidelberg (2013)

2. Young, S.J., Odell, J., Woodland, P.C.: Tree-based state tying for high accuracy acoustic modelling. In: ARPA Human Language Technology Workshop, pp. 307–312, Princeton (1994)
3. Jakovljević, N., Mišković, D., Janev, M., Pekar, D.: A decoder for large vocabulary speech recognition. In: 18th International Conference on Systems, Signals and Image Processing, IWSSIP, pp. 1–4, Sarajevo (2011)
4. Povey, D., et al.: The Kaldi speech recognition toolkit. In: IEEE Workshop on Automatic Speech Recognition and Understanding, ASRU, pp. 1–4, Waikoloa (2011)
5. Mohri, M., Pereira, F., Riley, M.: Weighted finite-state transducers in speech recognition. Comput. Speech Lang. **16**, 69–88 (2002)
6. Blackford, L.S., et al.: An updated set of basic linear algebra subprograms (BLAS). ACM Trans. Math. Softw. **28**(2), 135–151 (2002)
7. Anderson, E., et al.: LAPACK Users' Guide. Society for Industrial and Applied Mathematics (SIAM), Philadelphia (1999)
8. Popović, B., Pakoci, E., Ostrogonac, S., Pekar, D.: Large vocabulary continuous speech recognition for Serbian using the Kaldi toolkit. In: 10th Digital Speech and Image Processing, DOGS, pp. 31–34, Novi Sad (2014)
9. Veselý, K., Arnab, G., Lukáš, B., Povey, D.: Sequence-discriminative training of deep neural networks. In: International Speech Communication Association, Interspeech 2013, pp. 2345–2349, Lyon (2013)
10. Povey, D., Kanevsky, D., Kingsbury, B., Ramabhadran, B., Saon, G., Visweswariah, K.: Boosted MMI for model and feature-space discriminative training. In: 33rd International Conference on Acoustics, Speech and Signal Processing, ICASSP, pp. 4057–4060, Las Vegas (2008)
11. Povey D., Woodland, P.C.: Minimum phone error and i-smoothing for improved discriminative training. In: 27th International Conference on Acoustics, Speech and Signal Processing, ICASSP, pp. I-105–I-108, Orlando (2002)
12. Povey, D., Kuo, H-K.J., Soltau, H.: Fast speaker adaptive training for speech recognition. In: 9th Annual Conference of the International Speech Communication Association, INTERSPEECH, pp. 1245–1248, Brisbane (2008)
13. Povey, D., et al.: The subspace Gaussian mixture model - a structured model for speech recognition. Comput. Speech Lang. **25**, 404–439 (2011)
14. Carreira-Perpiñán, M., Hinton, G.: On contrastive divergence learning. In: 10th International Workshop on Artifitial Intelligence and Statistic, AISTATS, pp. 59–66, Barbados (2005)
15. Stolcke, A., Zheng, J., Wang, W., Abrash, V.: SRILM at sixteen: update and outlook. In: IEEE Workshop on Automatic Speech Recognition and Understanding, ASRU, Waikoloa (2011)
16. Kneser, R., Ney, H.: Improved backing-off for M-gram language modeling. In: 20th International Conference on Acoustics, Speech and Signal Processing, ICASSP, pp. 181–184, Detroit (1995)

DNN-Based Speech Synthesis: Importance of Input Features and Training Data

Alexandros Lazaridis$^{(\boxtimes)}$, Blaise Potard, and Philip N. Garner

Idiap Research Institute, Martigny, Switzerland
{alaza,blaise.potard,phil.garner}@idiap.ch

Abstract. Deep neural networks (DNNs) have been recently introduced in speech synthesis. In this paper, an investigation on the importance of input features and training data on speaker dependent (SD) DNN-based speech synthesis is presented. Various aspects of the training procedure of DNNs are investigated in this work. Additionally, several training sets of different size (i.e., 13.5, 3.6 and 1.5 h of speech) are evaluated.

Keywords: Text-to-speech synthesis · Statistical parametric synthesis · Deep neural networks · Hidden markov models

1 Introduction

Much of the text-to-speech (TTS) work at Idiap is in the context of speech-to-speech translation (S2ST). To this end, good quality speech recognition and synthesis are prerequisites. Further, the translation scenario requires both technologies to exist in multiple languages. Data can be scarce for some languages.

Hidden Markov model (HMM)-based TTS approaches have become dominant in TTS for S2ST, mainly due to their adaptation abilities and flexibility in changing voice characteristics (e.g. speaker, speaking style, emotional state, etc.), using a relatively small amount of data [10], occasionally outperforming even unit-selection approaches [13]. Nonetheless, various limitations and drawbacks occur in HMM-based TTS as listed in the work of Zen et al. [12].

Trying to address some of these deficiencies, deep neural networks (DNNs) have been introduced in speech synthesis over the last few years, outperforming HMM-based TTS approaches, such as Zen et al. [12] using 33k sentences of speech for training and Qian et al. [7] where a more modest database of approximately 5k sentences (approx. 5 h) was used. In an attempt to use an even smaller database, Lu et al. [5], used a training set of 1k sentences in a framework combining Vector Space Representation (VSR) [8] and DNN modelling without managing to outperform the HMM-based one. It seems that there is a data threshold below which HMMs are superior to DNNs.

In the following sections, we describe experiments aimed at evaluating whether recent DNN technology described above could be beneficial in our S2ST scenario. The main focus is on the amount of training data. We hypothesize that although the DNNs will clearly show their superiority over the HMMs when the

© Springer International Publishing Switzerland 2015
A. Ronzhin et al. (Eds.): SPECOM 2015, LNAI 9319, pp. 193–200, 2015.
DOI: 10.1007/978-3-319-23132-7_24

amount of training data is relatively large (i.e. more that 5 or 10 h of speech), this might not be the case when relatively small amount of data (i.e. approximately 1 h of speech) is used. Moreover, other aspects of the training procedure such as model order in terms of layers and nodes per layer, along with positional information in the input layer are also examined.

2 Framework

A DNN is a feed-forward artificial neural network with multiple hidden layers between the input and output layer, creating a mapping function between the input (i.e. linguistic features) vector and the output (i.e. acoustic features) vector. In the training phase, the input text is processed and transformed into labels, which contain linguistic features in an appropriate format for training the DNNs, i.e., containing binary and numerical features. Back-propagation is used for training the DNN using the input and output data.

In the synthesis phase, the input text is processed by the same front-end as in the training phase, creating the input vectors and the trained DNN is used in a forward-propagation manner for mapping them to output vectors. Consequently the acoustic features are created using maximum likelihood parameter generation (MLPG) trajectory smoothing [11] and finally, a vocoder is used for synthesizing the final waveform.

2.1 Database and Input/Output Features

For the experiments the blizzard-challenge-2011 [4] database was used. The speaker is known as "Nancy" and is a US English native female speaker. The database consists of 16.6 h of data, comprising around 12k utterances. The audio was re-sampled to a sampling frequency of 16 kHz for these experiments.

For the training of the DNNs, three different sizes of the *training* set were implemented, i.e. *T13.5*: 13.5 h (10k sentences), *T3.6*: 3.6 h (2.6k sentences) and *T1.5*: 1.5 h (1.1k sentences). The *development* set and the *evaluation* set consisted of 1.35 h (1k sentences) and 0.4 h (0.3k sentences) of speech respectively.

The text corresponding to each audio file has to be converted into a sequence of labels suitable for HMM and DNN training. A conventional and freely available TTS front-end was used for this [1].

The text is turned into a sequence of labels, which contain segmental information and rich contextual parameters such as lexical stress and relative position within syllables, phrases or sentences. The standard *"full"* labels generated by the scripts, i.e. quinphone segmental information, and a large number of categorical, numeric, or binary linguistic and prosodic information, was used [13]. These labels were aligned with the speech signal through a phone-based forced alignment procedure, using the Kaldi toolkit [6]. The models for the alignment were trained on the training plus development sets, and state-level labels force-aligned to acoustic frame boundaries were generated for the training, development and evaluation sets.

Concerning the output features, the STRAIGHT [13] vocoder was used for the acoustic analysis and feature extraction, essentially using the default settings from the EMIME [9] scripts: 5ms sampling step, STRAIGHT Mel-cepstral analysis with 40 coefficients, single f0 value, and 21 coefficients for band aperiodic energy, extracted by the STRAIGHT vocoder. For each acoustic feature, derivatives of first and second order are added. The overall acoustic vector dimension is 186.

2.2   DNN Setup

A slightly modified version of the Kaldi toolkit for the DNN training was used. An automatic procedure was used to convert the labels into numeric values: the categorical data (such as segmental information) was turned into arrays of binary values, while the numerical and binary data was preserved.

Since training requires a frame-level mapping between input labels and acoustic features, the segment-based labels have to be sampled so that we have an input label per acoustic frame. Based on this fact, various implementations were evaluated. Additionally, we hypothesize that the information concerning the input features included in the questions, which are used during the HMM-based TTS training procedure for building the decision tree [13] could be beneficial for training the DNNs. Based on this hypothesis, several sets of binary features were extracted from the questions. The different implementations are the following:

- **DNN$_{ba}$**: "baseline" DNN system trained using only the states within the phone in the input features, along with the standard "*full*" labels (i.e. a total of 424 input features).
- **DNN$_{mp}$**: "multi-pos" DNN system trained using the state position within the phone as categorical data, plus using two position features, i.e. numeric values corresponding to the frame position within the current state, and to the frame position within the current segment, plus the standard "*full*" labels (i.e. a total of 431 input features).
- **DNN$_{mpq}$**: "multi-pos plus phonological questions" DNN system trained using the previous implementation plus some additional phonological information for the current phone extracted based on the questions used in the HMM-based system (i.e. a total of 519 input features).

In some preliminary experiments other implementations of the input feature sets, adding more information extracted based on the question set, were investigated without being beneficial for the DNN-based system after all.

The DNNs were built implementing various combinations of the number of hidden layers (i.e. from 3 to 6 hidden layers), and nodes (i.e. 700, 1000, 1500 and 2000 nodes) in each layer. Each layer comprised an affine component followed by a sigmoid activation function. The input (label) data was further normalized for each component to be of zero mean and unit variance. The output (acoustic) data was normalized globally so that each component had values between 0.01 and 0.99; the output activation function was a sigmoid.

Unlike other approaches (such as Zen [12] or Qian [7]), we did not remove silent frames from the training. The training procedure was standard: we used a stochastic gradient descent based on back propagation. The minimisation criterion was the Mean Square Error (MSE). The training was run on the *training* set, and we used the *development* set for cross-validation.

2.3 HMM Setup

For comparison with state-of-the-art parametric systems, HMM-based synthesis models were built using the HTS v.2.1 toolkit [2]. More specifically, an implementation from the EMIME project [9], freely available online, was employed. We used standard five-state left-to-right Hidden Semi-Markov Models (HSMM), with no-skip.

2.4 Synthesis

The aligned label files from the evaluation set were used for synthesis. In the case of DNN-based synthesis, state-level alignments were used, while in the case of HTS, the alignment was only enforced up to the phone level. In the case of the DNN, synthesis was performed doing a forward pass through the network, followed by acoustic trajectory smoothing [2], through applying the "mlpg" tool from SPTK [3] and global variance computed on each acoustic component. This was followed by resynthesis using the STRAIGHT vocoder. For the HTS system, resynthesis is performed using "HMGenS" with global variance information, followed by STRAIGHT synthesis.

3 Results

In the following subsections, the objective evaluation on the different implementations of the input features and the various sizes of training sets used for training the DNN- and HMM-based systems, as described in the previous section, are presented, along with the subjective evaluation.

3.1 Objective Evaluation

In Fig. 1, the Mel-cepstral distortion (MCD) in dB and the F0 in root mean square error (RMSE) results on the evaluation set, for the different parameters concerning the number of hidden layers (i.e., 3, 4, 5 and 6) and the number of nodes per layer (i.e., 700, 1000, 1500 and 2000), using the full training set (T13.5), for the three DNN-based systems (i.e., DNN_{ba}, DNN_{mp}, DNN_{mpq}) can be seen. In all of the three systems both the MCD error and the RMSE of the F0 are decreasing with the increase of the number of nodes used. Concerning the DNN_{ba} system, the best performance in respect to both MCD error and RMSE, is achieved by the 4-hidden layers and 2000 nodes per layer implementation. The same trend can be seen in the case of the DNN_{mpq} system, while in DNN_{mp}

case, the best performance is achieve by the 5-hidden layers and 2000 nodes per layer implementation. In respect to the three systems, the DNN_{ba} managed to model F0 more accurate followed by the DNN_{mp} one, while in respect to the MCD error, the DNN_{mpq} slightly outperformed and DNN_{mp} one, followed by the DNN_{ba} one.

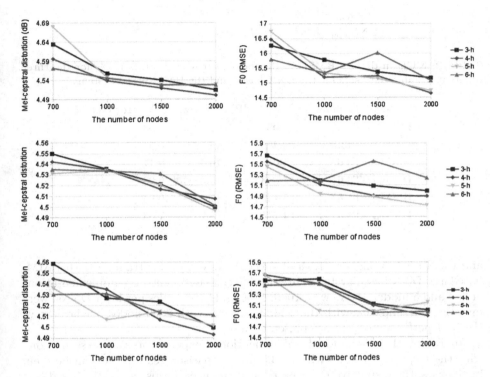

Fig. 1. MCD error in dB and RMSE of F0 in Hz, for the baseline DNN_{ba} (top), multi-pos DNN_{mp} (middle) and multi-pos plus phonological questions features DNN_{mpq} (bottom) systems (trained on T13.5 set), on evaluation set.

In Table 1 the results for the HMM-based system are presented. For comparison reasons, the results for three DNN-based systems are shown again. Along with the MCD error and the RMSE of the F0, the unvoiced/voiced (U/V) error, in percentage, is presented. As can be seen, all DNN-based systems outperform the HMM-based one, achieving around 11 % relative improvement (i.e., reduction) in MCD error, 8–9 % relative improvement (i.e., reduction) in RMSE of the F0 and 30–32 % relative improvement (i.e., reduction) in U/V error.

Based on the aforementioned objective results and an informal subjective one, the DNN_{mp} implementation was chosen for the second part of the experiments. For this, different size of training sets, i.e. the T3.6 training set (3.6 h of speech)

Table 1. MCD in dB, F0 RMSE in Hz and U/V decision errors in %, for the three DNN-based implementations and the HMM-based system (trained on T13.5 set).

System	MCD (dB)	F0 (Hz)	U/V error (%)
HMM	5.052	16.14	9.33
DNN$_{ba}$	4.501	14.65	6.39
DNN$_{mp}$	4.496	14.72	6.54
DNN$_{mpq}$	4.493	14.89	6.38

Table 2. MCD in dB, F0 RMSE in Hz and U/V decision errors in %, for the three different training data sets for the DNN-based and the HMM-based systems.

System	Training set	MCD (dB)	F0 (Hz)	U/V error (%)
HMM	T13.5	5.052	16.14	9.33
DNN$_{mp}$	T13.5	4.496	14.72	6.54
HMM	T3.6	5.089	16.94	9.17
DNN$_{mp}$	T3.6	4.563	16.58	6.98
HMM	T1.5	5.166	17.53	10.64
DNN$_{mp}$	T1.5	4.741	18.72	7.53

and the T1.5 training set (1.5 h of speech), were used for training both HMM-based and DNN-based systems. In some initial experiments, the implementations of 3, 4 and 5 hidden layers with 1000, 1500 and 2000 nodes per layer DNNs, were investigated. The case with the 4 hidden layers with 2000 nodes per layer gave the best performance and are presented next.

In Table 2 the results for the aforementioned experiments can be seen, along with the respective results with T13.5 for comparison reasons. As can be seen, in all cases, the respective DNN-based system outperforms the HMM-based corresponding one in terms of MCD error and U/V error. In respect to RMSE of the F0, only in the case of T1.5, the DNN-based system cannot manage to outperform the HMM-based one.

It should be mentioned here, that various implementations of pre-training were investigated. The deep belief network (DBN) framework [7] was used, trained on different size training sets and with or without splicing features along several frames, but none of them managed to help improve the DNN-based systems compared to the corresponding ones without pre-training.

3.2   Subjective Evaluation

In order to verify the objective evaluation results, a subjective preference listening (ABX) test was conducted. The subjective test was composed of two parts. In the first one, the listeners were asked to state their preference – in terms of the naturalness of the speech – between the DNN- and the HMM-based system, in respect to the three different training sets (i.e., T13.5, T3.6 and T1.5). In the second part, they were asked to compare each one of the three DNN-based systems (i.e., T13.5, T3.6 and T1.5) in respect to the other two. In the ABX preference test, for each sample, there were 5 preference choices: (1) the first sample sounds much closer to the reference, (2) the first sample sounds a bit closer to the reference, (3) no sample is significantly better than the other, (4) the second sample sounds a bit closer to the reference, (5) the second sample sounds much closer to the reference. Two sets of 7 samples were randomly selected from the evaluation set, and 11 and 19 listeners respectively, participated in the tests. In Table 3 the ABX results concerning the first part of the subjective test, are presented. As can be seen, in all three cases, the DNN-based systems clearly outperform the HMM-based ones.

Table 3. ABX preference test results (%) comparing the DNN-based system with the corresponding HMM-based one for the three different training sets, T13.5, T3.6 and T1.5.

Training set	Strong pref. DNN	Pref. DNN	Equal	Pref. HMM	Strong pref. HMM
T13.5	33.3	37.1	9.5	14.3	5.7
T3.6	20.5	41.9	16.7	17.6	3.3
T1.5	24.8	48.1	14.8	9.5	2.9

Table 4. ABX preference test results (%) comparing the DNN-based systems trained with the three different training sets with each other.

Strong pref. DNN (T13.5)	Pref. DNN (T13.5)	Equal	Pref. DNN (T3.6)	Strong pref. DNN (T3.6)
5.7	20.5	63.3	10.0	0.5
Strong pref. DNN (T3.6)	Pref. DNN (T3.6)	Equal	Pref. DNN (T1.5)	Strong pref. DNN (T1.5)
5.2	25.7	52.9	13.3	2.9
Strong pref. DNN (T13.5)	Pref. DNN (T13.5)	Equal	Pref. DNN (T1.5)	Strong pref. DNN (T1.5)
10.0	40.0	40.5	9.0	0.5

In Table 4 the ABX results concerning the second part of the subjective test, are shown. From these results, it can be seen that there is a preference on the DNN-based system trained using T13.5, over T3.6 and T1.5, nonetheless, in all cases the "no sample is significantly better than the other" choice in the ABX test gathers very high scores (i.e. 40–65 %). These results are in agreement with the objective results, which have shown the clear superiority of the DNN-based systems in respect to the HMM-based ones, even (to our surprise) when a relatively small amount of training data is used, and in parallel the relatively small differences among the three DNN-based systems.

4   Conclusions

Our attempt to explore features extracted from the question set, used in HMM-based techniques, turned out not to be as beneficial as expected. However, even without the contribution of these features, as both the objective and subjective results clearly show, the DNN-based systems managed to outperform the respective HMM-based ones, even when the smallest training dataset, i.e. 1.5 h of speech, is used for training the systems. Our future focus will be on the adaptation aspects of DNN-based speech synthesis, which is essential in the field of statistical parametric speech synthesis, especially in the area of S2ST.

Acknowledgements. This work has received funding from the Swiss National Science Foundation under the SIWIS project and was supported by Eurostars Programme powered by Eurostars and the European Community under the project "D-Box: A generic dialog box for multi-lingual conversational applications".

References

1. Black, A., Taylor, P., Caley, R.: The festival speech synthesis system: system documentation (1.3.1). Technical report HCRC/TR-83, Human Communication Research Centre (December 1998)
2. HTS: HMM-based speech synthesis system version 2.1 (2010)
3. Imai, S., Kobayashi, T.: Speech signal processing toolkit (SPTK) version 3.7 (2013)
4. King, S., Karaiskos, V.: The Blizzard challenge 2011 (2011)
5. Lu, H., King, S., Watts, O.: Combining a vector space representation of linguistic context with a deep neural network for text-to-speech synthesis. In: SSW8, pp. 281–285 (August 2013)
6. Povey, D., Ghoshal, A., Boulianne, G., Burget, L., Glembek, O., Goel, N., Hannemann, M., Motlicek, P., Qian, Y., Schwarz, P., et al.: The Kaldi speech recognition toolkit. In: Proceeding of ASRU (2011)
7. Qian, Y., Fan, Y., Hu, W., Soong, F.: On the training aspects of deep neural network (DNN) for parametric tts synthesis. In: ICASSP, pp. 3829–3833 (2014)
8. Watts, O.: Unsupervised Learning for Text-to-Speech Synthesis. Ph.D. thesis, University of Edinburgh (2012)
9. Wester, M., Dines, J., Gibson, M., Liang, H., Wu, Y.J., Saheer, L., King, S., Oura, K., Garner, P.N., Byrne, W., Guan, Y., Hirsimäki, T., Karhila, R., Kurimo, M., Shannon, M., Shiota, S., Tian, J., Tokuda, K., Yamagishi, J.: Speaker adaptation and the evaluation of speaker similarity in the EMIME speech-to-speech translation project. In: SSW7, pp. 192–197 (2010)
10. Yamagishi, J., Kobayashi, T., Nakano, Y., Ogata, K., Isogai, J.: Analysis of speaker adaptation algorithms for HMM-based speech synthesis and a constrained SMAPLR adaptation algorithm. Trans. Audio Speech Lang. Proc. **17**(1), 66–83 (2009)
11. Zen, H., Tokuda, K., Kitamura, T.: Reformulating the HMM as a trajectory model by imposing explicit relationships between static and dynamic feature vector sequences. Comput. Speech Lang. **21**, 153–173 (2006)
12. Zen, H., Senior, A., Schuster, M.: Statistical parametric speech synthesis using deep neural networks. In: Proceedings of the IEEE International Conference on Acoustics, Speech and Signal Processing, pp. 7962–7966 (2013)
13. Zen, H., Tokuda, K., Black, A.W.: Statistical parametric speech synthesis. Speech Commun. **51**(11), 1039–1064 (2009)

Emotion State Manifestation in Voice Features: Chimpanzees, Human Infants, Children, Adults

Elena Lyakso and Olga Frolova[✉]

The Child Speech Research Group, St. Petersburg State University,
St. Petersburg, Russia
lyakso@gmail.com, olchel@yandex.ru

Abstract. The goal of the study is to investigate how emotional states of human and chimpanzees are manifested in the voice features. The participants of this study were 5 infants aged 3 months and 12 months, 30 children from 3 years to 7 years old, 10 adult actors, 5 chimpanzees aged 3–17 years, and 360 adults listeners of vocalizations and speech. Perceptual and spectrographic analysis methods were used. The reflection of the discomfort state in the infants vocalizations, in the speech of 3–4 years old children, in actors meaningless speech, and state of anger, fear and sadness in vocalizations of chimpanzees and actors speech of different language were recognized by listeners better than reflection in the voice of comfort and joy state. The pitch values, its variability, the values of the third "emotional" formant, and duration are important acoustical features for the recognition of participants state of discomfort in the voice.

Keywords: Voice · Emotional state · Infants · Chimpanzees · Actors · Acoustic and perceptual analysis

1 Introduction

Emotions play a fundamental role in animal and human behavior. The voice is a rich source of emotional information and the most important sound in our environment.

Acoustic features of speech are used extensively to detect emotional coloring present in the speech signal by employing several pattern recognition techniques [4,5,7]. Most reviews consider information about acoustical features such as pitch, intensity, duration of sounds and voice quality of basic emotions like anger, fear, sadness and gladness [1,10]. Phoneme, syllable and word level statistics corresponding to pitch values, energy, duration, spectral parameters and voice quality parameters are among the features that have been mainly used for emotion recognition.

Model for study of the true reflection of the emotional state in the voice can serve vocalizations of infants and chimpanzees. The participants choice is determined by similarity in the vocal tract structure of newborn and human-like primates [6], brain regions involved in infants' and chimpanzee's vocalizations [8,11,13] and neuronal mechanism responsible for vocal production [2,3].

© Springer International Publishing Switzerland 2015
A. Ronzhin et al. (Eds.): SPECOM 2015, LNAI 9319, pp. 201–208, 2015.
DOI: 10.1007/978-3-319-23132-7_25

The social environment and learning make more impact in the expression of emotions with child's growth. Another model to study of the emotional state reflection in the voice could be an actor's speech from different languages environments. In studies it was shown that vocal expressions of anger, disgust, fear, sadness, and happiness/joy can be accurately recognized in foreign language [12]. These emotions possess discrete acoustic-perceptual properties in the voice which manifest in similar ways across languages [9]. Thus, based on the literature, we select to study emotional voice features of participants from four groups - chimpanzees, human infants and children, adults - actors.

The primary aim of the study is investigating how emotional states of human and chimpanzees are manifested in the voice features.

2   Method

The participants of the study were 5 infants aged 3 months and 12 months (longitudinally recorded), 30 children aged from 3 years to 7 years; 5 chimpanzees aged 3–17 years, 10 adult actors, and 360 adults - listeners of vocalizations and speech. Design of the study included: audio recording of vocalizations and speech, video recording of behavior; expert analysis of video records; perception analysis of audio records by listeners (auditors); spectrographic acoustical analysis; statistics.

The recordings were made by the digital recorder "Marantz PMD660" with external microphone "SENNHEIZER e835S". The emotional state of infants, children, actors, and chimpanzees were identified by experts on the basis of the context of the situation by video. Perceptual analysis of vocalizations and speech was carried out by adults ($n = 360$ auditors) when listening test sequences. The aim of the perceptual analysis was to estimate the possibility of recognition of the emotional state by voice features. All auditors reported normal hearing with no history of hearing loss. Vocalizations and speech were analyzed spectrographically. We defined vocalizations' and vowels' duration, vowels' pitch values (F0) and the third formant frequency (F3, "emotional formant"). The variability of pitch values was calculated as the difference between maximum and minimum pitch values (F0 max - F0 min). The median values are presented on the histograms.

Ethical approval was obtained from the Ethics Committees (Health and Human Services, HHS, IRB 00003875, St. Petersburg State University IRB#1-Behavioral) and Local Committee.

3   Results

3.1   Experiment 1

The goal of the first study is the review of the recognition of the infants' and childrens discomfort, neutral and comfort state on the base of vocalizations and speech. Audio records of 3 months and 12 months old infants' vocalizations

and 3–7 years old childs speech were analyzed. The test sequences were composed according to the age characteristics of infants and children: for 3 months
old infants, for 12 months old infants, for 3–4 years old children, for 5 years old
children and for 6–7 years old children, respectively. Vocalizations and speech
material included in the test sequences are designated as test samples. Every
test sequence contains test samples in discomfort, comfort and neutral (calm)
childs condition.

The improvement of recognition of infants and child's emotional state on the
base of their vocalizations and speech with age dynamic was shown (Fig. 1). The
greater trend of the recognition of the comfort state was revealed. The comfort,
neutral and discomfort state of 3 months old infants and 6–7 years old children
auditors were recognized with equal range. Recognition of all emotional states
improves to the childrens age of 6–7 years. The childrens discomfort state is
defined better than a comfort state from the age of 12 months to 5 years old.

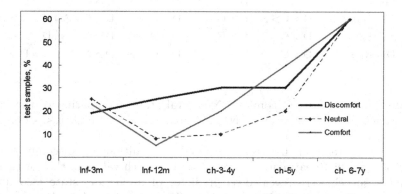

Fig. 1. Amount of children's emotional test samples recognized by auditors, %.

The acoustic features of test samples recognized by auditors (range 0.75–
1.0) was measured (Table 1). 3 months and 12 months old infants' vocalizations reflected discomfort state have the highest values of pitch, values of third
formants frequency (third spectra maxima in vocalizations - M3) and vowels
duration in comparison with corresponding features in comfort and neutral
vocalizations. Vowels from 3–4 years old children's words pronounced in discomfort state have higher values of third formant frequency and longer duration then
in comfort state. Pitch values and pitch variation values of vowels from words
pronounced by 3–4 years old children in discomfort state are higher than corresponding features in vowels from words pronounced in neutral state. The pitch
values, pitch variability and the duration of vowels from words pronounced by
5 years old children in discomfort state are higher than these features of vowels
from words pronounced in comfort and neutral state.

The pitch value differences are considered as a feature significant for detection
of distinctions between discomfort and neutral emotional states on the voice

characteristics for the children aged 3, 12 months and 5 years (Table 1). The pitch values of 6–7 years old children's speech in comfort, neutral and discomfort state are not differing significantly. Vowels duration was significant feature for detection of neutral state in voice. Based on the result of this study, we propose that the acoustic features make a less contribution in the recognition of emotional state of 6–7 years old children than in the younger age.

The pitch values and pitch variation values of infant's vocalizations as well as child vowels decrease for comfort state from 3 months to 6 -7 years.

Table 1. Differences in the acoustic features of vocalizations and speech signals correctly detected by the auditors as comfort, neutral and discomfort

No.	Features	Participants age				
		Infant 3m	Infant 12m	Child 3–4y	Child 5y	Child 6–7 y
1	F0	D > C > N	D > C > N	D = C > N	D > C > N	D = C = N
2	F0 (max-min)	D > C > N	D > C > N	D = C > N	D > C = N	D = C > N
3	M3/F3	D > C > N	D > C > N	C > D > N	D = C < N	D < N < C
4	Duration	D > C > N	D > N > C	D > C > N	D > N > C	C > D > N

Note: D-discomfort, C comfort, N-neutral state. Comparing of the corresponding features of states D, C, N. Measured values: > - higher, < - lower, = - equal.

Positive correlation between age and recognition of discomfort state $r = 0.9747$ (p < .05 Spearman) was revealed. The pitch values of the vowels from discomfort speech were revealed as predictor of discomfort state recognition: $F (1,3) = 12.308$, p < .03 (Beta = -0.896, $R2 = 0.80402$) Multiple Regression analysis. Changes of comfort and neutral state recognition with childrens age are bonded together: positive correlations between recognition of comfort and neutral test samples was revealed $r = 0,9$. The pitch values variability of the vowels from comfort speech was revealed as predictor of comfort state recognition: $F (1,3) = 13.283$, p < .035 (Beta = -0.9, $R2 = 0.815$) Multiple Regression analysis.

3.2 Experiment 2

The aim of the second study is to compare the reflection of the emotional state in infants and chimpanzees vocalizations. Participants of this study were infants (n = 5), investigated longitudinally from the age of 3 up to 12 months and chimpanzees (Pan Troglodytes) (n = 5) at age of 3 up to 17 years.

Audio and video recording of infants was made at home. Children interacted with their mothers in "face to face", "play", "book reading" situations. Records duration were 40–60 min. 133 auditors were invited to participate in the perceptual analysis. Test sequences were made for every child.

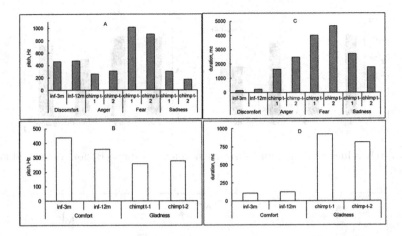

Fig. 2. The pitch values and the duration of vocalizations recognized by auditors as different emotional infants and chimpanzees states.

The recording of chimpanzees was carried out in laboratory condition during 2–4 h in interaction and feeding situations. Chimpanzee's vocalizations were included in two test sequences. The first test contains 10 vocalizations (3 chimpanzees). These vocalizations displayed anger, fear, gladness and sadness and were selected on the basis of situation context. The auditors were expected to determine the state of each vocalization. The auditors were Russian ($n = 10$) and Korean ($n = 10$) native speaking. The second test contains 30 vocalizations of 5 chimpanzees. The test includes aggressive, contact, play, food and exacting vocalizations. The auditors were expected to detect fear, anger, gladness and sadness vocalizations. Auditors ($n = 99$) were Russian ($n = 65$), Turkmen ($n = 16$) and other languages speaking Mongolian, Kabardian, Uzbek, Tatar ($n = 18$).

The results of the study showed the ability of adults to the proper recognition of the state of infants and chimpanzees in their vocalizations. More than 18 % of the auditors correctly determined the state of comfort and the state of discomfort of the infants vocalizations (with range 0.75) except the age of 12 months when only 5 % of auditors correctly recognized comfort vocalizations. Auditors correctly recognized (range 0.75) anger - 36.6 %, fear 47. 5 %, sadness 50 %, and gladness 10 % of chimpanzees. Auditors' "mistakes" was attributing comfort vocalization to discomfort vocalizations.

The pitch values and duration of infants discomfort vocalizations are higher than corresponding features of comfort vocalizations. Chimpanzee's vocalizations recognized as fear have higher pitch values then vocalizations recognized as anger, sadness and gladness. The pitch values of fear vocalizations are significantly ($p < 0.005$) higher than the pitch values of sadness vocalizations (Fig. 2).

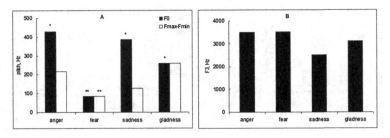

Fig. 3. Pitch values (A) and third formant frequency values (B) for recognized actors speech.

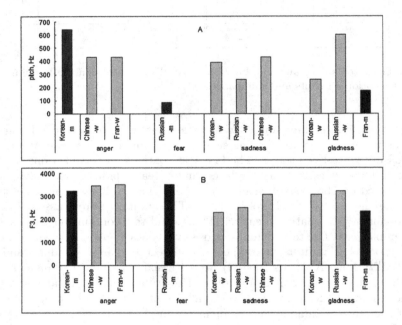

Fig. 4. The pitch values (A) and the values of third formant frequency of vowels from the words of the emotional actors speech referred by Korean and Russian auditors to anger, fear, sadness and gladness (range 0.75). Note: black columns for mens voices, gray columns for womens voices.

3.3   Experiment 3

The aim of the third study was to descript of different emotional states in adults voices. Emotional adults speech samples were selected from movies by native speakers. Participants of this study were adults - actors (n = 8): native Russian, Korean, Chinese and French speakers (men and women for every language). Selected fragments had the duration of two minutes. Russian (n = 10) and Korean (n = 10) native speakers were listeners.

The emotional state that demonstrated the actors was recognized by auditors when listening of speech samples. Korean and Russian native speakers (range 0.75–1.0) correctly recognized the anger state in voice of Korean, Chinese and French actors; fear only in Russian actors voice; sadness in Korean, Russian, and Chinese and gladness in Korean, Russian and French actor's voice. Auditors mistakes were in recognition of anger as fear, gladness as sadness. The differences in the recognition of the emotional state in the male and female voice were revealed.

The state of anger in voice is characterized by high values of pitch and third formant, intonation variability (Figs. 3 and 4).

The state of fear is characterized by low values of pitch and high values of the third formant. State of gladness in the voice is characterized by lower pith values than anger. Third formant frequency values in gladness are lower than in anger and fear, but higher than in sadness (Figs. 3 and 4). The actors speech was meaningful in the annotation study.

The speech of the Russian actors (n = 2) reciting a meaningless phrases were analyzed in the next part of this study. When actors pronounced these phrases they should represented the discomfort, neutral and comfortable states. 18 Russian-speaking adults attributed by listening these phrases to the category - discomfort, neutral, comfort. Recognition status was: 83 % of auditors correctly recognized discomfort by a man's voice, 88 % - by womens voice; for neutral state: 78 % - by mans voice and 55 % - by women voice; for comfort state: 78 % - by mans voice, 100 % - by womens voice.

4   Conclusion and Discussion

The reflection of the discomfort state in the vocalizations of infants aged 3 months and 12 months, in the speech of 3–4 years old children, in actors' meaningless speech, and state of anger, fear and sadness in vocalizations of chimpanzees and actors speech of different language were recognized by listeners better than reflection in the voice of a comfort and joy state. The improvement of recognition of child's emotional state on the base of their vocalizations and speech with age dynamic was shown. Acoustic features of vowels from discomfort vocalizations and discomfort speech of children aged before 5 years are characterized by highest pitch values and pitch variability values and the greatest length. Significant differences between acoustic features of vowels from discomfort, neutral and comfort speech of 6–7 years old children were not revealed. We supposed that the absence of visible differences in analyzed features of speech was caused by changes in childrens behavior in connection with the social environment, or the experimental conditions. Children tried to behave calmly and intently in the interaction with the experimenter, whereas younger children showed emotions more brightly and naturally. 6–7 years old childrens emotional expression in the voice could be reflected in other speech features, which were not included in this work. So in children of this age we have faced the problem that is present in adults. It is difficult to register true emotions in natural interaction. In our work this problem is solved in part by using actors speech. It was shown that the basic emotions in adult speech (actors speech) are recognized regardless of the language and the understanding of the message meaning.

We believe that obtained acoustic and perceptual features of emotional speech could be used to assess the emotional development and communication in healthy children and for detection of emotional disorders of children and adults.

Acknowledgments. The study is being performed with the financial support from the Russian Foundation for Humanities (projects # 13-06-00041a), the Russian Foundation for Basic Research (projects # 13-06-00281a, 15-06-07852a).

Thanks for collaboration - Tamara Kuznezova, Chief of the primate laboratory, Institute of Physiology Russian Academy of Science.

References

1. Drolet, M., Schubotz, R.I., Fischer, J.: Recognizing the authenticity of emotional expressions: F0 contour matters when you need to know. Front. Hum. Neurosci. **8**, 144 (2014)
2. Jürgens, U.: The neural control of vocalization in mammals: a review. J. Voice **23**(1), 1–10 (2009)
3. Jürgens, U.: Neural pathways underlying vocal control. Neurosci. Biobehav. Rev. **26**(2), 235–258 (2002)
4. Lee, C.M., Narayanan, S.S.: Toward detecting emotions in spoken dialogs. IEEE Trans. Speech Audio Process. **13**(2), 293–303 (2005)
5. Lee, S., Potamianos, A., Narayanan, S.: Acoustics of childrens speech: developmental changes of temporal and spectral parameters. J. Acoust. Soc. Am. **105**(3), 1455–1468 (1999)
6. Lieberman, P., Crelin, E.S., Klatt, D.H.: Phonetic ability and related anatomy of the newborn and adult human, neanderthal man, and the chimpanzee. Am. Anthropologist **74**(3), 287–307 (1972)
7. Lyakso, E., Grigorev, A., Kurazova, A., Ogorodnikova, E.: ≪INFANT. MAVS≫ - multimedia model for infants cognitive and emotional development study. In: Ronzhin, A., Potapova, R., Delic, V. (eds.) SPECOM 2014. LNCS, vol. 8773, pp. 284–291. Springer, Heidelberg (2014)
8. Owren, M.J., Amoss, R.T., Rendall, D.: Two organizing principles of vocal production: implications for nonhuman and human primates. Am. J. Primatol. **73**(6), 530–544 (2011)
9. Pell, M.D., Paulmann, S., Dara, C., Alasseri, A., Kotz, S.A.: Factors in the recognition of vocally expressed emotions: a comparison of four languages. J. Phonetics **37**(4), 417–435 (2009)
10. Scherer, K.R.: Vocal communication of emotion: a review of research paradigms. Speech Commun. **40**(1), 227–256 (2003)
11. Taglialatela, J.P., Russell, J.L., Schaeffer, J.A., Hopkins, W.D.: Chimpanzee vocal signaling points to a multimodal origin of human language. PLoS ONE **6**(4), e18852 (2011)
12. Thompson, W.F., Balkwill, L.L.: Decoding speech prosody in five languages. Semiotica **2006**(158), 407–424 (2006)
13. Wilson, B., Petkov, C.I.: Communication and the primate brain: insights from neuroimaging studies in humans, chimpanzees and macaques. Hum. Biol. **83**(2), 175 (2011)

Estimation of Vowel Spectra Near Vocal Chords with Restoration of a Clipped Speech Signal

Andrey Barabanov, Vera Evdokimova, and Pavel Skrelin[✉]

Saint Petersburg State University, Universitetskaya nab., 7/9,
Saint Petersburg, Russia
`Andrey.Barabanov@gmail.com`, {`postmaster,skrelin`}`@phonetics.pu.ru`

Abstract. Speech signals with Russian vowels were recorded simultaneously by two microphones. The first microphone was located in the larynx near the vocal chords and the second one was outside a mouth near the lips. A signal in the inner microphone is formed by the vocal chords and contains a weak reverberation echo. It is clipped to a half of the energy because of the sensitivity restrictions on the microphone. A new mathematical algorithm is proposed for restoration of the clipped signal part. The restored signal sounds better. The restored spectra of vowels contain the first formant that cannot be explained by a backward reverberation. A transfer function of the vocal tract is estimated by comparing spectra of the signals from the input and output microphones.

Keywords: Restoration of clipped signal · Vocal transfer function · Vocal chords

1 Problem Statement

A process of a speech phoneme signal generation is commonly divided into two stages: a generation a quasi periodic source signal by the vocal chords and transformation of this signal through the vocal tract. A conventional model of the output signal of the vocal chords is locally periodic function without formants. This means a function with a spectrum consisted of peaks at the mutiple fundamental frequencies and without local maxima of the spectral envelope. The vocal tract produces local maxima of the spectral envelope by suppression or intensification at corresponding frequency bands making formants at local maxima of the output spectrum [1–4].

Separation of the Pitch generation by the vocal chords and the formant generation by the vocal tract looks convenient for theoretical modelling and analysis. This assumption is difficult to be verified since a microphone attached to the neck near the vocal chords receives a strong reverberation from a mouth through bones and soft tissues. Recently, a new equipment became available for registering accurately a sound produced by vocal chords [5,6]. The miniature microphone QueAudio (with d = 2.3 mm, waterproof) is inserted through the nasal cavity and located in the proximity of vocal chords in the output air

© Springer International Publishing Switzerland 2015
A. Ronzhin et al. (Eds.): SPECOM 2015, LNAI 9319, pp. 209–216, 2015.
DOI: 10.1007/978-3-319-23132-7_26

stream. This microphone supplies records of a sound that will be called "input" to the vocal tract. The "output" signal is simultaneously recorded by another standard microphone located near the lips.

The following questions were supposed to be cleared by a superposition of sound spectra from the input and output signals: do vocal chords participate the formant generation, and what formants and other features are produced by the vocal tract?

2   Output Signals

The six Russian vowels were used in the experiments: /a/, /i/, /o/, /e/, /ɨ/, /u/. Each vowel was pronounced by the female speaker at a constant power for 1 s. The miniature microphone registered the sound near the vocal chords while the outer microphone registered the output speech signal.

The fundamental frequency was around 200 Hz. This gap between neighbouring frequencies of the signal harmonics appeared sometimes too big for precise location of formants. For instance, a typical spectrum of the output signal /o/ is shown in Fig. 1. The two first formants of /o/ cannot be separated in this picture while the sound /o/ is clearly recognised by a human ear.

For any vowel, an output signal containing this vowel was divided into frames of the duration of one period. All spectra of the frames are collected in Fig. 2.

The formants of each vowel are clearly indicated by local maxima of the spectral envelope. Similar spectral envelopes of the input signals indicate the place where a formant was formed: at the vocal chords or in the vocal tract.

3   Input Signals

The miniature microphone located inside the vocal tract near the vocal chords registers sound signals after the vocal chords but before the vocal tract. Unfortunately, the minimal sensitivity of the microphone is not enough to prevent overflow. All input signals were clipped, and this can influence their spectra.

However, there is enough information to calculate the Pitch period to a high accuracy and to divide the signal into frames of the Pitch period length. Special mathematical approach was developed for restoration of the clipped part of each frame. The approach is described below in Sect. 4. The initial clipped signals and

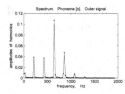

Fig. 1. Spectrum of /o/ registered outside near lips. The low frequency part

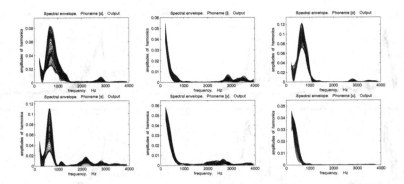

Fig. 2. Spectral envelopes of all vowels, from the left to the right, upper row: /a/, /i/, /o/; lower row: /e/, /ɨ/, /u/

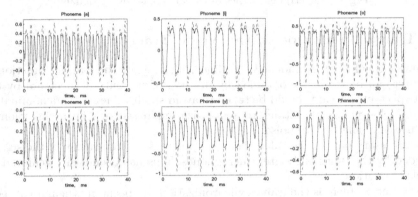

Fig. 3. The clipped signals (green) and the restored signals (blue) (Color figure online)

the restored signals are shown in Fig. 3 for all vowels. A short interval of 40 ms was taken to see the details.

The corresponding spectral envelopes of the restored signals are given in Fig. 4. The difference between them and the spectral envelopes of the input clipped signals appeared to be very small, the correlation coefficient is greater than 0.9. This difference can be important on the frequency bands with small spectral values when the transfer function of the vocal tract is calculated.

It follows from Fig. 4 that the low frequency formants of all vowels already exist in the input signals. Moreover, the second formant of the vowel /o/ looks much more evident than that in the output spectrum.

The output signal from the mouth can influence the sound near the vocal chords through a reverberation. But it seems impossible for the reverberation signal to have the more energy than the straight signal in the air stream directed to the mouth. Thus we have to conclude that the first formants are produced in the larynx but not in the mouth. The same conclusion was made in [7].

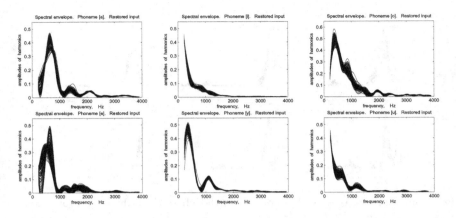

Fig. 4. Spectral envelopes of the unclipped input signals

4   Transfer Function of the Vocal Tract

Assume a vocal tract is modelled by a linear filter. Then the transfer function of the filter can be explicitly obtained by division of the output spectrum by the input spectrum. A care should be taken to avoid small value in the denominator. This is achieved by the standard regularization based on the assumption of presence of a small white noise.

A necessary part of the calculation is a precise synchronization of the signals recorded by the inner and outer microphones. This has been easily achieved by direct correlation.

Another problem is the frame synchronization. A special mathematical technique was implemented for precise estimation of Pitch periods [8,9]. A beginning sample of a period was not attached to a fixed point of the signal, for instance, to the zero intersection. A period was estimated by the precise global LS approach, and the next period starts at the time instant where the last period finished. The estimation error is less than a distance between samples.

The results of the Fundamental frequency estimation are shown in Fig. 5. The source input signals were clipped, and this is the reason for small random jumps in the input frequency estimates. The Pitch periods were calculated independently for each frame. Since this periods are around 5 ms, more than 140 independent procedures were made for each signal. A delay error is accumulated but the blue and the green lines do not diverge. Hence, the correspondence between frames of the input and output signals has been established to a high accuracy.

The transfer functions of the vocal tract model are shown in Fig. 6. The low frequency formants were changed insignificantly. An exception in the phoneme /o/ concerns the special case where the two formants of the input signal shown in Fig. 4 are merged in the output signal shown in Fig. 2.

The high frequency formants are clearly stressed for all phonemes. These formants cannot be found in Fig. 4. Thus, we have to conlude that high frequency

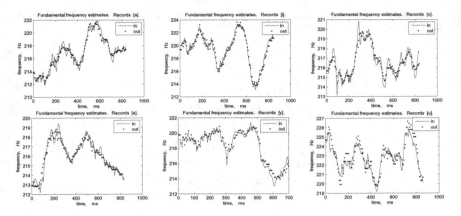

Fig. 5. Fundamental frequency curves for the input (blue) and output (green) signals (Color figure online)

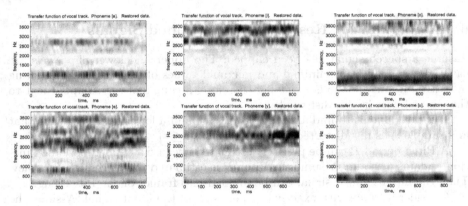

Fig. 6. The transfer functions of the vocal tract

formants are produced in the vocal tract and that the vocal chords do not participate this process.

5   Perception Tests

A group of 44 informants were involved into perception tests. The restored (unclipped) input signals were presented for recognition. Each record contains one phoneme and lasts for about 1 s. The records were randomly mixed. The informants were asked to identify the vowels as one of the six Russian phonemes for any stimulus. The "no detection" option was also available. The results are given in Table 1. The input vowels were not recognized correctly with a confidence but there is a correlation between close phonemes. The phonemes /i/, /u/ and /ɨ/ depend significantly on the high frequency formants which are absent in

Table 1. Any row contains percentage of recognition for an input vowel indicated in the first column.

	Decisions					
	a	i	o	e	ɨ	u
a	51	3	25	18	1	0
i	31	22	3	3	17	18
o	24	1	41	9	6	9
e	2	0	59	27	9	0
ɨ	13	10	8	9	33	20
u	9	23	9	2	16	39

the signal near the vocal chords. The wrong recognition of /o/ instead of /e/ in 59 % cases looks like an artefact because the opposite mistake appears rarely.

6   Algorithm for Restoration of Clipped Signals

Assume a speech signal has been clipped. The upper and lower clip levels are easily determined from minimal and maximal values of the signal. The cutting process in a microphone is dynamic, therefore, a couple of the samples next to the clipped part is also distorted.

It is not difficult to find an upper level $s_{\max}$ and a lower level $s_{\min}$ such that any sample s_t is not distorted by clipping if $s_{\min} \leq s_t \leq s_{\max}$.

A Pitch period P can be precisely estimated because a clipped periodic function remains periodic. Assume the Pitch P is estimated to a necessary accuracy. Then the input clipped signal can be divided into frames of the Pitch length.

Consider a frame with exactly one period P of the input signal. Assume the period P is measured in samples. It is a real number, not necessarily an integer. Denote a sequence of samples in this frame by $s = (s_t)_{t=0}^{N-1}$.

A voiced signal is modelled by the harmonic expansion

$$\widehat{s}_t = \sum_{m=-M}^{M} A_m e^{\frac{2\pi i}{P} tm}, \qquad 0 \leq n \leq N-1,$$

where A_m are the complex amplitudes and $A_{-m} = \bar{A}_m$ is a complex conjugate number. The number M of harmonics in the model is always less than $P/2$. The vector $A = (A_m)_{m=-M}^{M}$ is to be estimated.

Denote by T_d a set of all time instants t for which a sample s_t is distorted. It contains the set T_- with $s_t < s_{\min}$ and the set T_+ with $s_t > s_{\max}$.

The complementary set of t for which s_t is not distorted is denoted by T. Define the cost function for estimation as the squared error norm in the reliable samples

$$J(A) = \sum_{t \in T} |s_t - \widehat{s}_t|^2.$$

A direct minimization of $J(A)$ by A leads to the Least Squares method and is accomplished directly. Assume $\widehat{A}$ is the LS optimal vector and $\widetilde{s} = (\widetilde{s}_t)_{t=0}^{N-1}$ is the optimal sample sequence. The values $\widetilde{s}_t$ approximate s_t well in reliable samples, for $t \in T$. But for $t \in T_d$ the estimates s_t can be arbitrary.

It follows from the definition of the clip operation that $s_t \geq s_{\max}$ for $t \in T_+$ and $s_t \leq s_{\min}$ for $t \in T_-$. Therefore, minimization of $J(A)$ must be conditional with a set of linear inequalities

$$\widehat{s}_t \leq s_{\min} \, \forall t \in T_-, \qquad \widehat{s}_t \geq s_{\max} \, \forall t \in T_+.$$

This is a convex minimization problem, and it admits an effective numerical solution which combines the LS formula and an iterative gradient minimization.

Analysis of the clipped speech signals has shown that the information matrix of the Least Squares algorithm can be ill conditioned. This means that there are vectors δA such that a signal δs generated by the harmonic model with the complex amplitudes δA is almost zero in the reliable time instants $t \in T$. It follows that the vector δA can be added to any vector A almost without influence to the cost function $J(A)$.

These arbitrary vectors δA are easily computed. They can be used for regularization of the frame sequence when the optimal estimates $\widetilde{s}$ are obtained for all frames. A regularization can be formulated as a quadratic minimization of the difference between all neighbouring periods of the restored signal. The restored signals in Fig. 3 were obtained by an algorithm that combines a conditional LS minimization and a frame regularization.

7   Conclusion

Two sound signals were registered simultaneously when a speaker pronounced the Russian vowels. The first miniature microphone was inserted into the vocal tract and located in the proximity of the vocal chords. The second microphone registered a signal near lips. Analysis of the records obtained has led to the following conclusions.

1. The low frequency formants are formed near the vocal chords and do not change significantly in the vocal tract.
2. The high frequency formants are absent near the vocal chords and are formed by the vocal tract.
3. The inner microphone produces a clipped signal. An algorithm for the signal restoration is presented.
4. The low frequency formants formed by the vocal chords carry sufficient information for intelligibility of the phonemes that do not depend essentially from high frequency formants.
5. The voiced signal near the vocal chords can be represented by a sum of harmonics with multiple frequencies. A spectral envelope of this signal contains low frequency formants. In particular, the first harmonic with the Fundamental frequency has a relatively small amplitude if it is outside a formant.

Acknowledgments. The work was supported by Saint Petersburg State University, projects 6.37.349.2015 and 31.37.353.2015.

References

1. Bondarko, L.V.: Phonetics of Russian modern language, SPbSU (1998) (in Russian)
2. Kodzasov, S.V., Krivnova, O.F.: General Phonetics. Moscow (2001) (in Russian)
3. Fant, G.: Acoustic Theory of Speech Production. Mouton, Netherlands (1960)
4. Stevens, K.: Acoustic Phonetics. The MIT Press, Cambridge (1998)
5. Evgrafova, K., Evdokimova, V., Skrelin, P., Chukaeva, T., Shvalev, N.: A new technique to record a voice source signal. In: International Workshop on Models and Analysis of Vocal Emissions for Biomedical Applications (MAVEBA), Florence, pp. 181–182 (2013)
6. Evdokimova, V., Evgrafova, K., Skrelin, P., Chukaeva, T., Shvalev, N.: Detection of the frequency characteristics of the articulation system with the use of voice source signal recording method. In: Železný, M., Habernal, I., Ronzhin, A. (eds.) SPECOM 2013. LNCS, vol. 8113, pp. 108–115. Springer, Heidelberg (2013)
7. Galunov, V.I., Garbaruk, V.I.: Acoustic theory of speech production and a system of phonetic features. In: 100 Years of Experimental Phonetics in Russia, pp. 58–62 (2001)
8. Barabanov, A.E.: Fast identification of the voiced speech signal. In: Swedish-Russian Control Conference, St. Petersburg (2011)
9. Barabanov, A.E.: Parameter identification of the harmonic model of a speech signal. In: Transactions of the XII Russian Conference on Control Problems, pp. 3038–3049 (2014)

Fast Algorithm for Precise Estimation of Fundamental Frequency on Short Time Intervals

Andrey Barabanov, Alexandr Melnikov$^{(\boxtimes)}$, Valentin Magerkin, and Evgenij Vikulov

Saint Petersburg State University, Universitetskaya nab.,
7/9, Saint Petersburg, Russia
{Andrey.Barabanov,melnikov.alex.rus,magerkin93,jenyav94}@gmail.com

Abstract. Fast algorithms are proposed for precise estimation of the Fundamental frequency on a short time interval. The approach is a generalization of the unbiased frequency estimator. Its computational complexity is proportional to that of FFT on the same time interval. A trade-off between approximation error and numerical speed is established. The result is generalized to the linear trend model. The lower bound is obtained for the time interval length with a nonsingular information matrix in the estimation problem. The frequency estimation algorithm is not sensitive to big random noises.

Keywords: Frequency estimation · Fast algorithms · Harmonic model

1 Problem Statement

Accurate estimation of the Pitch period is necessary for correct calculation of harmonic amplitudes especially for the high frequency formants. An estimation error of the Fundamental frequency causes a multiple error for the high frequency harmonics. Assume a frame contains L periods of a speech signal recorded at the sample rate F_s kHz. Then a Pitch estimation error of ε samples causes a frequency error δ near the frequency F kHz which is equal to $\delta = -\varepsilon L F / F_s$ frequency samples of the spectrum. In particular, if a frame contains $L = 4$ periods, $F_s = 8$ kHz and $F = 2$ kHz then the error $\varepsilon = 1$ time sample causes a shift of one frequency sample of the signal spectrum near F. An amplitude of a harmonic with the frequency f is conventionally estimated by a spectrum value in f. Therefore, a Pitch estimation error of 1 sample can completely reject harmonics in the estimated model at the frequency band near 2 kHz.

The Least Squares approach is successfully implemented for estimation of the complex amplitudes of the harmonic polynomial model of a voiced signal [1,2]. But the Pitch estimation problem remains highly nonlinear with several local minima that can cause a standard multiple frequency error. An exhaustive search

---

The work was supported by Saint Petersburg State University, project 6.37.349.2015.

A. Ronzhin et al. (Eds.): SPECOM 2015, LNAI 9319, pp. 217–225, 2015.
DOI: 10.1007/978-3-319-23132-7_27

of admissible Pitch values makes a quadratic complexity of the numerical algorithm that is too expensive.

The novel "unbiased criterion" for Pitch estimation was proposed in [3]. Its complexity is proportional to $N \log_2 N$ where N is the frame window length. This criterion is also independent on the additive white noise. In this paper, the unbiased criterion is generalized to the affine model and to the short time intervals. It is shown that the complexity reduction is not easy for short frames. The value of the unbiased criterion has been also successfully implemented for the voice recognition in noises.

2   Model and Cost Function

Let $s = (s_t)_{t=-N/2}^{N/2-1}$ be a voiced signal of the length N. The affine model of the signal is

$$\widehat{s}_t = \sum_{k=-M}^{M} \left(A_k e^{\frac{2\pi i}{P} kt} + B_k \frac{t}{N} e^{\frac{2\pi i}{P} kt} \right), \qquad -\frac{N}{2} \le t \le \frac{N}{2} - 1,$$

where P is the Pitch period of the model, $M = [(P-1)/2]$ is the number of harmonics, A_k and B_k are the complex amplitudes and $A_k = \bar{A}_{-k}, B_k = \bar{B}_{-k}$ for all k. The Pitch period P corresponds to the Fundamental frequency $F = N/P$ calculated in periods per frame.

The full set of the model parameter contains the value of P and the vectors $A = (A_k)_{k=-M}^{M}$ and $B = (B_k)_{k=-M}^{M}$. All these values can be arbitrary. Accuracy of the model can be measured by the squared norm of the windowed estimation error

$$J(A, B, P) = \frac{1}{N} \sum_{t=-N/2}^{N/2-1} |w_t(s_t - \widehat{s}_t)|^2,$$

where $w_t = [1 + \cos(2\pi t/N)]2$ is the Hanning window. The estimation problem is then reduced to minimization of the function J by all variables.

It is numerically effective to make a successive minimization:

$$J_{\min}(P) = \min_{A,B} J(A, B, P), \qquad J_{\min}(P) \to \min_P.$$

The first minimization problem is to be solved for all P, and the last minimization in one variable P is made by a constrained search.

It is well known that minimization by A and B with a fixed P is reduced by the LS algorithm to a linear system of the dimension $2M+1 \approx P$. If this system is solved for any integer P in the range $[1, N/4]$ then the numerical complexity is proportional to N^2, and this is too long. In [3] an algebraic transform was found that calculates the values of $J_{\min}(P)$ in the stationary model with $B = 0$ for all integer P, and the number of operations is proportional to $N \log_2 N$. This result was not supplied by a strict mathematical proof but the idea was explained in detail. A careful analysis of the problem has shown that the proposed solution is correct for sufficiently long frames only.

In this paper the general case is studied. Short frames are necessary for precise modelling of an allophone containing 2–3 periods. It is also important on transitions between allophones.

3   Minimum of the Cost Function

Let $s = (s_t)_{t=-N/2}^{N/2-1}$ be a voiced signal of the length N. It is required to calculate the values of $J_{\min}(P)$ for all integer P. Let $w = (w_t)_{t=-N/2}^{N/2-1}$ be the Hanning window, as before.

The next assertion is a strict mathematical theorem that do not require any additional conditions.

Theorem 1. *For any positive $P < N$ the minimal cost function in the affine model is equal to*

$$J_{\min}(P) = \sum_{t=-N/2}^{N/2-1} w_t^2 s_t^2 - \sum_{m=0}^{P-1} y_m^* C_m^{-1} y_m,$$

where the 2×2 matrices C_m depend on m, N and P only,

$$C_m = \begin{pmatrix} C_m^0 & C_m^1 \\ C_m^1 & C_m^2 \end{pmatrix} = \sum_{n=\left[\frac{-N/2-m}{P}\right]+1}^{\left[\frac{N/2-1-m}{P}\right]} \begin{pmatrix} 1 & \frac{m+nP}{N} \\ \frac{m+nP}{N} & \left(\frac{m+nP}{N}\right)^2 \end{pmatrix} w_{m+nP}^2,$$

for $0 \le m \le P - 1$, the vectors $y_m = (y_m^A, y_m^B)^T$ are defined by

$$y_m = \sum_{n=\left[\frac{-N/2-m}{P}\right]+1}^{\left[\frac{N/2-1-m}{P}\right]} \begin{pmatrix} 1 \\ \frac{m+nP}{N} \end{pmatrix} \tilde{s}_{m+nP}, \qquad 0 \le m \le P - 1,$$

and $\tilde{s}_t = w_t^2 s_t$ for $-N/2 \le t \le N/2 - 1$.

Proof is pure algebraic and it is derived from the standard LS formulas.

The entries C_m^0, C_m^1, C_m^2 of the matrix C_m depend on m, P and N. But indeed they are determined by the values $x = m/N$ and $F = N/P$.

Recall that F is the number of signal periods in the frame window. The case $F < 2.8$ is not interesting because a signal and a noise are not distinguishable. If $F > 3.6$ then the matrix C_m is nearly the same for all m. This case corresponds to conditions under which the algebraic transformations from [3] are effective.

A similar expression can be derived for the class of stationary models with $B = 0$:

$$J_{\min}(P) = \sum_{t=-N/2}^{N/2-1} w_t^2 s_t^2 - \sum_{m=0}^{P-1} \frac{|y_{1,m}|^2}{C_m^0},$$

where $y_{1,m}$ is the first entry of y_m. The minimal admissible value of P in this case corresponds to $F = 1.6$. If the number of signal periods in the frame window is less than 1.6 then a signal cannot be distinguished from the white noise.

4   The Basic Algebraic Transformations

Assume $F \geq 3.6$. Then it can be shown that

$$J_{\min}(P) \approx \sum_{t=-N/2}^{N/2-1} w_t^2 s_t^2 - \frac{8}{3F} \sum_{m=0}^{P-1} |y_{1,m}|^2 - \frac{64\pi^2}{(2\pi^2 - 15)F} \sum_{m=0}^{P-1} |y_{2,m}|^2,$$

where $y_m = (y_{1,m}, y_{2,m})^T$.

Theorem 2. *Denote the autocorrelation function of the sequence* $(w_t^2 s_t)_{t=-N/2}^{N/2-1}$ *by* $r = (r_n)_{n=-N}^{N}$, *and denote the autocorrelation function of the sequence* $(w_t^2 s_t t/N)_{t=-N/2}^{N/2-1}$ *by* $q = (q_n)_{n=-N}^{N}$. *Then for any* $1 \leq P \leq N$

$$\sum_{m=0}^{P-1} |y_{1,m}|^2 = \sum_{n=-[F]}^{[F]} r_{nP}, \qquad \sum_{m=0}^{P-1} |y_{2,m}|^2 = \sum_{n=-[F]}^{[F]} q_{nP},$$

where $[F]$ *is the integer part of* F.

Proof is algebraic and it is omitted here. The number of summations in the assertion of Theorem 2 for all P is proportional to $N \log_2 N$. The same complexity operations are necessary for calculation of the autocorrelation through the Fast Fourier Transform.

The general case with $2.8 \leq F \leq 3.6$ appears to be much more complicated. The complexity of N^2 was not overcome for the precise calculation of $J_{\min}(P)$. However, there is a trade-off between accuracy and complexity. For brevity, consider a stationary case only. It is required to calculate the function

$$\phi(P) = \sum_{m=0}^{P-1} \frac{y_{1,m}(P)|^2}{C_m^0(P)}$$

for all integer P from the admissible interval $[P_{\min}, P_{\max}]$ where $P_{\min}$ is a fixed small integer and $P_{\max} \approx 5N/8$.

Theorem 3. *Let* $(S_n)_{n=-N/2}^{N/2-1}$ *be the FFT of the windowed input signal* $(w_t s_t)$. *There exist fast decaying sequences* $(C_{m,j})_{m=-N}^{N-1}$ *for* $j \geq 0$ *in both* m *and* j, *and the functions* α_F *from the interval* $[-0.4, 0]$ *such that for all* $P \leq N$

$$\phi(P) = r_P(0) + 2 \sum_{k=1}^{[N/P]} r_P(kP),$$

where

$$r_P(t) = \sum_{k=0}^{\infty} \sum_{m=0}^{\infty} \alpha_F^k \alpha_F^m \sum_{i=0}^{\infty} \sum_{j=0}^{\infty} x_{kF}^i x_{mF}^j \rho_{i,j}(t, \ell_{kF} - \ell_{mF}),$$

the function $\rho_{i,j}(t, \tau)$ is the inverse FFT of $(D_{n,i} \bar{D}_{n+\tau,j})_{n=-N}^{N-1}$ and $D_{n,j} = (S * C_{.,j})(n)$ is a convolution. The integer part ℓ_{kF} and the fractional x_{kF} are defined by $2kF = \ell_{kF} + x_{kF}$ and $|x_{kF}| \leq 1/2$.

Proof is omitted. The functions $C_{m,j}$ and α_F do not depend on the signal s. They can be tabulated. The series in the expression for $r_P(t)$ converge very fast. As a rule, it is sufficient to take two or three terms only. This is a trade-off between accuracy and complexity.

5   Unbiased Criterion

The function $J_{\min}(P)$ cannot be taken for the final decision of the Pitch estimate. The unbiased criterion $\mathcal{E}_{UB}(P)$ introduced in [3] corrects the two standard errors: the multiple frequency error and influence of the measurement white noise.

Assume a speech signal is locally represented by the model

$$s_t = \sum_{k=-M}^{M} \left(A_k^0 e^{\frac{2\pi i}{P_0} kt} + B_k^0 \frac{t}{N} e^{\frac{2\pi i}{P_0} kt} \right) + v_t, \qquad -\frac{N}{2} \leq t \leq \frac{N}{2} - 1,$$

where P_0 is the "true" Pitch period and (A_k^0, B_k^0) are the "true" complex amplitudes. The model error v_t can be considered as a measurement noise.

For the class of models $\widehat{s}_t$ with the estimate $P = P_0$ the optimal amplitudes $(\widehat{A}_k, \widehat{B}_k)$ minimize the cost function

$$J_{\min}(P) = \min_{(A_k),(B_k)} w_t^2 \left| \sum_{k=-M}^{M} \left((A_k^0 - A_k) e^{\frac{2\pi i}{P} kt} + (B_k^0 - B_k) \frac{t}{N} e^{\frac{2\pi i}{P} kt} \right) + v_t \right|^2.$$

Obviously, the residual amplitudes $(\delta A_k = \widehat{A}_k - A_k^0, \delta B_k = \widehat{B}_k - B_k^0)$ form the best estimate of the noise v_t. The unbiased criterion presented in [3] contains the following correction:

$$\mathcal{E}_{UB}(P) = \frac{J_{\min}(P)}{1 - \frac{\kappa}{F}},$$

where $F = N/P$ is the number of periods in the frame and the coefficient κ is determined by the window. For the Hanning window and the stationary model $(B = 0)$ with the white noise (v_t) considered in [3] this coefficient is $\kappa = 35/18 \approx 1.94$. For the affine model

$$\kappa = \frac{35}{216} \frac{48\pi^2 - 385}{2\pi^2 - 15} \approx 3.034.$$

For short time intervals the following theorem shows that the coefficient κ depends on F.

Theorem 4. *Let N be the frame length, P is a Pitch period and $F = N/P$ is the number of periods in the frame. Assume a signal is defined by the model*

$$s_t = \sum_{k=-M}^{M} \left(a_k \cos\left(\frac{2\pi i}{P} kt + \phi_k\right) + b_k \frac{t}{N} \cos\left(\frac{2\pi i}{P} kt + \psi_k\right) \right) + v_t$$

for $-N/2 \le t \le N/2 - 1$, where M the integer part of $P/2$, a_k and b_k are arbitrary amplitudes, ϕ_k and ψ_k are arbitrary phases, and v_t is the white noise with the variance σ^2.

Then the expectation of the minimal cost function is equal to

$$\mathsf{E} J_{\min}(P) = \frac{3}{8}\sigma^2 \left(1 - \frac{h_N(F)}{F}\right),$$

where the function $h_N(F)$ is approximated by the function

$$h_\infty(F) = \begin{cases} F, & F < 2.8, \\ -2.1967 + 2.8434 \cdot F - 0.3863 \cdot F^2, & 2.8 \le F \le 3.6, \\ 3.034, & F > 3.6, \end{cases}$$

to the accuracy less that 0.01 if $N \ge 128$.

The unbiased criterion in this problem coincides with the Maximum Likelihood criterion: to minimize the unbiased estimate of the noise variance σ^2:

$$\mathcal{E}_{UB}(P) = \frac{J_{\min}(P)}{1 - \frac{h_\infty(F)}{F}}.$$

It follows from definition of $h_\infty(F)$ that any value $F < 2.8$, or $P > N/2.8$ cannot provide an optimal estimate. For the stationary model this bound is near the value $F_{\min} = 1.6$. For $F > 3$ The unbiased criterion for the stationary model coincides with that in [3].

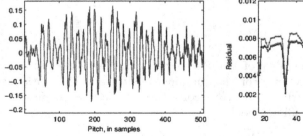
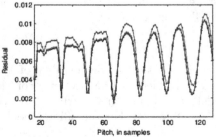

Fig. 1. A clean speech signal (left plot), and the functions $\mathcal{E}_{UB}(P)$ (right plot) for $P \in [16, 128]$ samples, and for SNR from $0\,\mathrm{dB}$ (pink) to $20\,\mathrm{dB}$ (blue) with a step $5\,\mathrm{dB}$ (Color figure online).

The criterion $\mathcal{E}_{UB}$ is not sensitive to big noises. A clean speech signal in Fig. 1 was taken from http://ecs.utdallas.edu/loizou/speech/noizeus/clean.zip. It contains 512 samples starting from the 11420'th sample of the file sp06.wav. The function $\mathcal{E}_{UB}(P)$ was calculated for the sum of this signal and a scaled airport noise. Clearly, the minimal value of $\mathcal{E}_{UB}(P)$ is achieved at $P = 66$ samples for all SNR values.

6   Example

A voiced speech signal in a frame window of the length 64 ms was taken as an example. It contains the allophone /a/ extracted from a long speech record. The sample rate is 8 kHz, the frame contains $N = 512$ samples. A correct value of Pitch is 52.7 samples.

For any integer value of P the LS approach was implemented for estimation of the complex amplitudes for the stationary model and for the affine model. A minimal admissible Pitch value was set to $P_{min} = 16$ because it corresponds the Fundamental frequency 500 Hz. The maximal bounds for the admissible Pitch values are determined in Theorem 4. These are $P_{max,stat} = [N/1.6] = 320$ samples, and $P_{max,stat} = [N/2.8] = 182$ samples, respectively.

The values of the function $J_{min}(P)$ for both stationary (green) and affine (blue) models are shown in Fig. 2 (left). There is an obvious decreasing trend of the minimal cost functions. An estimate of the Pitch value cannot be obtained by minimization of $J_{min}(P)$. The reason of this trend is the standard multiple frequency error together with the loss of the harmonic independency in the signal spectrum for big values of P.

A correction was made by Theorem 4. The unbiased criterion $\mathcal{E}_{UB}(P)$ is shown in Fig. 2 (right) for the stationary and affine models. The trend has been completely compensated that proves correctness of the regularization. The true value $P = 52$ is the best. The multiple periods $2P, 3P, \ldots, 6P$ also contain local minima but the Maximal Likelihood estimate $P = 52$ appeared to be better.

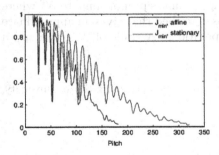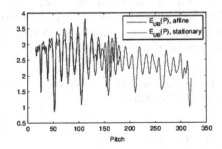

Fig. 2. The functions $J_{min}(P)$ (left plot) and $\mathcal{E}_{UB}(P)$ (right plot) for the stationary (green) and affine (blue) models (Color figure online).

7 Evaluation of the Algorithm

The proposed algorithm was called the Noise Variance Minimization (NVM). It was compared with the following pitch tracking algorithms: YAAPT [5], SWIPE [6], RAPT [7], PEFAC [8], and YIN [2]. The PTDB-TUG dataset [4] was chosen for evaluation. 300 voiced signal frames were extracted from various records of the database. Pitch value estimates P_0 were obtained for all frames by all algorithms. Then the values of $J_{\min}(P_0)$ were calculated, normalized by the signal energy, and averaged by frames. Pitch estimation errors generate mainly high frequency distortions. Table 1 contains the normalized residual energy after high-pass filtering shown in the first column.

Table 1. The normalized residual values $J_{\min}(P_0)$ after high-pass filtering.

Cut	PTDB	YAAPT	SWIPE	RAPT	PEFAC	YIN	NVM
0 Hz	0.3318	0.6025	0.2900	0.3147	0.3046	0.2781	0.2709
200 Hz	0.3531	0.6281	0.3092	0.3328	0.3221	0.2958	0.2885
400 Hz	0.3763	0.6467	0.3311	0.3534	0.3429	0.3163	0.3095
600 Hz	0.3895	0.6561	0.3445	0.3682	0.3577	0.3304	0.3241
1000 Hz	0.4082	0.6675	0.3635	0.3887	0.3795	0.3504	0.3450
2000 Hz	0.4300	0.6793	0.3861	0.4131	0.4049	0.3735	0.3693

8 Conclusion

Parameter identification problem was studied for the stationary and affine harmonic models of a voiced signal in short time intervals. Amplitudes and phases are successfully estimated by the conventional LS approach. The unbiased criterion from [3] for Pitch estimation was generalized to short time intervals. A general complexity of the identification algorithms is proportional to N^2 where N is the window length. A new algorithm is described that gives an approximate solution with a complexity of $N \log_2 N$ operations. A trade-off between speed and precision was established.

Acknowledgments. The work was supported by Saint Petersburg State University, project 6.37.349.2015.

References

1. Stylianou, Y.: Harmonic plus Noise Models for speech, combined with statistical methods, for speech and speaker modification. Ph.D. thesis. Ecole Nationale Superieure des Telecommunications, Paris (1996)

2. de Cheveigne, A., Kawahara, H.: YIN, a fundamental frequency estimator for speech and music. JASA **111**(4), 1917–1930 (2002)
3. Griffin, D.W., Lim, J.S.: Multiband excitation vocoder. IEEE Trans. Acoustic Speech Sig. Process. **36**(8), 1223–1235 (1988)
4. Pirker, G., Wohlmayr, M., Petrik, S., Pernkopf, F.: A pitch tracking corpus with evaluation on multipitch tracking scenario. In: INTERSPEECH, pp. 1509–1512 (2011)
5. Kasi, K., Zahorian, S.A.: Yet another algorithm for pitch tracking. IEEE Trans. Acoustic Speech Sig. Process. **1**, 361–364 (2002)
6. Camacho, A.: SWIPE: a sawtooth waveform inspired pitch estimator for speech and music. Doctoral dissertation, University of Florida (2007)
7. Talkin, D.: A robust algorithm for pitch tracking (RAPT). In: Kleijn, W.B., Paliwal, K.K. (eds.) Speech Coding and Synthesis, pp. 495–518. Elsevier, Amsterdam (1995)
8. Gonzalez, S., Brookes, M.: A pitch estimation filter robust to high levels of noise (PEFAC). In: IEEE 19th European Signal Processing Conference, pp. 451–455 (2011)

Gender Classification of Web Authors Using Feature Selection and Language Models

Christina Aravantinou[(✉)], Vasiliki Simaki, Iosif Mporas,
and Vasileios Megalooikonomou

Multidimensional Data Analysis and Knowledge Management Laboratory,
Department of Computer Engineering and Informatics, University of Patras,
26500 Rion, Greece
{aravantino,simaki,vasilis}@ceid.upatras.gr,
imporas@upatras.gr

Abstract. In the present article, we address the problem of automatic gender classification of web blog authors. More specifically, we employ eight widely used machine learning algorithms, in order to study the effectiveness of feature selection on improving the accuracy of gender classification. The feature ranking is performed over a set of statistical, part-of-speech tagging and language model features. In the experiments, we employed classification models based on decision trees, support vector machines and lazy-learning algorithms. The experimental evaluation performed on blog author gender classification data demonstrated the importance of language model features for this task and that feature selection significantly improves the accuracy of gender classification, regardless of the type of the machine learning algorithm used.

Keywords: Text classification · Gender identification · Feature selection

1 Introduction

The growth of social media and its users is impressive and the exploration of the available information in terms of topic, author, genre, etc., is a basic task. Every user of social media leaves his digital traces, makes transactions, expresses his opinion about things and describes moments of his life. Many trends have sprung up over tweets, blog posts and Facebook statuses. These trends express not only an individual user, but often an entire social group. Therefore, it is an interesting task to detect demographic characteristics, such as gender, in users' text data. Information about the gender can be derived not only from the data the user provides about himself, but also implicitly, from the linguistic choices he/she makes. The automatic extraction of information from the everyday enormously growing volumes of data related to the gender, age and other demographic characteristics of the user is essential in the e-government, security and e-commerce market.

The online user's attitude can be observed and explained from a social perspective and his/her "digital traces" [10] may be very informative about current

© Springer International Publishing Switzerland 2015
A. Ronzhin et al. (Eds.): SPECOM 2015, LNAI 9319, pp. 226–233, 2015.
DOI: 10.1007/978-3-319-23132-7_28

trends in any domain. The user's online activity reveals several elements, not only about his/her preferences or transactions, but also about his/her identity. The user, consciously or not, provides information about his/her social status, gender, age and even his/her educational level and profession.

User's gender detection can be perceived as a text classification task, where machine learning techniques are used to identify the author's gender [4,5]. Koppel et al. [9] propose text classification methods to extract the author's gender from formal texts, using features such as n-grams and function words that are more frequent in authorship attribution. They combine stylometric and text classification techniques, in order to extract the author's gender. In a subsequent study [2], Argamon et al., by applying factor analysis and machine learning techniques, contribute with gender and age information, in texts mined from the blogosphere. Ansari et al. [1] use frequency counting of tokens, tf-idf and part-of-speech (POS) tags to find the gender of blog authors. For gender recognition in Twitter, Burger et al. [3] exploit the content of the tweet combined with the username and other pieces of information related to the user.

Recent studies in gender estimation [8,12,13,18] deal with social media and propose methods that detect the gender and, in some cases, the age of the users. The experiments were implemented with gender-polarized words, POS tags and sentence length among other features. In Sarawgi et al. [15], they perform a comparative study of gender attribution, without taking into account the topic or the genre of the selected text. In [17] they use the Naive Bayes classifier, combined with text features and features such as the web page color. Holmgren and Shyu [6] applied machine learning techniques using a feature vector containing word counts, in order to detect the author's gender of Facebook statuses. Rangel and Rosso [14] introduced a set of stylistic features to extract the gender and age of authors, using a large set of documents from the social web, written in Spanish. Finally, Marquardt et al. [11] focused on detecting the best feature set towards age and gender prediction in social media.

In the present article, we perform feature ranking and subset selection, aiming to improve the accuracy of author gender classification on web blogs. The feature selection is performed over a large set of features, using statistical, part-of-speech tagging and language model based feature extraction methodologies. These text features were examined by machine learning classification algorithms, in order to evaluate the gender classification performance for different numbers of features.

The rest of the paper is organized as follows. In Sect. 2 we describe the proposed methodology for gender identification of web users from blog posts. In Sect. 3 we demonstrate and analyze the experimental results and finally, in Sect. 4 we conclude this work.

2   Proposed Gender Identification Methodology

For the feature selection on the task of blog authors' gender identification, we adopted a standard approach followed in most of the previous related work, i.e. pre-processing, feature extraction and classification structure was utilized, as shown in Fig. 1.

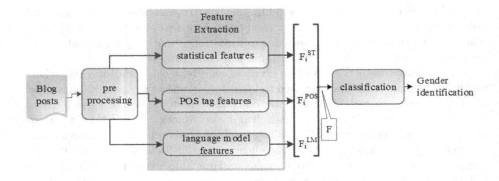

Fig. 1. Block diagram of the blog post users' gender identification scheme

Specifically, each blog post is initially preprocessed. During pre-processing, each post is split into sentences and each sentence is split into words. Afterwards, three feature extraction methodologies are applied in parallel and independently to each other to each post. In detail, statistical, part-of-speech (POS) tag and language model features are extracted constructing vectors F_i^{ST}, F_i^{POS} and F_i^{LM}, respectively. These features are consequently concatenated to a super vector $F = F_i^{ST}||F_i^{POS}||F_i^{LM}$. This results to one feature vector, F, per blog post, which is processed by a classification algorithm, in order to label each post with a gender class.

2.1   Feature Extraction

Three categories of features were computed for each blog post, namely the statistical features, the POS tag features and the language model features.

As far as the statistical features are considered, they consist of statistical values in character and word level. The statistical features that we employed are the following: the number of characters per web post; the normalized number of characters in capital; the normalized number of alphabetic characters; the normalized number of space characters; the normalized number of tab ("\t") characters; the number of occurrence of each alphabetic character; the normalized number of digit characters; the normalized number of occurrence of special characters ($\sim$,@,#,$,%,∧,&,*,−,_,=,+,>,<,[,],{,},/,\,|); the total number of words; the normalized number of words that consist of less than 4 characters (short words); the normalized number of characters per word; the average word length; the number of sentences; the number of paragraphs; the number of lines; the average number of characters per sentence; the average number of words per sentence; the normalized number of different words; the number of words that appear once in the document; the number of words that appear twice in the document; the number of punctuation symbols (".", ",", "?", "!", ":", ";", "'", " "); the number of function words; the average number of sentences per paragraph; the average number of characters per paragraph; the normalized number of words that start with a capital letter; the normalized number of emoticons; the normalized number of words whose letters are all capital; the standard deviation of the word length; the maximum word length; the minimum word length. All the above features compound the F_i^{ST} feature vector, which has dimensionality equal to 30.

POS tag features, which mainly represent a particular part of speech for every word in a given text, were then computed. These are: the number of nouns; the number of proper nouns; the number of adjectives; the number of prepositions; the number of verbs; the number of pronouns; the number of interjections; the number of adverbs; the number of articles. The F_i^{POS} feature vector comprises all these features and has dimensionality equal to 9.

Finally, for the language model features, we use 2 unigram, bigram and trigram language models, one for each gender class (female and male), in order to measure log likelihood and entropy as well as their normalized values for each model. These features are language independent. The F_i^{LM} feature vector contains all the above features and, therefore, is a 24-dimensional feature vector.

The concatenation of the three feature vectors results to F, as described above. Thus, for each blog post, one final feature vector, F, is constructed, which has dimensionality equal to $30 + 9 + 24 = 63$. For the estimation of the above text features we used the NLTK [19] open-source toolkit.

2.2 Feature Selection

For the evaluation of the importance of the features we relied on ReliefF algorithm [7]. ReliefF evaluates the worth of a feature by repeatedly sampling an instance and considering the value of the given feature for the nearest instance of the same and different class. ReliefF can operate on both discrete and continuous class data. In the present evaluation we used the Ranker [16] search method. Ranker method ranks features by their individual evaluations. For the feature selection step we used the WEKA machine learning toolkit software [20] implementation.

2.3 Classification

For the classification stage, we used a number of dissimilar machine learning algorithms, which are well studied and have been used extensively in several text classification tasks. In particular, we used a multilayer perceptron neural network (MLP), using the back-propagation algorithm for training and three layers, and support vector machines (SVMs) using the sequential minimal optimization algorithm, which were tested using radial basis kernel (rbf) and polynomial kernel (poly). In addition, we used four tree algorithms, namely the pruned $C4.5$ decision tree (J48), the random tree (RandTree), constructing a tree that considers K randomly chosen attributes at each node, the random forest (RandForest) constructing a forest of random trees and the fast decision tree learner (RepTree), that builds a decision tree using information gain or variance and prunes it using reduced-error pruning with back-fitting. Finally, we employed one lazy-learning algorithm, the k-nearest neighbor, IBk. All classifiers were implemented using the WEKA toolkit [20].

3 Experimental Setup and Evaluation

The feature selection methodology for blog post authors' gender classification described in the previous section was evaluated using the statistical, POS tag and language model features and the classifiers presented above. In order to avoid overlap between training and test subsets, a 10-fold cross validation evaluation protocol was followed.

For our evaluation we used the publically available "Blog author gender classification dataset", which was introduced in the work of Mukherjee and Liu [12]. It contains blog posts in English, 1390 written by female authors and 1546 written by male authors. The dataset includes 1319917 words and 6085202 characters. Each post was labeled as female or male, depending on the gender of its author, which was determined by the profile of each author.

At first, we tested the discriminative ability of the language model features, so we used only these features with the classifiers. The dimensionality of the feature vector is, therefore, 24. Table 1 shows the experimental results, in terms of percentages of correctly classified blog posts. SVM using polynomial kernel achieves the best accuracy, which is equal to 69.35 %.

As a second step, we evaluated the appropriateness of all the features on the task of web blog authors' gender identification, using the ReliefF criterion. As seen in Table 2, the language model based features were found to be the most relevant to gender classification, since sixteen out of the top-20 features derive from the language model based features we trained.

The absence of POS tag features from the top-20 list implies that these features are weakly correlated to the gender of an author. It is worth mentioning that the normalized number of characters per word, short words, different words and digits were found important for classifying a blog post as male or female, considering that they are ranked in the top-15, top-18, top-19 and top-20 features respectively.

In total, 62 out of the 63 text features were found to be to some degree relevant with the gender classification problem, i.e. they demonstrated positive attribute quality value. The remaining one, namely the normalized number of tab characters, obtained a negative value, which means that it is not a relevant attribute with respect to the gender classification problem.

The classification accuracy was evaluated in terms of percentages of correctly classified blog posts. The experimental results, in percentages, for the eight dif-

Table 1. Accuracy for gender classification using only the language model features.

J48	MLP	SVMrbf	SVMpoly	RandForest	RandTree	REPTree	IBk
68.19	68.02	67.91	**69.35**	67.92	60.42	67.40	68.66

Table 2. Ranking results for the top-20 features.

Rank	Score	Feature description	Feature type
1	0.00769	norm. entropy of female unigram lang. model	language model
2	0.00769	norm. entropy of male unigram lang. model	language model
3	0.00769	norm. log likel. for female unigram lang. model	language model
4	0.00769	norm. log likel. for male unigram lang. model	language model
5	0.00668	norm. entropy of female trigram lang. model	language model
6	0.00668	norm. entropy of male trigram lang. model	language model
7	0.00668	norm.log likel. for female trigram lang. model	language model
8	0.00668	norm. log likel. for male trigram lang. model	language model
9	0.00666	entropy for male trigram lang. model	language model
10	0.00489	norm. entropy for male bigram lang. model	language model
11	0.00489	norm. entropy for female bigram lang. model	language model
12	0.00489	norm. log likelihood for male bigram lang. model	language model
13	0.00489	norm. log likel. for female bigram lang. model	language model
14	0.00478	entropy for female trigram lang. model	language model
15	0.00354	norm. number of characters per word	statistical
16	0.00351	entropy for male bigram lang. model	language model
17	0.00309	entropy for female bigram lang. model	language model
18	0.00241	number of short words	statistical
19	0.00189	number of different words	statistical
20	0.00182	digits	statistical

ferent machine learning techniques and for each of the 6 different subsets of the top-n features with $n = \{10, 20, 30, 40, 50, 60\}$ are presented in Table 3. The last column presents the classification accuracy for each algorithm in the case that we do not perform feature selection ("All") and the dimensionality of the feature vector is 63. The best performing subset of features for each algorithm is indicated in bold. The top-10 features consist only of language model features. The top-20 features contain 16 language model features and so do the top-30 features. The top-40 features include 21 language model features; the top-50 features include 23 language model features and finally, the top-60 features contain all the language model features.

Comparing the results obtained with the use of feature selection to those using all 63 features, i.e. with no feature selection, we observe that for the all classification algorithms the former results are better compared to the latter. This fact verifies our initial hypothesis, namely that the feature selection is able to improve the accuracy of gender classification. As seen in Table 3, the improvement in accuracy varies from 0.51 % in SVM using rbf kernel to 7.12 %, in the case of Random Tree. The IBk shows a significant improvement in performance, which is approximately 6 %, followed by J48 and MLP, with improvements of 2.8 % and 1 % respectively.

Table 3. Accuracy for gender classification per feature subset and classification algorithm.

	top-10	top-20	top-30	top-40	top-50	top-60	All
J48	**68.32**	67.92	67.44	67.54	67.47	67.68	65.46
MLP	68.46	67.88	68.56	68.56	**68.66**	67.27	67.57
SVMrbf	68.02	68.26	68.32	**68.42**	68.36	68.32	67.91
SVMpoly	69.43	69.24	69.75	69.75	69.93	**70.27**	69.72
RandForest	69.52	68.46	69.41	**70.50**	70.03	69.96	69.69
RandTree	67.01	**68.43**	67.17	65.90	66.62	66.55	61.31
REPTree	67.23	**67.51**	66.49	66.79	66.38	67.34	66.62
IBk	68.12	68.29	**68.66**	68.56	68.56	68.49	63.01

The best classification accuracy, 70.50 %, was achieved by combining the top-40 features with Random Forest, followed by the 70.27 %, achieved using the top-60 features with SVM using polynomial kernel. It is worth mentioning that SVM using polynomial kernel performs better with a larger number of features. This is owed to the curse of dimensionality phenomenon, from which the SVMs do not suffer. One the other hand, J48 performs best when using only the top-10 features. In general, the top-10 and top-20 features obtain quite high results and specifically, Random Tree and REP Tree achieve their best performance using only the top-20 features. This shows the great impact of the language model features on the gender classification problem, since the top-20 features consist mainly of them. Finally, as can be seen in Table 1, the use of the language model features only, succeeded a quite high performance, having accuracy equal to 69.35 %.

4   Conclusion

In this article, we investigated the effectiveness of feature selection for improving the accuracy of web blog authors' gender identification. A combination of statistical, part of speech tagging and language model based features was used to represent each web post. We evaluated the gender identification performance using eight classification algorithms for different subsets of features according to ranking scores, produced by the ReliefF algorithm. Random Forest outperformed all the evaluated algorithms, when using the top-40 text-based features, with accuracy equal to 70.50 %. The experimental results showed that the use of subsets of features improved the overall gender identification accuracy for all the evaluated algorithms. Finally, the superiority of the language model features was proved, since the best classification results were obtained, mainly, due to their contribution.

References

1. Ansari, Y.Z., Azad, S.A., Akhtar, H.: Gender classification of blog authors. Int. J. Sustain. Dev. Green Econ. **2**(1) (2013). ISSN No: 2315–4721
2. Argamon, S., Koppel, M., Pennebaker, W., Schler, J.: Mining the Blogosphere: age, gender and the varieties of self-expression. First Monday **12**, 9 (2007)
3. Burger, J., Henderson, J., Kim, G., Zarrella, G.: Discriminating gender on Twitter. In: Proceedings of the Conference on Empirical Methods in Natural Language Processing, pp. 1301–1309. Association for Computational Linguistics, Stroudsburg (2011)
4. Cheng, N., Chandramouli, R., Subbalakshmi, K.P.: Author gender identification from text. Int. J. Digit. Forensics Incident Response **8**(1), 78–88 (2011)
5. Company, J.S., Wanner, L.: How to use less features and reach better performance in author gender identification. In: Proceedings of the 9th International Conference on Language Resources and Evaluation (LREC). Reykjavik, Iceland (2014)
6. Holmgren, J., Shyu, E.: Gender Classification of Facebook Posts (2013)
7. Kira, K., Rendell, L.A.: A practical approach to feature selection. In: Proceedings of the 9th International Workshop on Machine Learning, pp. 249–256 (1992)
8. Kobayashi, D., Matsumura, N., Ishizuka, M.: Automatic estimation of Bloggers' gender. In: Proceedings of International Conference on Weblogs and Social Media (2007)
9. Koppel, M., Argamon, S., Shimoni, A.R.: Automatically categorizing written texts by author gender. Literary Linguist. Comput. **17**(4), 401–412 (2003)
10. Lazer, D., Pentland, A.S., Adamic, L., Aral, S., Barabasi, A.L., Brewer, D., Van Alstyne, M.: Life in the network: the coming age of computational social science. Science **323**(5915), 721 (2009). (New York, NY)
11. Marquardt, J., Farnadi, G., Vasudevan, G., Moens, M., Davalos, S., Teredesai, A., De Cock, M.: Age and Gender Identification in Social Media. Author Profiling Task at PAN (2014)
12. Mukherjee, A., Liu, B.: Improving gender classification of blog authors. In: Proceedings of EMNLP (2010)
13. Peersman, C., Daelemans, W., Van Vaerenbergh, L: Predicting age and gender in online social networks. In: Proceedings of the 3rd Workshop on Search and Mining User-Generated Contents, Glasgow, UK (2011)
14. Rangel, F., Rosso, P.: Use of language and author profiling: identification of gender and age. In: Proceedings of the 10th International Workshop on Natural Language Processing and Cognitive Science (2013)
15. Sarawgi, R., Gajulapalli, K., Choi, Y.: Gender attribution: tracing stylometric evidence beyond topic and genre. In: Proceedings of the 15th Conference on Computational Natural Language Learning, pp. 78–86. Association for Computational Linguistics, Stroudsburg (2011)
16. Witten, I.H., Frank, E.: Data Mining: Practical Machine Learning Tools and Techniques. Morgan-Kaufman Series of Data Management Systems, 2nd edn. Elsevier, San Francisco (2005)
17. Yan, X., Yan, L.: Gender Classification of Weblog Authors. Computational Approaches to Analyzing Weblogs, AAAI (2006)
18. Zhang, C., Zhang, P.: Predicting gender from blog posts. Technical report. University of Massachusetts Amherst, USA (2010)
19. NLTK. http://www.nltk.org/
20. WEKA. http://www.cs.waikato.ac.nz/ml/weka/

Improving Acoustic Models for Russian Spontaneous Speech Recognition

Alexey Prudnikov[1,2], Ivan Medennikov[2,3]([⊠]), Valentin Mendelev[1],
Maxim Korenevsky[1,2], and Yuri Khokhlov[3]

[1] Speech Technology Center Ltd, St. Petersburg, Russia
{prudnikov,mendelev,korenevsky}@speechpro.com
[2] ITMO University, St. Petersburg, Russia
[3] STC-innovations Ltd, St. Petersburg, Russia
{medennikov,khokhlov}@speechpro.com

Abstract. The aim of the paper is to investigate the ways to improve acoustic models for Russian spontaneous speech recognition. We applied the main steps of the Kaldi Switchboard recipe to a Russian dataset but obtained low accuracy with respect to the results for English spontaneous telephone speech. We found two methods to be especially useful for Russian spontaneous speech: the i-vector based deep neural network adaptation and speaker-dependent bottleneck features which provide 8.6 % and 11.9 % relative word error rate reduction over the baseline system respectively.

Keywords: Speech recognition · Russian spontaneous speech · Deep neural networks · Speaker adaptation · I-vectors · Bottleneck features

1 Introduction

Recognizing spontaneous conversational speech is one of the most difficult tasks in the field of automatic speech recognition (ASR). There is a lot of literature on recognizing spontaneous English speech [1–3]. Systems proposed in these papers have high accuracy rates, which makes it possible to use them in commercial applications. The main source of data for such research is the Switchboard-1 corpus (SWB) [4], which comprises 300 h of telephone conversations in English. As far as we know, currently the best English spontaneous speech recognition system trained on the SWB corpus provides 10.4 % word error rate (WER) on the HUB5 2000 test dataset [1]. This result was achieved by combining convolutional neural network and speaker-dependent deep neural network (SD-DNN) in the acoustic model, as well as using Hessian-free sequence training.

Our task is to build a system for high-quality Russian spontaneous speech recognition with acceptable operation speed. At present no Russian spontaneous speech recognition systems provide recognition quality comparable with the above mentioned English systems. It is often impossible to understand the meaning of the original utterance from the output of the available systems.

© Springer International Publishing Switzerland 2015
A. Ronzhin et al. (Eds.): SPECOM 2015, LNAI 9319, pp. 234–242, 2015.
DOI: 10.1007/978-3-319-23132-7_29

The difficulties are due to the properties of Russian spontaneous conversational speech: high channel and speaker variance, additive and non-linear distortions, accents and emotional speech, diversity of speaking styles, speech rate variance, reductions and weakened articulation. One of the most obvious ways to deal with such variability is enlarging the training dataset. However, this method is expensive and labour-intensive. We focus on the search for algorithmic solutions for improving Russian spontaneous speech recognition quality.

In our experiments we used the open-source Kaldi toolkit [5], since it includes many effective state-of-the-art training methods for Gaussian mixture models (GMMs) (LDA, MLLT, fMLLR [6], MMI/MPE discriminative training [7], and others) and deep neural networks (DNNs) (training by the cross-entropy (CE) minimization criterion and sequence training [2] using graphics processor unit (GPU)). First of all, we tried the Kaldi SWB recipe, which produces excellent results (WER 12.6 % on HUB5 2000 and 13.0 % on HUB5 2001 [2]) for English spontaneous speech. We attempted to follow this recipe on our dataset. Analysing the SWB recipe and testing it on Russian spontaneous speech is the topic of Sect. 2. The results we obtained were unsatisfactory.

We performed a series of experiments and concluded that the most promising approach to recognition quality improvement is lowering sensitivity to acoustic variability of the speech signal. This approach is described in Sect. 3, which deals with DNN adaptation using i-vectors [3]. Then, similarly to the GMM training recipe, we used series of features transformations, which improves discriminative properties of the model, for improving DNNs. This was implemented by extracting bottleneck features from the trained DNN model. This approach is described in Sect. 4. Section 5 contains the description of the experiments and the analysis of their results.

2   Applying the SWB Recipe to Russian Data

As our starting point we took the Kaldi recipe for the Switchboard corpus. Our goal was to figure out which training steps contributes the most to performance of the resulting model. The recipe includes two stages: GMM-HMM training and DNN-HMM training. GMM-HMM training consists of the following main steps:

1. Training a monophone model on 10,000 utterances (mono).
2. Training the first triphone model on 30,000 utterances using mel-frequency cepstral coefficients (MFCC) with deltas (tri_deltas).
3. Training the second triphone model with LDA-MLLT normalization on 100,000 utterances (tri_mllt).
4. Training a fMLLR-SAT model on a full dataset using the LDA-MLLT features (tri_fmllr).
5. Training a discriminative model on the full dataset using the LDA-MLLT features adapted with fMLLR (tri_discr).

The DNN-HMM training includes the following steps:

1. Training with the cross-entropy criteria.
2. Additional training with one of sequence criteria (MMI/bMMI/MPE/sMBR).

We repeated the GMM-HMM training stages on the Switchboard corpus. At the DNN-HMM training stage we limited ourselves to cross-entropy training on 30,000 utterances in order to save time. We trained three DNNs using different input features, namely MFCC (dnn_mfcc), LDA-MLLT (dnn_mllt), and LDA-MLLT-fMLLR (dnn_fmllr). The results on the HUB5 2001 evaluation set are given in Table 1. One can see that different normalization (LDA-MLLT) and adaptation (fMLLR) techniques provide significant improvement in spontaneous speech recognition quality.

After that, we applied the same steps to a Russian spontaneous speech dataset (about 390 h). The results (see Table 2) proved to be significantly worse than those for English speech. The absolute difference between our results and the state-of-the-art results on Switchboard is over 15 % WER. That can be explained by the more spontaneous character of our recordings, as well as lower quality of the transcripts.

Despite the results obtained are not satisfactory, increasing the system's robustness to acoustic variability by means of normalization and adaptation led

Table 1. Results on English (HUB5 2001).

model	data set	WER, %	ΔWER, %	WERR, %
tri_deltas	30k utt	46.6	—	—
tri_mllt	100k utt	37.7	8.9	19.1
tri_fmllr	full	29.4	17.2	36.9
tri_discr	full	26.4	20.2	43.3
dnn_mfcc	30k utt	37.4	—	—
dnn_mllt	30k utt	31.1	6.3	16.8
dnn_fmllr	30k utt	26.4	11.0	29.4

Table 2. Results on Russian.

model	data set	WER, %	ΔWER, %	WERR, %
tri_deltas	90k utt	50.4	—	—
tri_mllt	90k utt	47.6	2.8	5.5
tri_fmllr	full	40.8	9.6	19.0
tri_discr	full	36.2	14.2	28.2
dnn_mfcc	full	32.2	—	—
dnn_mllt	full	32.0	0.2	0.6
dnn_fmllr	full	31.2	1.0	3.1

to a great improvement in GMM on Russian data as well. One can see that DNN models significantly outperform GMMs, so we focus on lowering DNN sensitivity to acoustic variability of the speech signal.

3   Lowering Sensitivity to Acoustic Variability

Channel and speaker variations are among the most important factors causing the acoustic variability of the speech signal. Traditional means of counteracting these variability types are adaptation and normalization algorithms. Many adaptation algorithms have been developed for CD-DNN-HMM acoustic models. They can be classified into the following approaches:

- Extraction and tuning of a subset of DNN parameters [8–11].
- Tuning all network parameters using an additional regularizing penalty in the target function, which does not allow the tuned parameters to deviate too strongly from the source model [12,13].
- Supplying the DNN with additional information reflecting some properties of the recording or its fragments [3,14].
- Using GMM-adapted features [15,16].

Second recognition pass is unaffordable due to speed constraints, so we applied the DNN i-vector based adaptation algorithm, which provides adaptation both to the speaker and to the acoustic environment [17]. An i-vector is a low-dimensional vector encoding the difference in feature distribution between a target speech fragment (normally the fragment corresponding to one speaker) and the distribution estimated over the whole training set. I-vectors are widely used in speaker identification and verification [18,19], and have recently been successfully applied to ASR tasks [3].

Our training set is characterized with low quality of speaker labeling and the presence of a large number of short files. These factors lead to lack of data for reliable i-vector estimation and to the ineffectiveness of the straightforward training procedure proposed in [3]. For this reason, we chose the solution proposed in [14], which is more robust to i-vector estimation noise. It consists of the following steps:

1. Training a speaker-independent DNN on the source features.
2. Expanding the input layer of the speaker-independent DNN trained at the first step.
3. Training the DNN with an expanded input layer using a penalty for parameters deviation from the source model.

Multiple experiments which are outside the scope of this paper showed that this training scheme provides significant advantages over a straightforward realization in our task.

4 Speaker-Dependent Bottleneck Features

State-of-the-art GMM models for spontaneous speech recognition employ a sequence of feature transformations. A conventional transformation series consists of successively applied LDA-MLLT and fMLLR transformations. Experimental results described in Section 2 demonstrate that application of such sequence of transformations leads to significant performance gains for both GMM and DNN in case of SWB. However, in case of Russian spontaneous speech, the effect of these transformations on the DNN turned out to be small.

The second approach examined in this paper is extracting high-level features from a well-trained DNN model and using them to train another model. Specifically we extracted bottleneck features from a SD-DNN model employed i-vector based adaptation. This training procedure can be interpreted as i-vector-based SAT DNN training.

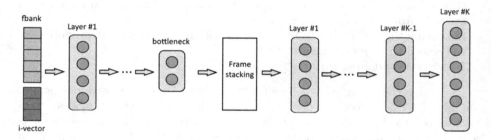

Fig. 1. DNN speaker-adaptive training scheme

The following steps were performed:

1. An SD-DNN was trained.
2. The last hidden layer was transformed into two layers. The first layer was a bottleneck with a linear activation function. The second was a non-linear layer with the original output dimension.

$$y = f(WX + B) \approx f(W_{out}(W_{bn}X) + B) \tag{1}$$

These layers were formed by applying SVD to the weight matrix W of the source layer:

$$W = USV^T \approx \tilde{U}_{bn}\tilde{V}_{bn}^T = W_{out}W_{bn} \tag{2}$$

Here bn designates reduced dimension.
3. The network formed on the step 2 was retrained using cross-entropy criterion with the L_2-penalty for parameters deviation from original values.
4. All layers after the bottleneck were discarded. The resulting DNN was used for feature extraction.

The described extractor training scheme showed a significant advantage in terms of WER compared to directly embedding a linear bottleneck layer into the DNN. For the SAT model training the obtained features were spliced, see Fig. 1.

We suppose that the better the basic DNN is, the better are the bottleneck features extracted from it. For this reason the scheme was adapted for use with models trained using the sequence training criterion. A straightforward solution of changing the training criterion for sequence training at step 4 did not work, so we applied cross-entropy training, using the probabilities generated by the original sequence-trained model as target probabilities.

5   Experiments

We performed experiments using the full training dataset of 390 h and 3-gram language model with modified Kneser-Ney smoothing [21] and a 200 k word lexicon. Test set perplexity is 360, out of vocabulary (OOV) rate is 1.8 %.

As input features for the basic DNN configuration we used 20-dimensional mel-frequency log-energies (FBANK) features with cepstral mean normalization (CMN) with the temporal context of 31 frames. As mentioned in Sect. 3, we decided not to use fMLLR adaptation due to the specific character of our task. The output softmax layer contained 13,000 neurons corresponding to the GMM-HMM senones. The best quality was obtained when using 6 hidden layers with 1024 sigmoidal neurons in each.

The speaker-dependent DNN was trained according to the scheme described in Sect. 3. We used 50-dimensional i-vectors because of lack of data for reliable i-vector estimation and bad speaker labeling.

Speaker-dependent bottleneck features of dimension 80 were extracted from speaker-dependent DNNs with FBANK+ivector features. We extracted bottleneck-features from CE and sequence-trained DNN (SD-BN and ST-SD-BN respectively, see Sect. 4).

We trained the GMM using SD-BN features (tri_sdbn), as well as two DNNs using SD-BN and ST-SD-BN features. Table 3 demonstrates GMM results.

DNN training with speaker-dependent bottleneck features was performed using the temporal context of 31 frames taking every 5th frame. The best results were obtained by the DNN configuration with 4 hidden layers with 2048 neurons per layer. DNNs were trained by the CE minimization criterion. Finally, we performed sMBR sequence training. The results of DNNs are presented in Table 4.

Our experiments demonstrate the following: first, DNN adaptation using i-vectors significantly improves the quality of the acoustic model. Second, using

Table 3. Experiments on GMM.

model	WER, %	ΔWER, %	WERR, %
tri_discr	36.2	—	—
tri_sdbn	32.1	4.1	11.3

Table 4. Experiments on DNNs.

features	criterion	WER, %	ΔWER, %	WERR, %
FBANK	CE	32.0	—	—
FBANK+ivec	CE	29.1	2.9	9.1
SD-BN	CE	28.4	3.6	11.3
ST-SD-BN	CE	27.9	4.1	12.8
FBANK	sMBR	28.5	—	—
FBANK+ivec	sMBR	26.0	2.5	8.6
SD-BN	sMBR	25.3	3.2	11.2
ST-SD-BN	sMBR	25.1	3.4	11.9

highly discriminative features provides an additional model quality improvement. This effect is substantial for both GMM and DNN models.

6   Conclusion

The methods described in the paper, namely i-vector based DNN adaptation and speaker-dependent bottleneck features, proved to be effective for Russian spontaneous speech recognition. The proposed scheme of bottleneck feature extraction from a DNN trained using the sequence-discriminative criterion provided additional improvement. The final system achieved 25.1 % WER. We plan to assess effectiveness of the presented approach on the Switchboard English task in the future.

Acknowledgements. The work was partially financially supported by the Government of the Russian Federation, Grant 074-U01, and by the Ministry of Education and Science of Russian Federation, contract 14.579.21.0057, ID RFMEFI57914X0057.

References

1. Soltau, H., Saon, G., Sainath, T.N.: Joint training of convolutional and non-convolutional neural networks. In: 39th International Conference on Acoustics, Speech and Signal Processing (ICASSP), pp. 5572–5576. Florence (2014)
2. Vesely, K., Ghoshal, A., Burget, L., Povey, D.: Sequence-discriminative training of deep neural networks. In: 14th Annual Conference of the International Speech Communication Association (Interspeech), pp. 2345–2349. Lyon (2014)
3. Saon, G., Soltau, H., Nahamoo, D., Picheny, M.: Speaker adaptation of neural network acoustic models using i-vectors. In: 13th Biannual IEEE Workshop on Automatic Speech Recognition and Understanding (ASRU), pp. 55–59. Olomouc (2013)

4. Godfrey, J.J., Holliman, E.C., McDaniel, J.: SWITCHBOARD: telephone speech corpus for research and development. In: 17th International Conference on Acoustics, Speech and Signal Processing (ICASSP), pp. 517–520. San Francisco (1992)
5. Povey, D. et al.: The Kaldi speech recognition toolkit. In: 12th Biannual IEEE Workshop on Automatic Speech Recognition and Understanding (ASRU), pp. 5572–5576. Big Island (2011)
6. Gales, M.J.F.: Maximum Likelihood Linear Transformations for HMM-Based Speech Recognition. Technical report, Cambridge University Engineering Department (1997)
7. Povey, D.: Discriminative training for large vocabulary speech recognition. Ph.D. dissertation. University of Cambridge, Cambridge, UK (2003)
8. Seide, F., Li, G., Chen, X., Yu, D.: Feature engineering in context-dependent deep neural networks for conversational speech transcription. In: 12th Biannual IEEE Workshop on Automatic Speech Recognition and Understanding (ASRU), pp. 24–29. Big Island (2011)
9. Gemello, R., Mana, F., Scanzio, S., Laface, P., De Mori, R.: Linear hidden transformations for adaptation of hybrid ANN/HMM models. Speech Commun. 49(10–11), 827–835 (2007)
10. Yao K., Yu, D., Seide, F., Su, H., Deng, L., Gong, Y.: Adaptation of context-dependent deep neural networks for automatic speech recognition. In: IEEE Spoken Language Technology Workshop (SLT), pp. 366–369. Miami (2012)
11. Ochiai, T., Matsuda, S., Lu, X., Hori, C., Katagiri, S.: Speaker adaptive training using deep neural networks. In: 39th International Conference on Acoustics, Speech and Signal Processing (ICASSP), pp. 6399–6403. Florence (2014)
12. Li, X., Bilmes, J.: Regularized adaptation of discriminative classifiers. In: 31st International Conference on Acoustics, Speech and Signal Processing (ICASSP). Toulouse (2006)
13. Yu, D., Yao, K., Su, H., Li, G., Seide, F.: KL-divergence regularized deep neural network adaptation for improved large vocabulary speech recognition. In: 38th International Conference on Acoustics, Speech and Signal Processing (ICASSP), pp. 7893–7897. Vancouver (2013)
14. Senior, A., Lopez-Moreno, I.: Improving DNN speaker independence with i-vector inputs. In: 39th International Conference on Acoustics, Speech and Signal Processing (ICASSP), pp. 225–229. Florence (2014)
15. Tomashenko, N., Khokhlov, Y.: Speaker adaptation of context dependent deep neural networks based on MAP-adaptation and GMM-derived feature processing. In: 15th Annual Conference of the International Speech Communication Association, pp. 2997–3001. Singapore (2014)
16. Liu, S., Sim, K.C.: On combining DNN and GMM with unsupervised speaker adaptation for robust automatic speech. In: 39th International Conference on Acoustics, Speech and Signal Processing (ICASSP), pp. 195–199. Florence (2014)
17. Rouvier, M., Favre, B.: Speaker adaptation of DNN-based ASR with i-vectors: does it actually adapt models to speakers? In: 15th Annual Conference of the International Speech Communication Association (Interspeech), pp. 3007–3011. Singapore (2014)
18. Kozlov, A., Kudashev, O., Matveev, Y., Pekhovsky, T., Simonchik, K., Shulipa, A.: SVID Speaker Recognition System for NIST SRE 2012. In: Železný, M., Habernal, I., Ronzhin, A. (eds.) SPECOM 2013. LNCS, vol. 8113, pp. 278–285. Springer, Heidelberg (2013)

19. Novoselov, S., Pekhovsky, T., Simonchik, K., Shulipa, A.: RBM-PLDA subsystem for the NIST i-vector challenge. In: 15th Annual Conference of the International Speech Communication Association (Interspeech), pp. 378–382. Singapore (2014)
20. Karafiat, M., Grezl, F., Hannemann, M., Cernocky, J.H.: But neural network features for spontaneous Vietnamese in BABEL. In: 39th International Conference on Acoustics, Speech and Signal Processing (ICASSP), pp. 5622–5626 (2014)
21. Chen, S.F., Goodman, J.: An empirical study of smoothing techniques for language modeling. Technical report search in Computing Technology (Harvard University) (1998)

Information Sources of Word Semantics Methods

Miloslav Konopík[(✉)] and Ondřej Pražák

Department of Computer Science and Engineering Faculty of Applied Sciences,
University of West Bohemia, Univerzitni 8, 30614 Plzen, Czech Republic
konopik@kiv.zcu.cz, ondfa@students.zcu.cz

Abstract. This paper studies quality and orthogonality of information sources used in methods for computing word semantics. The quality of the methods is measured on several hand-crafted comparison datasets. The orthogonality is estimated by measuring the performance increase when two information sources are linearly interpolated using optimal interpolation parameters. The experiment conclusions reveal both expected and contradictory results and offer a deeper insight into the information sources of particular methods.

Keywords: Word semantics · Distributional semantics · WordNet · CBOW · Skip-gram · GloVe · LSA · LDA

1 Introduction

The main purpose of speech is to transfer a meaning. Therefore, we believe that it is most cardinal to study how the meaning is captured in it. In this paper, we focus on the meaning that is encoded in words. We study computer algorithms designed to discover the context-independent meaning by finding semantically similar or related words.

Before we go any further, it is necessary to establish the difference between semantic *similarity* and *relatedness* and between context *dependent* and *independent* meaning. *Semantic similarity* of words indicates how big part of the meaning the words share. The higher similarity of the words, the higher probability is that the words can be replaced with one another in a sentence without changing the meaning of the sentence. On the other hand, *semantic relatedness* describes how much are the words related in meaning. The higher relatedness, the higher is the chance that the words appear in semantically similar texts. Some examples are shown in Table 1.

Context-dependent meaning is based upon the word context whereas *context-independent* meaning is considered regardless to the context. Table 1 shows some examples of context-dependent and independent meanings. "Car" and "automobile" are pretty similar in many contexts. "Automobile" is slightly more suitable for the formal register. "Puck" and "biscuit" carry similar meanings in ice hockey but the language style differs greatly. "To water" and "to irrigate" are similar only if they are of the same part of speech. Water can be verb or noun and

© Springer International Publishing Switzerland 2015
A. Ronzhin et al. (Eds.): SPECOM 2015, LNAI 9319, pp. 243–250, 2015.
DOI: 10.1007/978-3-319-23132-7_30

Table 1. Examples of semantically similar and related words.

Similar	Related
car – automobile	car – road
ground – soil	soil – crops
puck – biscuit	puck – hockey
water – irrigate	irrigate – field

the part of speech is determined by the sentence context. The direct neighbours often decide about the parts of speech (drink water VS water plants). Thus we can see that the determining context can be long (a whole document) or very short (direct neighbours).

In this paper we will deal with context-independent meaning. However, it does not imply that we do not use context information to derive the context-independent meaning. In fact, the latter is true for some of the best methods (see Sects. 2.2 and 2.3).

2   The Sources of Information

In this paper, we consider three different sources of information. We experiment with semantic networks, with local context, and with global context.

2.1   Semantic Networks

Semantic networks organize words in graph structures – trees and directed graphs (most often). Vertices represent words (called concepts) and edges semantic relations. The meaning of a word is defined by its position in the structure. Word-Net [10] is probably the best known example of a semantic network. Nouns, verbs, adjectives, and adverbs are grouped into sets of synonyms (synsets). Each synset represents a distinct concept. Among synsets, several semantic relations are defined: super-subordinate relation, meronymy relation, antonymy relation, etc. For us, the super-subordinate relation (sometimes called IS-A relation) is the most important. It links more abstract synsets (like activity, sport) with more specific synsets (e.g. hockey, football).

Path length (Path) is the simplest metric for computing semantic similarity based upon the shortest distance between two synsets containing the compared words. The distance is measured in the super-subordinate relation. The returned value is the reciprocal function of the distance. For words in the same synsets, it is defined as 1.

Wu-Palmer [16] distance (W+P) uses the LCS – Least Common Subsumer (the closest common hypernym) to measure the words similarity. The measure grows with the depth[1] of the LCS in the super-subordinate relation and decreases with the distance between the two synset. It thus includes the path length metric.

---

[1] The distance from the most abstract synset – the common root.

Resnik [13] measure (RES) is based upon measuring the information content of the LCS of the two synsets. The information content (IC) is computed as $IC(S) = -log(P(S))$, where $P(S)$ is the probability that a word belongs to the synset S. The $P(S)$ is estimated from a training corpus.

Lin [7] metric (LIN) extends the Resnik algorithm. The similarity is defined by the following formula:

$$sim_{Lin}(C1, C2) = \frac{2 \times IC(LCS)}{IC(C1) + IC(C2)}. \tag{1}$$

2.2   Global Context

Both local and global context methods for computing word semantics use the *distributional hypothesis*. The theoretical work on words distributional properties dates back to 1954 [5]. Harris observed that words with similar meaning tend to have similar distributional properties. In another words: "a word is characterized by the company it keeps"[2]. The company means the context of the word.

Nowadays, we distinguish between two types of contexts: local context and global context. The local context works with direct neighbours of the words whereas the global context is defined as the same document or paragraph. For example consider these two sentences: "the *ship* sank to the bottom of the sea" and "the *boat* sank to the bottom of the sea". The words *ship* and *boat* are pretty similar and thus tend to have similar words around them. This is an example of local context.

On the contrary, the global context methods focus on documents. For example words "ship" and "water" should occur in the same documents more likely than, let us say, "ship" and "air".

Now, we shortly describe two global context methods that are tested in this article. LSA (Latent Semantic Analysis) and LDA (Latent Dirichlet Allocation).

LSA. The LSA method [6] builds a matrix containing words (rows) counts per documents (columns) from large collections of text documents. The main principle of the method is the idea that latent semantic relations can be revealed by reducing the dimension of the matrix. In particular, the dimension of the matrix is reduced by using the singular value decomposition method and discarding the lowest eigenvalues. In order to distinguish informative and non-informative words, the tf-idf weighing is employed. In LSA, the meaning of words is compared by computing the angle of their respective vectors (cosine distance) in the matrix of the reduced dimension.

LDA. The LDA method [1] works also on the document level, however, the approach is radically different from the LSA method. Here the observed text is modeled using the following generative process. For a given document, generate a

---

[2] A quote by John Rupert Firth.

set of topics. For each topic, generate a word. The topics and words are generated according to the Dirichlet prior distribution. For some documents, some topics are more probable and for some topics, some words are more probable. The probabilistic distributions are estimated from large collections of data using either the EM algorithm (older approach) or the Gibbs sampling (newer approach). In LDA, the meaning of words is computed by comparing vectors of probabilities of the words across all topics. The words that have similar probabilities in the same topics are considered to be more related to each other.

2.3   Local Context

We selected the current state-of-the-art methods for this study: CBOW (Continuous Bag-of-Words Model) and GloVe (Global Vectors for Word Representation).

CBOW model [9] is based upon the idea that neural networks can be used to predict a word given its context (surrounding words). The network is trained on a large collection of texts. The word vectors are taken from the weighting matrix of a trained neural network and compared using the cosine distance.

GloVe model [11] extracts the meaning from a word-word co-occurrence matrix. This model compares ratios of word conditional probabilities (a probability of a word conditioned by one word of its context) extracted from the co-occurrence matrix. The word vectors are taken from the parameters of a weighted least squares regression model built upon the above mentioned probabilities. The cosine distance is again used to compare these word vectors.

3   Experiments

3.1   Evaluation Corpora

In order to measure how well the above mentioned methods compute semantic similarity/relatedness, we employ hand-crafted evaluation corpora listed in Table 2. The datasets contain scores created by human annotators. We measure the performance of the methods by computing Pearson and Spearman correction coefficients between dataset scores and scores produced by measured methods.

We distinguish whether the particular dataset captures semantic similarity or semantic relatedness (as defined in the introduction). Often, this information is not provided directly in the dataset description and we had to derive it from the annotation instructions provided with the dataset. One exception is the WS353 dataset which is divided into similarity (WS353-sim) and relatedness (WS353-rel) subsets. The former contains 153 word pairs and the later 200 pairs.

Table 2. Evaluation Datasets.

Acronym	Dataset	No. of pairs	S/R	Reference
RG65	Rubenstein Goodenough	65	S	[14]
WS353	Wordsim	353	S+R	[3]
MTurk	MTruk	287	R	[12]
RW	Rare Words	2034	R	[8]
MEN	MEN	3000	R	[2]

3.2 Training

The methods based upon the information content (Res, Lin) and the methods based upon word context information (LSA, LDA, CBOW, GloVe) require training on large corpora. Res and Lin algorithms are trained on the News Crawl corpus 2011[3]. LSA and LDA models are taken from the Similar toolkit[4]. CBOW and GloVe models come from the official model sites[5]. We have chosen the official models because these were selected by the authors in order to provide the best results.

However, in order to compare the models in the same conditions, we also trained LDA, CBOW a GloVe on one fairly large corpus – the official Wikipedia dump from March 7, 2015. We have not trained LSA, since the toolkit is unable to process such a large corpus. Res and Lin algorithm are not included in this comparison since their performance is not largely dependent on the corpus.

3.3 Results

In Table 3, we show the experimental results of all the methods described in Sect. 2. Table 4 shows the results for the optimal interpolation of selected methods pairs. In Table 5, the comparison of the methods trained on the same corpus is presented.

We can see several interesting outcomes in the tables. Firstly, the GloVe method dominates all the tests except the RG65 and the WS353-SIM in the single method comparison. Secondly, the methods based upon semantic networks (LIN) and global methods (LSA, LDA) combine well in the linear interpolation test. Thirdly, the performance of GloVe drops significantly when trained on a different corpus.

4 Discussion

We can confirm that the current state-of-the-art methods using local context as the information source perform exceptionally well on the evaluation datasets.

---

[3] http://www.statmt.org/wmt11/translation-task.html#download.
[4] http://www.semanticsimilarity.org/.
[5] https://code.google.com/p/word2vec/ and
http://nlp.stanford.edu/projects/glove/.

We can also see that the methods based upon the information source derived from semantic networks are significantly worse. We can explain that outcome by the following observation. Semantic network methods are very good when evaluated on the RG65 dataset and on the WS353-sim dataset. We know that these datasets are based upon semantic similarity (see Table 2). The other datasets are based upon semantic relatedness. Thus, the conclusion is that the methods that use information from semantic networks compute the semantic similarity rather that semantic relatedness. This conclusion can be crucial for some tasks

Table 3. Single models evaluation. PC = Person Correlation, SC = Spearman Correlation.

Information Source		Semantic Networks				Local C.		Global C.	
Dataset	Corr	LIN	Path	Res	W+P	CBOW	GloVe	LSA	LDA
RG65	PC	**0,840**	0,783	0,824	0,790	0,772	0,771	0,716	0,423
	SC	0,774	**0,785**	0,756	0,777	0,761	0,770	0,761	0,534
WS353	PC	0,308	0,371	0,306	0,314	0,653	**0,733**	0,586	0,502
	SC	0,323	0,302	0,323	0,357	0,700	**0,738**	0,594	0,564
WS353-sim	PC	0,577	0,582	0,567	0,574	**0,719**	0,574	0,552	0,583
	SC	0,572	0,576	0,563	0,616	**0,713**	0,563	0,556	0,562
MTurk	PC	0,475	0,467	0,455	0,432	0,692	**0,741**	0,516	0,490
	SC	0,389	0,380	0,384	0,392	0,633	**0,692**	0,529	0,449
RW	PC	0,018	0,013	0,024	-0,003	**0,438**	**0,440**	0,240	0,182
	SC	-0,020	-0,042	-0,029	-0,021	**0,453**	**0,451**	0,302	0,185
MEN	PC	0,240	0,286	0,231	0,197	0,736	**0,806**	0,601	0,511
	SC	0,189	0,205	0,182	0,201	0,743	**0,805**	0,603	0,587

Table 4. Comparison results for interpolated models (Pearson/Spearman).

Dataset	LIN+LSA	LIN+CBOW	CBOW+LSA	LIN+LDA	GloVe+LDA
RG65	**0,873/ 0,866**	0,872/0,848	0,762/0,780	0,850/0,846	0,532/0,609
WS353	0,624/0,645	0,625/0,665	**0,670/ 0,700**	0,544/0,594	0,587/0,628
MTurk	0,579/0,534	**0,726/ 0,674**	0,716/0,662	0,569/0,517	0,680/0,605
RW	0,251/0,237	0,230/0,260	**0,311/ 0,313**	0,182/0,191	0,228/0,234
MEN	0,616/0,617	0,712/ 0,718	**0,721/ 0,724**	0,518/0,594	0,643/0,659

Table 5. Comparison of models trained on the same corpora (Pearson/Spearman).

Dataset	RG65	WS353	MTurk	RW	MEN
LDA	0,423/0,534	0,502/0,564	0,490/0,449	0,182/0,185	0,511/0,587
CBOW	**0,687/ 0,706**	**0,600/ 0,601**	**0,715/ 0,661**	**0,277/ 0,260**	**0,706/ 0,711**
GloVe	0,556/0,575	0,484/ 0,456	0,664/0,592	0,209/0,196	0,607/0,617

where we do not want high scores for words that are related but not similar (e.g. words "ship" and "sea").

The results in Table 3 show an outstanding performance of the GloVe method. However, Table 5 indicates that this performance may not be entirely caused by the quality of the method itself. The original GloVe model is trained on a corpus consisting of 840 billion tokens gathered from the Internet. When the same corpus is used, the CBOW method clearly outperforms GloVe. This conclusion can be verified on Internet forums[6], thus we believe this was not caused by an improper training.

In Table 4, we tried to estimate the orthogonality of information sources. We can conclude that CBOW and GloVe seem to combine poorly with other methods in our tests. They provide the best performance, so we can say that these methods may contain the information present in other information sources (semantic networks, global context). On the other hand, methods based upon semantic networks and global context improve each other quite significantly. Thus, it is probable that it would be beneficial to use them together in practical tasks.

5   Related Work

To our best knowledge, there is no such a complete comparison of word semantics methods performance in the literature. Nevertheless, the following papers are worth mentioning.

The authors of [4] provide a nicely arranged overview of methods for computing word semantic similarity and relatedness. They include the following three top-level sources of information: string similarity, corpus co-occurrences and knowledge bases (e.g. WordNet). However, the article attempts no independent comparison of the approaches. The paper also lacks the description of the current state of the art (CBOW, GloVe).

Turney and Pantel deal with vector space models of semantics in [15]. They go deeper with their explanation and also show some possible applications. However, they focus only on corpus co-occurrences captured in vector space models. The paper was also written before the current state-of-the-art methods were published.

6   Conclusion

This article provides a comprehensive comparison of methods for computing semantic similarity/relatedness. We claim that GloVe might not be the really the current state-of-the-art method as stated in the GloVe article [11].

Also, we conclude that the information derived from semantic networks combines well with the information source gathered form global context.

---

[6] See http://radimrehurek.com/2014/12/making-sense-of-word2vec/.

Acknowledgements. This work was supported by grant no. SGS-2013-029 Advanced computing and information systems, by the European Regional Development Fund (ERDF) and by project "NTIS – New Technologies for Information Society", European Centre of Excellence, CZ.1.05/1.1.00/02.0090. The access to the MetaCentrum computing facilities provided under the programme "Projects of Large Infrastructure for Research, Development, and Innovations" LM2010005, funded by the Ministry of Education, Youth, and Sports of the Czech Republic, is highly appreciated. The access to the CERIT-SC computing and storage facilities provided under the programme Center CERIT Scientific Cloud, part of the Operational Program Research and Development for Innovations, reg. no. CZ. 1.05/3.2.00/08.0144 is acknowledged.

References

1. Blei, D.M., Ng, A.Y., Jordan, M.I.: Latent dirichlet allocation. J. Mach. Learn. Res. **3**, 993–1022 (2003)
2. Bruni, E.: The men test collection (2012). http://clic.cimec.unitn.it/elia.bruni/ MEN.html. Accessed 3 April 2015
3. Gabrilovich, E.: The wordsimilarity-353 test collection (2002). http://www.cs. technion.ac.il/gabr/resources/data/wordsim353/. Accessed 1 March 2015
4. Gomaa, W.H., Fahmy, A.A.: A survey of text similarity approaches. Int. J. Comput. Appl. **68**(13), 13–18 (2013)
5. Harris, Z.: Distributional structure. Word **10**(23), 146–162 (1954)
6. Landauer, T.K., Dutnais, S.T.: A solution to plato problem: the latent semantic analysis theory of acquisition, induction, and representation of knowledge. Psychol. Rev. **104**(2), 211–240 (1997)
7. Lin, D.: Extracting collocations from text corpora (1998)
8. Luong, M.T., Socher, R., Manning, C.D.: Better word representations with recursive neural networks for morphology. In: CoNLL. Sofia, Bulgaria (2013)
9. Mikolov, T., Chen, K., Corrado, G., Dean, J.: Efficient estimation of word representations in vector space. CoRR abs/1301.3781 (2013). http://arxiv.org/ abs/1301.3781
10. Miller, G.A.: Wordnet: a lexical database for english. Commun. ACM **38**(11), 39–41 (1995). doi:10.1145/219717.219748
11. Pennington, J., Socher, R., Manning, C.: Glove: global vectors for word representation. In: Proceedings of the 2014 Conference on Empirical Methods in Natural Language Processing (EMNLP), pp. 1532–1543. Association for Computational Linguistics (2014). http://aclweb.org/anthology/D14-1162
12. Radinsky, K.: The wordsimilarity-353 test collection (2010). http://tx.technion.ac. il/kirar/Datasets.html. Accessed 1 April 2015
13. Resnik, P.: Using information content to evaluate semantic similarity in a taxonomy. In: Proceedings of the 14th International Joint Conference on Artificial Intelligence, IJCAI 1995, vol. 1, pp. 448–453. Morgan Kaufmann Publishers Inc., San Francisco (1995)
14. Rubenstein, H., Goodenough, J.: Contextual correlates of synonymy. Commun. ACM **8**, 627–633 (1965)
15. Turney, P.D., Pantel, P.: From frequency to meaning : vector space models of semantics. J. Artif. Intell. Res. **137**, 141–188 (2010)
16. Wu, Z., Palmer, M.: Verbs semantics and lexical selection. In: Proceedings of the 32nd Annual Meeting on Association for Computational Linguistics, ACL 1994, pp. 133–138. Association for Computational Linguistics, Stroudsburg, PA, USA (1994). http://dx.doi.org/10.3115/981732.981751

Invariant Components of Speech Signals: Analysis and Visualization

Valeriy Zhenilo[1]($^{(\boxtimes)}$) and Vsevolod Potapov[2]

[1] Institute of Applied and Mathematical Linguistics,
Moscow State Linguistic University, Ostozhenka 38, Moscow 119034, Russia
zhenilo@yandex.ru
[2] Faculty of Philology, Lomonosov Moscow State University,
GSP-1, Leninskie Gory, Moscow 119991, Russia
rkpotapova@yandex.ru

Abstract. In real-world acoustic environment the speech signal is characterized by high variability. It is possible to transmit information only using invariant structures of the speech signal. Some of these invariant structures are formed directly in the speech production apparatus while some are generated by the human auditory perception system. It is shown experimentally that the latter is most sensitive to changes in the speech signal invariant components. Some analysis methods of speech signal harmonic components (invariant components of a speech signal) are proposed.

Keywords: Information · Structure · Invariant · Harmonic · Frequency · Resonance · Overtone · Sensitivity · Spectrum

1 Introduction

"Information is a primary concept in the science that has no satisfactory definition. Information is one of basic general scientific categories which reflects the structure of matter and ways of its cognition; it cannot be reduced to other, more basic notions" [3]. Such convergence of notions "information" and "structure" is so meaningful for describing sound wave features and those of speech waves in particular that a tentative definition *information is structure* will be used in this article.

In real-world conditions speech signals (and all types of signals in general) are quite variable because of numerous reflections and summation of the original speech signal with itself. The more reflective surfaces (even if they are as small as leaves in a forest), the more variable is the resulting signal. Thus, let us consider two waveforms of the same original speech signal recorded by two microphones Fig. 1. One microphone is located within 10 cm from the speakers lips; the second one is located within half a meter. Thus, if the audience listens to a lecturer, the lecturer's speech signal waveform is different for each ear of any listener [5,6].

It becomes clear that there are some invariants in the speech signal that make it possible to transmit linguistic and paralinguistic information to every listener

© Springer International Publishing Switzerland 2015
A. Ronzhin et al. (Eds.): SPECOM 2015, LNAI 9319, pp. 251–258, 2015.
DOI: 10.1007/978-3-319-23132-7_31

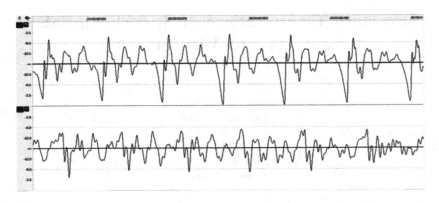

Fig. 1. The same speech signal recorded by two different microphones

without changes (e.g. ref. to: [8,9]). It is quite obvious that information can be transmitted only by some unchanged (invariant) structures. The waveform does not possess these features (according to its appearance). It is known that the main invariant elements of the speech signal are harmonic components [7].

2   Method and Experiment

If a sound source produces harmonic type signal for a considerable time, all reflections sum up to the same harmonic type signal in case of motionlessness of reflective surfaces of this harmonic signal. However, this output harmonic signal amplitude may vary from one point to another in space. It should be noted that the phase characteristic value varies quite considerably. It is well known that our listening perception [10] does not recognize phase value variations, but it recognizes amplitude variations quite well. However, our hearing perceives harmonic frequency variations the best.

Experiments conducted in this research have shown that the mean threshold sensitivity of human hearing to harmonic type signal amplitude modulations is less than one dB. However, the sensitivity to frequency modulation is about 10 music cents (about a tenth of a music semitone). If not acoustic units of measurement, but physical values of hearing sensitivity to harmonic type signal modulations are considered, it turns out that our hearing perceives frequency modulation much better than amplitude modulation. This is quite natural because harmonic type signal frequency is invariant to numerous reflections, while amplitude and phase especially are not. Averaged modulation values of lower threshold levels that can be perceived by our hearing are provided in Table 1.

Two last columns of the table describe well the fact that our hearing system perceives harmonic type signal frequency changes (variations) best of all; and it perceives amplitude modulations of the same harmonics much worse.

The obtained results show how well our hearing system is focused on perceiving invariant signal characteristics. Its perception of variations of non-invariant characteristics is much worse.

Table 1. Average lower threshold values of hearing sensitivity regarding different types of harmonic signal modulation.

Signal frequency (Hz)	Amplitude modulation (dB)	Frequency modulation (semitones)	Amplitude modulation (%)	Frequency modulation (%)
125	1.8 ± 1.0	1.9 ± 9.1	23 ± 12	6 ± 26
500	1.0 ± 0.8	0.5 ± 0.8	12 ± 10	1.4 ± 2.3
2000	0.8 ± 0.7	0.2 ± 0.3	10 ± 8	0.6 ± 0.9
8000	0.7 ± 0.5	0.3 ± 0.3	8 ± 6	0.9 ± 0.9

These facts explain why experts in the field of forensic phonetics and acoustics almost never analyse the speech signal waveforms, although the waveform is the primary form of the signal. They switch to spectrograms right away, where invariant dynamic structure (information) of the speech signals harmonic components is reflexed. For example, Fig. 2 shows waveforms and spectrograms of the same original speech signal passed through different electro-acoustic channels at the same time point.

It is almost impossible to build adequate Fourier series during a real speech signal spectral analysis. For example, in order to find the fundamental frequency (voice pitch), the exact period of the speech signal tone should be known. But it is actually the value sought. If the spectral structure of an explosive sound should be found, its boundaries should be known in advance.

The technology of cutting speech signal into frames using the so called weighing window functions provides a solution. But Heisenberg uncertainty principle starts working here. It is proven experimentally [12] that the Gaussian window suits this task the best. Chui has proven theoretically that the Gaussian window is the best window for spectral analysis from the informational point of view [2, 13].

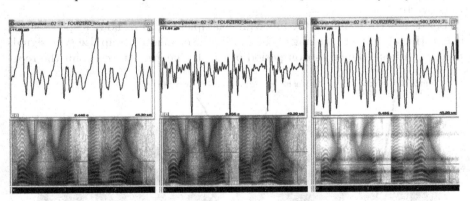

Fig. 2. The same speech signal (the original one is on the left) after differentiation (in the middle) and after the resonance effect (on the right)

2.1   Produced and Perceived Invariants

The only harmonic type signals produced in speech are free-decaying harmonic type signals, which occur in the vocal tract when it is excited separately by any voice impulse. However, these harmonic type signals are so short that they decay almost completely before the next vocal fold clap in the case of a deep male voice, while similar free-decaying oscillations last for seconds in sounding glasses, and for a minute or even longer in large bells.

Efforts to show the tracks of the speech path resonance frequencies as accurately as possible have led to the form of visualization that made other mysterious traces of the harmonic components of speech signals clearly visible on the spectrograms. They are shown in Fig. 3 at the very bottom of the spectrogram. V. N. Sorokin [11] has shown that this is not a kind of harmonic oscillations, but a trace of the form of a voice impulse exciting the air column of the vocal tract. The voice impulse form model shown in Fig. 4 was proposed by Ananthpadbanabha in 1984 [1].

As for what harmonic type signals a man produces when he speaks or sings, it turns out that the only signals of this type are free-decaying oscillations of the vocal tract air column. Those who are used to think that vocal folds "generate" a series of harmonic type signals called overtones, do not agree usually. Overtones are spaced equally from each other at an equal distance in frequency, during phonation of vowel sounds while speaking or singing. However, in reality the voice impulse and its shape do not contain or produce any harmonic signals, except for the free-decaying oscillations of the vocal tract. So how do overtones appear that are clearly visualized using a narrow-band spectrogram (Fig. 3)? In addition, as it is proven theoretically and experimentally - if harmonic type signals are synthesized with frequencies equal to the corresponding voice pitch frequency and all the overtones, there is virtually no difference between the real voice sounding (speaking or singing) and a synthesized voice model based on the same overtones.

Let us illustrate this by the following example. Figure 5 shows a spectrogram of an artificial signal consisting of the sum of the elementary impulse-type signals (delta impulses), the repetition period of which changes. At one point the repe-

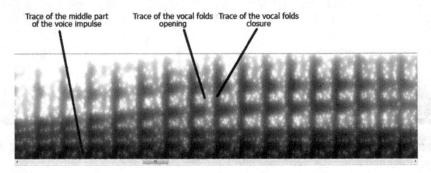

Fig. 3. A fragment of real speech signal with clearly visible traces of vocal folds clapping

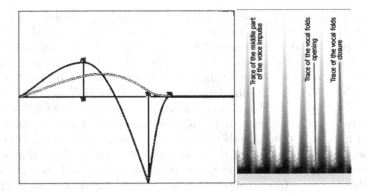

Fig. 4. Modelled shape of a voice impulse [1] (on the left) and a spectrogram of a sequence of such impulses (on the right)

tition period of these impulses is approximately equal to one second (1 Hz), then it gradually increases and reaches a periodicity (it is better to say "frequency") of 300 Hz. Visualization of a typical computer spectrogram - is actually a frame-by-frame spectral description of the signal. In Fig. 5 spectral information of one time frame of the signal corresponds to one vertical row of computer pixels. At the point where impulses are very rare, separate (isolated) vertical lines are seen on the spectrogram. These vertical lines on the spectrogram correspond to the time frame where a single impulse was captured. In other words, if only a single impulse is captured in the time frame, it will look on the spectrogram as a vertical black line isolated from its neighbors.

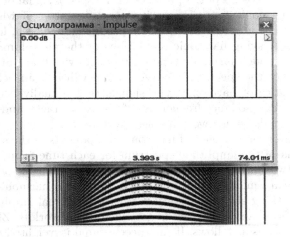

Fig. 5. The waveform (above) and the spectrogram (below) of frequency modulated impulses

But those time frames, where a pair or more adjacent impulses get captured, do not look like vertical lines, and we see a pattern, which is called a pattern of voice overtones. What is happening? Several sound impulses get into the time frame, and impulses with the same repetition period are located next to the frame outside of it. As a result, in this time frame it is possible to build an adequate Fourier model which is visualized in accordance with Heisenberg uncertainty principle. The essence of Heisenberg uncertainty principle is as follows. Inside the frame only one adequate model of decomposition of a periodic signal to the sum of harmonic type signals with multiple frequencies which are equal to the inverse repetition period of these impulses is possible. It is impossible to ideally visualize the frequencies of these harmonic type signals in the model. It is impossible to make frequencies of harmonic type signals appear in the form of ideal thin lines in the model. This is the essence of Heisenberg uncertainty principle for harmonic type signals.

A conclusion is drawn that overtones are not produced by vocal folds "piece-by-piece", but are formed in the auditory system (in the system of the spectral description of the signal). However, it should be noted that the primary cause of their formation is the fact of almost strict periodicity of the work of the vocal folds. If there is no high degree of periodicity of the work of the vocal folds, voice overtones will not appear. This phenomenon is found in those people whose vocal folds do not work strictly periodically, or when their vocal cords are removed, and the man tries to retrieve vowel sounds using vestibular folds, the physiology of which does not allow to achieve the desired periodicity.

2.2   Diagnostics of Invariant Sound Elements

Considering the diagnostics of the presence in the speech signal of the individual components of harmonic type signals, it does not matter of what type these harmonic oscillations are: whether they are produced in speech, for example, in the form of free-decaying harmonic oscillations of the air column of the vocal tract or they are model harmonic type components which are produced in the auditory system, or the spectrum analyzer. What will be said below is true for both the diagnostics of harmonic type signals that actually occur after each vocal folds clap (the resonance frequencies of the vocal tract), and for the model harmonic type signals, which we call voice overtones.

The indicator of the presence of harmonic components in the speech signal is the local maxima of the amplitude spectrum for each time frame of the speech signal. We give two simple diagnostic criteria to define that one or another local amplitude spectrum maximum is actually a trace of a harmonic type signal, rather than something else that is very common in the real amplitude spectra.

The first criterion for diagnostics is described in the work by Zhenilo [12, 13], the essence of which is as follows. If the speech signal is weighted by a Gaussian function with a parameter, the amplitude spectrum of each harmonic component (stationary, amplitude or frequency modulated) of the speech signal will have the form of a parabola on a logarithmic scale (e.g., a dB scale). As far as the fast Fourier transform gives us a spectrum of individual discrete frequencies going in sequence with the constant step Δ, then a simple differential Eq. (1) allows us to get a measure of closeness M of the measured amplitude spectrum lobe to the lobe trace which is left by any stationary harmonic type signal:

$$M = \left| \frac{y_{n+1} - 2y_n + y_{n-1}}{2\Delta^2} - \frac{20 \lg e}{2\sigma_f^2} \right| \tag{1}$$

However, this formula is valid only for unmodulated (stationary) speech signal harmonic components. If there is an amplitude or frequency modulation in the speech signal, then the value $b = \frac{20 \lg e}{2\sigma_f^2}$ is obtained from the amplitude and phase spectra in three stages:

1. First, a local amplitude spectrum maximum is found in the vicinity of the interested frequency.
2. Then the value of amplitude and frequency modulation is extracted from the phase spectrum [12,13];
3. The value of b is adjusted, and, thus, the final measure of closeness of the analyzed signal trace to the harmonic type signal is obtained (1).

Another simple - simple in terms of computational costs - criterion is a diagnostic criterion for the amplitude spectrum local maximum that exists in the peripheral nervous system of animals, namely, in the retina of the eye [4], where the problems of diagnostics (recognition) of visual objects are very similar to the problems of diagnostics (recognition) of the principal invariant components of the sound - the harmonic type signals.

3   Conclusion

In this paper the problem of transmission of information using sound waves was considered. Sound waves are highly variable in the reality. Information can be transferred only with the help of invariant structures, which may be represented by the frequency of the harmonic components of speech signals. Some of these invariant structures are formed directly in the speech production apparatus in the form of free-decaying oscillation frequencies of the air column of the vocal tract, while some are formed in the auditory system these are voice overtones. It is shown experimentally that the human auditory system is most sensitive to changes of the invariant components of speech sounds - the harmonic components of the speech signal. If it is impossible to perceive rapidly repeated voice impulses separately, the hearing perceives the rapid repetition of voice impulses as a set of voice overtones described by harmonic type signals. Diagnostics and visualization mechanisms of actually produced harmonics and audible model harmonics are the same.

Acknowledgments. The investigation is being carried out with the support of the Russian Science Foundation (RSF) in the framework of the project # 14-18-01059 at Moscow State Linguistic University (scientific head of the project R.K. Potapova).

References

1. Ananthapadmanabha, T.V.: Acoustic analysis of voice source dynamics. STL QPSR, pp. 2–3, 1–24 (1984)
2. Chui, C.K.: An Introduction to Wavelets. Academic Press, Boston (1992)
3. Encyclopedic Dictionary of Mathematics. Sovetskaya Entsiklopediya, Moskva (1988) (in Russian)
4. Hubel, D.H.: Eye, Brain, and Vision, 2nd edn. W.H. Freeman, New York (1995)
5. Kipyatkova, I., Ronzhin, A., Karpov, A.: Avtomaticheskaya Obrabotka Razgovornoy Russkoy Rechi. GUAP, St-Petersburg (2013). (in Russian)
6. Petrovskiy, A. (ed.): Analizatory Rechevyh i Zvukovyh Signalov: Metody, Algoritmy i Praktika (s MATLAB Primerami). Bestprint, Minsk (2009) (in Russian)
7. Potapova, R.K., Mikhailov, V.G.: Osnovy Rechevoy Akustiki. IPK MGLU "Rema", Moskva (2012) (in Russian)
8. Potapova, R., Potapov, V.: Auditory and visual recognition of emotional behaviour of foreign language subjects (by native and non-native speakers). In: Železný, M., Habernal, I., Ronzhin, A. (eds.) SPECOM 2013. LNCS, vol. 8113, pp. 62–69. Springer, Heidelberg (2013)
9. Potapova, R., Potapov, V.: Associative mechanism of foreign spoken language perception (forensic phonetic aspect). In: Ronzhin, A., Potapova, R., Delic, V. (eds.) SPECOM 2014. LNCS, vol. 8773, pp. 113–122. Springer, Heidelberg (2014)
10. Schacter, D., Gilbert, D., Wegner, D.: Sensation and Perception. In: Linsmeiser, C. (ed.) Psychology. Worth Publishers, pp. 158–159 (2011)
11. Sorokin, V.N.: Speech Processes. Narodnoe Obrazovanie, Moskva (2012). (in Russian)
12. Zhenilo, V.R.: Komp'yuternaya Fonoskopiya. Izdatel'stvo Akademii MVD Rossii, Moskva (1995). (in Russian)
13. Zhenilo, V.R.: Informatsiya, Zvuk i Preobrazovaniye Fourier-Gauss. In: Materialy XV Mezhdunarodnoy konferentsii "Informatizatsiya i Informatsionnaya Bezopasnost' Pravoohranitel'nyh Organov", Moskva, pp. 332–340 (2006) (in Russian)

Language Model Speaker Adaptation for Transcription of Slovak Parliament Proceedings

Ján Staš[(✉)], Daniel Hládek, and Jozef Juhár

Department of Electronics and Multimedia Communications,
Faculty of Electrical Engineering and Informatics, Technical University of Košice,
Park Komenského 13, 042 10 Košice, Slovak Republic
{jan.stas,daniel.hladek,jozef.juhar}@tuke.sk

Abstract. Language model and acoustic model adaptation play an important role in enhancing performance and robustness of automatic speech recognition, especially in the case of domain-specific, gender-dependent, or user-adapted systems development. This paper is oriented on the language model speaker adaptation for transcription of parliament proceedings in Slovak for individual speaker. Based on the current research studies, we have developed a framework combining multiple speech recognition outputs with acoustic and language model adaptation at different stages. The preliminary results show a significant decrease in the model perplexity from 45 % to 74 % relatively and the speech recognition word error rate from 29 % to 43 %, for male and female speakers respectively.

Keywords: Automatic speech recognition · Acoustic modeling · Language modeling · Slovak language · Speaker adaptation · Hypothesis combination

1 Introduction

In the previous research, we have developed a dictation software for automatic transcription of judicial readings in Slovak whose speech recognition performance reaches almost 95 % accuracy [1]. Recently, we are interested in building of an automatic subtitling system for broadcast news TV shows and transcription of parliament proceedings, educational talks and lectures. The increasing demand for the performance improvement and robustness of transcription of spontaneous speech in Slovak forces us to look for the advanced methods of adaptation of acoustic and language models to a specific topic, gender, or user.

Several previous works have been reported on adaptation of language models (LMs) to a specific topic or user with a small amount of adaptation data, including transcription of educational talks, lectures and academic presentations [2–4], live sports games [5], broadcast news [6], parliament proceedings [7], or business meetings [8,9], for many different languages like English, German, or Czech.

© Springer International Publishing Switzerland 2015
A. Ronzhin et al. (Eds.): SPECOM 2015, LNAI 9319, pp. 259–267, 2015.
DOI: 10.1007/978-3-319-23132-7_32

The basic idea of LM adaptation is to use a small topic- or user-specific text data to adjust the background LM to reduce the impact of language differences between the training and testing data and adjust the parameters of background LM to the correspond domain, either in supervised or unsupervised manner.

A number of algorithms have been recently proposed for adaptation of LMs to the target domain, a group of users, or a specific user, including fill-up models [10,11], unigram marginal adaptation [6,9,11,12], minimum discrimination information estimation [2,4,6], maximum a posteriori adaptation [4,6,13], linear and log-linear interpolation [3,6–9], mixture models [6], n-gram weighting [4], or discriminative re-ranking with positive or negative n-grams [9]. Many of them were tested regarding to the Slovak language modeling in our previous work [14].

Also, the initial recognition hypotheses from the first pass of speech recognition then can be used as adaptation data, either as queries for retrieving relevant articles from various of electronic resources and training component LM on these data [3,5,6], or directly as in-domain development data [2,8]. In some cases, the output hypotheses can be used to build an adaptation LM to be combined with baseline LM [4]. Since the output hypotheses change through LM adaptation, the process can be repeated iteratively for further improvements [2,4,13].

Regarding to parliament speech, the members of the parliament are not professional speakers. Spontaneous speech occurs more often than the read speech. The politicians are more expressive than in other domains, because they tend to persuade the listeners rather than inform them. There are some differences among the speakers in grammar, articulation and speaking style with frequent errors (hesitations, repetitions, or mistakes) in their pronunciation. Also, the acoustic environment in the parliament is much worse than in small offices or in studio [7]. Moreover, the most of the politician talks are relatively long, which makes the LM speaker adaptation possible.

In the following sections we describe the process of language model speaker adaptation for transcription of the Slovak parliament proceedings. User-specific LMs were trained on text corpora gathered from web using the text selection based on perplexity for each individual speaker. Parameters of user-adapted LMs were adjusted on the development data that have been formed either by a part of user-specific text data and/or by the initial speech recognition hypotheses. We have also used the gender-dependent acoustic modeling and appropriate combination of output hypotheses from multiple speech recognition setups to increase performance and robustness of the Slovak transcription system.

2   Language Model Adaptation to a Specific User

2.1   User-Specific Text Data

The user-specific text data are represented by the corpus of Slovak parliament proceedings, total size of about 33.5 M tokens in 1.8 M sentences. The text corpus was obtained from the Joint Czech and Slovak Digital Parliamentary Library[1] and consists of a collection of stenographic reports from the meetings

---

[1] www.nrsr.sk/dl/.

Table 1. Statistics on the training, development and evaluation data

Speaker ID	Train. text data		Dev. text data		Eval. speech utterances		
	#sent.	#words	#sent.	#words	#utt.	#words	duration
F1	1,089	22,941	396	8,849	64	684	06:47
F2	2,672	56,790	892	18,263	204	1,733	14:23
F3	2,915	57,177	935	19,045	143	1,319	09:14
F4	3,156	68,087	1,060	23,497	23	240	02:47
F5	4,992	45,012	1,635	14,428	37	386	02:57
M1	10,586	121,738	3,539	40,910	498	4,304	37:51
M2	6,498	123,618	2,149	42,288	123	1,130	09:19
M3	4,248	88,484	1,402	29,685	105	931	07:17
M4	10,631	116,038	3,536	39,278	249	1,921	14:40
M5	16,267	184,522	5,419	60,700	279	2,309	16:52
Total	63,054	884,407	20,963	296,943	1,725	14,957	02:01:32

of the National Council of the Slovak Republic and official press releases realized between 2010 and 2013 years. The text corpus was divided according to the speaker identified by his or hers name, surname and quotation marks indicating direct speech. Moreover, the text selection based on the model perplexity (similar to [3]) has been used for retrieving additional relevant documents for individual speakers. The user-specific raw text was preprocessed, tokenized and all punctuation was removed. The text data obtained from ten (5 male and 5 female) representative speakers were selected for training, adaptation and evaluation of LMs. The statistics on the number of tokens and sentences are summarized in the Table 1. The development data were compiled from 25 % of the text for each speaker that were not used in the training of the user-specific LMs.

2.2 Language Model Adaptation

Among the methods for combination and adaptation of LMs, discussed in our previous work [14], we have concluded that usage of linear interpolation (LI) for Slovak is more than sufficient. In this straightforward approach of LM adaptation, the adapted LM $P_{LI}(w|h)$ was obtained by linear interpolation of the user-specific (adaptation) LM $P_A(w|h)$ with the background LM $P_B(w|h)$ according to the equation:

$$P_{LI}(w|h) = \lambda P_A(w|h) + (1 - \lambda)P_B(w|h). \tag{1}$$

The adaptation weight λ can be adjusted on a development set or can be chosen empirically. An expectation-maximization (EM) algorithm is usually used to maximize the likelihood on a development set, as a function of λ.

2.3 Adjusting Interpolation Weights

We have chosen our newly-designed criterion based on the ratio of the language model perplexity (computed on the development data) for given LM in the set of all LMs for adjusting adaptation weight λ, as follows:

$$\lambda_i = \frac{1}{PPL_i} \left(\sum_i \frac{1}{PPL_i} \right)^{-1}, \qquad (2)$$

where PPL_i is the perplexity of i-th LM and sum is performed over all perplexities. Perplexity is defined as the reciprocal value of the geometric mean of the probability assigned by the LM to each word in the evaluation data and is related to cross-entropy. The calculation of λ using this criterion is not computationally expensive and takes into account the fact that there are particular LMs adapted to the development data. This criterion is a simplification to the EM algorithm and gives very similar results in many cases. In addition, it does not need iterative optimization of adaptation weights, but they are adjusted directly [14].

3 Speech Recognition Overview

The baseline trigram LM has been created using the SRILM Toolkit [15], restricted by the vocabulary size of 385 k words and smoothed by the Witten-Bell algorithm. Trigram LM has been trained on the preprocessed and classified web-based text corpora of more than 2,150 M of tokens contained in 120 M of Slovak sentences. The latent Dirichlet allocation has been used for dividing whole text corpus into 7 semantically similar subsets, ready for the training LMs. Resulting LM are composed from 7 independent LMs generated from the classified text corpora. Models are merged into the one and adapted to the domain of parliament speech using linear interpolation performed just between two models, continuing until all models were combined. Maximization of likelihood on a development set given by the proposed criterion of model perplexity proportion has been used for computing adaptation weights. Finally, the resulting domain-specific LM was reduced (to 700 MB in ARPA format) by relative entropy-based pruning in order to use it in a real-time application of the Slovak transcription system [14].

The speech transcription system makes use of triphone context-dependent acoustic modeling based on using hidden Markov models (HMMs) with 32 Gaussian mixtures. Acoustic models (AMs) have been generated from feature vectors with standard dimension of 39 mel-frequency cepstral coefficients (along with delta and acceleration coefficients and cepstral mean normalization enabled). A typical tree-based state tying for HMMs has been replaced by triphone mapping. Baseline AM has been trained on about 320 h of annotated speech recordings of judicial readings and real parliament proceedings. Gender-dependent AMs were created by splitting the training speech database with respect to each gender and building two separate AMs for female and male gender, respectively [1].

The decoding in our speech transcription system is performed with open-source large vocabulary recognition engine Julius [16] based on two-pass speech recognition strategy. In the first pass, the frame synchronous decoding is performed, where resulting word trellis represents candidates for the second pass. Bigram LM is used and the cross-word dependencies are handled approximately. The second pass rescores the candidates using the trigram LM with stack decoding and outputs the final word sequence as hypothesis.

We have used the ROVER system [17] for combination of hypotheses from multiple speech recognition setups, slightly modified to our needs to include confidence score context between words into consideration. The main algorithm consists of two components. The first component performs incremental alignment of the input hypotheses by aligning at most two hypotheses at time. In this step it uses the NULL word transition score $C(@)$ that allows to handle insertions and deletions when aligning. After that, two hypotheses are combined into one word search network for alignment with the next hypothesis. The second component is voting V. It uses confidence score for each different word $C(w_i)$ and the number of occurrences of each alternative $N(w_i)$ according to the equation:

$$V(w_i) = \alpha \frac{N(w_i)}{N_s} + (1 - \alpha)C(w_i).$$ (3)

The number of occurrences is normalized by the count of the combined systems N_s. The NULL word transition score $C(@)$ was set to 0.5 and α to 0.7 in order to control the balance between the number of word occurrences and its confidence score. However, the ROVER does not consider any context when performing the hypothesis combination. Therefore, we have modified this algorithm and included into each word score $C(w_i)$ some portion of the previous one $C(w_{i-1})$ as follows:

$$\bar{C}(w_i) = \beta C(w_{i-1}) + (1 - \beta)C(w_i).$$ (4)

The factor β was introduced to control the balance between previous and current word score and was set to 0.9 [18].

4   Experiments

The experiments are oriented on evaluation of the model perplexity and performance of the Slovak transcription system on an evaluation data set, after adaptation of LMs to a specific user. The test data, summarized in the Table 1, were represented by randomly selected speech utterances from the database of real parliament proceedings for each of ten (5 male and 5 female) speakers. These speech utterances have not been used in the training of AMs and contain 14,957 words in 1,725 sentences and short phrases, total length of about 2 h.

Word error rate (WER), computed by comparing reference text with recognized result taking into account insertion, deletion and substitution errors, was used to evaluate a contribution of user-adapted LMs to speech recognition.

Table 2. Evaluation of LM speaker adaptation for different adaptation weights λ

LMA	Female gender WER [%]				Male gender WER [%]				Together WER [%]			
	PPL	AM_B	AM_G	Δ_r	PPL	AM_B	AM_G	Δ_r	PPL	AM_B	AM_G	Δ_r
Baseline	351.61	13.89	12.72	−8.42	364.85	13.42	13.07	−2.61	358.23	13.55	12.97	−4.28
λ_S	91.78	8.85	8.55	−3.39	254.48	10.37	9.91	−4.44	173.13	9.93	9.51	−4.23
λ_D	90.87	8.87	8.30	−6.43	201.46	10.30	9.92	−3.69	146.17	9.89	9.44	−4.55
λ_R	99.56	9.26	8.57	−7.45	271.73	10.63	10.17	−4.33	185.64	10.23	9.70	−5.18
λ_{D+R}	90.64	8.85	8.34	−5.76	201.09	10.40	9.96	−4.23	145.87	9.95	9.49	−4.62

Table 2 summarize model perplexity and speech recognition results evaluated on the test data. For clarity, the WER results obtained from individual speakers were merged into single master label file (MLF) and the PPL values were averaged. Also, the contribution Δ_r of utilization the gender-dependent (AM_G) acoustic models to speech recognition task was evaluated.

The baseline LM achieves average model perplexity 364.85 and 351.61, and 13.42 % and 13.89 % WER, for male and female speakers respectively. The relative contribution of the gender-dependent acoustic modeling is −4.28 % WER in average. The initial recognition hypotheses were used for further improvement.

4.1 Language Model Adaptation to a Specific User

A small separate user-specific trigram LM was created for each speaker, trained on a part of text data summarized in the Table 1. The user-specific models were created and smoothed in a similar way and restricted by the same vocabulary size of 385 k words as the baseline LM. We did not consider adding the new words into the LM vocabulary and speech recognition dictionary.

As it was mentioned in the Sect. 2, we have used a linear interpolation of user-specific LMs with the baseline LM. For this purpose, we have created three types of the development data for computing adaptation weights. The PPL and WER results of user-adapted language models are summarized in the Table 2. The adaptation weights were computed as follows:

- λ_S - static adaptation weights ($\lambda_S = 0.2$);
- λ_D - adaptation weights were tuned on the user-specific development data;
- λ_R - weights were adjusted according to the initial recognition hypotheses;
- λ_{D+R} - adaptation weights were computed either on the user-specific development data and initial recognition hypotheses together.

We have achieved significant improvement in the model PPL and WER in all presented scenarios. The averaged results with the different development data and adaptation weights are very similar. Only if the initial recognition hypotheses from the first round of speech recognition with the baseline LM and gender-dependent AM were used as the development data, we observed a small deviation from these values. Therefore, the output hypotheses for this purpose (λ_R) were not considered in the next step of hypothesis combination.

In general, the best WER results we observed when interpolation weights for LM adaptation were tuned on the user-specific development data and gender-dependent AMs were used. As it can be seen in the Table 2, the speech recognition performance was relatively increased by using user-specific LMs from about 24.10 % to 34.75 %, for male and female speakers respectively.

If we look at the model perplexity, the best results were observed when the text data from initial recognition hypotheses were added to the development data. In this case we achieved the relative reduction in PPL from 44.88 % to 74.22 %, for male and female speakers respectively.

4.2 Combination of Hypotheses from Multiple Recognition Setups

We prefer a combination of several hypotheses from multiple speech recognition setups rather than multi-pass speech recognition with multiple times adapted AMs and LMs. The output hypotheses from several speech recognizers with combination of the different AMs and LMs were rescored and the final result has been composed. We have created five experimental settings as follows:

- setting 1–4 hyp. (AM_B + 4 × LM: baseline, λ_S, λ_D, λ_{D+R});
- setting 2–4 hyp. (AM_G + 4 × LM: baseline, λ_S, λ_D, λ_{D+R});
- setting 3–8 hyp. (2 × AM: AM_B, AM_G × 4 × LM: baseline, λ_S, λ_D, λ_{D+R});
- setting 4–4 hyp. (AM_B + baseline & λ_S LMs, AM_B + λ_D & λ_{D+R} LMs);
- setting 5–2 hyp. (AM_B + λ_S LM & AM_G + λ_D LM).

Table 3 summarizes the WER results after applying combination of hypotheses for these experimental settings. Other values are copied from Table 2 for comparison. The best results were obtained with the settings 4 and 5. In these settings we have achieved an additional relative decrease in WER from 4.03 % to 4.70 %, for males and females respectively. In practice, two appropriately chosen speech recognition hypotheses are sufficient to achieving such improvement.

Table 3. The WER results [%] after applying combination of N-best hypotheses

Gender	Baseline AM_B	Baseline AM_G	Setting 1	Setting 2	Setting 3	Setting 4	Setting 5	Single best
Female	13.89	12.72	8.83	8.25	8.07	7.98	7.91	8.30
Male	13.42	13.07	10.29	9.88	9.55	9.52	9.55	9.92
Together	13.55	12.97	9.86	9.39	9.11	9.07	9.07	9.44

5 Conclusion

This paper was oriented on the language model speaker adaptation for transcription of the talks of Slovak politicians. In the proposed approach for LM speaker adaptation we have achieved overall relative reduction in PPL of about 59 %

and 27 % in WER in average. Using multiple speech recognizers with gender-dependent AMs in various configurations and application of user-adapted LMs and combination of N-best hypotheses with rescoring can achieve overall relative decrease up to 33 % in WER in average for both genders. In our further research, we want to focus on adding the new words obtained from the individual speaker's text data to the vocabulary in the step of LM speaker adaptation.

Acknowledgments. The research presented in this paper was supported by the Ministry of Education, Science, Research and Sport of the Slovak Republic under the project VEGA 1/0075/15 (50 %) and the Research and Development Operational Programme funded by the ERDF under the project ITMS: 26220220182 (50 %).

References

1. Rusko, M., et al.: Slovak automatic dictation system for judicial domain. In: Vetulani, Z., Mariani, J. (eds.) LTC 2011. LNCS, vol. 8387, pp. 16–27. Springer, Heidelberg (2014)
2. Niesler, T., Willett, D.: Unsupervised language model adaptation for lecture speech transcription. In: Proceedings of ICSLP 2002, pp. 1413–1416 (2002)
3. Nanjo, H., Kawahara, T.: Language model and speaking rate adaptation for spontaneous presentation speech recognition. IEEE Trans. Speech Audio Process. **12**(4), 391–400 (2004)
4. Hsu, B.-J., Glass, J.: Language model parameter estimation using user transcriptions. In: Proceedings of ICASSP 2009, Taipei, Taiwan, pp. 4805–4808 (2009)
5. Ariki, Y., et al.: Live speech recognition in sports games by adaptation of acoustic and language model. In: Proceedings of EUROSPEECH 2003, pp. 1453–1456 (2003)
6. Chen, L., Gauvain, J.-L., Lamel, L., Adda, G.: Dynamic language modeling for broadcast news. In: Proceedings of ICSLP 2004, Jeju Island, Korea, pp. 997–1000 (2004)
7. Cerva, P., Nouza, J., Kolorenc, J., David, P.: Improved transcription of Czech parliament speeches by acoustic and language model adaptation. In: Proceedings of SPECOM 2006, St. Petersburg, Russia, pp. 103–106 (2006)
8. Tur, G., Stolcke, A.: Unsupervised language model adaptation for meeting recognition. In: Proceedings of ICASSP 2007, Honolulu, Hawaii, USA, pp. IV-173–IV-176 (2007)
9. Vergyri, D., Stolcke, A., Tur, G.: Exploiting user feedback for language model adaptation in meeting recognition. In: Proceedings of ICASSP 2009, pp. 4737–4740 (2009)
10. Besling, S., Meier, H.-G.: Language model speaker adaptation. In: Proceedings of EUROSPEECH 1995, Madrid, Spain, pp. 1755–1758 (1995)
11. Klakow, D.: Language model adaptation for tiny adaptation corpora. In: Proceedings of INTERSPEECH 2006, Pittsburgh, PA, USA, pp. 2214–2217 (2006)
12. Kneser, R., Peters, J., Klakow, D.: Language model adaptation using dynamic marginals. In: Proceedings of EUROSPEECH 1997, Rhodes, Greece, pp. 1971–1974 (1997)
13. Bacchiani, M., Roark, B.: Unsupervised language model adaptation. In: Proceedings of ICASSP 2003, Hong Kong, China, pp. I-224–I-227 (2003)

14. Staš, J., Juhár, J., Hládek, D.: Classification of heterogeneous text data for robust domain-specific language modeling. EURASIP J. Audio Speech Music Process. **2014**(14), 12 (2014)
15. Stolcke, A.: SRILM - an extensible language modeling toolkit. In: Proceedings of ICSLP 2002, Denver, Colorado, USA, pp. 901–904 (2002)
16. Lee, A., Kawahara, T., Shikano, K.: Julius - an open source real-time large vocabulary recognition engine. In: Proceedings of EUROSPEECH 2001, Aalborg, Denmark, pp. 1691–1694 (2001)
17. Fiscus, J.G.: A post-processing system to yield reduced word error rates: recognizer output voting error reduction (ROVER). In: Proceedings of IEEE ASRU Workshop, Santa Barbara, CA, USA, pp. 347–354 (1997)
18. Lojka, M., Juhár, J.: Hypothesis combination for Slovak dictation speech recognition. In: Proceedings of 56th International Symposium on ELMAR 2014, Zadar, Croatia, pp. 43–46 (2014)

Macro Episodes of Russian Everyday Oral Communication: Towards Pragmatic Annotation of the ORD Speech Corpus

Tatiana Sherstinova[✉]

St. Petersburg State University,
Universitetskaya Nab. 11, St. Petersburg 199034, Russia
sherstinova@gmail.com

Abstract. The ORD corpus is a representative resource of everyday spoken Russian that contains about 1000 h of long-term audio recordings of daily communication made in real settings by research volunteers. ORD macro episodes are the large communication episodes united by setting/scene of communication, social roles of participants and their general activity. The paper describes annotation principles used for tagging of macro episodes, provides current statistics on communication situations presented in the corpus and reveals their most common types. Annotation of communication situations allows using these codes as filters for selection of audio data, therefore making it possible to study Russian everyday speech in different communication situations, to determine and describe various registers of spoken Russian. As an example, several high frequency word lists referring to different communication situations are compared. Annotation of macro episodes that is made for the ORD corpus is a prerequisite for its further pragmatic annotation.

Keywords: Everyday Russian speech · Oral communication · Registers of spoken Russian · Communication situations · Speech corpus · Annotation · Statistics · Frequency word lists

1 The ORD Speech Corpus

The ORD corpus is a representative resource of everyday spoken Russian containing long time audio recordings of daily communication made in real life and supplied by sociological and psychological data about the speakers [1]. The participants recorded all oral communication in which they took part during one day. This explains the origin of the ORD abbreviation that means *Odin Rechevoy Den* (in English: *One Day of Speech*). As a result, the audio recordings – that include diverse everyday communication situations – form a valuable resource to study variants and registers of spoken Russian, to describe real communication situations, to carry out sociolinguistic and psycholinguistic studies, to perform discourse analysis, and to provide data to define and test statistical models for speech technologies.

© Springer International Publishing Switzerland 2015
A. Ronzhin et al. (Eds.): SPECOM 2015, LNAI 9319, pp. 268–276, 2015.
DOI: 10.1007/978-3-319-23132-7_33

Nowadays, the corpus contains more than 1000 h of speech recorded by 107 major participants (58 men and 49 women) that represent different social groups. Speech transcripts currently numbers about 500,000 words; and it is planned to extend this number up to 1,000,000 words.

Oral communication situations in the ORD corpus are described on two structural levels – *macro episodes* and *micro episodes* [2]. Thus, every "day of speech" of any particular individual may be divided into large communication episodes – called *macro episodes* – united by setting/scene of communication, social roles of participants and their general activity. Macro episodes are, in some way, similar to stages within acts in theatrical plot structure. The recordings of the ORD corpus are segmented into audio files in accordance with this approach. Therefore, macro episodes became the main objects of description on the macro level. According to the ORD data, each individual takes part in 20–50 macro episodes every 24 h, and the length of macro episodes varies from 15 to 90 min on average. Each macro episode is further divided into *micro episodes*, united by topic of communication or its main pragmatic task [3]. In this paper, we constrain ourselves to description of macro episodes.

It is well-known that individual speech features strongly depend on communication settings [4]. No existing corpus before had such a variety of authentic recordings made in different communication situations. The ORD corpus helps to eliminate this gap.

2 Annotation of Communication Situations in the ORD Corpus

At the stage of expert audition and segmentation of new recordings, each macro episode gets verbal description in three aspects: (1) *Where does the situation take place?* (2) *What are participants doing?* (3) *Who is (are) the main interlocutor(s).* This information is presented in the Table ORDSoundFiles of the database [5].

Then, these verbal descriptions are normalized to standard codes and may be given additional markers. In the result, annotation of communication situations includes information on scene and type of communication, social roles of participants, and a few other factors.

2.1 Setting/Scene of Communication

We distinguish the following common communication settings: (1) home that is a place of informant's permanent or temporal residence (e.g., apartment, house, hostel or hotel room), (2) someone else's home (formally the similar setting to the previous one, but the informant is here as a guest or a service staff), (3) office, (4) cafe (incl. restaurant, snack bar, cafeteria, pub, etc.), (5) store (incl. shopping center, supermarket, pharmacy, groceries, kiosk, etc.), (6) service center (commercial and government agencies, banks, studios, libraries, service stations, etc.), (7) educational institution (school, university, college, etc.), (8) medical center (clinic, hospital, first aid room, etc.), (9) military institutions (military school, military barrack), (10) public institutions and other public places (museum, theater, cinema, gym, church, etc.), (11) outdoors (on the street, in the park, etc.), (12) public and private transport (car, taxi, metro, train, etc.), (13) workshop (shed, garage, outbuildings), and (14) unidentified settings.

2.2 Speaker's Social Roles

We consider speakers' social roles to be an extremely important factor having influence on speech [6]. Hence, we use detailed categorization of this parameter:

1. **Close relatives:** (a) husband, (b) wife, (c) father, (d) mother, (e) son, (f) daughter, (g) sister, (h) brother, (i) grandmother, (j) grandfather, (k) grandson, (l) granddaughter.
2. **Other relatives:** (a) older relative (aunt, uncle, mother/father-in-law, godfather, etc.), (b) younger relative (son/daughter-in-law, nephew, niece, etc.), (c) relative of the same age (cousins, half cousins), (d) unidentified relative.
3. **Friends:** (a) male friend, (b) female friend, (c) romantic partner (boyfriend), (d) romantic partner (girlfriend).
4. **Colleagues:** (a) colleague, (b) boss or commander, (c) subordinate colleague, (d) colleague-friend.
5. **"Customer-service" roles:** (a) "customer" (client, patient, etc.), (b) "service staff" (seller, waiter, repairer, nurse, etc.), (c) student, pupil, (d) teacher, lecturer, instructor, trainer, etc.
6. **Group members:** (a) classmate, schoolmate, (b) partner or companion in some activity (hobby, sports, social work, church, etc.), (c) casual companion, the client of the same cafe, shop or some other public place.
7. **Others:** (a) master (in communication with pets), (b) talking to themselves.

2.3 General Types of Everyday Oral Communication and Other Circumstances

The following general types of oral communication are distinguished:

1. **Informal communication.** It was noticed that such conversations are common for participants of fairly different social roles, including colleagues in the office (the conversations does not refer to participants' professional duties).
2. **Professional communication** and other business-orientated official communication. Here, the conversational topic relates to professional duties.
3. **Customer-service communication** takes place in various situations, in which one participant (seller, waiter, concierge, social worker, doctor, librarian, etc.) is serving or helping another (customer, patient, client, etc.) on professional level.
4. **Educational communication** implies the variety of activities, such as university studies, practical training, instructing, private lessons, teaching children, etc.
5. **Public speeches** (public lectures, presentation, etc.).

Annotation of communication situations implies marking of the most typical communication circumstances. In particular, we have additional marks for the following situations: (1) *"kitchen"conversations* (since the Soviet times, the kitchen is a traditional place for domestic conversations and discussions), (2) *holidays and parties communication,* (3) *"drinking" conversations,* (4) *household or similar activities,* (5) *talking in motion,* when walking or driving, (6) *relaxation and leisure conversations,* (7) *communication by phone,* etc.

Additionally, some other labels for particular communication may be given when needed, e.g. *isolated cues, monologues, reading aloud, reciting, singing, prayer, positive and negative emotions, conflicts, humor,* etc.

In most cases, communication situations presented in the ORD corpus appeared to be complex phenomena. As a result, most of annotations include complex codes. Moreover, sometimes one may observe a mix of two general communication types within one episode. These situations are specially marked too.

3 Distribution of Communication Situations in the ORD Corpus

The ORD corpus is a developing resource; transcribing and annotation of its data are still in progress, as well as recordings of new audio material. By May 2015, annotation of communication situations on macro level is made for 1854 macro episodes of oral everyday communication got from 79 volunteers (informants). The total duration of these audio recordings is 483 h. Statistics presented below refer to this part of the corpus.

Table 1 presents the most frequent scenes of communication in the ORD macro episodes. Naturally, the considerable amount of everyday communication takes place *at home* or *in the office.* The other relatively frequent scenes are the following: *educational institution, someone else's home, center of customer service, hospitals and medical centers,* and *outdoors.*

Table 2 shows the ranked list of the most common social roles of informants in the corpus. The data presented here refer only to one-on-one communication situations. About 33 % of all recorded communication are situations, where participants have multiple roles.

Finally, Table 3 presents distribution of general types of communication situations. It is worth mentioning that informal communication takes up to 61 % of

Table 1. The most frequent scenes of communication in the ORD corpus

Scene	Perc.	Scene	Perc.	Scene	Perc.
home	22 %	outdoors	6 %	other public places	3 %
office	21 %	transport	5 %	military barracks	1 %
educational inst.	9 %	cafe	4 %	workshop	1 %
someone else's home	7 %	medical center	3.5 %	others	9 %
customer service c.	5 %	shop	3.5 %		

Table 2. Distribution of subjects' social roles in the ORD corpus

Social role	Perc.	Social role	Perc.	Social role	Perc.
colleague	18 %	customer	2.9 %	student	1.0 %
friend (female)	5.6 %	classmate	2.8 %	talking to himself	1.0 %
instructor/lecturer	5.6 %	colleague-friend	2.2 %	mother	0.7 %
service staff	5.2 %	familier	1.3 %	daughter	0.7 %
friend (male)	4.3 %	son	1.2 %	others	10.3 %
husband	3.1 %	father	1.1 %	multiple roles	33 %

all communication. Moreover, ORD recordings showed that even in offices one may find a considerable amount of informal communication.

Analysis of annotations enabled to get all combinatorial variants of communication situations presented in the corpus and helped to reveal the most typical macro episodes of everyday communication and examine their features.

All combinations for the *"social role"* + *"scene of communication"* pair were analysed during the research. According to these two parameters, the most typical situations in the ORD corpus turned out to be the following:

1. Communication between colleagues in the office (207 episodes, 11 %).
2. Communication at home between friends (74 episodes, 4 %).
3. Communication between instructor (professor, teacher) and student(s) in educational institution (72 episodes, 4 %).
4. Communication at home between husband and wife (55 episodes, 3 %).

The absolute and relative frequencies of other common conditions of communication are as follows: There are 230 (12 %) *"kitchen"* and 54 (3 %) *"drinking"* conversations in the corpus, *monologic* fragments are presented in 393 (21 %) episodes, *phone conversations* may be found in 420 (22 %) episodes, *positive emotions* are present in 60 (3 %) episodes, *negative emotions* – in 54 (3 %) episodes, *humor* elements characterize 222 (12 %) episodes.

Table 3. Distribution of types of commutation situations in the ORD corpus

Type of Commun. Situation	Perc.	Frequent Circumstances
1. Informal communication	61 %	(a) household activities, (b) "kitchen" conversations, (c) isolated cues, (d) "in motion"
2. Professional communication	23 %	professional activity
3. Customer-service communication	8 %	(a) doctor-patient communication, (b) product selection and purchase
4. Educational communication	6 %	university lectures, practical training, private lessons
5. Public speeches	2 %	presentations

In addition, all ORD informants were ranged according to a number of different communication situations, in which they took part during the recording period. The most diverse material had the following informants (mainly, female):

S24 (female, at age 63): 12 different social roles in 7 different types of scenes;
S35 (male, at age 70): 10 different social roles in 6 different types of scenes;
S30 (female, at age 20): 10 different roles in 8 different types of scenes;
S04 (female, at age 34): 9 different roles in 7 different types of scenes.

It is worth noticing that there are two female informants (*S11*, age 28, and *S05*, age 27) who demonstrated their skills in four general types of oral communication, taking place at 12 and 9 types of scenes correspondingly [2]. Their recordings may be regarded as a perfect material to study different registers of spoken Russian.

4 Functional Activity of Words in Different Communication Situations

In this section, we shall give a short example of how information presented above may be used to study different registers of spoken Russian on lexical level. Register is a "variety of language used in a particular social setting" [6]. To study functional activity of words in different registers (or styles) we need to compare the whole high frequency word list of the corpus with sub-corpora lists that refer to particular communication situations.[1] The study was performed on a sample of 235,000 words.

Tables 4, 5 and 6 present rank comparisons for the 10 most frequent words and discourse particles that cover 20.06 % of all words in speech transcripts.

Table 4. Rank comparison for the 10 frequent words depending on scene (Edu. = Education. Inst., M.C. = Medical Cent., S.C. = Service Cent., Outd. = Outdoors)

Word	In the whole sample			Ranks in different scenes							
	Num	%	Rank	Home	Office	Edu	M.C	S.C	Cafe	Outd	Shop
ja	5901	2.51	1	1	1	1	1	4(−)	3(−)	1	11(−)
vot	5369	2.28	2	4(−)	2	5(−)	2	1(+)	15(−)	2	1(+)
ne	5359	2.28	3	3	3	3	3	8(−)	1	4	4
nu	5272	2.24	4	2(+)	7(−)	6	7(−)	2(+)	2(+)	3	6
da	5016	2.13	5	5	6	2(+)	4	3	4	5	2(+)
a	4342	1.85	6	7	9	4	5	7	6	6	5
čto	4064	1.73	7	6	4	7	8	11(−)	8	10	10
i	4015	1.71	8	8	5	11	11	10	9	8	8
v	3979	1.69	9	9	10	10	10	5(+)	5	7	13
eto	3838	1.63	10	11	8	9	6(+)	6(+)	13	11	9

---

[1] For more information on how to use frequency word list structure in study of language styles see [8].

Table 5. Rank comparison for the 10 most frequent words depending on type of communication

Word	Rank in the whole sample	Ranks in different types of situations			
		Informal	Professional	Cust.-Service	Educational
ja	1	1	3(−)	3(−)	4(−)
vot	2	4(−)	1(+)	1(+)	1(+)
ne	3	2(+)	4	5(−)	9(−)
nu	4	3	5	4	5
da	5	5	2(+)	2(+)	2(+)
a	6	6	9(−)	6	10(−)
čto	7	8	8	10(−)	6
i	8	9	6	9	8
v	9	7	7	8	13
eto	10	11	10	7(+)	3(+)

Table 6. Rank comparison for the 10 most frequent words depending on social role

Word	Rank in the whole sample	Ranks for different social roles			
		Friend (female)	Friend (male)	Husband/Wife	Colleague
ja	1	1	1	3(−)	1
vot	2	4(−)	7(−)	2	2
ne	3	3	3	4	3
nu	4	2(+)	2(+)	1(+)	4
da	5	5	8(−)	8(−)	5
a	6	6	5	10(−)	7
čto	7	10(−)	10(−)	6	8
i	8	9	9	7	6
v	9	8	6	5(+)	9
eto	10	12	11	11	10

Table 4 also shows the absolute number and percentage of these words in the sample. The evident shifts of word ranks for particular situations are marked by symbols (+) (higher rank) and (−) (lower rank).

As shown in the tables, the most common shifts are observed for two discourse particles "*vot*" and "*nu*". Both of them are often regarded by linguists either as fillers or "parasite words". However, we may now assume that they can be indicators of a type of communication situation as well. Thus, "*vot*" is mainly used in *official* and *formal* situations (in the office, shop, medical or service centers), while its functional activity *at home* and especially in *cafés* is lower. On the contrary, the particle "*nu*" is used more often in *informal close relationships* (e.g., in *husband and wifes communication* and *between close friends*).

We can also mention higher activity of particle *"da"* (*"yes"*) in *formal* situations, whereas its opposite *"ne"* (*"not"*) is more frequent in *informal* communication.

The results of this preliminary research lead us to conclusion that there are some evident differences between analyzed settings on lexical level. Our next task is to investigate and describe these phenomena in detail and to expand these studies to other linguistic levels.

5   Conclusion

Annotation of macro episodes that is made for the ORD corpus is a necessary step for its further pragmatic annotation on the levels of micro episodes and speech acts [3]. Speech data recorded in different communication situations are analyzed on phonetic, lexical, and grammar levels in regard to psychological and social information about the speakers. As a result, we will get the descriptions of characteristic features that distinguish speech of one language register from another. Such data may be used in particular for solving current problems in speech technologies for speech synthesis and recognition systems, forensic linguistic and forensic phonetics.

Acknowledgements. The annotation principles for macro episodes tagging have been developed with support of the Russian Foundation for Humanities (project # 12-04-12017, "Information System of Communication Scenarios of Russian Spontaneous Speech"). The presented statistics were obtained within the framework of the project "Everyday Russian Language in Different Social Groups" supported by the Russian Scientific Foundation, project # 14-18-02070.

References

1. Asinovsky, A., Bogdanova, N., Rusakova, M., Ryko, A., Stepanova, S., Sherstinova, T.: The ORD speech corpus of Russian everyday communication "One Speaker's Day": creation principles and annotation. In: Matoušek, V., Mautner, P. (eds.) TSD 2009. LNCS, vol. 5729, pp. 250–257. Springer, Heidelberg (2009)
2. Sherstinova, T.: Communikativnyje macroepizody v korpuse povsednevnoj russkoj rechi "Odin rechevoj den'"': principy annotirovanija i rezul'taty statisticheskoj obrabotki. In: Zakharov, V., Mitrofanova, O., Khokhlova, M. (eds.) Proceeding of the International Conference "Corpus linguistics-2013", pp. 449–456. St. Petersburg State University, St. Petersburg (2013)
3. Sherstinova, T.: Pragmaticheskoe annotirovanie konnunicativnykh jedinic v korpuse ORD: mikroepisody i rechevye akty. In: Proceeding of the International Conference "Corpus linguistics-2015", pp. 436–446 (2015) (in Russian)
4. Potapova, R.K.: Rech: kommunikacija, informatika, kibernetika. URSS, Moscow (2003)
5. Sherstinova, T.: The structure of the ORD speech corpus of Russian everyday communication. In: Matoušek, V., Mautner, P. (eds.) TSD 2009. LNCS, vol. 5729, pp. 258–265. Springer, Heidelberg (2009)

6. Chebanov, S., Martynenko, G.: Semiotika opisatel'nykh tekstov: tipologicheskij aspekt. St. Peterburg State University, St. Petersburg (1999)
7. Ottenheimer, H.J.: The Anthropology of Language: An Introduction to Linguistic Anthropology. Wadsworth Cenage Learning, Belmont, CA (2006)
8. Martynenko, G.: Osnovy stilemetrii. Leningrad State University, Leningrad (1988)

Missing Feature Kernel and Nonparametric Window Subband Power Distribution for Robust Sound Event Classification

Tran Huy Dat$^{(\boxtimes)}$, Jonathan William Dennis, and Ng Wen Zheng Terence

Institute for Infocomm Research, A*STAR, Singapore, Singapore
hdtran@i2r.a-star.edu.sg

Abstract. Sound Event Classification (SEC) aims to understand the real life events using sound information. A major problem of SEC is that it has to deal with uncontrolled environmental conditions, leading to extremely high levels of noise, reverberation, overlapping, attenuation and distortion. As a result, some parts of the captured signals could be masked out or completely missing. In this paper, we propose a novel missing feature classification method by utilizing a missing feature kernel in the classification optimization machine. The proposed method first transforms audio segments into the Subband Power Distribution (SPD), a novel image representation where the pure signal's area is separable. A novel masking approach is then proposed to separate the SPD into reliable and non-reliable parts. Next, missing feature kernel (MFK), in forms of probabilistic distances on the intersection between reliable areas of the SPD images, is developed and integrated into SVM optimization framework. Experimental results show superiority of the proposed method for challenging tasks of SEC, when signals come out with severe noises and distortions.

Keywords: Sound event classification · Missing feature · Kernel machine classification · Subband power distribution · Non-parametric windows

1 Introduction

Sound Event Classification (SEC) is a major task of machine listening, which aims to understand real life events using sound information [1]. The biggest challenge of SEC is to deal with uncontrolled environments leading to severe noise conditions, multi-path and reverberation effects, as well as attenuation and distortions. As a result, the target sound information is partially masked out or missing. Missing Feature methods (MFM) have proven to be effective for the related task of automatic speech recognition [2]. Conventional MFM can be divided into two categories: (1) imputation: where the unreliable elements are imputed based on its reliable neighbors; (2) marginalization: where the classifier is modified to reduce the contribution from unreliable elements. The main

© Springer International Publishing Switzerland 2015
A. Ronzhin et al. (Eds.): SPECOM 2015, LNAI 9319, pp. 277–284, 2015.
DOI: 10.1007/978-3-319-23132-7_34

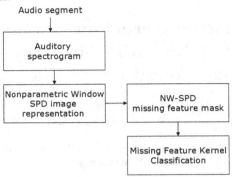

Fig. 1. Overview of proposed system.

drawback of conventional marginalization MFM in ASR is its need for modified HMM classifiers that incur high computation costs, thereby limiting its applications. The imputation method is normally implemented via distance based nearest neighbor (kNN) approach. A limitation of missing feature kNN classifier is that it is not optimized for classification accuracy, particular with an inhomogeneous dataset. A novelty of this work is that we utilize a novel framework of missing feature classifier (MFC) by introducing the missing feature kernel (MFK) and incorporating it into the kernel classification machine. Particularly, the sub-band probabilistic distance missing kernel support vector machine (MF-SPDSVM) has been developed. Together with the classifier, the missing feature mask, which separates reliable and non-reliable parts of the signal representation, is an extremely important component of MFM. In this paper, we introduce a novel nonparametric window subband power distribution (NW-SPD) masking method. The basic idea here is to transform the spectrogram into a new image representation, where the signal and noise regions are better localized and separable. Hence the missing feature mask could be effectively designed to distinguish between reliable and unreliable parts of the representation. In this paper, nonparametric windows (NW) is employed, as it is suitable for modeling the distribution of strongly correlated signals. The overview of our proposed system is illustrated in Fig. 1. We note that sound activity detection is not discussed in this paper, but in a live system a simple energy based detector could be employed. The rest of this paper is as follows: Sect. 2 introduces NW-SPD. Section 3 describes the proposed missing feature kernel classifier (MFK-SVM). Section 4 reports experimental results conducted on through-the-wall listening sound event classification. Finally, Sect. 5 concludes the work.

2   Non-parametric Windows SPD

2.1   Subband Power Distribution

The basic idea of the SPD is to transform the spectrogram into a new image representation, where the signal and noise are better localized and separable [3].

This is done by three steps. First, normalize the auditory spectrogram into a gray-scale image

$$G(f,t) = \frac{\log S(f,t) - \min\left(\log S(f,t)\right)}{\max\left(\log S(f,t)\right)}, \tag{1}$$

where f represents the center frequencies of the filters, t is the time index. Second, transform each subband power series into its distribution, putting them together to form a new image representation. One of simplest approach to model the distribution from its data is the Parzen kernel density estimation, denoted as:

$$H(f,z) = \frac{1}{T} \sum_{t=1}^{N} K_h(z - G(z,t)), \tag{2}$$

where T is the number of time samples in the segment and K_h is the kernel function. The resulting $H(f,z)$ matrix therefore represents the raw probability distribution information for each frequency subband over time, which is constrained to lie in the range $0 \leq H(k,b) \leq 1$. Finally, contrast stretching is employed to enhance the contrastness of the SPD image.

However, a limitation of histogram and Parzen window, is that it assumes observations to be identical independent distributed. For sound and speech, due to the nature of modulations, the signals are strongly correlated across the time.

2.2   Nonparametric Windows SPD

In this paper, we propose an effective way to overcome the above shortcoming of SPD by using nonparametric windows (NW) density estimation [4]. This approach treats the input as an analytical signal, approximated by interpolations between each consecutive pair of observation. The method to calculate the PDF using NP-Windows consists of two main steps:

1. Calculate the PDF for each piecewise section, such that the signal is considered a function of a uniform random variable representing its domain
2. Populate the appropriate bins for each piecewise section.

To estimate the PDF in each subband, first we connect each adjacent data input with a straight line in the form $l_{k,i}(x) = a_{k,i}x + b_{k,i}$ where i represents the piecewise index and k represents the subband. For each piecewise straight line, a PDF, g, is assigned scaled to its gradient:

$$g_{f,i}(z) = \begin{cases} \frac{1}{|a_{f,i}|} & b_{f,i} \leq z \leq a_{f,i} \\ 0 & otherwise \end{cases}. \tag{3}$$

Then, an arbitrary number of bins is chosen for the output histogram by summing up all the PDF that lies within the interval:

$$D(f,z) = \sum_i g_{f,i}(l_b \leq z \leq r_b), \tag{4}$$

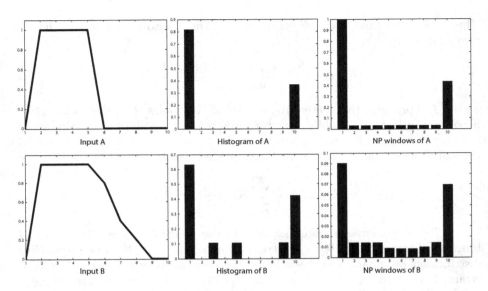

Fig. 2. The top row indicates input A and its density estimation using histogram and NP-Windows from left to right respectively. The bottom row indicates input B which is a reverberated version of signal B.

where l_b and r_b are the respective left and right edges of a particular histogram bin, b. Figure 2 illustrates an example of different density estimation of a clean input and its reverberated version. It suggests that the NW estimations are closer and hence less mismatch than that of conventional histogram estimation.

2.3 NW-SPD Missing Feature Mask

Figure 3 shows examples to illustrate the SPD representation of the following sounds: a bell ringing sound, noise from an air-conditioner, and the bell sound masked in the air-conditioner noise. The top row represents the spectrogram surface, which is transformed by taking its probability densities of the power across time in each subband to produce the SPD representation in the bottom row.

From Fig. 3 is can be seen that reliable, signal-represented, area are always positioned in the right side of the NW-SPD image [3] . Hence it can be seen that by choosing only the region containing the reliable image area (indicated by the area to the right of the yellow dotted line in Fig. 3), which matches the same region of a bell sound in high SNR condition from training as illustrated in Fig. 3. This provides motivation to find the boundaries of the noise mask, in order to perform classification using only the reliable area. To estimate the separation point in each frequency bin, we first utilize a SPD image from a segment containing only noise, denoted as $I_N(k, z)$, to generate a non-stationary noise estimation, based on the characteristic that many noise distributions remain the same across the time. The upper bound of the distribution in $I_N(k, z)$ forms an

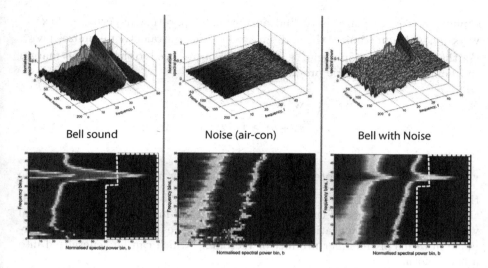

Fig. 3. Examples to illustrate the SPD representation of clean signal, noise and noisy, respectively. Top row represents the spectrogram surface and bottom row represents the SPD representation (bins-frequency). The dotted yellow lines show the reliable part of SPDs (Color figure online).

estimate of the noise boundary, $n_{max}(k)$, in the SPD and is estimated as the maximum occupied bin for each frequency subband:

$$n_{max}(k) = \operatorname*{argmax}_{z}(I_N(k, z) > 0). \tag{5}$$

Then, given a NW-SPD, $I(k, z)$ from a noisy sound event clip, we take the cross-correlation $(\star)$ between $I_N(k, z)$ and $I(k, z)$ to find the intensity difference, a_{max} with the highest correlation. Since $I(k, z)$ is a mixture of the noise and signal distributions, we perform the cross-correlation separately on each SPD-IF subband, k, such that the highest correlation should occur between two noise-dominated subbands:

$$a_{max} = \max_{a}\left[I(k, z) \star I_N(k, z + a)\right], \quad \forall k \tag{6}$$

The final SPD-IF noise estimate, $n(k)$ is then simply derived as:

$$n(k) = n_{max}(k) + a_{max}. \tag{7}$$

3   Missing Feature Kernel Classification

Starting with linear SVM, we consider the problem of designing a separating hyperplane for m vectors $\mathbf{x}_i \in \mathbf{R}^n$ $i = 1, 2, ..., m$. Each point $\mathbf{x}_i \in \mathbf{R}^n$ belongs to one of two classes, by its label $y_i \in \{1, -1\}$, $i = 1, 2, ..., m$. The goal of linear support vector machines is to find an optimal separating hyperplane $f(\mathbf{x}) = \mathbf{w}^T\mathbf{x} + b$, which maximizes the margin, i.e. $\frac{2}{\|\mathbf{w}\|^2}$, or equivalently minimizes $\|\mathbf{w}\|^2$. For the solution, the non-negative variable ξ_i is introduced so that the soft margin can be found by quadratic programming:

$$\min_{(\mathbf{w},b,\xi)} \left(\tfrac{1}{2}\mathbf{w}^T\mathbf{w} + C\sum_{i=1}^{n}\xi_i \right)$$
$$\text{s.t. } y_i\left(\mathbf{w}^T\mathbf{x}_i + b\right) \geq 1 - \xi_i \ ; i = 1, 2, ..., n \qquad (8)$$
$$\xi_i \geq 0,$$

where the term $\sum_{i=1}^{n}\xi_i$ denotes the upper bound of the misclassification from the training samples and C is a coefficient that regulates between the misclassification and the robustness of the classification (width of margin). There are several ways to solve this optimization problem, all return the form of separating hyperplane in terms of the inner product of vectors $\mathbf{x}_i$, which can be generalized into a kernel form as

$$f(\mathbf{x}) = \sum_{i=1}^{m}\alpha_i K(\mathbf{x}, \mathbf{x}_i) + b. \qquad (9)$$

In the implementation, all the classification optimization methods link to the calculation of the kernel matrix $K(\mathbf{x}_i, \mathbf{x}_j)$ [5].

The idea of this paper is to incorporate the missing feature mask into kernel SVM to allows both training and testing with missing feature samples. It can be done by introducing the intersection area of reliable parts in the kernel between each pair of samples noted as

$$K(\mathbf{x}_i, \mathbf{x}_j) \rightarrow K\left(\mathbf{x}_i^{R_i \cap R_j}, \mathbf{x}_j^{R_j \cap R_i}\right), \qquad (10)$$

where R_i and R_j denote the reliable parts of sample $\mathbf{x}_i$ and $\mathbf{x}_j$, respectively.

In the case, when training is carried out using the clean data, the intersection in the kernel calculation in testing phase will return the reliable part of the testing sample, i.e.

$$f(\mathbf{x}) = \sum_{i=1}^{m}\alpha_i K\left(\mathbf{x}^R, \mathbf{x}_i^R\right) + b. \qquad (11)$$

Without applying missing feature masking, NW-SPD is partitioned into 9×9 local sub-blocks and each block's image pixel distribution statistics are computed [3] to form the feature vector. In this work, under the framework of the missing feature kernel (MFK), first the masking (NW-SPD masking) is performed in each NW-SPD image. Then the intersection between reliable parts are computed. The MFK is then computed using Eq. 10. Particularly, the Hellinger distance, which has been successfully used in image retrieval tasks, is employed as a probabilistic distance between images block's pixels distribution [5].

$$d_H(x_i, x_j) = \sum_{k=1}^{N_R}\left(1 - \sqrt{\frac{2\sigma_{i,k}\sigma_{j,k}}{\sigma_{i,k}^2 + \sigma_{j,k}^2}}\, e^{-\frac{1}{4}\frac{(\mu_{i,k}-\mu_{j,k})^2}{\sigma_{i,k}^2 + \sigma_{j,k}^2}}\right)^{\frac{1}{2}}, \qquad (12)$$

where N_R is the number of reliable blocks, x_i and x_j is a couple of samples, μ and σ^2 are the distribution means and variance of the image pixel distribution.

4   Experiments

Task: The proposed method is evaluated for the through-the-wall (TTW) sound event classification which aims to classify events in enclosed environments from outside. Several ways of signal capturing are possible for the task. In this paper, the outside listening through wall attached contact microphones is investigated.

Sound Database: The original sound database includes sound clips from 5 classes: normal speech, crying, gunshot, explosion and footsteps [6]. These sound classes are chosen according to our interest in security surveillance applications. The original clips are at 44kHz sampling, manually balanced in advance with length varying from 2 to 5 s, respectively. For each sound class, 500 samples are chosen for the experiments.

Recordings: The original sound clips were played inside an enclosed room. A cold gold piezo contact microphone [7] is attached outside on a cement and brick wall of estimated 20 cm thickness, to record back the sounds at 16kHz sampling rate. The signals are observed rather weak with severe distortions and attenuations. Beside to attenuations and distortions, noises generated by other wall vibrations also contributed to the weakness of SNR whose estimates are varying from -3dB to 6dB SNR [8].

Experimental Methods: The TTW sound event classification is evaluated using proposed missing feature kernel with nonparametric windows subband power distributions. In the experiment evaluation, 10 run of trials are performed. During each trial, 200 samples from each sound class are randomly picked up for the training and the rest is used for test. To compare to conventional methods, following approaches are also evaluated:

1. : MFCC-GHM: both training and testing use the recorded TTW signals.
2. : AFE-GMM: TTW records with ITU's AFE Wiener filter.
3. : SPD-kNN: previous SPD with kNN classifier.
4. : SPD-MFK: proposed missing feature classifier with previous version SPD.
5. : nwSPD-MFK: proposed missing feature classifier with new version nwSPD.

Note that all the above methods do training and testing on the recorded signals. The performances of system with clean training and TTW testing did not achieve meaningful results on conventional methods and also worse on SPD methods and hence are not reported here. Since, the SPD has demonstrated its significant superiority compared to other missing feature for sound event classification in [3], we don't evaluate the later here anymore.

Discussions: Table 1 summarizes the classification results in terms of mean and standard variation through 10 runs of experiments. We can see that the conventional MFCC-GMM and AFE-GMM methods could not perform in this task.

Table 1. Classification accuracy results (%).

	MFCC-GMM-multi	AFE-GMM-multi	SPD-kNN	SPD-MFK	nwSPD-MFK
mean	38.66	42.33	75.66	79.66	**80.33**
std	5.12	5.74	3.25	3.46	**1.89**

It could be explained by that the attenuation and distortion are varying from sample to sample and hence the so-called matched condition training could not reduce enough the mismatch effects. The missing feature approaches using SPD image feature demonstrate its robustness and all of them yield reasonable classification accuracy. The proposed missing feature kernel (MFK) classifier has shown its promising results achieving statistical significant improvements compared to the SPD-kNN classification. Furthermore, the nonparametric windows gives additional improvements compared to the previous histogram-based SPD. It seems that NW-SPD as discussed above, is more invariant compared to the histogram-based SPD and hence yields better results in the task.

5   Conclusions

We propose a novel sound event classification method which includes two novelties: (1) the missing feature kernel method enabling optimizing the classification machine with noisy, attenuated, and distorted samples; (2) the nonparametric windows modeling of subband power distribution which together significantly improved the classification accuracy on a very challenging task of through-the-wall sound event classification.

References

1. Lozano, H., Hernáez, I., Picón, A., Camarena, J., Navas, E.: Audio classification techniques in home environments for elderly/dependant people. In: Miesenberger, K., Klaus, J., Zagler, W., Karshmer, A. (eds.) ICCHP 2010, Part 1. LNCS, vol. 6179, pp. 320–323. Springer, Heidelberg (2010)
2. Raj, B., Stern, R.M.: Missing-feature approaches in speech recognition. Sig. Process. Mag. **22**, 101–116 (2005)
3. Dennis, J., Dat, T.H., Chng, E.: Image feature representation of the subband power distribution for robust sound event classification. IEEE Trans. Audio Speech Lang. Process. **321**, 367–377 (2012)
4. Kadir, T., Brady, M.: Non-parametric estimation of probability distributions from sampled signals. Technical report, OUEL (2005)
5. Dat, T.H., Li, H.: Sound event recognition with probabilistic distance SVMs. IEEE Trans. Audio Speech Lang. Process. **19**, 1556–1568 (2011)
6. Sound Effect Collections. http://www.sound-ideas.com/
7. Cold Gold contact microphone. http://www.contactmicrophones.com/
8. Dat, T.H., Takeda, K., Itakura, F.: On-line Gaussian mixture modeling in the log-power domain for signal-to-noise ratio estimation and speech enhancement. Speech Commun. **48**, 1515–1527 (2006)

Multi-factor Method for Detection of Filled Pauses and Lengthenings in Russian Spontaneous Speech

Vasilisa Verkhodanova[1]([✉]) and Vladimir Shapranov[2]

[1] SPIIRAS, 39, 14th Line, St. Petersburg, Russia
verkhodanova@iias.spb.su
[2] Betria Systems Inc, 50, Building 11, Ligovsky Prospekt, St. Petersburg, Russia
equidamoid@gmail.com

Abstract. Spontaneous speech contains high rates of speech disfluencies, most common being filled paused and lengthenings (FPs). Human language technologies are often developed for other than spontaneous types of speech, and disfluencies occurrence is the reason for many mistakes in automatic speech recognition systems. In this paper we present a method of automatic detection of FPs using linear combination of statistical characteristics of acoustic parameters variance, basing on a preliminary study of FPs parameters across the mixed and quality-diverse corpus of Russian spontaneous speech. Experiments were carried out on a corpus, consisting of the task-based dialogue corpus of Russian spontaneous speech collected in SPIIRAS and on Russian casual conversations from Open Source Multi-Language Audio Database collected in Binghamton University.

Keywords: Speech disfluencies · Filled pauses · Sound lengthenings · Automatic speech processing · Russian spontaneous speech

1 Introduction

Almost all speech we produce and comprehend every day is spontaneous. This type of oral communication is likely to be one of the most difficult forms of speech communication among people: during very dense time interval speaker has to solve several laborious cognitive tasks. One has to form the utterance and to choose the exact linguistic form for it by selecting words, expressions, grammatical forms, etc. This process leads to different flaws in spontaneous speech production, so called speech disfluencies, like self-repairs, repetitions, filled pauses and lengthenings, slips of the tongue and other mispronunciations. These phenomena indicate the mental processes of underlying speech generation and have been viewed as a sign of word-searching problem [5] or difficulties in conceptualization at major discourse boundaries [3]. Speech disfluencies are breaks or irregularities that occur within the flow of otherwise fluent speech. These are self-repairs, repetitions, filled pauses, lengthenings etc. There are evidence that

© Springer International Publishing Switzerland 2015
A. Ronzhin et al. (Eds.): SPECOM 2015, LNAI 9319, pp. 285–292, 2015.
DOI: 10.1007/978-3-319-23132-7_35

they can affect up to one third of utterances [20]: for example, about 6 per 100 words are disfluent in conversational speech in American English [20,25].

In Russian speech filled pauses occur at a rate of about 4 times per 100 words, and at approximately the same rate inside clauses and at the discourse boundaries [11]. Though evidence on filled pauses differs across languages, genres, and speakers, it can be summarized that on average there are several filled pauses per 100 syllable [17]. They also are most frequent speech disfluencies: filled pauses occur more often than any other speech disfluencies (repetitions, word truncations, etc.) [17], signaling not only of breaks in speech production process, but also of explication of this process [11].

The need in coping automatically with speech disfluencies appeared along with the need of spontaneous speech processing, what brought up a lot of interesting challanges to speech science and engineering. Once seen as errors, along with other disfluencies filled pauses and lengthenings (jointly referred to as FPs in the rest of the paper) were acknowledged as integral part of natural conversation [11,21]. They may play a valuable role such as helping a speaker to hold a conversational turn or expressing the speaker's thinking process of formulating the upcoming utterance fragment [4,18,21]. According to [24] in the conversational Switchboard database [8], about 39.7 % of the all disfluencies contain a filled pause. Thus, the detection of vowel lengthening and filled pauses could be an important step towards locating the disfluent regions and evaluating the spoken fluency skills of a speaker. The problem of detecting filled pauses has been addressed from various perspectives. In computational linguistics speech disfluencies analysis is sometimes incorporated into syntactic parsing and language comprehension systems [6], as well as into automatic speech recognition systems [15]. However, FPs as well as other speech disfluencies, were always an obstacle for automatic processing of spontaneous speech as well as its transcriptions, because speech recognition systems are usually trained on the structured data without speech disfluencies, what decreases speech recognition accuracy and leads to inaccurate transcriptions [2,9,16,21]. The interest in automatic detection of fillers also has been raised by INTERSPEECH Computational paralinguistic challenge in 2013 [10]. Nowadays the most efficient methods coping with FPs can be roughly divided into those, that use only acoustic parameters and [2,9,16,26] and those, that combine language and acoustic modeling with the purpose of incorporating them into automatic speech recognition systems [13–15]. This division is caused by the unavailability of resources: the application of disfluencies detecting methods based on language modeling requires a large corpus with rich transcriptions, while for approaches based on acoustic properties there is no such need.

In this study we describe a method based on the gradient decent aimed to find the values of acoustic parameters of FPs that would maximize the harmonic mean of precesion and recall (F_1 score) for FPs detection for Russian spontaneous speech. The results of the experiments based on a mixed different quality corpus of Russian spontaneous speech are also presented.

2   Material

The material we have used in this study consists of two parts, one being the corpus of task-based dialogs (2/3 of the corpus) collected at SPIIRAS in 2012–2013 [27], and the other one being 5 casual conversations recordings (1/3 of the corpus) taken from the Russian part of Open Source Multi-Language Audio Database collected in Binghamton University in 2010–2012 [28]. The whole dataset we used for the experiments is about 1.5 h with 17 speakers, 8 men and 9 women.

First corpus was collected specially for analysis of speech disfluencies in Russian. The task methodology was chosen to elicit speech as close as possible to normal conversational spontaneous speech. This approach towards spontaneous speech eliciting is well-known and used. For example the HCRC corpus collected Edinburgh and Glasgow consists only of map-task dialogs [1], and half Kiel corpus of German speech consists of appointment tasks [12]. We consider the recorded speech to be spontaneous since it is informal and unrehearsed and also it is the result of direct dialogue communication [29]. In recording the two types of tasks were used: map tasks and appointment tasks. Map task dialogs represent a description of a route from start to finish, basing on the maps with different sometimes unmatched landmarks. This task was fulfilled twice by pair of speakers switching roles. In appointment task dialogs, a pair of participants tried to find a common free time for a telephone talk and for a meeting based on their individual schedules. Participants could not see maps or schedules of each other. Due to maps and schedules structure participants had to ask questions, interrupt and discuss the route or possible free time, what resulted in higher rates of FPs and artefacts. The recorded corpus consists of 18 dialogs from 1.5 to 5 min. All the recordings were made in St. Petersburg in the end of 2012 - beginning of 2013 in the sound isolated room by means of two tablet PCs Samsung Galaxy Tab 2 with Smart Voice Recorder. Participants were students: 6 women speakers and 6 men speakers from 17 to 23 years old with technical and humanitarian specialization. Corpus was manually annotated into speech disfluencies, with 222 filled pauses and 270 sound lengthenings.

The second part of the corpus we used is part of Multi-Language Audio Database [28]. This database consists of approximately 30 h of sometimes low quality, varied and noisy speech in each of three languages, English, Mandarin Chinese, and Russian. For each language there are 900 recordings taken from open source public web sites, such as http://youtube.com. All recordings have been orthographically transcribed at the sentence/phrase level by human listeners. The Russian part of this database consists of 300 recordings of 158 speakers (approximately 35 h). The casual conversations part consists of 91 recordings (10.3 h) of 53 speakers [28]. From this Russian part we have taken the random 5 recordings of casual conversations (3 female speakers and 2 male speakers) that were manually annotated into FPs. The number of annotated phenomena is 266 (186 filled pauses and 80 sound lengthenings).

3   Method for Automatic FPs Detection

We have based our method on acoustical features of FPs that are peculiar to these events in Russian. We used gradient decent method to get optimal parameters to maximize the F_1 score for FPs detection.

Acoustic features of hesitation pauses in Russian speech was studied in [23], where author has found that filled pauses in Russian differ in terms of F1 and F2 values from vowels in stressed positions. In our study we have analyzed duration, F0, three first formants, energy and stableness of spectra across our corpus. Similar approaches have been applied for FPs detection in other languages and proved the relevancy of these acoustic properties [2,7,9].

In the literature the most commonly observed feature of FPs is the long duration [9,11,20,26]. In our corpus the average duration of FPs is 400ms (minimum and maximum durations of FPs are 129 ms and 2.3 s respectively). 87 % of the whole set of 758 FPs are longer than 200 ms (Fig. 1).

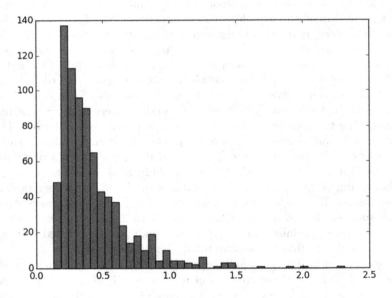

Fig. 1. The distribution of FPs duration

Another prominent feature of FPs is a gradual fall of fundamental frequency (F0). This tendency is a well-known fact, in [19] it has been shown that FPs tend to be low in F0 as well as displaying a gradual, roughly linear F0 fall [19]. To compare characteristics of FPs with surrounding signal, we have manually annotated the left and right context of each phenomena, marking at least one word (or two-three words) to gain minimum two syllables at either side of disfluency. We have checked the standard deviation for F0 and first three formants and the most obvious case of small variance of standard deviation in FPs were for F0 and energy (Figs. 2 and 3).

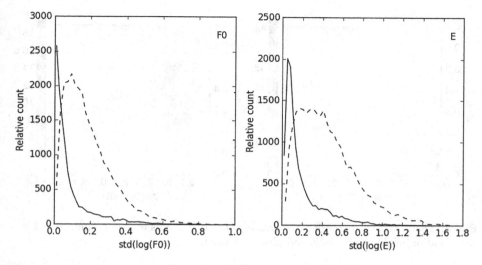

Fig. 2. The standard deviation of the logarithms of F0 (left) and energy (right) of FPs (thick line) and of neighboring words and phrases (dashed line).

The proposed algorithm has several parameters that should be optimized: w_n that are weights for stardard deviations of $log(E)$ and $log(F_N)$ and E_0 that is a minimal mean energy level. The following steps were performed:

- Calculate the standard deviations and means for the logarithms of F0, F1 and energy in 150-ms windows
- Obtain the optimal values of parameters w_n and E_0 for criterion $C = \sum_n w_n V_n < 1; E > E_0$ where w_n are weights for values V_n: stardard deviations of $log(E)$ and $log(F_N)$ and E_0 is a minimal mean energy level. The optimal values are those that maximize F_1score for the task of selection of 150ms windows that are part of the FPs.
- Find the consecutive intervals matching the criterion C.
- Compare the intervals with annotation.
- Calculate F_1score $= \frac{2 \cdot \text{true positive}}{2 \cdot \text{true positive} + \text{false negative} + \text{false positive}}$

The parameters were then optimized using gradient descent method [22].

At the stage of comparison with annotation, the intervals intersecting with the labeled ones are found. Here we calculate the intersection length $T_{int} = \text{len}(I \cap L)$ and length of non-matching part of the interval $T_{ext} = \text{len}(I \setminus S)$, where I is interval and L is label. If $T_{int} > 0.2\text{len}(L)$ and $3T_{ext} < T_{int}$ the pair of label and interval is considered matching. After processing the whole signal the amount of non-matched intervals is considered false positive count and the amount of non-matched labels is considered false negative count.

The experiments were conducted on 85 % of the corpus with 15 % used as a test-set. The test-set was randomly taken from the whole corpus and the results were averaged. The performance was compared to the annotation of 758 FPs. The obtained F_1score is 0.46. For two parameters (F0 and Energy) and with grid search instead of gradient decent the F_1 score was 0.43.

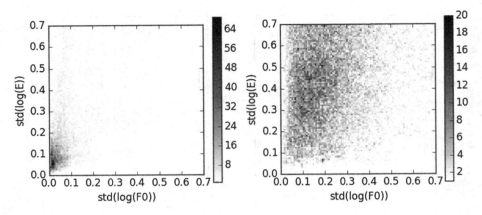

Fig. 3. The heatmap of standard deviation of the logarithms of energy and F0 of FPs (left) and of neighboring words and phrases (right).

The misses were mainly caused by the disorder of harmonic components in hoarse voice and the laryngealized filled pauses and lengthenings. In some cases the FP has an unstable expressive intonation contour, which was not flat or lowering, that it can be argued whether they are FPs or interjections. Few cases of misses were the result of small duration of annotated phenomena. Some false alarms were caused by lengthenings that were missing in the annotation. And noises (especially in the part from the open source multi-language database) and overlappings (in task dialogs part) caused number of false negatives.

4   Conclusions

This paper presents the method based on acoustic parameters of FPs in Russian spontaneous speech, that maximizes the F_1 score for FPs detection by the gradient decent method. As the acoustic parameters we have used standard deviations of F0, F1, F2, F3 and energy. This gave us F_1 score of 0.46, what, comparing to F_1 score obtained with only two parameters and grid search is a small improvement. This could be due to the challenging quality data (in the part from the open source multi-language database) or because of small influence of F1, F2 and F3 on the FPs detection for our data, that should be tested, since it is not comply with studies on other languages. We also plan to use non-linear expression to separate FPs from other signal to test whether it would improve the obtained F_1 score. The results of this study are also a step towards building a complex and reliable FPs search method, that could be used on data of different recording quality and conditions.

Acknowledgements. This research is supported by the grant of Russian Foundation for Basic Research (project No 15-06-04465) and by the Council of Grants of the President of Russia (project No MK-5209.2015.8).

References

1. Anderson, A., Bader, M., Bard, E., Boyle, E., Doherty, G., Garrod, S., et al.: The hcrc map task corpus. Lang. Speech **34**(4), 351–366 (1991)
2. Audhkhasi, K., Kandhway, K., Deshmukh, O., Verma, A.: Formant-based technique for automatic filled-pause detection in spontaneous spoken english. In: IEEE International Conference on Acoustics, Speech and Signal Processing, ICASSP 2009, pp. 4857–4860. IEEE (2009)
3. Chafe, W.L. (ed.): The Pear Stories: Cognitive, Cultural, and Linguistic Aspects of Narrative Production. Ablex, Norwood (1980)
4. Clark, H.: Using Language. Cambridge University Press, Cambridge (1996)
5. Eisler, F.G.: Psycholinguistics: Experiments in Spontaneous Speech. Academic Press, New York (1968)
6. Ferreira, F., Lau, E.F., Bailey, K.G.: Disfluencies, language comprehension, and tree adjoining grammars. Cogn. Sci. **28**(5), 721–749 (2004)
7. Garg, G., Ward, N.: Detecting filled pauses in tutorial dialogs (2006)
8. Godfrey, J.J., Holliman, E.C., McDaniel, J.: Switchboard: telephone speech corpus for research and development. In: 992 IEEE International Conference on Acoustics, Speech, and Signal Processing, ICASSP-92, vol. 1, pp. 517–520. IEEE (1992)
9. Goto, M., Itou, K., Hayamizu, S.: A real-time filled pause detection system for spontaneous speech recognition. In: Eurospeech, Citeseer (1999)
10. INTERSPEECH: computational paralinguistic challenge in 2013. http://emotion-research.net/sigs/speech-sig/is13-compare. Accessed 1 Apr 2015
11. Kibrik, A., Podlesskaya, V. (eds.): Rasskazy o snovideniyah: Korpusnoye issledovaniye ustnogo russkogo diskursa [Night dream stories: Corpus study of Russian discourse]. Litres (2014)
12. Kohler, K.: Labelled data bank of spoken standard german: the kiel corpus of read/spontaneous speech. In: Proceedings of Fourth International Conference on Spoken Language, ICSLP 96, vol. 3, pp. 1938–1941. IEEE (1996)
13. Lease, M., Johnson, M., Charniak, E.: Recognizing disfluencies in conversational speech. IEEE Trans. Audio, Speech Lang. Process. **14**(5), 1566–1573 (2006)
14. Liu, Y., Shriberg, E., Stolcke, A.: Automatic disfluency identification in conversational speech using multiple knowledge sources. In: 8th European Conference on Speech Communication and Technology Proceedings, INTERSPEECH, pp. 957-960 (2003)
15. Liu, Y., Shriberg, E., Stolcke, A., Hillard, D., Ostendorf, M., Harper, M.: Enriching speech recognition with automatic detection of sentence boundaries and disfluencies. IEEE Trans. Audio, Speech Lang. Process. **14**(5), 1526–1540 (2006)
16. Medeiros, H., Moniz, H., Batista, F., Trancoso, I., Nunes, L., et al.: Disfluency detection based on prosodic features for university lectures. In: 14th Annual Conference of the International Speech Communication Association, INTERSPEECH, pp. 2629–2633 (2013)
17. O'Connell, D., Kowal, S.: The history of research on the filled pause as evidence of the written language bias in linguistics (linell, 1982). J. Psycholinguist. Res. **33**, 459–474 (2004)
18. Ogden, R.: Turn-holding, turn-yielding and laryngeal activity in finnish talk-in-interaction. J. Int. Phonetics Assoc. **31**(1), 139–152 (2001)
19. O'Shaughnessy, D.: Recognition of hesitations in spontaneous speech. In: 1992 IEEE International Conference on Acoustics, Speech, and Signal Processing, ICASSP-92, vol. 1, pp. 521–524. IEEE (1992)

20. Shriberg, E.: Preliminaries to a theory of speech disfluencies. Ph.D. thesis, University of California at Berkeley (1994)
21. Shriberg, E.: Spontaneous speech: how people really talk and why engineers should care. In: 9th European Conference on Speech Communication and Technology, INTERSPEECH, pp. 1781–1784 (2005)
22. Kober, J., Peters, J.: Introduction. In: Kober, J., Peters, J. (eds.) Learning Motor Skills. STAR, vol. 97, pp. 1–6. Springer, Heidelberg (2014)
23. Stepanova, S.: Some features of filled hesitation pauses in spontaneous Russian. Proc. ICPhS. **16**, 1325–1328 (2007)
24. Stolcke, A., Shriberg, E., Bates, R.A., Ostendorf, M., Hakkani, D., Plauche, M., Tür, G., Lu, Y.: Automatic detection of sentence boundaries and disfluencies based on recognized words. In: ICSLP (1998)
25. Tree, J.E.F.: The effects of false starts and repetitions on the processing of subsequent words in spontaneous speech. J. Mem Lang. **34**(6), 709–738 (1995)
26. Veiga, A., Candeias, S., Lopes, C., Perdigão, F.: Characterization of hesitations using acoustic models. In: International Congress of Phonetic Sciences-ICPhS XVII, pp. 2054–2057 (2011)
27. Verkhodanova, V., Shapranov, V.: Automatic detection of filled pauses and lengthenings in the spontaneous russian speech. In: 7th Speech Prosody conference, pp. 1110–1114 (2014)
28. Zahorian, S.: Open-source multi-language audio database for spoken language processing applications. Technical report, DTIC Document (2012)
29. Zemskaya, E.: Russian spoken speech: linguistic analysis and the problems of learning. Moscow (1979)

Multimodal Presentation of Bulgarian Child Language

Dimitar Popov$^{(\boxtimes)}$ and Velka Popova

Laboratory of Applied Linguistics, Faculty of Humanities,
Konstantin Preslavsky University of Shumen, Shumen, Bulgaria
labling@shu-bg.net

Abstract. The holistic tradition in modern linguistics is characterized by integrated and corpus approaches towards the explored phenomena. In that way specific circumstances are established so that speech could be thoroughly examined in norm and pathology in exploiting contemporary multimedia equipment and software products. The present research work focuses on some of the possibilities of ones of the most frequently used interactive platforms such as TalkBank and CHILDES, which diverse corpora have an extremely broad specter of applications in different spheres of science and social life which on its part specifies them as socially valid and crucial. Additionally the paper dwells on a Bulgarian child language corpus created within the parameters of that multimodal paradigm presentation.

Keywords: Bulgarian child language · Computer corpora · TALK-BANK · CHILDES · CLARIN

1 Introduction

The holistic tradition in modern linguistics is characterized by integrated and corpus approaches towards the explored phenomena. In that way specific circumstances are established so that speech could be thoroughly examined in norm and pathology in exploiting contemporary multimedia equipment and software products. The present research work focuses on some of the possibilities of one of the most frequently used interactive platforms such as TalkBank and CHILDES [3], which diverse corpora have an extremely broad specter of applications in different spheres of science and social life which on its part specifies them as socially valid and crucial. Additionally the paper dwells on a Bulgarian child language corpus created within the parameters of that paradigm in the domain of the operating research program in the Laboratory of Applied linguistics in Konstantin Preslavsky University of Shumen. The data which are in a constant process of expanding are taken as default part of the databank of Bulgarian scientific consortium CLARIN (BG-CLARIN). They specifically are of great importance in the formation and creation of a national interdisciplinary e-infrastructure in the integration and development processes of Bulgarian language electronic resources.

A. Ronzhin et al. (Eds.): SPECOM 2015, LNAI 9319, pp. 293–300, 2015.
DOI: 10.1007/978-3-319-23132-7_36

2   Bulgarian Corpus of Child Speech Data

The creation of computerized Bulgarian corpus of child speech data is one of the crucial tasks in Applied Linguistics Laboratory at Konstantin Preslavsky University of Shumen. This corpus is already a fact, developed in the terms of CHILDES. It comprises two types of speech resources: CORPUS A, comprising spontaneous speech of four children at their early age (from 1 to 3 years old), and CORPUS B, comprising stories based on a series of pictures with 90 children at pre-school age (from 3 to 6 years old). This empirical material has not been included yet in the common bank of CHILDES system since it is still being loaded with new data as well as with raw materials which are still being collected and prepared.

Until now in the area of **CORPUS A** (Table 1) the collected and prepared computer based data have comprised audio recordings of spontaneous speech of four Bulgarian children ALE (*Alexandra* at age 1;01–2;04), TEF (*Stefany* at age 1;03–2;05), BOG (*Bogomila* at age 2;01–2;05) and IVE (*Ivelin* at age 2;07–2;10) (transformed in computer WAV-files) which are transcribed and coded in CHAT-format. This corpus consisting of the utterance data has been organised in two modules: basic corpuses (the longitudinal data of systematic continuous recordings of two of the children, Stephanie and Alexandra, presented in **7474 children's utterances (3871 of them belong to ALE and 3603 to TEF)**) and additional corpuses (the data of insufficient continuous non-systematic recordings of the other two children Ivelin and Bogomila).

The transcribing process is carried out in **Sonic Mode** (*This method focuses on use of a waveform drawn at the bottom of the editor screen for precise demarcation of utterances and insertion of begin-end times. Sonic Mode is the prime mode for highly detailed transcriptions* [5]) – this method requires more time but is rather accurate and precise. The links to the sound or video media are

Table 1. CORPUS A.

BASIC CORPUSES				ADITIONAL CORPUSES			
ALE (*Alexandra*)		TEF (*Stefany*)		BOG (*Bogomila*)		IVE (*Ivelin*)	
File Name	Age	File Name	Age	File Name	Age	File Name	Age
Al10129.cha	1;01.29	1St.cha	1;03.11	1bog.cha	2;01.08	1ive.cha	2;07.17
Al10506.cha	1;05.06	2St.cha	1;06.22	2bog.cha	2;02.27	2ive.cha	2;10.23
Al10621.cha	1;06.21	3St.cha	1;08.0	3bog.cha	2;04.05		
Al10720.cha	1;07.20	4St.cha	1;11.04	4bog.cha	2;05.19		
			1;11.08				
Al10822.cha	1;08.22	5St.cha	1;11.25				
Al10919.cha	1;09.19	6St.cha	2;0.09				
Al11012.cha	1;10.12	7St.cha	2;0.23				
Al11114.cha	1;11.14	8St.cha	2;01.16				
Al20013.cha	2;00.13	9St.cha	2;02.16				
Al20224.cha	2;02.24	10St.cha	2;03.23				
Al20312.cha	2;03.12	11St.cha	2;04.21				
Al20409.cha	2;04.09	12St.cha	2;05.25				

inscribed in the transcription under the form of bullets (Clicking on the bullet plays the segment referred to in the bullet. In addition to the playback of individual segments, CLAN also provides a method for continuous playback of the whole transcript. CLAN then highlights each utterance as it is played and turns the pages of the transcript when necessary. This playback can be halted by a mouse click in the transcript window.). Here are some examples that were extracted directly from a CHAT transcript (see the next two figures – Figs. 1 and 2).

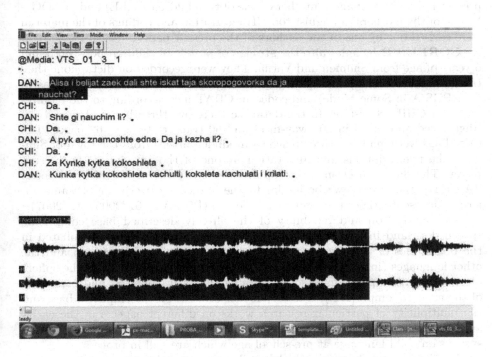

Fig. 1. Audio transcription from a waveform

In the core of the database there are 33 h of recordings (digitalized and saved in 32 *.wav-files) and transcribed in 355 pages. During the process of creating the *.cha-files the data from certain short-lived files were summarized in a single document. The corpus of data comprising the results given by the four children is saved in 30 files in CHAT-format. This database is part of a large study on early acquisition of Bulgarian Verb Morphology. The data collection and processing was supported by the Center for General Linguistics, ZAS (http://www.zas. gwz-berlin.de) to the Projects *Erwerb sprachlicher Markierungen zur Differenzierung von ±Begrenztheit* (DFG, ZAS - 01/2003 - 12/2005) and *Syntaktische Konsequenzen des Morphologieerwerbsn* (DFG, ZAS - 01/2000 - 12/2002).

The children in question were born and live in the town of Shumen, northeast part of Bulgaria. They were recorded in common situations (games, when dressing, eating, going to sleep, going through children's pictorial books, free playing with mother, free playing with father, free playing with other children, reading a book and others) in the process of their daily interaction surrounded by their relatives. All individuals who were signed in the database in their role as participants in dialogues are monolingual with their first language – Bulgarian. The adults in the surroundings have a sufficient level of proper education (either secondary or higher university education). The audio-recordings of the three of the children (ALE, TEF, IVE) were made by the researcher (the author of the present research work and a mother of one of the children – ALE) and of BOG – by one of the mothers (a linguist too). Transcription and codings of the material were carried out by one of the authors of the present paper.

CORPUS B includes also the **stories** of preschool children between 3 and 6 years of age from Shumen and Varna. They were recorded on dictaphone then transformed into computer WAV-files which were transcribed (the same as in CORPUS A in Sonic Mode) and coded in CHAT-files according to the requirements of CHILES system. In the database there are three hours of recordings (digitalized and saved in 30 *wav-files) and 60 transcriptions of 62 pages. The recordings were made by three teachers in kindergartens from the town of Shumen, the transcriptions and annotation by one of the authors of the present paper. The data collection was supported by the General Linguistics Center, ZAS (http://www.zas.gwz-berlin.de) to the Projects Erwerb und Disambiguierung intersententialer pronominaler Referenz (P5/ZAS - 01/2006 - 12/2007).

The application and reliability of the already described base comprising speech data and information by Bulgarian children is partially approbated in the boundaries of discussions and comparative analyses of Bulgarian and the other languages (in particular, German and Russian), carried out in the sphere of cross-linguistic programme for examining the early adoption and mastering of the aspect (comp.: [1,2]). The corpus also stresses on the empirical base and the multiplicity of particular research works on different aspects of the early-age ontogenesis of Bulgarian grammar (see: [6–8]) and others, as well as certain surveys on child language at pre-school age which are still in process.

The database in Bulgarian which is still in progress, also comprises video-data included in one ClassTalk session in the database of TalkBank which are easily integrated in the already prepared CHILDES corpora. They present Classroom interactions and take up a number of classes in the kindergarten. They are still in progress in a transcribing process (Video transcription follows the same basic principles as audio transcription. Figure 2 illustrates how video files are transcribed in CLAN (see an in-depth analysis [4]). These Bulgarian corpora could be used not only in the research process on the specifics of the speech interaction between the teacher and the children lasting one class hour but also as sample material in the process of teaching students-pedagogues.

CLAN supports additional methods for numerical analysis, such as *Analysis with Praat, Nested files* and others. By **Praat** analysis any bullet that refers to a sound file can be directly exported to Praat, where segmental and prosodic features of the speech can be analyzed and displayed. The Praat analyses can

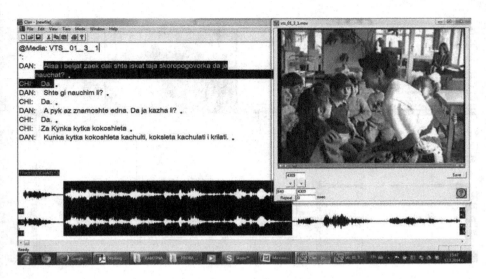

Fig. 2. Video transcription with an open Sound Panel

then be written to picture files, which can be attached to the transcript respectively. Within Praat, the user can select the spectrogram option and then Praat options to highlight the prosodic contour (See Fig. 3). By **Nested files** nested picture files are linked to a bullet in the transcript. The user inserts bullets for nested files by selecting the "Insert Bullet" function and then navigating to locate the relevant picture or text file. Bullets for nested files can be inserted at any relevant position in the transcript. *Nested text files can also support the detailed annotation of gestures* [5].

Another corpus is also in progress and namely the corpus comprising data of a free associative experiment with 140 respondents:

- 50 Bulgarian children of pre-school age among whom there are monolingual and bilingual children (Bulgarian-Turkish and Bulgarian-Russian). At present the digital audio-base is completely equipped and can implement the transcribing process of the speech material.
- 70 adults at the age of 20–70 among whom there are monolingual and bilingual children (Bulgarian-Turkish and Bulgarian-Russian). At present the digital audio-base is completely equipped and can implement the transcribing process of the speech material.
- 10 adults with light or average degree of mental retardation. At present the digital audio-base is completely equipped and can implement the transcribing process of the speech material.

Though it is a fact that the Bulgarian corpus has not been uploaded on the CHILDES net, as it was already mentioned above, it has been used numerous times in different publications and international projects under the form of empirical base focusing on the approbation of the cognitive models in speech

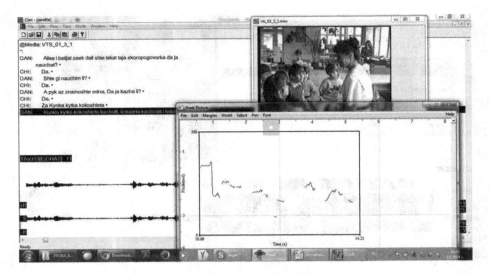

Fig. 3. Pitch contour in a segment exported to Praat

interaction. It could be further expanded and optimized by the creation of parallel and comparative corpora which on its part could be extremely important for the comparative research works in different languages and cultures.

In the last years the Bulgarian corpus of child speech presented in the paper has been incorporated as a sub-corpus in the new system BG-CLARIN, which is still in progress, and on its part is a segment of the European consortium CLARIN[1](Common Language Resources and Technology Infrastructure aiming to create an European infrastructure network). The mission of this pan-European infrastructure initiative (CLARIN-ERIC) is *to advance research in humanities and social sciences by giving researchers unified single sign-on access to a platform which integrates language-based resources and advanced tools at a European level. This shall be implemented by the construction and operation of a shared distributed infrastructure that aims at making language resources, technology and expertise available to the humanities and social sciences research communities at large* (See more on http://centres.clarin.eu/).

3   The Cooperation of TALKBANK from North America with CLARIN

In the paper hereby presented the authors attempt to dwell on the multimodal corpus perspective as a basic line in the tradition of research in language onto-

---

[1] Bulgaria is one of the founders of the European consortium CLARIN ERIC and has close connections to the rest countries-members in that infrastructural network. On 21st, September, 2010 the Ministry Council of the Republic of Bulgaria adopted "National scientific infrastructure road map", which additionally issues the construction of BG-CLARIN (http://www.mon.bg).

genesis. The accumulation of empirical data has always been, still is and will be domineering as it is provided with a great set of data. In the course of time and technical advance, however, the empirical products reach a new level of quality with respect to their processing. The card-files and registers are replaced with electronic speech arrays, the time-consuming and exhausting work regarding the registration, transcription and statistic processing of the data is provided by various modern technological devices and programme products. The climax of this evolutionary process was the creation of CHILDES. The typological diversity of the linguistic data included in the survey, the unified format of the transcription, the packet of CLAN programme resources for automatic processing turn this system into an extremely useful and convenient platform for research work. Additionally, the optimal empirical possibilities could guarantee the achievement of high level of objectivity and adequacy of the results as well as turn them into a solid set of database for approbation of the models of language ontogenesis. The unified available technical devices used in the process of annotation of the extra-linguistic data which go along with the speech of the individuals in question as well as the constant connection between the transcripts and the respective audio and video-files provide certain possibilities and perspectives not only for further research work in all aspects of speech interaction but also in interaction as a whole on the part of the other scientific fields. In that respect by using CHILDES explorers and researchers from different spheres of humanities could successfully fulfill and realize their searches and also join in the interdisciplinary projects. Following the logic of what has already been said it could be expected that the exchange data system CHILDES is highly likely to turn into one of the most successful professional ON-LINE networks for humanitarians which on its part could lead to stable and modern inter-disciplinary surveys.

We should point out here that in perspective one of the most significant factors in speech interaction research work could be the constant reintegration of multimodal scientific platforms, approaches and paradigms. The present paper has made an attempt to illustrate that phenomenon in the context of CHILDES and TalkBank which with their rationality and numerous possibilities and applications have found their way in the processes of cooperation and globalization in the studies of humanities as a whole. This could stand as a prerequisite for the broad social validity of the research results based on TalkBank data as well as for their integration in the actual work programmes in infrastructure creations for language data exchange which aim is to overcome the present lack of coordination in the scientific environment (a favourable example in this respect could be the cooperation of TalkBank from North America with CLARIN. This, on its part, could quite naturally be interpreted as a solid guarantee not only for the quality of the scientific products but also for their broad applicability in linguistics and other branches of science but also for their overall usefulness in society.

4   Conclusion

The presented multimodal contributions to the Bulgarian CHILDES database consist of transcripts that are linked to audio- and video-files. These multimedia files allow the researcher to systematically investigate new aspects of child language. For instance, although some of the standard CHAT transcripts include information on intonation and illocutionary force, it is impossible to systematically investigate these aspects without the linkage of transcripts and audio-recordings. Similarly, the linkage of transcripts and video-files makes it possible to study non-verbal communication and the influence of the pragmatic context on the child's speech.

References

1. Bittner, D., Gagarina, N., Popova, V., Kühnast, M.: Aspect before tense in the acquisition of Russian, Bulgarian, and German. In: Solovyev, V., Polyakov, V. (eds.) Text Processing and Cognitive Technologies, pp. 263–272. Ucheba, Moskow (2005)
2. Kühnast, M., Popova, V., Popov, D.: Erwerb der Aspektmarkierung im Bulgarischen. In: Gagarina, N., Bittner, D. (eds.) ZAS-Paper in Linguistics 33, 2004: Studies on the Development of Grammar in German, Russian and Bulgarian, pp. 63–87. ZAS-Berlin, Berlin (2004)
3. MacWhinney, B.: The CHILDES Project. Tools for Analyzing Talk: The Database, vol. II. Lawrence Erlbaum, Hillsdale (2000)
4. MacWhinney, B.: Opening up video databases to collaborative commentary. In: Goldman, R., Pea, R., Barron, B., Derry, S. (eds.) Video Research in the Learning Sciences, pp. 537–546. Lawrence Erlbaum Associates, Mahwah (2007)
5. MacWhinney, B., Wagner, J.: Transcribing, searching and data sharing: the CLAN software and the TalkBank data repository. Gesprächsforschung **11**, 154–173 (2010). Online-Zeitschrift zur verbalen Interaktion, Ausgabe. http://www.gespraechsforschung-ozs.de
6. Popova, V., Popov, D.: The emergence of verb grammar in two Bulgarian-speaking children. In: Solovyev, V., Polyakov, V. (eds.) Text Processing and Cognitive Technologies, pp. 236–248. Ucheba, Moskow (2007)
7. Popova, V.: Korpusno izsledvane na gramatichnata metamorfoza na rannija detski ezik. In: Ezik, kultura, identichnost. Faber, Veliko Tarnovo, pp. 101–115 (2010) (In Bulgarian)
8. Popova, V.: Roljata na onomatopeite v rannata glagolna ontogeneza. In: Litera et Lingua. Prolet 2011, Sofia (2011) (In Bulgarian). http://slav.unisofia.bg/lilijournal/index.php/bg/issues/spring2011

On Deep and Shallow Neural Networks in Speech Recognition from Speech Spectrum

Jan Zelinka[1]($\boxtimes$), Petr Salajka[2], and Luděk Müller[2]

[1] Faculty of Applied Sciences, Department of Cybernetics,
University of West Bohemia, Univerzitní 8, 30 614 Plzeň, Czech Republic
[2] Faculty of Applied Sciences, New Technologies for the Information Society,
University of West Bohemia, Univerzitní 8, 30 614 Plzeň, Czech Republic
{zelinka,salajka,muller}@kky.zcu.cz

Abstract. This paper demonstrates how usual feature extraction methods such as the PLP can be successfully replaced by a neural network and how signal processing methods such as mean normalization, variance normalization and delta coefficients can be successfully utilized when a NN-based feature extraction and a NN-based acoustic model are used simultaneously. The importance of the deep NNs is also investigated. The system performance was evaluated on the British English speech corpus WSJCAM0.

1 Introduction

This paper describes an application of Neural Networks (NNs) in a feature extraction and an acoustic model for a speech recognition system. Although methods such as the PLP [4] allow to reach high accuracy in a usual GMM-based modelling, they could be viewed as a limitation that prevents further progress in NN-based acoustic modelling. There are still only sparse attempts to apply NNs as the feature extraction for speech recognition [2,3,6,10–12] and there are even some papers reporting a slightly higher error for the raw signal [14]. Usually, convolutional neural networks are applied [1]. But standard neural networks are sufficient for this task. Our experiments showed that the methods such as the PLP could be successfully substituted with a relatively small NN. But above all, this paper shows that the PLP method could be significantly outperformed.

In the case of usual GMM-based acoustic models, using delta coefficients, mean and variance normalization significantly increases performance of speech recognition. This increasing is significant even in the case of usual NN-based models. In this paper, we didn't want to loose the advantages of these methods. Therefore, we implemented and tested possibility to incorporate these methods in our framework. The novelty of this paper is the demonstration how methods such as mean or variance normalization and delta coefficients can be beneficial when a NN-based feature extraction and a NN-based acoustic model are trained simultaneously.

In this paper, some experiment with deep NNs and relatively shallow NNs are done. Generally, deep NNs bring some difficulties during training. There

© Springer International Publishing Switzerland 2015
A. Ronzhin et al. (Eds.): SPECOM 2015, LNAI 9319, pp. 301–308, 2015.
DOI: 10.1007/978-3-319-23132-7_37

are many training process enhancements such as weight mean and variance normalization [5]. But in this paper, an enhancement that allows to initialize NN-based feature extraction by means of the PLP features. This enhancement is a modification of well-known method [13] that allows to train deep NN by means of additional gradients application. In our experiments, the contribution of this enhancement is investigated.

This paper is organized as follows: Sect. 2 describes our NN-based acoustic models. Section 3 deals with NNs for approximating the PLP method. The role of a mean normalization and some other methods is investigated in Sect. 4. Results of our experiments where the NNs are connected are shown in Sect. 5. Some conclusions and our future work descriptions are in Sect. 6.

2 Neural-Network-based Acoustic Models

A NN-based acoustic model computes posterior probabilities. In this paper, the posteriors are computed for context-independent phones. We used an English phonetic alphabet which has 43 phonemes. Because each phoneme is modeled as a three state HMM, the output layer provides estimates of 129 posterior probabilities.

In our experiments, we experimented with shallow and deep NNs. Standard NN-based acoustic models represent our baselines. In our previous works, a special long temporal spectral pattern feature processing technique was used in the hybrid NN/HMM systems. However in this paper, these features are replaced with a sequence of the PLP vectors (or some transforms of these features) constituting one large vector. In all presented NNs, activation functions in the hidden layers are sigmoid functions. The "shallow" NNs have one hidden layer (with 512 or 1024 neurons) and an output layer (with 129 neurons). The "deep" NNs have three hidden layer (with 512 neurons) and an output layer (with 129 neurons).

In this paper, NN-based acoustic models ware always trained by means of the Cross-Entropy (XENT) criterion. The employed training algorithm was a momentum method. The NN training algorithm was stochastic, i.e. a random subset is selected from a training set every cycle of the training process.

3 Neural-Network-based Feature Extraction

NN-based acoustic models which use the PLP features determine our baselines. Instead the PLP features, absolute spectrum (|FFT|) features are used in proposed connection of a NN-based feature extraction and a NN-based acoustic model. In the PLP computation, the used Hamming window and FFT are linear transforms without time-shifting. Hence, these transforms can be performed by a NN easily. Operations that are necessary for |FFT| computation (i.e. square and square root) can be provided by particular activation functions or can be approximated adequately by one layer with a relatively small number of neurons. Hence, using |FFT| is very similar to using a "raw" signal. We didn't want to increase the number of layers excessively and we also didn't want to use unusual activation function. Even though we admit that using a raw signal could improve precision of NN-based acoustic models, we decided to use |FFT| as a reasonable compromise between a raw sampled signal and the PLP features.

For computing the sequence of the PLP features or NN-based features, several time-shifting operations must be computed. Formally, the time-shift (TS) operation output is computed in the following way:

$$Y_t = \text{TS}(x_t, s) = \begin{cases} x_{t+s} & 1 \leq t + s \leq T \\ x_1 & t + s < 1 \\ x_T & T < t + s \end{cases}, \tag{1}$$

where s is the time-shift and T is the length of processed recording. In the back-propagation, a gradient $\frac{\partial \varepsilon}{\partial x_t}$ is computed using gradient $\frac{\partial \varepsilon}{\partial y_t}$ where ε is a criterion. The following equation holds:

$$\frac{\partial \varepsilon}{\partial x_t} = \begin{cases} \frac{\partial \varepsilon}{\partial y_{t-s}} & 1 < t + s < T \\ \sum_{i=1}^{s} \frac{\partial \varepsilon}{\partial y_i} & t = 1 \wedge s > 0 \\ \sum_{i=T+s}^{T} \frac{\partial \varepsilon}{\partial y_i} & t = T \wedge s < 0 \\ 0 & \text{otherwise} \end{cases}. \tag{2}$$

The role of the time-shifting operation is showed in Fig. 1. The gray module labeled as "Time Shifting" denotes the required sequence of time-shifting operations. In this module, each output vector Y_i is computed from its input x_t as follows: $Y_t = [\text{TS}(x_t, -s), \text{TS}(x_t, -s+1), \ldots, \text{TS}(x_t, 0), \text{TS}(x_t, 1), \ldots, \text{TS}(x_t, s)]$. In our experiments s was equal to five.

Our experiments show that a NN-based feature extraction and a NN-based acoustic model could be trained separately with satisfactory results. But, in this paper, another approach is also investigated. Well known approach to deep neural networks training is adopted. This approach is shown in Fig. 1. The depicted NN-based feature extraction and the depicted NN-based acoustic model are connected together before the training. Two gradients are computed: the gradient for the feature extraction part (with wights W) is computed by means of Mean Square Error (MSE) criterion (ε_{MSE}) and the gradient for the connection is computed according to the cross-entropy criterion (ε_{XENT}). Naturally, the resultant gradient is the sum $\frac{\partial \varepsilon}{\partial w} = \frac{\partial \varepsilon_{MSE}}{\partial w} + \frac{\partial \varepsilon_{XENT}}{\partial w}$, where W denotes a weight of a NN in a NN-based feature extraction. The motivation behind this approach is an assumption that although the approximation of the PLP is still not precise this approach leads to a more precise acoustic model (in comparison to the approach where both parts are trained separately) for a posteriors estimate.

In this paper, shallow NNs for feature extractions have one hidden layer with 256 neurons. These neurons have sigmoid activation functions. Deep NNs have three hidden layers. Each hidden layer has 256 neurons and sigmoid activation functions. Output layers have always 12 neurons with linear (diagonal) activation functions. After connection of a NN-based feature extraction and a NN-based acoustic model, the resultant "shallow" NNs have four layers and the resultant

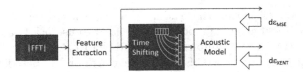

Fig. 1. The proposed alternative approach of a NN-based feature extraction and a NN-based acoustic model connection training.

deep NNs have eight layers. In our preliminary experiments, we noticed some training algorithm collapse due to a numerical issue in the linear layer of NN-based feature extraction. As a collapse prevention, weights of the output layers (but not the inputs) were limited. The maximal absolute value was one.

4   Signal Processing Methods in NN-based Acoustic Models

Mean normalization (MN), variance normalization (VN) and delta coefficients (Δ) are usual feature extraction methods with significant benefits. Therefore, these methods cannot be ignored. A common NN-based acoustic model could not perform MN or/and VN even if long temporal features are applied but it could use their approximation. However, this approximation is probably highly inaccurate. Thereby, in this paper, the output of the feature extractions are extended by Δ, MN and VN.

MN transforms an input x_t according to the formula $y_t = \mathrm{MN}(x_t) = \sum_{\tau=1}^{T} x_\tau$. During the backpropagation, it is necessary to compute a gradient $\frac{\partial \varepsilon}{\partial x_t}$, where ε is a criterion. MN is a linear transform therefore the gradient $\frac{\partial \varepsilon}{\partial x_t}$ can be computed from a gradient $\frac{\partial \varepsilon}{\partial y_t}$ by a linear transform too. After a short and simple derivation, the following surprisingly plain equation can be obtained: $\frac{\partial \varepsilon}{\partial x_t} = \mathrm{MN}\left(\frac{\partial \varepsilon}{\partial y_t}\right)$.

VN is computed as follows:

$$y_t = \frac{x_t}{\sigma}, \; \sigma = \sqrt{\frac{1}{T}\sum_{\tau=1}^{T}(x_\tau - \mu)^2}, \; \mu = \frac{1}{T}\sum_{\tau=1}^{T}x_\tau. \tag{3}$$

Although a gradient $\frac{\partial \varepsilon}{\partial x_t}$ computation is much less straightforward, with a little effort, one can see that the following equation holds:

$$\frac{\partial \varepsilon}{\partial x_t} = \frac{1}{\sigma}\frac{\partial \varepsilon}{\partial y_t} - \frac{1}{T}\frac{x_t - \mu}{\sigma^2}\sum_{\tau=1}^{T}\frac{\partial \varepsilon}{\partial y_\tau}y_\tau. \tag{4}$$

Delta coefficients computation is a linear transform. Hence, a gradient $\frac{\partial \varepsilon}{\partial x_t}$ computation is also a linear transform. Its formula is also simple, nevertheless not as short as the previous formulae.

Figure 2 shows a schema of the connection of a NN-based feature extraction and a NN-based acoustic model where only delta and delta-delta coefficients are computed. Figure 3 shows a schema of the connection where besides delta and delta-delta coefficients MN and VN are computed. Obviously, MN doesn't change delta coefficients. But VN does and therefore additional delta and delta-delta coefficients are computed from VN.

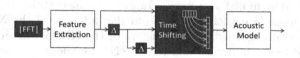

Fig. 2. The schema of a NN-based feature extraction and a NN-based acoustic model connection with delta and delta-delta coefficients

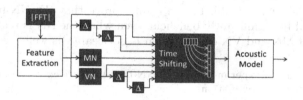

Fig. 3. The schema of a NN-based feature extraction and a NN-based acoustic model connection with mean normalization, variance normalization, delta and delta-delta coefficients

5   Experiments and Results

The British English speech corpus WSJCAM0 [9] is used for the system performance evaluation in the following experiments. This corpus includes 7861 utterances (i.e. approximately 15 h of speech) in the training set. Phonetic alphabet consists of 43 phones (including silence and inhale). The experiments were performed on the development sets si_dt5a and si_dt5b. In the corpus, a particular trigram language model for both sets is prescribed. The set si_dt5a is used to find the optimal word insertion penalty and the optimal language model weight. The set si_dt5b is used strictly as an evaluation set. Our proprietary real-time LVSCR decoder [7,8] was applied.

In the first seven experiments, the role of a NN-based feature extraction was investigated. The number of neuron in hidden layers in each NN-based acoustic models was 1024.

In the first experiment, the PLP features (with delta and delta-delta coefficients) and a usual acoustic GMM-based acoustic model were investigated. A forced alignment was performed using the GMM acoustic model to determined initial targets for training NN-based acoustic models. More convenient targets were determined during training the NN-based acoustic models by applying of a realignment. In the second experiment a hybrid NN/HMM was investigated. In the third experiment the front-end NN was trained by means of the MSE criterion as an approximation of the PLP. The training process were stopped when the accuracy reached almost the result from the previous experiment (on the development set si_dt5a). On the test set si_dt5b the accuracy significantly decreased but, naturally, we had to ignore this fact in the training process. The acoustic model was the same model as the acoustic model used in the second experiment (the model was fixed). In order to distinguish the influence of the NN-based acoustic model training from the influence of the NN-based feature extraction training we fixed parameters of the NN for the acoustic model in the third and fourth experiment where the NN for the feature extraction was trained. In the fifth experiment both NNs were trained together. In the sixth experiment, MN and VN were computed. In the seventh experiment, MN and VN were also computed and a NN-based feature extraction was tested. In this experiment, the additional gradient $\frac{\partial \varepsilon_{MSE}}{\partial w}$ was applied. The results (i.e. word accuracies) are shown in Table 1. The results prove that the NN-based feature extraction could be significantly beneficial even when the NN is relatively small. Contribution of MN and VN computation is noticeable as well.

Table 1. The results of experiments with a NN-based feature extraction where the NN was trained as PLP approximation.

No.	Feat. Ext	Signal Processing	Ac. Model	ε	si_dt5a	si_dt5b
1	PLP	Δ, $\Delta\Delta$	GMM	N/A	83.66 %	82.20 %
2	PLP	Δ, $\Delta\Delta$	NN	ε_{XENT}	87.06 %	85.93 %
3	init. NN	Δ, $\Delta\Delta$	fixed NN	ε_{MSE}	87.05 %	85.09 %
4	NN	Δ, $\Delta\Delta$	fixed NN	ε_{XENT}	88.02 %	86.71 %
5	NN	Δ, $\Delta\Delta$	NN	ε_{XENT}	88.63 %	87.56 %
6	PLP	Δ, $\Delta\Delta$, MN, VN	NN	ε_{XENT}	89.49 %	88.72 %
7	NN	Δ, $\Delta\Delta$, MN, VN	NN	$\varepsilon_{MSE} + \varepsilon_{XENT}$	91.64 %	90.87 %

In the next six experiments, shallow NNs, deep NNs and the proposed training algorithm were investigated. For the NN-based acoustic models, the number of neurons in a hidden layer was reduced form 1024 to 512. The reduction also slightly decreases the accuracies for the shallow NNs but the decreasing prevents overtraining of the deep NNs. In all these experiments, in addition to the PLP (or a PLP substitution), delta and delta-delta coefficients, MN, VN and its delta and delta-coefficients were computed. Unfortunately, in comparison with shallow NNs, training deep NNs is highly sensitive to weights initialization. Therefore, in each experiment three randomly initialized NNs were trained and the corresponding results is the result for a NN which was the most accurate on the training data set.

In the eighth experiment, a NN-based acoustic model with a shallow NN was trained. In the ninth experiment, a NN-based acoustic model with a deep NN was trained. In the tenth experiment, a NN-based feature extraction and a NN-based acoustic model were investigated. Both NNs were shallow. The same NN structures were applied in the ninth experiment. In the-eleventh experiment, additional gradient was computed during training. The twelfth and the thirteenth experiment are the same experiments as the tenth and the eleventh experiment where NNs with two layers were replaced by NNs with four layers.

The results are shown in Table 2. The results prove that the described training enhancement could be beneficial in the case of deep NN training. Not surprisingly, using deep NNs leads to more accurate speech recognition. The accuracy for the deep NN in the seventh experiment even reaches the accuracy for the connection in the eighth and the ninth experiment. Even in this case, the NN-based feature extraction is still significantly beneficial.

Table 2. The main results of experiments with shallow and deep NNs.

No.	Feat. Ext	Signal Processing	Ac. Model	ε	si_dt5a	si_dt5b
8	PLP	Δ, $\Delta\Delta$, MN, VN	NN (2 layers)	ε_{XENT}	85.27 %	84.38 %
9	PLP	Δ, $\Delta\Delta$, MN, VN	NN (4 layers)	ε_{XENT}	89.14 %	88.74 %
10	NN (2 layers)	Δ, $\Delta\Delta$, MN, VN	NN (2 layers)	ε_{XENT}	88.44 %	88.23 %
11	NN (2 layers)	Δ, $\Delta\Delta$, MN, VN	NN (2 layers)	$\varepsilon_{MSE} + \varepsilon_{XENT}$	88.41 %	87.64 %
12	NN (4 layers)	Δ, $\Delta\Delta$, MN, VN	NN (4 layers)	ε_{XENT}	89.69 %	88.67 %
13	NN (4 layers)	Δ, $\Delta\Delta$, MN, VN	NN (4 layers)	$\varepsilon_{MSE} + \varepsilon_{XENT}$	90.63 %	89.67 %

6   Conclusion and Future Work

In this paper, the NN-based feature extraction and the NN based acoustic model for the automatic speech recognition system were investigated. Our experiments showed that the NN-based feature extraction can sufficiently approximate methods such as the PLP and it could lead to more accurate results in the speech recognition when a machine learning is simultaneously applied on the NN-based feature extraction and the NN-based acoustic model. Moreover, this paper demonstrates that mean or variance normalization and delta coefficients could be utilized successfully when a NN-based feature extraction is used together with a NN-based acoustic model.

In the future, some experiments described in this paper will be done for context-dependent units. Also some NN-based speaker normalization or some speaker adaptation techniques will be integrated in the described system. Beside this we are going to make some experiments with the NN-based feature extraction in a non-hybrid speech recognition system.

Acknowledgement. This research was supported by the Ministry of Culture Czech Republic, project No.DF12P01OVV022.

References

1. Chang, S., Morgan, N.: Robust CNN-based speech recognition with Gabor filter kernels. In: 15th Annual Conference of the International Speech Communication Association (Interspeech 2014), pp. 905–909, Singapore, September 14–18 (2014)
2. Astudillo, R.F., Abad, A., Trancoso, I.: Accounting for the residual uncertainty of multi-layer perceptron based features. In: IEEE International Conference on Acoustics, Speech and Signal Processing (ICASSP), pp. 6859–6863, May 2014
3. Grézl, F., Karafiát, M.: Semi-supervised bootstrapping approach for neural network feature extractor training. In: ASRU, pp. 470–475. IEEE (2013)
4. Heřmanský, H.: Perceptual linear predictive (PLP) analysis of speech. J. Acoust. Soc. Am. **57**(4), 1738–1752 (1990)
5. Ioffe, S., Szegedy, C.: Batch normalization: accelerating deep network training by reducing internal covariate shift. In: CoRR abs/1502.03167 (2015)
6. Narayanan, A., Wang, D.: Ideal ratio mask estimation using deep neural networks for robust speech recognition. In: IEEE International Conference on Acoustics, Speech and Signal Processing (ICASSP), pp. 7092–7096, May 2013
7. Pražák, A., Psutka, J.V., Psutka, J., Loose, Z.: Towards live subtitling of TV ice-hockey commentary. In: Cabello, E., Virvou, M., Obaidat, M.S., Ji, H., Nicopolitidis, P., Vergados, D.D. (eds.) SIGMAP, pp. 151–155. SciTePress (2013)
8. Psutka, J., Švec, J., Psutka, J.V., Vaněk, J., Pražák, A., Šmídl, L.: Fast phonetic/lexical searching in the archives of the czech holocaust testimonies: advancing towards the malach project visions. In: Sojka, P., Horák, A., Kopeček, I., Pala, K. (eds.) TSD 2010. LNCS, vol. 6231, pp. 385–391. Springer, Heidelberg (2010)
9. Robinson, T., Fransen, J., Pye, D., Foote, J., Renals, S.: Wsjcam0: A british english speech corpus for large vocabulary continuous speech recognition. In: Proceedings of ICASSP 1995, pp. 81–84. IEEE (1995)
10. Sainath, T.N., Kingsbury, B., Mohamed, A.R., Ramabhadran, B.: Learning filter banks within a deep neural network framework. In: ASRU, pp. 297–302. IEEE (2013)
11. Sainath, T.N., Peddinti, V., Kingsbury, B., Fousek, P., Ramabhadran, B., Nahamoo, D.: Deep scattering spectra with deep neural networks for LVCSR tasks. In: 15th Annual Conference of the International Speech Communication Association (Interspeech 2014), pp. 900–904, Singapore, September 14–18 (2014)
12. Seps, L., Málek, J., Cerva, P., Nouza, J.: Investigation of deep neural networks for robust recognition of nonlinearly distorted speech. In: Interspeech, pp. 363–367 (2014)
13. Szegedy, C., Liu, W., Jia, Y., Sermanet, P., Reed, S., Anguelov, D., Erhan, D., Vanhoucke, V., Rabinovich, A.: Going deeper with convolutions. In: CoRR abs/1409.4842 (2014)
14. Tüske, Z., Golik, P., Schlüter, R., Ney, H.: Acoustic modeling with deep neural networks using raw time signal for LVCSR. In: Interspeech, pp. 890–894, Singapore, September 2014

Opinion Recognition on Movie Reviews by Combining Classifiers

Athanasia Koumpouri$^{(\boxtimes)}$, Iosif Mporas, and Vasileios Megalooikonomou

Multidimensional Data Analysis and Knowledge Management Laboratory,
Department of Computer Engineering and Informatics,
University of Patras, 26500 Rion, Greece
{koumpour,vasilis}@ceid.upatras.gr, imporas@upatras.gr

Abstract. In this paper we present a combined opinion recognition scheme based on discriminative algorithms, decision trees and probabilistic algorithms. The proposed scheme takes advantage of the information provided from each of the recognition models in decision level, in order to provide refined and more accurate opinion recognition results. The experimental results showed that the proposed combined scheme achieved an overall recognition performance of 87.90 %, increasing the accuracy of our best-performing opinion recognition model by 3.5 %.

Keywords: Opinion mining · Discriminative algorithms · Decision trees · Probabilistic algorithms

1 Introduction

The rapid growth of the web over the last decade has changed drastically the way people express opinion. Opinions can now be found almost everywhere i.e. in websites, blogs, social networking sites, forums and review sites. As a result, a vast amount of user-generated content has overwhelmed the World Wide Web. Capturing public opinion about social events, political movements, company strategies, marketing campaigns, and product preferences is garnering increasing interest from the scientific community to commercial applications and services [1].

Nowadays, it is common practice to review and share experience about a product or service. Hence, the need for detecting and understanding the opinions expressed in social web became crucial for twofold reason. For individuals, people can easily evaluate other's opinion and experience about it while purchasing a product or service. For market intelligence, knowing public opinion can be exploited in targeted advertising and product development. Thus, opinion mining has gained a considerable deal of attention from the research community in the past few years due to abundant challenging research problems and practical applications both in commerce and academic areas.

In opinion mining the target is to automatically detect and extract the opinion of writers about products, topics, problems, etc. The main challenge in this

© Springer International Publishing Switzerland 2015
A. Ronzhin et al. (Eds.): SPECOM 2015, LNAI 9319, pp. 309–316, 2015.
DOI: 10.1007/978-3-319-23132-7_38

area is the polarity classification, in which an opinion stated in a text document can be labeled as positive or negative and can be in the form of document, sentence or feature. The opinion mining task is based on technology from the area of data mining and of natural language processing (NLP) to retrieve and extract opinions from written input, mainly found on the web. Researchers have suggested several approaches and methodologies for opinion mining and have proposed different methods for performing this task. It should be mentioned that the general idea of sentiment classification from text is that of assigning a "positive" or "negative" (or "neutral") label to a text block (document, sentence, review, etc.).

In the present article we perform feature ranking and successive selection of features aiming to improve the accuracy of opinion classification on movie reviews. The feature selection is performed over a large set of features, i.e. statistical, part-of-speech tagging and language model based features. These text-based movie review descriptors were evaluated by machine learning classification algorithms in order to evaluate the opinion classification performance for different number of features.

The remainder of this paper is organized as follows. In Sect. 2, we present a brief description of the background of opinion mining. In Sect. 3, we describe the proposed methodology for opinion recognition from online movie reviews. Section 4 presents the experimental setup and the experimental results. Finally, in Sect. 5 we conclude this work.

2   Background

The methods proposed for extracting and classifying opinions from text can be roughly divided into two main approaches, namely the machine learning and the lexicon-based. The first approach considers opinion mining as a text classification problem using machine learning algorithms for classification and syntactic and/or linguistic features. The second approach relies on opinion lexicons using the prior polarity of words or phrases.

With respect to the machine learning approach, several methods have been employed that can be broadly divided into two major categories: supervised and unsupervised. Pang and Lee [8] reported an approach to classify movie reviews in two classes, positive and negative. They experimented with three classifiers (naive Bayes, maximum entropy, and support vector machines) and features like unigrams, bigrams, term frequency, term presence and position, and parts-of-speech. In [7] an approach based on the multinomial naive Bayes classifier that uses n-gram and part of speech (POS) tags as features, to classify tweets as positive, negative or neutral was reported. A recursive neural tensor network model, which takes as input phrases of any length and represents them through word vectors and a parse tree and computes vectors for higher nodes in the tree using the same tensor-based composition function was presented in [11].

Regarding unsupervised methods, in [12] classification of reviews as recommended (thumbs up) or as not recommended (thumbs down), was presented, where the algorithm calculated the pointwise mutual information of the candidate word for semantic orientation with two given seed words, i.e., "poor" and "excellent". The algorithm depended on patterns of two consecutive words where one word is an adverb or adjective used for orientation and the other word is used to represent the context. Adjectives and adverbs with different patterns of term categories were used for the semantic orientation, and each review was classified as recommended if the average semantic orientation of its phrases was positive and as not recommended if the average semantic orientation of its phrases was negative. In [10] an unsupervised technique to extract product features and opinions from unstructured reviews was proposed by introducing the OPINE system. OPINE is based on an unsupervised information extraction approach to mine product features from reviews. It uses syntactic patterns for the semantic orientation of words to identify opinion phrases and their polarity.

Except supervised and unsupervised methods, semi-supervised approaches have also been proposed. In [2], authors propose a semi-supervised approach where they first mine the unambiguous reviews using spectral techniques and based on this they classify them via a combination of active learning, transductive learning, and ensemble learning. Goldberg and Zhu [3] proposed a technique operating on a graph of both labeled and unlabelled data. Documents are represented with a graph, where vertices correspond to documents, and edges are drawn between similar documents using a distance measure computed directly from document features. In [14], authors describe a semi-supervised technique for feature grouping. As the same features can be expressed by different synonyms, words or phrases, these words and phrases were grouped. With respect to feature grouping, the process generated an initial list to bootstrap the process using lexical characteristics of terms.

On the other hand the lexicon-based approaches can be distinguished into two main categories: the dictionary-based and the corpus-based. The dictionary-based approaches use a prebuilt dictionary such as the General Inquirer, AFINN and Senti-WordNet, which is currently the most popular dictionary for sentiment analysis, that contains opinion polarities of words. Several research efforts have exploited these resources for the identification of opinionative words as well as for directly using polarity scores. Most of the dictionary methods aggregate the polarity values for a sentence or document, and compute the resulting sentiment using simple rule-based algorithms [15]. In [5,6] two dictionary-based approaches are presented, based on bootstrapping using a small set of seed opinion words (verbs and adjectives) with known orientations. The set is expanded by extracting from WordNet the synonyms and antonyms of the words of the seed list and by assigning them to appropriate lists (synonyms placed in the same list and antonyms in the opposite). Corpus based methods depend on syntactic or statistical techniques like co-occurrence of word with another word whose polarity is known. In [4] the orientation of adjectives was predicted by assuming that pairs of conjoined adjectives have same orientation (if conjoined by "and") and opposite orientation (if conjoined by "but").

3   Proposed Method for Automatic Recognition of Opinion

For the recognition of opinion expressed on movie reviews we relied on the combination of discriminative algorithms, decision trees and probabilistic algorithms. Specifically, we experimented with 3 discriminative algorithms, namely MLP, SVM and k-Nearest Neighbors algorithm (IBk), 3 decision trees, namely C4.5 algorithm (J48), random tree (RandTree), random forest (RandomForest) and 1 probabilistic algorithm, Bayesian network (BayesNet).

The opinion recognition is performed in two stages. In the first stage the text is pre-processed, parameterized and processed independently from each classifier. In the second stage the output recognition results from each classification model are combined by a fusion method in order to provide the final opinion recognition results. The block diagram of the proposed scheme is illustrated in Fig. 1.

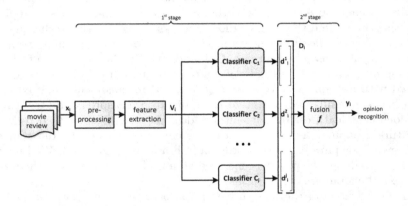

Fig. 1. Block diagram of the combined opinion recognition scheme.

As shown in Fig. 1 a movie review x_i with $1 \leq i \leq I$ is introduced to the opinion recognition scheme. The movie review is pre-processed by converting all words to lowercase and with each line in the text file corresponding to a single sentence. Additionally, each review is cleansed from rating information upon which the rating decision was based [9]. Sequentially, each pre-processed movie review x_i is driven to the feature extraction block where a feature vector V_i is computed by a text parameterization algorithm p, i.e. $V_i = p(x_i)$, with $1 \leq i \leq I$.

Specifically, for the decomposition of the movie reviews to feature vectors we initially relied on statistical values extracted from the text. We measured the number of characters and words, as well as the mean, minimum, maximum and standard deviation value for the length of all words resulting to 6-dimensional vectors. Moreover, we expanded the aforementioned feature vectors with 9 additional features derived after processing each movie review with part-of-speech tagger. Finally, we used n-gram language models, with $1 \leq n \leq 3$ one for each opinion class, in order to measure log-likelihood and entropy (as well as their normalized values), resulting in 24 additional features. Thus, through the entire process of decomposition we ended up with 39-dimensional feature vectors.

The output of the feature extraction block is forwarded in parallel to each of the classifiers, as illustrated in Fig. 1. Each of the classification models C_j, with $1 \leq j \leq J$ estimates whether the i-th incoming feature vector corresponds to positive or negative opinion, i.e. providing binary classification results d_i^j with the corresponding recognition score for each of the two classes, i.e. $d_i^j = C_j(V_i)$, with $1 \leq i \leq I$ and $1 \leq j \leq J$.

The second stage of the opinion recognition scheme exploits the results of the aforementioned classifiers, in order to combine them and provide a final decision for each feature vector V_i. Specifically, the recognition results d_i^j estimated at the first stage by each of the classification models, are concatenated in a single vector D_i with $1 \leq i \leq I$ as shown in Fig. 1. A fusion model f utilizes the results derived from the classification models, which are included in the D_i vector, in order to provide the final decision y_i for the i-th movie review, i.e. $y_i = f(D_i)$. In the present work, the fusion model f was implemented with SVM algorithm, MLP, RandomForest, J48 and BayesNet.

4   Experimental Setup and Evaluation

The opinion recognition scheme illustrated in Fig. 1 combines the recognition results produced by the classification models. As mentioned in Sect. 3, we experimented with various dissimilar machine learning algorithms, namely 3 discriminative algorithms, 3 decision trees, and 1 probabilistic algorithm, aiming to investigate whether different opinion recognition models have different recognition ability on different features. For the implementation of all the models we relied on the WEKA [13] machine learning software toolkit. Specifically, for the SVM algorithm we used the sequential minimal optimization (SMO) algorithm and RBF kernel. After grid search the C and γ parameters were empirically set to 4.0 and 0.06, respectively. The SMO algorithm with RBF kernel was also used for the implementation of the fusion model. Moreover, we utilized a multilayer perceptron neural network (MLP), using the back-propagation algorithm for training and three layers, also used for the implementation of the fusion model, and the k-nearest neighbour algorithm (IBk). For the decision trees, we used a pruned C4.5 decision tree (J48) and the random forest (RandForest) constructing a multitude of decision trees, both used for the implementation of the fusion model. Additionally, we used the random tree (RandTree), which constructs a tree that considers K randomly chosen attributes at each node. Finally, we used the BayesNet, a probabilistic graphical model that represents a set of random variables and their conditional dependencies via a directed acyclic graph, which is also used for the fusion model.

The proposed opinion detection methodology described in the previous section was evaluated using the Polarity Dataset v2.0 [9]. The dataset consists of 2,000 movie reviews extracted from the IMDB movie archive and the review posts are annotated as positive or negative. The distribution of the two opinion classes is balanced to 1000 positive and 1000 negative review posts. The average size of each review post is 3145 words and 749 characters, distributed to, in average, 30 sentences per post.

Table 1. Accuracy results for the opinion recognition models (percentage)

Algorithm	Accuracy
MLP	80.90 %
SVMpoly	**84.40 %**
SVMrbf	84.35 %
IBk	82.50 %
J48	81.60 %
RandForest	83.50 %
RandTree	81.35 %
BayesNet	82.60 %

We first investigated the performance of each of the 8 opinion recognition models separately. The performance, in terms of accuracy, of the opinion recognition models implemented with 8 different classifiers is shown in Table 1. The best performing classification algorithm is indicated in bold. Support vector machines using polynomial kernel outperformed all other classifiers achieving the highest accuracy, 84.40 % followed by the SVM with radial basis kernel with 84.35 % accuracy. Due to the fact that SVM does not depend on the dimensionality of the feature space, it achieved the two highest accuracies, while algorithms that are more sensitive to high dimensional data, i.e. IBk, RandTree showed lower accuracy, 82.50 % and 81.35 % respectively, in correctly classified movie reviews. The other two evaluated decision trees offered slightly lower recognition performance than the SVMs, which varies from 81.60 % to 83.50 % for J48 and RandomForest accordingly. In the case of BayesNet, opinion polarities were recognized with accuracy equal to 82.60 %, i.e. approximately 2 % lower than the SVM poly. Finally, the worst performing opinion recognition model was the one using MLP as classification algorithm, achieving the lowest accuracy of 80.90 %.

In a second step, we combined the results of the 8 opinion recognition models, using SVM, MLP, J48, RandomForest and BayesNet implementations for the fusion function. The opinion recognition performance is illustrated in Table 2.

As can be seen in Table 2, the combination of the 8 classifiers results significantly improved the opinion recognition accuracy. In particular, the accuracy achieved from the combined opinion recognition scheme varies from 84.90 % to 87.90 %, using BayesNet and RandomForest as fusion model respectively. Compared to the best-performing SVM poly model, as seen in Table 1, our proposed scheme improved the accuracy of correctly classified instances for all 5 fusion models. RandomForest outperformed the best-performing SVM poly model by 3.5 % in terms of accuracy. We assume that the boosted performance of the pro-

Table 2. Accuracy results for the combined opinion recognition scheme (percentage)

Algorithm	Accuracy
MLP	85.15
SVMrbf	86.70
J48	87.85
RandForest	**87.90 %**
BayesNet	84.90 %
Pang & Lee (2004)	87.15 %

posed combined scheme is owed to the exploitation of the information included in the 8 dissimilar classifiers recognition results by the fusion model.

Finally, we compared the results of our proposed opinion detection methodology to Pang and Lee [9] approach both evaluated using the Polarity Dataset v2.0. The experimental results are promising since we achieved to improve Pang and Lee's accuracy by 0.70 % and 0.75 % using J48 and RandomForest as fusion model respectively, as shown in Table 2.

5   Conclusions

In this study we evaluated a scheme for automatic recognition of opinion from online movie reviews. The proposed scheme combines the recognition results produced by different classification algorithms, in order to provide more accurate results. The experimental results showed that the fusion of the 8 opinion recognition models outcome achieved accuracy of 87.90 % improving the best-performing opinion recognition model by 3.5 % in terms of accuracy. The experimental results are encouraging regarding the fact that we achieved to boost Pang and Lee [9] best accuracy by 0.75 % evaluating our scheme using the same dataset.

To our knowledge, this is the first attempt to combine different classifiers and fusion at decision level aiming to accurate opinion recognition. We presume that different opinion recognition models have different recognition ability on different features. Thus, our proposed combined scheme is valuable in exploiting the underlying recognition ability of different models.

References

1. Cambria, E., Schuller, B., Xia, Y., Havasi, C.: New avenues in opinion mining and sentiment analysis. IEEE Intell. Syst. **2**, 15–21 (2013)
2. Dasgupta, S., Ng, V.: Mine the easy, classify the hard: a semi-supervised approach to automatic sentiment classification. In: Proceedings of the Joint Conference of the 47th Annual Meeting of the ACL and the 4th International Joint Conference on Natural Language Processing of the AFNLP, ACL 2009, vol. 2, pp. 701–709. Association for Computational Linguistics, Stroudsburg (2009)

3. Goldberg, A.B., Zhu, X.: Seeing stars when there aren't many stars: graph-based semi-supervised learning for sentiment categorization. In: Proceedings of the First Workshop on Graph Based Methods for Natural Language Processing, TextGraphs-1, pp. 45–52. Association for Computational Linguistics, Stroudsburg (2006)
4. Hatzivassiloglou, V., McKeown, K.R.: Predicting the semantic orientation of adjectives. In: Proceedings of the Eighth Conference on European Chapter of the Association for Computational Linguistics (EACL 1997), pp. 174–181. Association for Computational Linguistics, Stroudsburg (1997)
5. Hu, M., Liu, B.: Mining and summarizing customer reviews. In: Proceedings of the Tenth ACM SIGKDD International Conference on Knowledge Discovery and Data Mining, KDD 2004, pp. 168–177. ACM, New York (2004)
6. Kim, S.M., Hovy, E.: Determining the sentiment of opinions. In: Proceedings of the 20th International Conference on Computational Linguistics, COLING 2004. Association for Computational Linguistics, Stroudsburg (2004)
7. Pak, A., Paroubek, P.: Twitter as a corpus for sentiment analysis and opinion mining. In: Proceedings of the Seventh Conference on International Language Resources and Evaluation, pp. 1320–1326 (2010)
8. Pang, B., Lee, L., Vaithyanathan, S.: Thumbs up?: Sentiment classification using machine learning techniques. In: Proceedings of the ACL-02 Conference on Empirical Methods in Natural Language Processing, EMNLP 2002, vol. 10, pp. 79–86. Association for Computational Linguistics, Stroudsburg (2002)
9. Pang, B., Lee, L.: A sentimental education: sentiment analysis using subjectivity summarization based on minimum cuts. In: Proceedings of the 42nd Annual Meeting on Association for Computational Linguistics (ACL 2004), Article 271. Association for Computational Linguistics, Stroudsburg (2004)
10. Popescu, A.M., Etzioni, O.: Extracting product features and opinions from reviews. In: Proceedings of the Conference on Human Language Technology and Empirical Methods in Natural Language Processing, HLT 2005, pp. 339–346. Association for Computational Linguistics, Stroudsburg (2005)
11. Socher, R., Perelygin, A., Wu, J., Chuang, J., Manning, D.C., Ng, A., Potts, C.: Recursive deep models for semantic compositionality over a sentiment treebank. In: Proceedings of the 2013 Conference on Empirical Methods in Natural Language Processing, pp. 1631–1642. Association for Computational Linguistics (2013)
12. Turney, P.D.: Thumbs up or thumbs down?: Semantic orientation applied to unsupervised classification of reviews. In: Proceedings of the 40th Annual Meeting on Association for Computational Linguistics, ACL 2002, pp. 417–424. Association for Computational Linguistics, Stroudsburg (2002)
13. Witten, I.H., Frank, E., Hall, M.A.: Data Mining: Practical Machine Learning Tools and Techniques, 3rd edn. Morgan Kaufmann Publishers Inc., San Francisco (2011)
14. Zhai, Z., Liu, B., Xu, H., Jia, P.: Grouping product features using semi-supervised learning with soft-constraints. In: Proceedings of International Conference on Computational Linguistics (COLING- 2010) (2010)
15. Zhu, J., Zhu, M., Wang, H., Tsou, B. K.: Aspect-based sentence segmentation for sentiment summarization. In: Proceedings of the International CIKM Workshop on Topic-Sentiment Analysis for Mass Opinion Measurement, TSA 2009, pp 65–72. ACM, New York (2009)

Optimization of Pitch Tracking and Quantization

Oleg Basov[1], Andrey Ronzhin[2,3(✉)], and Victor Budkov[2]

[1] Academy of FAP of Russia, 35, Priborostroitelnaya, Orel 302034, Russia
oobasov@mail.ru
[2] SPIIRAS, 39, 14th Line, St. Petersburg 199178, Russia
{budkov,ronzhin}@iias.spb.su
[3] SUAI, 67, Bolshaya Morskaia, St. Petersburg 199000, Russia

Abstract. The article presents the results of the research focused on procedures for allocating and quantizing values of the pitch. Corresponding optimization tasks are set and accomplished. The results of experimental study of the developed algorithm for determining the pitch lag and its optimal quantizer are presented. The gain in noise immunity and signal to noise ratio compared to the known solutions is shown.

Keywords: Speech coding algorithms · Speech recognition · Pitch · Noise immunity · Dynamic programming · Quantization

1   Introduction

Determination and quantization of pitch period values are general procedures for most speech coding and recognition algorithms. Despite the large number of proposed algorithms [8], the task of practical constructing noise-resistant pitch analyzers, reliably functioning in the presence of acoustic noise or while limiting frequency range of speech, is far from the final solution.

At the same time, variation range, number of levels and method of pitch quantization in the existing speech coding algorithms are different [1,4,13,19]. Uniform quantization, occurring in most cases, assumes full use of quantization range, and if the signal swing (pitch melody) is very small, it is equivalent to using only a few quantization levels. If the variance of the quantized signal is only half of that for which the quantizer is designed, this leads to a deterioration by 6 dB of the signal to noise ratio (SNR) of quantization [15]. Quantization of logarithm of pitch period values [2,4,7] allows us to obtain a constant SNR over a wide range of pitch melody dispersions, but this is achieved at the cost of deteriorating the SNR in comparison with that one, which can be achieved if the quantization range is adjusted with the variance of the quantized signal. If the variance of the signal is known, it is possible to choose the quantization levels, so as to minimize noise power and thus maximize the SNR of quantization.

The aim of this work was to develop a noise-resistant algorithm for determining the pitch period and optimal quantizer for its values.

This paper is organized as follows. Section 2 describes the algorithm for determining the pitch. Section 2.1 presents the results of comparison of noise immunity

© Springer International Publishing Switzerland 2015
A. Ronzhin et al. (Eds.): SPECOM 2015, LNAI 9319, pp. 317–324, 2015.
DOI: 10.1007/978-3-319-23132-7_39

of different algorithms for determining the pitch. Section 2.2 describes the optimal pitch quantizer and the results of its calculation for the Russian language.

2   A Pitch Determination Algorithm

To determine the pitch period according to the developed algorithm [4,5] the following steps are implemented:

Step 1. Filtration of the original speech signal by a lowpass filter with a bandwidth of 0-500 Hz.
Step 2. The calculation in each interval of identification of the normalized auto-correlation function:

$$r(l) = \frac{c[0,l,l]}{\sqrt{c[0,0,l]c[l,l,l]}},$$ (1)

where

$$\tilde{n}[f,g,h] = \sum_{i=d1}^{d2} s[i+f]s[i+g], d1 = -[h/2] - T/2; d2 = -[h/2] + T/2,$$

for all pitch lag values $l = \overline{16,160}$, corresponding to frequencies from 50 to 500 Hz. If the speech frame were strictly periodic, acoustic noise - stationary, and the length of the analysis window T - - large enough, the problem of estimating the pitch period l_{max} would be reduced to finding the argument of the global maximum of the function (1):

$$l_{max} = \arg\max_l r(l).$$ (2)

For real speech signal frames (in view of its nonstrict periodicity), this rule causes a large number of errors.

Step 3. Determination of the arguments of positive local maximums of the function (1), forming a plurality $\{l_{cand}\}$ of possible values of pitch estimation. True pitch estimation will lie among the candidates of the above-mentioned plurality.

In the analysis of the function (1) different rules for sorting the candidates are usually used, e.g. the following [20]:

$$\forall l_{cand} \text{ if } r(l_{cand}) > c \cdot r(l_{cand}) \text{ then } l_{max} = l_{cand},$$ (3)

where c - a threshold, changing the balance of errors in the determination of the pitch and minimizing their total number. However, the number of gross errors of pitch analyzer for noisy signals is still significant. Especially many errors appear at the beginning and end of voiced regions, where the degree of vocalization (and, hence, the magnitude of the maximums of the function (1)) is small. Therefore, to estimate the most probable path of the pitch, it makes sense to conduct a cumulative analysis of groups of adjacent intervals of adaptation, allowing for the probability of possible candidates for pitch estimation for each segment lasting T [8]. At the same time, taking into account the estimations of various researchers [16], we should take $T = 40$ samples, (5 ms), and formulate the task of finding the pitch path as the problem of dynamic programming (DP) to find a way, maximizing the general probability of pitch estimation appearance for the group of segments of the speech signal.

Step 4. Solution of the DP problem. In the developed decision rule the problem of DP is formulated as follows: for interval of identification with number k we search for arguments of all positive local maximums of function (1) forming the plurality $\{l_{cand}^{(k)}\}$, consisting of $I^{(k)}$ candidates for pitch period estimation for the given interval (of duration T). Pluralities of candidates for adjacent intervals with the numbers $k.k+1, \ldots, k+K-1$ form grid columns, through nodes of which pitch path most likely passes. The cost of the node for the k-th interval and the candidate $l_{cand\,i}^{(k)} \in \{l_{cand}^{(k)}\}$ is selected proportionally to local maximum value:

$$d_U(l_{cand\,i}^{(k)}) = r(l_{cand\,i}^{(k)}). \tag{4}$$

The cost of the transition route of pitch path between the grid nodes from candidate $l_{cand\,i}^{(k)}$ for the i-th interval to the candidate $l_{cand\,t}^{(k+1)}$ for the t-th interval considers the distance between the candidates for the adjacent intervals and reflects the likelihood of changing pitch path:

$$d_T(l_{cand\,i}^{(k)}, l_{cand\,t}^{(k+1)}) \begin{cases} 0, & \text{if } |l_{cand\,i}^{(k)} - l_{cand\,t}^{(k+1)}| \le \mu \cdot l_{cand\,i}^{(k)}, \\ -\inf, & \text{if } |l_{cand\,i}^{(k)} - l_{cand\,t}^{(k+1)}| > \mu \cdot l_{cand\,i}^{(k)}, \end{cases} \tag{5}$$

while jumps of pitch path beyond the boundaries of permissible tolerance μ are not considered. Evaluation of the most probable pitch path during K intervals is carried out by choosing optimal path between grid nodes $l_{cand}^{(k)}, l_{cand}^{(k+1)}, \ldots, l_{cand}^{(k+K-1)}$, maximizing the functional of the total cost of the form:

$$D_P(l_{cand}^{(k)}, l_{cand}^{(k+1)}, \ldots, l_{cand}^{(k+K-1)}) = \sum_{i=0}^{K-2} (d_U(l_{cand\,i}^{(k)}) + d_T(l_{cand\,i}^{(k)}, l_{cand\,t}^{(k+1)})) + d_U(l_{cand\,i}^{(k+K-1)}), \tag{6}$$

where k - index of the interval of identification, K - number of adjacent intervals involved in smoothing pitch path.

Step 5. Determination of integer value of pitch period. Taking into account adopted value T, speech frame is divided into 4 subframes. At that point, pitch identification is performed through six such subframes in two stages. At first, we search for the most probable pitch path for the last subframe of the past and the first two subframes of the current speech frame (K). By found pitch estimation values (grid nodes), with regard to the rule (3), we can determine pitch period estimation $l_{max(1)}$ for the first half of the analyzed speech frame. Next, the functional (6) is determined for the third and fourth subframes of the current and the first subframe of the next speech frame, and the value $l_{max(2)}$ for the second half of the analyzed message. As an integer value l_{max} of pitch period for the entire speech signal frame one of the two evaluations ($l_{max(1)}$ and $l_{max(2)}$) is selected, belonging to the path with the largest value D_P (6).

Step 6. Calculation of the fractional value of the pitch period:

$$\eta = \frac{c[0, l_{max} + 1, l_{max}]c[l_{max}, l_{max}, l_{max}] - c[0, l_{max}, l_{max}]c[l_{max}, l_{max} + 1, l_{max}]}{c_1 + c_2}, \quad (7)$$

$$c_1 = c[0, l_{max} + 1, l_{max}](c[l_{max}, l_{max}, l_{max}] - c[l_{max}, l_{max} + 1, l_{max}]),$$

$$c_2 = c[0, l_{max}, l_{max}](c[l_{max} + 1, l_{max} + 1, l_{max}] - c[l_{max}, l_{max} + 1, l_{max}]).$$

Step 7. The final value, which represents a result of the pitch period determination, is defined as

$$X = l_{max} + \eta. \quad (8)$$

Distinctive features of the developed pitch determination algorithm in comparison with the existing solutions [3, 7] are:

- restriction of the search for pitch path by finite number of points in order to implement the analyzer in real time scale;
- use of combined method for independent pitch path estimation at intervals of the past and future speech signal frames with subsequent selection of the best result, which can effectively reduce errors at the beginning and end of voiced sounds;
- determination of fractional pitch period for its optimal integer value.

2.1 Comparison of Noise Immunity of Different Pitch Determination Algorithms

The results of evaluation of noise immunity of the developed pitch determination algorithm and its comparison with noise-immunity of the existing pitch extractors, according to the technique [3], are presented in Table 1.

Table 1. Comparison of different pitch determination algorithms

Characteristic of speech signal	GPE, %			
	G.729	G.723.1	FS 1017	Developed algorithm
User-defined text (duration 32 min, 3 speakers), the sampling frequency of 8 kHz, without acoustic noise	10.2	10.8	4.5	4.3
User-defined text (the same), the sampling frequency of 8 kHz, in mixture with white noise (SNR equal to 0 dB)	29.5	31.4	47.3	6.9

A quantitative measure of noise immunity of pitch analyzers is based on the calculation of the percentage of gross errors in the estimation of pitch lag of the total number of issued evaluations for the given test signals:

$$GPE = \frac{100}{F} \sum_{f}^{F} = 1 \begin{Bmatrix} 1, & \text{if } |NPE_f| \geq \varepsilon \\ 0, & \text{if } |NPE_f| < \varepsilon \end{Bmatrix} \%; \quad NPE_f = NP_f - 1; \quad NP_f = \frac{X^{(f)}}{X_{ctr}^{(f)}},$$
$$(9)$$

where F – number of pitch measurements; NPE_f – normalized pitch estimation error; ε – threshold for separating gross errors and small deviations in pitch estimation; NP_f - normalized pitch lag estimation; $X^{(f)}$ – pitch lag estimation at the output of the analyzer; $X_{ctr}^{(f)}$ – control pitch lag value for the f-th measurement point, known in advance.

As can be seen from Table 1, the developed algorithm surpasses known analogs in the quality of pitch determination, especially in the conditions of the effect of the acoustic noise. The obtained pitch period value is subjected to quantization.

2.2   Optimal Quantizer for Pitch

The first iterative method for calculating the characteristics of the quantizer, which are optimal according to the minimum mean square error criterion, was proposed by Max [12]. It provides for the solution of nonlinear equations:

$$\begin{cases} X(i) = (\tilde{X}(i) + \tilde{X}(i-1))/2 \text{ for } i = \overline{2, o_2}; \\ \int\limits_{X(i)}^{X(i+1)} (X - \tilde{X}(i))p(X)dX = 0 \text{ for } i = \overline{1, o_2}; \end{cases} \quad (10)$$

where $\tilde{X}(i)$, $i = \overline{1, o_2}$ - output levels of a quantizer, corresponding to the intervals of the input signal values from $X(i)$ to $X(i+1)$; $p(X)$ - the probability density function of pitch values. The results of statistical studies of a large amount of speech material allowed us at the critical level of significance $\alpha = 0,01$ to approximate function $p(X)$ by lognormal distribution with parameters $\mu = 4,0887$, $\sigma = 0,216752$, and the average value $M(X) \approx 61$. The obtained data harmonizes

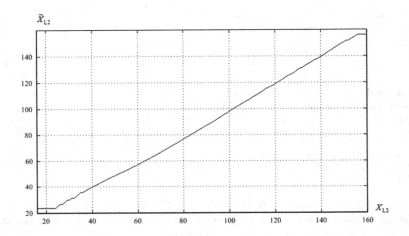

Fig. 1. Characteristic of the optimal 128-level quantizer for pitch period

well with the previously known approximations of the frequency distribution of pitch of the Russian language [9–11].

The calculation data of parameters of the optimal scalar quantizer for pitch lag for the lognormal distribution $p(X)$ is presented in Table 2 and Fig. 1. For a small number of quantization levels $o_2 < 60$ standard Maxs algorithm was used [15]. At the number of quantization levels $o_2 > 60$ a method based on the use of asymptotically optimal compression characteristic of the form was applied:

Table 2. Parameters of the optimal quantizers for pitch period

i	$o_2 = 2$		$o_2 = 4$		$o_2 = 8$		$o_2 = 16$	
	X	$\tilde{X}$	X	$\tilde{X}$	X	$\tilde{X}$	X	$\tilde{X}$
1	63,678	52,709	63,678	45,794	44,311	40,261	38,453	35,564
2			74,647	64,351	74,647	51,720	48,360	43,527	41,342
3					79,463	70,658	79,463	55,080	47,618	45,712
4					88,268	65,039	88,268	51,297	49,525
5							72,483	68,495	54,779	53,069
6							81,571	76,471	58,191	56,490
7							94,645	86,672	94,645	59,892
8								102,618	65,185	63,373
9									68,930	66,997
10									72,976	70,864
11									77,462	75,087
12									82,584	79,837
13									88,745	85,331
14									96,783	92,158
15									108,981	101,41
16										116,56

$$g(\tilde{X} = \left[\int_{-\infty}^{\infty} [p(X)]^{\frac{1}{3}} dX \right]^{-1} \int_{-\infty}^{\tilde{X}} [p(X)]^{\frac{1}{3}} dX). \tag{11}$$

At that point, approximations of the initial values of quantization levels were determined in accordance with the expression:

$$\tilde{X}(i) = g^{-1}\left(\frac{2i - 1}{2o_2}\right), \tag{12}$$

where $g^{-1}(\bullet)$ - characteristic of the expander, inverse 11.

3 Conclusion

The results presented demonstrate the possibility of optimizing the procedures for determining and quantizing values of the pitch period (lag) of the speech signal. Application of the developed tools will reduce errors in pitch determination in the Russian speech recognition systems, as well as improve the quality of low-rate encoding and transmitting a speech signal. The developed analyzer and the pitch quantizer in comparison with similar standard algorithms require increased efficiency of estimators, additional capacity of memory elements and would implemented in various telecommunication and cyber-physical systems [6,14,17,18].

Acknowledgments. This work is partially supported by the Russian Foundation for Basic Research (grants № 15-07-06744-a,13-08-0741-a).

References

1. Ayuso, A.J.R., Soler, J.M.L. (eds.): Speech Recognition and Coding: New Advances and Trends. Nato ASI Subseries F: vol. 147. Springer, Heidelberg (1995)
2. Azarov, E., Vashkevich, M.I., Likhachov, D.S., Petrovsky, A.A.: Pitch modification of speech signal using harmonic model with time-varying parameters. Tr. SPIIRAN **32**, 5–26 (2014)
3. Babkin, V.: Basic channels of interpersonal communication and their projection on the infocommunications systems. In: 7th International Conference of Moscow Institute of Control Sciences RAS, pp. 175–178. Moscow Institute of Control Sciences RAS (2005)
4. Basov, O.O., Nosov, M.V., Shalaginov, V.A.: Pitch-jitter analysis of the speech signal. Tr. SPIIRAN **32**, 27–44 (2014)
5. Basov, O.O., Saitov, I.A.: Basic channels of interpersonal communication and their projection on the infocommunications systems. Tr. SPIIRAN **30**, 122–140 (2013)
6. Basov, O.: Principles of construction of polymodal info-communication systems based on multimodal architectures of subscriber's terminals. Tr. SPIIRAN **2**(39), 109–122 (2015)
7. Chu, W.C.: Speech Coding Algorithms: Foundation and Evolution of Standardized Coders. Wiley, Hoboken (2004)

8. Huang, X., Acero, A., Hon, H.W.: Spoken Language Processing: A Guide to Theory, Algorithm, and System Development. Prentice Hall PTR, Upper Saddle River (2001). Foreword By-Reddy, R

9. Kocharov, D., Skrelin, P., Volskaya, N.: F0 declination patterns in russian. In: Ronzhin, A., Potapova, R., Delic, V. (eds.) SPECOM 2014. LNCS, vol. 8773, pp. 217–226. Springer, Heidelberg (2014)

10. Kondaurova, M.V., Francis, A.L.: The relationship between native allophonic experience with vowel duration and perception of the english tense/lax vowel contrast by spanish and russian listeners. J. Acoust. Soc. Am. **124**(6), 3959–3971 (2008)

11. Makarova, V.: Perceptual correlates of sentence-type intonation in russian and japanese. J. Phonetics **29**(2), 137–154 (2001)

12. Max, J.: Quantizing for minimum distortion. IRE Trans. Inf. Theory **6**(1), 7–12 (1960)

13. McCree, A., Stachurski, J., Unno, T., Ertan, E., Paksoy, E., Viswanathan, V., Heikkinen, A., Rämö, A., Himanen, S., Blöcher, P., et al.: A 4 kb/s hybrid melp/celp speech coding candidate for ITU standardization. In: IEEE International Conference on Acoustics, Speech, and Signal Processing (ICASSP), vol. 1, pp. 629–632. IEEE (2002)

14. Meshcheryakov, R., Bondarenko, V.: Dialogue as a basis for construction of speech systems. Cybern. Syst. Anal. **44**(2), 175–184 (2008)

15. Prokhorov, Y.: Statistical models and recurrent prediction of speech signals. Radio and Communications (1984)

16. Ramishvili, G.: Automatic speaker recognition by voice. Radio and Communications (1981)

17. Ronzhin, A.L., Budkov, V.Y., Karpov, A.A.: Multichannel system of audio-visual support of remote mobile participant at e-meeting. In: Balandin, S., Dunaytsev, R., Koucheryavy, Y. (eds.) ruSMART 2010. LNCS, vol. 6294, pp. 62–71. Springer, Heidelberg (2010)

18. Ronzhin, A., Budkov, V., Kipyatkova, I.: Parad-r: speech analysis software for meeting support. In: 9th International Conference on Information, Communications and Signal Processing (ICICS), pp. 1–4. IEEE (2013)

19. Ronzhin, A., Budkov, V.: Speaker turn detection based on multimodal situation analysis. In: Železný, M., Habernal, I., Ronzhin, A. (eds.) SPECOM 2013. LNCS, vol. 8113, pp. 302–309. Springer, Heidelberg (2013)

20. Vary, P., Martin, R.: Digital Speech Transmission: Enhancement, Coding and Error Concealment. Wiley, Chichester (2006)

PLDA Speaker Verification with Limited Speech Data

Andrej Ridzik$^{(\boxtimes)}$ and Milan Rusko

Institute of Informatics, Slovak Academy of Sciences, Dúbravská Cesta 9,
845 07 Bratislava, Slovakia
{andrej.ridzik,milan.rusko}@savba.sk

Abstract. In some speaker verification applications the amount of data available for enrolment and verification can be limited. One of the aims of this paper is to study the impact of the volume of enrolment and verification data on the performance of the system. The second aim is focused on the improvement of the speaker verification using PLDA. The PLDA is generally used to model the speaker and channel variability in the i-vector space using data from several recording sessions. In our experiment, only data from single-session per speaker was available. Therefore, we divided the development recordings into shorter segments and these segments were treated as if they were recorded in different sessions. This approach does not model the inter-session speaker variability, nor the channel variability. However, we assumed that statistical modelling of the intra-session speaker variability could bring an improvement to the results of the verification. Different granularity of segmentation was studied at various amount of enrolment and verification data.

Keywords: i-vector · Probabilistic linear discriminant analysis · Speaker verification

1 Introduction

The traditional speaker verification systems require a large volume of speech data, especially when the inter-session variability is high. This large amount of data is needed during the enrolment, verification, and development. However, in many applications this requirement is not tractable and the limited amount of speech data is becoming the key issue. Recently, many approaches have focused on the problem of limited amount of enrolment and verification data, but not many studies have been done to investigate the impact of limiting also the development data on the verification performance.

The main aim of recent studies has been focused on the usage of a variety of speaker verification methods to deal with the problem of reduced amount of enrolment and verification data and the combination of i-vector representation [2] and probabilistic linear discriminant analysis (PLDA) has become the state-of-the-art approach [5]. These studies have shown that the performance

© Springer International Publishing Switzerland 2015
A. Ronzhin et al. (Eds.): SPECOM 2015, LNAI 9319, pp. 325–332, 2015.
DOI: 10.1007/978-3-319-23132-7_40

of verification degrades considerably when utterances shorter than ten seconds are used for evaluation. One of the aims of this paper is to study the impact of limiting the enrolment and verification data to even shorter durations on the performance of the system.

In addition to the experiments limiting the amount of verification data, also some recent studies have been done to investigate the effect of limiting also the development data. It has clearly been established that a state-of-the-art speaker verification system requires a significant volume of development data covering multiple sessions across a large number of speakers [8]. However, the amount of sessions per speaker can be in many situations limited. Kanagasundaram et al. have studied the impact of reducing the number of sessions per speaker in the development data on the performance of the verification system [4]. In many languages, including the Slovak language, no speech databases with multiple recording sessions per speaker are available. Thus, the standard PLDA method cannot be used. In this paper, a method of splitting the development data into shorter segments in order to train the PLDA model is studied.

The rest of this paper is organized as follows: Sect. 2 gives a brief overview of a typical state-of-the-art PLDA speaker verification system; the experimental settings and corresponding results are given in Sects. 3 and 4; and Sect. 5 summarizes the results of this paper.

2   Speaker Verification Using PLDA

2.1   I-vector Extraction

The i-vector representation [2] is a fixed-length representation of speech utterances, which consists of several acoustic feature vectors. This is done by representing a Gaussian mixture model (GMM) mean super-vector by a single total-variability subspace. This approach was motivated by the fact that the channel space of the earlier Joint factor analysis (JFA) technique contained some speaker-discriminant information [1]. A speaker and channel specific super-vector **s** is assumed to be in the form

$$\mathbf{s} = \mathbf{m} + \mathbf{T}\mathbf{w}, \tag{1}$$

where **m** is a mean super-vector of a universal background model (UBM), which was trained beforehand over a large development set, **T** is a low-rank total-variability matrix whose columns span the major variability in the super-vector subspace of dimension R, and the total-variability factors **w** represent latent variables drawn from a standard normal distribution, i.e. $\mathbf{w} \sim N(\mathbf{0}, \mathbf{1})$. These factors are called *i-vectors* and their extraction can be done by maximum a posteriori estimation of **w** in the subspace defined by the i-vector extractor **T**. An efficient algorithm for the optimisation of the total-variability space **T** and also the subsequent i-vector extraction is described by Kenny et al. [7].

2.2   PLDA Modeling

The PLDA model is a generative model adapted from face recognition and used by Kenny et al. [6] to model the speaker and channel variability in the i-vector space. Two main approaches were introduced, while Heavy-tailed PLDA (HTPLDA) seemed to outperform the Gaussian PLDA (GPLDA) in the performance, but at the cost of higher time complexity [5]. However, Garcia-Romero et al. have shown that simple whitening followed by length-normalisation of the i-vectors can bring the performance of the GPLDA approach up to HTPLDA while still preserving its simplicity [3]. In this simplified variant of PLDA is the speaker and session dependent length-normalised i-vector represented as

$$\mathbf{w}_{s,i} = \bar{\mathbf{w}} + \mathbf{U}\mathbf{x}_s + \epsilon_{s,i}, \tag{2}$$

where for a given speaker s, having n_s sessions $i = 1, \ldots, n_s$, is $\bar{\mathbf{w}}$ the mean length-normalised i-vector, $\mathbf{x}_s$ are the speaker factors having a standard normal distribution, $\epsilon_{s,i}$ is a residual term representing the within-speaker variability which has a normal distribution, and $\mathbf{U}$ is the eigenvoice matrix trained during the PLDA modelling. Thus, the speaker specific part is represented as $\bar{\mathbf{w}} + \mathbf{U}\mathbf{x}_s$ and represents the inter-speaker variability.

2.3   PLDA Scoring

Scoring of the speaker verification system using the PLDA model consists of calculating the batch-likelihood ratio between test and target i-vectors [6]. Given two length-normalised i-vectors $\mathbf{w}_1$ and $\mathbf{w}_2$, the score of the verification can be calculated as

$$\frac{P(\mathbf{w}_1, \mathbf{w}_2 | H_1)}{P(\mathbf{w}_1 | H_0)P(\mathbf{w}_2 | H_0)}, \tag{3}$$

where the hypothesis H_1 indicates that both i-vectors represent the same speaker, and H_0 denotes that they come from two different speakers.

3   Experimental Configuration

Our PLDA experiments were evaluated using two datasets of speech, the Slovak part of the eastern European fixed-line telephone speech database SpeechDat(E) SK [9] and the mobile telephone speech database MobilDat-SK [11]. Both of these databases contain one recording session per speaker. SpeechDat contains utterances of 1000 speakers and MobilDat utterances of 1100 speakers. From these utterances the active speech was extracted by energy-based voice activity detector, what resulted in approximately 74 to 408 s for Speechdat and 72 to 446 s for MobilDat. Subsequently, all active speech data was truncated to a specific length for each speaker. The SpeechDat database was truncated to the length of 90 s per speaker and was used as the development data consisting of

888 speakers.[1] The MobilDat database was truncated to 60 s and was used as the enrolment data. Additionally, extra 10 s of active speech for each speaker was truncated from both mentioned databases and was used in our experiments as the verification data. Although the SpeechDat database consists of as many as 1000 speakers in total, in the verification data we included only utterances of the 888 speakers, being contained also in the development data. The verification data was excluded from all other data and was used only during the verification. Moreover, in our experiments we focused on evaluating the performance also on shorter than 10-second-long speech utterances. For this purpose, we have created several verification datasets by truncating the original verification data. In this way, several utterances of length from ten to one second were created.

In all proposed experiments were used 19-dimensional features of mel frequency cepstral coefficients (MFCC) with appended delta and delta-delta coefficients. A gender-independent UBM containing 1024 Gaussians was created from the development data and was subsequently used to calculate the total variability subspace of dimension $R = 400$, which was later used to calculate the i-vector representation of each speaker. The experiments were done using the full UBM in a combination of its diagonal version, which was used for the Gaussian selection. All tasks involving feature extraction, i-vector training, and scoring were performed using the Kaldi toolkit [10].

The PLDA speaker verification method requires more than one speech recording per speaker, but the SpeechDat database consists of only a single recording session per speaker. Therefore, in our experiments, we used a method of splitting a single longer speech recording into several shorter segments which were afterwards used to train the PLDA model. The data used for this training consisted of the first 60 s of each recording from the development data (i.e. 888 × 60 s of active speech) and also of additional 60 s of active speech from the 112 speakers not included in the development data, but contained in the SpeechDat database. Therefore, 60 s of active speech from each of the 1000 speakers were used for the training of the PLDA model. The process of splitting the data will be described in detail in the results section.

4   Experimental Results

Following is an experimental study regarding the impact of the length of enrolment data and PLDA-segment length on PLDA speaker verification. Our experiments are divided into two sections and in both of them we have evaluated the performance of verification using the equal error rate (EER). In the first section, a study of the verification of speakers, whose speech utterances were also included in the development is proposed, i.e. UBM training, i-vector extractor training, and also PLDA training. On the other hand, the second section focuses on experiments done on the MobilDat database, which was not used during the development. In this section, experiments on limited amount of verification data as well as enrolment data are discussed.

---

[1] Active speech data of the remaining 112 speakers was not used due to its insufficient length.

4.1 Analysis of Performance on Data from Speakers Used in the Development

Initially, the PLDA verification system was investigated with speech utterances from the same database as the development set, i.e. the SpeechDat database. In this experiment, the influence of different splitting of the PLDA data on EER of the system was studied. The data used for PLDA training was split into smaller segments of speech, while several different segment sizes were examined and for each splitting, a different PLDA model was created. In this experiment, the PLDA data was also used as the enrolment data, i.e. 60 s of active speech per speaker. For a specific segment size, the performance on verification data described in Sect. 3 has been evaluated. The results are shown in Table 1. For comparison, we also provide the results of an approach, when PLDA model is not used, since no splitting has been done, but a simple cosine distance scoring is applied. According to the results, the PLDA method clearly outperforms the cosine distance, even though segments of the same recording session were used during the training. From the table we also see that the lowest EER was overall achieved by using the splitting of the PLDA data into segments of one or two seconds. In comparison with the half-second splitting approach, the one-second splitting results in more than 13 % relative decrease of EER for every studied verification set. From this experiment, we can conclude that splitting the data into shorter parts, leading to more utterances being used during the PLDA training, results in better performance of the scoring. However, the splitting into shorter than one-second-long utterances results in quantitatively more, but less accurate i-vectors, and thus the EER starts to increase.

From the results we also see that decreasing of the amount of verification data results in increasing the EER exponentially, while a significant increase can be observed between three and two seconds of active speech used for verification. This observation holds for each PLDA model used.

4.2 Analysis of Performance on Limited Speech Data

In our second experiment, we used the previous models that had been trained on SpeechDat data and we evaluated their performance on MobilDat speech utterances. According to our previous experiment, we used the PLDA model being trained on the one-second-long speech segments, since this model resulted in one of the best performance. We studied the EER of the system while decreasing the amount of verification and also enrolment data. The results are shown in Fig. 1. From these results we see that providing more enrolment data brings better performance. However, according to our experiments, using 30 s of enrolment results in a performance comparable to using even twice as much data.

From these results we also see that in case of the worst scenario of using only five-second-long utterances of active speech for the enrolment, the verification of one-second-long utterances resulted in EER of 12.09 %. After these findings, we have investigated the performance of the system in its worst scenario, while not using only the best PLDA model according to our previous experiment, but all

Table 1. Comparison of EER values using different sizes of segments used for PLDA training. Values in rows represent the performance of verification of a corresponding PLDA model used on different duration of verification data. Best performing splits for each verification evaluation are highlighted across each column. In the last row, depicted as FULL, the results of the cosine distance scoring, i.e. no splitting was done, are provided.

Size of segment	Duration of verification data						
	1 s	2 s	3 s	4 s	6 s	8 s	10 s
0.5 s	4.08 %	2.14 %	0.90 %	0.56 %	0.45 %	0.42 %	0.28 %
1.0 s	**3.38 %**	**1.69 %**	0.78 %	**0.45 %**	0.35 %	0.34 %	**0.23 %**
2.0 s	3.49 %	**1.69 %**	**0.68 %**	0.56 %	**0.31 %**	**0.27 %**	**0.23 %**
2.5 s	3.49 %	1.91 %	0.79 %	0.56 %	0.35 %	0.33 %	**0.23 %**
5.0 s	3.49 %	2.03 %	0.79 %	0.68 %	0.41 %	0.34 %	**0.23 %**
FULL	7.68 %	4.39 %	2.27 %	1.91 %	1.01 %	0.92 %	0.79 %

studied models. In Fig. 2, we see the comparison of EER of the verification using several PLDA models trained on different segment sizes. We see that splitting the data into 0.5-second-long segments resulted in clearly the worst performance. However, in spite of the fact that the one-second splitting had been chosen as one of the best performing approach; in this experiment, it did not outperform the other PLDA models. We see that using the PLDA models, trained on segments

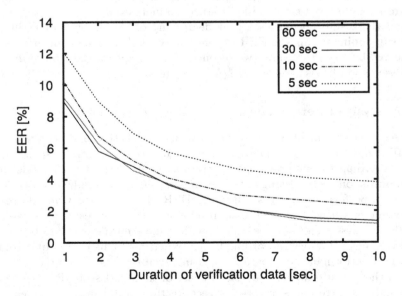

Fig. 1. Comparison of EER values using different duration of verification and enrolment data. Each line represents the performance of the system using different amount of enrolment data.

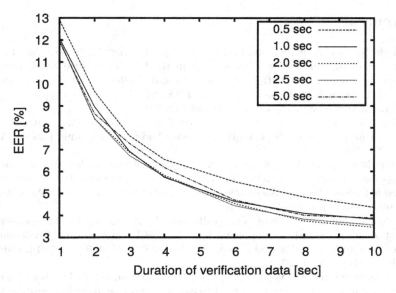

Fig. 2. Comparison of EER of the verification using five seconds of active speech for enrolment. Each line represents the performance of the system using PLDA model trained on a specific size of segments.

of length 2 or 2.5 s, resulted in even slightly lower values of EER. According to this observation and also the results from our first experiment, we can conclude that splitting the one-minute-long recording of active speech into segments of the length of two seconds results in a comparable performance, and thus can be used in our future experiments.

5   Conclusion

Creating a robust speaker verification system while providing only limited amount of speech data still remains a key issue. In this paper, we presented a study of PLDA speaker verification when encountering these limitations. We studied the performance using two databases of Slovak speech, while decreasing the amount of data used for verification as well as enrolment. We focused also on the problem of using the PLDA model when only a one session recording per speaker is provided and we compared the impact of different granularity of segmentation used for the PLDA training on the final performance of the verification. Our experiments found that splitting the PLDA data into shorter segments results in improving the performance; however, splitting one-minute-long recording of active speech into segments shorter than two seconds does not bring any significant improvement and starts to harm the system.

Acknowledgments. This research was supported by VEGA grant, number 2/0197/15.

References

1. Dehak, N., Dehak, R., Kenny, P., Brümmer, N., Ouellet, P., Dumouchel, P.: Support vector machines versus fast scoring in the low-dimensional total variability space for speaker verification. In: 10th Annual Conference of the International Speech Communication Association, INTERSPEECH 2009, 6–10 September 2009, Brighton, United Kingdom, pp. 1559–1562 (2009)
2. Dehak, N., Kenny, P., Dehak, R., Dumouchel, P., Ouellet, P.: Front-end factor analysis for speaker verification. IEEE Trans. Audio Speech Lang. Process. **19**(4), 788–798 (2011)
3. Garcia-Romero, D., Espy-Wilson, C.Y.: Analysis of i-vector length normalization in speaker recognition systems. In: 12th Annual Conference of the International Speech Communication Association, INTERSPEECH 2011, 27–31 August 2011, Florence, Italy, pp. 249–252 (2011)
4. Kanagasundaram, A., Dean, D., Sridharan, S.: Improving PLDA speaker verification with limited development data. In: IEEE International Conference on Acoustics, Speech and Signal Processing, ICASSP 2014, 4–9 May 2014, Florence, Italy, pp. 1665–1669 (2014)
5. Kanagasundaram, A., Vogt, R., Dean, D., Sridharan, S.: PLDA based speaker recognition on short utterances. In: The Speaker and Language Recognition Workshop, Odyssey 2012, 25–28 June 2012, Singapore, pp. 28–33 (2012)
6. Kenny, P.: Bayesian speaker verification with heavy-tailed priors. In: The Speaker and Language Recognition Workshop, Odyssey 2010, June 28–July 1, 2010, Brno, Czech Republic, p. 14 (2010)
7. Kenny, P., Ouellet, P., Dehak, N., Gupta, V., Dumouchel, P.: A study of interspeaker variability in speaker verification. IEEE Trans. Audio Speech Lang. Process. **16**(5), 980–988 (2008)
8. Kinnunen, T., Li, H.: An overview of text-independent speaker recognition: from features to supervectors. Speech Commun. **52**(1), 12–40 (2010)
9. Pollk, P., Boudy, J., Choukri, K., Heuvel, H.V.D., Vicsi, K., Virag, A., Siemund, R., Majewski, W., Staroniewicz, P., Tropf, H., Kochanina, J., Ostroukhov, E., Rusko, M., Trnka, M.: SpeechDat(E) - Eastern European telephone speech databases. In: Workshop on Very Large Telephone Speech Databases, XLDB 2000, pp. 20–25 (2000)
10. Povey, D., Ghoshal, A., Boulianne, G., Burget, L., Glembek, O., Goel, N., Hannemann, M., Motlek, P., Qian, Y., Schwarz, P., Silovsk, J., Stemmer, G., Vesel, K.: The Kaldi speech recognition toolkit. In: IEEE 2011 Workshop on Automatic Speech Recognition and Understanding (2011)
11. Rusko, M., Trnka, M., Darjaa, S.: MobilDat-SK - a mobile telephone extension to the SpeechDat-E SK telephone speech database in Slovak. In: Speech and Computer - 11th International Conference, SPECOM 2006, 25–29 June 2006, St. Petersburg, Russia, pp. 449–454 (2006)

Real-Time Context Aware Audio Augmented Reality

Gerasimos Arvanitis$^{(\boxtimes)}$, Konstantinos Moustakas, and Nikos Fakotakis

Electrical and Computer Engineering Department,
University of Patras, Rio, Patras, Greece
{gerarvanitis,fakotaki}@upatras.gr, moustakas@ece.upatras.gr

Abstract. The purpose of this paper is to present a method for real time augmented reality sound production from virtual sources, which are located in a real environment. In the performed experiments, we will initially emphasize on augmenting audio information, beyond the existing environmental sounds, using headphones. The main goal of the approach is to produce a virtual sound that has a natural result so that the user gets immersed and senses a context aware synthetic sound. The necessary data, such as spatial coordinates of source and listener, relative distance and relative velocity between them, room dimensions and potential obstacles between virtual source and listener are given as input to the proposed framework. Real time techniques are used for data processing. These techniques are fast and effective in order to achieve high performance requirements. The resulted sound gives the impression to the listener that the virtual source is part of the real environment. Any dynamic change of the parameters will have as a result the simultaneous real time change of the produced sound.

Keywords: Spatial sound · Audio augment reality · Real/virtual object interaction

1 Introduction

In recent years mobile devices like smartphones and tablets have become faster and more powerful. The technological development in this direction is significant, especially in the area of computer graphics. However, no special attention has been given in audio augmented reality environments. This has a negative consequence to the general audiovisual result and causes the loss of important information which disturbs the user's qualitative experience.

1.1 Related Works

Several applications that use sound in augmented reality environments have been presented over the years. In [3] a smartphone application uses spatialized audio to render nearby locations to blind users as they walk down the street.

© Springer International Publishing Switzerland 2015
A. Ronzhin et al. (Eds.): SPECOM 2015, LNAI 9319, pp. 333–340, 2015.
DOI: 10.1007/978-3-319-23132-7_41

Table 1.

Parameter	form	Description	Affected Effect
Source's Position	Spos(x,y,z)	Vector that describes the position of the virtual source expressed in coordinates	Sound's spatialization
Source's Velocity	Svel(x,y,z)	Vector that describes the velocity of the virtual source	Doppler effect, sound's pitch
Listener's Position	Lpos(x,y,z)	Vector that represents the position of the listener while he moves	Sound's spatialization
Listener's Velocity	Lvel(x,y,z)	Vector that represents the velocity of the listener	Doppler effect, sound's pitch
Listener's Orientation	Lori(xat, yat, zat, xon, yon, zon)	Vector that represents the position of the listener's head in two directions	Sound's spatialization
Room's Dimensions	Length, width, height	The dimensions of the room which determine if a room is small, medium, large	Reverberations and reflections
Environment's Type	ToR	Type of the environment which is determined by the main material of the room	Reverberations and reflections
Obstruction	Obstruction	Yes or No value that indicates the existence of an obstruction or not	Reverberations, reflections and lowpass filter
Obstruction's Type	ToO	Type of obstruction such as pillar, chair, curtain	Reverberations, reflections and lowpass filter

In application [7] the augmented reality audio combines virtual sound sources with the real sonic environment of the user. In [8] a 3D audio wearable system is developed that can be used to provide alerts and informational cues to a mobile user in such a manner as to appear to emanate from specific locations of the user's environment. In [9], another application developed for educational purposes to support different learning in different contexts using multimedia capabilities and location based service on smartphones. In [10], a 3D audio spatialization system is created. Its goal is to test user's experience of discovery in a purely exploratory environment that included multiple simultaneous sound sources. In [4], an audio-only augmented reality system for social interaction is described, where the music that users hear in their earphones based on their position changes dynamically. In [6], a wearable system is created that plays digital sound corresponding to the user's location and current state. In all of these papers the sound is not related to environmental parameters. Moreover, there is not a virtual source as object in the real environment and in most of them it is required extra wearable equipment.

1.2   Originality of This Work

The main originality of this study is reflected from the working hypothesis that the virtual object exists and augments the real world. Therefore, the sound that the virtual object produces does not have the acoustic characteristics of a virtual space but the acoustic characteristics of the real world in which the object is part of. The features that we study in this paper are divided into two categories. The first category concerns characteristics such as the location of the source and the listener, the velocities and the orientation of the listener. In the second category, parameters related to the morphology of the area in which the virtual source is displayed are examined. These features depend on many factors, such as the size of the room, potential obstacles between virtual source and listener, building materials etc. The used parameters are presented in Table 1.

2   Room's Dimensions and Large Object Clustering

Before starting audio processing we need to know the values of some environmental parameters that affect the augmented sound. These values will be received by scanning the room with a Kinect camera and creating a point cloud that represents the room. For the cloud processing we use Point Cloud Library (PCL) [1]. Since the original point cloud carries useless, redundant information increasing the mathematical complexity of the processing, we apply statistical methods to filter and downsample the original cloud in order to remove the outlier values that are mainly related to noise (Fig. 1).

In a real-time scanning we do not have every detail of the room because it is difficult and time consuming to capture it. At least two projections are required to calculate the room's dimensions. For the projection we need to know the mathematical equations of the plane on which the point cloud will be projected. In general case the mathematical equation of a plane in a $\mathbb{R}^3$ space is described by the formula below:

$$ax + by + cz + d = 0 \qquad (1)$$

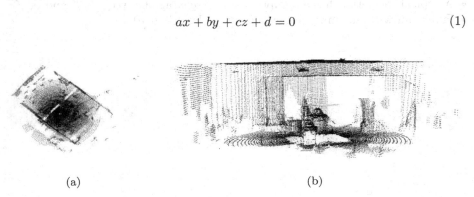

(a)   (b)

Fig. 1. (a) Filtered and downsampled point cloud from above (b) the same point cloud from another point of view

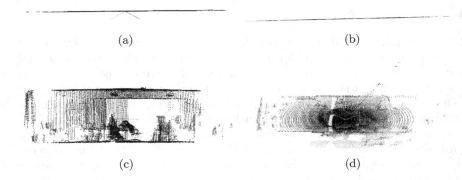

(a)   (b)

(c)   (d)

Fig. 2. (a) wall projection from above, x, y axes are vertical to this projection (b) floor projection from sideways, z axis is vertical to this projection (c) wall projection from another point view (d) floor projection from above

Because some areas have an incomplete scanning, the system chooses the two vertical projections (walls, floor, ceiling) with the most information(Fig. 2). In this example the mathematical equations of the chosen planes are the following:

$$cz = 0 \text{ for one wall projection} \tag{2}$$

$$ax + by = 0 \text{ for floor projection} \tag{3}$$

Moreover, we find the position and dimensions of large objects by searching only the objects that satisfy specific dimensional requirements (Fig. 3). For this reason, a lower and upper threshold of points is chosen.

One other parameter that is investigated and affects the produced sound result is the percentage fullness. We recognize three general types of rooms:

- Almost empty room whose empty space percentage is over 90 %
- A typical room that has an empty space percentage between 70 % and 90 %
- Full room with an empty space percentage less than 70 %

(a)   (b)

Fig. 3. (a) All object clusters appear together, (b) object clusters after planes removal.

3   Context-Aware Augmented Reality Audio Rendering

The audio processing starts with the creation of a localized sound, without special effects. Firstly, we assume that source and listener exist in an open area without walls or objects, the only parameters we need to know at this phase are the source's and listener's position as well listener's orientation. This simplification is described by the following hypothesis. Let Xs be the source position, Xl the corresponding value of the listener and Ol the listener's orientation. Then the localized sound is:

$$\widehat{sound} = \Gamma(sound, Xs, Xl, Ol) \tag{4}$$

where Γ defines the processing technique and $\widehat{sound}$ the localized sound.

3.1   Attenuation and Relative Velocity - Doppler Effect

The sound intensity from a point source of sound will obey the inverse square law if there are no reflections or reverberation. In a closed space, like a room, the sound intensity does not obey to a specific mathematical law and the phenomena that are affecting the final aural result are more complicate. For our experiments we used the default distance model that is described by the following relation. This mode is equivalent to the IASIG I3DL2 distance model [9] (Fig. 4).

Another very important issue that affects the produced sound is relative velocity. The sound effect that is directly associated with velocity is the Doppler Effect. The amount of frequency shift is proportional to the speed of listener and source along their line of sight.

3.2   Dimensions and Position of Real Objects

In an ideal and simplified case, source and listener exist in an empty room. However, in real life a room is not always empty. Furthermore, it is possible that an object exists between the listener and the source. This hypothetical case affects

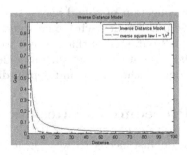

Fig. 4. Inverse Distance Model that we used. The parameters can change on demand depending on the type of the area.

Fig. 5. Surface of object's projection in a different listener's and source's relative position

the sound result. In this scenario the direct path between the sound source and the listener is blocked. So when the obstruction scenario is detected for a sound source, the source's direct path should have attenuation and filtering applied. The tonal effect of transmission through the obstacle or diffraction around an obstacle is similar because materials are typically less transmissive at high frequencies than at low: in both cases, the direct-path sound is low-pass filtered (Fig. 5).

The surface of the obstacle that listener "sees" when source is hidden behind them, depends on relative location between listener and source. Moreover, the relevant thickness of the obstacle depends also on relative location. The relevant surface and thickness affect the transmitted sound in a different manner. We find these values in real time when the position of the listener or source changes. To create a quick and effective algorithm we compute only the objects that exist between listener and source.

3.3   Type of Environment

Reverberation comprises all the different reflections produced by a sound in an environment, in our case a room. Assuming that a direct path exists between the listener and the sound source, the direct sound will be heard first. This will be followed by reflections of nearby surfaces, called early reflections, within the first 80 ms after the sound starts [2]. After a few tenths of a second, the number of reflected waves becomes very large and the resulting reverberation is characterized by a dense collection of sound waves travelling in all directions, called the late reverberation. Different environment types have different acoustic characteristics. There are 22 parameters that we use to produce the expedient sound result regarding the type of the room such as reflection's gain and delay, reverberation's gain and delay, echo's time and depth, diffusion and others.

4   Experimental Procedure and Results

The user of this application just needs to wear headphones in order to hear the produced sound. The first time the application runs it takes 2-3 seconds for variable initialization. In this step the objects of interest are enumerated and the variables such as room's type and dimensions, object's position and dimensions are received. After this process, we assume that the room is a static environment and all parameters remain steady until the Kinect camera recognizes a difference in the background. While the listener or virtual source is moving a new relative distance, relative velocity and obstacles between them are identified and their effect in the sound synthesis is computed in real time. The result of this procedure is the creation of a real-time context aware augmented reality sound. Every dynamic change of a parameter will change the produced sound rapidly in order for the listener to have the impression of hearing a sound from a real source. For the creation of special sound effects we use the OpenAL library [5], which is capable of managing all this information and producing reliable sound results depending on the parameters we study. Some examples of produced sound are shown in Fig. 6. Different aural cases for easiest comparison of results are chosen.

Moreover, in the experimental phase we developed a simulative application that allows the creation of a wide range of different environmental cases concerning room's size, different materials, relative distance and velocity between listener and source and even any type of obstacles. The advantage of the simulation is that it allows the use of special cases that would be very difficult to test in real environment.

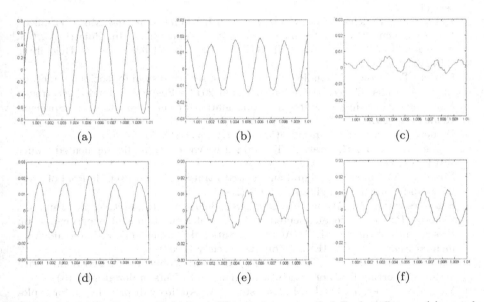

Fig. 6. (a) Original sinusoidal sound (b) sound in a small, full of stuff room (c) sound in a small, full of stuff room with obstacle (d) sound in a large room with relative velocity (e) sound in a large room with reverberation (f) sound in a large room with opposite orientation of listener

5 Conclusions

In this paper we described a method for augmented reality sound that is real time and context aware. The main task on which we focus is the creation of a sound that depends on the environmental parameters of the room where the virtual source appears. The necessary data are received from a Kinect sensor and are processed in order to fine-tune the parameters of the virtual source. Data processing techniques are effective and take place rapidly in real time, creating a believable augmented reality sound and making listener feel that virtual source is actually in the room.

Acknowledgments. This work has been supported by the Greek Secretariat for Research and Technology Bilateral Collaboration Project MOMIRAS (ISR3215).

References

1. The point cloud library (pcl). http://pointclouds.org/
2. Begault, D.R., et al.: 3-D sound for virtual reality and multimedia, vol. 955. Citeseer (1994)
3. Blum, J.R., Bouchard, M., Cooperstock, J.R.: What's around Me? spatialized audio augmented reality for blind users with a smartphone. In: Puiatti, A., Gu, T. (eds.) MobiQuitous 2011. LNICST, vol. 104, pp. 49–62. Springer, Heidelberg (2012)
4. Gurion, T., Jacoby, N.: Audio-only augmented reality system for social interaction. In: Stephanidis, C. (ed.) HCI International 2013 - Posters' Extended Abstracts. Communications in Computer and Information Science, pp. 322–326. Springer, Heidelberg (2013)
5. Hiebert, G.: Openal 1.1 specification and reference (2005)
6. Lyons, K., Gandy, M., Starner, T.: Guided by voices: an audio augmented reality system (2000)
7. Rämö, J., Välimäki, V.: Digital augmented reality audio headset. Journal of Electrical and Computer Engineering 2012 (2012)
8. Sundareswaran, V., Wang, K., Chen, S., Behringer, R., McGee, J., Tam, C., Zahorik, P.: 3D audio augmented reality: implementation and experiments. In: Proceedings of the 2nd IEEE/ACM International Symposium on Mixed and Augmented Reality, p. 296. IEEE Computer Society (2003)
9. Ternier, S., De Vries, F., Börner, D., Specht, M.: Mobile augmented reality with audio, supporting fieldwork of cultural sciences students in florence (2013)
10. Vazquez-Alvarez, Y., Oakley, I., Brewster, S.A.: Auditory display design for exploration in mobile audio-augmented reality. Pers. Ubiquit. Comput. **16**(8), 987–999 (2012)

Recurrent Neural Networks for Hypotheses Re-Scoring

Mikhail Kudinov[(✉)]

Dorodnicyn Computing Centre of RAS,
Institution of Russian Academy of Sciences,
Vavilov St. 40, 119333 Moscow, Russia
mikhailkudinov@gmail.com

Abstract. We present our first results in applications of recurrent neural networks to Russian. The problem of re-scoring of equiprobable hypotheses has been solved. We train several recurrent neural networks on a lemmatized news corpus to mitigate the problem of data sparseness. We also make use of morphological information to make the predictions more accurate. Finally we train the Ranking SVM model and show that combination of recurrent neural networks and morphological information gives better results than 5-gram model with Knesser-Ney discounting.

Keywords: Recurrent neural networks · Hypotheses re-scoring · Inflective languages

1 Introduction

The problem of statistical language modelling of inflectional languages is known to be more complicated than in case of English [12]. The main difficulties emerge because of the great number of morphological forms of the same word (lemma) and a frier word order [15]. Both reasons effectively lead to aggravation of data sparseness and degradation of efficiency of n-gram models.

While using n-gram models for the first pass of the recognition process is still a common practice [4], the options for the following passes made by multi-pass speech recognition algorithm are much wider. For example, the process of re-scoring of the hypotheses returned by the beam search procedure may be based on different morphological, syntactic and semantic information. The latter one has been represented by means of different word or text embeddings: LSA [1], Probabilistic Topic Modelling [6] or Neural Networks [2]. In 2010 the so-called Recurrent Neural Network language model (RNNLM) was proposed [10]. The model has shown the new state-of-the-art results both in perplexity and WER in LVCSR task. Although the model was proposed for English in [9] there is evidence of some promising results in a small speech recognition task for Czech. As structures of Czech and Russian have much in common using RNN for predicting words for Russian seems tempting. Although Recurrent Neural Network Model has been tested on Russian material in [14] as a result of suboptimal

© Springer International Publishing Switzerland 2015
A. Ronzhin et al. (Eds.): SPECOM 2015, LNAI 9319, pp. 341–347, 2015.
DOI: 10.1007/978-3-319-23132-7_42

hyperparameters (small number of hidden layers and large number of classes) poor results were obtained. At the same time, training RNNLM model directly on word forms seems to be too difficult because of large vocabulary size and parameters number.

However, the problem of learning the RNNLM for a morphologically rich language is more challenging at least if the original approach is adopted [10]. In addition to the abovementioned difficulties with data sparseness the learning of the model with the vocabulary designed as a simple word list is prohibitevely time-consuming. Thus, we decided to begin with the simpler problem of sentence re-scoring based on interpolation of the lexical model which is RNN and a separate morphological model.

The remainder of the paper is organized as follows. In Sect. 2 we give some basics of the Recurrent Neural Network Model. In Sect. 3 we discuss applicability of the original Recurrent Neural Network to inflective languages and propose several solutions to the problems connected with it. Finally, in Sect. 3.1 we describe our experiments and next present brief discussion.

2   Recurrent Neural Network Language Model

Recurrent Neural Network (RNN) was first proposed in [5] by Elman in 1990. In this pioneering research also the idea of word prediction based on the left context by means of RNN was proposed. However, the computational complexity and the lack of large available linguistic corpora didn't let the model become popular in the language modelling community.

In 2003 in [2] the idea of the Neural Network language model of n-th order was proposed. Essentially the model behaved like the n-gram model i.e. the prediction was made according to the $(n-1)$ long left context but each word was replaced by the unique embedding of the word into a M-dimensional vector space. Each word input (say with index l) in the vocabulary of $|V|$ words was represented as a $|L|$-dimensional vector $< 0_1, \ldots, 1_l, 0_{l+1}, \ldots, 0_{|L|} >$ with all coordinates equal to 0 except the l-th which was equal to 1. The vector was multiplied by matrix $W_{M \times L}$ that effectively corresponds to taking the l-th column of W.

The same technique was taken by T. Mikolov in [10] where the recurrent layer from Elman's architecture was used. The resulting model calculated probability distribution of the next word according to the formula:

$$P(w_t|w_{t-1}, h_{t-1}) = y_{w_t}. \tag{1}$$

$$y_t = s(U \cdot h_t). \tag{2}$$

$$h_t = W \cdot x + V \cdot h_{t-1}, \tag{3}$$

where

$$\sigma(x) = \frac{1}{1 + e^{-x}}$$

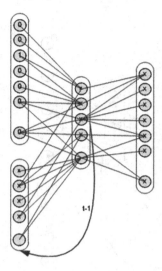

Fig. 1. Recurrent Neural Network language model

is the logistic activation function and

$$s(y_k) = \frac{e^{y_k}}{\sum_i e^{y_i}}$$

is softmax function. h_t is a recurrent hidden layer; y is an output layer with each k-th element corresponding to the probability $P(w_k|w_{t-1}, h_{t-1})$, $V_{H \times H}$ is the recurrent matrix, $W_{H \times |L|}$ is the vocabulary matrix or lookup table, $U_{|L| \times H}$ is the output matrix; H is the number of elements in the recurrent layer.

As far as h_t potentially depends on the whole previous context such model seems more attractive than n-gram models or its modifications. Unfortunately, in fact it is not totally right because the gradient $\frac{\partial h_t}{\partial h_k}$, $k < t$ of the activation vanishes (or explodes) exponentially fast on $(t - k)$ [3,13]:

$$\frac{\partial h_t}{\partial h_k} = \prod_{k < i \leq t} \frac{\partial h_i}{\partial h_{i-1}} = \prod_{k < i \leq t} V^T diag(\sigma'(h_{i-1})).$$

Behaviour of the gradient above is determined by the matrix V but it is proved to be either vanish or explosion [2].

Although there are several methods to circumvent the vanishing gradients problem [2,7], it is claimed in [10] that this problem is not so important for word prediction. So we will try to adapt this model to inflective languages.

3   Recurrent Neural Networks and Inflective Languages

In addition to the well known problems of data sparseness training the Neural Network language model with a reasonably large vocabulary for an inflective language

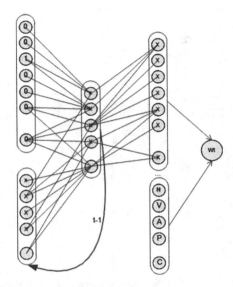

Fig. 2. Recurrent Neural Network Language Model with external classifier for word form prediction

presents another technical challenge. A large amount of different word forms leads to proportionally larger vocabulary. From (3) it is easy to see that complexity of backpropagation is linear on the amount of words in the vocabulary.

To circumvent this problem we could use the scheme at the Figs. 1 and 2 Each word is lemmatized with an external lemmatizing tool. The lemmas are used for lemma prediction. Then for each lemma the logistic regression classifier is launched with morphological and lexical features. This approach would reduce the problem of data sparseness without dramatic growth in the vocabulary size.

But in the present research we begin with a smaller problem whose goal is to test if a simpler combination of RNN with morphological model outperforms n-gram models with Knesser-Ney discounting.

3.1 Experiments

We trained our language models on a news corpus of approximately 2 million tokens collected from Lenta.ru website. For training RNNLM 10 % of texts were used as validation set. Each text was processed by the lemmatization tool for Russian [11] with a large vocabulary of approximattely $2 \cdot 10^6$ word forms. We processed the data to make two datasets. The first dataset was the output of the lemmatizer i.e. the text where each known word was replaced with its normalized form (lemma). Each unknown word was replaced with "UNK" label. We used vocabulary of 10^4 most frequent lemmas so all lemmas outside the list were also replaced with "UNK". In the second dataset the only change was the replacement of each word form whose lemma was not present in the vocabulary with "UNK".

As a result we prepared two train and test pairs with lemmas and word forms respectively. These corpora were used for training and perplexity tests.

For the re-scoring tests we used the hypotheses returned by Nuance speech recognition engine. We had a corpus of speech of studio quality with transcripts. Selected audio files were fed to the engine with up to 10 hypotheses retrieved. As a result we collected a corpus of unsorted recognition hypotheses. Usually, the hypotheses list did not contain the right one and we added it manually.

Then each hypothesis was processed by the tools we used for preparation of the training corpus. As a result we had a lemmatized and tokenized corpora with "UNK" replacements. These corpora were processed by the models we used in our experiments. Finally we had train and test sets containing sentences and sentence scores from KNn and RNN models we were going to test. Totally there were 1300 phrases in the training set with approximately 5 hypotheses per phrase and 300 in the test set with 5 average number of hypotheses per phrase. This dataset was used for training the reranking model.

We tested the n-gram models with the Knesser-Ney discounting of order 3, 4 and 5 trained on both lemmas and word forms. We also had scores retrieved by our lemmatizer and scores by Recurrent Neural Networks with 100, 200, 300, 400 and 500 hidden units. All RNNs were trained on the lemmatized corpus. The lemmatizer score is essentially a probability of the best decoding hypothesis $P(Y_1^t|X_1^T)$ where Y is the sequence of morphological labels and X is the sequence of observed features of each token.

Totally each sentence had 12 scores.

The re-scoring was made by means of the ranking SVM [8] model with model scores used as features. The model was trained to retrieve the right hypothesis according to the scores. Effectively, it leads to interpolation. We used word and sentence error rates as basic perfomance measures for the reranking model.

3.2   Results

The performance of the models is shown in Tables 1 and 2. In Table 1 perplexities of all trained models are presented. In Table 2 performance of the modelss and their combinations in terms of word error rate and sentence error rate is presented. Sentence error rate (SER) is the portion of wrong answers given by the model trying to predict 1 best hypothesis.

It should be noted that the perplexity results for models trained on lemmatized and non-lemmatized corpora are not truly comparable because of the different number of unknown words in train and test sets. This fact accounts for a considerable difference in perplexity results for lemmatized and tokenized corpora: number of unknown words in the latter case is much greater. Thus, the promising result of the experiment is that RNN models perform considerably better than best performing KN5.

Consider the results on the re-scoring task. On the 3.2 **KN5** is the model with only 5-gram Knesser-Ney predictions are used. **KN all** is the model with 3,4,5-gram predictions taken as features. Subscripts *lem* and *tok* stand for models trained on lemmas and tokens correspondingly. Model with **morph** addition had

Table 1. Perplexities of different models on test set.

Model	Perplexity	Model	Perplexity
KN3$_{lem}$	272.8	**RNN100**	240.13
KN4$_{lem}$	272.2	**RNN200**	230.45
KN5$_{lem}$	273	**RNN300**	231
KN3$_{tok}$	128.72	**RNN400**	231.87
KN4$_{tok}$	130.76	**RNN500**	231.21
KN5$_{tok}$	132		

Table 2. Performance of models and their combinations on the re-scoring task.

Model	WER%	SER%	Model	WER%	SER%
KN5$_{lem}$	16.62	40.8	**RNN100**	17.55	43.67
KN5$_{tok}$	18.09	42.72	**RNN200**	15.35	40.5
KN5$_{lem}$ + **morph**	15.58	43.98	**RNN300**	17.09	43.98
KN$_{lem}$ **all**	17.05	40.82	**RNN400**	16.58	41.77
KN$_{lem}$ **all + morph**	15.74	43.67	**RNN500**	17.43	43.67
KN$_{lem+tok}$ **all**	15.74	39.24	**RNN all**	**15.35**	**38.29**
KN$_{lem+tok}$ **all + morph**	15.89	43.35	**RNN all + morph**	14.58	41.45
all models	14.78	40.5			

additional feature from morphology/lemmatization tool. *Ex:* **KN**$_{lem+tok}$ **all + morph** is the model using predictions of all Knesser-Ney models learned on lemmas and tokens and also morphological probabililty as features.

There are several points to notice here. The first one is the superiority of the RNN-based model over the n-gram based. The second point is a strange influence of the morphological score which favours parses with a better WER but more likely votes for actually wrong hypotheses. This can be explained by the fact that the morphological score is actually the probability of the best parse $P(tag_1^T|word_1^T)$. For this reason it tends to choose parses with less parse entropy. It should be admitted that this score is not fully appropriate when we want to interpolate it with a language model. The third point is a somehow volatile behaviour of the RNN models: some of them demonstrate rather poor performance by themselves but interpolation of all of them gives the best performance.

Recognition experiments have shown the superiority of the RNN models. The best performing combination uses RNNs and the lemmatizer score effectively combining lexical and morphological information. This result suggests that the following research in this direction will be productive.

3.3 Discussion

We have proposed a simple experiment for testing the performance of the Recurrent Neural Network language model on the re-scoring task. The results suggest that the Recurrent Neural Network language model performs better than the n-gram model with the Knesser-Ney discounting in both terms of perplexity and recognition accuracy. However, for the sake of research correctness the standard recognition experiments are still needed. Also the current model must be adapted to the word form prediction task for Russian.

References

1. Bellegarda, J.R.: Exploiting latent semantic information in statistical language modeling. Proc. IEEE **88**(8), 1279–1296 (2000)
2. Bengio, Y., Ducharme, R., Vincent, P., Janvin, C.: A neural probabilistic language model. J. Mach. Learn. Res. **3**, 1137–1155 (2003)
3. Bengio, Y., Simard, P., Frasconi, P.: Learning long-term dependencies with gradient descent is difficult. IEEE Transact. Neural Netw. **5**(2), 157–166 (1994)
4. Deoras, A., Mikolov, T., Kombrink, S., Church, K.: Approximate inference: a sampling based modeling technique to capture complex dependencies in a language model. Speech Commun. **55**(1), 162–177 (2013)
5. Elman, J.L.: Finding structure in time. Cogn. Sci. **14**(2), 179–211 (1990)
6. Gildea, D., Hofmann, T.: Topic-based language models using em. History (1999)
7. Hochreiter, S., Schmidhuber, J.: Bridging long time lags by weight guessing and long short-term memory. In: Silva, F.L., Príncipe, J.C., Almeida, L.B. (eds.) Spatiotemporal Models in Biological and Artificial Systems, vol. 37, pp. 65–72. IOS Press, Amsterdam (1996)
8. Joachims, T.: Optimizing search engines using clickthrough data. In: Proceedings of the Eighth ACM SIGKDD International Conference on Knowledge Discovery and Data Mining, pp. 133–142. ACM (2002)
9. Mikolov, T.: Statistical language models based on neural networks. Ph.D. thesis, Brno University of Technology (2012)
10. Mikolov, T., Karafiát, M., Burget, L., Cernocký, J., Khudanpur, S.: Recurrent neural network based language model. In: INTERSPEECH 2010, 11th Annual Conference of the International Speech Communication Association, Makuhari, Chiba, Japan, pp. 1045–1048, 26–30 September 2010 (2010)
11. Muzychka S.A., Romanenko A.A., Piontkovskaja I.I.: Conditional random field for morphological disambiguation in Russian. In: Conference Dialog-2014 (2014)
12. Oparin, I.: Language models for automatic speech recognition of inflectional languages. Ph.D. thesis, University of West Bohemia (2008)
13. Pascanu, R., Mikolov, T., Bengio, Y.: On the difficulty of training recurrent neural networks (2012). arXiv preprint arXiv:1211.5063
14. Vazhenina, D., Markov, K.: Evaluation of advanced language modeling techniques for Russian LVCSR. In: Železný, M., Habernal, I., Ronzhin, A. (eds.) SPECOM 2013. LNCS, vol. 8113, pp. 124–131. Springer, Heidelberg (2013)
15. Whittaker, E.W.D.: Statistical language modelling for automatic speech recognition of Russian and English. Ph.D. thesis, University of Cambridge (2000)

Review of the Opus Codec in a WebRTC Scenario for Audio and Speech Communication

Michael Maruschke, Oliver Jokisch$^{(\boxtimes)}$, Martin Meszaros, and Viktor Iaroshenko

Leipzig University of Telecommunication (HfTL), Leipzig, Germany
{maruschke,jokisch}@hft-leipzig.de
http://www.hft-leipzig.de

Abstract. The Internet Engineering Task Force (IETF) – the open Internet standards-development body – considers the Opus codec as a highly versatile audio codec for interactive voice and music transmission. In this review we survey the dynamic functioning of the Opus codec within a Web Real-Time Communication (WebRTC) framework based on the Google Chrome browser. The codec behavior and the effectively utilized features during the active communication process are tested and analyzed under various testing conditions. In the experiments, we verify the Opus performance and interactivity. Relevant codec parameters can easily be adapted in application development. In addition, WebRTC framework-coded speech achieves a similar MOS assessment compared to stand-alone Opus coding.

Keywords: Opus codec · WebRTC · Google Chrome · Audio and speech quality

1 Introduction

The world-wide internet-based communication is accompanied by a steadily increasing popularity of web technologies. This so called "webification" encompasses the browser-based real-time communication as one of essential feature in new web applications. The upcoming WebRTC technology enriches ordinary web browsers by real-time communication functionality [6]. For voice and audio communication, the multifunctional Opus codec is an inherent component of the WebRTC capable browser. Our contribution presents a survey of the Opus codec characteristics in a real WebRTC scenario. By using the Google Chrome web browser for audio and speech communication, the implemented (default) parameters of Opus are identified, and the possible configuration settings are ascertained and tested. The outcome is reviewed in the current article. To verify the voice and audio performance of the Opus codec in a real WebRTC environment, we conducted a listening test as well as instrumental assessments. The assessment results are discussed in a corresponding publication [7].

Section 2 is summarizing the previous work related to the Opus codec. Section 3 investigates the properties of the embedded Opus codec in a WebRTC scenario, and Sect. 4 discusses the achieved results and provides an insight into the next research steps.

© Springer International Publishing Switzerland 2015
A. Ronzhin et al. (Eds.): SPECOM 2015, LNAI 9319, pp. 348–355, 2015.
DOI: 10.1007/978-3-319-23132-7_43

2 Previous Studies on Opus Codec

Standardized in RFC 6716 [2] by the IETF, Opus is designed as an all-purpose interactive speech and audio codec. Applicable in multiple use cases, Opus is suitable for scopes like Voice over IP, videoconferencing, online-gaming or audio on demand. It comprises low bit rate speech as well as very high quality stereo music. To realize high quality and dynamic characteristics, Opus combines the linear prediction-based SILK codec [8] with the Modified Discrete Cosine Transform (MDCT)-based Constrained Energy Lapped Transform (CELT) codec [9]. For a flexible use, the Opus codec supports the frequency band types Narrowband (NB), Wideband (WB), Super-Wideband (SWB) and Fullband (FB). As documented in [10,11], Opus operates in the following three modes:

- SILK mode (NB and WB speech),
- CELT mode (music, SWB and FB speech),
- Hybrid mode (SILK and CELT synchronously for SWB and FB speech).

Consequently, the Opus codec provides speech and music (alternatively mono or stereo) within a bit rate range from 6 kbit/s to 510 kbit/s and low delay coding (2,5 ms to 60 ms) for all relevant sample rates, from 8 kHz (NB) up to 48 kHz (FB). The codec offers several control parameters that are changeable during a running communication. The most common dynamic encoder parameters are as follows [2]:

1. Sample rate (samples per second/kHz),
2. Audio bandwidth (frequency band: NB, WB, FB),
3. Used encoder bit rate (kbit per second),
4. Used channels (mono/stereo),
5. Opus working mode (CELT/SILK/Hybrid),
6. Frame duration(frame size/length in milliseconds),
7. Complexity (integer to indicate CPU complexity, from lowest value "0" up to highest value "10").

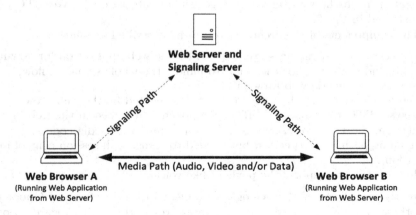

Fig. 1. WebRTC triangle architecture

On encoder side, well-formed Opus packets enclose a so called Table-Of-Contents (TOC) header that indicates the Opus parameters: working mode, audio bandwidth and frame size [2].

Since its introduction in 2010/2011, the Opus codec has passed several listening test campaigns – supplemented by comparison to other speech and audio codecs (Speex NB/WB, iLBC, G.722.1/G.722.1C, AMR NB/WB, HE-AAC, Vorbis). The results are examined and summarized in Hoene et al. [4] in which Opus outperformed all codecs – in particular in the wider bands if applicable. Nevertheless, the mentioned tests were carried out without disruptions on standalone codec.

3 Opus Codec in a Web-Based Real-Time Communication

3.1 WebRTC Principles

WebRTC adds new communication functionality to regular web browsers which can interact among each other via a so called "Triangle Architecture" as shown in Fig. 1. The signaling path through the network is linked involving a signaling server as relay point. In contrast, the media data are sent directly to the other web browser (peer-to-peer-connection).

WebRTC is an open project initiated by Google Inc. which is still under development respectively in the standardization process [3]. Therefore, the standardization body World Wide Web Consortium (W3C) is responsible for the web developer Application Programming Interface (API) and the IETF for all corresponding protocols.

Current relevant standard documents are the W3C working draft "WebRTC 1.0: Real-time communication between browsers" [6] describing the Javascript based WebRTC APIs, and also the IETF draft "Real Time Protocols for Browser-based Applications" [1].

Before initiating a WebRTC session, the web browsers download the web application from the web server. The generic architecture of a WebRTC client is illustrated in Fig. 2.

The components of the architecture can be described as follows:

- Web server and signaling server – provides the web application for download and includes a server for the client to handle the whole signaling flow,
- Browser – a generic web browser,
- Web application – application source code executed by the web browser,
- Browser RTC function – WebRTC component embedded in the web browser with transport, video and voice engines including the media codecs,
- Signaling path – not specified but needed to transfer all session control information,
- Media path – transports the payload like voice or video data.

Currently, web browsers like Google Chrome, Mozilla Firefox and Opera provide these components by default. There are restrictions with regard to other operation systems (Apple's iOS or Microsoft's Windows Phone).

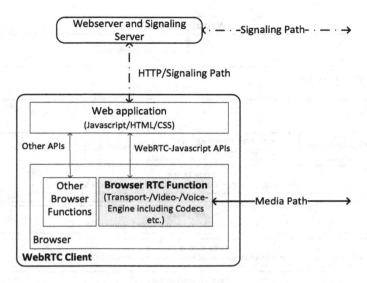

Fig. 2. WebRTC client based on [1]

3.2   Characteristics of Google Chrome Implementation

In our review we focus on the implementation and operation of the Opus codec in a real-world communication scenario – namely using the RTC function of the Google Chrome browser. Our testing environment consists of two x64 processor-based laptops (2.70 GHz clock rate) with OS Windows 7. Usually, the payload data are generated by using a microphone and the computers sound card which processes the A/D converting at a predefined sample rate. In contrast, we pre-generate the test files with a sample rate of 48 kHz and load them to the browser using Javascript functions.

The Opus characteristics and capabilities are described in [2]. We want to find out which functional features of this interactive codec are effectively used – the default values in a Google Chrome WebRTC framework that include the Opus codec control parameters (see also Sect. 2) but furthermore the Opus working mode (CELT/SILK/Hybrid mode) and the sample rate (samples per second/kHz).

The WebRTC framework is based on the source code "libopus" provided by the Xiph.Org foundation [12]. We developed and integrated a logging function into the Opus encoder to measure the Opus control parameters (cf. Sect. 2) which protocols internal values of the encoder state in real time while encoding the audio frames.

The Fig. 3 illustrates how the audio codecs are integrated in the browsers' RTC function framework:

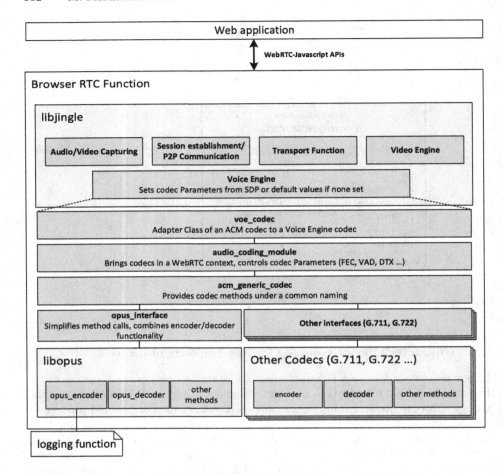

Fig. 3. Implementation of audio codecs in the browsers' RTC function

- *opus_interface* summarizes the functions delivered by Libopus and simplifies function calls. It sets the default values for the frame size and the audio bandwidth – depending on the sampling rate,
- *acm_generic_codec* combines the standardized encoder and decoder method calls to a generic codec class. It sets default values for all codecs (e.g. maximal sample rate 48,000 samples per second) and provides some codec-specific configuration (e.g. frame size calculations),
- *audio_coding_module* brings codec payload data in a WebRTC adequate context by combining it with the Libjingle transport functions,
- *voe_codec* represents a codec class for the voice engine and serves as an adapter between the audio coding module (ACM) notation and the voice engine notation,

– *webrtc_voice_engine* defines codec default parameters or uses those given by session description during the call control procedure using Session Description Protocol (SDP).

4   Results and Discussion

4.1   Runtime Functioning of Opus Codec

By utilizing the implemented logging function, in default the following Opus codec parameters were detected running a WebRTC communication with the Google Chrome browser:

1. Sample rate: 48 kHz,
2. Audio bandwidth: Fullband (FB),
3. Used encoder bit rate: 32 kbit/s,
4. Used channels: 1 (mono),
5. Opus working mode: CELT and Hybrid,
6. Frame duration: 20 ms,
7. Complexity: 9.

Two parameter values define the complexity (based on language C and Libjingle software part): value 5 for Android, iOS or ARM based end devices and value 9 for all others (like laptop or desktop PC). All parameters except for Opus working mode and audio bandwidth can directly be modified by the *Voice Engine* module if requested by the SDP-based session description. The Opus working mode depends on the used encoder bit rate while the bit rate tightly depends on the sample rate. While analyzing the internals of the Opus encoder function, another important encoder_state parameter (*voice_ratio*) – which directly influences the current working mode – can be observed. *Voice_ratio* means the probability (in %) of being a voice signal in the given audio input.

The Fig. 4 shows a concatenated voice/music example which consists of the German utterance "Die roten pfelchen sind fr.." (The little red apples are for..) and a piece of Ska music from "Take one down" (Sounds Like Chicken, 2004). Regarding a dynamically modified working mode, the *voice_ratio* threshold for a switch-over from a voice-optimized mode to a non-voice (music) favored mode is about 25 %. Vice versa, from music to voice mode one can observe a threshold of about 50 %.

4.2   Manipulation of Codec Parameters

Table 1 illustrates the practical results which were achieved by changing the Opus codec parameters effective sample rate and channel count. For various audio bandwidth types the shifting of the operating mode as well as the TOC header value is evident.

It is obvious that the encoder bit rate is doubled when using stereo instead of mono mode. Using the default parameters, the Opus working modes CELT and Hybrid were monitored (see also last line of Table 1). In this context, Opus codec operates conform to its definition (cf. [2]).

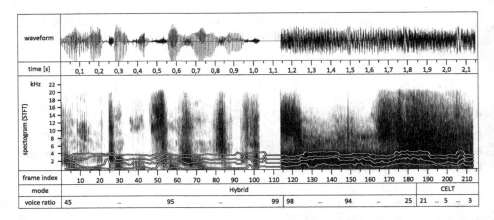

Fig. 4. Seamless switch-over in Opus working mode: audio stream excerpt with voice part left and music part right (frame length 10 ms, spectrogram incl. formant curves)

Table 1. Opus encoder operating mode in dependence of the sample rate.

Sample rate [kHz]	Audio bandwidth	Used encoder bitrate [kbit/s]		TOC header	Operating mode	Parameters
		Mono	Stereo			
8	Narrowband	12	24	1	SILK	Manipulated
12	Mediumband	20	40	5	SILK	Manipulated
16	Wideband	20	40	9	SILK	Manipulated
24	Super-wideband	32	64	13 & 27	Hybrid & CELT	Manipulated
48	Fullband	32	64	15 & 31	Hybrid & CELT	Default

4.3   Audio Performance

To verify the audio performance within the WebRTC involving the specific runtime parameters, we conducted a listening test. Furthermore, we proceeded an instrumental assessment via Perceptual Objective Listening Quality Assessment (POLQA) [5] as a novelty in the WebRTC and Opus context [7]. The POLQA method is standardized for the quality assessment in NB and SWB speech. In addition and as a second novelty, we utilized the tool for the assessment of SWB speech and FB music. Beside speech signals we tested with singing voice and mixed music-voice signals. The corresponding results are discussed in [7].

Compared to the previous Opus experiments, WebRTC framework-coded speech achieves similar POLQA results if we provide natural reference signals: MOS = 4.73 in male and MOS = 4.64 in female samples. A perceptual assessment of FB speech scores up to MOS ≈ 4.8 normally.

5   Conclusion

We surveyed the Opus codec behavior in a real-world scenario of Web-based Real-Time Communication. The given default parameter setting (sample rate of 48 kHz/FB and bit rate of 32 kbit/s) limits the potential range of applications. Otherwise, for high definition audio services like stereo music or audio on demand, the adequate Opus characteristics can be configured by the application developer via changing the session description parameters (SDP) in WebRTC. The codec functioning in the exemplary WebRTC environment of Google Chrome is well-implemented and allows various new audio and speech communication applications in near future. With regard to the resulting audio quality, there is no significant difference compared to the stand-alone performance of Opus.

References

1. Alvestrand, H.: Overview: real time protocols for brower-based applications draft-ietf-rtcweb-overview-11. Internet-Draft. http://tools.ietf.org/id/draft-ietf-rtcweb-overview-11.txt. Accessed August 2014
2. Falin, J., Vos, K., Terriberry, T.: Definition of the Opus audio codec. RFC 6716 (Proposed Standard), September 2012. http://www.ietf.org/rfc/rfc6716.txt
3. Google Inc.: Webrtc, September 2014. http://www.webrtc.org/
4. Hoene, C., Valin, J., Vos, K., Skoglund, J.: Summary of Opus listening test results draft-ietf-codec-results-03. Internet-Draft, May 2013. http://tools.ietf.org/html/draft-ietf-codec-results-03. Accessed April 2015
5. ITU-T: Methods for objective and subjective assessment of speech quality (POLQA): perceptual objective listening quality assessment. REC P.863, International Telecommunication Union (Telecommunication Standardization Sector), September 2014. http://www.itu.int/rec/T-REC-P.863-201409-I/en
6. Jennings, C., Narayanan, A., Burnett, D., Bergkvist, A.: WebRTC 1.0: real-time communication between browsers. W3C Editor's Draft, W3C, March 2015. http://w3c.github.io/webrtc-pc/. Accessed April 2015
7. Jokisch, O., Maruschke, M., Meszaros, M., Iaroshenko, V.: Audio and speech quality survey of the opus codec in web real-time communication, October 2015 (to be published)
8. Vos, K., Jensen, S., Sorensen, K.: SILK speech codec: draft-vos-silk-02. Internet-Draft, September 2010. http://tools.ietf.org/html/draft-vos-silk-02. Accessed April 2015
9. Valin, J.M., Terriberry, T.B., Montgomery, C., Maxwell, G.: A high-quality speech and audio codec with less than 10 ms delay. IEEE Trans. Audio Speech Lang. Process. **18**(1), 58–67 (2010)
10. Valin, J.M., Maxwell, G., Terriberry, T., Vos, K.: High-quality, low-delay music coding in the opus codec. AES Convention, October 2013
11. Valin, J.M., Maxwell, G., Terriberry, T., Vos, K.: Voice coding with opus. AES Convention, October 2013
12. Xiph.Org: libOpus, September 2014. http://www.opus-codec.org/downloads/

Semantic Multilingual Differences of Terminological Definitions Regarding the Concept "Artificial Intelligence"

Rodmonga Potapova and Ksenia Oskina[(✉)]

Institute of Applied and Mathematical Linguistics,
Moscow State Linguistic University, Moscow, Russia
RKPotapova@yandex.ru, ksenia.oskina@gmail.com

Abstract. The current use of information technology in terminography gives rise to a fundamentally new lexicographical paradigm as compared to classical concepts of ordering the semantic constituents of natural language units. This article presents the concept of formalization of semantic representation of lexis on the example of the "Artificial Intelligence" term. An attempt is also made to develop an optimal strategy for the construction of a context-oriented terminological electronic translation dictionary.

Keywords: Lexical semantics · Contrastive linguistics · Corpus-based linguistics · Terminography · Context · Relational database (RDB) · Artificial intelligence · Machine translation (MT)

1 Introduction

At present the development of optimal methods for semantic constituent extraction and fixation comes to the fore as these methods make it possible to solve a variety of applied problems, which arise due to "people's practical activity needs" [10].

"For the moment rule systems for the automatic analysis of the whole sentence structure have been created. However, this analysis is carried out without considering the sense and lexical meaning of separate words < ... > Despite the fact that a number of syntactic problems have already been solved, complex semantic problems remain, which, being settled, would determine the ultimate success of the case" [10]. Thus, the primary objective in solving the problems, which arise during the machine translation (MT) system development as well as during artificial intelligence (AI) component development, is the formal description of the semantic and lexical layer of a natural language. Moreover, the formalization of semantics will help solve such a wide-spread problem in the area of Natural Language Processing as ambiguousness which acts through different language levels.

A number of attempts have been undertaken in order to represent and process the semantic level in machine translation system development. In particular,

© Springer International Publishing Switzerland 2015
A. Ronzhin et al. (Eds.): SPECOM 2015, LNAI 9319, pp. 356–363, 2015.
DOI: 10.1007/978-3-319-23132-7_44

D. Kan in his work points out that a word's semantics is required for a success-ful final resolution of a sentence meaning. He solves the problem of semantics representation by building a model of translation on the basis of a phrase trans-lation dictionary, which is made up of phrase pairs generated from a parallel corpus [4]. The CLT-ROM (Cross-Language Transformation based on Recur-sive Object Model) method has also been proposed, where a natural language sentence is transformed into a source ROM diagram and a corresponding tar-get ROM diagram in another language is generated by a transformation algo-rithm [14]. These examples illustrate multiple attempts to analyze the semantic level in Natural Language Processing. They do have their strong points. How-ever, the concept, presented in this article, is likely to be more effective, though complicated to implement.

2 Method and Procedure

The statement that determination of adequacy/ inadequacy of language expres-sions depends only on the described reality and the speaker's actual knowledge and is not connected with any specific language [6], turns to be misleading. One can talk about the absence of connection between the extralinguistic reality and a specific language for as long as one refers to some material object, whereas abstraction can be expressed only due to the word meanings, predetermined by a particular language. Drawing upon the ideas of W. von Humboldt, E. Coseriu presumes that there cannot be found any word in one nation's language which would entirely correspond to some word of another nation's language [2]. Conse-quently, when one tries to formalize the semantic representation of some language or to convey the meaning of one term by the means of another language, the analysis of word meanings on the domain of lexis becomes the task of prime importance. It should be noted that the term "lexis" is used in linguistics to refer to the vocabulary of a language and it is used adjectivally in a variety of technical phrases [3].

E. Coseriu distinguishes three sides of a "content" notion which include "meaning", "designation" and "sense". Meaning (according to E. Coseriu) is lin-guistic "content", which is created in a particular language on the base of gram-matical and vocabulary oppositions which exist there. Designation is an extralin-guistic "reference" regarding an "object" of extralinguistic reality (a different one in every particular case) or to extralinguistic reality itself. Sense in its turn is determined as some particular cultural frameworks which can be expressed both by linguistic (question, answer, greeting, compellation) and extralinguistic (extralinguistic knowledge of cultural frameworks) means [2].

The foregoing is illustrated by E. Coseriu using the German preposition "mit". In German language the lexical unit "mit x" (assuming that x = "Messer") has at least two meanings: the meaning of co-presence and the instru-mental meaning.

According to E. Coseriu "The designation in every particular case is considered to be uncertain and is specified only in the context or in a certain situation" [2].

The following two examples illustrate the designation of the presented above meanings of the lexical unit "mit":

1. Der Mann mit dem Messer ist hier (the meaning of co-presence).
2. Er hat Papier mit dem Messer geschnitten (instrumental meaning).

Thus, it can be seen that the context potentially complements the meaning, i.e. certain elements of meanings may acquire different shades of meaning, which should also be taken into consideration when developing MT systems as well as working upon AI components. Therefore, the semantic unit can be formed only in the context [8].

To optimize the operation of MT systems it is essential to compile a multilingual context-oriented translation dictionary specialized in the analysis of equivalent meanings. This article would cover the basics of the concept, which is supposed to optimize the compilation of such a dictionary considering Russian, English and German languages.

A collection of domain-specific terms can be represented by three sets: X, Y and Z, where X represents a set of terms and their meanings in Russian, Y represents a set of terms and their meanings in English, while Z represents a set of terms and their meanings in German (the idea belongs to R.K. Potapova).

The union of these sets, represented in the Euler-Venn diagram (Fig. 1), illustrates a set of domain-specific terms together with their meanings in languages x, y and z.

The union of three sets $X \cup Y \cup Z$ forms a set of all domain-specific terms. The intersection of the three sets $X \cap Y \cap Z$ forms a set of semantic invariants Inv of all the terms in the three languages, while the symmetric difference of the three sets $(X \vartriangle Y) \vartriangle Z$ describes the set of "variforms"[1] of the terms. The set $XY = (X \cap Y) \vartriangle Inv$ represents the invariant of terms typical for the languages x and y. Similarly, $XZ = (X \cap Z) \vartriangle Inv$ and $YZ = (Y \cap Z) \vartriangle Inv$.

Thus, the invariant of meanings forms a set of tuples, which turn to be the subsets of the Cartesian product of four domains. These domains include such

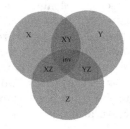

Fig. 1. Euler-Venn diagram illustrating the relations among the sets of terms and their meanings in three languages

---

[1] The notion of "variform" has been proposed in this article by R.K. Potapova to determine the scope of meanings different from the invariant of the term.

Table 1. Meanings of the "Artificial Intelligence" term in Russian, English and German languages.

	Language x (x = Russian) **The number of meanings (M) n = 6**
M_{x1}	Совокупность средств, обеспечивающих диалог между пользователем и технической системой, например компьютером.
M_{x2}	Совокупность некоторых свойств машины, обеспечиваемых её структурным оборудование, к которому относится и внутреннее матобеспечение. Эти свойства следующие: восприимчивость к языкам программирования высокого уровня; набор сведений (знаний), способность к его пополнению, к обучению и оперированию знаниями; способность к организации вычислительного процесса и взаимодействия с пользователями; эффективность способов обработки информации, определяемая аппаратными и микропрограммными средствами.
M_{x3}	Научное направление, в рамках которого ставятся и решаются задачи технического или программного моделирования тех видов человеческой деятельности, которые традиционно считаются интеллектуальными.
M_{x4}	Искусственно созданная система, проявляющая свойство интеллекта, т.е. способность выбора и принятия целесообразного решения при большом многообразии целей на основе ранее полученного опыта или рационального анализа внешних воздействий.
M_{x5}	Способность машинной программы выполнять функции, обычно считающиеся элементами интеллектуальной деятельности человека.
M_{x6}	Часть информатики, занимающаяся разработкой методов решения задач, для которых не удаётся разработать формальных алгоритмов, таких как понимание естественного языка, обучение, доказательство теорем, распознавание изображений.
	Language y (y = English) **n = 2**
M_{y1}	A part of computer science, aimed at exploring the range of tasks over which computers can be programmed to behave intelligently.
M_{y2}	A part of the new field of cognitive science, aimed at programs that simulate the actual processes that human beings use in their intelligent behaviour.
	Language z (z = German) **n = 1**
M_{z1}	Ein Teilgebiet der Informatik, das Intelligenz erfordernde Tätigkeiten des Menschen wie das Verstehen natürlicher Sprache, das Sehen und Erkennen von Gegenständen, das Planen von Handlungsfolgen, das Entwerfen technischer Systeme oder das Erstellen medizinischer und technischer Diagnosen analysiert.

attributes as "Language", "Object domain", "Term", "Meaning" and the scope of their meanings.

As an illustration of the foregoing the "Artificial Intelligence" term can be regarded in three languages: Russian [1], English [12] and German [5], the meanings of which are presented in Table 1.

These meanings have been analyzed manually and automatically with the aim of determining the invariant of the term.

In order to manually determine the invariant of the term, the meanings have been broken down into components (C). The results of the manual analysis are included in Table 2.

The second component of the invariant in German is italicized in order to show the absence of this component in the dictionary meaning of the term.

Along with this, the meanings of this term have been analyzed by software-based methods. The analysis has been conducted using the Perl scripting language, whereby the meanings of the terms in Russian, English and German have been compared pairwise. The meanings in a language other than English have

Table 2. Results of the manual analysis of the term's meanings in three languages.

M_{x6} C_{1mx6}	Часть информатики,	M_{y1} C_{1my1}	A part of computer science,	M_{z1} C_{1mz1}	Ein Teilgebiet der Informatik,
M_{x3} C_{2mx3}	в рамках которого ставятся и решаются задачи технического или программного моделирования тех видов человеческой деятельности, которые традиционно считаются интеллектуальными.	M_{y1} C_{2my1}	aimed at exploring the range of tasks over which computers can be programmed to behave intelligently.		*das auf die Aufgabenlösung gezielt wird, den Computer auf solche Weise zu programmieren, dass er sich intelligent verhalten könnte.*

been previously transferred into it using the Google translation service https://translate.google.ru/. After that the procedure of lemmatization has been carried out. The obtained lexemes have been compared to each other. Equal lexemes for two languages and their number have been retrieved. The results of the automatic analysis are presented in Fig. 2 (the results are presented only for the significant words) (Fig. 2).

The scope of meanings of the "Arificial Intelligence" term can be represented schematically. T_l stands for a term in language l, M_l is the meaning of the term in language l, C_l is the component of the meaning of the term in language l and, finally, Res_{invl} is the resulting invariant of the term in language l, which can consist of components of different meanings of the same term (Table 3).

The assignment of values to these variables would make it possible to visualize the structure of the meanings of the "Artificial Intelligence" term.

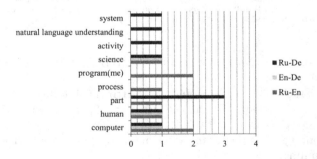

Fig. 2. Results of the automatic analysis of the term's meanings in three languages

Table 3. Schematic representation of the meanings of the "Artificial Intelligence" term.

T_x								T_y		T_z	
M_{x1}	M_{x2}	M_{x3}		M_{x4}	M_{x5}	M_{x6}		M_{y1}	M_{y2}	M_{z1}	
		C_{1mx3}	C_{2mx3}			C_{1mx6}	C_{2mx6}			C_{1mz1}	(C_{2mz1})
Res_{invx}								M_{y1}		Res_{invz}	

3   Results and Discussion

The invariant is formed by adding up three components: Res_{invx} (as a result of the sum of components C_{2mx3} and C_{1mx6}) + M_{y1} + Res_{invz} (as a result of the sum of component C_{1mz1} and the second component C_{2mz1} of the meaning, which is absent in German language). Thus, due to breaking down the meanings into components, the invariant can be singled out, which would characterize the term in the above languages.

The "Artificial Intelligence" term contains the following semantic components:

1. part of computer science;
2. analyzes the human intellectual activity;
3. simulates human intelligence through the use of computers.

The structure of this term can be represented as a tree graph, whose vertices correspond to the invariant and to "variforms" of the term while the edges marked in bold represent the equivalence of the term's meanings in the above languages (Fig. 3). Correspondingly, the resulting meaning (equivalent to the meaning M_{y1}) in language x Res_{invx} consists of a conjunction of the components of the meanings M_{x3} and M_{x6}. In a similar way for the language z, Res_{invz} consists of conjunction of the components of the meaning M_{z1}. However, it should be borne in mind that the component C_{2mz1} is absent in the definition of the term. Therefore, the graph edge, leading to this component, is indicated by a dotted line (Fig. 3). Thus, the presented graph reflects the cognitive mechanism of semantic information processing in neural networks.

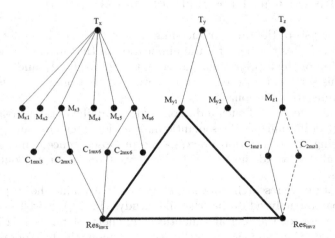

Fig. 3. Representational schema of the "Artificial Intelligence" term in the form of a tree graph

Furthermore, proceeding from the graph, it can be seen that "variform" has no analogues in the languages under examination. Consequently, the meaning, which some "variform" carries, should be conveyed by means of the target language, i.e. if language z is missing meaning M_x, this meaning cannot be expressed by the term T_z, since there is no correlation between this meaning and the term itself.

Thus, the comparative analysis of the meanings of the "Artificial Intelligence" term in languages x, y and z has revealed that the a priori equivalence of the initial term demolishes. The hypothesis about the need to analyze the terms' meanings makes it possible to eliminate this vulnerability and to convey the meaning from the source language into the target one the most accurate way possible.

Moreover, it should be taken into account that while analyzing the terms' meanings, one should consider the context of usage of the terms. According to E. Coseriu "In the course of translation the question is not about the correspondences among the meanings (as functional units of certain languages), but always among the way they are used" [2]. The study of the context was made possible due to formation and active development of corpus linguistics: "Corpus linguistics deals with language as a social phenomenon. The meaning is manifested in words and texts. Corpus linguistics is not interested in meanings of isolated words outside their relevant contexts. The quote provides more information than the dictionary definition of a word" [7]. To put it differently, corpus linguistics makes it possible to move on to the next stage of term analysis and by considering the dictionary definition of the term to describe its semantic constituent the fullest way possible.

4   Conclusion and Prospects of Investigation

Thus, the analysis of the range of meanings of the "Artificial Intelligence" term clearly demonstrates the need for the application of the current concept due to the demolition of the a priori equivalence of the terms T_x, T_y and T_z. Vulnerabilities of this sort confirm the need to create a context-oriented terminological electronic translation dictionary.

The defining feature of such a dictionary is its applied orientation. The current strategy of formalizing the semantic information opens up new possibilities for automating the translation process. The proposed concept makes it possible to minimize or avoid the retrieval of irrelevant results on the output of the MT systems.

As part of future research work it is supposed to examine the corpora (which have been partly analyzed during the pilot study [15–18]) as well as to provide a full description of the lexical-semantic component of terms relating to the Information and Communication Technologies domain (the ICT domain) taking into account contextual nuances in relation to texts, whose implementation in an MT system would increase the percentage of semantically correct translation.

Acknowledgments. The survey is being carried out with the support of the Ministry of Education and Science of Russian Federation in the framework of the project

№34.1254.2014K at Moscow State Linguistic University (the project is implemented under the supervision of R.K. Potapova).

References

1. Averkin, A.N., Gaaze-Rapoport, M.G., Pospelov, D.A.: Tolkovyiy slovar po iskusstvennomu intellektu. Radio i svyaz, Moskva (1992). (in Russ.)
2. Coseriu, E.: Kontrastivnaya lingvistika i perevod: ih sootnoshenie. In: Novoe v zarubezhnoy lingvistike, vol. 25, pp. 63–81. Progress Publishers, Moskva (1989). (in Russ.)
3. Crystal, D.A.: Dictionary of Linguistics and Phonetics. Blackwell Publishing, USA (2008)
4. Kan, D.: Method for an automatic generation of a semantic-level contextual translational dictionary. In: ICSOFT 2011 Proceedings of the 6th International Conference on Software and Data Technologies, vol. 2, pp. 415–418. Seville, Spain (2011)
5. Koble, W.: Künstliche Intelligenz : engl.-dt., dt.-engl.; mit je etwa 6500 Wortstellen. Verl. Technik, Berlin (1990)
6. Melchuk, I.A.: Opyit teorii lingvisticheskih modeley. Yazyiki russkoy kulturyi, Moskva (1999). (in Russ.)
7. Potapova, R.K.: Osnovnyie tendentsii razvitiya mnogoyazyichnoy korpusnoy lingvistiki (Part 1). Rechevyie tehnologii **2**, 92–114 (2009). (in Russ.)
8. Potapova, R.K.: Osnovnyie tendentsii razvitiya mnogoyazyichnoy korpusnoy lingvistiki (Part 2). Rechevyie tehnologii **3**, 93–112 (2009). (in Russ.)
9. Potapova, R.K.: Phonetische Datenbasen als Grundlage der modernen Sprechtechnologien. In: Bose, I., Neuber, B. (eds.) Sprechwissenschaft: Bestand, Prognose, Perspective, vol. 51, pp. 191–198. Peter Lang, Frankfurt Am Main (2014)
10. Potapova, R.K.: Rech: kommunikatsiya, informatsiya, kibernetika. Knizhnyiy dom "Librokom", Moskva (2010) (in Russ.)
11. Potapova, R.K., Potapov, V.V.: Pragmaphonetische Typologie der sprechsprachlichen Wissenschaftsstilgenres (Russisch). In: Doleschal, U., Mertlitsch, C., Rheindorf, M., Wetschanow, K. (eds.) Writing across the Curriculum at work: Theorie, Praxis und Analyse, pp. 281–291. LIT Verlag, Wien (2013)
12. Shapiro, S.C.: Encyclopedia of Artificial Intelligence. Wiley-Interscience Publication, Buffalo (1990)
13. Tumanov, V.E.: Osnovyi proektirovaniya relyatsionnyih baz dannyih. Internet-Universitet Informatsionnyih Tehnologiy, Moskva (2012). (in Russ.)
14. Wen, K., Tan, S., Wang, J., Li, R., Gao, Y.: A model based transformation paradigm for cross-language collaborations. Adv. Eng. Inform. **27**(1), 27–37 (2013)
15. Russian National Corpus. http://www.ruscorpora.ru/
16. British National Corpus. http://www.natcorp.ox.ac.uk/
17. Corpus of Contemporary American English. http://corpus.byu.edu/coca/
18. DWDS Korpora. http://www.dwds.de/ressourcen/korpora/

SNR Estimation Based on Adaptive Signal Decomposition for Quality Evaluation of Speech Enhancement Algorithms

Sergei Aleinik[1]([✉]) and Mikhail Stolbov[1,2]

[1] ITMO University,
49 Kronverkskiy Pr., St. Petersburg 197101, Russia
[2] Speech Technology Center,
Krasutskogo-4, St. Petersburg 196084, Russia
{aleinik,stolbov}@speechpro.com

Abstract. This paper presents a new method for estimating signal-to-noise ratio based on adaptive signal decomposition. Statistical simulation shows that the proposed method has lower variance and bias than the known signal-to-noise ratio measures. We discuss the parameters and characteristics of the proposed method and its practical implementation.

Keywords: Signal-to-noise ratio · SNR · Speech processing · Speech enhancement

1 Introduction

Signal-to-noise ratio (SNR) is one of the objective measures of speech quality. SNR is widely used for efficacy estimation of noise reduction algorithms (NRA) [9,10] and other signal processing applications [5–8,12,13,16]. The evaluation procedure includes the creation of a test mixture of speech signal + noise with a predetermined SNR value ("input SNR"), its processing by the NRA and the subsequent evaluation of the SNR of the output mixture ("output SNR"). Input SNR is easy to calculate [7], since the signal and noise are separate at the NRA input during simulation. Output SNR estimation is more difficult. There are two types of SNR estimation: "output based" estimation and "input-output based" estimation [9,10,13]. Output based estimation is based on blind output signal and noise power estimation when input processes are unknown; input-output based estimation uses the known input signal and noise [5,6,8]. Both methods have their own restrictions.

In this paper we propose a new input-output based method of SNR estimation that has better characteristics (lower bias) than the known signal-to-noise ratio measures.

2 Problem Formulation

The classic [7,10] definition of signal-to-noise ratio is: "The SNR is defined as signal power divided by noise power". Hence, if the signal $s(i)$ has the power P_s

© Springer International Publishing Switzerland 2015
A. Ronzhin et al. (Eds.): SPECOM 2015, LNAI 9319, pp. 364–371, 2015.
DOI: 10.1007/978-3-319-23132-7_45

and the noise $n(i)$ has the power P_n, SNR in logarithmic (dB) scale is written as

$$SNR = 10\log_{10}\left(\frac{P_s}{P_n}\right).\tag{1}$$

In real life, P_s and P_n are often unknown and replaced with their estimates, so (1) for the zero mean of $s(i)$ and $n(i)$ (often the true condition) can be rewritten as

$$SNR = 10\log_{10}\left(\frac{\sum_{i=0}^{N-1}s^2(i)}{\sum_{i=0}^{N-1}n^2(i)}\right),\tag{2}$$

where N is the number of samples. If (2) is calculated using the total number of samples in the analyzed data, the corresponding SNR is usually called the "global SNR" [12]. In speech processing, in order to account for the non-stationary nature of speech, so-called "segmental SNR" (SSNR) is used. In this case (2) is calculated using short (normally 15–30 ms) segments of signal and noise data, with the following averaging of the results [7, 13]:

$$SSNR_1 = \frac{1}{K}\sum_{i=0}^{K-1}\left(10\log_{10}\frac{\sum_{j=0}^{M-1}s_i^2(j)}{\sum_{j=0}^{M-1}n_i^2(j)}\right),\tag{3}$$

$$SSNR_2 = 10\log_{10}\left(\frac{1}{K}\sum_{i=0}^{K-1}\frac{\sum_{j=0}^{M-1}s_i^2(j)}{\sum_{j=0}^{M-1}n_i^2(j)}\right),\tag{4}$$

where K and i are the number of segments and the segment index; M and j are the segment length and the time index in the segment. The subscripts "1" and "2" indicate the differences in the order of logarithm and summation and are discussed in [7]. Input SNR is calculated as follows. First, speech segments (frames) and pauses of $s(i)$ are marked using any of the known voice activity detectors (VAD). Then (2), (3) or (4) are calculated using the speech frames of $s(i)$ and the corresponding frames of noise $n(i)$.

Now let us suppose that our input test dataset includes the zero-mean speech signal $s_{inp}(i)$ and the zero-mean noise $n_{inp}(i)$, $i = 0, N-1$ (signal and noise are assumed to be independent). To simulate a realistic situation we create the "noised speech" mixture $x(i)$ at the input of the NRA:

$$x(i) = s_{inp}(i) + n_{inp}(i).\tag{5}$$

Let $y(i)$ denote the output signal of the NRA: $y(i) = NRA\{x(i)\}$. In general, $y(i)$ can be divided into two types of segments: the first is the segments where only processed noise $n_{out}(i)$ is present (they correspond to the pause frames in $s_{inp}(i)$). The second is the segments where the processed mixture of signal + noise is present. So we have "pure processed noise" but we have no "pure processed signal" $s_{out}(i)$ to use (2–4) directly. There are two common estimations of SNR^{out} in this case. In the first SNR^{out} is evaluated as [12].

$$SNR_1^{out} = 10 \log_{10} \left(\frac{\frac{1}{L_{n+s}} \sum_{i=0}^{L_{n+s}-1} y^2(i)}{\frac{1}{L_n} \sum_{j=0}^{L_n-1} n_{out}^2(j)} - 1 \right), \tag{6}$$

where L_n is the number of samples in $y(i)$ frames where only $n_{out}(i)$ is present; L_{n+s} is the number of samples in $y(i)$ where the processed mixture is present.

The second estimation of SNR^{out} [5,6,8] is based on the assumption that the processing algorithm does not change the speech signal. In this case we can calculate $n_{out}(i)$ as the difference between the input speech and the output mixture. So it is possible to estimate the output SNR using the corresponding speech frames directly as

$$SNR_2^{out} = 10 \log_{10} \frac{\sum_{i=0}^{N-1} s_{inp}^2(i)}{\sum_{i=0}^{N-1} (s_{inp}(i) - y(i))^2}. \tag{7}$$

Both Eqs. (6) and (7) can be easily transformed to the "segmental" modification (see [10] for (6) and [5,6] for (7)). We also note that (7) requires precise (up to a single sample) alignment of input speech and the output mixture.

Both Eqs. (6) and (7) give adequate results when NRA does not change the speech signal and there is no mutual interference of $s_{inp}(i)$ and $n_{inp}(i)$ during the enhancement process. But in real life this assumption is not correct, especially when adaptive or nonlinear NRAs are used. It is known, for example, that the spectral subtraction method leads to nonlinear speech distortion and additional music noise [11,15] in $y(i)$, which is not taken into account in (6–7). In [2] it is claimed that microphone array (MA) postprocessing algorithms lead to the fact that SNR gain depends on the input SNR, i.e. noise power estimation using only noise frames of $y(i)$ as in (6) is also incorrect. In [4,14] it is reported that Zelinski postfiltering as well as the Multichannel alignment method in MAs leads to output speech signal attenuation. Consequently, the denominator is no longer equal to the estimated noise power, and (7) gives a shifted value.

3   The Proposed Method

In this paper we propose a novel method that gives more stable and adequate SNR estimates. The idea of the method is based on a preliminary separation of output mixture $y(i)$ into two components: $s_{out}(i)$, corresponding to the processed speech, and $n_{out}(i)$, corresponding to the processed noise. Such separation can be performed by an adaptive filter (AF). Then the output SNR is calculated using Eqs. (2–4) and these components as $s(i)$ and $n(i)$.

The main two steps in the proposed method are: (1) input speech signal and noise creation; (2) adaptive filter and adaptation algorithm selection.

We propose to construct a test clean speech signal that includes speech frames and pauses of the same length, connected sequentially: speech frame, pause, speech frame, pause, etc. (we suggest choosing the frame length equal to several seconds). The power of every frame has to be normalized so that their powers are equal. The input noise power must be equal to speech power. Hence, the input mixture with the desired SNR^{inp} can be constructed as

$$x(i) = s_{inp}(i) + \beta n_{inp}(i); \quad \text{where} \quad \beta = \left(10^{(SNR^{inp}/10)}\right)^{-1/2}. \tag{8}$$

At the second step we used AF [17] to separate the output mixture $y(i)$ that can be formally written as

$$y(i) = s_{out}(i) + \Delta s_{out}(i) + n_{out}(i) + \Delta n_{out}(i), \tag{9}$$

where: $s_{out}(i)$ is correlated with the $s_{inp}(i)$ speech component (enhanced speech); $\Delta s_{out}(i)$ is uncorrelated with the $s_{inp}(i)$ "distorted speech" component; $n_{out}(i)$ is correlated with the $n_{inp}(i)$ noise component (suppressed noise); $\Delta n_{out}(i)$ is uncorrelated with the $n_{inp}(i)$ noise component (musical noise, etc.).

For the output mixture separation we used a modified adaptive filter with normalized least-mean squares (NLMS) adaptation [3,17]. The modification is that we add the norm of the main signal in the denominator as follows:

$$W(k+1) = W(k) + \frac{\mu}{\delta + 0.5(\|Y(k)\|^2 + \|D(k)\|^2)} X(k)\xi(k), \tag{10}$$

where $W(k)$ is the filter coefficient vector; k is the step number; μ is the adaptation coefficient; $Y(k)$ is the reference input signal vector; $\xi(k)$ is the so-called prediction error; δ is the small regularization constant; $\|Y(k)\|^2$ and $\|D(k)\|^2$ are the norms of the reference and the main signal vectors, respectively. Our experiments showed that (10) converges faster than the "classic" NLMS algorithm (without the main signal norm in the denominator) when the input signals are highly non-stationary processes. The separation scheme is given in Fig. 1.

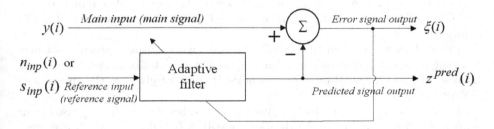

Fig. 1. Flow-chart of the adaptive separation.

So if we set the main signal as $y(i)$ and the reference signal as $n_{inp}(i)$ or $s_{inp}(i)$ we will have the output signals showed in Table 1.

The signals $s_{out}(i)$ and $n_{out}(i)$, obtained at the predicted signal output of AF, are our desired separated estimates of the speech and noise, processed by the NRA. Using these signals and Eqs. (2–4) we can estimate the output SNR.

Table 1. Output error and predicted signals as functions of reference signal

Reference signal	Error signal output	Predicted signal output
$n_{inp}(i)$	$s_{out}(i) + \Delta s_{out}(i) + \Delta n_{out}(i)$	$n_{out}(i)$
$s_{inp}(i)$	$n_{out}(i) + \Delta s_{out}(i) + \Delta n_{out}(i)$	$s_{out}(i)$

4   Experiments and Results

For the experiments we generated a 10-min length test clear speech signal, where the length of the speech and pause frames was 5 s and the sampling rate was 16 kHz. The AF parameters were as follows: the filter length was 512 samples; $\mu = 0.05$; $\delta = 1$. When the reference signal was clear speech, adaptation was provided only for the speech frames of the reference signal. The first two seconds of every frame of the output signals were omitted to avoid AF transient processes. The input signals, the output NRA signals and the output AF signals were manually aligned.

In the first experiments we calculated the distribution densities of five SNR^{out} estimates: (6); (7); two segmental modifications of (7): "the sum of logarithms" and "logarithm of the sum" (designated below as "sum(log)" and "log(sum)", respectively and corresponding to (3) and (4)); and our method using (2). All calculations (except (6)) were provided for the $s_{out}(i)$ and $n_{out}(i)$ frames that correspond to the speech frames of $s_{inp}(i)$. The number of trials was 10000. The simulation results for the artificial $y(i)$ are shown in Figs. 2 and 3. Figure 2 demonstrates the result for $SNR^{inp} = 0$ dB when noise was suppressed by 10 dB but there was also output speech suppression by 1 dB, i.e. the theoretical $SNR^{out} = 9$ dB. Eq. (6) as well as the proposed method give adequate results: mean values are equal to the theoretical values.

In contrast, all the methods that have subtraction in the denominators, i.e. (7), (7) sum(log) and (7) log(sum) are shifted down. The worst method is (7) sum(log).

Figure 3 shows the result for $SNR^{inp} = 0$ dB when output speech was equal to input speech, but the output noise suppression was 10 dB on the "pure noise frames" of $y(i)$ and 6 dB on "speech+noise frames" of $y(i)$, i.e. the theoretical $SNR^{out} = 6$ dB.

In this case (6) is dramatically shifted upwards, because of the increase of the numerator due to the noise; (7) sum(log) is still shifted down; (7), (7) log(sum) and the proposed method give adequate values.

Figure 4 depicts the result of the second experiment: real NRA, provided by Adobe Audition CS 5.5 [1] software package testing. This NRA is spectral subtraction with a preliminary captured noise print (we choose the following parameters: "Noise reduction" = 100 %; "Reduce by" = 10 dB). In this NRA we discovered the "output signal attenuation" as well as "noise increasing in speech frames" phenomenon. Input SNR varied from −18 to 18 dB, and the SNR gain:

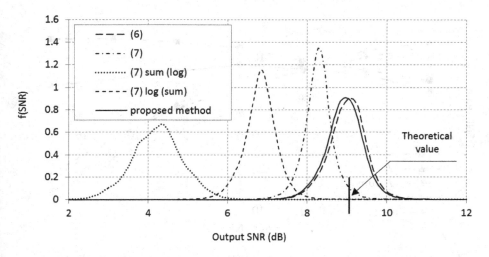

Fig. 2. Output SNR distributions for "additional output speech suppression" test.

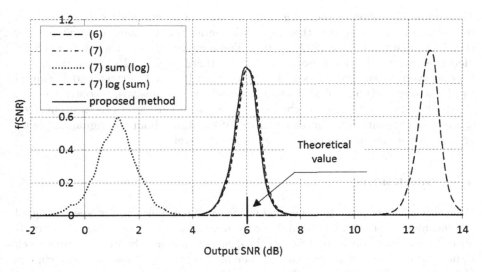

Fig. 3. Output SNR distributions for "output noise increases in the speech frames" test.

$SNRgain = SNR^{out} - SNR^{inp}$ was calculated using the total 6 min of data (10 min of signals minus transient processes).

Figure 4 shows that the most straight curve is the SNR gain for the proposed method. The SNR gain calculated using (6) is shifted upwards for high input SNR. This behavior, in our opinion, is caused by the increase of noise in speech frames (since this method is sensitive to this phenomenon) which is especially noticeable for high input SNR.

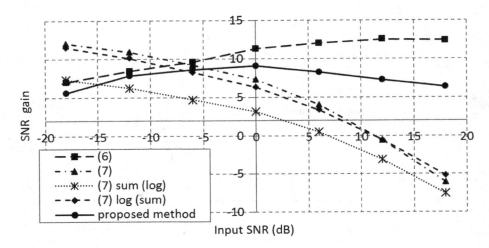

Fig. 4. SNR gain as function on input SNR. Spectral subtraction method test.

Completely different behavior is demonstrated by the SNR gain curves cor-responding to the methods that use "subtraction in the denominator", i.e. for the (7), (7) sum(log) and (7) log(sum). These curves go down when input SNR increases. Such behavior is noted in many articles (e.g. [11,15]) on various top-ics and even considered normal. In our opinion it is not correct and is caused by the wrong methods of SNR estimation which are sensitive to output target signal attenuation. In fact, on the basis of physical considerations, if input SNR is large, the algorithm has more accurate information about the signal and noise and, therefore, should suppress noise more effectively.

5   Conclusions

We propose a method for the evaluation of NRA efficacy for speech signal enhancement that can be used in different areas of speech processing. This input-output based method is used for artificial mixtures when the input clean speech signal and the input noise are known. The method takes into account the change of speech signal as well as the change of noise in the speech+noise segments dur-ing the enhancement process.

The proposed method is based on the decomposition of the NRA output signal into two components, one of which is correlated with the input speech, and the other with the input noise. This decomposition is based on the use of a two-channel adaptive noise canceller. We also propose a method for creating input test signals with different values of SNR.

Adaptation of the method for multichannel NRA used in microphone array processing is a task for future work.

Acknowledgements. This work was financially supported by the Ministry of Education and Science of the Russian Federation, contract 14.575.21.0033 (RFMEFI57514X0033), and by the Government of the Russian Federation, Grant 074-U01.

References

1. Adobe audition. https://creative.adobe.com/products/audition
2. Abad, A., Hernando, J.: Speech enhancement and recognition by integrating adaptive beamforming and wiener filtering. In: INTERSPEECH, pp. 2657–2660
3. Bitzer, J., Brandt, M.: Speech enhancement by adaptive noise cancellation: problems, algorithms, and limits. In: Audio Engineering Society Conference: 39th International Conference: Audio Forensics: Practices and Challenges. Audio Engineering Society (2010)
4. Borisovich, S.M., Vladimirovich, A.S.: Improvement of microphone array characteristics for speech capturing. Modern Appl. Sci. **9**(6), p. 310 (2015)
5. Grundlehner, B., Lecocq, J., Balan, R., Rosca, J.: Performance assessment method for speech enhancement systems. In: Proceedings of 1st Annual IEEE BENELUX/DSP Valley Signal Process Symposium (2005)
6. Hansen, J.H., Pellom, B.L.: An effective quality evaluation protocol for speech enhancement algorithms. In: ICSLP, vol. 7, pp. 2819–2822. Citeseer (1998)
7. Kieser, R., Reynisson, P., Mulligan, T.J.: Definition of signal-to-noise ratio and its critical role in split-beam measurements. ICES J. Marine Sci.: J. du Conseil **62**(1), 123–130 (2005)
8. Kondo, K.: Subjective Quality Measurement of Speech: Its Evaluation, Estimation and Applications. Springer, Heidelberg (2012)
9. Martin, R.: An efficient algorithm to estimate the instantaneous snr of speech signals. Eurospeech. **93**, 1093–1096 (1993)
10. Mattila, V.: Objective measures for the characterization of the basic functioning of noise suppression algorithms. In: Proceedings of Online Workshop Measurement Speech Audio Quality Networks (2003)
11. Nomura, Y., Lu, J., Sekiya, H., Yahagi, T.: Spectral subtraction based on speech/noise-dominant classification. In: International Workshop on Acoustic Echo and Noise Control (IWAENC2003), pp. 127–130 (2003)
12. Plapous, C., Marro, C., Scalart, P.: Improved signal-to-noise ratio estimation for speech enhancement. IEEE Transact. Audio Speech Lang. Process. **14**(6), 2098–2108 (2006)
13. Stolbov, M.: Algorithm of signal-to-noise estimation of speech signals. Izvestiya VUZ. Proborostroenye **6**(82), 67–72 (2012)
14. Stolbov, M., Aleinik, S.: Speech enhancement with microphone array using frequency-domain alignment technique. In: Audio Engineering Society Conference: 54th International Conference: Audio Forensics. Audio Engineering Society (2014)
15. Vaseghi, S.: Advanced Digital Signal Processing and Noise Reduction, 2nd edn. Wiley, Chichester (2000)
16. Vondrášek, M., Pollak, P.: Methods for speech snr estimation: evaluation tool and analysis of vad dependency. Radioengineering **14**(1), 6–11 (2005)
17. Widrow, B., Stearns, S.D.: Adaptive signal processing, vol. 1, p. 491. Prentice-Hall Inc., Englewood Cliffs (1985)

Sociolinguistic Factors in Text-Based Sentence Boundary Detection

Anton Stepikhov[✉]

The Russian Language Department, St. Petersburg State University,
11 Universitetskaya emb., 199034 St. Petersburg, Russia
a.stepikhov@spbu.ru

Abstract. The paper explores the correlation between perception of spontaneous speech based on textual information and original speech in sound recording. We investigate factors which may affect the extent of a reader's 'guesstimate' of prosodic characteristics of the original speech. To explore a reader's prosodic competence, we focused on pause as the most prominent cue of prosodic boundaries and performed statistical analysis to find out, on the one hand, whether there is a correlation between an annotator's estimation of a sentence end and a real pause in these positions and, on the other hand, if the type of text and sociolinguistic characteristics of a speaker influence this estimation.

Keywords: Sentence boundary detection · Segmentation · Pause · Annotation · Spontaneous speech · Unscripted speech · Sociolinguistics · Russian

1 Introduction

Nowadays, both linguistics and natural language processing use expert manual annotation to define sentence boundaries in spontaneous speech which in contrast to written texts does not contain any evident information about the beginning and the end of a sentence. This method may be applied to both recordings of unscripted speech and its transcripts or transcripts only, i.e. an expert may draw upon prosodic and textual information or upon textual information exclusively [1,2]. The latter case raises the question of the correlation between prosodic annotation based on speech recording and annotation based on textual information only.

In our studies on Russian spontaneous speech, we earlier argued that text-based sentence boundaries reflected segmentation in the inner speech of the annotator while she or he was reading the transcription [3]. In this case a reader's prosodic competence helps to compensate for the lack of information about a speaker's intonation, thus allowing the reader to feel the rhythm and melody of sentences without hearing the actual speech [4]. In the present study, we try to verify this assumption and to define whether the type of text and sociolinguistic factors such as a speaker's age, gender and profession have any effect on the extent of an annotator's estimation of the prosodic characteristics of the original speech.

© Springer International Publishing Switzerland 2015
A. Ronzhin et al. (Eds.): SPECOM 2015, LNAI 9319, pp. 372–380, 2015.
DOI: 10.1007/978-3-319-23132-7_46

Traditionally, sentence boundaries in speech are associated with pause [5] which is one of the acoustic boundary marks both in Russian and many other languages, e.g. Swedish, English, European Portuguese, French, Finnish, Thai [5–7]. Thus, to explore the reader's prosodic competence, we focused on pause as the most prominent (though not the only) cue of prosodic boundaries. For the analysis, we used the corpus of Russian spontaneous monologue described in [8] and compared two types of annotation: expert manual annotation of unscripted speech based on textual information, and prosodic annotation. Based on these data, we performed statistical analysis to find out, on the one hand, whether there is a correlation between annotator's estimation of a sentence end and a real pause in these positions and, on the other hand, if sociolinguistic characteristics of the speaker influence this estimation.

2 Data and Method Description

2.1 Corpus

The study is based on the corpus of Russian spontaneous monologues described in [8]. This corpus contains manual transcriptions of different types of monologues recorded by 32 native speakers of Russian. Each speaker was presented with several tasks: (1) to read a story with a plot and subsequently retell it from memory ('story'), (2) to read a descriptive narrative without a plot and retell it from memory ('description'), (3) to describe a series of pictures in a cartoon ('picture story'), (4) to describe a landscape painting ('picture description'), and finally (5) to comment on one of the suggested topics ('free comment').

The corpus consists of 160 texts (~55k words), with an overall duration of about 9 h. The corpus data is balanced with respect to speakers' social characteristics (e.g. gender, age, use of speech in everyday life) and text types.

2.2 Texts for Analysis

For this study, we used two types of monologues from the corpus – picture story and free comment, since these types of text are opposed in terms of inter-annotator agreement. As we showed in [8], the agreement is highest for picture story and lowest for free comment.

We investigated 48 texts produced by 24 speakers (2 texts by each) whose background ranged across 3 dimensions (the speaker groups are shown in Table 1):

– gender (12 male and 12 female speakers);
– age (17–24, 25–45, 45–65 years old);
– profession (linguists and non-linguists).

The total duration of the analysed monologues is 3 h 10 min (1 h 10 min for picture story and 2 h for free comment) or ~22k words (7,152 words for picture story and 14,930 for free comment). Summary statistics is shown in Table 2.

Table 1. Distribution of the speakers between groups according to their social characteristics

Profession	Age		
	17–24	25–44	45–65
Linguists	2 m, 2 f	2 m, 2 f	2 m, 2 f
Non-linguists	2 m, 2 f	2 m, 2 f	2 m, 2 f

Table 2. Summary statistics of analysed texts by text type

Type of Text	Duration		Words	
	Mean (sec)	SD	Mean (count)	SD
Picture story	174.2	215.3	298.0	420.9
Free comment	301.2	280.3	622.1	648.6

2.3 Expert Manual Annotation

The corpus of Russian spontaneous monologues also includes manual annotations of sentence boundaries. These were collected using orthographic transcriptions of recorded speech (see [8] for further detail). The transcription did not contain any punctuation. To make text reading and perception easier, graphic symbols of hesitation (like *eh, uhm*) and other comments (e.g. [sigh], [laughter]) were also excluded.

These transcripts were then manually segmented into sentences by a group of experts consisting of 20 native speakers of Russian, mostly women, with a background in linguistics who were asked to mark sentence boundaries using conventional full stops or any other symbol of their choice (e.g. a slash). The annotation was performed based on textual information only. The experts were presumed to have a native intuition of what a sentence is and, thus, it was left undefined. There were no time-constraints.

2.4 Prosodic Annotation

For prosodic annotation, we identified all positions in the transcriptions where at least one annotator marked a sentence boundary. We then identified whether the actual recording contained a pause in those positions and if so what the duration of the pause was. Hesitations were considered to be part of the pause. This annotation was done manually by an expert in Russian phonetics.

3 Data Analysis

Following [3] for each position in the text we computed the number of experts who had marked the boundary at this position. This number is interpreted as a "boundary confidence score" (BCS) which ranges from 0 (no boundary marked by any of the experts) to 20 (boundary marked by all experts = 100 % confidence).

The total amount of positions with BCS > 0 in the analysed texts is 4129: 1204 positions in picture stories and 2925 positions in free comments.

3.1 Difference Between Types of Text

Table 3 shows average BCS and average duration of corresponding pauses in each type of the text.

Table 3. Summary statistics of analysed text types with regard to BCS and pause length

	Picture story		Free comment	
	BCS	Pause duration (ms)	BCS	Pause duration (ms)
Minimum	1	0	1	0
Median	6	428	4	104
Mean	8.18	716	6.35	547
Maximum	20	11211	20	20227
SD	6.48	966	5.47	1077
N	1204		2925	

We found that there was a statistically significant correlation between pause duration and BCS: Spearman's $r = 0.43$ for free comment and $r = 0.41$ for picture story $(p < 0.0001)$.

It is worth mentioning that in both text types there is a substantial share of marked positions without pause in the signal but the analysis reveals that the text types differ in this regard (Table 4). In picture story the number of positions with pause is significantly higher than in free comment – 66.2 % vs 52.2 % $(\chi^2(1, N = 4129) = 67.9, p < 0.0001)$.

Table 4. Marked positions and presence or absence of pause in picture story and free comment

	Picture story		Free comment	
	Count	Percentage	Count	Percentage
Pause	797	66.2 %	1527	52.2 %
No pause	407	33.8 %	1398	47.8 %

We also explored whether BCS depends on the presence or absence of pause in analysed texts. Since the data is not normally distributed we used non-parametric Mann-Whitney U test for the analysis. It revealed that BCS is significantly higher in places where there is also a pause in spoken speech $(p < 0.0001)$.

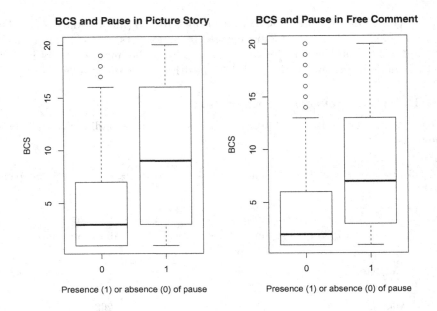

Fig. 1. BCS and presence or absence of pause in picture story and free comment

Figure 1 shows that, on average, BCS is higher for pauses in picture story than in free comment.

3.2   BCS, Pause and Gender

For further analysis, we combined the data of different text types. First, we explored whether the number of marked positions corresponding to pause (of any length) differs in male and female speech. Table 5 shows that there is significant difference in prosodic annotation of male and female speech. BCS in female speech corresponds to pause in the actual signal more regularly than in male speech 63.8 % vs 54.0 % ($\chi^2(1,\ N = 4129) = 29.3,\ p < 0.001$).

Table 5. Marked positions and presence or absence of pause in male and female speech

	Male speakers		Female speakers	
	Count	Percentage	Count	Percentage
Pause	1702	54.0 %	622	63.8 %
No pause	1452	46.0 %	353	36.2 %

Then we performed correlation analysis which did not reveal any significant difference between BCS and pause length depending on a speaker's gender:

Spearman's $r = 0.43$ for male speech and $r = 0.42$ for female speech ($p < 0.0001$ in both cases). Multiple regression analysis with pause length, speaker's gender and the interaction between the two as predictors showed significant main effect of both these variables as well as their interaction on BCS ($p < 0.0001$ for all effects, multiple $R^2 = 0.15$, adjusted $R^2 = 0.15$, $p < 0.0001$).

The analysis of only those positions in which BCS corresponded to pause showed that the correlation between BCS and pause length is slightly higher in female speech than in male though the correlation is weak in both cases: Spearman's $r = 0.31$ and $r = 0.28$ respectively ($p < 0.0001$). Multiple regression model in this case also showed a significant main effect of gender and pause length as well as their interaction ($p < 0.001$ in all cases), but the total variance explained by the model was about half of the previous model (multiple $R^2 = 0.08$, adjusted $R^2 = 0.08$, $p < 0.0001$).

3.3 BCS, Pause and Age

There is a statistically significant difference between the three age groups regarding the presence or absence of pause in annotated positions ($\chi^2(1, N = 4129) = 8.53$, $p = 0.014$). However, this difference does not exceed 6 %, with the highest correspondence in perception of speech of the second (25–45 years old) age group (see Table 6).

Table 6. Marked positions and the presence or absence of pause in speech of speakers of different age groups

	17–24		25–45		46–65	
	Count	Percentage	Count	Percentage	Count	Percentage
Pause	815	56.1 %	1073	58.3 %	436	52.2 %
No pause	637	43.9 %	769	41.7 %	399	47.8 %

The correlation between BCS and pause length is highest in the first group: Spearman's $r = 0.48$. For the other two groups Spearman's $r = 0.41$ ($p < 0.0001$). A multiple regression model showed a significant main effect of pause length and age on BCS ($p < 0.001$). Furthermore, the interaction between age and pause length for younger speakers was significantly different from the other two age group ($p < 0.001$). The model explained about 14 % of variance in BCS (multiple $R^2 = 0.14$, adjusted $R^2 = 0.14$, $p < 0.0001$).

In positions with BCS accompanied by pause the correlation between BCS and the pause length is the following: for the first age group Spearman's $r = 0.36$, for the second group $r = 0.25$, and for the third group $r = 0.27$ ($p < 0.0001$). Multiple regression analysis revealed the same trends as those for pause length mentioned in the previous paragraph, save for the total variance explained by the model which was smaller (multiple $R^2 = 0.08$, adjusted $R^2 = 0.08$, $p < 0.0001$).

3.4   BCS, Pause and Profession

The analysis reveals that the extent of association of BCS with pause is significantly higher in linguists' speech than in non-linguists' speech. Almost 60 % of all marked positions in transcripts of linguists' speech corresponded to pause. For non-linguists this connection was about 8 % weaker ($\chi^2(1, N = 4129) = 28.5$, $p < 0.0001$) (Table 7).

Table 7. Marked positions and presence or absence of pause in linguists' and non-linguists' speech

	Non-linguists		Linguists	
	Count	Percentage	Count	Percentage
Pause	862	51.3 %	1462	59.7 %
No pause	818	48.7 %	987	40.3 %

The correlation between BCS and pause length for linguists' and non-linguists' speech is approximately the same: Spearman's $r = 0.44$ for linguists and $r = 0.43$ for non-linguists ($p < 0.0001$). Multiple linear regression model showed significant main effect of pause length ($p < 0.001$) and a speaker's profession ($p < 0.001$) on BCS, as well as their interaction ($p < 0.001$) (multiple $R^2 = 0.14$, adjusted $R^2 = 0.14$, $p < 0.0001$).

4   Discussion and Conclusions

In this paper we explore whether speakers' prosodic competence allows them to reconstruct pauses in spontaneous speech based on transcription only without hearing the speech itself. We then examine whether their annotation is affected by the type of an annotated text and sociolinguistic factors. To achieve our goal, we compared (1) whether sentence boundaries marked by expert annotators in textual transcriptions of Russian spontaneous speech corresponded to pauses in speech in actual recording; (2) whether boundary confidence score (BCS), i.e. the number of annotators who marked sentence boundary in a given position, is correlated with the duration of the pause; (3) whether the type of text and sociolinguistic characteristics of a speaker influence an annotator's estimation of prosodic characteristics of the original speech.

Our results showed that there was significant difference between BCS depending on the presence or absence of pause in the recording. In other words, more annotators marked sentence boundaries in places where the speaker made a pause. Therefore the annotators are able to use their prosodic competence to correctly identify at least some of the prosodic boundaries. We also found a significant, but rather moderate correlation between pause duration and BCS (Spearman's $r = 0.43, p < 0.0001$). Thus, boundaries with higher inter-annotator agreement have a slight tendency to be accompanied by longer pauses. The multiple regression model showed that, first, 15 % of variability in BCS can be explained by pause length and speaker's gender and, second, the relationship between BCS and pause length is different between the two genders.

Data analysis with regard to text type revealed that in picture story the number of positions with pause is significantly higher than in free comment. This may be explained by picture story's simpler syntactic structure. On the other hand, in Russian, as in other languages, pause is not the only cue to prosodic segmentation. Although pauses are often used as a convenient way to establish boundaries between prosodic units [9,10], prosodic boundaries can also be indicated by other acoustic cues such as pitch movement, intensity or duration of preceding segments. Sometimes these may not be accompanied by a pause [6,7]. Since our analysis was limited to pause length, it does not take into account prosodic boundaries indicated by other acoustic cues. However, strong prosodic boundaries are usually indicated by the combination of all prosodic cues while our results showed that even boundaries with very high inter-annotator agreement were not necessarily accompanied by a pause.

Analysis of association between BCS, presence or absence of pause in speech and speakers' social characteristics showed that there is a significant difference between the perception of male and female speech. BCS in female speech corresponds to pause in the actual signal more regularly than in male speech, which may indicate that female speech is more coherent and has a more transparent structure. We also found a statistically significant difference between age groups and speakers' profession with regard to the presence of pause at the sentence end. The annotated boundaries correspond to pauses more regularly among speakers of the middle age group and linguists. Moreover, multiple regression analysis revealed that the association between BCS and pause length is affected not only by speakers' gender, but also by their age and profession. The effect of speakers' age on the interaction between BCS and pause length was observed for the first and second age groups (young and middle age).

Thus, we argue that the type of text and sociolinguistic factors have an impact on perception of spontaneous speech regarding sentence boundaries in annotated texts and pauses in real speech. The correlation between syntax and prosody is explained by annotators' prosodic competence, as well as their communicative competence in general. In the same time, ambiguous sentence boundaries and individual speech perception impose limitations on this correlation.

Acknowledgments. This study was supported by the Russian Foundation for Humanities, project No. 15–04–00165. We thank Dr. Anastassia Loukina for her valuable comments and suggestions.

References

1. Vannikov, Y., Abdalyan, I.: Eksperimental'noe issledovanie chleneniya razgovornoj rechi na diskretnye intonacionno-smyslovye edinicy (frazy). In: Sirotinina, O.B., Barannikova, L.I., Serdobintsev, L.J. (eds.) Russkaya Razgovornaya Rech, Saratov, pp. 40–46 (1973). (in Russian)
2. Guaïtella, I.: Rhythm in speech: what rhythmic organizations reveal about cognitive processes in spontaneous speech production versus reading aloud. J. Pragmatics **31**, 509–523 (1999)
3. Stepikhov, A.: Resolving ambiguities in sentence boundary detection in Russian spontaneous speech. In: Habernal, I., Matoušek, V. (eds.) TSD 2013. LNCS, vol. 8082, pp. 426–433. Springer, Heidelberg (2013)
4. Gasparov, B.M.: Yazyk, pamyat', obraz. Lingvistika yazykovogo sushchestvovaniya. Novoe literaturnoe obozrenie, Moscow (1996). (in Russian)
5. Bolinger, D.: Intonation in American English. In: Hirst, D., Di Cristo, A. (eds.) Intonation Systems. A Survey of Twenty Languages, pp. 45–55. Cambridge University Press, Cambridge (1998)
6. Svetozarova, N.: Intonation in Russian. In: Hirst, D., Di Cristo, A. (eds.) Intonation Systems. A Survey of Twenty Languages, pp. 264–277. Cambridge University Press, Cambridge (1998)
7. Hirst, D., Di Cristo, A.: A survey of intonation systems. In: Hirst, D., Di Cristo, A. (eds.) Intonation Systems. A Survey of Twenty Languages, pp. 1–44. Cambridge University Press, Cambridge (1998)
8. Stepikhov, A.: Analysis of expert manual annotation of the Russian spontaneous monologue: evidence from sentence boundary detection. In: Železný, M., Habernal, I., Ronzhin, A. (eds.) SPECOM 2013. LNCS, vol. 8113, pp. 33–40. Springer, Heidelberg (2013)
9. Kochanski, G., Shih, C., Jing, H.: Quantitative measurement of prosodic strength in Mandarin. Speech Commun. **41**(4), 625–645 (2003)
10. Aylett, M., Turk, A.: The smooth signal redundancy hypothesis: a functional explanation for relationships between redundancy, prosodic prominence, and duration in spontaneous speech. Lang. Speech **47**(1), 31–56 (2004)

Sparsity Analysis and Compensation for i-Vector Based Speaker Verification

Wei Li[1(✉)], Tian Fan Fu[2], Jie Zhu[1], and Ning Chen[3]

[1] Department of Electronic Engineering, Shanghai Jiao Tong University,
Shanghai 200240, China
liweisjtu@126.com, zhujie@sjtu.edu.cn
[2] Department of Computer Science and Engineering (CSE),
Shanghai Jiao Tong University, Shanghai 200240, China
futianfan@gmail.com
[3] School of Information Science and Engineering,
East China University of S&T, Shanghai 200237, China
nchen@ecust.edu.cn

Abstract. Over recent years, i-vector based framework has been proven to provide state-of-art performance in speaker verification. Most of the researches focus on compensating the channel variability of i-vector. In this paper we will give an analysis that in the case that the duration of enrollment or test utterance is limited, i-vector based system may suffer from biased estimation problem. In order to solve this problem, we propose an improved i-vector extraction algorithm which we term Adapted First order Baum-Welch Statistics Analysis (AFSA). This new algorithm suppresses and compensates the deviation of first order Baum-Welch statistics caused by phonetic sparsity and phonetic imbalance. Experiments were performed based on NIST 2008 SRE data sets, Experimental results show that 10 %–15 % relative improvement is achieved compared to the baseline of traditional i-vector based system.

Keywords: Speaker verification · i-vector · Phonetic sparsity · Adapted first order Baum-Welch statistics analysis (AFSA)

1 Introduction

In the last decade, Gaussian Mixture Model based on Universal Background Model (GMM-UBM) framework has demonstrated strong performance. It is commonly believed that the set of mean vector of Gaussian component contains most information to discriminate speaker identity [11]. Extended from GMM-UBM framework, Factor Analysis (FA) techniques [7,9] jointly model the speaker Gaussian components. The mean vectors of a speaker are concatenated to generate a new long vector named *supervector*. Each speaker is represented by the *mean supervector* which is a linear combination of the set of *eigenvoices*. Based on FA technique, *Joint Factor Analysis (JFA)* [5,8] decomposes GMM Supervector into a linear combination of speaker component and channel component. Derived

© Springer International Publishing Switzerland 2015
A. Ronzhin et al. (Eds.): SPECOM 2015, LNAI 9319, pp. 381–388, 2015.
DOI: 10.1007/978-3-319-23132-7_47

from JFA, i-vector framework proposes a *Total Space* modelling which contains the mixture information of speaker and channel effects [4]. Each utterance is represented by a low dimensional feature vector called *i-vector*. Optimization and compensation are performed on this i-vector space [2–4,6]. Both JFA and i-vector have demonstrated superior performance for Text-Independent speaker verification tasks in the past NIST Speaker Recognition Evaluation (SREs).

However, despite the success of FA based techniques, in this paper we will give a description that in the real world application, phonetic sparsity and imbalance are intrinsic attributes of utterance especially when the duration of utterance is very limited. Conventional FA based techniques may encounter a biased estimation problem in the case that sparse enrollment and test data is available.

To cope with this problem, we propose an improved i-vector extraction algorithm termed Adapted First order Baum-Welch Statistics Analysis (AFSA). Firstly a sufficient first order Baum-Welch statistics space is constructed. Zero order and first order Baum-Welch statistics of each utterance are projected onto this space to get a modified reference statistics, final Baum-Welch statistics of an utterance feeding into i-vector extraction are adapted from the reference statistics. Experimental results show that AFSA suppresses the deviation of first order Baum-Welch statistics caused by phonetic sparsity and imbalance.

Evaluation experiments were carried out on the core condition of NIST 2008 SREs. Experimental results show that by applying AFSA algorithm in the phase of i-vector extraction, a most 10 %–15 % relative improvement is obtained compared with the baseline system adopting traditional i-vector algorithm and following channel compensation techniques.

This paper is organized as follow. Section 2 gives a brief description of the paradigm of i-vector extraction. Section 3 we analyzes the phonetic sparsity and imbalance from experimental perspective and gives an explanation that why phonetic sparsity will lead to biased estimation problem and degenerate the performance of verification system. In Sect. 4, we state our AFSA algorithm applied in the i-vector extraction phase. Experiments and results are given in Sect. 5. Section 6 concludes the paper.

2   Total Factor Space and i-Vector

In the context of i-vector framework, speaker variability and channel variability are jointly modelled by a *Total Factor Matrix*, total variability is restricted in this linear manifold, hence each utterance can be projected onto this total factor space and be represented by a low dimensional feature vector.

The basic idea of i-vector approach is that each speaker- and channel- dependent GMM supervector $\mathbf{M}$ can be modelled as:

$$\mathbf{M}(s) = \mathbf{m} + \mathbf{T} * \mathbf{w}(s) . \tag{1}$$

where s denotes a target speaker, $\mathbf{m}$ is a speaker and channel independent supervector, which is often taken from UBM supervector. $\mathbf{T}$ is the total factor matrix with low rank, which expands a subspace containing speaker and channel dependent information (The process of training total factor matrix is detailedly explained in [7]). $\mathbf{w}(s)$ is the i-vector adapted from the training utterance. For a same utterance, supervector and i-vector are mutual one-to-one mapping, but the length of i-vector is much shorter that supervector, so optimization and compensation techniques can be simply manipulated on the i-vector space.

3   Phonetic Sparsity Analysis

3.1   Baum-Welch Statistics and Adapted Gaussian Mean Vectors

In order to estimate i-vector, the first and zero order Baum-Welch statistics for an utterance should be extracted beforehand, conventionally the Baum-Welch statistics are extracted from the UBM model. Suppose we have a sequence of L frames $\{\mathbf{y}_1, \mathbf{y}_2, \ldots, \mathbf{y}_L\}$ and a UBM Ω composed of C Gaussian components defined in some feature space of dimension F. The Baum-Welch statistics for a given speech utterance u are obtained by

$$N_c = \sum_{t=1}^{L} P(c|\mathbf{y}_t, \Omega) . \tag{2}$$

$$\mathbf{F}_c = \sum_{t=1}^{L} P(c|\mathbf{y}_t, \Omega)\mathbf{y}_t . \tag{3}$$

where $c = 1, \ldots, C$ is the Gaussian index and $P(c|y_t, \Omega)$ corresponds to the posterior probability of mixture component c generating the frame vector $\mathbf{y}_t$. (2) and (3) are named zero order and first order Baum-Welch statistics (we drop out speaker parameter s for brevity).

In the traditional MAP adaptation approach, The adapted mean vector of a Gaussian component can be written as:

$$\mathbf{M}_c = \frac{r}{N_c + r}\mathbf{m}_c + \frac{N_c}{N_c + r}\left(\frac{\mathbf{F}_c}{N_c}\right) . \tag{4}$$

where $\mathbf{M}_c$ denotes the c th component of $\mathbf{M}$, $\mathbf{m}_c$ denotes the c th component of UBM $\mathbf{m}$, $(1/N_c)\mathbf{F}_c$ is the normalized first order Baum-welch statistics, r is termed *Relevance Factor* which is an empirical value has to be manually tuned. From Eq. (4) we can see that the posterior mean vectors of the c th Gaussian component $\mathbf{M}_c$ is an interpolation between the mean of UBM Gaussian component $\mathbf{m}_c$ and the normalized first order Baum-Welch statistics $(1/N_c)\mathbf{F}_c$. N_c can be regarded as a conditioning factor, as the amount of speaker frames observed by the component c increases, $\mathbf{M}_c$ will get closer to the real statistical mean vectors $(1/N_c)\mathbf{F}_c$.

In the i-vector approach, the adapted mean vector of a Gaussian component can be written as:

$$\mathbf{M}_c = \mathbf{m}_c + \mathbf{T}_c * \mathbf{w} . \tag{5}$$

where $\mathbf{T}_c$ denotes the c th component of $\mathbf{T}$. $\mathbf{T}_c$ can be regarded as the total basis for the c th Gaussian component. From Eq. (5) we can see that in the context of i-vector framework, adapted mean vector for a Gaussian component is no longer tuned by zero order Baum-Welch statistics, in other word, all Gaussian components are adapted in the same degree, which are conditioned by i-vector.

3.2   Deviation of First Order Baum-Welch Statistics on Sparse Training Data

Suppose the distribution of speaker frames is approximately uniform or stationary, the first order Baum-Welch statistics will not deviate exaggeratedly from the mean vectors of UBM Gaussian components. Unfortunately, in the real world condition, as the duration of training utterance is limited, phonetic sparsity and imbalance will become obvious.

we randomly pick out 20 speakers (IDs) from the conditions of *10sec*, *short2* and *8conv* of NIST SRE 2008 corpus sets respectively, adding up to 60 speakers, all of which are *telephone* utterances. For each speaker zero order Baum-Welch statistics are firstly normalized to ensure the maximum value of zero order Baum-Welch is equal to 1, then we take the average among speakers in the same condition to remove statistical fluctuation. The configuration of feature extraction and UBM model are identical with experiment section. Above process could be written as:

$$N_c^{cond} = \frac{1}{S} \sum_{s=1}^{S} \frac{N_c^{cond}(s)}{\{\max(N_c^{cond}(s))|c \in 1, 2, \ldots, C\}} . \qquad (6)$$

where $N_c^{cond}(s)$ denotes the *sorted* zero order Baum-Welch statistics in ascending order corresponding to the s th speaker, *cond* denotes one of the conditions mentioned above.

As indicated in Fig. 1, the distributions of short2 and 8conv have similar gradients, as a comparison, the gradient of 10sec condition is far steeper than the others, which means that it is more prone to get stuck into phonetic imbalance. Considering the average duration of 10sec portion is no more than 10 s, hence it could be concluded that in the 10sec condition, quite a number of Gaussian components do not have authentic speaker frame observations.

In order to evaluate the degree of deviation, Euclid distance between UBM Gaussian mean vectors and corresponding fist order Baum-Welch statistics is adopted as the metric to measure the deviation of first order Baum-Welch statistics, which can be written as:

$$d_c = \|(\mathbf{F}_c/N_c) - \mathbf{m}_c\|_2 = ((\mathbf{F}_c/N_c) - \mathbf{m}_c)^T((\mathbf{F}_c/N_c) - \mathbf{m}_c) . \qquad (7)$$

where $c = 1, \ldots, C$ denotes the sorted Gaussian index which is coordinate with Eq. (6). Figure 2 is curves of the mean and variance of d_c across various conditions, from Fig. 2 it could be concluded that in the case that the utterance is sparse and limited, $\mathbf{F}_c/N_c$ deviates out of "rational" range from corresponding UBM mean vector and encounters obvious oscillation.

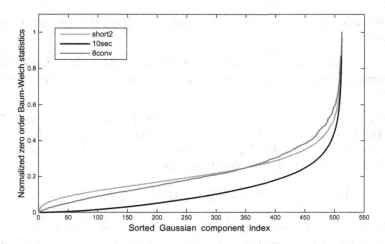

Fig. 1. Sorted distribution of zero order Baum-Welch statistics. X axis denotes the sorted Gaussian component index, Y axis denotes corresponding value of zero order Baum-Welch statistics, it could be concluded that sparse utterance is more prone to suffer from phonetic imbalance problem

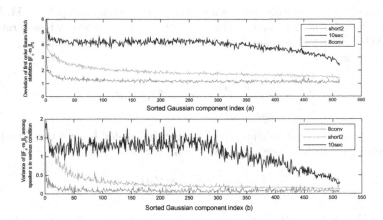

Fig. 2. Distribution of the statistics of d_c among speaker s in accordance with the order of N_c^{cond} in Fig. 1. The mean of 10sec condition in (a) deviates obviously in comparison with short2 and 8conv, also $d_c(s)$ oscillates much among speakers in the same condition as depicted in (b) (high variance)

4   Adapted First Order Baum-Welch Statistics Analysis

One of the criterions that a first order Baum-Welch statistics could be trusted is that as a Gaussian component observes more sufficient speaker frames, then the first order Baum-Welch statistics corresponding to that Gaussian component is more authentic, hence the objective to compensate phonetic sparsity comprised of two aspects:

1. Retain the information of Gaussian components with sufficient statistics.
2. Suppress the deviation of first order Baum-Welch statistics caused by phonetic sparsity.

Firstly large quantity of sufficiently estimated zero and first order Baum-Welch statistics are collected, the 8conv condition from NIST 2005, 2006, 2008 SREs are appropriate as development corpus sets. We use $\mathbf{H}$ to denote normalized sufficient first order Baum-Welch Matrix:

$$\mathbf{H} = \left((\tfrac{\widetilde{\mathbf{F}}(1)}{N(1)} - \mathbf{M}), (\tfrac{\widetilde{\mathbf{F}}(2)}{N(2)} - \mathbf{M}), \ldots, (\tfrac{\widetilde{\mathbf{F}}(s)}{N(s)} - \mathbf{M}) \right) . \qquad (8)$$

where $\widetilde{\mathbf{F}}(s)$ denotes the sufficient first order statistics from development sets. $\mathbf{M}$ denotes the super mean vector of speaker independent model, usually derived from UBM. Then Singular Value Decomposition (SVD) is applied to construct the eigen column space, which is denoted by $\mathbf{F}_{eig}$:

$$\mathbf{F}_{eig} = \mathbf{H} * (\boldsymbol{\Sigma} * \mathbf{D})^{-1} . \qquad (9)$$

where $\boldsymbol{\Sigma}$ is diagonal singular value matrix, $\mathbf{D}$ is the eigen row space of $\mathbf{H}$. For an utterance from target speaker (either for enrollment or test), whose first order Baum-Welch statistics is denoted by $\mathbf{F}(u)$, then the objective optimizing function is to minimize

$$\sum_{c=1}^{C} N_c(u) \| \frac{\mathbf{F}_c(u)}{N_c(u)} - \mathbf{m}_c - \mathbf{F}_{eig} * \varphi(u) \|_2 . \qquad (10)$$

where $\mathbf{w}(u)$ is the linear coefficients of projection, which is a vector. Final referential first order Baum-Welch statistics can be written as:

$$\mathbf{F}_{ref}(u) = \mathbf{F}_{eig} * \varphi(u) . \qquad (11)$$

$$= \mathbf{F}_{eig} [\sum_{c=1}^{C} N_c(u) * \mathbf{F}_{eig}^{T} * \mathbf{F}_{eig}]^{-1} \sum_{c=1}^{C} (\mathbf{F}_{eig})_c^{T} * (\mathbf{F}_c(u) - N_c(u) * \mathbf{m}_c) . \qquad (12)$$

Compared with traditional i-vector extraction algorithm mentioned in [4], improved i-vector extraction can be written as:

$$\mathbf{w}(u) = (\mathbf{I} + \mathbf{T}^t \boldsymbol{\Sigma}^{-1} \mathbf{N}(u)\mathbf{T})^{-1} \mathbf{T}^t \boldsymbol{\Sigma}^{-1} * N_c(u)*$$

$$[\frac{r}{N_c(u) + r} \mathbf{F}_{ref}(u) + \frac{N_c(u)}{N_c(u) + r}(\frac{\mathbf{F}_c(u)}{N_c(u)} - \mathbf{m}_c)] . \qquad (13)$$

in formula (13) the only parameter that needs to be manually tuned is r, as $r \to 0$, formula (13) will be identical to the traditional i-vector extraction form in [4].

5 Experiments

All experiments were carried out on the core condition (short2-short3), short2-10sec and 10sec-10sec of NIST 2008 SREs. NIST 2005 and NIST 2006 were used as development datasets. Our experiments are based on English-only male telephone data (det7) for enrollment and testing.

Mel Frequency Cepstral Coefficients (MFCCs), speech/silence segmentation was performed according to the index of transcriptions provided by the NIST with its automatic speech recognition (ASR) tool. The MFCC frames are extracted using a 25 ms Hamming window, every 10 ms step, 19 order coefficients together with log energy, 20 first order delta, and 10 second order delta were appended, equal to a total dimension of $F = 50$, where we follow the configuration of [1]. All frames were subjected to feature warping normalization [10].

A male UBM containing 512 Gaussians is trained and the order of total factor matrix T is 400, the corpus from the 2005 1conv4w transcription index and 2006 1conv4w transcription index was used to train the UBM with a total length of 17 h speech from about 550 speakers. The corpus from the 2005 8conv4w and 2006 8conv4w transcription index was used as the development datasets to train the total factor matrix and normalized sufficient first order Baum-Welch matrix. Linear Discriminant Analysis (LDA) was applied to compensate channel effects. Cosine scoring was taken as scoring method. All the decision scores were given without normalization.

Table 1. Comparison of cosine scoring of baseline system and improved system applying AFSA, best results are obtained in the 10sec-10sec condition when $r = 0.4$.

	LDA(270) + Cosine scoring							
	Baseline		AFSA, r = 0.1		AFSA, r = 0.4		AFSA, r = 1.0	
	EER(%)	DCF	EER(%)	DCF	EER(%)	DCF	EER(%)	DCF
short2-short3	2.77	0.0251	2.77	0.0251	2.77	0.0251	2.82	0.0257
short2-10sec	8.36	0.0402	8.30	0.0395	**7.54**	**0.0369**	7.96	0.0374
10sec-10sec	17.09	0.0703	16.51	0.0671	**14.31**	**0.0644**	15.98	0.0624

As indicated in Table 1, in the short2-short3 condition, little improvement was obtained, this is because in the short2-short3 condition, both enrollment and testing utterance are relative adequate (about 2 min duration), so the effect of phonetic sparsity is negligible. As the duration of training utterance was getting limited, the effect of phonetic sparsity gradually became significant, Best result was obtained in the 10sec-10sec condition, which gave a minimum EER of 14.31 and minimum DCF of 0.0644.

6 Conclusion

In this paper we propose an improved i-vector algorithm to compensate the biased estimation caused by phonetic sparsity. Although significant improvement was obtained in the sparse training conditions, in the real world, channel effects and short training utterance are still the main challenges to degenerate the performance of the speaker verification system. In the future work, we will continue to focus on phonetic sparsity problem, and we aim at a combination of PLDA [6] and AFSA.

Acknowledgments. This article was supported by the National Natural Science Foundation of China (NSFC) under Grants No. 61271349, 61371147 and 11433002.

References

1. Bonastre, J.F., Scheffer, N., Matrouf, D., Fredouille, C., Larcher, A., Preti, A., Pouchoulin, G., Evans, N.W., Fauve, B.G., Mason, J.S.: Alize/spkdet: a state-of-the-art open source software for speaker recognition. In: Odyssey, p. 20 (2008)
2. Bousquet, P.M., Larcher, A., Matrouf, D., Bonastre, J.F., Plchot, O.: Variance-spectra based normalization for i-vector standard and probabilistic linear discriminant analysis. In: Speaker and Language Recognition Workshop (IEEE Odyssey) (2012)
3. Bousquet, P.M., Matrouf, D., Bonastre, J.F.: Intersession compensation and scoring methods in the i-vectors space for speaker recognition. In: INTERSPEECH, pp. 485–488 (2011)
4. Dehak, N., Kenny, P., Dehak, R., Dumouchel, P., Ouellet, P.: Front-end factor analysis for speaker verification. IEEE Trans. Audio Speech Lang. Process. **19**(4), 788–798 (2011)
5. Kenny, P.: Joint factor analysis of speaker and session variability: Theory and algorithms. CRIM, Montreal, (Report) CRIM-06/08-13 (2005)
6. Kenny, P.: Bayesian speaker verification with heavy-tailed priors. In: Odyssey, p. 14 (2010)
7. Kenny, P., Boulianne, G., Dumouchel, P.: Eigenvoice modeling with sparse training data. IEEE Trans. Speech Audio Process. **13**(3), 345–354 (2005)
8. Kenny, P., Boulianne, G., Ouellet, P., Dumouchel, P.: Joint factor analysis versus eigenchannels in speaker recognition. IEEE Trans. Audio Speech Lang. Process. **15**(4), 1435–1447 (2007)
9. Kenny, P., Ouellet, P., Dehak, N., Gupta, V., Dumouchel, P.: A study of inter-speaker variability in speaker verification. IEEE Trans. Audio Speech Lang. Process. **16**(5), 980–988 (2008)
10. Pelecanos, J., Sridharan, S.: Feature warping for robust speaker verification (2001)
11. Reynolds, D.A., Quatieri, T.F., Dunn, R.B.: Speaker verification using adapted gaussian mixture models. Digital Sig. Process. **10**(1), 19–41 (2000)

Speaker Identification Using Semi-supervised Learning

Nikos Fazakis$^{(\boxtimes)}$, Stamatis Karlos, Sotiris Kotsiantis, and Kyriakos Sgarbas

University of Patras, Patras, Greece
fazakis@ece.upatras.gr,{stkarlos,sgarbas}@upatras.gr,
sotos@math.upatras.gr

Abstract. Semi-supervised classification methods use available unlabeled data, along with a small set of labeled examples, to increase the classification accuracy in comparison with training a supervised method using only the labeled data. In this work, a new semi-supervised method for speaker identification is presented. We present a comparison with other well-known semi-supervised and supervised classification methods on benchmark datasets and verify that the presented technique exhibits better accuracy in most cases.

Keywords: Semi-supervised learning · Speaker identification · Classification using labeled · Unlabeled data

1 Introduction

Labeled examples are often costly and time consuming to obtain, since labeling examples requires the effort of a human expert. On the other hand, unlabeled data is relatively easy to obtain in a number of domains. Semi-supervised classification methods use the available unlabeled data, along with a small set of labeled instances, to reduce the error rate in comparison with training a supervised classifier using only the labeled data [22]. To the best of our knowledge, there is no study that examines the efficiency of semi-supervised learning techniques in speaker identification that uses as base learners support vector machines and local based models.

The most known models for extracting useful characteristics for speech recognition are the source-filter model, which lead to extraction of Mel-frequency Cepstral coefficients (MFCC), Linear Predictive Codes (LPC), Perceptual Linear Prediction (PLP), PLP-Relative Spectra (PLP-RASTA) [2]. The reason why such various sets of features exist, is that Digital Speech Processing can be performed at three different levels so as to parameterize the speech. The first one examines the anatomy of human auditory system and tries to adjust its features to the average physical model of this. The second one considers speech phonemes, which constitute the basic component of speech, and the last one is associated with the linguistic nature of speech [14]. However, because of the

© Springer International Publishing Switzerland 2015
A. Ronzhin et al. (Eds.): SPECOM 2015, LNAI 9319, pp. 389–396, 2015.
DOI: 10.1007/978-3-319-23132-7_48

non-linear behavior of speech, there is a need for converting the field of frequency into another one, which may fit to human ear scale in a better way and can exploit the frequency domain features of speech. Consequently, the MFCCs features have been proved more efficient for this concept [32].

Grimaldi and Cummins [2] presented an experimental evaluation of different MFCC features for use in speaker identification. Those features were produced using speech data provided by the chains corpus, in a closed-set speaker identification task. The same wav files are used in our work. In this work, a new semi-supervised method for speaker identification is presented. We performed a comparison with other well-known semi-supervised and supervised classification methods and the presented technique had best accuracy in the tested data.

2   Speaker Identification Using Machine Learning

Mel-frequency Cepstral coefficients (MFCC) are popular features extracted from speech data for speaker identification. The speech signal is fragmented into frames and the MFCC features extracted from each frame show some temporal redundancy which forms the basis of fuzzy nearest neighbor classifier proposed in [19]. Khaled [1] used techniques of wavelet transform (WT) and neural network for speech based text-independent speaker identification. Lan et al. [6] examined extreme learning machine (ELM) on the text-independent speaker verification task and compared with SVM classifier. Empirical results showed that ELM classifiers performed better than SVM classifiers.

Pal et al. [28] illustrated, with the help of a bilingual speech corpus, how the well-known principal component transformation, in conjunction with the principle of classifier combination can be used to enhance the performance of the MFCC-GMM speaker recognition systems. Conventional speaker Identification systems use Gaussian mixture models and support vector machines (SVM) to model a speakers voice based on the speakers acoustic characteristics. Whereas GMMs needs more data to perform adequately and is computationally inexpensive, SVM on the other hand can do well with less data and is computationally expensive. Bourouba et al. [27] proposed a novel approach that combines the power of generative GMMs and discriminative support vector machines.

Dileep et al. [4] proposed to use the pyramid match kernel (PMK) based SVM classifier for speaker identification from the speech signal of an utterance represented as a set of local feature vectors. The main issue in building the PMK-based SVM classifier is the construction of a pyramid of histograms. Results of their studies show that the dynamic kernel SVM-based approaches give better performance than the state-of-the-art GMM-based approaches. Manikandan and Venkataramani [3] used modified One against All Support Vector Machine (SVM) classifier for speaker identification.

3   Semi-supervised Techniques

Sun [15] reviews theories developed to understand the properties of multi-view learning and gives a taxonomy of approaches according to the supervised and semi-supervised machine learning mechanisms involved. Self-training is a wrapper method usually used for semi-supervised classification [2]. In this process a classifier is first trained using the small set of labeled examples. Then unlabeled examples are classified using the trained learner. The classified unlabeled examples, for which the learner is high confident about its prediction (e.g. the first instances after the ranking of class probability values), are added to the training set along with their predicted class labels. In this way, the amount of training data increases due to the inclusion of the high-confidence unlabeled examples in the training set. Re-training of the classifier is done using the new enlarged training set and this process is repeated a fixed number of iterations until stopping criteria to be satisfied.

Co-Training is based on the assumption that the attribute space can be split into two disjoint subsets, and that each subset can produce correct classification [8]. Thus, a single learner is trained on each subset. Initially, both learners are trained only on labeled data. Then each learner is asked to classify a small number of unlabeled instances and the most confident predictions of each one learner are added to the training set of the other one. This procedure re-iterates for a number of times until a stopping criteria to be satisfied. Didaci et al. [21] evaluated co-training performance as a function of the size of the labeled training set. Results on real data sets, showed that co-training performance seems not be affected a lot by the training set size. On the other hand, Du et al. [25] made a number of experiments and concluded that based on small labeled training sets, verifying the sufficiency and independence assumptions or splitting single view into two views are unreliable.

Jiang et al. [20] proposed a co-training style algorithm which employs Naive Bayes and Support Vector Machine as base learners. The final prediction is given by the combination of base learners. Wang et al. [9] proposed to combine the probabilities of class membership with a distance metric between unlabeled instances and labeled instances. If two instances have the same class probability value, the one with the smaller distance will have larger chance to be selected.

Li and Zhou [11] proposed Co-Forest algorithm. According to this algorithm, a number of Random Trees are trained on bootstrap sample data from the data set. Then each Random Tree is refined with a small number of unlabeled instances during the training process and the final prediction is produced by majority voting. Deng and Guo [16] proposed a new Co-Forest algorithm named ADE-Co-Forest [7] which uses a data editing technique to identify and discard probably mislabeled instances during the iterations. RASCO [17] uses random attribute splits in order to train different learners. The unlabeled data are labeled and added to the training set based on the combination of decisions of the learners trained on different attribute splits. Tri-training algorithm has been proposed by [7]. In each round of tri-training algorithm, an unlabeled instance is labeled for a learner if the other two learners agree on the labeling.

Democratic co-learning [13] also uses multiple classifiers. Initially, each classifier is trained with the same data. The classifiers are then used to label the unlabeled data. Each instance is then labeled with the majority voting, and the labeled instance is added to the training set of the classifier whose prediction disagree with the majority.

4   Proposed Algorithm

The proposed method begins with a transformation of the speech signal to the feature space model in order to apply semi-supervised machine learning techniques. To be more specific, the procedure of extracting the MFCCs is based on a short-term spectral analysis method, in which speech signals are divided into short frames using mainly the Hamming window of length equal to either 1024 points or even less for less stationary signals, or bigger ones for the rest. Also, the choice of 50 % overlap between consecutive frames, seems to satisfy the majority of the different scenarios. Furthermore, the calculation of these parameters includes the computation of Fast Fourier Transform (FFT) of all the windowed speech segments. Then, the logarithmic Mel-scaled filter bank is applied to each one. The main characteristic of this scaling is that it combines both linearly spaced filter bank for frequencies lower than 1kHz and logarithmically spaced one for higher frequencies, without the temporal resolution in every frequency band being affected. The output of this stage is the mel spectrum coefficients which are strictly real numbers. Finally, Discrete Cosine Transformation (DCT) of any filter bank is performed during the last phase, computing the desired amount of MFCC coefficients for every frame. It is necessary ·to refer that in the most automatic speech recognition systems, the 0th coefficient of the MFCC cepstrum is ignored because of its unreliability [2]. This assumption will be supported during our experiments in this work. Also, the values of Min and Max Frequency that are inserted in MFCC extraction procedure, have been set to 0 Hz and 4 kHz, in order to cover the whole spectrum of speech signals. Self-training models do not make any specific assumption for the training data, but they accept that their own high-confident predictions are correct. However, it can lead to wrong predictions if noisy instances are classified as the most confident instances and merged into the training set. Of course, self-training will also fail if the small number of labeled examples cannot at all represent the underlying structure of the space, because the initial trained learner will produce bad predictions for the unlabeled data.

Most often speaker Identification systems use support vector machines (SVM) to model a speakers voice based on the speakers acoustic characteristics. SVMs [18] revolve around the notion of a "margin" - either side of a hyperplane that separates two data classes. Self-training cannot straightforward be applied to support vector machines. The confident examples are not too informative since most of them would have large distance from the decision boundary.

Naive Bayes classifier [24] is among the most popular learners used in the machine learning community. In this work, we combine the power of Naive Bayes and instance base learners. Combining instance-based learning with Naive Bayes is motivated by improving Naive Bayes through relaxing the conditional independence assumption using lazy learning. It is expected that there are no strong

```
Input: An initial set of labeled instances L and a set of unlabeled
instances U

Initialization:
 1) Initialize a shared training set EL by initial set of labeled instances
 2) Initialize a Support Vector Machines (SVM) classifier
 3) Initialize a Logistic Regression classifier
For a number of iterations do:
 4) Find the k(=100) nearest neighbors in EL using the selected distance
 metric (Euclidean in our implementation). Using as training instances
 the 100 instances train the simple Bayes classifier. Use local simple Bayes
 classifier to give the probabilities for each instance in U
 5) Use SVM classifier to give the probabilities for each instance in U
 6) Use Logistic Regression classifier to give the probabilities for each
 instance in U
 7) Average the probabilities of the three classifier and select the
 instances with the most confident predictions, remove them from U and
 add them to EL. In each about 1-2 instances per class are removed
 from U and added to EL

Output: Built the same ensemble of classifiers in the final labeled set
to predict the class labels of the test cases.
```

Fig. 1. The SelfSSL algorithm

dependences within the k nearest neighbors of the test instance, although the attribute dependences might be strong in the whole data [24]. Essentially, they are looking for a sub-space of the instance space in which the conditional independence assumption is true or almost true. Logistic regression [10] measures the relationship between the categorical dependent variable and one or more independent variables, which are usually continuous, by estimating probabilities. Logistic regression is not as accurate method as SVMs but exports more reliable probabilities for each instance classification.

Finally, the proposed algorithm (SelfSLL) is presented in Fig. 1. Combining the power of SVMs, Local Naive Bayes and Logistic Regression, the model predicts more accurate the class probability values. As a result, a number of most confident predictions of unlabeled instances can be added into the training set and the ensemble is retrained. The process is repeated until a stopping criterion is met.

For the implementation, it must be mentioned that we made use of the free available code of WEKA [22] and KEEL [31].

5   Experiments

The experiments are based on datasets extracted from the CHAINS Corpus (http://chains.ucd.ie/). The dataset consists of 16 different speakers who read 33 different sentences at a comfortable rate. In order to study the influence of the amount of labeled data, we take two different ratios when dividing the training set: 20 % for 8 speakers problem and 40 % for 16 speakers problem. These datasets have been partitioned using the 10-fold cross-validation procedure. For each generated fold, a given algorithm is trained with the examples contained in the rest of folds (training partition) and then tested with the current fold. It is noteworthy that test partitions are kept aside to evaluate the performance of the learning algorithm. Each training partition was divided into two parts: labeled and unlabeled examples. For the experiments, the proposed method has been compared with other state of the art algorithms integrated into the KEEL (Knowledge Extraction based on Evolutionary Learning) tool http://sci2s.ugr. es/keel/ [31]. For the tested algorithms the default parameters of KEEL and WEKA have been used. The classification accuracy of each supervised and semi-supervised learning algorithm tested in our study is presented in Tables 1 and 2 respectively.

The proposed method performs better than the tested state of the art algorithms. The presented approach can utilize automatically labeled data to augment a smaller, manually labeled dataset and thus improve the performance.

Table 1. Accuracy of each tested supervised learning method.

Algorithms	20 % Instances of 8 speakers	40 % Instances of 16 speakers
SupervisedNN	0.6401	0.5875
SupervisedNB	0.6997	0.6032
SupervisedC45	0.4561	0.3467
SupervisedSMO	0.8001	0.7685
SupervisedSLL	0.7968	0.7696
SupervisedLogistic	0.6921	0.6877
SupervisedLNB	0.7433	0.6942

Table 2. Accuracy of each tested semi-supervised learning method.

Algorithms	20 % Instances of 8 speakers	40 % instances of 16 speakers
SelftrainNN	0.6233	0.5718
SelftrainNB	0.6004	0.5354
SelftrainC45	0.4399	0.3639
SelftrainSMO	0.7808	0.7455
SelfSLL	0.8145	0.7819
TriTrainC45NBNN	0.6569	0.5415
CoTrainNNC45NN	0.6348	0.5844
CoForest	0.5553	0.4657
Rasco	0.2712	0.2821

6   Conclusion

In this work, a new semi-supervised method for speaker identification was presented. We performed a comparison with other well-known semi-supervised classification methods on standard benchmark datasets and the presented technique had the best accuracy in the specific datasets. Due to the encouraging results obtained from these experiments, we can expect that the proposed technique can be effectively applied to the classification task in the real world case giving slightly better accuracy than the traditional semi-supervised approaches. In spite of these results, no general method will work always.

References

1. Khaled, D.: Wavelet entropy and neural network for text-independent speaker identification. Engg. Appl. Artif. Intell. **24**, 796–802 (2011)
2. Grimaldi, M., Cummins, F.: Speaker identification using instantaneous frequencies. IEEE TASLP **16**(6), 1097–1111 (2008)
3. Manikandan, J., Venkataramani, B.: Design of a real time automatic speech recognition system using modified one against all SVM classifier. Microproc. Microsyst. **35**(6), 568–578 (2011)
4. Dileep, A., Chandra, C.: Speaker recognition using pyramid match kernel based support vector machines. Int. J. Speech Technol. **15**(3), 365–379 (2012)
5. Friedhelm, S., Edmondo, T.: Pattern classification and clustering: a review of partially supervised learning approaches. Pattern Recogn. Lett. **37**, 4–14 (2014)
6. Lan, Y., Hu, Z., Soh, Y.C., Huang, G.-B.: An extreme learning machine approach for speaker recognition. Neural Comput. Appl. **22**(3–4), 417–425 (2013)
7. Zhi-Hua, Z., Li, M.: Tri-training: exploiting unlabeled data using three classifiers. IEEE TKDE **17**(11), 1529–1541 (2005)
8. Chapelle, O., Schlkopf, B., Zien, A.: Semi-supervised learning. MIT Press, Cambridge (2006)
9. Shuang, W., Linsheng, W., Licheng, J., Hongying, L.: Improve the performance of co-training by committee with refinement of class probability estimations. Neurocomputing **136**, 30–40 (2014)
10. Xu, J., He, H., Man, H.: DCPE co-training for classification. Neurocomputing **86**, 75–85 (2012)
11. Li, M., Zhou, Z.: Improve computer-aided diagnosis with machine learning techniques using undiagnosed samples. IEEE TSMC **37**, 1088–1098 (2007)
12. Hady, M., Schwenker, F.: Co-training by committee: a new semi-supervised learning framework, In: Proceedings of the IEEE International Conference on Data Mining Workshops, pp. 563–572 (2008)
13. Zhou, Y., Goldman, S.: Democratic co-learning. In: 16th IEEE International Conference on Tools with Artificial Intelligence (ICTAI'04), pp. 594–202 (2004)
14. Hyon, S., Dang, J., Feng, H., Wang, H., Honda, K.: Detection of speaker individual information using a phoneme effect suppression method. Speech Commun. **57**, 87–100 (2014)
15. Sun, S.: A survey of multi-view machine learning. Neural Comput. Appl. **23**(7–8), 2031–2038 (2013)
16. Deng, C., Guo, M.Z.: A new co-training-style random forest for computer aided diagnosis. J. Intell. Inf. Syst. **36**, 253–281 (2011)

17. Wang, J., Luo, S., Zeng, X.: A random subspace method for co-training. In: IEEE International Joint Conference on Computational Intelligence, pp. 195–200 (2008)

18. Cristianini, N., Shawe-Taylor, J.: An Introduction to Support Vector Machines and Other Kernel-Based Learning Methods. Cambridge University Press, Cambridge (2000)

19. Susan, S., Sharma, S.: A fuzzy nearest neighbor classifier for speaker identification. In: 4th International Conference on Computational Intelligence and Communication Networks, CICN 2012, pp. 842–845 (2012)

20. Jiang, Z., Zhang, S., Zeng, J.: A hybrid generative/discriminative method for semi-supervised classification. Knowl.-Based Syst. **37**, 137–145 (2013)

21. Didaci, L., Fumera, G., Roli, F.: Analysis of co-training algorithm with very small training sets. In: Gimel'farb, G., Hancock, E., Imiya, A., Kuijper, A., Kudo, M., Omachi, S., Windeatt, T., Yamada, K. (eds.) SSPR &SPR 2012, vol. 7626, pp. 719–726. Springer, Berlin (2012)

22. Hall, M., Frank, E., Holmes, G., Pfahringer, B., Reutemann, P., Witten, I.: The WEKA data mining software: an update. SIGKDD Explor. **11**(1), 10–18 (2009)

23. Frank, E., Hall, M., Pfahringer, B.: Locally weighted naive Bayes. In: 19th Conference on Uncertainty in Artificial Intelligence. Mexico (2003)

24. Domingos, P., Pazzani, M.: On the optimality of the simple Bayesian classifier under zero-one loss. Mach. Learn. **29**, 103–130 (1997)

25. Du, J., Ling, C.X., Zhou, Z.-H.: When does cotraining work in real data? IEEE TKDE **23**(5), 788–799 (2011)

26. Goldberg, X.: Introduction to semi-supervised learning. In: Synthesis Lectures on Artificial Intelligence and Machine Learning. Morgan Claypool (2009)

27. Bourouba, H., Korba, C.A., Djemili, R.: Novel approach in speaker identification using SVM and GMM. Control Engg. Appl. Inf. **15**(3), 87–95 (2013)

28. Pal, A., Bose, S., Basak, G.K., Mukhopadhyay, A.: Speaker identification by aggregating Gaussian mixture models (GMMs) based on uncorrelated MFCC-derived features. Int. J. Pattern Recogn. Artif. Intell. **28**(4), 25 (2014)

29. Zhao, X., Wang, Y., Wang, D.: Robust speaker identification in noisy and reverberant conditions. IEEE TASLP **22**(4), 836–845 (2014)

30. Alcal-Fdez, J., Fernandez, A., Luengo, J., Derrac, J., Garca, S., Snchez, L.: KEEL data-mining software tool: data set repository, integration of algorithms and experimental analysis framework. J. Multi.-Valued Logic Soft Comput. **17**(2–3), 255–287 (2011)

31. Triguero, I., Garca, S., Herrera, F.: Self-labeled techniques for semi-supervised learning: taxonomy, software and empirical study. Knowl. Inf. Syst. **42**(2), 245–284 (2015)

32. Namrata, D.: Feature extraction methods LPC, PLP and MFCC in speech recognition. Int. J. Adv. Res. Engg Technol. **1**(6), 1–4 (2013)

Speaker Verification Using Spectral and Durational Segmental Characteristics

Elena Bulgakova[1], Aleksei Sholohov[1], Natalia Tomashenko[1,2][✉] , and Yuri Matveev[1,2]

[1] ITMO University, St. Petersburg, Russia
[2] Speech Technology Center, St. Petersburg, Russia
{bulgakova,sholohov,tomashenko-n,matveev}@speechpro.com

Abstract. In the present paper we report on some of the results obtained by fusion of human assisted speaker verification methods based on formant features and statistics of phone durations. Our experiments on the database of spontaneous speech demonstrate that using segmental durational characteristics leads to better performance, which shows the applicability of these features for the speaker verification task.

Keywords: Spectral formant features · Segmental durations · Speaker verification

1 Introduction

Information contained in speech signal makes it possible to solve one of the most important problems of modern speech technology - the problem of speaker verification. This task involves comparing test and model recordings to confirm the identity of speakers' voices in the presented recordings. At the present time, automatic and human assisted methods are widely used for solving the problem of speaker verification. While automatic methods usually give superior performance, human assisted methods make it possible to clarify and correct the work of automatic methods. They are also applied in cases where the work of automatic methods is restricted, for example, under high noise conditions.

Earlier studies into forensic speaker recognition which include the speaker verification task are often concerned with the statistical analysis of the distribution of such acoustic and prosodic features as fundamental frequencies [1–3], formant frequencies [4–7] and temporal suprasegmental characteristics [8,9]. Relatively little attention has been given to speaker specific segmental durations. However, such information is valuable in distinguishing speakers [10].

These features are especially useful for verification of speakers with a similar vocal tract, when some other features (*e.g.* spectral characteristics) are not sufficiently trustworthy. In this paper we study the applicability of durational characteristics for the speaker verification task as well as the possibility to use them with the other features. To this aim we implement a fusion of the phone durations method and the method based on formant features [7] and compare the obtained results with the performance of the human assisted pitch method [3].

© Springer International Publishing Switzerland 2015
A. Ronzhin et al. (Eds.): SPECOM 2015, LNAI 9319, pp. 397–404, 2015.
DOI: 10.1007/978-3-319-23132-7_49

2 Speaker Verification Methods

2.1 Formant Method

The main spectral peaks (formants) are influenced by the anatomical structure of the vocal tract and the sizes of the resonant cavities. For this reason such features may be useful for speaker discrimination. We extract the values of the first four formants for 6 Russian vowels (/i/, /e/, /a/, /u/, /o/, /y/).

Since formant values are usually not independent from each other, there is a need for modeling of complex statistical relationships of formants values in speech for each speaker. Currently, one of the most common approaches to modeling complex multivariate distributions for speaker recognition is GMM-UBM framework [7]. The key idea of this approach is to construct so-called *universal background model* (UBM), which approximates the feature distribution of a large number of speakers to represent the whole population. Both UBM and speaker models are implemented by means of a Gaussian mixture model (GMM), which is a weighted sum of K multivariate Gaussian distributions:

$$p(\boldsymbol{x}|\theta) = \sum_{k=1}^{K} \pi_k g(\boldsymbol{x}|\boldsymbol{\mu}_k, \boldsymbol{\Sigma}_k), \tag{1}$$

where $\boldsymbol{\mu}_k$ is the mean vector and $\boldsymbol{\Sigma}_k$ is the covariance matrix of k-th component, π are mixture weights summing to 1 and the tuple $\theta = \{\pi_k, \boldsymbol{\mu}_k, \boldsymbol{\Sigma}_k\}$ represents all the GMM parameters.

Given a set of feature vectors $X = \{\boldsymbol{x}_1, ..., \boldsymbol{x}_N\}$ assumed to be statistically independent and a speaker model θ, the *likelihood* function measures how well the model θ fits the data $\boldsymbol{X}$:

$$P(\boldsymbol{X}|\theta) = \prod_{n=1}^{N} p(\boldsymbol{x}_n|\theta), \tag{2}$$

where $p(\cdot|\theta)$ is Gaussian mixture density (1) representing the speaker model θ. Given a speaker model $\theta_{speaker}$, UBM – θ_{UBM} and the set of fetures $\boldsymbol{X}_{test}$ extracted from a test recording, the decision of the identity or difference of the two speakers can be made on the basis of the following rule:

$$\frac{P(\boldsymbol{X}|\theta_{speaker})}{P(\boldsymbol{X}|\theta_{UBM})} < \Lambda, \tag{3}$$

where Λ is the decision threshold value set in advance. Since numenator represents the hypothesis that the test feature vectors originate from the model $\theta_{speaker}$, higher likelihood ratio (3) favors this hypothesis. Otherwise, it is more likely that $\boldsymbol{X}_{test}$ comes from different speaker.

In our experiments we used UBM with 16 mixture components.

2.2 Phone Durations Method

The main stages of the algorithm based on statistics of phone durations include:

1. *Automatic phonetic segmentation* on the basis of recordings and text contents of these files. In the course of the segmentation, temporary boundaries of each phone are defined. After carrying out automatic segmentation the expert can correct the boundaries of the allocated phones if necessary.
2. *Calculation of average durations* for each phone in the phonetic segmentation.
3. *Calculation of a matching score* of speakers' voices and decision-making.

We produce forced alignment of speech audio files with its transcription at the phone level. The number of phone classes is 53, they correspond to 52 (17 vowels and 35 consonants) phones of the Russian language and a silence model. The six vowel symbols (i, e, a, u, o, y) acquire a numerical index specifying vowel position in relation to the stressed syllable: "0" denotes a vowel in a stressed syllable, "1" denotes a prestressed vowel (for vowel /a/ – only the 1st pre-stressed syllable or the initial word position), "2" stands for a second pre-stressed position of vowel /a/, while "4" indicates any post-stressed position of all vowels. The 3rd degree of vowel reduction indicated by "3" in some notation systems is excluded from our vowel classification. For producing phonetic segmentation we trained a Hidden Markov Model (HMM) acoustic model on 150 h of audio data from a Russian speech dataset. The training set consists of reading, spontaneous conversational speech and records of TV broadcasts. The acoustic model is a standard tandem GMM-HMM with tied-state context-dependent triphones, where each model, except the silence, has left-to-right, 3-state topology [12]. The silence model has one state. The total number of tied states is 13700 with, on average, 14 Gaussians per state. Acoustic features are LC-RC [11]. In practice, available transcriptions for some speakers may be poor, for example, when they do not correspond exactly to the audio content. A traditional approach to segmentation, such as forced-alignment with Viterbi algorithm, fails to work under these conditions. Hence, we implement a two-stage segmentation algorithm, similar to that, proposed in [13,14]. Figure 1 shows an example of phonetic segmentation.

Thus, unlike the formant-based method, training a statistical model of the speaker's voice requires transcription as well as speech recording. If a sufficiently large number of training files are available we can in principle apply the generic GMM-UBM approach. Otherwise, UBM would significantly differ from the actual statistical distribution of features in the population, leading to very poor performance as a result of overfitting because of a large number of model parameters. In our case, due to lack of transcribed utterances, we define a simple matching score as follows:

$$s(\boldsymbol{x}_1, \boldsymbol{x}_2) = -\sum_{t=1}^{T} w_i (x_1^t - x_2^t)^2, \tag{4}$$

where $\boldsymbol{x}_1, \boldsymbol{x}_2$ are the vectors of mean durations representing a trial, T is the total number of phones and w_i are the nonnegative weights. These weights should con-

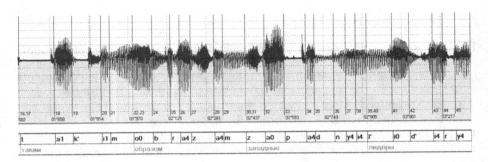

Fig. 1. Screenshot of phonetic segmentation of the utterance "takim obrazom zapadnye lidery"

form to the importance of a phone for speaker discrimination. Following the intuition that phones with greater discriminating ability should have lower *within-speaker variability* and higher *between-speaker variability* at the same time, we define the weights in the following way[1]:

$$w = \frac{\sigma^b}{\sigma^b + \sigma^w}. \tag{5}$$

We define the notion of between- and within-speaker variability as between-$\sigma^b = \frac{1}{S} \sum_s (m^s - m)^2$ and within-speaker $\sigma^w = \frac{1}{N} \sum_s \sum_r (x^{sr} - m^s)^2$ variances respectively, where s runs over all the S speakers in training set, r stands for the session index for each speaker. Here $m^s = \sum_r x^r$ is within-speaker mean, $m = \sum_s m^s$ is the mean of means and N is the training set size.

2.3 Pitch Method

The pitch method allows the expert to analyze and compare the main characteristics of intonation structures presented as sets of pitch parameter values for comparable units of melodic contour. The possibility of comparison of melodic structures is provided with their relative stability within-speaker variability in comparable contexts. Pitch analysis consists of finding of the same intonation structures in the studied recordings and comparing their characteristics. The data analysis includes obtaining and correcting the pitch files for neutral declarative utterances and building the tables containing the values of pitch parameters for the structural intonation units of the utterances (prosodic phrase, head, prehead, nuclear tone, nucleus + tail). Because of the high labour intensity of this method we performed segmentation of speech material based on prosodic phrases of 10–15 s duration. Such procedure is possible as this intonation structure is considered to be the most informative. After that we performed statistical analysis of basic intonation structures used by speakers. The following characteristics were taken as pitch parameters: minimum, maximum and average frequency

---

[1] Superscript t is omitted for the sake of presentation clarity.

values, F0 interval measured in Hz and semitones, pitch change speed, second irregularity coefficient [3].

3 Experiments

3.1 Database

For training we recorded a database consisting of 194 Russian native speakers. The speech data include quasi-spontaneous Russian speech of 124 male speakers and 70 female speakers recorded through the telephone channel. During the recording each informant answers the questions of the questionnaire. Every speaker takes part in five recording sessions of 3–5 min duration and there is a gap of at least one week between two sessions. For testing we recorded a database of 1–3 min natural spontaneous telephone conversations between two Russian native speakers. This evaluation set consists of 1037 target and 9397 non-target trials for males and 507 target and 2233 non-target trials for females.

3.2 Experiment – Speaker Verification

Here we describe experiments in speaker verification using the database, as described above. We report speaker verification performance in the form of *equal error rate* (EER,%) [15]. In the first experiment, we compared performance of three human assisted methods. Two of them (the formant and phone methods) were compared in a completely automatic mode, *i.e.* without hand-correcting formant tracks and phone boundaries. Trials using the pitch method were conducted in the semi-automatic way as discussed in Sect. 2.3. Because of the high labour intensity of the pitch method, we did not have the possibility to use the full test set. Therefore, we selected a subset consisting of 50 targets and 50 impostors.

Table 1 presents the results of comparison. As can be seen from Table 1, the formant method is the most accurate of all.

Table 1. Results for speaker verification on toy test (EER, %)

Method	EER, %	
	male	female
Pitch	12.5	13.6
Phones	31.3	33.8
Formants	2.0	2.0

To study the possibility of joint use of the compared methods we carried out their fusion. As the pitch method demands considerable time for data preparation, it was excluded from fusion.

For two matching scores s_1 and s_2 fusion was performed at the score-level using simple convex combination with a weight α to get the final score:

$$s = \alpha s_1 + (\alpha - 1)s_2$$

The optimal value of α was found using a subset of training set. It was close to 0.9.

Table 2 shows that fusion of methods based on formant features and statistics of phone durations decreases EER and results in sharp gains in performance. It means that using segmental durational characteristics improves the speaker verification performance.

Table 2. Results for speaker verification (EER, %)

Method	EER,%	
	male	female
Formants	3.2	4.8
Formants+Phones	2.4	4.5

3.3   Experiment – Informative Phones

Here we set the task of finding the most informative phones in terms of their ability of speaker discrimination. As discussed in the previous section, the formula (5) may be an indicator of the discriminative ability. According to this definition of informativity we can list the phones having the largest values of (5): /t/, /n/, /r/, /v/, /p/, /a0/, /l/, /k/, /o0/, /a1/ for females and /l'/, /l/, /ch/, /n'/, /r/, /t'/, /n/, /r'/, /a0/, /a1/ for males. Figure 2 shows weights for the case of female gender.

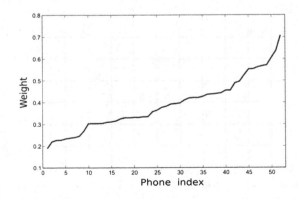

Fig. 2. Weights calculated on female data and sorted in ascending order.

Experimental results allow us to draw the conclusion that the majority of phones found with the greatest weight represent vowels and sonants. Interestingly, such phones as vowel /a/ in the pre-stressed syllable, sonants /n/, /r/, /l/ have the best discriminative ability both for male and female speakers. However, it is possible to note some gender distinctions. For example, vowels, /a/, /o/ in the stressed position as well as voiceless stops /p/, /t/, /k/ and voiced labiodental fricative /v/ are especially important for discrimination of female speakers while affricate /ch/, sonants /n'/, /r'/, /l'/ and voiceless dental stop /t'/ belong to informative phones found for male speakers.

To visualize this method of phone importance ranking, we conducted the following experiment. Starting from the one most informative phone we gradually added one by one all remaining phones ordered according to their relevance for speaker discrimination. At each step k we measured speaker verification performance for the top-k most informative phones. In other words, only a subset of phones was used to compute the sum (4).

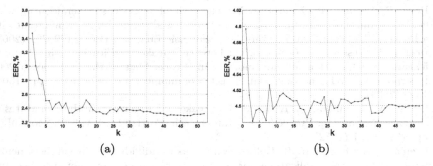

(a)   (b)

Fig. 3. Speaker verification performance with a subset of the top-k most informative phones for males (a) and females (b).

We can see that the first few phones make it possible to reach the performance comparable to the best performance using larger subsets of phones. Interestingly, including the rest of less informative phones leads to slight degradation (Fig. 3).

4   Conclusion

In this paper we approved the applicability of segmental durational characteristics for the speaker verification task. We also demonstrated that fusion of human assisted methods based on phone durations and formant features decreased equal error rate obtained by the best of these methods. We found a subset of phones with the highest speaker discriminative ability which gives a performance comparable to the case of using the full set of phones. This finding can be useful when carrying out verification on recordings of small duration that do not contain larger subsets of phones.

Acknowledgments. This work was financially supported by the Government of the Russian Federation, Grant 074-U01.

References

1. Kunzel, H., Masthoff, H., Koster, J.: The relation between speech tempo, loudness, and fundamental frequency: an important issue in forensic speaker recognition. Sci. Justice **35**(4), 291–295 (1995)
2. Nolan, F.: Intonation in speaker identification: an experiment on pitch alignment features. Forensic Linguist. **9**(1), 1–21 (2002)
3. Smirnova, N., et al.: Using parameters of identical pitch contour elements for speaker discrimination. In: Proceedings of the 12th International Conference on Speech and Computer, SPECOM 2007, Moscow, Russia, pp. 361–366 (2007)
4. Morrison, G.: Likelihood-ratio-based forensic speaker comparison using representations of vowel formant trajectories. J. Acoust. Soc. Am. **125**, 2387–2397 (2009)
5. Nolan, F., Grigoras, C.: A case for formant analysis in forensic speaker identification. J. Speech Lang. Law **12**(2), 143–173 (2005)
6. Rose, P., Osanai, T., Kinoshita, Y.: Strength of forensic speaker identification evidence: multispeaker formant-and cepstrum-based segmental discrimination with a Bayesian likelihood ratio as threshold. Forensic Linguist. **10**(2), 179–202 (2003)
7. Becker, T., Jessen, M., Grigoras, C.: Forensic speaker verification using formant features and Gaussian mixture models. In: Proceedings of the Interspeech 2008 Incorporating SST, International Speech Communication Association, pp. 1505–1508 (2008)
8. Dellwo, V., Leemann, A., Kolly, M.-J.: Speaker idiosyncratic rhythmic features in the speech signal. In: Proceedings of Interspeech, Portland, USA, 9–13 September, pp. 1584–1587 (2012)
9. Leemann, A., Kolly, M.-J., Dellwo, V.: Speaker-individuality in suprasegmental temporal features: implications for forensic voice comparison. Forensic Sci. Int. **238**, 59–67 (2014)
10. Van Heerden, C., Barnard, E.: Speaker-specific variability of phoneme durations. S. Afr. Comput. J. (SACJ) **40**, 44–50 (2008)
11. Schwarz, P.: Phoneme recognition based on long temporal context. Ph.D. thesis, Brno University of Technology (2009)
12. Chernykh, G., Korenevsky, M., Levin, K., Ponomareva, I., Tomashenko, N.: State level control for acoustic model training. In: Ronzhin, A., Potapova, R., Delic, V. (eds.) SPECOM 2014. LNCS, vol. 8773, pp. 435–442. Springer, Heidelberg (2014)
13. Moreno, P., Joerg C., Van Thong, J.-M., Glickman, O.: A recursive algorithm for the forced alignment of very long audio segments. In: Proceedings of ICSLP 1998, Sydney, Australia, pp. 2711–2714. IEEE Press (1998)
14. Tomashenko, N.A., Khokhlov, Y.Y.: Fast algorithm for automatic alignment of speech and imperfect text data. In: Železný, M., Habernal, I., Ronzhin, A. (eds.) SPECOM 2013. LNCS, vol. 8113, pp. 146–153. Springer, Heidelberg (2013)
15. The NIST year 2010 Speaker Recognition Evaluation plan (2010). http://www.itl.nist.gov/iad/mig/tests/sre/2010/NIST_SRE10_evalplan.r6.pdf

Speech Enhancement in Quasi-Periodic Noises Using Improved Spectral Subtraction Based on Adaptive Sampling

Elias Azarov$^{(\boxtimes)}$, Maxim Vashkevich, and Alexander Petrovsky

Department of Computer Engineering,
Belarusian State University of Informatics and Radioelectronics, Minsk, Belarus
{azarov,vashkevich,palex}@bsuir.by

Abstract. The paper presents a speech processing method based on spectral subtraction that is effective for reduction of specific rate-dependent noises. Such noises are produced by a variety of different rotation sources such as turbines and car engines. Applicability of convenient spectral subtraction for such noises is limited since their power spectral density (PSD) is connected with rotation rate and therefore constantly changing. The paper shows that in some cases it is possible to compensate variation of PSD by adaptive sampling rate. The signal can be processed in warped time domain that makes noise parameters more stable and easy to estimate. Stabilization of PSD leads to more accurate evaluation of noise parameters and significantly improves result of noise reduction. For de-termination of current rotation rate the proposed method can either use external reference signal or the noisy signal itself applying pitch detector to it. Considering that the noise typically consists of deterministic and stochastic components narrow-band and wide-band components of the noise are removed separately. The method is compared to the recently proposed maximum a posteriori method (MAP).

Keywords: Noise reduction · Spectral subtraction · Time warping

1 Introduction

The paper addresses the problem of cleaning speech signals from time-varying quasi-periodic noises typically generated by rotating machines. The problem is characterized by the following tough points: unsteadiness of the noise that requires fast tracking of the noise parameters; extremely low signal-to-noise ratios (SNRs) that can be below $-10\,\mathrm{dB}$, the hybrid structure of the noise that combines deterministic (tonal or narrow-band) with stochastic (non-periodic wide-band components).

Among approaches that have been applied to the problem are spectral subtraction, Weiner filtering, MAP and others [1–5]. Majority of the methods use additional reference information such as engine or vehicle speed in order to find frequency locations of engine harmonic noise components. When rotation rate

© Springer International Publishing Switzerland 2015
A. Ronzhin et al. (Eds.): SPECOM 2015, LNAI 9319, pp. 405–412, 2015.
DOI: 10.1007/978-3-319-23132-7_50

changes both deterministic and stochastic components shift their frequency, but speed-dependent filtering is actually applied only to the deterministic part which is typically done by notch filtering. Notch filters are applied to suppress individual harmonics [1,5] as long as it is not possible to obtain sufficient frequency resolution for such non-stationary periodic components using a filter bank, or short-time Fourier transform (STFT). The stochastic part is processed regardless of the rotation speed information that results in a high engine noise residue in the processed speech.

The paper presents a noise reduction technique based on spectral subtraction. Noise is processed in warped time domain which makes possible to process noise spectrum with high frequency resolution and apply speed-dependent filtering both to deterministic and stochastic noise components.

The method can use external reference information or estimate rotation rate from the noise using a pitch detector assuming that engine speed cannot change very rapidly. The obtained experimental results are rated in terms of objective and subjective values.

2   Method Outline

The method can be shortly described by the following steps (Fig. 1): (1) acquisition of rotation rate using external source or noised signal; (2) warping of the signal accordingly to estimated fundamental frequency; (3) detection of tonal components and narrow-band filtering; (4) estimation of unvoiced regions and estimation of PSD of the noise; (5) spectral subtraction of the noise using gathered noise statistics; (6) inverse signal warping of the processed signal in order to return it into original time domain.

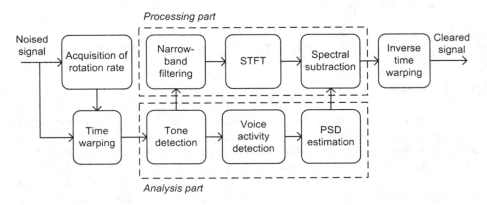

Fig. 1. Signal processing scheme

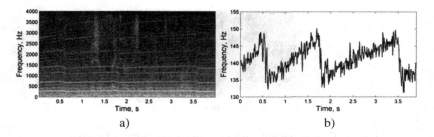

Fig. 2. Acquisition of rotation rate from noised signal using the fundamental frequency estimation algorithm. (a) – noised signal, (b) – estimated fundamental frequency

The steps of the algorithm are detailed and illustrated below.

2.1 Acquisition of Rotation Rate

If no reference signal available rotation rate is estimated using fundamental frequency of the noised signal. Fundamental frequency is estimated in three steps: subband signal decomposition, calculation of period candidate generation function and frequency tracking [6]. In order to make accurate estimation we use instantaneous harmonic parameters. First the signal is decomposed into overlapping subband analytic signals using Discrete Fourier Transform (DFT)-modulated filter bank. Then series of complex samples are transformed into instantaneous harmonic parameters [7,8] and the values of period candidate generation function $\phi_{inst}(m, k)$ is calculated [6]:

$$\phi_{inst}(m, k) = \frac{\sum_{p=1}^{P} A_p^2(m) \cos(F_p(m)k)}{\sum_{p=1}^{P} A_p^2(m)},$$

where $A_p(m)$ – instantaneous amplitude, $F_p(m) \in [0, \pi]$ – instantaneous frequency, P – number of channels, m – signal sample number and k – lag in samples. The local maximum values of the function are traced from sample to sample using dynamic programming technique in order to impose constraints on fundamental frequency deviation speed. The estimation technique has inherent delay of 50 ms. An example of fundamental frequency contour estimation for speech degraded by a formula 1 car noise is given in Fig. 2.

2.2 Time-Warping

In order to stabilize frequencies of tonal components and PSD of the noise we eliminate pitch modulations using time-warping [6,9]. Discrete signal $s(n)$ is interpolated in new time moments m so each rotation period corresponds to an equal number of samples N_{f_0}. Each time sample $s(n)$ is associated with a phase mark $\phi(n)$ using instantaneous pitch values $f_0(n)$:

$$\phi(n) = \sum_{i=0}^{n} f_0(i)$$

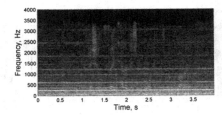

Fig. 3. Warped signal with constant fundamental frequency

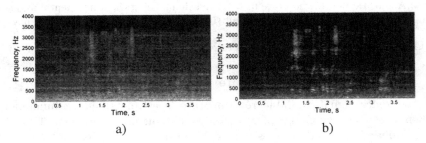

a)   b)

Fig. 4. Results of two-step noise reduction: (a) – tone removal, (b) – spectral subtraction

Interpolation moments m are obtained as:

$$m = \phi^{-1}(q/N_{f_0})$$

where q is sample index in warped time (phase) domain. The samples of the warped signal $s(q)$ are recalculated using sinc-interpolation. The result of time-warping of the same signal is given in Fig. 3.

2.3   Noise Reduction

The time-warped signal is much more suitable for noise reduction. Noise reduction itself consists of the following operations: tone removing and noise subtraction. Both operations are implemented on short-time Fourier spectrum of the signal, however we use analysis windows of different lengths. For tone detection and removing an long-size (about 100 ms) STFT is used. Considering that the signal contains tonal noise components with constant frequencies their locations in the spectrum emerge as clear sharp peaks. The tone detector analyzes time-averaged amplitude spectrum to find frequency bins with relatively high energy (in comparison with adjacent bins). Speech harmonics are not detected as tonal noise because due to frequency variations its energy smoothed on the long analysis frame. Narrow-band components of the detected tones are removed from the spectrum. After removing tonal noise components wideband noise are attenuated using spectral subtraction technique [10]. We use short STFT windows (about 20 ms).

Considering that due to time-warping the noise spectral envelope becomes less dependent on pitch variations the noise reduction technique works very effectively. The PSD of noise is updated in silent regions where no voice is present. We use the voice activity detector described in [11]. After spectral subtraction the original time scale of the signal is restored by inverse time warping. The processing results for the time-warped signal are shown in Fig. 4.

3   Experimental Result

This section provides performance evaluation of the proposed algorithm. First, accuracy of fundamental frequency estimation is evaluated using synthetic quasi-periodical signals with different harmonic-to-noise ratios. Secondly spectrogram analysis is provided in order to compare obtained processing result with the method of maximum a posteriori estimation of noise from non-acoustic reference signals in very low signal-to-noise ratio environments [2]. Finally results of listening tests are presented.

3.1   Fundamental Frequency Estimation Accuracy

In the context of the target application there are three main characteristics important for estimation of fundamental frequency: robustness against noise, robustness against tone modulations and frequency resolution. These characteristics are evaluated using three error measures: (1) gross pitch error (GPE); (2) mean fine pitch error (MFPE) and (3) root-mean square-error (RMSE) on signals with different amounts of noise and frequency modulations. Percentage of GPE is calculated as

$$\text{GPE}(\%) = \frac{N_{\text{GPE}}}{N_v} \times 100$$

where N_{GPE} – the quantity of frames with estimated fundamental frequency error more than $\pm 20\%$ of the true value, N_v – overall quantity of frames.

Mean fine pitch error is calculated on frames where no gross pitch errors occur.

$$\text{MFPE}(\%) = \frac{1}{N_{\text{FPE}}} \sum_{n=1}^{N_{\text{FPE}}} \frac{|F_0^{true}(n) - F_0^{est}(n)|}{F_0^{true}(n)} \times 100,$$

where N_{FPE} – number of frames without GPE, $F_0^{true}(n)$ – true fundamental frequency and $F_0^{est}(n)$ estimated value. Root-mean square-error is evaluated in the following way:

$$\text{RMSE}(\%) = \sqrt{\frac{1}{N_{\text{FPE}}} \sum_{n=1}^{N_{\text{FPE}}} \left[\frac{F_0^{true}(n) - F_0^{est}(n)}{F_0^{true}(n)} \times 100 \right]^2},$$

Table 1. Fundamental frequency evaluation GPE (%), MFPE(%) and RMSE(%).

	Fundamental frequency change rate, Hz/ms				
	0	0.5	1	1.5	2
	$HNR = 0\,$dB				
GPE	0	0	0	0	0
MFPE	0.14	0.13	0.2	0.21	0.44
RMSE	0.15	0.16	0.24	0.32	0.69
	$HNR = -10\,$dB				
GPE	0	0	0	1.31	1.52
MFPE	0.34	0.52	0.86	1	1.68
RMSE	0.58	0.64	1.12	1.77	2.42

Test signals are generated using different fundamental frequency change rates and harmonic-to-noise rates (HNR)

$$HNR = 10\lg\frac{\sigma_H^2}{\sigma_e^2},$$

σ_H^2 – the energy of the harmonic signal and σ_e^2 – the energy of the noise. Fundamental frequency is changes from 100 to 350 Hz. The performance of fundamental frequency evaluation is summarized in Table 1.

The proposed algorithm showed a good robustness against noise and frequency modulations that makes possible to use it instead of the reference signal in motor noise processing.

3.2 Performance Analysis

The following picture gives results of the proposed technique and the method of maximum a posteriori estimation of noise from non-acoustic reference signals (MAP) for the signal we used in the previous section – Fig. 5.

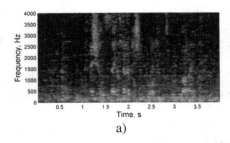 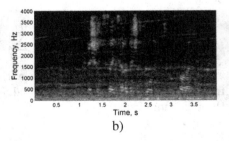

a)   b)

Fig. 5. Comparison of MAP and the proposed processing technique (a) – MAP output, (b) – output of the proposed algorithm

As can be seen the proposed algorithm provides a good average noise attenuation (18 dB) that is slightly better compared to MAP (17 dB). Moreover, in the high frequency band (higher than 2 kHz) the proposed method retains lesser amount of noise. The harmonic structure of the speech signal is a bit clearer perceived and less degraded than in MAP. However because of fully automatic harmonic noise detection due to absence of non-acoustic reference signals a small amount of harmonic noise has been left in the result.

Listening tests were carried out using the same subjective measures as in [2], where Comparative Mean Opinion Score (CMOS) scale was used. The speech quality improvement is evaluated from source/processed speech pairs on a scale of -3 to $+3$, where -3 corresponds to a significant loss of quality, 0 to no perceived difference and $+3$ to significant quality improvement.

A group of 10 listeners participated in the listening. In each test every listener was listening to 3 pairs of speech samples and rated quality change. The averaged listening results for MAP filtering is 1.62 and for the proposed algorithm 1.71.

4   Conclusion

A method for racing car noise reduction has been proposed. The noise processing is made on a warped signal with constant fundamental frequency that makes it easier to estimate and remove noise components because of their stationarity. During noise reduction the narrow-band and wide-band noise components are processed separately. The method can be applied directly to one-channel noised signals and does not utilize any non-acoustic reference information. The method has provided good results with comparison to the MAP technique that utilize external engine speed measurements. The main drawback of the method is increased inherent delay which is about 100 ms.

Acknowledgments. This work was supported by Belarusian Republican Foundation for Fundamental Research (grant No F14MV-014).

References

1. Hadley, M., Milner, B., Harvey, R.: Noise reduction for driver to pit-crew communication in motor racing. In: IEEE International Conference on Acoustics, Speech and Signal Processing, vol. 1, pp. 165–168. IEEE Press, Toulouse (2006)
2. Milner, B.: Maximum a posteriori estimation of noise from non-acoustic reference signals in very low signal-to-noise ratio environments. In: 12th Annual Conference of the International Speech Communication Association (Interspeech), pp. 357–360. Florence (2011)
3. Gomez, P., Alvarez, A., Nieto, V., Martinez, R.: Speech enhancement for a car environment using LP residual signal and spectral subtraction. In: 8th European Conference on Speech Communication and Technology (Eurospeech), pp. 1373–1376. Geneva (2003)

4. Vaseghi, S., Chen, A., McCourt, P.: State based sub-band LP Wiener filters for speech enhancement in car environments. In: IEEE International Conference on Acoustics, Speech and Signal Processing, pp. 213–216. IEEE Press, Istanbul (2000)
5. Puder, H., Steffens, F.: Improved noise reduction for handsfree car phones utilizing information on vehicle and engine speeds. In: 10th European Signal Processing Conference (EUSIPCO), pp. 1851–1854. Tampere (2000)
6. Azarov, E., Vashkevich, M., Petrovsky, A.: Instantaneous pitch estimation based on RAPT Framework. In: 20th European Signal Processing Conference (EUSIPCO), pp. 1851–1854. Bucharest (2012)
7. Petrovsky, A.L., Azarov, E., Petrovsky, A.: Hybrid signal decomposition based on instantaneous harmonic parameters and perceptually motivated wavelet packets for scalable audio coding. Signal Process. **91**(6), 1489–1504 (2011)
8. Azarov, E., Petrovsky, A.: Instantaneous harmonic analysis: audio and speech processing in multimedia systems. Lambert Academic Publishing (2011) (in Russian)
9. Petrovsky, A., Stankevich, A., Balunowski, J.: The order tracking front-end algorithms in the rotating machine monitoring systems based on the new digital low order filtering. In: International Congresses on Sound and Vibration, pp. 2985–2992. Copenhagen (1999)
10. Loizou, P.: Speech Enhancement: Theory and Practice. CRC Press, Inc., Boca Raton (2007)
11. Puder, H.: Single channel noise reduction using time-frequency dependent voice activity detection. In: International Workshop on Acoustic Signal Enhancement, pp. 68–71, USA, Pocono Manor (1999)

Sub-word Language Modeling
for Russian LVCSR

Sergey Zablotskiy$^{(\boxtimes)}$ and Wolfgang Minker

Institute of Communications Engineering, University of Ulm,
Albert-Einstein-Allee 43, 89081 Ulm, Germany
{sergey.zablotskiy,wolfgang.minker}@uni-ulm.de

Abstract. Russian is a highly inflected language with rich morphology. It is characterized by the low lexical coverage, high out-of-vocabulary (OOV) rate and perplexity. Therefore, the large vocabulary continuous speech recognition (LVCSR) of Russian and languages with similar morphology still remains to be a challenging task. Augmenting the full-word language model by fragments is a well-known approach targeting this challenge which also allows us to recognize missing words in the lexicon (open vocabulary recognition). In this paper we suggest a novel "double-sided" approach for marking word fragments, which reduces the WER by up to 3.7 % absolute (20.8 % relative) compared to the full-word baseline and by up to 1.1 % absolute (7.2 % relative) compared to the corresponding sub-word baseline, tested on evaluation set. Moreover, the type of word decomposition (syllables or morpheme-like units), their smallest size and optimal number of non-fragmented words were also investigated for Russian LVCSR.

Keywords: Russian speech recognition · Double-sided marking · Syllables · Morphemes · Morphs

1   Introduction

Similarly to the other Slavic languages Russian is a highly inflected language with a complex mechanism of word formation. Five basic parts of Russian speech (a noun, a verb, an adjective, a numeral and a pronoun) are inflected according to different grammatical categories: 6 cases, 3 genders, etc. There are no articles and almost no auxiliary words. The entire grammatical information is embedded into a word itself by the use of various grammatical affixes. This leads to the abundance of word forms.

The loose word order of Russian language also sophisticates the process of LVCSR contributing to the data sparsity and up to several times higher perplexities comparing to English [8].

There are different approaches in literature addressing the same problem for Russian and other highly inflected or agglutinative languages. Thus, in [17] two advanced language modeling techniques for Russian were investigated: factor

© Springer International Publishing Switzerland 2015
A. Ronzhin et al. (Eds.): SPECOM 2015, LNAI 9319, pp. 413–421, 2015.
DOI: 10.1007/978-3-319-23132-7_51

language models (LMs) and recurrent neural networks (RNNs). The factor LM is the N-gram model extended by word features. Trained on an entire text corpus, the RNNs outperformed significantly the factor LMs. However, an aggregation of the factor LMs, RNNs and trigrams showed further improvement compared to the standalone RNNs. A syntactico-statistical method was suggested in [9], which estimates more accurate N-gram models for synthetic languages like Russian.

A very popular approach to reduce the lexicon size and increase an average frequency of its elements [15] is the employment of sub-word units. In [8,15] morphemes are used as the smallest linguistic components with semantic meaning. Syllables [15,18] are often chosen from the speech production point of view. Various statistically derived units and elements augmented by their pronunciation (graphones) are successfully exploited as well [2,6,15]. The use of graphones allows to capture diverse sub-lexical pronunciation on the LM level rather than the lexical level [15]. Several attempts are made to automate the word decompounding [12] or optimize the lexicon (e.g. by using the discriminative learning method exploiting the perceptron algorithm [1]).

In this work we focused on the word decomposition approach, since it has already proven its efficiency for multiple languages with rich morphology. It is able to recognize OOV-words as a combination of sub-words (so called open vocabulary recognition [2,7]). Moreover, this approach is highly portable and, therefore, does not cost much efforts and code changes if moving from one ASR system to the other. In this paper we suggested a novel approach for sub-word marking, which does not sophisticate the process of backward full-word synthesis, but significantly improves the word recognition accuracy.

2   Methodology

2.1   Sub-lexical Units

Syllables. The algorithm of the full-word division into syllables is quite straightforward and absolutely deterministic according to the principle of rising sonority. Each syllable consists of one vowel and null to several consonants.

Morphs. For decomposing of full-words into morphemes or morpheme-like units there exist dictionary-based and unsupervised approaches [6]. The disadvantage of the former one is the necessity to have the decomposition mapping for all the words. Even large existing dictionaries for Russian can not guarantee the availability of every single word.

Therefore, the data-driven tool *Morfessor* [5] for unsupervised decomposition into pseudo-morphemes (later called "morphs" as in [5]) was used. For its training an unannotated raw text is required only. Words appeared more than five times in the text corpus were used for training as it was recommended in [6]. Nevertheless, the resulted model was used for decomposing rare words as well.

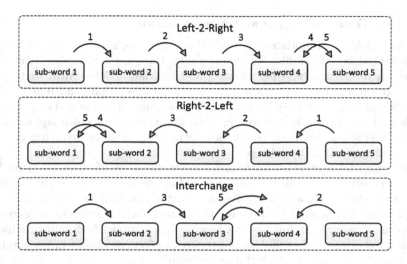

Fig. 1. Joining algorithms.

Sub-word Joining. For improving of the final WER it is recommended in [15] to adapt the word decomposition so as to avoid the very short units. Hence, here we investigated the optimal size of the smallest units for different sub-words types (syllables and morphs) as well as the algorithm of small elements' concatenation. Thus, three different joining algorithms for small sub-words were suggested: left-to-right (L2R), right-to-left (R2L) and interchange (INT). These algorithms are presented in Fig. 1. The L2R algorithm starts from the most left sub-word: if its length in letters is shorter than a threshold "min size" - join it with the neighbor to the right. The most right sub-word (if shorter than "min size") should be joint with its left neighbor. This procedure stops if all sub-words gain the required minimum size or the word boundary is reached. The R2L case is exactly inversed. The direction change for the INT happens only after reaching "min size" of the current unit. Otherwise, all transition numbers are subtracted by one. For the L2R algorithm - the largest sub-word tends to be located at the end of the word; for R2L - at the beginning, for INT - closer to the middle.

Sub-word Marking and Synthesis. Appending the "+" marker to non-terminal sub-words for easy recovery [15] ("single-sided" marking) does not take into account relative sub-word positions. Our suggestion is to use the "double-sided" marking for non-boundary sub-words. This makes the sub-word LM more context specific and more sensitive to the position of sub-units in a word.

For example, the word "прекрасное" will be decomposed as "пре+ +кра+ +сно+ +е" in the "double-sided" marking scheme and as "пре+ кра+ сно+ е" in the "single-sided" one. The "double-sided" scheme allows us to distinguish between three positional types of sub-words on the LM level. During recombination the pluses in front of sub-words are just ignored.

2.2   Text Data Collection and Normalization

To train a LM an abundance of textual resources is necessary, especially for such inflected languages like Russian. Usually the largest available digital text sources are e-books, newspaper archives and Internet articles. Most texts, especially those from newspapers, comprise lots of abbreviations and numbers. For less inflected languages they do not pose any serious challenge and can easily be substituted by full-words performing some minor grammatical adaptation. For Russian this substitution turns into a multi-step procedure involving morphological and syntactical knowledge.

Omitting such sentences causes undesired statistics falsification and such LMs poorly represent almost all the numbers and abbreviations in diverse contexts.

The rule-based algorithm for Russian text normalization *NormyRiUS* [19] is implemented as a single Perl-script available at https://gitlab.com/serjosch/normyrius. Currently it invokes the morphological tool *Mystem* [14], which is even able to estimate morphological properties of words absent in its database. Alternatively, any morphological analyzer could be exploited, e.g. *Pymorphy2*, available at https://pymorphy2.readthedocs.org/en/latest/index.html.

In this work the text data for Russian LVCSR was collected from the following sources: books of Moshkov's library (www.lib.ru), electronic scientific magazine "Наука и жизнь" (www.nkj.ru), political and non-political articles of the newspapers "АиФ" (www.aif.ru) and "Лента.ру" (www.lenta.ru).

The collected corpus of normalized texts consists of 714 M running words. It was also used for the selection of the most frequent words to be included into vocabularies.

2.3   Phonetic Transcription

Russian is a language with a close grapheme-to-phoneme relationship. There are strict pronunciation rules [8,10] with negligibly small amount of exceptions. However, the pronunciation of each word strongly depends on the position of the emphasis. For example, the word "молоко" is pronounced as /м а л а к о!/, since the first two vowels (letters) "о" are non-emphasised.

The determination of the emphasis' position is a challenge, which is normally solved by the employment of the emphasis dictionary. However, despite of its tremendous size (2.3 M), the lexicon is still missing lots of word-forms (about 100 k words out of 500 k most frequent ones are absent in the emphasis dictionary).

To our best knowledge there are no tools for the automatic Russian emphasis detection publicly available. Therefore, for the pronunciation generation of the unknown words the data-driven grapheme-to-phoneme converter *Sequitur G2P* [3] was used. It exploits data in the form "word - phonetic transcription" to train the pronunciation model and can be applied to any arbitrary language.

For a full-word Russian lexicon two different strategies were suggested and proved empirically to have very similar efficiency (±0.1 % WER for 500 k full-word vocabulary on the Development set with different parameters). Both strategies require a rule-based transcriber. In our case it was provided by the Speech and Multi-Modal Interfaces Laboratory of the St. Petersburg Institute for Informatics and Automation of Russian Academy of Science [10]. This transcriber requires information regarding stressed vowel(s) as well as proper recognition of a letter "ё", since it is mostly omitted in written.

The difference between two approaches is in the order of two steps: either the rule-based transcriber is applied first and the Sequitur G2P is trained on the phonetic representations including emphasized phonemes or the Sequitur G2P is trained first on the words with stress markers (emphasized letter form) and the rule-based transcriber is applied to unknown words with emphases, preliminary predicted by the Sequitur G2P. The second scenario was used in this work for the sub-word lexicon generation, since it allows us to make a rule-based grapheme-phoneme alignment (transcriber property). The advantage of the rule-based alignment is the exact pronunciation borders between sub-words after splitting of full words. The same scenario was used for syllables and morphs.

3   Experimental Setup

The ISABASE-2 [4] is one of the largest high-quality continuous read speech corpora for Russian. It was created and provided for our experiments by the Institute of System Analysis of the Russian Academy of Science. A lexical material of the database consists of three non-intersecting sets:

- R-set: 70 sentences with sufficient allophone coverage for training.
- B-set: 3060 sentences, also used for training.
- T-set: 1000 sentences for testing.

The sets B and T were chosen from newspaper articles and Internet pages of different domains.

Sentences from the sets R and B were spoken by 100 speakers: 50 male and 50 female. Each speaker has uttered all 70 sentences from R-set and 180 sentences from B-set. For any two speakers the B-subsets either coincide or do not intersect at all. Therefore, each sentence from the R-set was spoken by all 100 speakers and each sentence from the B-set was pronounced by several males and females.

The test set was uttered by other 10 speakers: 5 male and 5 female. Each of them read 100 unique sentences from the T-set. The utterances of the T-set were split into 2 equal parts (with non-intersecting speakers) for the development (Dv) and evaluation (Ev) SR sets. All speakers were non-professional speakers living in Moscow and having mostly the Moscow pronunciation accent.

Every utterance is presented as a separate Wav-file (22050 Hz, 16 bit, downsampled to 16 kHz) along with its information file. The total duration of speech is more than 34 h including 70 min of the development and test material.

In all experiments the word is considered to be an OOV only if it is absent in the vocabulary and can not be composed from in-vocabulary fragments [15].

The acoustic modeling is performed according to [7] (re-estimation of CART, LDA with fastVTLN). The *SRILM toolkit* [16] was used to estimate the backoff 5-gram LMs with Kneser-Ney Smoothing [11] for full-word and hybrid vocabularies. SR results were obtained using the *RWTH ASR system* [13].

4 Evaluation

More than 10000 recognition experiments (minimum one hour long each on a state-of-the-art desktop computer) with different acoustic and language model parameters were carried out on the Dv set to achieve the results presented here.

The performance of a baseline full-word Russian LVCSR is shown in Table 1.

Table 1. Baseline WERs - full word 5-gram LMs (voc: vocabulary, Dv: development, Ev: evaluation, RTF: real time factor on Intel® Xeon® E3-1245, 3.40 Ghz machine)

Voc size	ISABASE-2 (Dv)			ISABASE-2 (Ev)		
	WER[%]	OOV[%]	RTF	WER[%]	OOV[%]	RTF
100 k	16.9	5.52	1.55	17.8	4.52	1.45
200 k	12.7	2.25	1.75	14.1	1.63	1.86
300 k	11.1	1.11	1.84	13.4	0.93	2.02

Table 2 shows the comparison between the morph baseline and its "double-sided" counterpart. Each row corresponds to the best parameters found on Dv set (including the type of joining and smallest element size). As can be seen, the suggested "double-sided" version outperforms significantly the morph baseline: 1.0 % WER absolute (7.1 % relative) for 300 k vocabulary on Ev set.

Table 2. WERs - morph based 5-gram LMs

Voc size	#full words	min size	join type	ISABASE-2 (Dv)			ISABASE-2 (Ev)		
				WER[%]	OOV[%]	RTF	WER[%]	OOV[%]	RTF
Single-sided marking									
100 k	50 k	1	-	11.9	0.00	2.42	14.6	0.00	2.31
200 k	150 k	1	-	10.6	0.00	2.50	14.1	0.00	2.32
300 k	200 k	1	-	10.3	0.00	2.51	14.0	0.00	2.63
Double-sided marking									
100 k	50 k	1	-	11.2	0.00	2.40	14.4	0.00	2.42
200 k	150 k	1	-	10.1	0.00	2.65	13.2	0.00	2.60
300 k	150 k	1	-	10.0	0.00	2.98	13.0	0.00	3.00

The number of full-words means the number of the most frequent originally non-split words. After the text enrichment with resulted sub-words, the most frequent (sub-)words were selected again and, therefore, the number of full-words may deviate.

The comparison to the syllable baseline is given in Table 3. Again, the syllable "double-sided" modification outperforms not only the full-word baseline, e.g. by

Table 3. WERs - syllable based 5-gram LMs

Voc size	#full words	min size	join type	ISABASE-2 (Dv)			ISABASE-2 (Ev)		
				WER[%]	OOV[%]	RTF	WER[%]	OOV[%]	RTF
Single-sided marking									
100 k	30 k	4	R2L	11.8	0.72	1.86	15.2	0.63	1.77
200 k	150 k	4	R2L	10.7	0.40	2.01	13.5	0.25	1.88
300 k	150 k	4	INT	10.4	0.13	2.23	13.6	0.05	2.08
Double-sided marking									
100 k	70 k	3	R2L	11.6	0.27	1.94	14.1	0.25	1.87
200 k	150 k	3	R2L	10.7	0.08	2.24	13.1	0.08	2.19
300 k	150 k	4	INT	10.3	0.13	2.21	13.1	0.08	2.07

3.7 % absolute (20.8 % relative) for 100 k vocabulary, but also the syllable "single-sided" baseline, e.g. by 0.5 % absolute (3.7 % relative) for 300 k on Ev set.

For morph models the optimal size of the smallest unit is equal to one, i.e. joining of even one-letter morphs decreases the recognition accuracy of Russian LVCSR (as opposed to the results reported for German [6] and Polish [15]).

5 Conclusions and Future Work

Suggested "double-sided" marking method improves significantly the recognition accuracy without remarkable sophistication to conventional sub-word models. For 100 k and 200 k vocabularies, syllable modifications outperform morph ones on Ev set, taken into account, that the minimum syllable size is equal to 3.

It is worth noting that the sub-words with differently located markers are counted as separate elements. As a result, the "double-sided" LMs have a priori slightly smaller variety of vocabulary entries. Nevertheless, the "double-sided" variation outperforms its "single-sided" counterpart.

It was figured out, that all OOVs should be split, even if appeared once.

A comprehensive testing of suggested methods on the other corpora is currently ongoing. Investigation of Russian graphones is also referred to future work.

Acknowledgements. This work was partly supported by the DAAD (German Academic Exchange Service).

References

1. Ablimit, M., Kawahara, T., Hamdulla, A.: Lexicon optimization based on discriminative learning for automatic speech recognition of agglutinative language. Speech Commun. **60**, 78–87 (2014)

2. Bisani, M., Ney, H.: Open vocabulary speech recognition with flat hybrid models. In: Proceedings of the European Conference on Speech Communication and Technology (Eurospeech), Lisbon, Portugal, pp. 725–728 (2005)
3. Bisani, M., Ney, H.: Joint-sequence models for grapheme-to-phoneme conversion. Speech Commun. **50**(5), 434–451 (2008)
4. Bogdanov, D., Bruhtiy, A., Krivnova, O., Podrabinovich, A., Strokin, G.: Tekhnologiya formirovaniya rechevykh baz dannykh. In: Organizatsionnoe upravlenie i iskusstvennyy intellekt, pp. 239–258. Editorial URSS (2003). [Technology for Creation of Speech Corpora. In: Administration and Artificial Intelligence] (in Russian)
5. Creutz, M., Lagus, K.: Unsupervised morpheme segmentation and morphology induction from text corpora using Morfessor 1.0. Technical report A81, Helsinki University of Technology (2005). http://www.cis.hut.fi/projects/morpho
6. El-Desoky Mousa, A., Shaik, M., Schluter, R., Ney, H.: Sub-lexical language models for German LVCSR. In: Spoken Language Technology Workshop (SLT), pp. 171–176 (2010)
7. Hahn, S., Rybach, D.: Building an open vocabulary ASR system using open source software. In: Interspeech, Florence, Italy (2011). http://www-i6.informatik.rwth-aachen.de/rwth-asr/manual/index.php/Open_Vocabulary_Tutorial
8. Karpov, A., Kipyatkova, I., Ronzhin, A.: Very large vocabulary ASR for spoken Russian with syntactic and morphemic analysis. In: Proceedings of the 12th Annual Conference of the International Speech Communication Association (Interspeech), Florence, Italy (2011)
9. Karpov, A., Markov, K., Kipyatkova, I., Vazhenina, D., Ronzhin, A.: Large vocabulary Russian speech recognition using syntactico-statistical language modeling. Speech Commun. **56**, 213–228 (2014)
10. Kipyatkova, I., Karpov, A.: Creation of multiple word transcriptions for conversational Russian speech recognition. In: Proceedings of the 13th Conference "Speech and Computer" (SPECOM), St. Peterburg, Russia, pp. 71–75 (2009)
11. Kneser, R., Ney, H.: Improved backing-off for m-gram language modeling. In: International Conference on Acoustics, Speech, and Signal Processing. ICASSP, vol. 1, pp. 181–184 (1995)
12. Pellegrini, T., Lamel, L.: Automatic word decompounding for ASR in a morphologically rich language: application to Amharic. IEEE Trans. Audio Speech Lang. Process. **17**(5), 863–873 (2009)
13. Rybach, D., Hahn, S., Lehnen, P., Nolden, D., Sundermeyer, M., Tüske, Z., Wiesler, S., Schlüter, R., Ney, H.: RASR - the RWTH Aachen University open source speech recognition toolkit. In: IEEE Automatic Speech Recognition and Understanding Workshop, Hawaii, USA (2011)
14. Segalovich, I.: A fast morphological algorithm with unknown word guessing induced by a dictionary for a web search engine. In: MLMTA, pp. 273–280 (2003)
15. Shaik, M.A.B., El-Desoky Mousa, A., Schlüter, R., Ney, H.: Using morpheme and syllable based sub-words for Polish LVCSR. In: IEEE International Conference on Acoustics, Speech and Signal Processing (ICASSP), pp. 4680–4683 (2011)
16. Stolcke, A., Zheng, J., Wang, W., Abrash, V.: SRILM at sixteen: update and outlook. In: Proceedings of the IEEE Automatic Speech Recognition and Understanding Workshop, Waikoloa, Hawaii (2011)
17. Vazhenina, D., Markov, K.: Evaluation of advanced language modeling techniques for Russian LVCSR. In: Železný, M., Habernal, I., Ronzhin, A. (eds.) SPECOM 2013. LNCS, vol. 8113, pp. 124–131. Springer, Heidelberg (2013)

18. Xu, B., Ma, B., Zhang, S., Qu, F., Huang, T.: Speaker-independent dictation of Chinese speech with 32K vocabulary. In: Fourth International Conference on Spoken Language Processing ICSLP, vol. 4, pp. 2320–2323 (1996)
19. Zablotskiy, S., Zablotskaya, K., Minker, W.: Automatic pre-processing of the Russian text corpora for language modeling. In: Proceedings of the XIV International Conference "Speech and Computer" (2011)

Temporal Organization of Phrase-final Words as a Function of Pitch Movement Type

Tatiana Kachkovskaia[✉]

Department of Phonetics, Saint Petersburg State University,
Saint Petersburg, Russia
tania.kachkovskaya@gmail.com

Abstract. It is well known that the type of pitch movement has an influence on segments' (at least the stressed vowel's) duration, and so does the position of the word within the phrase. The Corpus of Professionally Read Speech was used here to study the interaction between these two factors. Statistical analysis has allowed us to obtain a description for 14 frequent pitch movement types (following the classification used in the Corpus) in terms of their temporal characteristics, namely the duration of the stressed vowel and the duration of the post-stressed vowel and the final consonant (if there were any), for words ending in -cV, -cVc, -cVcv, -cVcvc, -cVccv, and -cVccvc.

Keywords: Phrase-final lengthening · Segmental duration · Pitch movement type

1 Introduction

In most cases nuclear stress is placed on the last content word before the end of the utterance or intonational phrase. At the same time, the last word or clitic group (at least, its last vowel and the following consonants, and to some extent the last stressed vowel) is the locus of phrase-final lengthening [1–6]. Since both of these influence the duration of the final clitic group's segments, it is of particular interest how they interact.

There have been some studies on the effect of pitch movement type on the degree of phrase-final lengthening. For Russian some results are reported in [3]: in phrase-final position words are shorter for rising contours and longer for falling contours, which might be due to the fact that falling contours are more often used in final phrases (in most cases, for "full stop" intonation), while rising contours are used for questions and non-final phrases. This might be the result of an interaction between two separate factors: pitch movement type and boundary depth, since final phrases correspond to larger prosodic units—utterances. It is therefore necessary to treat separately as many factors as possible.

The present study deals with the influence of pitch movement type on the duration of stressed and post-stressed vowels and final consonants in clitic groups immediately preceding major prosodic boundaries necessarily followed

© Springer International Publishing Switzerland 2015
A. Ronzhin et al. (Eds.): SPECOM 2015, LNAI 9319, pp. 422–428, 2015.
DOI: 10.1007/978-3-319-23132-7_52

by a pause. We distinguish between two types of prosodic boundaries: signalling the end of the utterance (utterance-final) and signalling the end of the intonational phrase but not the end of the utterance (IP-final).

We have also tried to control for other factors. To account for the clitic group's accentual and syllable structure, we decided to process only clitic groups ending in -cV, -cVc, -cVcv, -cVcvc, -cVccv, and -cVccvc, which are the most frequent CV-patterns occurring word-finally in Russian; thus, word CV-pattern was one of the parameters considered in the analysis. Factors such as segment type and tempo were eliminated by means of using normalized duration values; we have also imposed some conditions on the length of prosodic unit and on its internal structure (for more detail see section "Method").

As soon as we decide to take into account the large number of factors influencing segment duration, we come across the issue of how much data are needed. The solution we have chosen is to use a speech corpus.

2 Material

For the present study the Corpus of Professionally Read Speech (CORPRES) [7] was chosen. The corpus comprises texts of different speaking styles recorded from 4 male and 4 female speakers and contains 60 h of recorded speech, 40 % of which has been manually segmented (into phrases, words and sounds) and fully annotated, both phonetically and prosodically. Prosodic information includes the pitch movement type in the intonation center, pause type, and prominence.

For the present study 14 frequent pitch movement types (contours) have been selected (see Tables 1 and 2). It is worth noting that in utterance-final and IP-final positions different sets of pitch movement types are used. The system adopted for prosodic annotation of CORPRES is described in detail in [8]. For our analysis we have chosen 4 speakers, 2 male and 2 female, who had recorded more material than others—approximately 5 h each.

3 Method

In order to get all the necessary information about the segments (vowels and consonants) in question, a Python script was written to process the annotation files of the corpus. For each segment we obtained information about its duration and context. Contextual parameters included the length of prosodic units (accentual phrase and intonational phrase) where the segment occurs and the position of each prosodic unit within the higher one; the CV-pattern of the clitic group where the segment occurs (e.g. "cVccv" for /ˈmaska/, "mask"; uppercase "V" stands for the stressed vowel; phoneme /j/ is treated as a vowel or a consonant according to its realization); the presence of a pause after the intonational phrase; pitch movement type and the position of nuclear stress within the phrase.

Despite the fact that the corpus is manually segmented, it is important to pay special attention to the right boundaries of vowels followed by a pause or a

Table 1. The intonation contours frequently occurring in utterance-final position.

Contour	Description and *usage*
01	falling to very low
	end of a paragraph
01a	falling to low
	end of a sentence
01b	falling to non-low
	as a link to the next sentence
01c	falling from high to low
	establishing contact with the listener
02	falling from higher level + intensity
	emphasis
03a	falling from higher level + intensity
	wh-questions
04	falling from higher level + intensity
	exclamations
09	falling to low or non-low
	parenthetical clauses
07	rising-(falling)
	yes/no questions

voiceless consonant. For our study we analysed only those parts of vowels where pitch periods could be seen clearly, thus excluding breathy and creaky endings.

As mentioned in the Introduction, only frequently occurring CV-patterns have been analysed. Since the CV-pattern might influence the duration values, these patterns were treated separately, although in some cases statistical analysis allowed us to analyse two CV-patterns together (e.g., the difference in vowel duration between cVcvc and cVccvc was never statistically significant).

Based on the frequency data, we have selected only intonational phrases containing from 2 to 6 clitic groups and at least 5 syllables. We also limited our choice to intonational phrases with no internal pauses and the nuclear stress on the last clitic group.

In order to be able to compare duration values for different types of segments it is reasonable to calculate *normalized* duration values. Here the formula given in [9, formula (4)] was used, which allowed us to compensate for the average duration of the segment, its standard deviation, and tempo:

$$\tilde{d}(i) = \frac{d(i) - \alpha\mu_p}{\alpha\sigma_p}, \tag{1}$$

where $\tilde{d}(i)$ is the normalized duration of segment i, $d(i)$ is its absolute duration, α is the tempo coefficient, and μ_p and σ_p are the mean and standard deviation

Table 2. The intonation contours frequently occurring in intonational-phrase-final position.

Contour	Description and *usage*
10	falling to low or non-low
	non-finality
02	falling from higher level + intensity
	emphasis
11	rising-(falling)
	non-finality
11b	rising-(falling) + intensity
	non-finality + emphasis
12	high-rising
	non-finality
13	low (falling)-rising
	non-finality

of the duration of the corresponding phone p. The tempo coefficient (α) was calculated using formula provided in [9, formula (6)]:

$$\alpha = \frac{1}{N} \sum_{i=1}^{N} \frac{d_i}{\mu_{p_i}}, \tag{2}$$

where d_i is the duration of segment i, and μ_{p_i} is the mean duration of the corresponding phone.

Such method enables us to put duration values for different segment types (e.g., closed and open vowels, which differ in inherent duration, or consonants of different types) on the same scale.

To estimate the influence of different factors on segment duration, statistical analysis was carried out using R. For normally distributed data ANOVA and pairwise t-tests were used with Welch's correction for unequal variance if necessary; for non-normally distributed data Kruskal-Wallis test was used instead.

4   Stressed Vowels

Based on statistical analysis of the influence of CV-pattern on vowel duration, we have found it necessary to analyse duration values separately for different CV-patterns; the only 2 patterns which could be grouped together were cVccvc and cVcvc.

4.1   IP-final Position

The difference in stressed vowel duration for rising vs. falling contours was found *significant* for at least 2 speakers for each CV-pattern. For the rising contours these duration values were lower than for the falling contours. However, for clitic groups ending in cV and cVc the results were highly speaker-specific, with direction of inequality changing from speaker to speaker. Statistical analysis provided the following relations between contours in terms of normalised stressed vowel duration (significant for at least 2 speakers at $p < 0.05$).

- cVcvc and cVccvc: $02 > 11$, $02 > 12$, $10 > 11$;
- cVccv: $02 > 11$, $02 > 12$, $02 > 13$, $10 > 11$;
- cVcv: $02 > 11$, $02 > 12$, $10 > 11$, $10 > 12$, $11b > 11$.

It seems clear that here contour types can be clearly divided into two groups: falling (10 and 02) and rising (11, 11b, 12 and 13), where the former group shows higher duration values of stressed vowels. Within these groups the duration values do not differ, the only exception being $11 < 11b$.

As mentioned above, clitic groups with stress on the last syllable (patterns cV and cVc) showed contradictory results. For some speakers, higher vowel duration values have been observed for the rising contours compared to those for the falling contours, while for some speakers the opposite held true; what is more, all the differences were statistically significant. We are unable to provide any explanation for these results so far. Such difference might be speaker-specific, although in order to clarify this question a much larger speech corpus is needed.

4.2   Utterance-final Position

The difference in stressed vowel duration for rising vs. falling contours was found *non-significant* for all CV-patterns and all speakers but pattern cVc, where the rising contours showed lower values than the falling contours for 2 of 4 speakers.

A more detailed comparison revealed some relations between contours in terms of normalised stressed vowel duration. Here we provide only those results which were found significant for at least 2 speakers at $p < 0.05$.

- cVcvc and cVccvc: $01 < 01c$, $01 < 02$, $01 < 04$;
- cVccv: $01a < 01c$, $01a < 02$;
- cVcv: $01 < 01b$, $01 < 03a$, $09 < 01b$, $09 < 01c$, $09 < 02$;
- cVc: $01 < 01c$, $01 < 02$, $09 < 01a$, $09 < 01b$, $07 < 01c$, $09 < 01c$, $09 < 02$;
- cV: $01 < 01b$, $01a < 01b$, $01c < 01b$, $02 < 01b$.

In general, for stressed vowels we observe a tendency for contour types 01, 01a, and 09 to show the lowest vowel duration values, while 01b, 01c and 02 seem to show the highest values. The values for the only rising contour 07 lie somewhere in the middle, which is why the direction of pitch movement had almost no influence on vowel duration.

5   Post–stressed Vowels

According to statistical analysis, for post-stressed vowels it was possible to group patterns cVcv and cVccv together; the same goes for cVcvc and cVccvc.

5.1   IP-final Position

In IP-final position normalised duration of post-stressed vowels was significantly higher for rising contours compared to falling contours. For patterns cVcv and cVccv the difference was significant for 3 speakers, for patterns cVcvc and cVccvc—for all 4 speakers. The relations between contour types in terms of normalised duration of post-stressed vowels are as follows (significant at $p < 0.05$):

- cVcvc and cVccvc: $02 < 11$, $02 < 12$, $10 < 11$;
- cVccv and cVcv: $02 < 11$, $02 < 12$, $02 < 13$, $10 < 11$, $10 < 11b$, $10 < 12$, $10 < 13$, $11b < 12$.

Interestingly, for post-stressed vowels the results are opposite to those for stressed vowels: falling contours (02 and 10) show lower duration values than rising contours (11, 11b, 12 and 13).

5.2   Utterance-final Position

In utterance-final position normalised duration of post-stressed vowels was significantly higher for rising contours compared to falling contours only for patterns cVcv and cVccv ($p < 0.01$ for 2 speakers).

A comparison of contour types revealed the following relations in terms of normalised duration of post-stressed vowels (significant for at least 2 speakers at $p < 0.05$):

- cVcvc and cVccvc: $01 < 01b$, $01 < 09$;
- cVcv and cVccv: 01b and 07 have longer post-stressed vowels than any other contour types.

The results seem to show that in utterance-final position post-stressed vowels reveal the same tendencies as stressed vowels (see above): low duration values for 01 and high for 01b.

6   Final Consonants

It appears rather difficult to compare intonation contour types in terms of final consonant duration. As shown by statistical analysis, final consonant duration in clitic groups ending in cVccvc does not depend on contour type for all 4 speakers for utterance-final position and for 3 speakers in IP-final position. For clitic groups in IP-final position other CV-patterns (cVcvc and cVc) showed non-significant influence of contour type on final consonant duration for 2 speakers, while other speakers failed to reveal any conformity.

For clitic groups in utterance-final position the only CV-pattern which yielded some results was cVc ($p < 0.05$ for 2 speakers):

- cVc: $01 < 01a$, $01 < 01b$, $01 < 01c$, $01 < 03a$, $01 < 09$.

The absence of interaction between final consonant duration and intonation contour type leads us to a conclusion that the final consonant does not contribute to the organisation of the intonation contour.

7   Conclusions

The results of statistical analysis applied to normalized duration values for stressed and post-stressed vowels and consonants in utterance-final and IP-final clitic groups allow us to make the following conclusions.

1. In intonation-phrase-final clitic groups
   - stressed vowels have *higher* normalized duration values for the falling contours (10 and 02) compared to the rising contours (11, 11b, 12, 13);
   - post-stressed vowels have *lower* normalized duration values for the falling contours (10 and 02) compared to the rising contours (11, 11b, 12, 13).
2. In utterance-final clitic groups
   - the direction of pitch movement does not have influence on the stressed vowel duration;
   - both the stressed and post-stressed vowels have the highest normalized duration values for contour types 01b (used to express a link to the next sentence), 01c (used to establish contact with the listener), and 02 (used for emphasis);
   - the lowest values are realised in contours 01 (signalling the end of a paragraph), 01a (signalling the end of a sentence), and 09 (used in parenthetical clauses).
3. In most cases normalized duration of final consonants does not depend on the intonation contour.

Acknowledgements. The research is supported by Saint Petersburg State University (grant 31.37.353.2015).

References

1. Turk, A., Shattuck-Hufnagel, S.: Multiple targets of phrase-final lengthening in American English words. J. Phonetics **35**, 445–472 (2007)
2. Cambier-Langeveld, T., Nespor, M., van Heuven, V.J.: The domain of final lengthening in production and perception in Dutch. In: Kokkinakis, G., Fakotakis, N., Dermatas, E. (eds.) Proceedings of Eurospeech 1997, pp. 931–934 (1997)
3. Volskaya, N.B., Stepanova, S.: On the temporal component of intonational phrasing. In: Proceedings - SPECOM 2004, pp. 641–644 (2004)
4. Berkovits, R.: Durational effects in final lengthening, gapping, and contrastive stress. Lang. Speech **37**(3), 237–250 (1994)
5. Oller, D.K.: The effect of position in utterance on speech segment duration in English. JASA **54**, 1235–1247 (1973)
6. Cho, T., Kim, J., Kim, S.: Preboundary lengthening and preaccentual shortening across syllables in a trisyllabic word in English. JASA **133**, 384–390 (2013)
7. Skrelin, P., Volskaya, N., Kocharov, D., Evgrafova, K., Glotova, O., Evdokimova, V.: CORPRES - Corpus of Russian professionally read speech. In: Sojka, P., Horák, A., Kopeček, I., Pala, K. (eds.) TSD 2010. LNCS, vol. 6231, pp. 392–399. Springer, Heidelberg (2010)
8. Volskaya, N.B., Skrelin, P.A.: Prosodic model for Russian. In: Proceedings of Nordic Prosody X, pp. 249–260. Peter Lang, Frankfurt am Main (2009)
9. Wightman, C.W., et al.: Segmental durations in the vicinity of prosodic phrase boundaries. JASA **91**, 1707–1717 (1992)

The "One Day of Speech" Corpus: Phonetic and Syntactic Studies of Everyday Spoken Russian

Natalia Bogdanova-Beglarian, Gregory Martynenko,
and Tatiana Sherstinova[(✉)]

St. Petersburg State University,
Universitetskaya Nab. 11, St. Petersburg 199034, Russia
nvbogdanova_2005@mail.ru, {g.martynenko,sherstinova}@gmail.com

Abstract. The studies described in the paper are made on the base of the ORD – "One day of speech" – corpus of Russian everyday speech which contains long-term audio recordings of daily communication. The ORD corpus provides rich authentic material for research in phonetics and syntax of spoken Russian, and may be used for adjustment and improvement of speech synthesis and recognition systems. Current phonetic investigations of the ORD corpus relate to temporal studies, study of speech reduction, phonetic realization of words and affixes, investigation of phonetic errors and mondegreens, studies of rhythm structures and hesitation phenomena. Syntactic studies primarily deal with linear word order of syntactic groups, syntactic complexity of spoken utterances, and specific syntactic phenomena of spontaneous speech. In this paper, we summarize main achievements in phonetic and syntactic studies made on the base of the ORD corpus and outline some directions for further investigations.

Keywords: Everyday spoken Russian · Speech corpus · Phonetics · Syntax

1 Introduction: The ORD Corpus

Everyday spoken Russian has been the subject of scientific analysis since the works of E. Zemskaja, O. Sirotinina, O. Lapteva, N. Rozanova, M. Kitajgorodskaja, and other linguists. However, up to present, there were not enough linguistic resources of Russian real-life spontaneous speech. For example, the Spoken Speech Subcorpus in Russian National Corpus does not contain any audio data at all, consisting just of speech transcripts [1]. The other well-known Night Dream Stories corpus contains both texts and thoroughly annotated speech recordings. However, this corpus is relatively small (about 2 h of recordings, 14000 words in transcripts) and contains a restricted number of spoken genres (mainly narratives) [2]. There are also other Russian speech corpora that should be mentioned: RuSpeech corpus [3], an annotated corpus of Russian

© Springer International Publishing Switzerland 2015
A. Ronzhin et al. (Eds.): SPECOM 2015, LNAI 9319, pp. 429–437, 2015.
DOI: 10.1007/978-3-319-23132-7_53

speech [4], corpus of emotion Russian speech [5] and some other resources. However, all these corpora either contain no everyday speech recordings or are limited just to few communicative situations (like the latter one).

The only Russian corpus containing spoken everyday speech recorded in natural and diverse communicative situations is the "One Day of Speech" (ORD) corpus that has its origin in St. Petersburg State University. The recordings are made by participants-volunteers who spend a whole day with switched-on voice recorders and record all their audible communication [6]. The similar methodology of long-term recordings had been earlier used for collecting data for the British National Corpus [7] and the JST ESP corpus in Japan [8].

Speech is transcribed and selectively annotated on different levels – phonetic, lexical, grammatical, and pragmatic levels. Transcribing and most annotations are made in ELAN [9]. Phonetic annotation is made in Praat [10]. Quantitative data processing is made for annotations on each level [11].

Nowadays, the ORD corpus is one of the most representative collections of everyday spoken Russian. It contains more than 1000 h of recordings gathered from 110 main participants and hundreds of their interlocutors. The ORD volunteer participants represent various professional and status strata. The age of participants rangers from 18 to 77 years with an average value of 37 years. Speech transcripts comprise about 500000 words.

The ORD corpus provides rich authentic material for research in phonetics and syntax of spoken Russian, and for solving applied linguistic problems in speech technologies (e.g., it may be used for adjustment and improvement of speech synthesis and recognition systems, and for forensic phonetics). In this paper we summarize main achievements in phonetic and syntactic studies made on the base of this corpus and outline some directions for further investigations.

2   Phonetic Studies

The initial goal of the ORD corpus was to conduct phonetic studies of Russian everyday speech. Nowadays, we may list the following phonetic aspects that are being successively investigated on the ORD data: temporal studies, study of speech reduction, phonetic realization of words and affixes, investigation of phonetic errors in speech production and mondegreens in speech perception, studies of rhythm structures and hesitation phenomena.

2.1   Temporal Studies

All multimedia annotations of speech signal are made in linguistic annotator ELAN, therefore each annotated phenomenon (sound, morpheme, word, phrase, turn, etc.) refers to a particular segment in correspondent sound file and has particular duration. Thus, temporal study of elements is possible on all linguistic levels. For example, on phonetic level we study speech rate, rhythmic patterns, temporal registers of Russian everyday speech, and other temporal phenomena.

In our phonetic studies, first of all, we obtained the frequency distribution of utterance length in words. Based on the ORD data, the average utterance length for spoken Russian is 4.35 words (SD = 4.02). Most of all utterances consist of a single word or a word-like particle (25.26 %). Two-word utterances make 15.58 % of the whole data, three-word utterances have the third rank that makes 12.45 %. Four-word utterances make 10,98 %, five-word utterances – 8.74 %, etc. [12].

If to measure utterance length in syllables, it turns out that the most frequent Russian utterances consist of one or two syllables and represent 11.0 % and 11.7 % of all utterances respectively. Three-syllable utterances are ranked third (8.7 %), four-syllable utterances take 7.7 %, five-syllable – 6.88 % and six-syllable utterances – 6.50 %. Utterances longer than 20 or more syllables take up less than 1 % of the whole. Thus, more than half of all spoken communication consists of short utterances with a length up to 6 syllables [12].

Therefore, the majority of Russian spoken interaction consists of one or a few word utterances that contain one or few syllables. As for the dependency of average utterance duration on their length in syllables, it is well described by the following linear function: $y = 133.28x + 367.5$, where x is a number of syllables, and y is an average duration of such utterances in milliseconds [12].

An average tempo of ORD informants is 5.31 syllables per second (syl/s). The variation among informants begins from the slowest 3.6 syl/s till the fastest 6.7 syl/s. These numbers are on average higher than, for example, in Norwegian (3.5–4.5 syl/s), in standard northern Dutch (5.2 syl/s), or in French (according to some data, 4.31 syl/s). However, they are significantly lower than in Spanish (7.81 syl/s) or in Brazilian Portuguese (6.57 syl/s). As Russians in Russia, with approximately the same tempo, people speak English in the UK (3.16–5.33 syl/s), as well as in the USA (3.1–5.4 syl/s) [13].

It was determined that there are several factors that influence speech tempo in Russian: gender (men speak faster than women), age (the older a speaker, the slower he or she speaks), level of language competence (the higher the competence level, the slower is the speech), and social role of speakers (speech is faster when communicating with friends than in work settings) [13, 14].

Finally, the hypothesis on existence of two temporal registers of speech was proposed: (1) the "regular" (or dialogue) register is used for producing utterances whose length does not exceed 15 syllables. Its distinctive feature is a strong interrelation between an average syllable duration (syllable rate) of utterances and their length in syllable (in this case the average syllable duration is a function from utterance length in syllables, ranging from 450 ms to 150 ms) and (2) the "speedy" (or monologue) register is used for producing longer utterances (exceeding 15 syllables). In contrast to a dialogue register, the average syllable duration (or an average utterance rate) of a "speedy" register does not depend on utterance length in syllables and is equal to approximately 150 ms [12].

2.2   Study of Reduction. Phonetic Realization of Words and Affixes

Reduced forms of different words and phrases, especially the most commonly used in everyday Russian, are analyzed. Many of these forms have already got correspondent written forms, which may be found in modern Russian literature and which are frequent in electronic communication. Current analysis touched on all possible features of reduced forms: (1) pronunciation (i.e., detailed phonetic transcription), (2) spelling (common variants of written forms), (3) semantic features, and (4) pragmatic features. Based on the results, the multimedia dictionary of reduced forms in Russian is created [15]. The study of spontaneous speech reduction may be used for building an authentic lexicon of word pronunciations.

In search for the correlation between grammatical meanings of morphemes and their phonetic realization, the real phonetic transcription of inflectional affixes for different speakers in various communication situations was obtained [16]. Statistical tables are drawn with correspondence of orthography, real phonetic transcription, and grammatical categories. These data provided the basis for the Audio dictionary of Russian inflectional affixes.

2.3   Studying the "Weak Points" in Speech Perception and Production

The lists of common mistakes of hearing (mondegreens or incorrect attribution of words) that were made by linguists-experts while transcribing the ORD recordings were compiled [17]. Based on these lists, the analysis of significant perceptive elements of word forms that are essential for their proper attribution was made. The following elements turned out to be invariant despite incorrect recognition of words: stressed syllable position, segmental parts of the stressed syllable (both consonants and vowels), number of syllables, consonantal "skeleton" of word form, its either initial or final segmental fragment.

The analysis of the phonetic mistakes that are typically done by Russian speaking people in everyday speech was made, too. Most common mistakes are the following: incorrect stress position in words and phrases, the alignment of phonetic features in neighboring words, palatalization errors, substitution of proper words by not-existing quasi-words, which are phonetically similar to the prototype words. However, we should point out that phonetic mistakes occur comparatively less than other type of errors, which have been also analyzed. Cf.: phonetic errors – 17 %, lexical errors – 28 %, morphology errors – 31 %, and syntactic errors – 24 % [18].

2.4   Russian Speech Rhythm Studies

Empirical investigation of the ORD recordings has revealed a tendency towards the usage of symmetrical rhythmical structures built of isochronic or quasi-isochronic segments in Russian everyday speech [19]. The most typical are structures consisting of two, three, four, etc. quasi-isochronic segments. Moreover, it was observed that phenomenon of isochronism of speech rhythmic structures can simultaneously appear on different structural levels. We have a hypothesis that the lower quasi-isochronic level performs the role of some kind of inner metronome, which organizes our speech flow. It may change its tempo on borders of rhythmic groups. However, these structural levels do not correlate with linguistic levels. We may suggest that the distribution of linguistic units onto "isochronic boxes" is determined mainly by pragmatics: the more important the segment is the more "boxes" it may take [19].

The use of fillers and other discourse markers in spontaneous speech may be explained in many cases just by unconscious desire of speakers to reach this temporal pattern. The examples of such cases are given and explained in [20]. This hypothesis is to be tested on representative ORD data.

2.5 Hesitation Phenomena

Speech hesitations are a common feature of spontaneous speech production. According to the ORD data, both filled and silent hesitation pauses are among the most frequent elements of spoken Russian. They naturally occur in all types of speech and by all speakers. Different types of hesitations found in the corpus have been analyzed. The classification model of hesitation phenomena was proposed. The most frequent hesitations are the following: silent pauses, stretching of sounds, interruptions, repetitions, filler-words, other kinds of fillers, and paralinguistic actions. The new term "verbal hesitation" has been introduced for denotation of verbal fillers of hesitation nature [21].

3 Syntactic Studies

Syntax is a part of grammar where the features of spoken language are most clearly revealed in a variety of ways (for example, cf. [22]). Syntactic studies of spontaneous speech are very important for ASR systems. Nowadays, language models of the most speech recognition systems are trained on the corpora of written texts. However, written Russian and spoken Russian differ greatly from each other in respect to some fundamental syntactic features, as it is shown below. Therefore, n-gram models that are built for written language cannot be efficiently applied to LVCSR tasks. That particularly refers to recognition of spontaneous real-life speech. Speech transcriptions of the ORD corpus form a valuable resource for creating a language model of spoken Russian.

Several syntactic studies have been already made on the base of the ORD corpus. One of them is a pilot research of verbal groups in Russian spontaneous speech. Based on the random sample of 550 verbal branches represented in the formal way, the following models of left- and right-branching subordinations were found:

1. Verbs without dependents (V): 13.64%;
2. Symmetrical verbal groups (*1V1, 2V2, 3V3*): 14.00%;
3. Generally left-branching verbal groups (*1V, 2V, 3V, 4V, 5V, 2V1, 3V1, 3V2, 4V1*): 59.27%;
4. Pure left-branching verbal groups (*1V, 2V, 3V, 4V, 5V*): 50.36%;
5. Generally right-branching verbal groups (*V1, V2, V3, V4, V5, 1V2, 1V3, 1V4, 2V3*): 12.90%;

6. Pure right-branching verbal groups (*V1, V2, V3, V4, V5*): 7.45 %.

We have calculated the averages, characterizing left- and right- branching in verbal groups. Thus, the average left-width of the branch equals to 1.195, the average right-width of the branch is 1.565. Their ratio (L/R) equals to 1.309, therefore we observe in spoken Russian an evident trend towards left-branching asymmetry.

These results are very different from data obtained on the material of written texts. For example, in [23] is shown that in written Russian texts the ratio of left-branching structures to right-branching ones is close to 1 (i.e., almost symmetrical) with the slight tendency to right-branching:

Fiction: $(L/R)=0.974$
Scientific texts: $(L/R)=0.984$
Poetry: $(L/R)=0.983$
Spoken speech: $(L/R)=1.310$

Therefore, written Russian in this aspect leans towards the mirror symmetry, while everyday spoken Russian is left asymmetrical [23].

Amazingly, the difference in branching preference between written and spoken Russian is even greater than that between different languages. Thus, we may claim that in this aspect the difference between written and spoken Russian is larger than that between written Russian and written English.

The other syntactic studies made on the ORD data include the analysis of repetitions, interruptions, self-corrections, "plug-in" constructions, and the ways of reporting someone else's speech [24]. Elements of meta-communication that are common for spontaneous speech and that depend on the type of communication and speaker's characteristics have been studied as well.

4   Some Directions for Further Research

Recently, we have started a large sociolinguistic project with an aim to analyze special characteristics of everyday Russian used by different social groups, and to reveal how the language actually functions and what modifications does it have in a nowadays society. Speech of the major social groups of a contemporary Russian city (age-, gender-, professional-related, etc.) has to be analyzed on different linguistic levels in regard to social information about the speakers. In light of this task, it has became necessary to extend the volume of speech data gathered from particular social groupings [25] and to make correspondent adaptation of the corpus itself. Thus, "one day of speech" recordings are continued in 2015.

The study of speech of different social groups from the population of the second biggest Russian city – St. Petersburg – is to be conducted on phonetic, lexical, morphological and syntactic levels. For example, the following parameters are to be analyzed on phonetic level: (a) temporal characteristics of speech (overall speech tempo, duration of speech elements, typical rhythmic structures); (b) phonetic realization of frequently reduced forms, discursive markers and fillers; and (c) prosodic models for particular types of utterances. Regular studies of intonation have not been earlier conducted on the ORD data.

As for syntactic studies, it is planned to carry out syntactic analysis for the following parameters: (a) linear word order of verbal and noun syntactic groups, (b) syntactic complexity of spoken utterances (e.g., height and width of linearized trees, left-branching structures vs. right-branching ones, syntactic discontinuity) [26], (c) specific syntactic phenomena of spontaneous speech (parcellation, ellipsis, breaks, incompleteness, self-correction, etc.), and (d) the usage of syntactic markers (prepositions, conjunctions, introductory words, etc.).

Besides, it is planned to conduct studies of paralinguistic phenomena and psycholinguistic studies (dependency of speech characteristics from speaker's psychological type) on all linguistic levels.

In this review, we intentionally skipped the description of lexical and morphological studies made on the ORD data. These investigations are actively performed as well (for example, cf. [11,16,24]) and deserve a separate review.

Sociolinguistic extension of the corpus allows to increase the volume of speech transcripts up to 1 million words during the next 1.5 years. Therefore, the ORD corpus will be a representative resource of everyday spoken Russian, suitable for solving both theoretical and applied linguistics problems.

Acknowledgements. The research is made within the framework of the project "Everyday Russian Language in Different Social Groups" supported by the Russian Scientific Foundation, project # 14-18-02070.

References

1. Grishina, E.: Ustnaja rech v Nacionalnom korpuse russkogo jazyka. Nacionalnyj korpus russkogo jazyka: 2003–2005, pp. 94–110. Indrik Publication, Moscow (2005) (in Russian)
2. Kibrik, A., Podlesskaya, V. (eds.): Rasskazy o snovidenijakh. Korpusnoe issledovanie ustnogo russkogo diskursa. Yazyki slavyanskikh kul'tur, Moscow (2009) (in Russian)
3. Krivnova, O.: Russkij rechevoj korpus RuSpeech. In: Proceedings of the VII International Scientific Conference "Fonetika segodnia", pp. 54–56 (2013)
4. Skrelin, P., Volskaya, N., Kocharov, D., Evgrafova, K. et al.: A fully annotated corpus of Russian speech. In: Proceedings of LREC 2010, pp. 109–112, Malta (2010)
5. Kotov, A., Gopkalo, O.: Russkojazychnyj emocional'nyj korpus: kommunikativnoe vzaimodejstvie v real'nykh emocional'nykh situaciajkh. In: Proceedings of the International Conference "Corpus linguistics-2013", pp. 211–216. St. Petersburg State University, St. Petersburg (2013) (in Russian)
6. Asinovsky, A., Bogdanova, N., Rusakova, M., Ryko, A., Stepanova, S., Sherstinova, T.: The ORD speech corpus of Russian everyday communication "One Speaker's Day": creation principles and annotation. In: Matoušek, V., Mautner, P. (eds.) TSD 2009. LNCS, vol. 5729, pp. 250–257. Springer, Heidelberg (2009)

7. Reference Guide for the British National Corpus. http://www.natcorp.ox.ac.uk/docs/URG.xml

8. Campbell, N.: Speech and expression; the value of a longitudinal corpus. In: Proceedings of LREC 2004, pp. 183–186 (2004)

9. ELAN - Linguistic Annotator. Version 4.9.0. http://www.mpi.nl/corpus/html/elan/

10. Praat: Doing Phonetics by computer. http://www.praat.org

11. Sherstinova, T.: Quantitative data processing in the ORD speech corpus of Russian everyday communication. In: Grzybek, P., Kelih, E., Mačutek, J. (eds.) Text and Language: Structures, Functions, Interrelations, pp. 195–206. Praesens Verlag, Wien (2010)

12. Sherstinova, T.: Russian everyday utterances: the top lists and some statistics. In: Thielemann, N., Kosta, P. (eds.) Approaches to Slavic Interaction. Dialogue Studies, vol. 20, pp. 105–116. John Benjamins Publication Company, Amsterdam/Philadelphia (2013)

13. Stepanova, S.: Speech rate as reflection of speakers social characteristics. In: Thielemann, N., Kosta, P. (eds.) Approaches to Slavic Interaction. Dialogue Studies, vol. 20, pp. 117–129. John Benjamins Publishing Company, Amsterdam/Philadelphia (2013)

14. Metlova, V.: Temp rechi v svobodnoj kommunikacii: sociolingvisticheskij aspekt. Vestnik Permskogo universiteta. Rossijskaja i zarubezhnaja filologija 4(28), pp. 58–65 (2014) (in Russian)

15. Bogdanova, N., Palshina, D.: Reducirovannye formy russkoj rechi (opyt leksikograficheskogo opisanija). In: Proceedings of Sc. Conference "Slovo. Slovar'. Slovesnost': Tekst slovaria i kontekst leksikografii", pp. 491–497. RGPU imeni A. Gerzena, St. Petersburg (2010) (in Russian)

16. Stepanova, S., Asinovsky, A., Ryko, A., Sherstinova, T.: Zvukovaja real'nost' slovoizmenitel'nykh affiksov (po dannym Zvukovogo korpusa russkogo jazyka). In: Proceedings of the International Conference "Dialog 2010", pp. 41–46, Bekasovo (2010) (in Russian)

17. Stepanova, S.: Oslyshki i peresprosy kak baza dlia issedovanija vosprijatija rechi. In: Aktual'nye voprosy teoreticheskoj i prikladnoj fonetiki, pp. 383–397, BukiVedi, Moscow (2014) (in Russian)

18. Bogdanova-Beglarjan, N. (ed.): Zvukovoj korpus kak material dlja analiza russkoj rechi. Chast 1. Chtenie. Pereskaz. Opisanie. Philological Faculty of St. Petersburg State University, St. Petersburg (2013) (in Russian)

19. Sherstinova, T.: Ob izokhronnosti strukturnykh jedinic v spontannoj rechi (k postanovke problemy). In: Asinovsky, A.S., Bogdanova N.V. (eds.) Proceedings of XXXVII International Philological Conference, Issue 23, pp. 109–118. St. Petersburg State University, St. Petersburg (2010) (in Russian)

20. Bogdanova-Beglarian, N., Sherstinova, T., and Kisloshchuk, A.: O ritmoobrazujushchej funkcii diskursivnykh jedinic. Vestnik Permskogo universiteta. Rossijskaja i zarubezhnaja filologija 2(22), pp. 7–17 (2013) (in Russian)

21. Bogdanova-Beglarian, N.: Kto ishchet - vsegda li najdet? (o poiskovoj funkcii verbalnykh khezitativov v russkoj spontannoj rechi). In: Proceedings of the International Conference "Dialog-2013", pp. 125–136 (2013) (in Russian)

22. Lapteva, O.A.: Russkij razgovornyj sintaksis. Nauka, Moscow (1976) (in Russian)

23. Martynenko, G.: Sintaksis zhivoj spontannoj rechi: simmetrija linejnykh poriadkov. In: Proceedings of the International Conference "Corpus linguistics-2015" pp. 307–314 (2015) (in Russian)

24. Bogdanova-Beglarjan, N. (ed.): Zvukovoj korpus kak material dlja analiza russkoj rechi. Chast 2. Teoreticheskie i prakticheskie aspekty analiza. Vol. 1. O nekotorykh osobennostjakh ustnoj spontannoj rechi raznogo tipa. Zvukovoj korpus kak material dlja prepodavanija russkogo jazyka v inostrannoj auditorii. Philological Faculty of St. Petersburg State University, St. Petersburg (2014) (in Russian)
25. Baeva, E.M.: O sposobax sociolingvisticheskoj balansirovki ustnogo korpusa (na primere "Odnogo rechevogo dn'a"). Vestnik Permskogo universiteta. Rossijskaja i zarubezhnaja filologia, 4(28), pp. 48–57 (2014) (in Russian)
26. Martynenko, G.: Osnovy stilemetrii. Leningrad State University, Leningrad (1988) (in Russian)

The Multi-level Approach to Speech Corpora Annotation for Automatic Speech Recognition

Igor Glavatskih, Tatyana Platonova[✉], Valeria Rogozhina, Anna Shirokova,
Anna Smolina, Mikhail Kotov, Anna Ovsyannikova, Sergey Repalov,
and Mikhail Zulkarneev

Stel - Computer Systems Ltd, Moscow, Russia
{glavatskih_ia,platonova_ts,rogozina_vs,smolina_aa,
anna_a,kotov,anna}@stel.ru, repalov@gmail.com, zulkarneev@mail.ru
http://www.stel.ru

Abstract. In the paper the multi-level approach to audio files annotation is briefly summarized. The emphasis is mainly placed on the development of annotation rules. Firstly, some general requirements are outlined and more specific markers are listed, which may or may not be included in a particular rule set depending on the given practical task. Then software tools used for creating annotations and its spell-checking are described, and an example of a database created on the basis of the multi-level approach to annotation is given. Lastly, the application of tag sorting in ASR training and testing is discussed.

Keywords: Speech annotation · Speech corpus · Speech data · Speech recognition · Annotation guidelines · Orthographic transcript

1 Introduction

Speech corpora creation plays an essential role in language processing and is vastly used in practical tasks of speech technology such as automatic speech recognition. The quality of these systems' output strongly corresponds with the quality of the database used for their training.

As highlighted in [1], there are several steps in speech corpus development, and the most important of them are speech data collection and annotation. The techniques and methods used here mostly depend on the purpose a database is intended for. Thus, data can be collected online via mobile devices and web applications as in [2], or recorded in a studio as in [1,3]. Speech itself can be either read or spontaneous. In case of read speech balanced phonetically rich sentences of optimal length, produced either manually [1] or automatically [2,4], can be used. This method simplifies the process of annotation to some degree, since the real utterances are usually not very different from the text. However, it must be pointed out that although it is helpful for some problems' solutions, the ASR systems' performance on spontaneous speech data would not be of a high quality in this case.

© Springer International Publishing Switzerland 2015
A. Ronzhin et al. (Eds.): SPECOM 2015, LNAI 9319, pp. 438–445, 2015.
DOI: 10.1007/978-3-319-23132-7_54

At the same time, spontaneous speech has recently become one of the speech technology's main focuses due to the need of enabling natural human-machine communication. State-of-the-art ASR tasks (such as voice web search, voice dictation applications, etc.) are not generally performed on high-quality noise-free signals produced by qualified speakers. So for better output the training material should match the type of speech and the environment the speech recognizer would run in. Therefore, speech corpora annotation method should provide a means to reflect not only linguistic content, but also some extralinguistic information within the utterance.

In consideration of the foregoing, a multi-level approach to annotation was designed, which covers several levels of information about speech data: broad orthographic transcription (word sequence actually pronounced and speech/nonspeech events within utterances), the information about the signal as a whole and the recording environment, the speaker information. This method is used to collect large corpora of spontaneous speech on different languages for developing multilingual ASR [5].

It the present paper characteristics of this approach are discussed in details. Furthermore, the program tool used in the annotation process is described and an example of a database created is given.

2   Multi-level Method of Speech Material Annotation

2.1   General Requirements

The design of annotation rules depends on several issues. First of all, it is the audio data submitted for annotation. For instance, if the audio file is long, it is reasonable to mark out the speech fragments for further annotation. Besides, if experts are dealing with noisy signals, the preliminary automatic processing should be recommended to exclude signals not valid for any annotation.

The language of annotation should be taken into account as well (especially in the case of adapting existing rules to a new language), since each language has its own peculiarities and phonetic phenomena that do not occur in other languages and are worth marking (e.g. accents, umlauts and other diacritical signs; apostrophes).

All annotations are created with a view of a particular practical goal, which determines specific features of the rule set. However, there are some general guidelines that are to be followed irrespective of the annotation task (e.g. the speech material that is to be annotated):

- All words are written correctly in the context of the language's orthographic system (for some tasks an exception is made for regional variants that are spelled as pronounced in those cases and have special marks);
- The orthographic transcriptions are to be comprehensive: all the speech fragments and elements should be transcribed successively, all speech and nonspeech events should be marked in accordance with the developed rules;

- All words are to be written in lower case in order to speed up the annotation process (the exceptions include spelled letters and abbreviations that are written in capitals);
- No punctuation marks or symbols are allowed; hyphens within words should be substituted by spaces;
- Numerals, money amounts and measures should be written down as words;
- Meaningful fillers (e.g. "well", "say") are to be transcribed;
- The use of contracted constrictions is not allowed (e.g. "october" and not "oct");
- The speech cut off by truncation of the wave form at the beginning or the end of the signal should be marked.

2.2 Specific Marks

Alongside with general rules our experts register a number of speech and non-speech events that could be detected in sound files. This requirement arises from the necessity of training an ASR system not to confuse them with words.

- In-speech events:
  - noise;
  - music;
  - applause;
  - IVR speech;
  - side speech (speech by any person not intended for the recognizer);
  - overlapped speech (speaker's speech that occurs at the same time as ome other person's speech);
  - fragmented or interrupted word;
  - target speaker's noise, breath sound, yawning, laughter, cough;
  - shouted phrases;
  - hesitation words.
- Speech anomalies:
  - unclear pronunciation;
  - wrongly stressed syllables;
  - reduced words;
  - mispronounced words;
  - words in the non-target language;
  - overlong sound quantity;
  - syllable-by-syllable pronunciation.

Furthermore, under our annotation rules the following signal and speaker features could be outlined (when occur):

- bad audio;
- harmonic background noise;
- inharmonic background noise;
- foreign (non-target) language;

- acoustic environment: speaker in studio, speech via telephone, prerecorded speech, voice-over translation, live commentary, film fragment, jingle;
- no speech;
- gender: male, female;
- age group: 5–8 years, 8–13 years, 13+ years, 20+ years;
- native/non-native.

2.3   Software Tools

In general the process of sound material annotation is a hard and time-consuming task since it is performed manually by human experts. Still some program tools could help to solve the problem. That is why Speech_Utility, a special data processing software, was designed. Speech_Utility simplifies the process to some degree, providing a means of creating an annotation, setting time labels for speech and tags, as well as marking some peculiar characteristics of signal (e.g. bad quality, harmonic/inharmonic noise, language, etc.) and speaker (e.g. male/female, age, native/non-native, etc.) by simply checking the boxes. The software interface (see Figs. 1, 2) allows the user to choose the type of image that is more appropriate for their task. Moreover, it has several additional plugins which contribute to the automation of preliminary processing. They automatically spot voice activity and mark its boundaries on the timescale; detect signals that are too noisy and exclude them from the material for annotation;

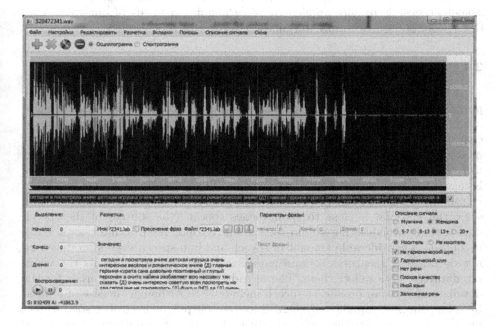

Fig. 1. Speech_Utility software interface, oscillogram

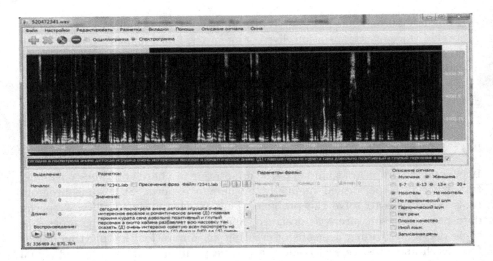

Fig. 2. Speech_Utility software interface, spectrogram

generate phonetic transcriptions, setting time labels for each phoneme, reducing the experts' task to manual correction. Thus, Speech_Utility gives an opportunity to create a structured database that consists of audio signals, corresponding orthographic transcriptions and information about signals and speakers.

It must be mentioned that to ensure the consistency in spelling of all experts, a spell-checker is usually applied to every annotated word. In our work Yandex.Speller is used (for more information about this tool see [6]).

2.4 Example

As it has been already mentioned, annotation rules are typically framed for the purpose of corpora build-up. At the moment our research group has several ongoing projects related to this task. One of them is the speech database of broadcast speech. It is being created for the purposes of training and adapting acoustic models for automatic recognition of speech on different languages (Russian, English, German) obtained from various mass media sources. The Russian material is taken from web pages of different stations' TV and radio programs (e.g. from Euronews, Business FM, NTV, Russia Today, etc.). It should be mentioned that since the material is close to spontaneous speech (the sources of the speech data include broadcasting studio speech, on-the-spot reports, interviews, etc.), it contains a considerable amount of speech and non-speech events produced by a wide range of speakers. To gain more accurate recognition results the training database is to reflect them. The already annotated audio materials for the database of Russian broadcast speech include 75 h. Although the size of a database influences the quality of an ASR system output, it is correct speech data pre-processing that counts the most. For that reason all annotations are created manually by our experts on the basis of a particular rule set. For this task the Speech-Utility program is used and the main rules are:

- the following speaker categories are marked: male, female, child;
- the following types of acoustic environment are specified: speaker in studio, speech via telephone, prerecorded speech, voice-over translation, live commentary, film fragment;
- the following non-speech events are marked: music, inharmonic noise, target speaker's noise, breathing, coughing and laughter;
- the following speech events are marked: speech in a foreign language, unclear pronunciation, hesitation;
- the following speech events are marked and annotated: overlapped speech, shouted phrases, incorrect pronunciation, reduced words.

The resulting speech database includes annotation files containing orthographic transcriptions and information about the signal and speaker (see Fig. 3).

668453125 1206936875 ЖТ_ могу понять почему цискаридзе я не (Д) я сама ничего не понимаю понимаете (Д) почему именно цискаридзе я действительно я не могу скрывать от вас что я (Д) собиралась уходить да собиралась уходить и об этом говорю уже целый год (Д) я говорила о том что (X) вот %щас я двухсотсемидесяти летие отмечу (Д) и наверное буду уходить ну потом *двухсот* прошло двухсотсемидесяти летие потом (X) ну это ни для кого было не секрет что я собираюсь уходить (Д) понимаете секрета из этого и я не делала и никто не делал из этого секрета (Д) но для меня было полной неожиданностью да что именно в такое в такое время именно так и почему цискаридзе а никто другой (Д) у нас есть свой коллектив (Д) мы тоже готовили себе я также готовила себе замену к примеру правильно из нашего же коллектива

Fig. 3. An example of an annotation file containing an orthographic transcription

The acoustic models that were trained on the database of mass media language are incorporated in the Audioprotocol software system [8].

3   Tag Sorting for ASR

In respect to ASR the process of sound files annotation is mainly applied to build databases for training and testing. The relevancy of tags in annotations hugely varies depending on task requirements. Tag sorting of annotated data is used to form either test set or training set.

Test sets are framed with regard to the following points:

- All the words should be spelled orthographically correctly, regardless of the way they were pronounced; this condition is important since ASR systems are expected to output valid transcriptions.
- Annotation marks are used to exclude particular signals from the test set and to create a test sample that meets certain requirements; that is why tags that describe the whole signal (e.g. speaker's gender, age, type of acoustic environment or back-ground noise, etc.) are more appropriate for the task. Training sets should fit specific requirements as well:
- Speech and non-speech events should be marked, since training sets are usually grouped on the basis of these tags.
- Signal features that make it invalid for ASR processing should be marked (e.g. speech overlapped by music or by speech, etc.).
- Wrongly stressed syllables should be marked, so that rule-based letter-to-sound converter [7] could build the right phonetic transcription (since stressed syllables do not follow the same pattern in pronunciation as non-stressed ones they should be treated separately).
- Transcriptions with incorrect spelling that imitates speaker's pronunciation are used for acoustic models' training in order to make ASR system understand and identify different regional variants of the same word.
- For the purpose of preventing statistic distortion only orthographically correct transcriptions should be applied to language modeling.

4   Conclusion

The present paper describes basic aspects of our approach to speech annotation, applied in ASR systems development. The method could be referred to as multi-level, since it implies covering several levels of information concerning speech data. Thus, the annotations include text transcriptions along with special markers for various speech/non-speech events as well as the information about signal and speaker features.

It should be pointed out that the developed approach meets two fundamental requirements that arise in relation to speech annotating. On the one hand, it enables creating adequate annotations that represent all the basic parameters relevant for ASR systems; on the other hand, the approach facilitates and speeds up the process of annotation, making it more convenient for experts.

Acknowledgments. Research is conducted by Stel - Computer Systems Ltd. with support of the Ministry of Education and Science of the Russian Federation (Contract #14.579.21.0058) Unique ID for Applied Scientific Research (project) RFMEFI57914X0058. The data presented, the statements made, and the views expressed are solely the responsibility of the authors.

References

1. Bogdanov, D.S., Brukhtii, A.V., Krivnova, O.F., Podrabinovich, A.Ya., Strokin, G.S.: The technology of speech databases formation. Collected papers of system

Analysis Institute of RAS, pp. 238–259. Editorial URSS, Moscow (2003–2004) (in Russian)

2. Lane, I., Wailbel, A.: Tools of collecting speech corpora via mechanishanical-truk. In: 11th NAACL HLT 2010 Workshop on Creating Speech and Language Data with Amazon's Mechanical Truck, California, pp. 184–187 (2010)

3. Matoušek, J., Romportl, J.: Recording and annotation of speech corpus for Czech unit selection speech synthesis. In: Matoušek, V., Mautner, P. (eds.) TSD 2007. LNCS (LNAI), vol. 4629, pp. 326–333. Springer, Heidelberg (2007)

4. Anumanchipalli, G., Chitturi, R., Joshi, S., Kumar, R., Singh, S.P., Sitaram, R.N.V., Kishore, S.P.: Development of Indian language speech databases for large vocabulary speech recognition systems. In: 10th SPECOM International Conference on Speech and Computer, Patras, pp. 245–254 (2005)

5. Zulkarneev, M., Grigoryan, R., Shamraev, N.: Acoustic modeling with deep belief networks for Russian speech recognition. In: Železný, M., Habernal, I., Ronzhin, A. (eds.) SPECOM 2013. LNCS, vol. 8113, pp. 17–24. Springer, Heidelberg (2013)

6. YandexSpeller. https://tech.yandex.ru/speller/

7. Krivnova, O.F., Zakharov, L.M., Strokin, G.S.: Automatic transcriber of russian texts: problems, structure and application. In: 6th SPECOM International Conference on Speech and Computer, Moscow, pp. 408–409 (2001)

8. Audiprotocol. http://speech.stel.ru:8080 (online access: login guest, password 1)

The Role of Prosody in the Perception of Synthesized and Natural Speech

Maja Marković, Bojana Jakovljević$^{(\boxtimes)}$, Tanja Milićev, and Nataša Miliević

Faculty of Philosophy, University of Novi Sad, Novi Sad, Serbia
majamarkovic@ff.uns.ac.rs, bjn.jakovljevic@gmail.com

Abstract. This paper presents the results of research of perception of synthesized and natural speech, and investigates the role of the prosodic characteristic of pauses in the process of speech comprehension. The research involved a series of perception tasks, including quality assessment, an intelligibility task and comprehension tests of ten shorter and one longer text in Serbian produced by the AlfaNum speech synthesizer and a professional actor, and a follow-up comprehension task of synthesized speech with modified pauses. The results of the intelligibility task show similar performance by both groups of subjects, while the comprehensibility tasks indicate better performance for natural than for synthesized speech. The results of the follow-up task show that the modified prosody contributed to the better performance of the subjects. The quality assessment task revealed the subjects preference for natural speech mainly on the basis of the prosodic characteristic of pauses.

Keywords: Prosody · Serbian language · Speech perception

1 Introduction

With the advent of new speech technologies, there has been a constant advancement in the development of new speech synthesizers and speech recognition systems. Apart from technological requirements, text-to-speech systems (TTS) also need to incorporate a number of significant linguistic features and are highly language dependent, i.e. they have to be developed for a specific language in order to reach a necessary level of naturalness and comprehensibility. With the goal of improving TTS system synthesizers for various languages, their performance has to be evaluated from different aspects, such as intelligibility, naturalness, and preference of the synthetic speech [1–3]. Intelligibility, i.e. segmental recognition is undoubtedly a significant factor which affects the comprehension of the message conveyed [4]. While the evaluation of intelligibility is a relatively easy task, and therefore successfully researched in a number of studies [5,6], measuring comprehension is a serious challenge, since it involves a number of cognitive processes that are rather difficult to be captured and accounted for on the basis of speech quality alone. In recent studies post-perceptual comprehension tests have been used to measure listeners, comprehension, but many have failed to distinguish between TTS systems and natural speech. As recently as in 2011,

© Springer International Publishing Switzerland 2015
A. Ronzhin et al. (Eds.): SPECOM 2015, LNAI 9319, pp. 446–453, 2015.
DOI: 10.1007/978-3-319-23132-7_55

Chang [6] claims that an appropriate strategy for evaluating the comprehension is still not found. Our research aims to investigate the relationship between intelligibility and comprehension for the TTS developed for the Serbian language, as well as to come up with an adequate comprehension test for speech synthesis evaluation. Bearing in mind the high quality of the speech synthesizer investigated, we expected that intelligibility tasks designed for synthesized and natural speech would result in rather similar scores in the experiments conducted, while due to certain prosodic features, which still seem to pose difficulty to listeners, we expected different results in comprehension scores, i.e. we expected that the subjects would encounter difficulties understanding the linguistic content delivered by synthesized speech.

The paper is organized as follows. The second section describes the factors which affect the comprehensibility of spoken language, including the role of prosody in processing speech. Section 3 gives the experimental setup and results obtained. The final section discusses some of the implications of the findings and gives the conclusions reached, including some guidelines for future research.

2   Speech Comprehension: Problems

The process of understanding spoken language is still insufficiently understood by cognitive psychology. It is a very complex cognitive process which relies on the encoding of auditory sensory information, based on short-term memory, but then requires the retrieval of previously stored information from long-term memory, and the interpretation and integration of various sources of knowledge at the listeners disposal. The common assumption is that listeners primarily rely on the raw acoustic signal in the process of decoding the message, which enables them to do appropriate phonetic/phonological segmentation of the incoming signal, and then proceed to the higher levels of linguistic knowledge (bottom-up model of speech perception). Therefore, one of the factors that certainly plays a crucial role in listening comprehension is the quality of the initial acoustic-phonetic signal that is, segmental intelligibility of the speech, assumed to affect the earliest stage of processing, the encoding stage. However, it is well-known that higher levels of linguistic knowledge also affect the encoding stage, attested in experiments on phonemic restoration effect [7,8], which point to top-down processing of speech comprehension. Thus, it has long been known that the acoustic-phonetic properties of the signal are only one source of information used by listeners in speech perception and spoken language understanding.

Apart from the quality of the segments, another significant feature of spoken language is its prosody, including appropriate stress, pitch and pausing strategies. Their appropriate usage enables the listener to interpret the message with relative ease. Pausing strategy is important for proper syntactic segmentation of the message [9,10], for signaling information structure (focus/topic, old/new information) [11–13], as well as generally organizing discourse in spoken language [14]. Pauses of varying length are also an important perceptual cue to the listener, as they tend to increase listeners perception of the information delimited by longer pauses [15].

Spoken language is organized in prosodic units, commonly referred to as intonation phrases (IP), which are delimited by boundaries, usually including pauses of varying lengths[1]. According to [16], the duration of IPs is generally between one and two seconds. This, however, does not reflect the physiological necessity of the speaker, but seems to be a tool facilitating the listener to process the message fluently. The duration of IPs, as suggested in [16], seems to coincide with the capacity of short-term memory, which has been recognized as an important stage in the general comprehension of spoken language [17].

3   Methodology: Experiments and Results

The subjects of the experiments conducted were initially 60 speakers of Serbian. They were divided into two groups of 30, one of which was exposed to synthesized speech, and the other to the same materials read by a professional actor. The subjects were undergraduate students (38), M.A. students (13) or Ph.D. (9) students. In the follow-up experiment, involving modified synthesized speech, another group of 30 subjects were tested. In this group, there were 25 undergraduate students, 4 M.A. students, and 1 Ph.D. student. Each of the groups consisted of approximately the same number of male and female subjects. In the first group there were 17 were female and 13 male subjects, in the second there were 16 female and 14 male subjects, and in the third, there were 15 subjects of both genders.

None of the subjects reported any hearing impairment, and their participation in the experiment was voluntary. The group which was exposed to synthesized speech had undergone a training session in order to get familiarized with the speech produced by the synthesizer used in the experiments.

The materials used for the comprehension tasks included one longer text (512 words) and 10 shorter texts (80 115 words). The same texts were produced by the AlfaNum speech synthesizer for the Serbian language and presented to the first group of subjects, and by a professional actor, presented to the second group. The texts were carefully chosen so as to be rich in facts, to reduce the familiarity to the listeners, to be relatively easy to follow and contain as few story line cues as possible. The subjects were also asked to fill in a questionnaire in which they were to assess the quality of the spoken language they listened to (on a scale from 1 to 5), and suggest the areas of difficulties they encountered. Since the results of their answers showed that the main difficulty was in the temporal organization of the longer text[2], pausing strategy in particular, we also designed a follow-up task in which we modified the pauses in synthesized speech. The follow-up task examined the comprehension of the same longer text produced

---

[1] Pauses in the form of silence are not the only significant indicators of IP boundaries; the other common cues of IP boundaries are the lengthening of final segments (pre-boundary lengthening) and the presence of a specific boundary tone.

[2] The results will be reported in detail in Sect. 3.

by the synthesizer, but pauses were inserted between IPs so as to approximate the pauses in natural speech (recorded in the production of the professional actor).

The longer text was followed by 10 comprehension questions, and each of the short texts by 4 questions. The questions after the longer text included one fill-in and 9 were multiple-choice questions. The questions following the short texts included 1 fill-in question, while the other 3 were multiple-choice questions. The answers to the questions were designed with the assumption that there was no global or general knowledge to the articles. In other words, participants could not learn the answers to questions without listening. The types of questions were factual high proposition questions, examining whether listeners could get a general idea from the speech content; low proposition questions asking detailed information about the speech content and inference questions, measuring whether the listeners could draw a conclusion from the speech.

In the task of measuring intelligibility, we used 10 semantically unpredictable sentences (SUS), which are grammatically correct, but without any semantic cues which might facilitate understanding.[3] The subjects were asked to write down the sentences upon hearing them. All the sentences had the same syntactic structure: (Adjective) + (Noun) plural + (Verb) + (Aux) past tense + (Adjective) + (Noun) singular.

The words chosen in the SUS sentences are all low in frequency, in order to prevent the listeners from predicting the meanings easily. The listeners were informed in advance that the sentences in the intelligibility task might not be meaningful to them.

The listeners were allowed to listen to the texts and sentences only once.

Since the whole experiment was rather time consuming and required high concentration, we included two 10 min breaks between the tasks to allow the subjects to recuperate.

The study took place in the computer lab at the Faculty of Philosophy in Novi Sad. Each participant used a set of headphones, and the experiment was carried out by applying an online webpage in which the test was created.

3.1 Results

(a) Quality Assessment

The results of the quality assessment of natural and synthesized speech are given in Table 1 (based on Mann-Whitney U test). The analysis of the results obtained points to a statistically significant difference between natural and synthesized speech for both long and short texts ($p < 0,001$). In the question asking the subjects about the potential causes of difficulty, the most frequent comments were: "too short pauses", "there are no pauses between words", "the words sound as if they were glued together" and "she speaks without breathing", thus pointing to an insufficient number or duration of pauses.

---

[3] SUS is the methodology proposed as the most appropriate for assessing segmental intelligibility in [6] and references therein.

Table 1. The quality assessment of synthesized (S) and natural (N) for different types of texts.

Type of text	N(N) = N(S)	Mean rank (N)	Mean rank (S)	U	Z	Exact p (2-tailed)
Long	30	44,20	16,80	**39**	6,37	**0,000**
Short	30	42,77	18,23	**82**	5,75	**0,000**
Sentences	30	34,20	26,80	**339**	1,87	**0,076**

(b) Comprehension Tests

The analysis of the results of the comprehension task based on the ten short texts (Table 2) points to a statistically significant difference between natural and synthesized speech ($p < 0,001$). T-test showed that the subjects listening to the longer text produced by the actor (Table 3a), performed significantly better than the subjects exposed to the synthesized text. The analysis of the follow-up task, involving the synthesized text with modified pauses, showed that the group who listened to the modified text also performed significantly better than the group exposed to unmodified synthetic speech ($p < 0,001$), which corroborates the importance of pauses in speech comprehension (Table 3b). The significance of pauses in speech comprehension is also supported by the absence of statistically significant difference between the results of the comprehension test based on the natural and modified synthesized longer piece of text (Table 3c).

Table 2. Comparison of the comprehension test results for short texts between natural (N) and synthesized (S) speech.

N(N) = N(S)	Mean(N)	Mean(S)	Mean difference	t	p (2-tailed)
30	29,26	25,67	3,59	**3,79**	**0,000**

Table 3. Comparison of the comprehension test results for a long text between: (a) natural (N) and synthesized (S) speech, (b) modified synthesized (MS) and synthesized speech, and (c) natural and modified synthesized speech.

	N(N) = N(S)	Mean(N)	Mean(S)	Mean difference	t	p (2-tailed)
(a)	30	7,72	6,12	1,60	5,86	0,000
(b)	N(MS) = N(S)	Mean(N)	Mean(S)	Mean difference	t	p (2-tailed)
	30	7,63	6,12	1,51	4,13	0,000
(c)	N(N) = N(MS)	Mean(N)	Mean(S)	Mean difference	t	p (2-tailed)
	30	7,72	7,63	0,09	0,23	0,819

(c) Intelligibility

The results of the intelligibility task point to the absence of a statistically significant difference between natural and synthesized speech (Table 4). Subjects of both groups made similar types of errors, including repetition of words, segmental errors, word omissions or replacements. The number of errors between the groups showed no statistical difference either.

Table 4. Comparison of intelligibility between natural (N) and synthesized (S) speech

N (N) = N (S)	Mean(N)	Mean(S)	Mean difference	t	p (2-tailed)
30	5,40	5,33	0,007	**0,13**	**0,894**

4   Discussion and Conclusions

The results of the scores of the SUS sentences indicate that segmental intelligibility is rather high in the synthesized speech analyzed, since there are no significant differences in the performance of the groups of subjects who listened to synthesized and natural speech. This indicates that the quality of segments of the AlfaNum synthesized speech is sufficiently high and comparable to the segments of natural spoken language. Although in a number of earlier studies segmental intelligibility was generally found to correlate with comprehensibility of synthesized speech [6], our findings point to different results. In our study, overall comprehension scores are significantly higher for the subjects who listened to natural speech than for those exposed to synthesized speech. The difference between our findings and those of similar studies in the past may be the consequence of our experimental design, and the types of questions asked about the texts. Since longer texts are generally more cognitively demanding for the listener, we hypothesized that this may be due to the temporal prosodic structure of longer stretches of speech. The fact that the change in prosody of synthesized speech, achieved by modifying the distribution, number and duration of pauses, contributed to the performance of the subjects in the follow-up test corroborates our hypothesis about the crucial role of pause strategies in spoken language. Another confirmation of this is found in the feedback obtained in the qualitative assessment of synthesized speech, in which the subjects subjective judgment was mainly affected by the prosodic properties of the text, notably, pauses.

To conclude, we may say that inappropriate pausing strategies in synthesized speech obviously make too heavy a load on the listeners short-term and working memory, since the listeners capability to process information is not harmonized with the sizes of intonational chunks delivered by the synthesizer. In other words, new pausing algorithms should take the cognitive demands of the listener in consideration as well.

The questions and problems that we encountered during the experiments conducted indicated guidelines for future research. Such issues mainly involve the types of texts and questions appropriate for this type of research, since the subjects performance does not necessarily need to be related to the quality of the speech tested, but can be attributed to various other factors (familiarity, disposition to the topic/voice, fatigue of the listener, lack of concentration, etc.). In order to test more precisely how the prosodic structure of spoken language correlates with the capacity of processing the semantic content of the message, different test designs should also be thought of, including simultaneous, rather than post-perceptual evaluation of the process of comprehension. Response latencies should also be measured in order to give us more fine-grained and in-depth insights into the questions of spoken language cognition.

Another question that awaits thorough investigation is the question of pauses in the Serbian language, which should be researched on a vast corpus of spoken language, and include the measurement of silent periods, as well as the other prosodic cues that indicate intonational boundaries - fundamental frequency changes, final lengthening and boundary tone types. This research should give answers about the relation of prosody and syntax, but also, about the role of prosodic segmentation in structures above the sentence level - i.e. the prosodic organization of discourse.

Acknowledgments. The presented study was financed by the Ministry of Education and Science of the Republic of Serbia under the Research grant TR32035.

References

1. Pisoni, D.B.: Perception of synthetic speech. In: van Santen, J.P.H., Sproat, R.W., Olive, J.P., Hirschberg, J. (eds.) Progress in Speech Synthesis, pp. 541–560. Springer, New York (1997)
2. Pisoni, D.B.: Some measures of intelligibility and comprehension. In: Allen, J., Hunnicutt, M.S., Klatt, D.H. (eds.) From Text to Speech: The MITalk System, pp. 151–171. Cambridge University Press, Cambridge, UK (1987)
3. Pisoni, D.B.: Speeded classification of natural and synthetic speech in a lexical decision task. J. Acoust. Soc. Am. **70**, S98 (1981)
4. Pisoni, D.B., Nusbaum, H., Greene, B.G.: Perception of synthetic speech generated by rule. In: Proceedings of the IEEE, pp. 1665–1676 (1985)
5. Pols, L.C.W., Santen, J.P.H. van, Abe, M., Kahn, D., Keller, E.: The use of large text corpora for evaluation text-to-speech systems. In: Proceedings of the First International Conference on Language Resources and Evaluation, pp. 637–640. Granada, Spain (1998)
6. Chang, Y.Y.: Evaluation of TTS systems in intelligibility and comprehension tasks. In: ROCLING, Proceedings of the 23rd Conference on Computational Linguistics and Speech Processing, Taipei, Taiwan, pp. 64–78 (2011)
7. Warren, R.M.: Perceptual restoration of missing speech sounds. Science **167**, 392–393 (1970)
8. Warren, R.M., Obusek, C.: Speech perception and phonemic restorations. Percept. Psychophys. **9**, 358–363 (1971)

9. Selkirk, E.: Phonology and Syntax: The Relation Between Sound and Structure. MIT Press, Cambridge (1984)
10. Kjelgaard, M.M., Speer, S.R.: Prosodic facilitation and interference in the resolution of temporary syntactic closure ambiguity. J. Mem. Lang. **40**, 153–194 (1999)
11. Swerts, M., Geluykens, R.: Prosody as a marker of information flow in spoken discourse. Lang. Speech **37**, 21–45 (1994)
12. Hirschberg, J.: Communication and prosody: functional aspects of prosody. Speech Commun. (Special Issue on Dialogue and Prosody) **36**, 31–43 (2001)
13. Shriberg, E., Stolcke, A., Hakkani-Tür, D., Tür, G.: Prosody-Based Automatic Segmentation of Speech into Sentences and Topics. Speech Commun. **32**, 127–154 (2000)
14. Cutler, A., Dahan, D., van Donselaar, W.: Prosody in the comprehension of spoken language: a literature review. Lang. Speech **40**, 141–201 (1997)
15. Swerts, M., Geluykens, R.: Local and global prosodic cues to discourse organization in dialogues. In: Proceedings of the ESCA Workshop on Prosody, pp. 108–111. Lund, Sweden (1993)
16. Tench, P.: The Intonation System of English. Cassell, London (1996)
17. Jonides, J., Lewis, R.L., Nee, D.E., Lustig, C.A., Berman, M.G., Moore, K.S.: The mind and brain of short-term memory. Annu. Rev. Psychol. **59**, 193–224 (2008)

The Singular Estimation Pitch Tracker

Daniyar Volf[✉], Roman Meshcheryakov, and Sergey Kharchenko

Tomsk State University of Control Systems and Radioelectronics,
40, Lenina Pr., Tomsk, Russia
runsolar@mail.ru, mrv@keva.tusur.ru

Abstract. A model of singular estimation process of speech fundamental pitch frequency is reviewed. Existing solutions for the known classes of mathematical problems (Singular spectrum analysis, fast Fourier transform, and convolution) are used to develop a numerical implementation of the model. The evaluation of the fundamental pitch frequency with existing algorithms.

Keywords: Singular spectrum analysis of speech · Fundamental pitch frequency · Model · Numerical implementation · Evaluation

1 Introduction

Analysis of speech signals is one of today's promising research topics. The present paper presents a model, a numeric implementation and a programmatic implementation of a process of singular estimation of vocal cord oscillation frequency, or pitch ($F0$) one of the major parameters of speech. Pitch estimation has an important role in a number of applications, including speech synthesis, recognition and as metadata in multimedia applications [1–4]. It is also used as a feature in many objective speech quality assessment algorithms. The area of pitch estimation has attracted a lot of interest resulting in a number of algorithms for pitch estimation. At present, popular algorithms for the estimation of pitch, or fundamental frequency of speech, include RAPT [5], YIN [6], SWIPE' [7], SHS [8], etc.

The principal shortcoming of this family of algorithms is their dependency on peak detection accuracy. The presence and amplitude of peaks depend on the length and type of analysis window and on the nature of sound, which gives rise to frequent errors. Furthermore, the accuracy also depends on pitch frequency and sampling frequency [9]. One more limitation is imposed by the underlying model assuming the signal to be periodic (stationary), which implies the pitch period to be repeat exactly, with no variations within the analysis window. For example, modulations of the fundamental frequency substantially decrease the estimation accuracy. Thus, estimation of the fundamental frequency of a speech signal from the speech waveform alone is a challenging problem due to the quasi-periodic nature of pitched speech and mixed nature of the excitation [10]. Speech studies usually employ the mathematical tools of Correlation, Fourier spectral

© Springer International Publishing Switzerland 2015
A. Ronzhin et al. (Eds.): SPECOM 2015, LNAI 9319, pp. 454–462, 2015.
DOI: 10.1007/978-3-319-23132-7_56

analysis or wavelet analysis, etc. The present paper relies on the Caterpillar-SSA singular spectrum analysis formalism, developed and validated at the end of last century at St. Petersburg State University [11]. Recent foreign publications also describe a fairly broad class of methods algorithmically and ideologically similar to the Caterpillar method, mostly known as Singular Spectrum Analysis (SSA) [12]. The method is based on an analysis of fundamental components and is applicable to both stationary and non-stationary time series. A relationship between the classical methods of stationary time series analysis and the fundamental component method is reviewed by Brillinger [13]. Bagshaw [14] asserts that time-domain methods have a lower voicing decision error rate (max. 17 %) compared to other (frequency-domain) methods. In [15], these methods are also shown to be the most robust with respect to voiced-unvoiced decision, distortions and external noises in the signal. The present paper aims to derive a voice pitch estimation technology taking amplitude and frequency modulations into account. The novelty of the proposed approach is the application of the mathematical formalism of singular spectral analysis to speech signals. The principal problem being solved is one of automated selection of quasi-harmonic components corresponding to the pitch of voiced segments, assuming the frequencies of speech overtones to be multiples of the fundamental pitch frequency.

2   Singular Estimation Fundamental Pitch Frequency

Let us define the estimation process as a set of interrelated operations using the singular estimation methods to convert the input speech signal into output mismatch parameters for the purpose of assessing match quality. In mathematical terms, the problem is equivalent to deriving a quasi-periodic component $T0$ from an N-element time series S, where $[f_{min} \le F0 \le f_{max}]$, assuming the frequencies of speech overtones to be multiples of the pitch frequency. Consider a generalized model of the singular estimation process using the SEPT (Singular Estimation Pitch Tracking) technology to solve the principal problem at hand:

(1) Input data: S_N an N-element discrete series of speech vowels with a sampling frequency of Fd kHz;
(2) Output data: $F0$ pitch frequency; Amp mean amplitude of the harmonic corresponding to the pitch frequency; $T0_N$ a time series corresponding to the pitch frequency quasi-harmonic component.

A conceptual model can be obtained by decomposing the generalized model (Figs. 1 and 2):

(1) A one-dimensional array of equally spaced data points S_N (quantized by level) obtained by sampling of the continuous set $S(t)$ is fed into a system decomposing the time series into an elementary spectrum of quasi-harmonics generated by each resonator in the vocal tract. The system thus outputs a multidimensional array of equally spaced data points $T_{L,N}$ (a quasi-harmonic spectrum).

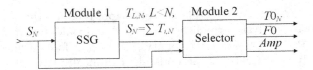

Fig. 1. Conceptual model of SEPT: S_N - input signal; $T_{L,N}$ - time-dependent spectrum; SSG - singular spectrum generator; S_N - input signal; $T0_N$ - pitch track; $F0$ - pitch frequency; Amp - amplitude.

(2) The quasi-harmonic spectrum $T_{L,N}$ along with the input signal SN is fed into a selector and stored in a time-dependent spectrum matrix controller (TSMC). As speech overtone frequencies are known to be multiples of the pitch frequency and the pitch frequency limits are known, we are to solve the problem of decimating the quasi-harmonic spectrum L to K elements, narrowing down the search limits of $f_0 \in [f_{min}, f_{max}]$. A time-dependent spectrum frequency analyzer (TSFA) uses a fast Fourier transform to analyze the frequency characteristics of the data points in the quasi-harmonic spectrum $T_{L,N}$. The time-dependent spectrum frequency analyzer thus outputs a set of M frequencies $f_{min} \leq \{f_1, f_2,\ldots,f_M\} \leq f_{max}$, which is then fed to the pitch frequency selector (PFS). The pitch frequency is then to be selected from the frequency set thus obtained. The pitch frequency is selected as the least multiple of $f_0 \in \{\min(f_i),\ 2\min(f_i),\ldots,\ M\min(f_i)\}$, where $f_i \in \{f_{min} \leq \{f_1, f_2,\ldots,f_M\} \leq f_{max}\}$.

The series $T0_n$ is computed as a mathematical convolution. Then, a mean pitch frequency $F0$ and an amplitude Amp are computed for the given time interval (defined by N and the sampling frequency).

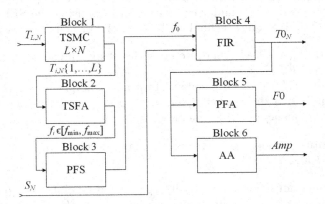

Fig. 2. SEPT model selector decomposition: TSMC - time-dependent spectrum matrix controller; TSFA - time-dependent spectrum frequency analyzer; PFS - pitch frequency selector; FIR - filter; PFA - pitch frequency analyzer; AA - amplitude analyzer.

This conceptual model can be reduced to known classes of mathematical problems:

– singular spectrum analysis;
– discrete Fourier transform;
– mathematical convolution.

This allows for a numerical implementation in the form of the following systems (1) and (2).

$$
\begin{cases}
A = \begin{pmatrix} S_0 & S_1 & \dots & S_{K-1} \\ S_1 & S_2 & \dots & S_K \\ \vdots & \vdots & \ddots & \vdots \\ S_{L-1} & S_L & \dots & S_{N-1} \end{pmatrix}; \\
C = A^T A; \\
V_A^T = U_C^T A D_C^{-1}; \\
T_n^j = \begin{cases} \frac{1}{j+1} \sum_{i=0}^{j} \sqrt{\lambda_i} \left[uv^T \right]_{iK+j-i}^{<n>}, 0 \le j < L, \\ \frac{1}{L} \sum_{i=0}^{L-1} \sqrt{\lambda_i} \left[uv^T \right]_{iK+j-i}^{<n>}, L \le j < K, \\ \frac{1}{N-j} \sum_{i=0}^{L-1-(j-K)} \sqrt{\lambda_i} \left[uv^T \right]_{(j-K+i)K+K-1-i}^{<n>}, \\ K \le j < N. \end{cases}
\end{cases}
\tag{1}
$$

$$
\begin{cases}
f_n = \frac{p}{N \Delta t}, \\
p = \left\{ k, \left| \left[\frac{1}{N} \sum_{j=0}^{N-1} T_j^{<n>} e^{-\frac{2\pi i}{N} kj} \right]_k \right| \subseteq MAX, k = \overline{0, N-1} \right\}, \\
n = \overline{0, L-1}; \\
f_j = f_n \in [f_{min} \le f_n \le f_{max}], n = \overline{0, L-1}, j = \overline{1, M} < L; \\
f_0 \in \{ min(f_i), 2\,min(f_i), \dots, M\,min(f_i) \}, j = \overline{1, K}; \\
f_c = f_0 + \Delta f; \\
W_i = 0.42 - 0.5 \cos\left(\frac{2\pi i}{N-1} \right) + 0.08 \cos\left(\frac{4\pi i}{N-1} \right), i = \overline{0, N-1}; \\
H_i = \left\{ 2\pi f_c W_i, i = 0; \frac{\sin(2\pi f_c i)}{2\pi f_c i} W_i, i > 0 \right\}, i = \overline{0, N-1}; \\
T0_n = \sum_{i=0}^{N-1} H_i \times S_{n-i}, n = \overline{0, N-1}; \\
F0 = \frac{1}{m-1} \sum_{i=1}^{m} \frac{1}{(k_i - k_{i-1})\Delta t}, k_i = \{ n, T0_n \subset MAX, n = \overline{0, N-1} \}, \\
i = \overline{1, m}; \\
Amp = \frac{1}{m} \sum \max(T0_n), n = 1, 2, \dots, m.
\end{cases}
\tag{2}
$$

where system (1) is the singular spectrum generator (SSG) and:
  S_N is the input time series;
  N is the length of this series;
  L is the spectral window size;
  A is the trajectory matrix of observations, which is a Hankel matrix;
  C is a bisymmetric matrix;

U_C is a left-singular rotation matrix;

V_A^T is a right-singular rotation matrix;

$u^{<n>}$ is a left-singular vector;

$v^{<n>}$ is a right-singular vector;

D_C is a diagonal matrix composed of eigenvalues λ_i of the bisymmetric matrix C and the spectral edge of the initial matrix A;

T_i^n is the spectrum of the time series (quasi-harmonic spectrum).

Where system (2) is the "selector" and:

f_n is a one-dimensional frequency representation of the time series spectrum T_n^i with $f_0 \in [f_{min}, f_{max}]$, where f_0 is the unknown pitch frequency such that $f_0 \in \{\min(f_i), 2\min(f_i), \ldots, M\min(f_i)\}$ is the least multiple;

p is the index of an element in T_n^i corresponding to the maximum amplitude of a Fourier transform for the n-th quasi-harmonic;

Δt is an inverse of the sampling frequency;

f_c is the cut off frequency;

W_i is a series numerically describing the Blackman window;

H_i is a series numerically describing the finite impulse response characteristic of the low-pass filter (LPF);

$T0_N$ is a time series corresponding to the quasi-harmonic component with the pitch frequency;

$F0$ is the mean pitch frequency such that

$$F0 = \frac{f_0^1 + f_0^2 + \ldots + f_0^m}{m - 1},$$

where $(m - 1)$ is the total number of inverse values (periods) in the series $T0_N$ ($f0_i$ being the local tone frequency)

$$f_0^1 + f_0^2 + \ldots + f_0^m = \frac{1}{(k_2 - k_1)\Delta t} + \frac{1}{(k_3 - k_2)\Delta t} + \ldots$$
$$+ \frac{1}{(k_m - k_{m-1})\Delta t} = \sum_{i=1}^{m} \frac{1}{(k_i - k_{i-1})\Delta t},$$

where k_i is the index at the maximum $k_i = \{ n, T0_n \subset MAX, n=\overline{0, N-1} \}$, $i=\overline{1,m}$;

Amp is the mean amplitude of the harmonic corresponding to the pitch frequency (averaged over maxima in $T0_N$).

The system (1) provides a mathematical description of the singular pitch frequency estimation model, where is solves the problem of decomposing the input speech signal S_N (a one-dimensional series) into a quasi-harmonic component spectrum T_i^n, $[i=0,1,\ldots,N-1; n=0,1,\ldots,L-1]$.

The system (2) solves the problem of selecting the quasi-harmonic component corresponding to the pitch frequency:

– picking a one-dimensional series $T0_N$ corresponding to the pitch frequency from the multidimensional series T_i^n describing the time-series spectrum;

- estimating the mean pitch frequency $F0$ (with modulations) contained in the time series $T0_N$;
- calculating the mean amplitude in the time series $T0_N$.

The singular matrices U_C and V_A define a basis in a linear space from the columns and rows of the initial matrix A.

3   Experiment

The Singular estimation pitch tracker (SEPT) algorithms are compared with another algorithms RAPT, YIN, SWIPE', SHS and SEPT, using natural speech samples from the speech databases: KPD - Keele Pitch Database Keele Pitch Database [16], PBD - Paul Bagshaws Database for evaluating pitch determination algorithms [17] and DVD - Disordered Voice Database [18]. Laryngograph data was recorded simultaneously with speech, and was used to produce estimates of the fundamental frequency.

The algorithms were asked to produce a pitch estimate every millisecond. The search range was set to 70–500 Hz for speech. The algorithms were given the freedom to decide if the sound was pitched or not. However, to compute our statistics, we considered only the time instants at which all the algorithms agreed that the sound was pitched. Special care was taken to account for time misalignments. Specifically, the pitch estimates were associated to the time corresponding to the center of their respective analysis windows, and when the ground truth pitch varied over time (i.e., for PBD and KPD), the estimated pitch time series were shifted within a range of $+/-100$ms to find the best alignment with the ground truth. The performance measure used to compare the algorithms was the gross pitch error rate (GPER). A gross pitch error occurs when the estimated pitch is off from the reference pitch by more than 20 %. In Table 1 shows the GPERs for each of the algorithms over each of the speech databases. Both the rows and the columns are sorted by average GPER: the best algorithms are at the top, and the more difficult databases are at the right. The best algorithm overall is SEPT, followed by SWIPE' and SHS.

Table 1. Gross pitch error rates for natural speech

Algorithm	GPER (%)			
	PBD	KPD	DVD	Average
SEPT	0.11	0.62	0.74	0.49
SWIPE'	0.14	0.87	0.80	0.60
SHS	0.16	1.03	1.34	0.84
RAPT	0.78	1.08	2.7	1.52
YIN	0.35	1.43	4.9	2.22

Table 2. Performance comparison using artificial signals

		Pitch change rate Hz/ms				
		0	0.5	1	1.5	2
HNR 25 dB						
RAPT	GPER	0.000	0.000	0.000	3.10	8.31
	MFPE	0.052	0.189	0.523	1.245	2.208
YIN	GPER	0.000	0.000	0.000	0.000	1.38
	MFPE	0.041	0.173	0.452	0.802	1.219
SWIPE'	GPER	0.000	0.000	0.000	0.000	0.000
	MFPE	0.035	0.14	0.289	0.413	0.712
SHS	GPER	0.000	0.000	0.000	0.000	0.110
	MFPE	0.033	0.161	0.344	0.618	1.0
SEPT	GPER	0.000	0.000	0.000	0.000	0.000
	MFPE	0.014	0.014	0.014	0.014	0.014
HNR 15 dB						
RAPT	GPER	0.000	0.000	0.000	8.12	12.75
	MFPE	0.162	0.271	0.859	2.425	4.814
YIN	GPER	0.000	0.000	0.000	0.000	4,82
	MFPE	0.147	0.238	0.615	1.513	3.101
SWIPE'	GPER	0.000	0.000	0.000	0.000	0.000
	MFPE	0.098	0.201	0.358	0.559	0.977
SHS	GPER	0.000	0.000	0.000	0.057	0.152
	MFPE	0.139	0.226	0.402	0.716	1.53
SEPT	GPER	0.000	0.000	0.000	0.000	0.000
	MFPE	0.019	0.019	0.019	0.019	0.019
HNR 5 dB						
RAPT	GPER	0.000	0.000	0.000	11.31	19.01
	MFPE	0.283	0.482	1.341	3.78	7.514
YIN	GPER	0.000	0.000	0.000	0.000	4.11
	MFPE	0.245	0.349	0.913	2.513	4.101
SWIPE'	GPER	0.000	0.000	0.000	0.000	0.000
	MFPE	0.154	0.28	0.498	0.932	1.89
SHS	GPER	0.000	0.000	0.002	0.103	0.389
	MFPE	0.227	0.32	0.577	1.659	2.734
SEPT	GPER	0.000	0.000	0.000	0.000	0.000
	MFPE	0.027	0.027	0.027	0.027	0.027

In order to evaluate true performance of the proposed algorithm a set of artificial signals with predefined instantaneous pitch is used for mean fine pitch error rate (MFPE, %) [10]. The pitch change rate differs from 0 to 2 Hzms. The pitch values are within the range of 100–350Hz. The signals are sampled at 44.1kHz and corrupted with additive white noise of different intensity HNR (Table 2). The experimental results in Table 2 show that the SEPT algorithm is robust for frequency modulation because MFPE does not depend on pitch change rate (MFPE is constant). However, as with other algorithms, estimation accuracy depends on the noise. Thus, the singular evaluation the fundamental frequency of the speech signal accounts for a non-periodic (non-stationary) models of the speech signal, which is available in a natural signal.

4   Conclusion

The new method of singular evaluation also proved to be robust against frequency modulation and additive noise, but not completely freed from dependence noise. Experiments with natural speech show that the proposed algorithm is applicable to applications of speech processing. The experimental results using synthetic signals show that the new measurement technology solves the problem of the fundamental frequency estimation of frequency modulation of the pitch.

The singular estimation of fundamental frequency can be used in real-time applications where latency of 10–20 ms can be tolerated. The proposed new technology for speech pitch frequency estimation addresses the problem of assessing the amplitude and frequency modulations. Generalizing the above, one can declare a new class of pitch frequency estimators, Singular Estimator Pitch Tracker (SEPT), to have been developed.

References

1. Cheveigne A., Kawahara H.: Comparative evaluation of F0 estimation algorithms. In: Proceedings Eurospeech (2001)
2. Karpov, A., Ronzhin, A., Kipyatkova, I.: An assistive bi-modal user interface integrating multi-channel speech recognition and computer vision. In: Jacko, J.A. (ed.) Human-Computer Interaction, Part II, HCII 2011. LNCS, vol. 6762, pp. 454–463. Springer, Heidelberg (2011)
3. Budkov, V.Y., Ronzhin, A.L., Glazkov, S.V., Ronzhin, A.L.: Event-driven content management system for smart meeting room. In: Balandin, S., Koucheryavy, Y., Hu, H. (eds.) NEW2AN 2011 and ruSMART 2011. LNCS, vol. 6869, pp. 550–560. Springer, Heidelberg (2011)
4. Ronzhin, A.L., Budkov, V.Y., Karpov, A.A.: Multichannel system of audio-visual support of remote mobile participant at e-meeting. In: Balandin, S., Dunaytsev, R., Koucheryavy, Y. (eds.) ruSMART 2010. LNCS, vol. 6294, pp. 62–71. Springer, Heidelberg (2010)
5. Talkin D. A.: Robust algorithm for pitch tracking (RAPT). In: Entropic Research Laboratory Suite 202, 600 Pennsylvania Ave. 20003, pp. 495–518 (1995)

6. Cheveigne, A., Kawahara, H.: YIN, a fundamental frequency estimator for speech and music. JASA **111**(4), 1917–1930 (2002)
7. Camacho, A., Harris, J.G.: A sawtooth waveform inspired pitch estimator for speech and music. JASA **123**(4), 1638–1652 (2008)
8. Hermes, D.J.: Measurement of pitch by subharmonic summation. JASA **83**, 257–264 (1988)
9. Bondarenko, V.P., Konev, A.A., Meshcheryakov, R.V.: Segmentation and para-metrisation of a speech signal. Izvestiya Vysshikh Uchebnykh Zavedenii **50**(10), 3–7 (2007). (in Russ.)
10. Azarov E., Vashkevich M., Petrovsky A.: Instantaneous pitch estimation based on RAPT framework. In: Proceedings of the 20th European Signal Processing Conference (EUSIPCO 2012), Bucharest, pp. 2787–2791 (2012)
11. Golyandina, N., Zhigljavsky, A.: Singular Spectrum Analysis for Time Series. Springer Briefs in Statistics, p. 120. Springer, Heidelberg (2013)
12. Golub, G.H., Van Loan, C.F.: Matrix computations, 3rd edn. The Johns Hopkins University Press, Baltimore (1996)
13. Brillinger, D.R.: Time Series Data Analysis and Theory. Society for Industrial and Applied Mathematics (SIAM), Philadelphia (2001)
14. Bagshaw P.C.: Automatic prosodic analysis for computer aided pronunciation teaching. Ph.D. thesis, University of Edinburgh, Edinburgh (1994)
15. Rabiner, L.R., Cheng, M.J., Rosenberg, A.E.: A comparative study of several pitch detection algorithms. IEEE Trans. Acoust. Speech **24**, 399–423 (1976)
16. Keele Pitch Database Keele Pitch Database. http://www.icocla.it/keele.html
17. Paul Bagshaw's Database for evaluating pitch determination algorithms. http://www.cstr.ed.ac.uk/research/projects
18. Disordered Voice Database. http://www.kayelemetrics.com

Voice Conversion Between Synthesized Bilingual Voices Using Line Spectral Frequencies

Young-Sun Yun$^{(\boxtimes)}$, Jinman Jung, and Seongbae Eun

Department of Computer, Communications, and Unmanned Technology,
Hannam University, Daejeon 306-791, Republic of Korea
{ysyun,jmjung,sbeun}@hnu.kr

Abstract. Voice conversion is a technique that transforms the source speaker individuality to that of the target speaker. We propose the simple and intuitive voice conversion algorithm not using training data between different languages and it uses text-to-speech generated speech rather than recorded real voices. The suggested method reconstructed the voice after transforming line spectral frequencies (LSF) by formant space warping functions. The formant space is the space consisted of representative four monophthongs for each language. The warping functions are represented by piecewise linear equations using pairs of four formants at matched monophthongs. In this paper, we applied LSF to voice conversion because LSF are not overly sensitive to quantization noise and can be interpolated. From experimental results, LSF based voice conversion shows good results for ABX and MOS tests than the direct frequency warping approaches.

Keywords: Voice conversion · Weighted frequency warping · Formant space · Piecewise linear warping · Line spectral frequencies

1 Introduction

Accessibility describes the degree of which a product, device, service, or environment is available to as many people as possible. It has become a significantly greater issue, as computers can now handle various types of information, including interaction with audio-visual interfaces on the Internet or actual life. There are some assistive devices and programs to assist computer operation. A popular assistive tools is the screen reader, using which the visual interfaces and information on the computer screen are converted to speech for the disabled, particularly low-vision and blind people. The screen reader plays a very important role for the disabled using computers, but is limited in that it depends on platforms and generally it serves only one language speech. If the system supports only one language, the user should switch the screen reader to another when he/she wants to access other pages in different languages. Therefore, to navigate the different language document/information, a text-to-speech (TTS) system must support different language outputs based on one or multiple speakers. In this

© Springer International Publishing Switzerland 2015
A. Ronzhin et al. (Eds.): SPECOM 2015, LNAI 9319, pp. 463–471, 2015.
DOI: 10.1007/978-3-319-23132-7_57

paper, we propose a voice conversion algorithm to transform speech as if it were generated by the same person, even though the TTS system is developed based on multiple speakers.

Voice conversion is a technique that modifies a speaker's individuality. That is, speech uttered by one speaker is transformed to different speech as if another speaker had generated it [10]. Many works of transforming voice individuality have been done using various parameters inflecting a speaker's characteristics. They assume that the source and target speakers are in the same language environments. In other words, with the same language, the voice conversion system transforms the source speech to the target speech. The voice conversion system is generally implemented with the speech synthesis technology. However, in this paper, we considered the case in which the speech synthesis system cannot be modified or just only the synthesized results are used.

It is known that any single specific acoustic parameter alone does not carry all of the individuality information, and various parameters affect the characteristics of speech. In these parameters, the formant frequency is considered to be one of the most important parameters characterizing speech and a speaker's individuality [8,10]. There are many approaches to manipulate the formant frequency by subspace codebook mapping [10], transformation using artificial neural networks [12], and vocal tract length normalization (VTLN) techniques [3,15]. VTLN attempts to normalize the speaker-dependent vocal tract lengths by warping the frequency axis of the phase and magnitude spectrum. In speech recognition, VTLN removes the speaker's individuality and improves the recognition performance [13]. The same techniques are introduced in voice conversion [18] and modify source speech as it is uttered by a target speaker [16]. The frequency warping approaches based on VTLN are implemented in various techniques, such as bilinear transformation [14] and piecewise linear transformation [3,15]. Some of these methods are performed under text-dependent conditions for the same language [3,10,12,14,15], whereas others are performed text-independent or in different language environments [16,17].

The outline of the paper is as follows. We described formant space that represents the speaker's individuality in Sect. 2, and presented frequency warping and our proposed algorithms in Sect. 3. In Sect. 4, we showed the experiments and their results and analysis. We end with conclusion in following Section.

2   Formant Space

The vocal tract can be modeled as a linear filter with resonances. The formants correspond to the harmonics of the fundamental frequency at natural resonances of the vocal tract cavity position for the vowels. We can easily find the formants by showing dark horizontal bands in the spectrogram of the given speech. The major resonances of the oral and pharyngeal cavities for vowels are called F1 and F2, the first and second formants, respectively. They are determined by tongue placement and oral tract shape in vowels and determine the characteristic timbre or quality of the vowel [5]. Figure 1 shows the average F1-F2 diagrams of

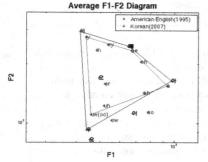

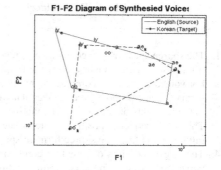

Fig. 1. Average F1-F2 diagrams for American English, and Korean women.

Fig. 2. F1-F2 diagrams of synthesized voices for four representaive monoph-thongs (*/iy, oo, a, ae/*).

American English monophthongs [4], and Korean monophthongs [11] produced by women. In this figure, we found that there are some similar monophthongs and others are not. Therefore, we choose the four representative monophthongs to find matched pair between two different language monophthongs. The four monophthongs are */ iy, oo, a, ae/* and it is called formant space that consists of the four representatives. Even though the average diagrams of four monoph-thongs are similar together, the formant spaces of individuals are very different. The F1-F2 diagrams of the synthesized speech used in this paper are shown in Fig. 2.

In general, F1 and F2 are considered sufficient to differentiate vowels, F3 is important in determining the phonemic quality, and F4 and higher formants are significant for voice qualities. Therefore, we used four formants in this work to construct the *formant space* of each speaker. These formants are used to build piecewise linear warping functions [16] of the frequency from the source speaker to the target speaker.

3   Frequency Warping

As shown in Fig. 2, the formant spaces of the source and target speakers are dif-ferent because of the speaker's individuality and language environment. Unlike previous studies [3, 16, 18], our system does not depend on the text and does not use phonemic clusters by segmentation or speech units obtained by speech recog-nition. Therefore, it requires reference features to transform the frequencies of the source speaker to those of the target speaker. We selected four monophthongs that are commonly found in both the English and Korean languages.

The frequency warping steps are briefly described as in Table 1. As in the previous studies [3, 12], it is known that the transformation of the voiced sounds is significantly more important than that of unvoiced sounds. Thus, our system transform only voiced frames, whereas unvoiced frames are not modified.

Table 1. Basic algorithm of frequency warping

1. The source speaker's speech, which is generated from a TTS system, is divided into frames, which are transformed to the frequency domain.
2. For voiced frames, we compute the relative position of the input frequency from the formant space of the source speaker. The relative position is represented as weights to the formants of each monophthong in the formant space.
3. The target frequency position is interpolated by applying weights to frequency warping functions from the source formant space to the target formant space.
4. The target speech is obtained by combining time domain samples along to the reverse processing of frequency tranformation.

3.1   Weighted Frequency Interpolation

In this section, we summarize the previous weighted frequency warping approach [19]. To compare formants of the given frame with those of reference monophthongs, they modified the distance measures to avoid endpoint restrictions of the general dynamic programming method in formant comparison. Because it is difficult for reliable formants to be extracted from the speech waveform, the first and last formants could be inaccurate.

To find the location of a given frame in the formant space, the weights of the input frame are calculated by comparison with the monophthong's formants organizing the formant space. The weights are easily obtained by (1), and the formant location can be represented in a source speaker's formant space.

$$W(\mathbf{f}, \mathbf{S}_j) = \begin{cases} \alpha \cdot \min D(\mathbf{f}, \mathbf{S}_k) + (1 - \alpha) \cdot \mathbf{I} & \mathbf{f} \notin \mathcal{S}_{fs} \\ \alpha \cdot \min_1 D(\mathbf{f}, \mathbf{S}_k) + \beta \cdot \min_2 D(\mathbf{f}, \mathbf{S}_k) + (1 - \alpha - \beta) \cdot \mathbf{I} \\ \text{one of } \mathbf{f} \in \text{one of axis ranges of } \mathcal{S}_{fs} \\ D(\mathbf{f}, \mathbf{S}_j)/\sum_{k=1}^{4} D(\mathbf{f}, \mathbf{S}_k) & \mathbf{f} \in \mathcal{S}_{fs} \end{cases} \quad (1)$$

where $\mathbf{f}$ is a formant vector of the input frame, and $\mathbf{S}_j$ denotes the jth reference formant vector of the source speaker. α and β are the weights contributing to each monophthong, $\mathcal{S}_{fs}$ is the formant space comprising four monophthongs, $\mathbf{I}$ is the identity transform function, and $\min_k$ denotes the kth minimum value. $D(\cdot)$ is the modified distance measure defined in [19]. In (1), if formant $\mathbf{f}$ is far from the formant space of the source speaker, the weights are calculated by interpolation of the nearest monophthong's formant and the identity transform function. If formant is partially overlapped in the range of each formant axis, the new formant is estimated by a combination of the nearest two monophthongs formants and the identity warping function.

If weights $W(\mathbf{f}, \mathbf{S}_k), k = 1, \ldots, 4$ of the input formant $\mathbf{f}$ are obtained, we can estimate the frequency warping function $\mathcal{T}(\mathbf{f})$, weighted average of piecewise linear functions, is obtained.

$$\mathcal{T}(\mathbf{f}) = \sum_{k=1}^{4} W(\mathbf{f}, \mathbf{S}_k) \cdot \mathbf{T}(\mathbf{S}_k, \mathbf{T}_k), \tag{2}$$

where $\mathbf{T}(.)$ is the transform function from the source formant vector $\mathbf{S}_k$ to the target formant vector $\mathbf{T}_k$. The transform function is a piecewise linear warping function, which has line segments corresponding to the frequency pairs of four formants.

3.2   Line Spectral Frequency Warping

In the previous work [19], the direct frequency warping (DFW) is done using weighted interpolation of piecewise linear functions. The DFW has an advantage of good voice quality if the frequency transformation functions are well estimated since the speech samples are exactly matched with the frequency with appropriate condition. Furthermore, it can separate the magnitude and the phase information from the source information. For example, the conversion system is able to use the source speaker's phase information whereas it uses the transformed magnitude information. However, if the magnitude information is only used for conversion, the system has a possibility that it cannot represent the target speaker's individuality sufficiently.

We present the frequency warping approach using line spectral frequencies (LSF) information based on linear prediction analysis. LSF are an alternate parameterization of the matched filter with the linear predictor coefficients. The concept of an LSF was introduced by Itakura [6]. In linear prediction analysis, a segment of speech signal can be modelled by time invariant linear all pole filter $H(z) = 1/A(z)$ where $A(z)$ is the response of the prediction error filter with P coefficients

$$A(z) = 1 - \sum_{k=1}^{P} a(k)z^{-k}. \tag{3}$$

A minimum phase prediction error filter has a corresponding synthesis filter $1/A(z)$ which is stable [7]. The prediction error filter $A(z)$ can be decomposed into a symmetric polynomial $P(z)$ and an antisymmetric polynomial $Q(z)$. The $A(z)$ can be easily reconstructed by the addition of both polynomials. The $P(z)$ and $Q(z)$ are called the line spectral pairs and the roots of both polynomials are a set of line spectral frequencies $(w_1, w_2, \ldots, w_p)$ [9]. The comparison of FFT spectrum, LPC spectrum and LSF parameters is shown in Fig. 3.

McLoughlin also described the possibility of modifications of LSF's position and amplitude by citing Paliwal's work [9]. In this article, the modification of lines (LSF parameters) is predominantly confined to the frequency region of original spectrum and amplitude change will cause compensatory power redistribution in other spectral regions of LSF parameters. From the inspiration of

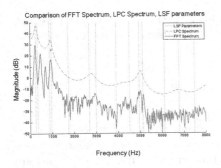

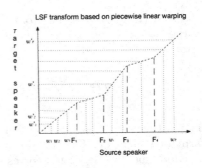

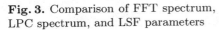

Fig. 3. Comparison of FFT spectrum, LPC spectrum, and LSF parameters

Fig. 4. Transformation from source speaker's LSF to target speaker's LSF by piecewise linear function

McLoughlin's review, we applied the weighted frequency warping to LSF parameters along to piecewise linear functions between the formants. The schematic transformation of LSF parameters is shown in Fig. 4. As shown in the figure, the piecewise linear warping function is obtained along to F1-F4 formants. The source LSF parameters are transformed to target LSF parameters along to the piecewise linear functions.

4   Experiments

Some experiments have been performed to evaluate the validity and potential of the proposed algorithm.

4.1   Environments

The speech samples utilized in this work are generated by the Voiceware TTS system [2]. English and Korean voices were recorded in 2008 and 2003, respectively. The English woman was born in Pennsylvania in 1974. The Korean speaker was born in 1971 and speaks the standard Korean language. The English and Korean speech samples are generated by a pitch synchronous overlap and add (PSOLA) TTS system at a sampling frequency of 16 kHz.

To obtain the frequency warping function, formants based on linear prediction coefficients (LPCs) are calculated for English monophthongs and the corresponding Korean monophthongs. Because phonemes are not exactly matched between two languages, similar vowels are used.

To transform the source speaker's individuality (English) to the target speaker's individuality (Korean), each frame of the English speech is transformed to the frequency domain, and its formants are calculated. The relative formant location of the given frame is obtained, and the frequency warping function is estimated by the weighted summation of each transform function of the four representative monophthongs /iy, oo, ae, a/. Finally, the source LSF parameters are transformed along to the weighted frequency warping function.

Table 2. Average results of the ABX test (speech preference) for speaker individuality and MOS test for voice quality with different approaches. (FS means formant space.)

Conditions	ABX (%)			MOS	Previous [19]	
	English	Korean	None		ABX (Korean)	MOS
DFW, Magnitude and Phase	**37**	33	30	1.85	50	2.00
DFW, Magnitude	**61**	32	7	2.56	50	3.14
DFW, Magnitude in FS	**58**	40	2	3.60	33	4.29
LSF	37	**58**	5	**3.98**	-	-
LSF in FS	46	**51**	3	3.67	-	-

4.2 Results and Discussion

In the previous study [19], the voice conversion experiments were performed in three cases: (1) both magnitude and phase information are used, (2) only magnitude information is used, and (3) transform the satisfied frame with the condition that it is placed within the source formant space. It is reported that many formants are placed outside of the source formant space. This phenomenon causes a degradation in speech quality in voice conversion. Therefore, for considering qualities, if the formants are placed in the formant space, the frame is converted by the estimated frequency warping function [19].

In this paper, we also use same three sentences for experiments, 20 Korean participants (1 woman and 19 men, most are 20 s.) evaluated the preferences and quality of the transformed speech for LSF based conversions. At first, each participant saw the bilingual speaker's interview [1] to understand the subtle differences between Korean and English voices. Next, each participant listened to the target speech (Korean), the source speech (English), and five converted recordings. He/she determined whether the transformed speech was close to Korean, English, or "none of these" (ABX evaluation for speaker individuality) for each recordings. The five converted recordings are obtained along to the feature conditions including DFW (same to the previous study), LSF features and LSF features within formant space. Furthermore, they were asked to evaluate the voice quality of the converted speech on a mean opinion score (MOS) scale between 1 (very poor) and 5 (excellent, very good). Table 2 shows the average results of the ABX test and MOS rating for each case and compares those with the previous study.

From the experimental results, voice conversion with LSF features show the better results than the DFW approaches. However, the LSF features in the formant space has not good voice quality than those without considering formant space. We also found that the MOS (voice quality) of DFW decreased comparing to the previous results. This is the reason that the relative voice quality is not good than LSF parameters. We suppose that the formant space with DFW has more effect than one with LSF parameters. The formant space is more directly related to the DFW than LSF approaches. LSF is obtained in time domain samples and the partial modification of LSF (4th case) is felt unnatural than full modification of LSF (3rd case).

5 Conclusion

A simple and intuitive voice conversion algorithm has been proposed. The presented algorithm uses weighted piecewise warping functions based on formant space information. The formant space consisted of matched vowels between the source and target speech. Our method estimated the warping functions by the weighted summation of each transform function between corresponding monophthongs based on the interpolation method. We applied the LSF features to the voice conversion and found that the LSF parameters are effective on voice conversion than the DFW approaches. The LSF based voice conversion transforms the LSF along to piecewise linear functions has bending points at formants. From the experimental results, LSF based voice conversion shows good results for ABX and MOS tests than the previous study [19].

Acknowledgments. This work was supported by 2015 Hannam University Research Fund.

References

1. Jenniffer clyde interview. https://youtu.be/Q7SgJCqY0Ws
2. Voiceware co.: http://www.voiceware.co.kr/english/index.html
3. Erro, D., Moreno, A., Bonafonte, A.: Voice conversion based on weighted frequency warping. IEEE Trans. Audio Speech Lang. Proces. **18**(5), 922–931 (2010)
4. Hillenbrand, J., Getty, L.A., Clark, M.J., Wheeler, K.: Acoustic characteristics of american english vowels. J. Acoust. Soc. Am. **97**(5), 3099–3111 (1995)
5. Huang, X., Acero, A., Hon, H.W.: Spoken Language Processing: A Guide to Theory, Algorithm, and System Development. Prentice Hall PTR, Upper Saddle River (2001). Foreword By-Reddy, R
6. Itakura, F.: Line spectrum representation of linear predictor coefficients of speech signals. J. Acoust. Soc. Am. **57**(S1), S35–S35 (1975)
7. Kabal, P., Ramachandran, R.P.: The computation of line spectral frequencies using chebyshev polynomials. IEEE Trans. Acoust. Speech Signal Process. **34**(6), 1419–1426 (1986)
8. Kuwabara, H., Sagisak, Y.: Acoustic characteristics of speaker individuality: control and conversion. Speech Commun. **16**(2), 165–173 (1995)
9. McLoughlin, I.V.: Line spectral pairs. Signal Process. **88**(3), 448–467 (2008)
10. Mizuno, H., Abe, M.: Voice conversion algorithm based on piecewise linear conversion rules of formant frequency and spectrum tilt. Speech Commun. **16**(2), 153–164 (1995)
11. Moon, S.J.: A fundamental phonetic investigation of korean monophthongs. Malsori **62**, 1–17 (2007)
12. Narendranath, M., Murthy, H.A., Rajendran, S., Yegnanarayana, B.: Transformation of formants for voice conversion using artificial neural networks. Speech Commun. **16**(2), 207–216 (1995)

13. Pye, D., Woodland, P.: Experiments in speaker normalisation and adaptation for large vocabulary speech recognition. In: IEEE International Conference on Acoustics, Speech, and Signal Processing, ICASSP 1997, vol. 2, pp. 1047–1050. IEEE (1997)

14. Saheer, L., Dines, J., Garner, P.N.: Vocal tract length normalization for statistical parametric speech synthesis. IEEE Trans. Audio Speech Lang. Process. **20**(7), 2134–2148 (2012)

15. Sundermann, D., Bonafonte, A., Ney, H., Höge, H.: Time domain vocal tract length normalization. In: Proceedings of the Fourth IEEE International Symposium on Signal Processing and Information Technology, pp. 191–194. IEEE (2004)

16. Sundermann, D., Ney, H., Hoge, H.: Vtln-based cross-language voice conversion. In: IEEE Workshop on Automatic Speech Recognition and Understanding, ASRU 2003, pp. 676–681. IEEE (2003)

17. Sündermann, D., Höge, H., Bonafonte, A., Ney, H., Black, A., Narayanan, S.: Text-independent voice conversion based on unit selection. In: Proceedings of 2006 IEEE International Conference Acoustics, Speech and Signal Processing, ICASSP 2006, vol. 1, pp. I-I. IEEE (2006)

18. Sündermann, D., Strecha, G., Bonafonte, A., Höge, H., Ney, H.: Evaluation of vtln-based voice conversion for embedded speech synthesis. In: Interspeech, pp. 2593–2596 (2005)

19. Yun, Y.-S., Ladner, R.E.: Text, speech, and dialogue. In: Habernal, I. (ed.) TSD 2013. LNCS, vol. 8082, pp. 137–144. Springer, Heidelberg (2013)

Voicing-Based Classified Split Vector Quantizer for Efficient Coding of AMR-WB ISF Parameters

Merouane Bouzid$^{(\boxtimes)}$ and Salah-Eddine Cheraitia

Speech Communication and Signal Processing Laboratory, USTHB University,
P.O. Box 32, El Alia, Bab ezzouar, Algiers, Algeria
mbouzid@usthb.dz, cher.salah@yahoo.fr

Abstract. Modern speech coders necessitate efficient coding of the linear predictive coding (LPC) coefficients. Line spectral Frequencies (LSF) and Immittance Spectral Frequencies (ISF) parameters are currently the most efficient choices of transmission parameters for the LPC coefficients. In this paper, we present a voicing-based classified split vector quantization scheme developed for efficient coding of wideband AMR-WB G.722.2 ISF (Immittance Spectral Frequencies) parameters under noiseless channel conditions. It was designed based on the classified vector quantization (CVQ) structure combined with the split vector quantization (SVQ). Simulation results will show that the new ISF coding scheme, called ISF-CSVQ coder, performs better than the conventional non classified ISF-SVQ, while saving several bits per frame.

Keywords: Source coding · Classified quantization · Wideband speech · ISF parameters · AMR-WB coder

1 Introduction

Most of modern speech coders are based on the so-called linear-predictive coding (LPC) model in which the short-term speech spectrum is approximated by the transfer function of an all-pole filter $H(z) = 1/A(z)$ where $A(z) = 1 + a_1 \ z^{-1} + \ldots + a_p \ z^{-p}$ [1]. The p LPC filter coefficients are derived from the input signal through a pth order linear prediction (LP) analysis of each speech signal frame. Efficient quantization of LPC coefficients is very important to preserve both intelligibility and natural quality of reconstructed speech. Therefore, the challenge in the quantization of these parameters is to achieve the transparent quantization quality [2], with a minimum bit-rate while maintaining the memory and computational complexity at a low level. In practice, these coefficients are not directly quantized because they have poor quantization properties. The Line Spectral Frequencies (LSF) and the Immittance Spectral Frequencies (ISF) have been shown to be more efficient to represent the LPC coefficients of modern speech coders based on autoregressive model.

© Springer International Publishing Switzerland 2015
A. Ronzhin et al. (Eds.): SPECOM 2015, LNAI 9319, pp. 472–479, 2015.
DOI: 10.1007/978-3-319-23132-7_58

In this work, we focused on the quantization of ISF parameters of wideband speech coders such as the Adaptive Multi-Rate Wide-Band (AMR-WB) speech coder, recommendation ITU-T G.722.2 [3]. The ISF parameters (ISFs) are a representation of Immittance Spectral Pairs (ISPs) in the frequency domain. For a 16th order wideband LP filter, the ISPs are defined as the poles and zeros of an immittance function at the glottis [4]:

$$I_{16}(z) = \frac{A(z) - z^{-16}A(z^{-1})}{A(z) + z^{-16}A(z^{-1})} \tag{1}$$

We obtain 16 ISP parameters and the sixteenth ISP is a reflection coefficient.

Compared to narrowband speech (300–3400 Hz) coders, the wideband coders have improved naturalness and intelligibility of speech due to the added bandwidth (50–7000 Hz). However, they require a higher number of LPC coefficients, typically $p = 16$, for representing the speech spectral envelope. Hence, using the conventional full-search vector quantizer (VQ) for ISF coding needs to operate at higher rates and on larger dimension vectors which leads to an exponential increase in the computational complexity and memory requirement.

In the past, several forms of structurally-constrained vector quantizers (VQs) have been developed for wideband ISF/LSF coding, which reduce complexity with a moderate loss of quantization performance. One of the widely reported schemes is the split vector quantizer (SVQ), which was initially developed by Paliwal and Atal [2] for narrowband speech coding and then further explored for wideband speech coding [5]. In [6], Chang et al. designed a classified VQ (CVQ) with class-dependent splitting for narrowband LSF quantization. In [7], Guibé et al. showed that the family of so-called Safety-Net Vector Quantization (SNVQ) schemes, which combines the memoryless and the predictive approaches, can improve the wideband LSF coding performance both over noisy and noiseless channels. In [8], Biundo et al. used a MA predictor split multistage vector quantizer (S-MSVQ) which combines SVQ and MSVQ. The same scheme is used to code the ISFs of the AMR-WB [3]. Other new wideband LSF/ISF quantizers were further developed. For example, So and Paliwal in [9] designed the switched split vector quantizer (SSVQ) and the multi-frame Gaussian mixture model (GMM) based block quantizer. In [10], Xiaochen, et al. proposed an efficient ISF parameter quantization algorithm based on GMM where the ISFs are quantized by a Gaussian lattice VQ. In [11], Z. Ma et al. developed a new VQ method based on Dirichlet mixture model (DVQ) for wideband LSF coding.

In this paper, we present a classified split vector quantization scheme developed for efficient coding of wideband G.722.2 ISF parameters under noiseless channel conditions. It's about a hybrid scheme based on a CVQ scheme combined with many split vector quantizers. In the design of our ISF system, called "ISF-CSVQ coder", we investigate the voiced/unvoiced classifier which classifies the ISF parameters of each frame according to specific phonetic (voiced/unvoiced) classes of speech. We will show that using a voiced/unvoiced classification of input ISF vectors before coding them yields significant improvement in spectral distortion (SD) performance.

2   Classified Split Vector Quantization

The classified split vector quantizer (CSVQ) is a hybrid scheme based on a CVQ combined with many split vector quantizers (SVQs). Before presenting the CSVQ scheme, let us first review briefly the basics of the SVQ and CVQ.

An N part k-dimensional SVQ (noted N-SVQ) is composed of N classical VQs of smaller sizes and dimensions [2]. Its basic principle consists of partitioning the set of the training base vectors x of dimension k in N subsets of sub-vectors of smaller dimension k_i (with $\sum_{i=1}^{N} k_i = k$). Then, for each part, the corresponding VQ codebook will be designed by using the well-known LBG algorithm [12].

In other hand, a CVQ consists of a classifier and separate VQ codebooks for each class. Figure 1 illustrates the conventional CVQ scheme of N classes. The input vector x is first determined to belong to a certain class out of a predetermined number of classes. Each class j ($j = 1,\ldots, N$) is represented by a corresponding VQ codebook C_j. Then, a full-search is conducted over the selected class VQ codebook in order to find the best matching nearest codevector for the input vector x. The codeword i sent by the CVQ coder consists of the index j specifying the selected codebook C_j and $log_2||C_j||$ bits specifying the selected nearest codevector of C_j.

The CSVQ is a kind of product code VQ method, where the training vector space is divided into several non-overlapping classes (regions) and a separate corresponding SVQ is designed for each class [6]. The design of an accurate classifier is the main issue in any CVQ scheme. Sophisticated classifiers partition the space very efficiently, resulting in small class sets. In the context of wideband speech ISF quantization, the objective is to assign the ISF vectors into classes having a particular statistical behavior, in an effort to improve the coding efficiency. In the design of our CVSQ coder, we investigate the voicing classification [13] approach which distinguishes between ISFs of a voiced (V) and an unvoiced (UV) speech frame. Indeed, Hagen et al. showed in [13] that a significant gain can be attained by designing VQ codebooks separately for voiced and unvoiced speech rather than using a single VQ codebook.

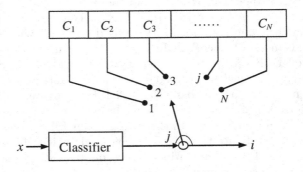

Fig. 1. Classified VQ scheme.

3   Efficient Coding of Wideband ISF Parameters

Using the CSVQ technique, an efficient coding scheme was developed to quantize wideband speech ISF parameters. The objective of this system, named "ISF-CSVQ coder", is to achieve a transparent quantization quality of the ISFs for transmissions over an ideal noiseless channel.

The ISF-CSVQ was designed based on a voiced-based CSVQ where each V/UV class is represented by a correspondent N-SVQ. Thus, the ISF vectors of the training database are classified in two V/UV classes using a phonetic classifier and a separate corresponding N-SVQ is designed for each class in order to preserve the phonetic feature associated with each region. In our work, we used the integrated Voice Activity Detector (VAD) procedure [3,14] of the G.722.2 to carry out the classifier voicing detection. It is about using the Boolean VAD flag which indicates presence ("1") or not ("0") of voiced frame.

Figure 2 shows a block diagram of the ISF-CSVQ coding procedure. Each input ISF vector is first classified to ISF vector of a V or UV speech frame. After that, the vector will be quantized by the corresponding N-SVQ selected by the V/UV classifier. The CSVQ coder transmits to the decoder an index i composed of $N + 1$ concatenated binary indices. The first index i_m of one bit/frame is used to indicate explicitly the V/UV mode selection. The remaining N indices i_n ($n = 1 \ldots N$) are provided by the corresponding N-SVQ. For a b bits/frame ISF-CSVQ, we require $i_m = 1$ bit to specify the V/UV class. The remaining ($b - i_m$) bits will be shared in N partial bit rates to code the N ISF sub-vectors by the corresponding N-SVQ. The partial rates are denoted by b_j ($j = 1 \ldots N$).

To further improve the performance of our ISF-CSVQ coders and to get transparent quantization quality at lower bit rate, an appropriate distance measure was selected. It is about the weighted Euclidean distance which is performed in the frequency ISF domain. In this work, we used the weighted distance given by [2,15,16]:

$$d(f, \hat{f}) = \sum_{i=1}^{16} \left[w_i(f_i - \hat{f}_i) \right]^2 , \qquad (2)$$

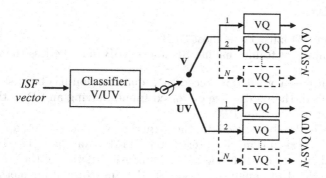

Fig. 2. ISF-CSVQ coding.

where f_i and $\hat{f}_i$ are respectively the ith coefficients of the original f and quantized $\hat{f}$ ISF vectors, and w_i represent the spectral weight assigned to the ith ISF coefficient. It is given by [2]:

$$w_i = [P(f_i)]^r, \tag{3}$$

where $P(f)$ is the power spectrum of the LPC original vector as a function of frequency f and r is an empirical constant determined experimentally. A value of $r = 0.15$ has been found satisfactory.

The quantization performance of our ISF coders operating at different bit-rates is evaluated by the average spectral distortion (SD). The spectral distortion of each frame i is given, in decibels, by [2,15,16]:

$$SD_i = \sqrt{\frac{1}{n_1 - n_0} \sum_{n=n_0}^{n_1-1} \left[10log_{10} \frac{S(e^{j2\pi n/N})}{\hat{S}(e^{j2\pi n/N})} \right]^2} \tag{4}$$

where $S(e^{j2\Pi n/N})$ and $\hat{S}(e^{j2\Pi n/N})$ are respectively the original and quantized power spectra of the LPC synthesis filter, associated with the ith frame of speech signal.

Generally, we can get transparent quantization quality if we maintain the three following conditions [2]:

1. The average spectral distortion (SD) is about 1 dB,
2. No Outliers frames with SD greater than 4 dB,
3. The percentage of Outlier frames having SD within the range of 2-4 dB must be less than 2 %.

According to Guibé et al. [7] and Cheraitia and Bouzid [16], listening tests have shown that these conditions for transparency, which are often quoted in the narrowband speech coding literature, also apply to the wideband case. In other hand, experiments done by Hagen et al. [13] showed that this transparency rule is not valid for unvoiced LPC quantization. Hence, transparency criteria should be defined individually for the voiced and unvoiced classes. The new transparency rule for UV frame is:

– The average SD must be at most 2 dB,
– The percentage of frames having SD above 4 dB must be less than 1 %.

Also, the transparency rule for voiced LPC quantization has been slightly modified [13]. Indeed, the percentage of voiced frames having an SD in the range of 2–4 dB should be less than 1 %.

The speech database used in the experiments consists of approximately 85 min of speech taken from the international TIMIT database [17]. To construct the ISF database, we used the same LPC analysis function of the AMR-WB [3], where a 16-order LPC analysis, based on the autocorrelation method, is performed on every analysis frame of 20 ms. Notice that in our experiments, we used the G.722.2 in mode 12.65 kbits/s where the speech signals are initially low pass filtered to 6.4 kHz, and then down sampled to 12.8 kHz. One part of the constructed ISF database, consisting of 208363 ISF vectors, is used for training. The remaining part of 48606 ISF vectors (not contained in the training set) is used for testing. The training and test databases were further separated into unvoiced and voiced sub-databases by using the G.722.2 VAD procedure. In training database, 39 % of frames were classified as voiced and 61 % were classified as unvoiced whereas for the test database 32 % of frames were classified as voiced and 68 % were classified as unvoiced.

In the ISF-CSVQ design, we used a N-SVQ schemes of different bit-rates for V/UV classes coding where a lower bit-rates N-SVQs are used to quantize the UV class. The ISF-CSVQ coder is characterized by its average bit rate, depending on the proportion of ISF vectors quantized by the UV class N-SVQ and V class N-SVQ, respectively [7]. The average number of bits per frame is thus calculated by:

$$b_{Av} = 1 + b_V N_V + b_{UV} N_{UV},\qquad(5)$$

where b_V and b_{UV} are respectively the bit rates of voiced and unvoiced class N-SVQs, and N_V and N_{UV} are the percentage of V and UV frames, respectively.

For different bit-rates, the performances of the ISF-CSVQ coders for the voiced and unvoiced frames are shown respectively in Tables 1 and 2. In these examples of simulation, we used a 5-part SVQ for each class where the wideband ISF vectors of dimension 16 are divided into 5 parts with (3 - 3 - 3 - 3 - 4) division. The bits are uniformly allocated to individual parts wherever possible. Notice that different distance (unweighted and weighted) measures were used in the design and the operation of the ISF-CSVQ coding systems.

We can see clearly that the weighted Euclidean distance measure improves the ISF-CSVQ coder performance in terms of both average SD and number of Outlier frames. In other hand, these simulation results show that the ISF-CSVQ coder (with weighted distance) achieves the transparent quantization quality at 49 bits/frame and 28 bits/frame for voiced and unvoiced frames, respectively. Thus, the ISF-CSVQ coder achieves the transparent quantization at an average bit rate b_{Av} of $1 + 0.32\,(49) + 0.68\,(28) = 35.72$ bits/frame.

Table 1. Performance of the ISF-CSVQ coders for voiced frames class

Bits/frame $b(b_1 + \ldots + b_5)$	ISF-CSVQ coder (Weighted distance)			ISF-CSVQ coder (Unweighted distance)		
	Average SD (dB)	Outliers (in %) 2-4 dB	> 4 dB	Average SD (dB)	Outliers (in %) 2-4 dB	> 4 dB
49(10+10+10+10+9)	1.084	0.534	0.00	1.100	0.737	0.000
48 (10+10+10+9+9)	1.120	0.610	0.00	1.140	0.883	0.000
47 (10+10+9+9+9)	1.159	0.922	0.00	1.182	1.182	0.000
46 (10+9+9+9+9)	1.201	1.284	0.00	1.226	1.742	0.000

Table 2. Performance of the ISF-CSVQ coders for unvoiced frames class

Bits/frame $b(b_1 + \ldots + b_5)$	ISF-CSVQ coder (Weighted distance)		ISF-CSVQ coder (Unweighted distance)	
	Average SD (dB)	Outliers (in %) > 4 dB	Average SD (dB)	Outliers (in %) > 4 dB
28 (6+6+6+5+5)	1.973	0.596	1.987	0.666
27 (6+6+5+5+5)	2.064	1.113	2.081	1.210
26 (6+5+5+5+5)	2.168	1.703	2.185	1.776
25 (5+5+5+5+5)	2.228	1.876	2.245	1.931

Table 3. Performance of the conventional 5-part ISF-SVQ as function of bit rate

Bits/frame $b(b_1 + \ldots + b_5)$	Average SD (dB)	Outliers (in %)	
		2-4 dB	>4 dB
46 (10+9+9+9+9)	1.080	1.113	0.00
45 (9+9+9+9+9)	1.107	1.158	0.00
44 (9+9+9+9+8)	1.156	1.818	0.00
43 (9+9+9+8+8)	1.198	2.501	0.00
42 (9+9+8+8+8)	1.248	3.489	0.00

For a comparative evaluation between the ISF-CSVQ coder and the non-classified ISF-SVQ coder designed by the conventional SVQ, we present in Table 3 the performance of the 5 parts ISF-SVQ coder operating under the same conditions of transmission. Notice that the 5-parts ISF-SVQ coders were designed with the same entire training database of non-classified wideband 208363 ISF vectors where each vector is divided also according to (3 - 3 - 3 - 3 - 4) division.

By comparing these results with those reported in Tables 1 and 2, we clearly notice that the CSVQ yields significant improvement to the ISFs coding performance. Indeed, the conventional 5-part ISF-SVQ needs 46 bits/frame to achieve the transparent quality whereas an average rate around 36 bits/frame is sufficient for the ISF-CSVQ to ensure the transparent coding. This gain in SD performance is the result of using a voiced/unvoiced classification of input ISF vectors before coding them by a separate corresponding N-SVQ rather than using a conventional single non-classified N-SVQ.

4   Conclusion

In this work, a phonetic classified split vector quantization scheme was developed for efficient coding of the wideband ISF parameters in the case of transmissions over noiseless channel. Compared to the conventional non-classified ISF-SVQ, the ISF-CSVQ coder can provide better performance, while saving several bits per frame. The performance of the ISF-CSVQ coder in the presence of channel errors re-mains to be studied. Also a more careful study of the coder robustness with respect to changes in recording conditions is necessary.

References

1. Kleijn, W.B., Paliwal, K.K.: Quantization of LPC parameters. Speech Coding Synth. 433–466 (1995). Elsevier Science B.V. Amsterdam, Netherlands
2. Paliwal, K.K., Atal, B.S.: Efficient vector quantization of LPC parameters at 24 bits/frame. IEEE Trans. Speech Audio Process. 1, 3–14 (1993)
3. Bessette, B., Salami, R., Lefebvre, R., Jelnek, M., Rotola-Pukkila, J., Vainio, J., Mik-kola, H., Jrvinen, K.: The adaptive multirate wideband speech codec (AMR-WB). IEEE Trans. Speech Audio Process. 10, 620–636 (2002)
4. Bistritz, Y., Peller, S.: Immittance spectral pairs (ISP) for speech encoding. In: 1993 IEEE International Conference on Acoustics, Speech, and Signal Processing (ICASSP 1993), vol. 2, pp. 9–12, Minneapolis, Minnesota (1993)
5. Chen, J.H., Wang, D.: Transform predictive coding of wideband speech signals. In: 1996 IEEE International Conference on Acoustics, Speech, and Signal Processing (ICASSP 1996), pp. 275–278, Atlanta, USA (1996)
6. Chang, D., Ann, S., Lee, C.W.: A classified vector quantization of LSF parameters. Signal Process. 59, 267–273 (1997)
7. Guibé, G., How, H.T., Hanzo, L.: Speech spectral quantizers for wideband speech coding. Eur. Trans. Telecommun. 12, 535–545 (2001)
8. Biundo, G., Grassi, S., Ansorge, M., Pellandini, F., Farine, P.A.: Design techniques for spectral quantization in wideband speech coding. In: 3rd COST 276 Workshop on Information and Knowledge Management for Integrated Media Communication, pp. 114–119, Budapest (2002)
9. So, S., Paliwal, K.K.: Efficient product code vector quantisation using the switched split vector quantiser. Digit. Signal Process. J. 17, 138–171 (2007)
10. Xiaochen, W., Yong, Z., Ruimin, H., Xi, D.: An immittance spectral frequency parameters quantization algorithm based on gaussian mixture model. In: International Conference on Multimedia Information Networking and Security (MINES 2009), pp. 324–328 (2009)
11. Ma, Z., Leijon, A., Kleijn, W.B.: Vector quantization of LSF parameters with a mixture of dirichlet distributions. IEEE Trans. Audio Speech Lang. Process. 21, 1777–1790 (2013)
12. Gersho, A., Gray, R.M.: Vector Quantization and Signal Compression. Kluwer Academic Publishers, New York (1992)
13. Hagen, R., Paksoy, E., Gersho, A.: Voicing-specific LPC quantization for variable-rate speech coding. IEEE Trans. Speech Audio Process. 7, 485–494 (1999)
14. ITU-T Recommendation G.722.2.: Wideband coding of speech at around 16 kb/s using Adaptive Multi-rate Wideband (AMR-WB) (2003)
15. Bouzid, M., Djeradi, A., Boudraa, B.: Optimized trellis coded vector quantization of LSF parameters: application to the 4.8 Kbps FS1016 speech coder. Signal Process. 85, 1675–1694 (2005)
16. Cheraitia, S., Bouzid, M.: Robust coding of wideband speech immittance spectral frequencies. Speech Commun. 65, 94–108 (2014)
17. Garofolo, J.S., et al.: DARPA TIMIT Acoustic-phonetic Continuous Speech Database. Gaithersburg, National Institute of Standards and Technology (NIST) (1988)

Vulnerability of Voice Verification System with STC Anti-spoofing Detector to Different Methods of Spoofing Attacks

Vadim Shchemelinin[1,2]([envelope]), Alexandr Kozlov[2], Galina Lavrentyeva[2], Sergey Novoselov[1,2], and Konstantin Simonchik[1,2]

[1] ITMO University, St. Petersburg, Russia
http://www.ifmo.ru
[2] Speech Technology Center Limited, St. Petersburg, Russia
{shchemelinin,kozlov-a,lavrentyeva,novoselov,simonchik}@speechpro.com,
http://www.speechpro.com

Abstract. This paper explores the robustness of a text-independent voice verification system against different methods of spoofing attacks based on speech synthesis and voice conversion techniques. Our experiments show that spoofing attacks based on the speech synthesis are most dangerous, but the use of standard TV-JFA approach based spoofing detection module can reduce the False Acceptance error rate of the whole speaker recognition system from 80 % to 1 %.

Keywords: Spoofing · Anti-spoofing · Speaker recognition · TV · SVM

1 Introduction

Speaker verification systems become widespread in recent time. They are used in different areas of our lives: forensic research, physical access control systems, banking, as well as on the web. The two main roles that such systems have in every-day life are usability enhancement and security. So to perform its functions a voice verification system has to have high robustness, especially if it is used for access to a bank account or personal information. For this reason, it is important to continuously assess the stability of voice verification systems against to spoofing attacks.

The greatest threat are automatable methods of spoofing based on the synthesis of speech or voice conversion techniques. In the works [1,2] it is shown that such attack mehods may raise a false error rate to unacceptable values.

Together with the increased security threat there were developed detection methods of similar attacks. However, the question of their reliability and performance evaluation is still open.

The aim of our study was to determine the most dangerous methods of spoofing for modern verification system working together with the spoofing detection module.

© Springer International Publishing Switzerland 2015
A. Ronzhin et al. (Eds.): SPECOM 2015, LNAI 9319, pp. 480–486, 2015.
DOI: 10.1007/978-3-319-23132-7_59

2   Voice Verification System with Anti-spoofing

2.1   Voice Verification Module

One of the standard use-cases of text-independent voice verification systems is the client voice model creation and its comparison with his etalon model during user interaction with the IVR (Interactive Voice Response) systems in call-centers. The user calls to the call-center and uses voice commands to go through the IVR menu. Throughout the call session, clients speech is sent to verification system for voice model creation and estimation if the access to the confidential information should be denied or not.

In our experiments the i-vector based speaker recognition system was used.

Before features extraction signal preprocessing module was applied. It included energy based voice activity detection, clipping [3], pulse and multi-tonal detection. The pre-emphasizing was also done and speech signal was divided into 22 ms window frames with a 50 % overlap, and, similarly to spoofing detection, multiplied by Hamming window function. As front-end features 13 MFCC features of each frame with first and second derivatives were selected. The derivatives were estimated over a 5-frame context and we also applied a cepstral mean subtraction (CMS) for the cepstral coefficients.

For the acoustic space modelling we used Total Variability super-vectors with Probabilistic LDA approach (TV-PLDA) to achieve better performance [4,5]. According to this approach, the distribution of the i-vectors can be expressed as following:

$$\mu = m + T\omega + \epsilon,$$

where μ is the super-vector of the Gaussian Mixture Models (GMM) parameters of the speaker model,

m is the super-vector of the Universal Background Model(UBM) parameters,

T is the TV matrix defining the basis in the reduced feature space,

ω is the i-vector in the reduced feature space, $\omega \in N(0,1)$,

ϵ is the error vector.

In our system the dimension of TV space was 600 and UBM was gender-independent with 512 component. UBM was obtained by standard ML-training on the telephone part of the NIST's SRE 1998-2010 datasets (all languages, both genders) [6,7].

In our study we used more than 4000 training speakers in total. We also used a diagonal, not a full-covariance GMM UBM.

The i-vector extractor and PLDA matrix were trained on more than 60000 telephone and microphone recordings from the NIST 1998-2010 comprising more than 4000 speakers' voices.

2.2   Spoofing Detection Module

Spoofing detection method was used in considered speaker verification system as preliminary step. It was firstly introduced in the ASVspoof Challenge 2015 [8]

and achieved 3.922 % EER for unknown types of spoofing attacks and 0.008 % EER for known spoofing attacks. It should be mentioned that for the HMM-based spoofing attacks of the ASVspoof Challenge evaluation base zero error of spoofing detection was achieved. That was the motivation to include this method to ASV system.

Anti-spoofing method consists of four main components:

- Pre-detection
- Acoustic feature extractor
- TV i-vector extractor
- SVM classifier

Pre-detector was used to check if the input signal had zero temporal energy and in this cases declared signal as spoofing attack. Otherwise acoustic features were extracted from signal.

As front-end acoustic features we used: 12 Mel-Frequency Cepstral Coefficients (MFCC), 12 Mel-Frequency Principal Coefficients (MFPC) and 12 Cos-Phase Principal Coefficients (CosPhasePC) based on phase spectrum with its first and second derivatives. To obtain these coefficients Hamming windowing was used with 256 window length and 50 % overlap.

For the acoustic space modelling we used the standard TV-JFA approach, which is the state-of-the-art in speaker verification [7,9,10]. According to this version of the joint factor analysis, the i-vector of the Total Variability space is extracted by means of JFA modification, which is a usual Gaussian factor analyser defined on mean super-vectors of the Universal Background Model (UBM) and Total-variability matrix T. UBM was represented by the Gaussian mixture model (GMM) of the described features. The diagonal covariance UBM was trained by the standard EM-algorithm.

For anti-spoofing method UBM was represented by a 1024-component Gaussian mixture model of the described features, and the dimension of the TV space was 400.

2.3 Fusion Decision Module

Fusion Decision Module was based on fusion on speaker recognition module output and spoofing detection module output as shown on Fig. 1. The decision made by verification and spoofing detection modules was expressed as a mentioned below

$$P = P_{verification} * (1 - P_{spoofing}),$$

where:

$P_{verification}$ is the probability that the speaker in the test recording is the same as the speaker in the etalon,

$P_{spoofing}$ is probability that the test recording is spoofing.

To calculate probabilities from scores, we used the BOSARIS toolkit [18].

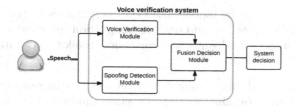

Fig. 1. Voice verification system with anti-spoofing sheme

3   Experiments with Different Types of Spoofing

For examining vulnerability of Voice Verification System to different methods of spoofing attacks we used ASVspoof development dataset [11]. It includes free and spoofed speech of 35 speakers, 15 male and 20 female. There are 3497 genuine and 49875 spoofed trials. Spoofed speech is generated according to one of the five spoofing methods ($S1$ - $S5$) as follows:

- $S1$ - Based on voice conversion, simplified frame selection algorithm [12,13]. The converted speech is generated by selecting target speech frames.
- $S2$ - The simplest voice conversion algorithm [14] which adjusts only the first mel-cepstral coefficient in order to shift the slope of the source spectrum to the target.
- $S3$ - The Hidden Markov model based speech synthesis system using speaker adaptation techniques [15] and only 20 adaptation utterances.

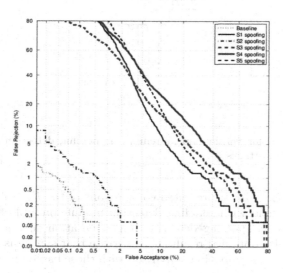

Fig. 2. DET curves for verification system without spoofing detection module against different methods of attacks

- $S4$ - The Hidden Markov model based speech synthesis system using speaker adaptation techniques [15] and only 40 adaptation utterances.
- $S5$ - The method based on voice conversion toolkit and with the Festvox system [16].

At first, we checked how strong FA error rate was increased if voice verification system didn't contain spoofing detection module. Also in this step, we wanted to make sure that proposed for ASVspoof Chalenge 2015 spoofing techniques were a threat to a system of verification.

As the baseline we used only free speech of all speakers from previous described dataset.

It is interesting to note that $S2$ based on conversion of the first mel-cepstral coefficient gives the greatest detection error [17], while this method has the least impact on verification system without spoofing detector as shown on Fig. 2.

The results of experiments with enabled spoofing detection module are presented on Fig. 3.

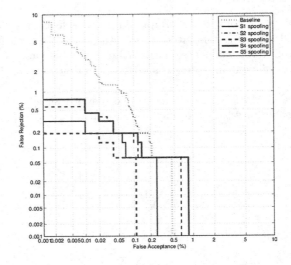

Fig. 3. DET curves for verification system with spoofing detection module against different methods of attacks

Additionally in Table 1, presented comparisons of the FA values at baseline EER point threshold with spoofing detection module on and off. As it can be seen from the table, spoofing detection implementation significantly improves FA error rate. Also obtained results demonstrate that synthesis based spoofing methods are more dangerous in comparison with those based on voice conversion techniques.

Table 1. FA verification error for spoofing the verification system based on different algorithms.

Voice verification system	FA for threshold in EER point				
	S1	S2	S3	S4	S5
Without spoofing detection module	52.5 %	1.7 %	68.5 %	77.1 %	63.7 %
With TV-JFA based spoofing detection module	0.36 %	0 %	0.23 %	1.35 %	0.98 %

4 Conclusions

In this paper we analyzed the vulnerability of voice verification system based on state-of-the-art speaker recognition and spoofing detection methods against different spoofing methods based on text-to-speech and voice conversion algorithms. As it was demonstrated by the experiments, spoofing using a TTS voice is more treatful than other methods. For instance, the Hidden Markov model based speech synthesis spoofing method gave 1.35 % False Acceptance error, comparing to the 0.98 % of method based on voice conversion toolkit.

Also, it can be sum up that it is important to evaluate spoofing detection methods together with voice verification systems. Firstly, spoofing detector can be reliable on the not effective spoofing attacks. Secondly, the system EER can be increased by false acceptances error of spoofing detector.

However, our results showed once again that it is highly necessary to test verification systems against spoofing by different methods, and to develop anti-spoofing algorithms reliable in real use-cases.

Acknowledgments. This work was partially financially supported by the Government of Russian Federation, Grant 074-U01.

References

1. Shchemelinin, V., Simonchik, K.: Examining vulnerability of voice verification systems to spoofing attacks by means of a TTS system. In: Železný, M., Habernal, I., Ronzhin, A. (eds.) SPECOM 2013. LNCS, vol. 8113, pp. 132–137. Springer, Heidelberg (2013)
2. Shchemelinin, V., Topchina, M., Simonchik, K.: Vulnerability of voice verification systems to spoofing attacks by TTS voices based on automatically labeled telephone speech. In: Ronzhin, A., Potapova, R., Delic, V. (eds.) SPECOM 2014. LNCS, vol. 8773, pp. 475–481. Springer, Heidelberg (2014)
3. Aleinik, S., Matveev, Y.N.: Detection of clipped fragments in speech signals. Int. J. Electr. Electron. Sci. Eng. **8**(2), 74–80 (2014)
4. Kenny, P.: Bayesian speaker verification with heavy tailed priors. In: Proceedings of the Odyssey Speaker and Language Recognition Workshop (2010)
5. Simonchik, K., Pekhovsky T., Shulipa, A., Afanasyev, A.: Supervized mixture of PLDA models for cross-channel speaker verification. In: Proceedings of the 13th Annual Conference of the International Speech Communication Association, Interspeech 2012 (2012)

6. Matveev, Yu., Simonchik, K.: The speaker identification system for the NIST SRE 2010. In: Proceedings of the 20th International Conference on Computer Graphics and Vision, GraphiCon 2010, pp. 315–319 (2010)
7. Kozlov, A., Kudashev, O., Matveev, Y., Pekhovsky, T., Simonchik, K., Shulipa, A.: SVID speaker recognition system for NIST SRE 2012. In: Železný, M., Habernal, I., Ronzhin, A. (eds.) SPECOM 2013. LNCS, vol. 8113, pp. 278–285. Springer, Heidelberg (2013)
8. Wu, Z., et al.: ASVspoof 2015: Automatic Speaker Verification Spoofing and Countermeasures Challenge Evaluation Plan, Training, 10(15), 3750 (2014). http://www.spoofingchallenge.org
9. Novoselov, S., Pekhovsky, T., Simonchik, K.: STC speaker recognition system for the NIST i-Vector challenge. In: Proceedings of Odyssey 2014 - The Speaker and Language Recognition Workshop (2014)
10. Kinnunen, T., Li, H.: An overview of text-independent speaker recognition: from features to supervectors. Speech Commun. **52**, 12–40 (2010)
11. Wu, Z., et al.: ASVspoof 2015: the First Automatic Speaker Verification Spoofing and Countermeasures Challenge (2015). http://www.spoofingchallenge.org/is2015_asvspoof.pdf
12. Dutoit, T., et al.: Towards a voice conversion system based on frame selection. In: Proceedings of IEEE International Conference on Acoustics, Speech, and Signal Processing (ICASSP) (2007)
13. Wu, Z., et al.: Exemplarbased unit selection for voice conversion utilizing temporal information. In: Interspeech (2013)
14. Fukada, T., Tokuda, K., Kobayashi, T., Imai, S.: An adaptive algorithm for mel-cepstral analysis of speech. In: Proceedings of IEEE International Conference on Acoustics, Speech, and Signal Processing (ICASSP) (1992)
15. Yamagishi, J., et al.: Analysis of speaker adaptation algorithms for HMM-based speech synthesis and a constrained smaplr adaptation algorithm. IEEE Trans. Audio Speech Lang. Process. **17**(1), 66–83 (2009)
16. Festvox project. http://festvox.org/
17. Novoselov, S., et al.: STC Anti-spoofing Systems for the ASVspoof 2015 Challenge. http://ris.ifmo.ru/wp-content/uploads/2015/06/Technical_report_ASVspoof2015_STC.pdf
18. BOSARIS Toolkit. https://sites.google.com/site/bosaristoolkit/

WebTransc — A WWW Interface for Speech Corpora Production and Processing

Tomáš Valenta[✉] and Luboš Šmídl

Department of Cybernetics, Faculty of Applied Sciences,
New Technologies for Information Society, University of West Bohemia,
Technická 8, 306 14 Plzeň, Czech Republic
{valentat,smidl}@ntis.zcu.cz

Abstract. This paper describes a web application that was designed to prepare and process speech corpora, key data sources for automatic speech recognition (ASR), natural language processing (NLP), speech synthesis (TTS) and many other tasks. The application allows users to process the corpora with no other equipment than a web browser with internet connection. The application has been used, upgraded and improved for several years and its history is also described here. During that time, many valuable experiences with speech corpora processing have been gained and they are also mentioned as some good practices.

Keywords: Speech corpora · Natural language processing · Transcription · Annotation · Web applications · Automatic speech recognition

1 Introduction

A speech corpus is any collection of speech records that is accompanied by an annotation (a symbolic representation of speech) and documentation sufficient enough so that the data can be used in the future [6].

Speech corpora can be divided by many criteria into various categories. For example, by the use:

- For *technical applications*, e.g. for automatic speech recognition system (ASR), text-to-speech (TTS), speaker verification and identification system (SVI) or dialogue system development.
- For *scientific purposes*, e.g. for research in fields of phonetics, sociolinguistics, psycholinguistics or audiology.

The use of a corpus, i.e. its target application or field of study, strongly affects its properties such as selection of speakers, whether the speech is dictated or spontaneous, preparation of source texts or scenarios (if needed at all), choice of recording environment and, above all, specification of transcription/annotation rules and strategy.

While the design of corpus properties in preparatory phase (before the recording is started) is entirely up to the corpus designer and his decision, recording and annotation phases can be assisted by software applications which can make the phases faster and more efficient.

© Springer International Publishing Switzerland 2015
A. Ronzhin et al. (Eds.): SPECOM 2015, LNAI 9319, pp. 487–494, 2015.
DOI: 10.1007/978-3-319-23132-7_60

The choice of the recording software depends on a device used for recording and metadata needed to be recorded with the speech signal. The device is usually a microphone recording audible sound, but it can be for example electroglotograph, electromagnetic articulograph etc. The metadata collected with the recording usually consist of synchronization timestamps, segmentation labels etc. In this work, we will assume that the recordings are sound wave files with no special metadata.

The key phase of corpus production consists of transcription or annotation. Transcription usually means an exact rewrite of what was said/heard including non-standard words, stumblings etc. Annotation rather denotes a record of how an utterance was pronounced. It consists of phonetic symbols, non-speech events (e.g. coughing, sigh), background noises, semantic labels and many other tags. It can also contain orthographic transcription. Transcription and annotation are usually produced at the same time and are often used as synonyms.

Annotations can be made in general-purpose or specialized software. General purpose software include word processors or general crowdsourcing tools, e.g. Mechanical Turk [3]. Examples of a tool specialized for phoneticians is Praat [2] which also includes many machine learning algorithms. A less specialized application is Transcriber [1] which is a "thick application" (requires installation) for annotating wave files. It does not, however, help with organization, such as distribution of recordings, collection of transcriptions, accounting rewards etc.

In the next Sect. 2 we are going to introduce our application WebTransc and its data organization. In Sect. 3 we will describe technical implementation of the application and its advanced features. Penultimate Sect. 4 will give an example of data preparation and import. Finally, Sect. 5 summarizes the application history giving some interesting figures.

2   WebTransc

The application with whole name *WebTransc — A WWW Interface for Speech Corpora Production and Processing* came into existence in 2007. The main goal, as its name suggests, was to make Transcriber's features accessible via a web browser. It should run in any browser with no special requirements on both client side and server side. Therefore the set of technologies that could be used was very limited compared to today's situation. But it was worth the effort, the application can be successfully used today (see Fig. 1) and we believe that in the future too.

The data is organized into *projects*. Each project consists of *sentence sets* which are pieces of work that a user can do — record, annotate or check. Sentences in sets can have a primary transcription. It can be used for recording or labelling. Each sentence set (the sentences in the set) can have one or more *recordings*, i.e. it can be recorded by one or more speakers. Each recording is then annotated one or more times yielding several *annotations* of the same recording. It can be useful for examining agreement among annotators [7]. Finally, all the annotations for a recording are *checked* together yielding single "most correct" annotation. Figure 1 shows two annotations and their alignment, comparison (diff) and agreement score.

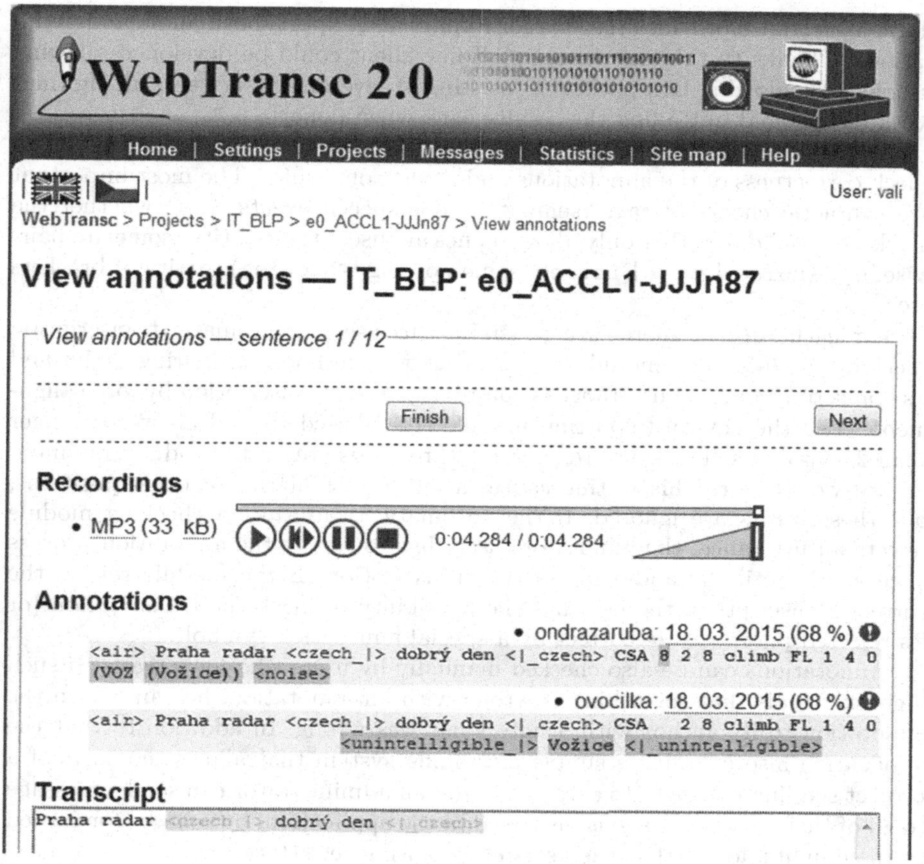

Fig. 1. WebTransc application layout.

Projects are homogeneous units in the sense of annotation rules, user rules and other things. Annotation rules consist of instructions, tags (semantics, non-speech events, timestamps etc.) and phonetic alphabet (on-screen keyboard). User rules are rights/roles (recorder, annotator, checker and admin) and properties/fields the users must or may fill in. The fields may be speaker's properties (gender, age, dialect; useful for recording), contact address and payment details. WebTransc contains sophisticated accounting system for rewarding users for their work. The rewards are calculated by formula:

$$reward = \text{set-rate} \times \textit{sets-annotated} +$$

$$\text{sent-rate} \times \textit{sentences-annotated} + \text{hour-rate} \times \textit{hours-annotated},$$

where the *hours-annotated* quantity refers to the duration of the recorded data not the time spent by annotating.

All data can be entered, modified and accessed through the web interface. This is necessary for regular work sentence by sentence, but for large amounts of data, WebTransc provides services for import and export, both audio and annotations. Thanks to this interface, an off-line client could be developed allowing users to download a data package consisting of several sentence sets, doing their work off-line and uploading the results back when done.

To make all the work as automatic as possible, several policies can be set to check correctness of the annotations and assert some rules. The most important are syntactic checks of tags (semantics, non-speech events, ...), whether the mark-up is valid, whether only allowed ones are used, their parity (some are pairwise, e.g. `<noise_|>...<|_noise>`, some not, e.g. `<sneeze>`), parity of brackets etc.

For each project there is a possibility to use an automatic transcription checking module. The module is based on two methods comparing audio and its transcription. Each utterance is compared to the transcription by force alignment. Also the keyword spotting module [10] is used to find all words longer than 2 characters. The keyword spotting thresholds are set to produce minimum missed word error. This setting causes a lot of false alarms at other positions, but these errors are ignored. If the automatic transcription checking module rejects an utterance, the annotator (user) has to repeat the annotation process once again until the audio meets the transcription. If the module rejects the correct transcription, the user has the possibility to mark the transcription (or its rejected part) as sure correct by a special annotation symbol.

Annotations can be also checked manually by users who have rights. If such a checker finds that something is wrong with an annotation, he can return the annotation to its author with a note what was wrong. In addition to that the application also contains a simple messaging system that allows the users of a project sending messages to each other and an administrator can send a message to all of them. The message is displayed in the application, but can be forwarded to the e-mail address that the users enter during registration.

Virtually everything in the projects can be monitored. Number of sets, sentences, recordings and annotations, their state (empty, in-progress, completed), user activity (time spent working on 1-h recording, real-time factor, work done in a time period) and some others.

Not only audio recordings can be processed in WebTransc. It also allows annotating pictures, videos (e.g., annotation of cuts by automatic time stamp insertion) or just texts (for example semantic labelling). The text editing field highlights syntax and allows to hide certain annotation streams (e.g. phonetic or prosodic annotations [4] in square brackets). Keyboard shortcuts that control player and tags insertion are customizable for annotator's efficient and convenient work.

3 Technical Details

WebTransc was designed to have minimal demands both on server and client side. Then it meant the choice of XHTML 1, CSS 2, a small subset of ECMAScript 5 features and Adobe Flash Player on the client side. Today Flash can be switched

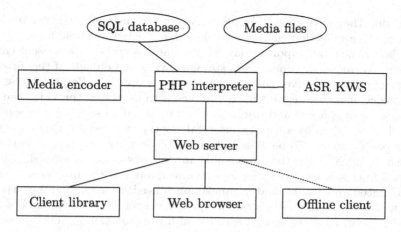

Fig. 2. Components participating in WebTransc infrastructure.

off in favour of HTML5 audio/video features. Users that want to do their work off-line need Python to run the off-line client. User-friendly library that utilizes the import/export API is also written in Python.

The server side of the application is written in PHP. It depends on no particular webserver nor particular operating system. MySQL database backend is preferred but not required. Therefore it can run on a webhosting where we cannot change server's configuration. To enable automatic audio/video conversion/compression, appropriate software must be installed on the system. For automatic transcription checking, a speech recognition software with appropriate interface [5] must be accessible. See the application organization in Fig. 2.

Entire application can be translated into any language. All texts are in a spreadsheet table which can be easily edited by any speaker of the language of interest. The spreadsheet is then compiled into the application PHP module.

3.1 Security

Often the data in a speech corpus is confidential, so the security is a very important feature. It can be sliced into several layers.

Transport layer (HTTP) can be secured by SSL/TLS (HTTPS) protocol. Alternatively the application can be run on a virtual private network (VPN) which only allowed users can access.

Second layer is user authentication and authorization. By default users are authenticated by own html-form-based password authentication. User passwords are never transferred nor stored in plain text. Very secure and convenient way of authentication can be set up using client SSL certificates. User authorization is determined by their rights/roles in the projects. Above roles in projects there are two application-wide roles, *admin* that can control everything in the application and *project admin* that can establish and control own projects. Ordinary users can do what they were allowed by administrators/owners of particular projects. Access to the application can be also allowed/restricted by IP address.

Probably the most important layer is the data security in the sense it cannot be stolen, downloaded, mined. Data storage always lays outside of the directory published by the web server and there is a broker script that allows to access only one sentence at a time. Each time a sentence is to be played (provided the user has access to the project and works on a certain sentence set; only one sentence set can be worked on by a user), ephemeral key is generated for it which is valid for just one playback. To be allowed to work on another set, the previous must be finished which means that reasonable annotations must be entered. Number of tasks (processed sets) per user can be also limited in the project so that an unexperienced annotator could not make much needless work, and if everything seems well and the annotator's output quality is good enough, the limit can be relaxed to allow more work. Packages for off-line annotation are encrypted by a key derived from user's credentials.

4   Data Preparation and Import

During the history of the application, its recording functions were used only seldom. The reasons for that were: limited audio recording abilities of web browsers (although the situation is much better today); and simply the fact that some domains cannot be recorded in browser, e.g. spontaneous telephony speech [7] or air–ground communication in air traffic control [8]. Instead of recording in-application, external data was prepared and imported.

Experiences show that most convenient way of data preparation is to divide the emerging corpus into some logical units (e.g. single phone calls) that do not exceed 10 min. They would become sentence sets. The set is divided into sentences either implicitly (it was recorded sentence by sentence) or it must be done explicitly, e.g. to segment a continuous phone call at speaker changes. Convenient length of such artificial sentences is up to about 30 seconds; longer sentences are harder to transcribe. From the segmented phone call, silence is removed from both channels and then the segments are ordered by time so that the annotator could hear them almost sentence by sentence as they occurred in the continuous call.

The import is done according to an index file, which is a list of sentence sets and their sentences (files) with optional primary transcriptions. WebTransc then handles the rest (import metadata, convert media) automatically.

5   Summary

Throughout the history of WebTransc since 2007, huge amounts of speech (and some visual) data has been processed, see Table 1. It would be almost impossible (or very inconvenient) to achieve such numbers with general text processing application, thick client or just general crowdsourcing solutions, because WebTransc helps a lot with organization, distribution, reward calculation, . . .

Table 1. WebTransc history since 2007 in figures

Users participated:	177	
Projects processed:	44	
Sentence sets:	42,403	
Sentences:	2,459,626	
Recordings time:	2,395:11:39	(almost 100 days)
Played time:	8,622 h	(cca 1 year; 3.6 × RT)
Annotating time:	19,519 h	(over 2 years; 8.1 × RT)

Many users spent a lot of time annotating speech recordings from various sources (quality microphone vs. telephone), domains (dictation vs. spontaneous speech) and environments (recording studio vs. busy street), for different purposes (speech synthesis, acoustic modelling, language modelling, natural language processing, semantic analysis), in several languages (Czech, Slovak, Russian, English, Armenian). Some corpora processed in WebTransc are private, for custom speech recognizer and synthesizer development, whereas some of them were made publicly available (e.g. Air Traffic Control Communication [8] or Czech political discussion broadcast "Otázky Václava Moravce" [9]) or were used as a dataset for research purposes [7, 12].

Table 1 shows overall numbers of WebTransc eight-year history. In case of the real-time (RT) factors, the numbers are averages over all projects, but for example annotations for acoustic modelling of spontaneous telephony speech would be very time-demanding and the annotator would have to play the recording several times to get correct transcription. On the other hand, semantic labelling [11] is quite easy and it is sufficient to play the recording once if at all.

WebTransc has become a mature project, an application with high customizability, easy installation and maintenance. Currently it is running in three installations and has been translated into two languages (Czech and English). It can be obtained under a permissive licence by contacting the developers.

Acknowledgements. This research was supported by the Technology Agency of the Czech Republic, project No. TE01020197, and by the grant of the University of West Bohemia, project No. SGS-2013-032.
The data used in this paper are available in the LINDAT/Clarin repository [8,9].

References

1. Barras, C., Geoffrois, E., Wu, Z., Liberman, M.: Transcriber: development and use of a tool for assisting speech corpora production. Speech Commun. **33**(1–2), 5–22 (2001). http://www.sciencedirect.com/science/article/B6V1C-41SBGXX-2/2/6e7ee46d45ac6bc627f6ae738ca95461
2. Boersma, P.: Praat, a system for doing phonetics by computer. Glot Int. **5**(9/10), 341–345 (2001)

3. Burch, C.C., Dredze, M.: Creating speech and language data with Amazon's Mechanical Turk. In: Proceedings of the NAACL HLT 2010 Workshop on Creating Speech and Language Data with Amazon's Mechanical Turk, CSLDAMT 2010, pp. 1–12. Association for Computational Linguistics, Stroudsburg (2010). http://portal.acm.org/citation.cfm?id=1866697

4. Grüber, M.: Acoustic Analysis of Czech Expressive Recordings from a Single Speaker in Terms of Various Communicative Functions. In: Proceedings of the 11th IEEE International Symposium on Signal Processing and Information Technology, pp. 267–272. IEEE, New York (2011). http://www.kky.zcu.cz/en/publications/GruberM_2011_AcousticAnalysisof

5. Müller, L., Psutka, J.V., Smíd, L.: Design of speech recognition engine. In: Sojka, P., Kopeček, I., Pala, K. (eds.) TSD 2000. LNCS (LNAI), vol. 1902, pp. 259–264. Springer, Heidelberg (2000). http://link.springer.com/chapter/10.1007/3-540-45323-7_44

6. Psutka, J., Müller, L., Matoušek, J., Radová, V.: Mluvíme s počítačem česky. Academia, Praha (2006)

7. Valenta, T., Šmídl, L., Švec, J., Soutner, D.: Inter-annotator agreement on spontaneous Czech language. In: Sojka, P., Horák, A., Kopeček, I., Pala, K. (eds.) TSD 2014. LNCS, vol. 8655, pp. 390–397. Springer, Heidelberg (2014). http://link.springer.com/10.1007/978-3-319-10816-2_47

8. Šmídl, L.: Air Traffic Control Communication, LINDAT/CLARIN digital library at Institute of Formal and Applied Linguistics, Charles University in Prague (2011). http://hdl.handle.net/11858/00-097C-0000-0001-CCA1-0

9. Šmídl, L., Pražák, A.: OVM – Otázky Václava Moravce, LINDAT/CLARIN digital library at Institute of Formal and Applied Linguistics, Charles University in Prague (2013). http://hdl.handle.net/11858/00-097C-0000-000D-EC98-3

10. Šmídl, L., Psutka, J.: Comparison of keyword spotting methods for searching in speech. In: Interspeech 2006, pp. 1894–1897 (2006). http://www.kky.zcu.cz/en/publications/SmidlL_2006_Comparisonofkeyword

11. Švec, J., Hoidekr, J., Soutner, D., Vavruška, J.: Web text data mining for building large scale language modelling corpus. In: Habernal, I., Matoušek, V. (eds.) TSD 2011. LNCS, vol. 6836, pp. 356–363. Springer, Heidelberg (2011). http://www.kky.zcu.cz/en/publications/JanSvec_2011_Webtextdatamining

12. Švec, J., Šmídl, L.: Prototype of Czech spoken dialog system with mixed initiative for railway information service. In: Sojka, P., Horák, A., Kopeček, I., Pala, K. (eds.) TSD 2010. LNCS, vol. 6231, pp. 568–575. Springer, Heidelberg (2010). http://dx.doi.org/10.1007/978-3-642-15760-8_72

Word-External Reduction
in Spontaneous Russian

Yulia Nigmatulina[(✉)]

Department of Phonetics, St. Petersburg State University, St. Petersburg, Russia
julia.nigmatic@yandex.ru

Abstract. Among many types of phonetic modifications in casual speech, those that occur across word boundaries can affect two words simultaneously. If inter-word penetration is considerable and accompanied with lack of other sources (semantic, syntactic) of information, the differentiation of two words can be confused. The present study, based on the data from spontaneous Russian, investigates word-external quantitative reductions. The classification of all examples is given in order to reveal what patterns of modified realizations can occur in sloppy Russian and what their probability is.

Keywords: Spontaneous speech · Acoustic reduction · Word joints

1 Introduction

Investigation of spontaneous speech is necessary to get a proper notion of the language we use in everyday life. Spontaneous speech realization including reductions and different phonetic modifications is highly variable that is observed in many languages [1,2,5,6,8,11]. Reductions vary from the qualitative change of a sound to the strong alteration of the whole word (e.g. yesterday [jɛʃei] in [7]) when the loss of phonetic information could be probably compensated by other sources of information (i.e. syntactic, semantic). However, mechanisms underlying the processes of speech reduction are not evident. To study regularities of speech realisation its detailed description is required.

[8,9,11] present phonetic alterations in spontaneous Russian, but mostly a word is taken in the focus as a research item. Yet, speech reduction can be word-internal as well as word-external. Here under word-external reduction I mean phonetic change that involves the end or the onset of a wordform. In sound sequences across word joints with no pause inside the process of sound interaction and modification should be about the same as it is within word-internal sound strings [11]. However, external reduction at word joint (two words with no pause between) modifies not only the word itself but also word boundary: *на_ ужасные_ условия* /na uˈʒasnɨje uˈslovʲia/ → [nuʒaslʲyslovʲæ] ('on terrible conditions'-ACC.PL). It is possible to assume that such inter-word diffuseness with no clear word-separation would complicate lexical identification in the

© Springer International Publishing Switzerland 2015
A. Ronzhin et al. (Eds.): SPECOM 2015, LNAI 9319, pp. 495–503, 2015.
DOI: 10.1007/978-3-319-23132-7_61

spoken word recognition process: listeners have to recognize two words from the sound string where is no evident delimitation between the words.

Study of cross-boundary phonetic realisation in spontaneous Russian is undertaken in order to collect reliable data on the phenomena hardly described before and to follow regular changes if there are any. In the present paper, firstly, the Materials and Methods will be described and then a classification of all quantitative sound modifications found in the material is presented.

2   Material

All data came from the Speech Subcorpus of Corpus of Standard Written Russian (www.narusco.ru), which consists of 90 min (10488 items) of spontaneous speech. All records from the Speech Subcorpus have orthographic as well as phonetic transcriptions. Trained phoneticians from St. Petersburg State University manually made transcriptions. Experts analysed the material by small 1-syllable fragments in order to avoid the influence of grammatical and lexical knowledge on the results of phonetic transcription. Along with auditory estimation, spectrogram and waveform displays were consequently used. Two records of spontaneous speech (65 min, or 8786 items overall) were analyzed for the current study. They are TV talk shows with many people participating in conversation.

3   Method

Absence of a sound leads to more significant modification in speech than the change in the quality of a sound, as it can cause syllable loss or resyllabification. In the present study, only the quantitative type of reduction when at least one sound is absent is taken into account.

All two words (W1 and W2) combinations with no pause between the words were taken for the analysis. "No pause" means that all cases with pause, inhalation, sigh, laugh, pause of hesitation or glottal stop between two words were excluded from the analysis. 6936 examples of pure word junctions were divided into 6 groups of quantitative external reduction (see Fig. 1 for their distribution):

1. final sound deletion of W1: *нашиx_ детей* /'naʃɨx dʲi'tʲej/ → [naʃɨ dʲitʲi] ('our children'-GEN);
2. initial sound deletion of W2: *свои_ взгляды* /svai vzglʲadɨ/ → [tsvae zglʲædə] ('one's'-POSS.REFL‿'view'-ACC.PL.);
3. final part (more than one sound) deletion of W1: *важный_ момент* /vaʒnɨj ma'mʲent/ → [vaʒ manet] ('important moment');
4. final sound deletion of W1 and initial sound deletion of W2: *конфликт_ мне* /kan'flʲikt mnʲe/ → [kamflʲik nʲæ] ('conflict'‿'me'-DAT.SG.);
5. external sound contraction: *должны_ опираться* [doʒnɛpʲerats] instead of /dalʒ'nɨ apʲi'ratsa/ ('must'-PL‿'base'-INF.MED.);

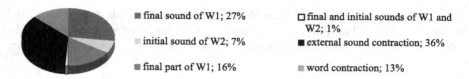

- ■ final sound of W1; 27%
- ▨ initial sound of W2; 7%
- ■ final part of W1; 16%
- ☐ final and initial sounds of W1 and W2; 1%
- ■ external sound contraction; 36%
- ▨ word contraction; 13%

Fig. 1. The distribution of types of quantitative external reductions.

6. word contraction: *страшное_ действительно* [straʃn sʲitna] instead of /ˈstraʃnaji dʲejstˈvʲitʲelʲna/ 'ugly'-Sg.N._'actually'.

In groups (1)–(3) the quantitative sound modification occurs only in one of two adjacent words; in (4)–(6) – both words undergo reduction. Groups (5) and (6) implicate overlapping of two words. The term 'sound contraction' is used for an interaction of only two external sounds when one new sound is pronounced instead of two. Under 'word contraction' I mean an interpenetration of two words including more than two sounds: e.g., *реальная_ альтернатива* /rʲiˈalʲnajaalʲternaˈtʲiva/ → [rʲænatərətʲy] ('real'-SG.F._alternative'-SG.NOM.), (Fig. 2).

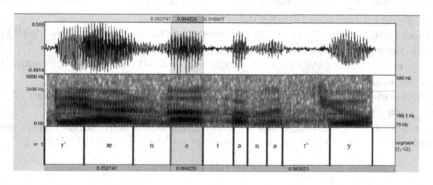

Fig. 2. Word-contraction (реальная_ альтернатива /rʲænatərətʲy/); the highlight fragment is a mutual part.

The method of continuous comparing of acoustic transcription (available from the Corpus) and phonemic transcription was applied to detect the absence of sounds at the position between two words. The phonemic transcription reflecting what phonemes a word consists of reproduces full and unreduced type of pronunciation, but unlike the ideal transcription considers some regular variants of speech realization (e.g., the drop of /j/ in an intervocalic position in the endings of nouns, adjectives and participles in standard Russian) [10].

In the analyzed records the comprehension between speakers never failed. The fact that some sounds were not realized in the speech signal did not prevent successful communication and, therefore, such 'loss' of sounds can be admitted by the language. What kind of sound loss is a norm for spontaneous speech? The following part gives the analysis of external reductions in spontaneous Russian.

4   Analysis of External Reductions

According to the results, 875 (13 %) of all word junctions undergo quantitative external reduction and only 6 % - simultaneous reduction of two words. As a word boundary is more faded with two words externally reduced, the groups (4)-(6) are of bigger interest for the present description.

4.1   'Word Contraction'

Classification. The 'word contraction' group with more sufficient external reduction than the other groups have was divided into six classes (see Fig. 3):

- Similar syllable contraction (22 %): *коллега_ говорил* [kaᴵegɨvarʲil] instead of /ka'lʲega gava'rʲil/ ('colleague'-SG.NOM_ 'say'-PST.3SG.M) (Fig. 4).
- Consonant drop in the intervocalic position with further vowel contraction (42 %): *давали_ возможность* /da'valʲi vaz'moʒnasʲtʲ/ → [dəvalʲæzmoʒnəsʲtʲ] ('give'-PST.PL_ 'opportunity'-ACC.SG).
- Vowel contraction (15 %): *к сожалению_ учителя* /k saʒi'lʲenʲiju utɕitʲi'lʲa/ → [k səʒenʲytɕtʲirʲæ] ('unfortunately'_ 'teacher'-ACC.SG).
- Fragment deletion (8 %): *из уст_ взрослых* /iz 'ust_'vzroslɨx/ → [ɨz uzroslɨx] ('from adults' lips').
- Vowel and sonorant contraction (only if a sonorant is not intervocalic) (7 %): *но_ если_ эта* /no 'jesʲi 'eta/ → [nesʲeta] (but if this-F).
- Vowel loss in the position between two consonants with further consonant contraction (6 %): *надо_ для* /'nada dlʲa/ → [nədlʲɨ] ('need'-IMPRS_'for').

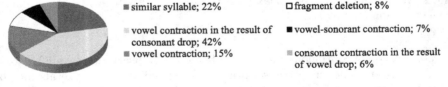

Fig. 3. The distribution of word contraction classes.

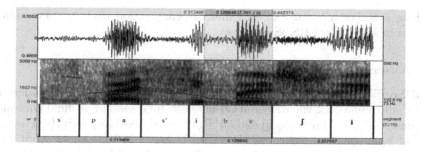

Fig. 4. Syllable-contraction (спасибо_большое /spaˈsʲiba balʲˈʃoe/ → [spasʲibeʃi] – 'thanks much'); the highlight fragment is a mutual syllable.

Discussion. The classification shows that the most frequent (almost 50 % of all instances) pattern of reduction in word-contraction type is vowel contraction as a result of the loss of an intervocalic consonant. In all instances, the dropped consonant was either a sonorant or a /v/-consonant with the following distribution: /j/ - 55 %, /v/ - 40 %, /m/ - 7 %, /r/ - 3 %, /n/ - 2 %[1]. This could be explained by the fact that the acoustic realization of sonorants as well as /v/ is closer to vowels' one than the other consonants have. Therefore, sonorants and /v/ prevent less vowel interaction and are easier to fall out.

The second-most common reduction pattern is the realization of only one syllable instead of two. All contracted syllables had CV structure with identical consonants and mostly but not necessary identical vowels. In 50 % of all instances, the consonant of the contracted syllable was sonorant /n/.

The class "fragment deletion" got few word combinations with more significant reduction than the other ones had. Several instances included the whole morpheme deletion (of W1 mostly): e.g., in three words it is an imperfective verb suffix *-iva-/-yva-*, dropped along with a verb ending, and in one word, with a reflexive suffix as well. Morpheme augmentation makes a word longer and its final part deletion more probable comparing with shorter words. The initial part of W2 was highly reduced (more than one sound) mostly when the syllable contraction pattern took place or if the word itself was frequent and had the typical for sloppy speech reduced variant of realization (e.g., *сейчас*-'now' is often pronounced as [ɕːæs] instead of full variant /sʲijtɕas/.

4.2 Absence of W1 Final Fragment (More Than One Sound)

The analysis of (3) group, which is 16 % of all external reductions, confirms that the deletion of the final part usually means the deletion of functional morpheme(s). In Russian, there is a tendency of distribution of grammatical and lexical meanings between vowels and consonants respectively [12]. Functional morphemes in Russian are mostly formed with vowels, sonorants, /v/ consonant,

---

[1] The general sum exceeds 100 %, as in some instances two consonants were deleted.

which as was shown before can easy undergo contraction, and /t/ consonant as well, which is used in PRS.3SG forms.

4.3   Absence of External Sound of a Word

Final Sound Deletion. Instances when only final sound of W1 was lost are 27 % of all reductions: the distribution between final vowel and final consonant deletions is 44 % (104 instances) and 56 % (130 instances) respectively. The most frequent final sound absence was the final /j/ loss – 118 instances – but as its final drop is regular in spoken Russian, all examples of final /j/-deletion were taken out from the general account. /t/ and /tʲ/ consonants prevail over the other final deleted consonants (see Fig. 5). There are 523 instances altogether of final /t/ and /tʲ/ consonants in the texts, 46 of which (or 7 %) were not realized.

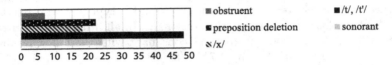

Fig. 5. Sound distribution for final consonant deletion (the data is absolute value).

Instances of the absence of single-consonant preposition were also included into the group; they made 8 % of all prepositions in texts (22 of 266). Yet, preposition loss differs from the loss of final consonant. A preposition is usually a part of grammatical construction and has its grammatical weight. With natural redundancy of language communication, preposition loss is not often critical for understanding: it can be with high probability predicted by the left context or reconstructed within the phrase: *ходили {к} нам* [xaˈdʲilʲæ ˈnam] ('they went to us'); *небезразличен {к} процессу* [nʲibʲezrazˈlʲiçən praˈtsɛsu] ('he is not indifferent about the process').

Initial Sound Deletion. Initial sound of W2 was absent in 7 % (60 instances) of all external quantitative reductions. There is significant prevalence of /v/ and /f/ consonants deletion among all deleted initial sounds – 62 % (in 37 combinations) (Fig. 6). At the same time, with a glance at all words with initial /v/s and /f/s in the texts these deleted consonants make 7 % only: 37 word of 515.

Final Sound of W1 and Initial Sound of W2 Deletion. This reduction pattern is less represented comparing with others – 1 % only of all external reductions in the material, but it supports the tendencies displayed in the two last subheads: the predominance of the initial /v/, /f/ and the final /t/, /tʲ/ loss.

The most prominent qualitative loss tends to take place in frequent words. Final fragment loss: *извините* /izvʲiˈnʲitʲi/ → [iʥ] ('excuse (me)'), *говорят*

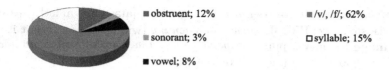

Fig. 6. Percentage of sound distribution for initial deletion.

/gava'rʲat/ → [gɛ] ('say'-PRS.3PL), человек /ʨila'vʲek/ → [ʨe] ('man'); initial sound loss: 59 % of all instances of the type are 12 instances are with a pronoun всё /vsʲo/ ('all') and 10 instances are with a particle вот /vot/ ('here').

4.4 Sound Contraction

Identical consonants contractions and vowel contractions of only two word-external sounds are included into the group. In the present data, sound contraction keeps 36 % (315 instances) of all word-external reductions: 225 instances (26 %) of external vowel contraction and 87 instances (10 %) of external consonant one. To state vowel contraction, the information from F1 and F2 was used. If there was any visible change in formants, the sound was considered a diphthong or a sequence of two sounds; if there was no change, a monophthong as the result of contraction was adopted. Vowel combinations are contracted (55.4 %) or not contracted (44.6 %) with about the same probability. Yet, stress seems to affect contraction process: the previous study [3, 4] showed that if both vowels at word joint have no stress, they undergo contraction in 70.1 %: говорили_ уже [gəvarʲilʲуʒɛ] instead of /gavarʲilʲi uʒe/ ('they already talked').

Combinations of identical consonants only (the same place and manner of articulation; no distinction between voiced/voiceless and palatalized/non-palatalized ones) were taken into account for the contraction group: садовник_который /sa'dovnʲik ka'torij/ → [saduvnʲəketorɨ] ('gardener who'). Realization of one sound at the place of 'different' consonants combinations was considered as a deletion.

4.5 Three Word Contraction

Finally, it is worth to mention instances of several words contraction, when reduction occurs across the joints of several successive words, fusing them together into one unit: сказать_ одну_ очень /ska'zatʲ ad'nu otɕinʲ/ → [(s)kezadnəʨ] ('to say one very'); почему_ они_ не_ осваивают /paʨi'mu anʲi nʲi as'vaivajut/ → [pɨʨymanʲæsəvej] ('why they do not learn'); осколок_ каждому_ учителю /as'kolak 'kaʒdamu u'ʨitʲelʲu/ → [askolkaʒmutɕitʲlʲy]('a splinter to every teacher').

As there is no regular rules to predict realization of pauses in continuous speech, words fusions can theoretically occur at any word joint. It happens sometimes even at the joint of words, which belong to different clauses: суме-

ет правильно к этому **отнестись,_ сумеет** [atəsʲtʲəsʲymʲiet] (instead of /atnʲisʲtʲisʲ sumʲeit/) PAUSE *показать ученику* (will manage to **treat** it right, **will manage** to show a pupil); *хорошо_ это_ или* **плохо,_ он** *естъ* [ploxun] (instead of /'ploxa 'on/) ('good it or **bad, he** is').

5   Discussion

Acoustic modifications are widespread in spontaneous speech. Yet, word-external reductions on the present data from spontaneous Russian occurred in 13 % of all word joints and in 10 % of all word boundaries. As word boundaries are still important for word differentiation, the results reveal them to be quite resistant to quantitative reduction: two simultaneously reduced words are 6 % only.

All variants of acoustic realization met in casual speech are only "...the possible result, in the majority of cases ..." [1]. With unpredictability of speech variations, we can assume only that some alterations are more plausible to happen, when some phonetic information is more stable than other is.

The results received for word-external positions correspond to the general tendencies of word-internal sound reductions in spontaneous Russian [8]. (1) vowels, (2) identical consonants, (3) sonant consonants and /v/ in combination with vowels, (4) consonant clusters and (5) similar syllables are more contraction-prone across word joints comparing with other sound combinations. Therefore, contraction across word joints should be primarily expected for these sound combinations, given stress realisation of both adjacent words.

Multiple sources of information cooperate to carry out the goal of speech recognition. As a result, even strongly externally reduced words are usually recognized due to the context support. Nevertheless, the role of phonetic and phonological information in this process is important to be defined in order to find relevant features of speech signal that could be crucial for its recognition.

References

1. Ernestus, M.: Voice assimilation and segment reduction in casual dutch: a corpus-based study of the phonology-phonetics interface (lot, Utrecht) (2000)
2. Johnson, K.: Massive reduction in conversational american english. In: Spontaneous speech: Data and analysis. Proceedings of the 1st session of the 10th international symposium, pp. 29–54. Citeseer (2004)
3. Nigmatulina, Y.O.: Sound contraction in russian spontaneous speech and its implication for spoken word recognition. In: New Perspectives on Speech in Action. Proceedings of the 2nd SJUSK, pp. 127–139 (2013)
4. Nigmatulina, Y.O.: St'azheniya udarnyx i bezudarnyx glasnyx na stykax slovoform. In: Cherdakov, D.N. (ed.) VXVI Mezhdunarodnaya konferenciya studentov-philologov. Izbrannyey trudy. Saint-Petersburg, Copenhagen (in publish)
5. Riekhakaynen, E.: Vzaimodestviye kontekstnoy predskazuyemosti i chastotnosti v protsesse vospriyatiya spontannoy rechi (na material russkogo yazyka) [interaction of context and frequency in the process of spontaneous speech recognition (evidence from russian)]. Linguistic Theory and Raw Sound, Saint-Petersburg (2010)

6. Schachtenhaufen, R.: Looking for lost syllables in danish spontaneous speech. In: Linguistic Theory and Raw Sound, pp. 61–88 (2010)
7. Schuppler, B., Ernestus, M., Scharenborg, O., Boves, L.: Acoustic reduction in conversational dutch: a quantitative analysis based on automatically generated segmental transcriptions. J. Phonetics **39**(1), 96–109 (2011)
8. Svetozarova, N.D.: Phonetika spontannoy rechi. Leningrad University, Leningrad (1988)
9. Tananaiko, S., Vasilieva, L.: Proiznositelnaya norma i eyo variant. Vestnik of St. Petersburg State University 3, Saint-Peterburg (2005)
10. Verbitskaya, L.: Davajte govorit' pravi'no. Vysshaya shkola, Moscow (1993)
11. Zemskaya, E.A.: Russkaya razgovornaya rech: Linguisticheskii analiz i problemy-obucheniya. Nauka, Moscow (1979)
12. Zubkova, L.: Phonetica i grammatical: k obosnovaniyu grammaticheskoy motivirovannosti russkogo zvukovogo stroya. Moscow (1999)

Author Index

Aleinik, Sergei 34, 121, 364
Aravantinou, Christina 113, 226
Arisoy, Ebru 11
Arvanitis, Gerasimos 333
Azarov, Elias 405

Barabanov, Andrey 209, 217
Basov, Oleg 65, 317
Bobrov, Nikolay 55
Bogdanova-Beglarian, Natalia 429
Bordás, Csaba 105
Bouzid, Merouane 472
Budkov, Victor 317
Bulgakova, Elena 397

Campbell, Nick 96
Chen, Ning 381
Cheraitia, Salah-Eddine 472
Chernykh, Irina 161
Chistikov, Pavel 161

Dat, Tran Huy 277
Delić, Vlado 186
Demri, Lyes 178
Dennis, Jonathan William 277
Dikici, Erinc 11
Djendi, Mohamed 51
Dmitrieva, Evgeniya 144

Epimakhova, Natalia 161
Eun, Seongbae 463
Evdokimova, Vera 209

Fakotakis, Nikos 129, 333
Falek, Leila 178
Fazakis, Nikos 389
Fegyó, Tibor 105
Frolova, Olga 144, 201
Fu, Tian Fan 381

Gakis, Panagiotis 170
Garner, Philip N. 193
Glavatskih, Igor 438
Grigorev, Aleksey 144

Hládek, Daniel 259
Huang, Yuyun 96

Iaroshenko, Viktor 348
Ivanko, Dmitry 121

Jakovljević, Bojana 446
Jakovljević, Nikša 186
Jedlička, Pavel 81
Jokisch, Oliver 348
Juhár, Jozef 259
Jung, Jinman 463

Kachkovskaia, Tatiana 422
Karlos, Stamatis 389
Karpov, Alexey 42, 144
Kaya, Heysem 144
Kharchenko, Sergey 454
Khemies, Feriel 51
Khokhlov, Yuri 234
Khomitsevich, Olga 25, 161
Kipyatkova, Irina 42
Koit, Mare 73
Komalova, Liliya 55, 89
Konopík, Miloslav 243
Korenevsky, Maxim 234
Kotov, Mikhail 438
Kotsiantis, Sotiris 389
Koumpouri, Athanasia 309
Kozlov, Alexandr 137, 480
Krivosheeva, Tatiana 161
Krňoul, Zdeněk 81
Kudinov, Mikhail 341
Kudubayeva, Saule 25

Lavrentyeva, Galina 121, 137, 480
Lazaridis, Alexandros 193
Li, Wei 381
Lyakso, Elena 144, 201

Madzlan, Noor Alhusna 96
Magerkin, Valentin 217
Marković, Maja 446

Martynenko, Gregory   429
Maruschke, Michael   348
Matveev, Yuri   397
Medennikov, Ivan   25, 234
Megalooikonomou, Vasileios   113, 226, 309
Melnikov, Alexandr   217
Mendelev, Valentin   25, 234
Meshcheryakov, Roman   454
Meszaros, Martin   348
Mihajlik, Péter   105
Milićev, Tanja   446
Miliević, Nataša   446
Minker, Wolfgang   413
Morsli, Amina   51
Moustakas, Konstantinos   333
Mporas, Iosif   113, 129, 226, 309
Müller, Luděk   301

Nigmatulina, Yulia   495
Novoselov, Sergey   137, 480

Oskina, Ksenia   356
Ostrogonac, Stevan   186
Ovsyannikova, Anna   438

Pakoci, Edvin   186
Panagiotakopoulos, Christos   170
Petrovsky, Alexander   405
Platonova, Tatyana   438
Popov, Dimitar   293
Popova, Velka   293
Popović, Branislav   186
Potapov, Vsevolod   153, 251
Potapova, Rodmonga   55, 89, 153, 356
Potard, Blaise   193
Pražák, Ondřej   243
Prudnikov, Alexey   234

Repalov, Sergey   438
Ridzik, Andrej   325
Rigoll, Gerhard   3
Rogozhina, Valeria   438
Ronzhin, Alexander   65
Ronzhin, Andrey   65, 317
Rusko, Milan   325
Rybin, Sergey   25

Salah, Albert Ali   144
Salajka, Petr   301
Saraclar, Murat   11
Saveliev, Anton   65
Sgarbas, Kyriakos   170, 389
Shapranov, Vladimir   285
Shchemelinin, Vadim   137, 480
Sherstinova, Tatiana   268, 429
Shirokova, Anna   438
Sholohov, Aleksei   397
Simaki, Vasiliki   113, 226
Simonchik, Konstantin   121, 137, 480
Skrelin, Pavel   209
Šmídl, Luboš   487
Smolina, Anna   438
Staš, Ján   259
Stepikhov, Anton   372
Stolbov, Mikhail   34, 364
Szaszák, György   105

Tarján, Balázs   105
Teffahi, Hocine   178
Terence, Ng Wen Zheng   277
Theodorou, Theodoros   129
Tobler, Zoltán   105
Tomashenko, Natalia   25, 397
Tsalidis, Christos   170

Valenta, Tomáš   487
Varga, Ádám   105
Vashkevich, Maxim   405
Vasilios, Verykios   170
Verkhodanova, Vasilisa   285
Vikulov, Evgenij   217
Volf, Daniyar   454

Yun, Young-Sun   463

Zablotskiy, Sergey   413
Železný, Miloš   81
Zelinka, Jan   301
Zhenilo, Valeriy   251
Zhu, Jie   381
Zulkarneev, Mikhail   438